D1603007

The Lives of Sri Aurobindo

The Lives of *Sri Aurobindo*

PETER HEEHS

Columbia University Press New York

Columbia University Press
Publishers Since 1893
New York   Chichester, West Sussex
Copyright © 2008 Columbia University Press
All rights reserved

Library of Congress Cataloging-in-Publication Data
Heehs, Peter.
The Lives of Sri Aurobindo / Peter Heehs.
    p.   cm.
Includes bibliographical references and index.
ISBN 978-0-231-14098-0 (cloth : alk. paper)
ISBN 978-0-231-51184-1 (electronic)
1. Ghose, Aurobindo, 1872–1950. 2. Gurus—India—Biography.
3. Philosophers—India—Biography. 4. Nationalists—India—Biography.
I. Title.
BL1273.892.G56H43   2008
294.5092—dc22
[B]   2007018739

Columbia University Press books are printed on permanent
and durable acid-free paper.
This book was printed on paper with recycled content.

Printed in the United States of America
c 10 9 8 7 6 5 4 3 2 1

Contents

Illustrations

All photographs reproduced with the permission of Sri Aurobindo Ashram Trust, Pondicherry, India.

Preface

Some generations count more than others. The United States owes an enormous debt to the men and women born between 1730 and 1760 who took part in the events of 1770 to 1790. Modern India owes as much to its own revolutionary cohort, men and women born between 1860 and 1900 who prepared and participated in the Struggle for Freedom. In popular memory, both groups are represented by a small number of exemplars: in America, the more important founders; in India, a dozen or so political, cultural, and spiritual leaders, among them Mahatma Gandhi, Jawaharlal Nehru, B.R. Ambedkar, Rabindranath Tagore, Swami Vivekananda, and Sri Aurobindo. Of these, Aurobindo is the most difficult to categorize. He was, for a moment, the most important political leader in the country, the first to say clearly that the goal of the national movement was independence. But he was also a scholar, a poet, a philosopher, and above all, a yogi and spiritual leader. His diverse achievements at various times can make it seem as though he led four or five different lives in a single lifetime.

I have called this book *The Lives of Sri Aurobindo* to highlight his many-sidedness. In each of the book's parts, one of his personas predominates. Part One, "Son," covers his early years in India. The next part, "Scholar," deals with his education in England and his intellectual, administrative, and academic life in Baroda. "Revolutionary," the third part, begins with his entry into the national movement and ends with his sudden departure from politics. Part Four, "Yogi and Philosopher," charts his early practice of yoga and examines his major works. The last part, "Guide," deals with his final years, during which an ashram grew up around him. The transitions are often abrupt, the demarcations sharp, but his five lives were not sealed off from one another. His relations with his family continued until 1920; his scholarly life went on until the late 1940s; his career as a revolutionary began before he left Baroda and continued after his departure from Calcutta; he took up yoga while still a politician, and began guiding others before he accepted the role of guru. Five lives, but in the end, only one.

I FIRST ENCOUNTERED Aurobindo in 1968 in a yoga center on 57th Street in Manhattan. The teacher was an elderly Polish Jew with a suitably Indian name. He gave instructions in postures and breathing for a fee, dietary and moral advice gratis. Between lessons, he told stories about his years of wandering in India. Among the artifacts he brought back were photographs of people he called "realized beings," which covered the walls of his studio. One of them was of Aurobindo as an old man. I did not find it particularly remarkable, as the subject wore neither loincloth nor turban, and had no simulated halo around his head.

A few months later, after a brief return to college and a stopover in a wild uptown "ashram," I found myself living in another yoga center housed, improbably, in a building on Central Park West. Here there were just three pictures on the wall, one of them the standard portrait of Aurobindo (figure 1). I was struck by the peaceful expanse of his brow, his trouble-free face, and fathomless eyes. It would be years before I learned that all of these features owed their distinctiveness to the retoucher's art.

The center had the most complete collection of Aurobindo's writings in New York. I started with a compilation of his philosophical works, which I could not understand. Undeterred, I tried some of his shorter writings, which seemed to make a lot of sense to me. By then I had read a number of books by "realized beings" of the East and West. Most of them consisted of what I now would call spiritual clichés. This is not to suggest that bits of advice like "remain calm in all circumstances" or "seek the truth beneath the surface" are not valid or useful. But if they do not form part of a coherent view of life, they remain empty verbiage. Aurobindo's view of life seemed to me to be coherent, though not always easy to grasp. His prose was good, if rather old fashioned, and he had a wry sense of humor that came out when you least expected it.

I lived in or near New York for the next four years, missing out on several events that were thought important at the time. I did a lot of reading, primarily of Aurobindo, but also writers he got me interested in: Shelley, Dante, Nietzsche, Ramakrishna, Plato, Homer, the Buddha, Kalidasa, Wordsworth, Whitman, and dozens of others, in no particular order. I learned enough Sanskrit to struggle through the *Gita*, and tried to meditate as long as I could, which was not very long. All the while I was helping out at the yoga center, and at the same time working as an office assistant, stock boy, or taxi driver. Now and then I thought about traveling to India, and eventually bought a ticket for Bombay. A week after my arrival, I found myself living in the ashram Aurobindo had founded.

I might not have stayed if I had not been asked to do two things I found very interesting: first, to collect material dealing with his life; second, to organize his manuscripts and prepare them for publication. The facts of his life were rather well known; after all, he was one of the most famous men in India

Figure 1. Aurobindo, circa 1915–16 (the "standard portrait").

when he died. But it had never occurred to anyone to search systematically for biographical documents. I spent parts of the next few years digging (sometimes literally) in archives and private collections in Delhi, Calcutta, Baroda, and Bombay. I was able to find material that might have lain unnoticed for years, or even been thrown out when an attic was cleaned. Later trips to London and Paris were less strenuous but equally productive.

Most of the documents I found in public archives dealt with Aurobindo's life as a politician. They confirmed that he had been an important figure in the Struggle for Freedom, but fell short of proving what his followers believed: that he was the major cause of its success. Nevertheless, his contribution was significant and, at the time, not very well known. Accounts that had been written to correct this deficiency were so uncritical that they undermined their own inflated claims.

Aurobindo retired from politics at the age of thirty-seven and devoted the rest of his life to yoga and literature. Going through his papers in the ashram's archives, I was amazed by the amount he had written. It took several years for me and my colleagues just to organize his manuscripts. While engaged in this work, we were surprised and delighted to find much that had not been published. The most remarkable discovery was a diary he had kept for more than nine years, in which he noted the day-to-day events of his inner and outer life. Most biographies of Aurobindo have made his *sadhana,* or practice of yoga, seem like a series of miracles. His diary made it clear that he had to work hard to achieve the states of consciousness that are the basis of his yoga and philosophy.

The genre of hagiography, in the original sense of the term, is very much alive in India. Any saint with a following is the subject of one or more books that tell the inspiring story of his or her birth, growth, mission, and passage to the eternal. Biographies of literary and political figures do not differ much from this model. People take the received version of their heroes' lives very seriously. A statement about a politician or poet that rubs people the wrong way will be turned into a political or legal issue, or possibly cause a riot. The problem is not whether the disputed statement is true, but whether anyone has the right to question an account that flatters a group identity.

Aurobindo has been better served by his biographers than most of his contemporaries have. But when I began to write articles about his life, I found that there were limits to what his admirers wanted to hear. Anything that cast doubt on something that he said was taboo, even if his statement was based on incomplete knowledge of the facts. Almost as bad was anything that challenged an established interpretation, even one that clearly was inadequate.

Figure 2 is a photograph of Aurobindo that was taken around the same time as figure 1. Note the dark, pockmarked skin, sharp features, and undreamy

Figure 2. Aurobindo, circa 1915.

eyes. As far as I know, it did not appear in print before 1976, when I published it in an ashram journal. To me it is infinitely more appealing than figure 1, which has been reproduced millions of times in its heavily retouched form. I sometimes wonder why people like figure 1. There is hardly a trace of shadow between the ears, with the result that the face has no character. The sparkling eyes have been painted in; even the hair has been given a gloss. As a historical document it is false. As a photograph it is a botched piece of work. But for many, figure 1 is more true to Aurobindo than figure 2. In later life, his complexion became fair and smooth, his features full and round. Figure 2 thus falsifies the "real" Aurobindo. It is the task of the retoucher to make the photograph accord with the reality that people want to see.

Hagiographers deal with documents the way that retouchers deal with photographs. Biographers must take their documents as they find them. They have to examine all sorts of materials, paying as much attention to what is written by the subject's enemies as by his friends, not giving special treatment even to the subject's own version of events. Accounts by the subject have exceptional value, but they need to be compared against other narrative accounts and, more important, against documents that do not reflect a particular point of view.

Such an approach is possible and necessary when dealing with public events. But what about mystical experiences? In trying to trace the lines of Aurobindo's *sadhana*, a biographer can use the subject's diaries, letters, and retrospective accounts. There are also, for comparison, accounts by others of similar mystical experiences. But in the end, such experiences remain subjective. Perhaps they are only hallucinations or signs of psychotic breakdown. Even if not, do they have any value to anyone but the subject?

Those who have had mystical experiences have always held that they are the basis of a kind of knowledge that is more fundamental, and thus more valuable, than the relative knowledge of words and things. Absorbed in inner experience, the mystic is freed from the problems that afflict men and women who are caught in the dualities of knowledge and ignorance, pleasure and pain, life and death. A mystic thus absorbed often is lost to the human effort to achieve a more perfect life. But this is not the only possible outcome of spiritual practice. Aurobindo's first major inner experience was a state of mystical absorption, but he was driven to return to the active life, and spent the next forty years looking for a way to bring the knowledge and power of the spirit into the world. In this lies the value of his teaching to men and women of the twenty-first century.

Acknowledgments

Special thanks to the late Jayantilal Parekh of the Sri Aurobindo Ashram Archives and to Michael Murphy of the Esalen Institute.

Thanks to Ashok Acharya, Rukun Advani, Duncan Bazemore, Francis Bertaud, Anuradha Bhattacharya, Liviu Bordas, Ratan Lal Chakraborty, A.K. Dutta, P.L. Dutta, Leela Gandhi, Aloka Ghosh, Ela Ghosh, Medha Gunay, Leslie Kriesel, Jeffrey Kripal, Marcel Kvassay, Julian Lines, Wendy Lines, Wendy Lochner, Raphael Malangin, Alka Mishra, Arup Mitra, the late Joya Mitter, Janine Morisset, Ajit Neogy, Neela Patel, Ramesh Patel, Madhumita Patnaik, Shanti Pillai, Olivier Pironneau, Stephen Phillips, Jacques Pouchepadass, Raman Reddy, Lalita Roy, Niharendu Roy, the late Ratnalekha Roy, Dhir Sarangi, the late Ambapremi Shah, Maurice Shukla, Brian Slattery, Chaitanya Swain, and Bob Zwicker.

Thanks also to the librarians, archivists, and staff of the Archives Nationales, Asiatic Society of Bangladesh, Bibliothèque Nationale de France, Baroda Record Office, India Office Library and Records, Institut Français de Pondichéry, National Archives of India, Nehru Memorial Museum and Library, Sri Aurobindo Ashram Archives, Sri Aurobindo Library, West Bengal State Archives, and the other institutions listed in the bibliography; and to the Sri Aurobindo Ashram, Pondicherry; Sri Aurobindo Ashram Branch, New Delhi; Sri Aurobindo Bhavan, Kolkata; Sri Aurobindo Institute of Culture, Kolkata; and Sri Aurobindo Society, Vadodara.

Apologies to any individual or institution whose name I have inadvertently omitted from the above lists.

Works of Sri Aurobindo are quoted with the kind permission of the Sri Aurobindo Ashram Trust. My thanks to Manoj Das Gupta, Managing Trustee and head of the Ashram's Publication Department, for granting this permission. The Sri Aurobindo Ashram is in no way responsible for the selection, arrangement, interpretation, or presentation of material in this biography. The author alone is responsible for the contents of the book.

Note on Proper Names

Indian personal names, when spelled with the Latin alphabet, take many different forms. These variants reflect regional differences in pronunciation and personal preferences in transliteration. The Sanskrit word *aravinda*, used as personal name, can be spelled Aravinda, Aravind, Arvind, Arabinda, Aurobindo, and so forth. Sri Aurobindo (Aurobindo Ghose) spelled his name Aravinda when he lived in England, Aravind or Arvind while he was in Baroda, and Aurobindo when he settled in Bengal. In the interest of consistency, I have used Aurobindo throughout except when quoting from source materials or suggesting the usage of a particular period. A similar variation exists in the spelling of the names of many other people referred to in this book. To give one example, the name of the novelist Bankimchandra Chattopadhyaya is also spelled Bankim Chandra Chattopadhyay, Bankimchandra Chatterjee, Bunkim Chundra Chatterji, and so on almost indefinitely. In this book I use the spelling that the person preferred if he or she wrote in English; otherwise I choose a single, recognizable form. When quoting I of course leave the spelling as it occurs in the document.

Many place names that were spelled to suit the British tongue during the colonial period have recently been changed to what are presumed to be the original forms: Mumbai, not Bombay; Vadodara, not Baroda; Chennai, not Madras. In this book I use the old forms for important cities, particularly those in which Aurobindo lived, because to do otherwise would be anachronistic. Moreover, the old forms are still in common use. For places mentioned in passing, I generally use the modern forms, as the British spellings (e.g., Trichinopoly for Tiruchirapalli) are often obsolete.

The Lives of Sri Aurobindo

PART ONE: *Son*

I may be son of my father or mother in certain respects, but most of me is as foreign to them as if I had been born in New York or Paraguay.

1. Early Years in India

Bengal, 1872–1879

The nineteenth century in India was imitative, self-forgetful, artificial. It aimed at a successful reproduction of Europe in India. . . . If we had succeeded in Europeanising ourselves we would have lost for ever our spiritual capacity, our intellectual force, our national elasticity and power of self-renovation.

Aurobindo Acroyd

Rangpur means "city of delight," but the town of Rangpur, in Bengal, was so unhealthy in the nineteenth century that people called it Yampur, or "city of death." The summer of 1872 was particularly bad. The annual outbreak of malaria was followed by a cholera epidemic.[1] No one in the town knew more about the situation than its energetic civil surgeon, Dr. Krishna Dhun Ghose. As the father of two small children and the husband of a pregnant wife, he had personal as well as professional reasons for concern.

Swarnalotta Ghose was due to give birth in August. As her time approached, her husband decided to send her to the comparatively healthy environment of Calcutta. When she reached the metropolis, she went to stay in the home of Mano Mohan Ghose, a friend of her husband's who lived in the best part of town. Fourteen South Circular Road was situated just off Chowringhee Avenue, which faced the town's *maidan,* or park.[2] The neighborhood, distinguished by its elegant mansions, had given Calcutta the name the City of Palaces. The opulence did not go very deep: The windows in the front of Mano Mohan's house looked out on similar mansions, but the windows in the back looked down on a pond where the local people fished, bathed, washed, and drew their drinking water.

Just before dawn on the morning of August 15, 1872, in this house that straddled two worlds, the nineteen-year-old mother gave birth to her third son. When the time came to name him, her husband, "in a sudden inspiration," chose Aurobindo, a Sanskrit word for lotus.[3] At some point the doctor added an English-style middle name in honor of his friend Annette Akroyd. Annette came to Calcutta from England in December 1872. By that time Aurobindo Acroyd Ghose and his mother had left the city.[4]

BEFORE RETURNING TO RANGPUR, Swarnalotta doubtless spent some time with her parents, who were then living in Calcutta. Rajnarain Bose had passed most of his working life as a teacher in the provincial town of Midnapore, but his writings and speeches had made his name well known throughout Bengal. A leading member of the Brahmo Samaj, or Society of God, a religious reform group, he also was an early promoter of what was called national culture. In his prospectus for "A Society for the Promotion of National Feeling among the Educated Natives of Bengal" (1861), he urged his countrymen to speak and write in Bengali, establish schools of indigenous medicine and music, revive national forms of greeting, diet, exercise and dress, and shun social reform "unless it comes in a national shape."[5] The society was never organized, but it was the precursor of dozens of national institutions that mushroomed in the following years. Many of them—the *National Paper*, the National Gathering, the National Society, the National School, the National Gymnasium—were founded by Rajnarain's friend Nabagopal Mitter. No wonder people began to call him National Nabagopal. More seriously, some referred to him as the Father of Indian Nationalism. When Rajnarain heard this, he commented wryly that if Nabagopal was the father of Indian nationalism, then he was its grandfather. The epithet stuck after the joke had been forgotten, and it is as the Grandfather of Indian Nationalism that Rajnarain is remembered.

Swarnalotta was Rajnarain's eldest child. Born in Midnapore in 1852 and educated at home by her father, she grew up in what, for the age, was an unusually enlightened atmosphere. Still, Rajnarain found it necessary to get Swarnalotta married soon after she reached the age of twelve. The girl's wedding was a memorable event in the annals of the Brahmo Samaj. All of the principal members of the society were there, notably its leader, Devendranath Tagore, and its rising star, Keshub Chunder Sen.[6] The bride's party was swelled by numerous members of the Bose clan. The groom's party contained few, if any, of the young man's relatives, for Krishna Dhun Ghose came from an orthodox Hindu family. He had not even told his mother that he was taking a Brahmo bride. What prompted him to defy custom was not the attractions of the girl; "I went to the length of offending a dear mother by marrying as I did," he later wrote, "to get such a father as Rajnarain Bose."[7]

Krishna Dhun's own father, Kali Prosad Ghose, had died when Krishna Dhun was twelve. Little is known of Kali Prosad. His native village was Konnagar, in the Hooghly district, but he passed at least part of his career in Patna, where his wife Kailaskamini gave birth to Krishna Dhun in 1844.[8] When Kali Prosad died, he left his widow and children no more than a month's salary. During the boy's youth the family was "very poor, living almost entirely by the charity of friends."[9] Kailaskamini went to Benares as a Hindu widow was supposed to. Krishna Dhun and his brother continued their studies in an English-medium school. For young men without money, the profession of choice was government service, but Krishna Dhun decided in his teens to become a doctor. His mother must have been distressed, as dissecting a cadaver meant losing caste. Krishna Dhun persisted, got hold of some money, entered the Calcutta Medical College, and in 1865 became a licentiate in medicine and surgery. In June he began his internship in the Medical College Hospital.

The next year the young doctor was sent to Bhagalpur and given charge of the government dispensary. His salary, a hundred rupees a month, allowed him and his wife to live in reasonable comfort. In 1867 their first child, Benoybhusan, was born. Another boy, Manmohan, followed two years later. The hundred-rupee salary was now less satisfactory, but there were few chances for promotion, as the higher posts were all reserved for members of the Indian Medical Service. If he wanted to enter that exclusive corps, Krishna Dhun would have to go to England. In November 1869 he took leave from his work, and three months later, he and a group of young Brahmos, among them Keshub Chunder Sen, embarked from Calcutta.[10]

The travelers reached London at the end of March 1870. While Krishna Dhun and most of the others looked for ways to advance their careers, Keshub embarked on a lecture tour that became a triumphal progress. He addressed large audiences in a dozen cities, spoke privately with John Stuart Mill and Prime Minister William Gladstone, and even had an audience with Queen Victoria. Although he was scorned by old India hands and ridiculed by *Punch*, he made a generally good impression on the British public—the first Indian with flowing robes and an agile tongue to captivate a credulous West.

Krishna Dhun encountered disappointment followed by success. He was unable to enter the Indian Medical Service, but he got himself admitted to King's College, Aberdeen, and in 1871 received the degree of M.D. with honors.[11] To study medicine in Scotland at that time meant taking sides in the greatest intellectual controversy of the century: *The Descent of Man* was published in 1871, twelve years after *The Origin of Species*. Throughout Krishna

Dhun's stay, Darwinians and their rivals proclaimed their views from platform and pulpit. Wherever his sympathies may have been before his arrival, by the time he left, they were firmly on the side of the evolutionists. He ended up becoming, as Aurobindo later remarked, "a tremendous atheist."[12] But he had his own ethical religion, which he explained in a letter to his brother-in-law: on one hand a Darwinian urge "to improve my species by giving to the world children of a better breed," and on the other an altruistic desire "to improve the children of those who do not have the power of doing it themselves." This was his kind of devotion, rather than "empty prayers which mean inaction and worship of a God of your own *creation*." The "real God" was the universe with its creatures, "and when I worship that by action I worship Him."[13]

Keshub Sen also was influenced by Darwin, and ended up, like many other nineteenth-century thinkers, formulating a theory of spiritual evolution. During his tour of England, however, he spoke mostly about religion and social reform. In August 1870 he appealed to the women of the Victoria Discussion Society of London "to do all in your power to effect the elevation of Hindu women."[14] Annette Akroyd, a Unitarian with an interest in women's education, was touched by Keshub's plea, and decided to go to India a year later. By then she had met a number of Indian students, among them Surendranath Banerjea (later a nationalist leader) and Krishna Dhun Ghose. During the summer of 1871, she and her Bengali friends visited Kew Gardens, attended a Handel festival, and otherwise improved themselves. By the time Dr. Ghose returned to Calcutta, he and Annette had become close friends.[15]

Dr. Ghose's homecoming was not a happy one. Rajnarain was crushed when he found that his son-in-law had rejected the ideals of the Brahmo Samaj in favor of Western science. To make things worse, Dr. Ghose's disavowal came when the Samaj was embroiled in internal conflict. Keshub and his followers were encouraging the government to recognize the group as a separate religion, while Rajnarain and other traditionalists continued to insist that Brahmoism was the pristine core of Hinduism. In a speech in 1872, Rajnarain went so far as to proclaim that the Hindu *dharma* was superior to all other religions. Dr. Ghose was not in Calcutta to hear his father-in-law's speech. Soon after his return from England, he was given a new post as assistant surgeon in charge of the civil station of Rangpur. He and his family arrived in the remote northern town around the end of October, ten months before Aurobindo's birth.

In the Shadow of the Himalayas

Sometime between August and December 1872, Swarnalotta and Aurobindo journeyed from Calcutta to Rangpur, where Aurobindo passed the first five years of his life. Although it was the headquarters of a fairly large district, Rangpur was little more than an overgrown village in the midst of a vast alluvial plain. The only part at all townlike was the British civil station, "a colony which has settled down round the walls of the Government offices and courts."[16] The doctor's house certainly was there, doubtless of brick and reasonably well furnished; but even the best buildings in town leaked copiously during the rains. Outside of the civil station, most structures were of bamboo and thatch. All around was open country. Fields of rice in various stages of growth were interspersed with plots of tobacco, mustard, sugarcane, and jute. The variegated green of the crops met the blue of the sky at the horizon. On a clear day in winter, one could see the Himalayas in the distance.

In February 1873 Dr. Ghose was named the district's civil surgeon.[17] This meant that he was responsible for the health of 2 million people. Most managed to eke out a precarious living, provided the monsoon did not fail. In 1873 a drought led to a famine that, in the shorthand of official reports, left Rangpur "very distressed"; in fact the district lost 4 percent of its population between 1872 and 1892.[18] Much of the decline was due to Rangpur's endemic diseases, cholera and malaria. Dr. Ghose spent much of his professional life fighting against them. While working with patients in different parts of the district, he noted that "malaria, whatever it may be"—at the time, no one knew what caused it—was most prevalent in areas with "undrained, waterlogged soils." Accordingly he recommended draining the swamps around Rangpur.[19] Surveying the land and drawing up plans were relatively easy, but it took five years of lobbying to get the funds required to begin work. Finally, in December 1877, Dr. Ghose had the pleasure of driving in the first stake in the town's drainage works.[20] The result, completed several years later, became known as Ghose's canal.

The doctor's struggles to raise money got him involved in local politics. In 1876 he became a member of the Rangpur Municipality; the next year he was elected its vice-chairman. His position, his training, and his mastery of English brought him close to the two top Britons, Edward Glazier, the magistrate and collector, and Henry Beveridge, the district judge. Beveridge had married the doctor's old friend Annette Akroyd in 1875. A year later he was transferred to Rangpur, and he and Annette often invited the Ghoses for dinner. At one such meeting, Annette remarked to the doctor that one hardly could expect the Bengalis to like the English. "Why not," he replied. "*We* know they are as a race superior and can teach us much."[21] Dr. Ghose was so convinced of the superiority of British culture that he discouraged the use of Bengali in his house. Aurobindo grew up speaking, thinking, and dreaming in English. The only other language he learned was Hindustani, apparently to use with the servants.[22]

At the Beveridges' parties and at home with the doctor, the Europeans of Rangpur got to meet the doctor's wife. They were not unfavorably impressed. Swarnalotta could make small talk in English, look comfortable in a frock, and stay in the saddle when she went riding. Her creamy complexion won her the epithet the Rose of Rangpur.[23] But she suffered from an emotional disturbance that, during her stay in Rangpur, began to reveal itself as madness. The first symptoms seem to have appeared in 1867, shortly after the fifteen-year-old mother gave birth to her first child. Seven years later, six months after Aurobindo's birth, Annette wrote to her sister that Dr. Ghose was in "worlds of trouble" because his wife was "ill with a most alarming illness—fits of some kind." This may have been a temporary episode. But as time passed, Swarnalotta's condition worsened. In October 1877, a month after a daughter, Sarojini, was born, Dr. Ghose told Beveridge "that his wife's eccentricity has entered a new stage & that she is always laughing at herself."[24] One day she became so enraged by something Manmohan had done that she began to beat him with a candlestick. Seeing his brother's plight, Aurobindo said that he was thirsty and left the room.

There is no way to know what effect his mother's illness had on Aurobindo, but a letter of Manmohan's shows how much Aurobindo's brother felt the lack of maternal affection: "You may judge the horror of this," he wrote a friend in 1888, "how I strove to snatch a fearful love, but only succeeded in hating and loathing, and at last becoming cold. Crying for bread, I was given a stone." Manmohan summed up his feelings in four words: "I had no mother." This seems a bit exaggerated, as Swarnalotta was comparatively normal during much of her stay in Rangpur. It is true, however, that as the boys grew older, she became incapable of giving them ordinary love and care. Perhaps in compensation, the three brothers worshipped their father. But Dr. Ghose, again according to Manmohan, was "kind but stern." He spent a good deal of his time touring the district and his sons "never saw much of him."[25]

To IMPROVE THE BOYS' ENGLISH and prepare them for greater things—and perhaps also to get them away from their mother—Dr. Ghose sent Benoy, Mano, and Ara to school in Darjeeling in 1877. Magnificently situated on a 7,000-foot ridge in the foothills of the Himalayas, Darjeeling was acquired by the British at gunpoint and developed as a health resort. Missionaries followed; planters discovered that its hillsides produced incomparable tea. It became a little piece of England in India, similar to the home country in climate and vegetation as well as in architecture and social life. The Loretto House boarding school, which the Ghose boys entered, was run by Irish nuns. As non-Christians, the boys may have been exempted from religious training, but they certainly were exposed to the symbols and stories of Christianity.

In October 1877, Annette Beveridge went to Darjeeling to escape the heat of the plains. After her arrival, she went to the Loretto House to look in on the doctor's sons. Led into "a room where flowers were arranged like Dutch flower pieces in quaint latticework dishes," she sat and chatted with some of the nuns while the boys were summoned. One of the nuns remarked that they "were very good & industrious & that the little one [Aurobindo] is now quite happy." The five-year-old clearly had not been overjoyed to leave home. When she met the boys, Annette was glad to find them "all grown & looking so well-dressed in their blue serges & scarlet stockings. The little fellow had a grey suit—very becoming—& is greatly *aged*—grown tall and boyish. I was struck particularly by the broadening of his forehead. He was pleased to see me I think but all were quite silent except for an extorted yes! or no!"[26]

Aurobindo retained few memories of his two years in Darjeeling. In later years he recalled walks along paths overhung with golden ferns. Across the valleys he could see forests of pine, deodar, and oak. Above the hills towered Kangchenjunga, the third-highest mountain in the world. Another memory was of a curious inner experience. "I was lying down one day," he said in 1926, "when I saw suddenly a great darkness rushing into me and enveloping me and the whole of the universe." This "darkness" stayed with him for the next fourteen years, most of which were spent in England.[27]

DARWINIAN DR. GHOSE WAS PROUD to have brought "children of a better breed" into the world, and he aspired to make "giants of them."[28] The first step was to give them a British education. The highest eminence an Indian could aspire to was the Covenanted Civil Service of India, better known as the ICS. There were only about a thousand Civilians in the country. Enormous salaries—the ICS was the highest-paying service in the world—helped prevent the unrestrained corruption that turned early British officials into fabulously rich nabobs back home. A stiff examination assured some degree of competence, but it also kept the service almost completely white. In principle, even an Indian boy whose father had the money to send him to England could take it. But no candidate could pass without mastering the English school curriculum. A few college-age Indians managed to do this after 1863; this caused some concern in Whitehall, and the maximum age was lowered. If Dr. Ghose's sons were going to make the grade, he had to get them ready while they were young. School in Darjeeling was not sufficient; he would have to send them to England. Edward Glazier agreed to help. While on furlough in 1877, Glazier arranged with one of his relatives, a clergyman named William H. Drewett, to act as the boys' guardian while they pursued their studies.[29]

In 1879 Dr. Ghose and his family sailed for England. It may have become less unusual by then for Indian men to cross the ocean, but for Indian women, it was almost unheard of. Swarnalotta was again pregnant. Concerned about her mental state and apprehensive about the effects of another confinement, Dr. Ghose decided to take her to England for examination and treatment. Leaving his sons with Mr. Drewett in Manchester and his wife in the care of a London physician, he returned to India alone. In January 1880, Swarnalotta gave birth to a son, whom she called Emmanuel Matthew Ghose. This name was never taken seriously. After she and the boy got back to Bengal, he became known as Barindrakumar.

There is a photograph of the family taken in England before the doctor returned to India. He stands in the rear, a protective arm around Manmohan's shoulder. To their right, staring nervously at the camera, is Benoybhusan. Swarnalotta also stares, but the fixity of her gaze expresses not so much nervousness as alienation. On her lap sits Sarojini, plump and cheerful. To her left, sitting on a rock or log (a studio prop) is Aurobindo. He wears a little-boy suit—jacket, vest, and knickers. The jacket is fastened by one big button at the top. The seven-year-old looks shy but not ill at ease. Leaning forward, his hands on his knees, he looks out on a new world.

PART TWO: *Scholar*

Up to the age of fifteen I was known as a very promising scholar at St. Paul's. After fifteen I lost this reputation. The teachers used to say that I had become lazy and was deteriorating.

How was that?

Because I was reading novels and poetry. Only at the examination time I used to prepare a little. But when now and then I wrote Greek and Latin verse my teachers would lament that I was not using my remarkable gifts because of laziness.

2. Growing up English

England, 1879–1893

> I spent six years in the great city [London], and I got quite used to the place, but I did not like it. I thought it a wonderful place at first, but the rush and the turmoil and the struggle of it, it is truly dreadful. I soon longed for the peaceful life of my native land.

A Very Promising Boy

Manchester, where the Ghose boys went to stay, was the center of the most industrialized and densely populated region of England. Rapidly expanding, the city had swallowed up neighboring townships such as Ardwick, where the Reverend William Drewett lived. Minister of the Stockport Road Congregational Church, Drewett stayed with his family in a two-story house at 84 Shakespeare Street. The neighborhood was new and entirely residential. Similar brick houses with similar gardens behind them stood all around.[1] It was an average English townscape, tidy and dreary, that Aurobindo looked back on without affection: "Mean and clumsy were the buildings, or pretentious and aimed at a false elegance. Miles of brick, with hardly a bit of green here and there." The speaker is a character in a fictional dialogue, but his words evoke the residential parts of Manchester, just as what follows evokes the town's enormous mills: "Ever a raucous roar goes up from them, the glint of furnaces and the clang of metal; a dull, vicious smoke clouds the sky."[2]

Dr. Ghose had brought his sons to England because he wanted them to "receive an entirely European upbringing." He gave the Drewetts "strict instructions that they should not be allowed to make the acquaintance of any Indian or undergo any Indian influence." The couple carried out these instructions to the letter, and the boys "grew up in entire ignorance of India, her people, her religion and her culture."[3] When Dr. Ghose went to Britain nine years earlier, he became an Anglicized Bengali. His sons grew up English.

Quickly forgetting the little Hindustani they knew, they spoke only the language of their new country. Meat, fish, and the rest of what passes for British cuisine was their normal fare. Even their relations with one another took on an English cast. Although thrown together most of the time, they never developed the family attachments that are the rule in India. They got along well enough, but "were not so passionately fond of each other."[4]

After a year or two on Shakespeare Street, the Ghose boys moved along with the Drewetts to a similar house at 29 York Place in Chorlton-on-Medlock, a neighboring residential district. The census returns of 1881 provide a glimpse of the household: William Drewett, aged 39; his wife Mary, 38; her sister Edith Fishbourne, 22; Drewett's mother Elizabeth, 68; the three Ghose boys; and two maids.[5]

The boys had come to Manchester to study in English schools. To be admitted, they had to learn Latin. Drewett spent two years teaching them the rudiments; then, in 1881, he enrolled Benoybhusan and Manmohan in the Manchester Grammar School. Aurobindo, still only nine, remained at home. Very much the baby of the family, he was "sent to bed much earlier" than his brothers, and used to lie there "in a sort of constant terror of the darkness and phantoms and burglars" until his brothers also went to bed.[6] Apparently because of his youth, the Drewetts decided to tutor him at home instead of sending him to school. William taught him Latin and history while Mary taught him French, geography, and arithmetic. Dr. Ghose had asked the Reverend Mr. Drewett not to give his sons any religious training, but the boys inevitably absorbed much of the intellectual and moral atmosphere of Christianity. Aurobindo later wrote that Christianity was "the only religion and the Bible the only scripture with which he was acquainted in his childhood."[7] When he began to reflect, he was repelled by Calvinist doctrines such as eternal damnation. Otherwise he found the whole thing rather tedious. Once, when he was ten, he was taken to an evangelical prayer meeting. He "was feeling completely bored" when "a minister approached me and asked me some questions. I did not give any reply. Then they all shouted, 'He is saved, he is saved,' and began to pray for me and offer thanks to God. I did not know what it was all about. Then the minister came to me and asked me to pray. I was not in the habit of praying. But somehow I did it in the manner in which children recite their prayers before going to sleep." He was much relieved when he got back to Manchester. Years later he wrote that the Bible always gave him a sense of "imprecision in the thought-substance," but he always considered the King James version a masterpiece of English prose.[8]

English poetry also absorbed him. Percy Bysshe Shelley became his special favorite. "The Cloud" made such an impression on the ten-year-old Aurobindo that he wrote a poem, "Light," in the same meter. This was published in January 1883 in an English family magazine.[9] Another poem by Shelley that he loved was *The Revolt of Islam*, in which the poet told the story of a struggle for freedom set in a mythic East, but patterned on the French Revolution. Aurobindo read it "again and again," and resolved to dedicate his life "to a similar world change and take part in it."[10] He had by then "received strongly the impression that a period of general upheaval and great revolutionary changes was coming in the world and he himself was destined to play a part in it." At first vague, this feeling was "canalised into the idea of the liberation of his own country" when his thoughts turned in that direction.[11] Dr. Ghose, less Anglophile than he once was, nurtured his son's interest by sending cuttings from a Calcutta newspaper "with passages marked relating cases of maltreatment of Indians by Englishmen." In his infrequent letters to his sons—Aurobindo received only a dozen during his fourteen years in England—Dr. Ghose denounced the British Raj as a "heartless government."[12]

Drewett resigned the pastorate of the Stockport Road Church in 1881, and for the next three years he remained in Manchester "without pastoral charge."[13] Then, apparently in 1884, he immigrated to Australia. Before his departure, he left the Ghose boys in the care of his mother, who went with them to London. The elderly Mrs. Drewett took a flat at 49 St. Stephen's Avenue, Shepherd's Bush. That autumn, Aurobindo and Manmohan were enrolled in St. Paul's School.

THE SCHOOL BUILDING the Ghose boys entered in September 1884 had been opened just two months earlier, but the school itself was 375 years old. Founded in 1509 by John Colet, a friend of Thomas More and Erasmus, St. Paul's helped to introduce the "new learning" of the Renaissance into England. During the seventeenth century it was the school of John Milton, Samuel Pepys, and the first Duke of Marlborough. Later it declined, but after Frederick William Walker was appointed headmaster in 1877, it regained its reputation as one of the leading schools in England. Its new building in Hammersmith was just at the edge of London's built-up area, and there was still open country around. St. Stephen's Avenue, where the Ghose boys lived, was about a mile to the north. The two boys came and went on foot.

Aurobindo found London "a wonderful place."[14] With a population approaching 5 million, it was the largest metropolis that ever had existed. Capital of the British Empire and the center of world trade, it was home to glittering wealth and unspeakable poverty. The Ghose boys saw little of either extreme. Most of their classmates were solidly middle class, the sons of local business-men and professionals. The way up for such boys was a scholarship to Oxford or Cambridge, and St. Paul's was just the place to secure one. As Aurobindo's younger contemporary G.K. Chesterton wrote, the school was "chiefly cel-ebrated for winning scholarships at the Universities, rather than for athletics or other forms of fame."[15] St. Paul's itself offered 153 "foundation scholarships" that exempted their holders from entrance and tuition fees. Aurobindo was awarded one in September 1884. Assigned to the upper fifth—the same form as his older brother—he spent his first months learning the elements of Greek under Walker's guidance. By Autumn 1885, the headmaster thought him ready for the upper school. Aurobindo went to the "classical side." Walker had in-troduced the teaching of science to St. Paul's, but "in those days," as Edmund Clerihew Bentley observed, science "did not really count."[16] For a university-bound boy, school meant learning Greek and Latin. Once grounded in the ba-sics, he plunged, or was pushed, into the works of the greatest authors. When Aurobindo entered the seventh form at the age of thirteen, he read Virgil and Cicero in Latin, Euripides and Xenophon in Greek. In addition he read "di-vinity"—the Greek New Testament, Anglican doctrine, and church history—as well as French literature and the works of William Shakespeare. Somewhat unusually for a boy studying classics, he also took mathematics. As for science, he once wrote—putting on the attitude that went with the opinion—"Never learned a word of chemistry or any damned science in my school. My school, sir, was too aristocratic for such plebeian things."[17]

In the beginning Aurobindo did exceptionally well. For the 1886 Christ-mas term, all of his masters gave him positive reports. Summing up, the form master wrote that he was "a very promising boy, one of the best in history."[18] Aurobindo's reports remained good for a number of years, though he could not be considered a prodigy on the basis of his class work. Only once was he near the top of his form, and he never came close to surpassing the head boy—a certain Cyril Bailey. This shows how high the standard was, however: Bailey became an internationally known classicist. Although not so much of a "swot" that he always pleased his masters, Aurobindo did impress his class-mates. In later years, several recalled his scholarly attainments. Most used the same word—"brilliant"—to describe him.[19]

In Autumn 1887, after only three years of school, Aurobindo reached the highest form. Up to this point his masters had found him hard-working and promising. Now they wrote comments such as "hardly maintains his old level" and "takes less pains, I think, than formerly."[20] Aurobindo later recalled that he was by then at ease in his classical studies and "did not think it necessary to labour over them any longer."[21] Instead, he read books not assigned in class: English and French poetry and fiction, European history. His English master was struck by the extent of his reading, and commented favorably on his writing style, "extraordinarily good" in 1887, "remarkably good" in 1888. In contrast he thought the essays of Laurence Binyon, the future poet and critic, to be "far below what was expected—often rather clap-trap."[22]

Walker and the other masters placed great importance on English style, but they thought that the right way to acquire it was to read the Greek and Latin classics and to translate them into English. This method had surprisingly good results. A number of St. Paul's students went on to become writers, and several achieved some fame. *The New Oxford Book of English Verse* includes eight poets born after William Butler Yeats (1865) and before James Joyce (1882).[23] Three of them—Binyon, Chesterton, and Edward Thomas—were contemporaries or near-contemporaries of Aurobindo's at St. Paul's.

Binyon and Manmohan, who were best friends, decided to become poets while still in school. Manmohan's efforts inspired Aurobindo to write poetry too. Most of his early attempts went into the wastepaper basket, but before he left school he produced a number of poems that he included in his first collection years later. His other activities outside the classroom were equally cerebral. He took part in the activities of the English and French debating societies, and joined the school's literary society when it was founded in 1889. At its inaugural meeting he took part in an exchange on Jonathan Swift, pointing out the inconsistencies in the satirist's political opinions. The next week the subject was Milton, and he spoke again.[24] As a rule, however, he kept to himself. Most of his classmates were too much older than he to be his friends. A few patronized him on account of his childishness; the rest paid him scant attention. He had few of the qualities that English schoolboys find interesting. Weak and inept on the playing field, he was also—by his own account—a coward and a liar. Years later, when he became known as a revolutionary leader, his former classmates could hardly believe the reports. "It would have been difficult in those days to regard him as a firebrand!" one exclaimed.[25] Another went to the trouble of informing the government that if either of the Ghose boys was involved in revolution, it must be Manmohan.[26] More demonstrative than his younger brother, Manmohan broadcast his political views, but his ardor soon cooled off. Aurobindo rarely spoke, but his conviction that he had a role in the coming transformation of India grew stronger. By the time he left school he had made a "firm decision" to work for India's liberation.[27]

While admitting in his later life that he was subject as a boy to "all human imperfections," Aurobindo drew the line at one thing: he was "not a serious prig." Neither was he a "budding yogi"; he was not even religious. He and Manmohan "were understood [by their classmates] to be Christians," but they had by then become indifferent if not openly hostile to Christianity. For a while Aurobindo considered himself an atheist before adopting an agnostic attitude. At home, he and his brothers were increasingly put off by Mrs. Drewett's "fervently Evangelical" notions. One day, after Bible reading, Manmohan let slip an injudicious comment about Moses. Outraged, the old lady cried that "she would not live with an atheist as the house might fall down on her."[28] She found another place to stay and the brothers were left alone, delighted by this turn of events. They kept the flat at 49 St. Stephen's Avenue until 1887, when they were obliged to find something cheaper.

During their first years in London, the brothers passed their summer vacations at holiday resorts. In 1885 they went to St. Bees, a place on the west coast of England renowned for its rosy cliffs. The next year, they returned to Cumberland for an extensive tour of the Lake District. To walk through the countryside immortalized by Wordsworth was a risky affair for Manmohan, who, in Aurobindo's diagnosis, suffered from "poetic illness." Once he fell behind and walked oblivious of precipices while "moaning out poetry in a deep tone." Aurobindo and Benoybhusan were glad when he made it back safely.[29] In 1887 the three brothers went to Hastings and strolled on the cliffs above the English Channel. Manmohan complained that it was "too hot to go for longer walks" and was ready to return to London earlier than planned, but as he wrote to Binyon, he and his brothers had to stay back because "money has to come from my father, before we can pay our rent here."[30]

More and more, money was becoming a problem. When Dr. Ghose left his sons in England, he arranged to provide funds for their maintenance. For some time he sent regular remittances, but he fell into arrears even before Mr. Drewett left England. In 1887 he got himself "in some financial straits," with the result that his sons' bank balance fell below ten pounds.[31] That autumn, just after the boys returned from Hastings, they moved from 49 St. Stephen's Avenue to 128 Cromwell Road, the building that housed the offices of the South Kensington branch of the Liberal Club. The club's secretary, James Cotton, brother of their father's friend Henry Cotton of the Bengal ICS, let the brothers stay in a large drafty room above the club's premises. Manmohan soon went up to Oxford, where he spent most of the money their father provided. Cotton gave Benoybhusan five shillings a week to do clerical work and odd jobs at the club. Five shillings a week was what a domestic servant earned; one needed three times as much to stay above the poverty line. Aurobindo was thus not exaggerating when he remarked years later that he and Benoy lived very spartan lives at that time. "During a whole year [1888–89] a slice or two of sandwich bread and butter and a cup of tea in the morning and in the evening a penny saveloy formed the only food."[32] For growing teenagers, this was almost a starvation diet. Aurobindo and Benoy had no wood for the fire and no overcoats to wear in what turned out to be the coldest winter in memory. As time went by, the boys at St. Paul's noticed that Aurobindo's clothing "grew more and more dirty and unkempt" and that he himself "looked more and more unhealthy and neglected."[33]

AUROBINDO WAS THE ONLY ONE of the brothers who had any hope of fulfilling his father's ambitions by entering the ICS. Manmohan was preparing himself for a career as a writer; Benoybhusan, whose education ended in Manchester, was not up to the entrance examination. Aurobindo's prospects of passing were excellent; his problems were financial, not academic. If selected for the ICS, he would have to pass his two-year probationary period as a student in an English university. He could not think of doing this without winning a full scholarship. During 1888 and 1889 he carried an unusually heavy load in the hope of scoring a double jackpot: ICS selection and an Oxbridge scholarship.

The challenge spurred him to renewed efforts. Between Autumn 1888 and Autumn 1889 his performance in every subject improved. A comment by his Greek master is typical: "Doing more & better work in every way." But this last-minute exertion was not enough to earn him a glorious exit from school. He won none of the dozen or so prizes offered in classics, and in other subjects only minor distinctions: an honorable mention in the history prize competition and a second in the contest for the Butterworth Prize, awarded "for knowledge of English literature, especially of Shakespeare."[34]

In December 1889 Aurobindo went to Cambridge to sit for the King's College scholarship examinations. Morning and evening he wrote translations from English into Latin and Greek and from Latin and Greek into English. There were also questions on classical grammar and history and an essay in English. On December 19, back in London, he learned that he had stood first. He later was told that he had "passed an extraordinarily high examination" with the best papers that the examiner, the noted scholar Oscar Browning, had ever seen.[35] Assured of a university scholarship, Aurobindo returned to school after Christmas for a last term of study before taking the ICS examination in June. The civil service commissioners would be testing the candidates' "proficiency

in subjects which . . . are included within the ordinary range of English education," meaning classics and mathematics along with English, history, European languages, and a bit of science.[36] The deck clearly was stacked in favor of
English public school boys, which was why Dr. Ghose had brought his sons
to England eleven years earlier. It was up to Aurobindo to see that his father's
financial sacrifice was not in vain.

The open competition was a monstrous, thirteen-day affair. There were two
three-hour sessions every day but the last, with oral as well as written questions in every subject but English composition. Aurobindo took ten: English
composition, English literature, English history, Greek, Latin, French, Italian, mathematics, logic, and political economy. The results were announced
in the middle of July. Aurobindo passed easily, standing 11th out of the 250
candidates.[37] Arthur Wood, a St. Paul's classmate, conceded that Aurobindo's
success was the more remarkable in that he passed "direct from school at his
first attempt." Most candidates took private tutoring after school and many
had to take the exam two or three times before they passed. Wood, who did
not get in that year, murmured that Aurobindo had succeeded "on little else
but Greek and Latin."[38] This was true—and a nice bit of irony that he shone
in the very subjects that kept most Indians out. He scored "record marks" in
the two languages, obtaining 557 out of a possible 600 in Greek and standing
second in Latin. In addition, his English composition was the eighth best and
his score in French ninth from the top. He also picked up marks in mathematics, Italian, political economy, English history, and English literature.[39]

Aurobindo left St. Paul's in July. At this time or a little earlier, he found
himself a separate flat, apparently at 28 Kempsford Gardens, Earls Court,
South Kensington.[40] Here he passed two gloriously unoccupied months before going up to Cambridge in October.

A Man and a Gentleman

When he arrived at Cambridge in October 1890, Aurobindo had lived in
England for eleven years. He had passed more than half of that time at a first-
rate public school, learning all that a well-bred Englishman was supposed to
learn. He was well prepared for his classes but, like many before and after, he
was not altogether prepared for the transition from school to university life.
Speaking to an audience of Indian students a decade later, he recalled what it
was like for a boy who left "the restricted life of his home and school," and found
himself "in surroundings which with astonishing rapidity expand his intellect,

strengthen his character, develop his social faculties, force out all his abilities and turn him in three years from a boy into a man. . . . The result is that he who entered the University a raw student, comes out of it a man and a gentleman, accustomed to think of great affairs and fit to move in cultivated society."[41]

The "surroundings" that helped transform schoolboys into gentlemen included the physical setting. At Cambridge and Oxford, Aurobindo told his audience, one "moves among ancient and venerable buildings, the mere age and beauty of which are in themselves an education."[42] This was more true of King's than most other colleges. Its grassy front court was bounded on the north by King's College Chapel, the most beautiful Gothic building in England. Opposite stood the Gothic Revival Wilkins Building, where students met their tutors, attended lectures, and dined. To the west, past the neoclassical fellows' building, was a lawn sloping down to the Cam. Across the Cam lay the Backs with their ancient elms. All around stood the twenty-odd colleges that, together with King's, made up the University of Cambridge.

As an open scholar, Aurobindo was a member of King's academic elite. The scholarship entitled him to certain privileges, such as wearing a special gown, and also to free tuition and eighty pounds a year.[43] For him this was not a token payment, but a vital source of income. His dependence on his scholarship meant that he was excluded from much of the social life of the college. The "best set" at King's came from families of wealth and standing by way of Eton. Their style of life was far beyond Aurobindo's means, and for the most part outside his interests.

Aurobindo was lodged in a building across King's Lane, which was known as the Drain because it was always wet and puddled. Shortly after he moved in, he mentioned his address while conversing with Oscar Browning, the tutor who was "the feature par excellence of King's." Hearing that Aurobindo was staying in the King's Lane building, Browning exclaimed, "That wretched hole!" and turning to another newcomer, "How rude we are to our scholars! We get great minds to come down here and shut them up in that box! I suppose it is to keep their pride down."[44] In fact, the rooms were not that bad. There was a bedroom doubling as a study, a storeroom, and a "gyp room," or kitchen, shared by two neighbors.[45] This was looked after by a gyp or servant; another attendant made sure the beds were made. Whatever an Etonian might have thought about the place, it certainly was an improvement over 128 Cromwell Road.

Although Aurobindo had come to Cambridge primarily to study the ICS curriculum, the terms of his scholarship obliged him to take the full classical course and to sit for the bachelor of arts honors examination, known at Cambridge as the Tripos. His classical studies were the sort he was familiar with from St Paul's. Twice a week he called on his tutor and received assignments, generally translations to and from Greek and Latin. He also attended lectures by members of the classical faculty. He did this less frequently than most of his classmates because his ICS subjects kept him busy. For his class on general jurisprudence he had to read theoretical texts, from Justinian's *Institutes* to Jeremy Bentham's *Theory of Legislation*. To pass in the law of evidence, he had to go through standard textbooks and attend and write up cases in London. Finally he had to master India's Hindu and Muslim codes, as well as the civil and criminal procedure of British India.[46] He also had to learn Bengali, the vernacular of the province he had been assigned to. His early efforts in the language of his parents were as clumsy as his classmates', and the teaching was not much help. The lecturer, R.M. Towers—Pundit Towers to the students—could barely speak Bengali and used outdated books as texts. Once Aurobindo and his friends brought him a work by the contemporary novelist Bankim Chandra Chatterjee. After a vain attempt to read it, the Pundit shook his head and declared, "This can't be Bengali."[47] In Sanskrit, Aurobindo could dispense with classroom instruction. He learned the language on his own "by reading the Naladamayanti episode in the *Mahabharata*," one of the assigned texts, "with minute care several times."[48] This gave him a direct initiation into the literary culture of his homeland. In history and geography he was force-fed the colonial version, reading works by James Mill, Mountstuart Elphinstone, and the like, but not one Indian. His last subject, political economy, was taught by John Neville Keynes, the father of John Maynard, who was then a child at Cambridge. His assigned reading was works by Adam Smith, J. S. Mill, and David Ricardo.[49]

The civil service commissioners required all probationers, university scholars included, to take the full ICS course and to sit for periodic and final examinations. Aurobindo had to pass these or risk being dropped from the service. This would have meant financial ruin for him and his brothers. Like other probationers, he was granted an allowance totaling £300, half given in two installments after the periodic examinations, the other half after the final. This became the Ghose brothers' principal source of income. After Dr. Ghose learned that Aurobindo had won a scholarship, he all but stopped sending money. In a letter written to his brother-in-law around this time, he boasted that Aurobindo, soon to "glorify his country by a brilliant administration," was at Cambridge, "borne there by his own ability."[50] Aurobindo had to use every penny of his scholarship money and ICS stipend to pay for meals, books, and other expenses, and to cover his brothers' needs. As a result, he was often short of funds. G.W. Prothero, a prominent historian who got to know him well, wrote in a letter of 1892:

He has had a very hard and anxious time of it for the last two years. Supplies from home have almost entirely failed, & he has had to keep his two brothers as well as himself, and yet his courage and perseverance have never failed. I have several times written to his father on his behalf, but for the most part unsuccessfully. It is only lately that I managed to extract from him enough to pay some tradesmen who would otherwise have put his son into the County Court. I am quite sure that these pecuniary difficulties were not due to any extravagance on Ghose's part: his whole way of life, which was simple and penurious in the extreme, is against this: they were due entirely to circumstances beyond his control.[51]

DESPITE HIS HEAVY LOAD and relative poverty, Aurobindo passed two happy years at Cambridge. Ten years later, he told an Indian audience: "I think there is no student of Oxford or Cambridge who does not look back in after days on the few years of his undergraduate life as, of all the scenes he has moved in, that which calls up the happiest memories."[52] Though no more outgoing at Cambridge than at St. Paul's, he did make a number of friends. Many of them were Indians, notably Keshav Ganesh Deshpande, a Maharashtrian undergraduate at St. John's College. Most of the others had Irish or continental backgrounds. One of the Irishmen, Robert Stewart Lepper, had this to say about Aurobindo: "I knew him in those days quite well, and have happy recollections of him as a brilliant young classical scholar . . . of marked literary and poetic taste, and as far as I ever saw a young man of high character and modest bearing, who was liked by all who knew him." Another fellow-student painted a less sunny picture, and also gave a hint as to why Aurobindo had few Anglo-Saxon friends:

> With regard to his life at Cambridge, a complete lack of interest in games must have lessened his enjoyment of the life of the place. His interests were in literature: among Greek poets for instance he once waxed enthusiastic over Sappho, and he had a nice feeling of English style. Yet for England itself he seemed to have small affection; it was not only the climate that he found trying: as an example, he became quite indignant when on one occasion I called England the modern Athens. This title, he declared, belonged to France: England much more resembled Corinth, a commercial state, and therefore unattractive to him.[53]

Aurobindo just did not like the English. Though he kept up cordial relations with individuals, he developed "a strong hatred" of Englishmen in general.[54] His contempt for a culture he considered philistine and shallow was only part of the reason. More important was his growing understanding of the nature of British rule in India. At Cambridge he began to express the nationalist feelings he had kept hidden at St. Paul's. As a member of the Indian Majlis, a club for students from the subcontinent, he delivered what he later termed "revolutionary speeches" decrying British imperialism.[55] If some jottings found in one of his notebooks are any indication, his "revolutionary" thoughts were rather temperate:

> The patriot who passes judgment on a great movement in an era of change and turmoil, should be very confident that he has something worth saying before he ventures to speak; but if he can really put some new aspect on a momentous question or emphasize any side of it that has not been clearly understood, it [is] his bounden duty however obscure he may be to ventilate [it.][56]

AUROBINDO'S READING AT CAMBRIDGE went far beyond the confines of his classical and ICS courses. Fluent in four languages and proficient in three or four others, he ranged over the whole of Western literature: Homer, Aeschylus, Catullus, Virgil, Dante, Racine, Shakespeare, Milton. He also read some Greek philosophers, notably Plato and Epictetus. Years later he still considered two of the Platonic dialogues he read at Cambridge, the *Republic* and the *Symposium,* to be among humanity's "highest points of thought and literature." Despite this, he read "only extracts" from Plato's other works, "and made no study of Greek philosophy" as a whole.[57] Modern philosophy interested him even less. The German Idealists, particularly Hegel, were in vogue at that time, attracting, among others, Trinity College undergraduate Bertrand Russell.[58] Aurobindo did not share in the general enthusiasm. He once "read, not Hegel, but a small book on Hegel, but it left no impression" on him. He also "tried once a translation of Kant but dropped it after the first two pages and never tried again." What little he learned of Western philosophy he "picked up desultorily in [his] general reading."[59]

Prothero noted that Aurobindo "possessed a knowledge of English Literature far beyond the average of undergraduates" and, perhaps as a result, "wrote a much better English style than most young Englishmen."[60] Among English poets, he continued to prefer the early nineteenth-century Romantics: William Wordsworth, Lord Byron, Shelley, John Keats.[61] He also read the works of Alfred Tennyson and Robert Browning and other Victorian poets such as William Morris. His favorite contemporary writer was George Meredith, who then was approaching the crest of a reputation that would soon decline sharply. In those days, recalled E.M. Forster—a Kingsman seven years Aurobindo's junior—Meredith was looked on as "a spiritual power," before whom "much of the universe and all Cambridge trembled."[62] Aurobindo was among his votaries. He considered him a "supreme genius" among novelists on the strength of *The Ordeal of Richard Feverel* and, after reading *Modern Love*, ranked him high as a poet as well.[63] Aurobindo also admired the works of Stephen Phillips, once thought of as one of England's leading poets though now completely forgotten. Phillips was a cousin of Manmohan's friend Laurence Binyon. Through this connection Aurobindo got to read Phillips's blank-verse narratives *Marpessa* and *Christ in Hades* in manuscript. They made a "considerable impression" on him while he was developing his own style.[64]

Many of the poems Aurobindo published in *Songs to Myrtilla* (1898) must have been written at Cambridge, though only one has a date that makes this certain. "Charles Stewart Parnell" was written in 1891, just after the Irish leader's death. "Hic Jacet: Glasnevin Cemetery" commemorates the same event. Both poems laud Parnell as an enemy of the British, and lament the vagaries of fate that cast him down at the height of his power. "The Lost Deliverer" similarly blames fate, and a woman's betrayal, for the death of Ferdinand Lassalle, the German socialist leader.[65]

Women brought disaster to Parnell and Lassalle just as they brought suffering to Meredith's heroes. But woman, in the abstract, was an object of adoration for the writer of *Songs to Myrtilla*. A good half of the poems in *Songs to Myrtilla* are on the theme of love, but it was a rarefied sort of eros that Aurobindo celebrated. Poems like "The Lover's Complaint" and "Love in Sorrow," conventional in form and language, are clearly not the records of actual attachments. One would be ill-advised to read them, as one of Aurobindo's biographers did, as confessions of infatuations with a half-dozen girls.[66] Still, memory may sometimes have cued his imagination. "Edith," whom he addresses in "Night by the Sea" ("Kiss me, Edith. Soon the night / Comes and hides the happy light"),[67] was the name of Mr. Drewett's young sister-in-law, who lived with the family in Manchester. Aurobindo had ample occasion to meet women at Cambridge, in London, and at holiday resorts, but he does not seem to have spent much time with them. He was attracted by feminine beauty, however, praising it lavishly in poems like "Estelle": "Turn hither for felicity," he tells the lady with the star-like eyes, "My body's earth thy vernal power declares."[68] A prose-poem from a Cambridge notebook is even more sensuous, but it is a stylized literary sensuousness, in the manner of the Song of Solomon:

Like a white statue made of lilies
Her eyes were hidden jewels beneath scabbards of black silk. Her shoulders
moonlit mountain-slopes when they are coated with new-fallen snow: her
breasts two white apples odoπrous with the sweet fragrance of girlhood,
her body a heap of silk in a queen's closet, her legs were marble pillars very
clear-cut, her face ivory flushed by the dawn.[69]

The same notebook contains the beginnings of a philosophical dialogue
on love with a capital L. Borrowing the scene as well as the theme of Plato's
Symposium, Aurobindo brought together a group of young Europeans—some
dull English men and women, a couple of Frenchmen, and two representatives
of the Celtic fringe—at a banquet with "the wine in lively progress around the
table." The talk turns to love. Powell the Welshman rhapsodizes on the subject.
The others trade witty aphorisms. Finally mysterious silent Ella blurts out that
love "is the sole motive of man's existence." The company laughs tenderly "as
of disillusioned September lenient to the emerald hopes of April." The women
leave, and the dialogue breaks off.[70]

Aurobindo returned to the same theme and form in his most considerable
Cambridge work, an incomplete dialogue called *The Harmony of Virtue*. In this
Platonic imitation, a Cambridge undergraduate named Keshav Ganesh Desai converses with three British fellow students. Aurobindo borrowed his chief
character's name from his friend Keshav Ganesh Deshpande, but Desai's opinions and wit clearly are Aurobindo's. The brilliant and charming Indian leads
his obtuse English companions on a "voyage of discovery" in search of "some
law, or should I not say rather some indicating tendency by which we may arrive
at a principle of life." His aim is to find the basis of morality ("virtue"), and the
path he follows is that of beauty. After considering the then-fashionable doctrine of utilitarianism—he had read Bentham "very carefully" but rejected the
facile notion of the greatest good for the greatest number—Desai goes on to
explore the ethical implications of beauty. Along the way he indulges in much
high thinking, but has a habit of getting lost on discursive bypaths. His conclusions, however, are clear. Men are to seek "virtue," not conventional morality but
"the perfect evolution by the human being of the inborn qualities and powers
native to his personality." These, "in their evolved perfection," are both beautiful
and harmonious. It is the task of each individual to develop them "and acquire
by a life of perfect beauty the peace of God that passeth all understanding."[71]

IN THE FIRST PERIODIC EXAMINATION, held in March 1891, Aurobindo
stood twenty-third of the forty-six ICS candidates. This was enough to keep

him a probationer in good standing, but it was a sharp drop from his entering rank. Six months later, in the second periodic examination, a dramatic improvement in Sanskrit brought his overall position to nineteenth. Meanwhile he was doing well in his classical studies. In 1891 he was named joint winner of the annual Rawley Prize for the best composition in Greek iambics.[72] The next year he shared the same prize with another student, carried off singly the prize for Latin hexameters, and was awarded forty pounds' worth of books for his performance in the college examinations. He won even greater distinction in the far more important university honors examinations: a first class (third division).[73] Even an unfriendly fellow-student had to admit that it was "probably only the fact that, to satisfy the regulations of the Indian Civil Service, he had to take the University Tripos after two years (instead of the usual three) prevented him from being in the top division of the First Class in the final test."[74] With the Tripos behind him, all that remained for him to do was to finish the ICS formalities. Then he would be given his first posting in India.

Transitions

Aurobindo left King's with a first class in the Tripos but no degree. He could have received one simply by residing at Cambridge for another year but, as a successful ICS candidate, he had neither the time nor the need to continue his studies. He seems nevertheless to have considered staying on. Had he done so, one of his classmates wrote, he was "certain of a very good degree and a fellowship, with which prospect he was understood to be quite content."[75] A fellowship, followed by an academic career, would certainly have been more to his liking than the ICS grind he seemed doomed to. His interests lay not in administration, but "in poetry and literature and the study of languages and patriotic action."[76] He would have to put all of it aside if he entered the ICS. As a magistrate or judge, he would pass his days making rounds, writing reports, and trying petty cases. His superiors and most of his colleagues would be Britons who had been educated solely to pass the ICS examinations. Successful candidates were reputed to be "the pick of the young men who qualify for our Civil Service at home as well as abroad."[77] Looking around him in the classroom, Aurobindo arrived at a different assessment:

A shallow schoolboy stepping from a cramming establishment to the command of high and difficult affairs, can hardly be expected to give us anything magnificent or princely. Still less can it be expected when the sons of small tradesmen are suddenly promoted from the counter to govern great provinces.... Bad in training, void of culture, in instruction poor, it is in plain truth a sort of education that leaves him with all his original imperfections on his head, unmannerly, uncultivated, unintelligent.[78]

Aurobindo the classicist, poet, and patriot evidently felt superior to the mediocre representatives of the philistine race he found himself among. Yet he might have been willing to toil in the ICS if he believed that it was the best way an Indian could serve his country, as members of his father's generation believed. So far he had never questioned his father's choice of career for him. He was, he later said, "too young to understand" what the ICS was all about. Now, a few months from his first posting, he discovered he had "a disgust for [the] administrative life."[79] But he could not disappoint his father. Dr. Ghose had already arranged with his friend Henry Cotton to get Aurobindo posted in the desirable district of Arrah, and was looking forward impatiently to his third son's return.

When Aurobindo went down to London in May or June 1892, it was with the idea of going through the last ICS formalities and booking his passage to India. He had a month and a half to prepare for the final examination, which was held in mid-July. He does not appear to have used the time to his advantage, for he did badly, falling to thirty-seventh place out of forty-four. Even in Sanskrit he finished in the lower half of his class, and in Bengali he did worse than all but one of his classmates.[80] Still he passed, and at this point that was all that mattered.

One last hurdle remained. The printed table of the results of the final examination has this footnote: "Those candidates opposite whose names the letter P occurs have passed the examination in Riding in a satisfactory manner. Mr. Aravinda Acroyd Ghose had not passed this Examination at the time of going to press."[81] His is the only name without a P. This deficiency, and another one, were also noticed in a departmental letter of August 24: "Messrs MacIver and A.A. Ghose have still to satisfy the Commissioners of their eligibility in respect of health and the latter gentleman has still to pass in riding."[82] According to a classmate, Aurobindo failed to pass his medical examination the first time around on account of "something found wrong with his urinary organs." He was "given a year's grace to improve," and when he was reexamined his health was judged acceptable.[83] Now all that remained was the riding examination.

Aurobindo did not know how to ride. He had taken a few lessons at Cambridge, but never learned much. As a result, he failed his first two trials, once by falling off the horse and once by not presenting himself.[84] After the final examination, he and the other bad horsemen were given one last trial. He again failed to appear, but two days later sent a medical certificate by way of explanation. Twice in August 1892, the civil service commissioners wrote to ask him when he wished to be examined. He left both letters unanswered, and for a month and a half, heard nothing more from them.

ONCE HE HAD PASSED the final ICS examination, Aurobindo had few responsibilities and could spend much of his time reading. His growing interest in his homeland made him turn more and more to books about Indian culture. In one of his Cambridge ICS courses he had read "a brief and very scanty and bare statement of the 'six philosophies' of India."[85] He was particularly interested in Vedanta, a philosophy based on the Upanishads. Intrigued by the Vedantic concept of *atman,* the individual self that is one with the transcendent spirit, or *brahman,* he turned to the Upanishads themselves. The archaic language in which they are written was too much for his ICS Sanskrit, so he had to rely on the English translations of the Oxford professor F. Max Müller.[86] Reading Müller's rendering of the *Isha Upanishad,* Aurobindo came across this classic explanation of the self:

> It stirs and it stirs not; it is far, and likewise near. It is inside all this, and
>   it is outside all this.
> And he who beholds all beings in the Self, and the Self in all beings, he
>   never turns away from it.
> When to a man who understands, the Self has become all things, what
>   sorrow, what trouble, can there be to him who once beheld that
>   unity?[87]

In Müller's preface, Aurobindo read: "Beyond the Aham or Ego, with all its accidents and limitations, such as sex, sense, language, country, and religion, the ancient sages of India perceived, from a very early time, the Âtman or the self, independent of all such accidents."[88] An admirer of Plato, even an agnostic one, could not but be attracted to this idea. Years later Aurobindo remarked that after reading Müller's translations, he had a "mental realisation" of the truth behind the concept of the self: "It was borne in upon his mind that here might be a true clue to the reality behind life and the world. He made a strong and very crude mental attempt to realize what this Self or Atman might be, to convert the abstract idea into a concrete and living reality in his own consciousness."[89]

If he found much to admire in Müller's renderings, Aurobindo was infuriated by the professor's asides on Indian civilization. As Müller wrote in his introduction, "I confess it has been for many years a problem to me . . . how the Sacred Books of the East should, by the side of so much that is fresh, natural, simple, beautiful, and true, contain so much that is not only unmeaning, artificial, and silly, but even hideous and repellent."[90] To which Aurobindo replied,

> Now I am myself only a poor coarseminded Oriental and therefore not disposed to deny the gross physical facts of life & nature. . . . This perhaps is the reason why I am somewhat at a loss to imagine what the Professor found in the Upanishads that is hideous and repellent. Still I was brought up almost from my infancy in England and received an English education, so that sometimes I have glimmerings.[91]

He was aware that European claims of cultural superiority went hand in hand with Europe's political domination of Asia. His own belief that Asian and particularly Indian culture was superior to anything in Europe grew in tandem with his conviction that India had to throw off the British yoke. He had no time for those who believed that radical political change could come about by parliamentary means. That summer, the Indian student community was excited about the campaign of Dadabhai Naoroji, a Bombay businessman turned Liberal politician, who was contesting a parliamentary seat. Aurobindo was unmoved when Naoroji pipped his rival in the election that brought Gladstone back to power. More to his taste was a meeting held a short while later, when he, his brothers, and some of their friends established a secret society called the Lotus and Dagger. Each member "vowed to work for the liberation of India"—but the group had no second meeting.[92]

IN OCTOBER, the ICS commissioners wrote Aurobindo asking him to fix a date to take his riding examination. He agreed to go on October 26, but did not turn up. An official then asked him to meet the riding instructor to make another appointment. He did not bother to see the man. Called to the office to explain, Aurobindo told a series of lies. The senior examiner heard him out, then said that he would give him one more chance: Aurobindo had to meet him on the platform of Charing Cross Station at 2:15 on November 15. The two would go to Woolwich, where Aurobindo would be examined. Aurobindo went neither to Charing Cross nor to Woolwich. Two days later he was told that he had been rejected from the service.[93]

There the matter would have ended if two English well-wishers had not taken up his case. Family friend James Cotton went to the Civil Service Commission, where he learned that Aurobindo's only hope was to write the secretary of state for India. His letter, stiff and formal, reads as though it had been dictated by Cotton. Aurobindo concluded that if given another chance, it would be "the object of [his] life to remember it in the faithful performance of my duties in the Civil Service of India"[94]—a phrase that must have stuck in his craw. Cotton sent this letter to the secretary of state, along with one of his own and one from Aurobindo's tutor G.W. Prothero. The file then made the rounds: from the secretary of state's office to the civil service commissioners to the India Office to the secretary of state and back again to the commissioners, who refused to reconsider the case. Finally, on the recommendation of George W.E. Russell, the parliamentary under-secretary of state for India, the case went before the secretary of state, John Wodehouse, First Earl of Kimberley. A powerful member of Gladstone's cabinet, Kimberley had many more important matters to deal with that day. He knew nothing about Aurobindo, but had clear views about the importance of riding. Informed the previous June about the poor horsemanship of some ICS recruits, he had written: "No candidate ought to be allowed to go out to India who cannot ride."[95] After leafing through Aurobindo's file, he declined to intervene, noting: "If the Sec^y of State sets a precedent of interfering with the Commissioners' discretion nothing but confusion can result. I rest my decision solely on this ground." He added, however, "I should very much doubt whether Mr Ghose w^d be a desirable addition to the Service and if Mr Prothero or anyone else is under the impression that a Hindoo ought to have a special exemption from the requirement of being able to ride, the sooner he is disabused of such an absurd notion the better."[96] That was the end of it. On December 7, Russell wrote to Aurobindo informing him officially that he would not be appointed to the ICS.

Aurobindo's rejection from the ICS was much commented on during his lifetime and has been much analyzed since. Trying to clear up the controversy fifty years after the event, he wrote that he managed "by certain manoeuvres," to "get himself disqualified for riding without himself rejecting the Service, which his family would not have allowed him to do."[97] This is consistent with his behavior in October and November 1892, in particular his failure to go to Charing Cross. He spent that afternoon, he explained on another occasion, "wandering in the streets of London to pass the time." Returning home, he announced to Benoybhusan: "I am chucked." Benoy proposed playing a game of cards. When Manmohan came in, he found his brothers thus engaged. Learning what had happened, he began to berate them for playing cards when such a calamity had happened. But it was not a calamity to Aurobindo, who was, he later wrote, "greatly relieved and overjoyed by his release from the I.C.S."[98]

To these accounts dating from the 1940s must be added an earlier one that is less well known. Asked about his rejection by a newspaper reporter in 1909, Aurobindo replied candidly: "I failed in the final for the Civil Service ... because I could not ride." He added: "If I was not actually glad, I was certainly not disappointed because the Civil Service was barred to me. I have never been fond of constraint of any sort and I was really not sorry to forego the service."[99] This suggests that Aurobindo's "manoeuvres" may have been less premeditated than they appear in his later accounts, but it supports his assertion that he had no desire to join the ICS.

When Aurobindo became famous as a revolutionary politician, many Britons assumed that it was his rejection from the ICS that "turned him against government."[100] This certainly was not so. His opposition to British rule took form long before he was rejected. Equally unfounded is the claim that his radical views contributed to his rejection. Aurobindo was once informed that the "revolutionary speeches" he made at Cambridge "were recorded as a black mark against him by the India Office" and "had their part in determining the authorities to exclude him from the Indian Civil Service."[101] There is no hint of any such black mark in the India Office correspondence. He was rejected simply because he did not pass the riding examination. He was not given another chance to pass because he did not follow instructions, keep appointments, or tell the truth. That said, it must be added that few men in Whitehall wanted "natives of India" to join the ICS. Less than a year after turning down Aurobindo's petition, Lord Kimberley wrote: "It is indispensable that an adequate number of the members of the Civil Service shall always be Europeans." Lord Lansdowne, the incumbent Viceroy, agreed with him on "the absolute necessity of keeping the government of this widespread Empire in European hands, if that Empire is to be maintained."[102]

In late November 1892, when it seemed likely that Aurobindo would be rejected, James Cotton learned that Sayajirao Gaekwar, the maharaja of the state of Baroda, would be stopping briefly in London. Using his India Office connections, Cotton obtained an interview with the Gaekwar, as he was called. Toward the end of the month, Cotton, Benoybhusan, and Aurobindo met the young prince at the Savoy. Cotton did most of the talking. The Gaekwar asked what sort of salary they were thinking of. Cotton proposed 200 rupees per month. The Gaekwar accepted, and later "went about telling people that he had got a Civil Service man for Rs. 200."[103] A week or so later, Aurobindo learned that his petition to Kimberley had been rejected. The Gaekwar's offer was now his best option.

Dr. ghose knew nothing about the events of November and December that would change the course of his son's life. Certain that Aurobindo would soon be coming to India, he took leave from his work in the beginning of September and in the words of his friend Brajendranath De, went to "meet him in Bombay and bring him back in triumph." The doctor was away for more than a month, "but he could not get any definite news as to when [Aurobindo] was coming," and toward the end of October, he "returned from Bombay in a very depressed frame of mind."[104] De, the magistrate and collector of Khulna, Bengal, where Ghose was then posted, had a great deal of admiration for the doctor. An excellent civil surgeon with a practice extending into neighboring districts, Dr. Ghose had in addition "considerable administrative ability," serving as chairman of the Khulna municipality, vice-chairman of the district board, and honorary magistrate. All in all, he was as active in local government as an Indian man could be, and the people of the district respected and loved him. On the other hand, De observed, the doctor had "made rather a mess of his [personal] life." To begin with, he was separated from his wife. After returning to India in 1880, Swarnalotta had gone to live in Deoghar, a hill resort in Bihar where her parents had settled the previous year. Too eccentric to stay in the family home, she was given a cottage in Rohini, a village a few miles outside of town. Here she lived with her daughter Sarojini and son Barin, both of whom she mistreated. Swarnalotta seems to have suffered from what we now would call manic-depressive psychosis.[105] "Storms of rage and storms of joy came alternately to the madwoman," Barin later wrote. "During her happy moods she would laugh and laugh to herself and babble uncontrollably. In her rage she would pace around the room like a caged tigress roaring at someone."[106] When her anger became intense, she beat the children mercilessly. Her husband managed to persuade her to give up Sarojini, but she kept possession of Barin until Dr. Ghose stole him away. He placed the two children in the care of a woman he had set up in a house in Calcutta. Such arrangements were common among men of his class, but this did not make it any more acceptable to his in-laws. They went so far as to blame Swarnalotta's insanity on his unfaithfulness, though it clearly was the other way around.[107] Every week or so, Dr. Ghose came into town to see his lady-friend and his children, but he remained a lonely, unhappy man, and tended to drink too much.

Sometime around the beginning of December, Dr. Ghose received a telegram from his agents in Bombay that contained bad news about his son. According to De, it was something "to the effect that his son's name did not appear on the list of the passengers by the steamer on which he had been expecting his son to come out to India." Another version, communicated later to Aurobindo, was that the telegram announced that the steamer the doctor expected Aurobindo to be traveling by had sunk and Aurobindo had drowned. This story is at least possible. A steamer bound for Bombay went down off Portugal on October 28, with the loss of all but nine of her passengers and crew.[108] Whatever the contents of the telegram, they were fatal to the doctor. De, who expected him for dinner that evening, was called to his bedside and found him "very ill and quite unconscious." He "lingered on for a day or two" before dying, probably on December 11, at the age of forty-eight.[109]

It is impossible to gauge the effect of the news of his father's death on Aurobindo. One can get a hint from a passage in a letter written fourteen years later: Aurobindo could not doubt his father's "affection for me, since it was the false report of my death which killed him." Four decades after that, he wrote that his father had died "uttering his [Aurobindo's] name in lamentation."[110] This anecdote, which Aurobindo must have heard on his return from England, is almost certainly fictitious. No member of the family was present in Khulna. De, who left the only eyewitness account, does not mention any last words. But it is interesting that Aurobindo accepted the story and recounted it as fact a half-century later.

If Aurobindo had given any thought to returning to Cambridge and getting a degree, his father's death ended that possibility. With what was left of his ICS stipend, he booked passage on the *Carthage*, a mail-steamer of the Peninsular and Oriental line. On January 11, 1893 he boarded the ship at the Royal Albert Dock.[111] Two weeks later, after a sometimes stormy crossing of the Mediterranean, the ship reached Port Said. To travelers of the time, the seaport at the head of the Suez Canal marked the beginning of the Orient. It also marked an invisible social frontier: "the social estrangement between the two races rapidly increases after Port Said is left," remarked one contemporary traveler.[112] In Victorian England there was comparatively little racial discrimination. Once or twice Aurobindo had been followed through the streets by rowdies crying "Blackie, Blackie," but he had always been treated as a gentleman by well-bred Englishmen.[113] The English in India went by a different code. A native was a native, whether he had a university education or not.

One cannot say whether Aurobindo got his first taste of Anglo-Indian condescension while the *Carthage* sailed from Egypt to Bombay. If he did, he may have found it surprising, but not painful. He did not care for the British or their island, and had no regrets on leaving. He had no ties to the country other than his attachment to "English and European thought and literature,"[114] but even this he was ready to put behind him. In a poem marking what he later called the "transition from one culture to another," he wrote of turning from "Sicilian olive-groves," "Athenian lanes," and the slopes of Parnassus to "regions of eternal snow" and the "Ganges pacing to the southern sea."[115]

Before leaving India for England in 1879, Aurobindo had had a dream in which a mantle of darkness descended on him. As the *Carthage* neared India, it seemed to him that this darkness was lifted away. A few days later, when he stood on Indian soil for the first time in fourteen years, he felt, amid the hustle and bustle of the pier, a "sense of calm and vastness pervading everywhere."[116]

3. Encountering India

Baroda, 1893–1906

.

In England he had received, according to his father's express instructions, an entirely occidental education without any contact with the culture of India and the East. At Baroda he made up the deficiency, learned Sanskrit and several modern Indian languages, assimilated the spirit of Indian civilisation and its forms past and present.

Mr. Ghose

Aurobindo arrived at Bombay on February 6, 1893 and reached Baroda two days later.[1] He found that the capital of the Gaekwar's realm was a thoroughly Indian city. A contemporary British visitor strolling through the town's bazaar was struck by "the open booths, the all but nude men, women and children squatting amongst the merchandise, the crowds, the noise." It all bore, he noted with some surprise, "no trace of the British Raj."[2] Aurobindo would have been equally bemused on his first shopping expedition. He did not know any of the local languages and was just as unaccustomed to seeing lightly clad people sitting on the ground selling vegetables. But he would have found the lack of British influence refreshing. From the very beginning of his stay, he discovered that he had a "natural attraction to Indian culture and ways of life and a temperamental feeling and preference for all that was Indian."[3] Entering slowly into the flow of Indian life, he felt no need to consciously "renationalize" himself. He kept his suit, his shoes and socks, his public-school accent—but he did drop his English middle name. From the time of his arrival in Baroda, he became known as Mr. Arvind A. Ghose.

Baroda was able to keep its Indian character because it was under Indian rule. The Gaekwar's domain was one of the largest of the country's 600-odd "native states," semi-independent principalities that recognized the suzerainty of the British crown. The arrangement was mutually beneficial. Lacking the manpower to administrate a subcontinent ten times its size, Britain imposed so-called subsidiary alliances on most Indian territories that came under its sway after 1766. The affected states were allowed to conduct their internal affairs as they pleased, but they were forced to accept the protection of the paramount power. Free from the threat of external aggression and internal intrigue, the maharajas, rajas, ranas, and nawabs passed their days in a bejeweled time warp. They held *darbars* to receive the nobility's pledges of fealty, rode during festivals on the backs of caparisoned elephants, played polo, shot tigers, ran after women, and spent their household funds with an extravagance that few millionaires could equal. All the while, their impoverished subjects never ceased to adore them.

The Gaekwar family had ruled much of Gujarat since the eighteenth century, but Sayajirao III had not been born a prince. His predecessor, Malharrao, was deposed by the government of India for gross mismanagement and misconduct. Adopted by the dowager maharani, Sayajirao was placed on the throne at the age of twelve. Before assuming full powers in 1881, he studied with an English tutor while a British-appointed minister ran the state. Overseas journeys introduced him to the efficiency and luxury of the West. During his third European trip, the thirty-year-old ruler met and employed Aurobindo Ghose.

In his first work order, dated February 18, 1893, Aurobindo was "instructed to work as an attaché in the Settlement Department."[4] He passed his first year in undocumented obscurity, learning the basics of land assessment and plowing through piles of routine paperwork. In the beginning of 1894 he spent some time in a village called Gojaria, which he described in a letter as "an exceedingly out of the way place, without any post-office within fifteen miles of it."[5] He was glad when he returned to the more civilized grind of Baroda. In March 1894 he was transferred to the revenue department. Still a probationer, his salary remained at two hundred rupees. For the next two years he moved around the department, from the revenue stamps office to the central revenue office, with a spell in the office of the local administrator.[6] He found the work in all of these places exceedingly boring. By the end of 1894 he was so fed up that he applied, unsuccessfully, for the post of principal of a college in another state.[7]

UNINTERESTED IN HIS WORK, he found stimulation in his studies. On March 18, 1893, just a month after his return from England, he began a verse translation of the *Mahabharata*. Before breaking off the next month, he had completed two chapters and part of a third. That is rather quick translation, and the result is both readable and faithful to the text. His next important writings of the period are a series of essays on Indian politics. It did not take him long to find out that few people in India shared his passion for radical political change. The public life of the country, such as it was, was dominated by opportunistic members of the emerging middle class. These men knew as little about the life of the masses as did the Britons they imitated in speech, manners, and dress. Innocent of the realities of British political life, they spoke of the British parliament in terms that would have made an English schoolboy smile. "The British House of Commons," proclaimed Surendranath Banerjea, was "the palladium of English Liberty, the sanctuary of the free and brave," upon whose "liberty-loving instincts" the Indian people could rely.[8] Aurobindo had followed English politics for almost a decade, watching the Tories, then the Liberals, make a mess of the Irish problem, and he knew that what Banerjea said was bunk. In Summer 1893 he was given an opportunity to share his insights with others.

K.G. Deshpande, his best friend at Cambridge, had become the editor of the English pages of *Indu Prakash*, a "weekly journal of literature, politics, commerce and news" published from Bombay. Deshpande invited Aurobindo to contribute an essay. He agreed, and his "India and the British Parliament" was published in June. At that moment, people in India were ecstatic over a snap parliamentary vote that favored simultaneous examinations for the ICS in India and England. Aurobindo explained that this was simply "a chance vote snatched by a dexterous minority from a meagre and listless House," which no more expressed "the real feeling of the English people than a decree of the Chinese Emperor would express it."[9] After throwing a little light on the way parliament worked, he concluded with a statement of his own political gospel: "We must no longer hold out supplicating hands to the English Parliament, like an infant crying to its nurse for a toy, but must recognise the hard truth that every nation must beat out its own path to salvation with pain and difficulty, and not rely on the tutelage of another."[10]

Deshpande was delighted with Aurobindo's piece and persuaded him to write more. A month later, Aurobindo submitted the first of a series of essays entitled *New Lamps for Old*. He took as his subject the institution that in theory embodied the political life of the country: the Indian National Congress. Conceived in 1885 by Allan O. Hume, a former British Civilian, the Congress was meant to be, in Hume's words, a "safety valve for the escape of great and growing forces" of discontent in the country.[11] Each year, the English-educated elite assembled at the end of December and let off steam for a few days. A typical session of Congress consisted of a ceremonial opening with a welcoming speech by a local dignitary, followed by an immensely long address by the president of the session. The next day a batch of resolutions formulated by the subjects committee were proposed, seconded, and approved by a passive assembly. Another round of speeches brought the proceedings to a pompous close. The resolutions were meant for the consideration of the government, but the rulers took no notice of them and held the Congress in contempt. During the first twenty years of its existence, the organization passed scores of resolutions, but with one exception, "not even a courteous reply was vouchsafed to any of them," as onetime Congress president A.C. Mazumdar admitted.[12] The exception was a superficial restructuring of the legislative councils in 1892, characterized by Aurobindo in "India and the British Parliament" as "nothing short of an insult to the people of India."[13]

Aurobindo returned to the same topic in the first installment of *New Lamps for Old*, describing the enlarged councils—the Congress's great success—as a "conjuring trick." "Over the rest of our political action," he continued, "the only epitaph we can write is 'Failure.'" It was time for Indians to drop their naïve ideas about the unselfishness of British politicians, stop fawning over the Queen-Empress ("an old lady so called by way of courtesy") and Prime Minister ("an astute and plausible man"), and deal squarely with the problems confronting them. "Our actual enemy," he insisted, "is not any force exterior to ourselves, but our own crying weakness, our cowardice, our selfishness, our hypocrisy, our purblind sentimentalism." Brushing aside the objection that public criticism would weaken the movement, he came out with this indictment: "I say, of the Congress, then, this,—that its aims are mistaken, that the spirit in which it proceeds towards their accomplishment is not a spirit of sincerity and whole-heartedness, and that the methods it has chosen are not the right methods, and the leaders in whom it trusts, not the right sort of men to be leaders." The Congress was not a popular body and had never tried to become one. The "real key of the situation" was not the "educated class" but "the proletariate"—by which he meant the lower classes in a general, not a Marxist, sense. Against stock Congress arguments favoring British-style constitutional agitation, he held up the example of the French Revolution. Seven centuries of glacial parliamentary development in England had done less than five years of "blood and fire" in France.[14]

The content and tone of Aurobindo's articles would not have been out of place in a London newspaper, but in the timid little world of Indian journalism, they stood out too much. One of Deshpande's predecessors as English editor of *Indu Prakash* was Mahadev Govind Ranade, a High Court judge and social reformer who was the éminence grise of the Congress movement. After reading one or two installments of *New Lamps for Old*, Ranade told the owner of the newspaper that the articles could land him in jail. Alarmed, the owner told Deshpande to stop the series. Deshpande argued in support of Aurobindo, and "it was finally concluded that the tone [of the articles] should be moderated, the substance made more academic and the thus moderated articles could then continue."[15] Aurobindo cooperated for a while, but soon lost interest. His articles came out less and less frequently, and finally stopped.

The last installment of *New Lamps for Old* was published in March 1894. For the next sixty years the articles languished unread in the files of *Indu Prakash*. Rediscovered and republished in the 1950s, they have been cited by historians as early examples of the aggressive nationalism that eventually turned Congress into an effective political instrument. Reading such appraisals, it is easy to forget that the articles attracted only fugitive notice in Bombay and had little direct impact on the development of Indian political discourse. Nevertheless, they are of great historical interest because they anticipate some of the most important strands of Indian nationalist thought. Indians had to "cease to hanker after the soiled crumbs which England may cast to us from her table," and take the reins of their destiny in their own hands. This demand for self-help, as it later would be called, was not associated with exclusionary chauvinism, but a broadminded cosmopolitanism. "Even if we are ambitious to conserve what is sound and beneficial in our indigenous civilization," Aurobindo wrote, "we can only do so by assisting very largely the influx of Occidentalism." But the primary need was for action. Aurobindo could not be explicit about the sort of action he was thinking of in a newspaper article, but his repeated references to eighteenth- and nineteenth-century France make it clear that he favored revolution. Finally, he identified the masses as the agent of the needed change. With the proletariat, he wrote "resides, whether we like it or not, our sole assurance of hope, our sole chance in the future."[16] Few other members of the educated middle class were willing to give any serious thought to the importance of the lower classes. But it was not until the masses entered the Congress a quarter-century later that the Indian national movement began to produce results.

AUROBINDO HAD TO WAIT until the beginning of 1894 to become acquainted with his family in Bengal. Leaving Baroda toward the end of January, he went to Ajmer to spend a day with Benoybhusan. From there he continued his journey across the Rajasthan plateau into the fertile plains of the north. Reaching Bihar, he changed to a small branch line that ascended the Rajmahal Hills to Deoghar. In this small town his grandfather Rajnarain was passing the evening of his life. Devoted to the Upanishads, he took equal delight in the poetry of Hafiz and the meditations of Madame Guyon. Pilgrims on the way to Deoghar's Baidyanath temple often stopped at the house of this "Hindu Brahmo," as he sometimes was called, to pay their respects.[17]

Aurobindo was surrounded on his arrival by a horde of female relatives, most of whom he never had met. He stood abashed until rescued by Rajnarain, who gave him a bear hug and led him to safety. Aurobindo was, his sister Sarojini concluded, a "very shy person." After he had settled in, he was taken to the village of Rohini to meet his mother. At first Swarnalotta did not recognize him. "My Aurobindo was small," she said, "he wasn't so big." Then suddenly she remembered: "My Aurobindo had a cut on his finger." Aurobindo had a scar on his finger where he had cut himself as a child; this was shown to her, and she recognized her son.[18]

For all intents and purposes Aurobindo was an orphan. It would not have been surprising if he had gradually lost contact with his family, but instead, he developed warm relations with his grandfather, his sister Sarojini, and his younger brother Barin, as well as aunts, uncles, nieces, nephews, cousins, and other relatives for which English has no name. Fourteen-year-old Barin found his *sejda* (third-eldest brother) "a strange friend . . . at once a playmate and a guide, with a quiet and absorbed look and almost always lost in deep study." Sarojini was captivated by his "delicate face" and "long mane of hair cut in the English fashion," but she found it hard to penetrate his reserve, and harder to communicate when she did.[19] He had received a letter in Bengali from her before he left Baroda, but could make out only its general sense. After he returned to Gujarat, Sarojini wrote him again, and he sent her a charming reply in English that she could hardly have understood:

It will be, I fear, quite impossible to come to you again so early as the Puja [autumn holidays], though if I only could, I should start tomorrow. Neither my affairs, nor my finances will admit of it. Indeed it was a great mistake for me to go at all; for it has made Baroda quite intolerable to me. There is an old story about Judas Iscariot, which suits me down to the ground. Judas, after betraying Christ, hanged himself and went to Hell where he was honoured with the hottest oven in the whole establishment. Here he must burn for ever and ever; but in his life he had done one kind act and for this they permitted him by special mercy of God to cool himself for an hour every Christmas on an iceberg in the North Pole. Now this has always seemed to me not mercy, but a peculiar refinement of cruelty. For how could Hell fail to be ten times more Hell to the poor wretch after the delicious coolness of his iceberg? I do not know for what enormous crime I have been condemned to Baroda, but my case is just parallel.[20]

Back in Gujarat, Aurobindo made an effort to learn the language of his family. Following his usual practice, he started with literary masterpieces: the poetry of Madhusudan Dutt and the novels of Bankim Chandra Chatterjee. Bankim, the greatest Bengali writer of the age, died that April at the age of fifty-five. This impelled Aurobindo to write a series of essays on his life and writings, which were published in *Indu Prakash* in July and August. Aurobindo began with an account of the writer's education. Bankim's "intellectual habits were irregular," he noted approvingly. "His spirit needed larger bounds than a school routine could give it, and refused, as every free mind does, to cripple itself and lose its natural suppleness." Drawn into an administrative career, Bankim passed a good part of his life in "thankless drudgery." The work by which he would be remembered was his literary output and not his toil in the lower ranks of government service. Aurobindo assigned Bankim the highest place in Bengali letters—"there is no prose-writer, and only one poet who can compete with him"—but he simply catalogued Bankim's works and excused himself from the task of evaluating the writer's style. He had more to say about the effect of Bankim's and Madhusudan's writings on the cultural life of Bengal. They had given the world three great gifts: the Bengali language, Bengali literature, and the Bengali nation. The third item in this list was the most important. If Bengal was destined for preeminence, it was "largely due to the awakening and stimulating influence of Bankim on the national [that is, the Bengali] mind."[21]

In Aurobindo's view, the previous generation of Bengali intellectuals had been too much influenced by European thought and too inclined to express itself in English. Not with them lay "our hope in the future," but with the young generation, "a generation national to a fault, loving Bengal and her new glories, and if not Hindus themselves, yet zealous of the honour of the ancient religion and hating all that makes war on it." Aurobindo was a member of this new generation, but not free from the habits of the old. His Western-trained eye could find nothing to admire in Indian art. For him the only decent contemporary painter was the Bengali Sasi Hesh, who "has been winning noble renown . . . in Italy, the native land of painting, the land of Raphael, Da Vinci and Angelo." In evaluating Bengali literature too he fell back on European models. Madhusudan at his best was comparable to Shakespeare or Thucydides. (Somewhat inconsistently, Tagore and other contemporary writers were inferior to Madhusudan, because they were "too obviously influenced by Shelley and the English poets.") In prose fiction, Bankim was deeper than Fielding and more subtle than Scott, though inferior to Aurobindo's favorite, George Meredith.[22]

Aurobindo's efforts to learn Bengali were not matched by an equal enthusiasm to master Marathi and Gujarati, the languages, respectively, of Baroda's ruling family and of the majority of its people. On the day he reported for duty in the state in 1893, he had been asked to learn Gujarati within six months. This was not much to ask of a scholar who already knew Sanskrit, but he would not play along. Ignoring frequent reminders from his superiors and even the threat of a cut in his pay, he refused to learn a language that did not interest him. Eventually he picked up enough Gujarati to read and summarize documents, enough Marathi to chat with friends, and enough Hindi to read books and newspapers. By the turn of the century he knew at least twelve languages: English, French, and Bengali to speak, read, and write; Latin, Greek, and Sanskrit to read and write; Gujarati, Marathi, and Hindi to speak and read; and Italian, German, and Spanish to read.

IN 1894 AND 1895 Baroda was rocked by protests against its land policy. V.S. Bapat, an officer in the survey settlement department, was made a scapegoat and indicted for corruption and extortion.[23] The Gaekwar returned from Europe in 1895 to this confused situation. For some time the ruler had been watching Aurobindo. Now he decided to see what the young man could do. On May 24, 1895 the head of Baroda's revenue department received a telegram asking him to send Aurobindo to Ootacamund, where the Gaekwar was vacationing.[24] Ooty, as it was known, was South India's answer to Darjeeling, a resort in the hills where the governor of Madras, his staff, and hangers-on repaired during the torrid summer months. Its scenery and climate had won it the name Queen of the Hill-Stations; its stuffy society earned it the epithet Snooty Ooty. The Gaekwar's bungalow was situated just across a wooded valley from the governor's mansion. But the Bapat case, which was giving the state a bad press, made it difficult for him to relax. He needed to have someone go through the material and write a précis of the case, and he gave the task to Aurobindo.

To reach Ootacamund, Aurobindo had to travel nine hundred miles to the south. He got no farther than Bombay's Parel station before he ran into trouble. "Must have an intelligent peon send one immediately to Parel," he wired to his office. His superior, nonplussed, wired back that he could engage a peon in Bombay and continue on his way. After reaching his destination four days later, Aurobindo wrote that he had met His Highness, who wished "to keep me with him for some time further." He added: "I have also the honour to state that as I desired a peon rather at Ootie than on the journey and even so it was not *absolutely* necessary, I did not think myself justified in taking advantage of your kind permission to engage one at Bombay as far as Ootie." His superior was indulgent enough not to question this. He wrote back: "I hope the climate at Ooty agrees with you, and that you are getting on smoothly with your work."[25]

The Gaekwar must have been satisfied with Aurobindo's précis, for when he returned to Baroda he gave him a fifty-rupee raise and ordered the dewan, or prime minister, to assign him "responsible work." He also began to summon Aurobindo to write official letters in English.[26] By the end of 1895 Aurobindo had a post in the dewan's office and was spending much of his time working directly under the Gaekwar. The ruler appreciated his abilities but could not use them as much as he wanted without provoking a revolt among his officers. The officers need not have worried, for Aurobindo was not interested in their jobs. What he wanted was to teach in Baroda's college. The British principal of the institution was anxious to add Aurobindo to his staff, and in January 1897 requested the dewan to "spare him for an hour daily to teach French in the College."[27] The Gaekwar agreed, but continued to call Aurobindo to the palace. The idea of giving him a regular position at the college had to be dropped, though he did begin to do a bit of teaching on the side. Then, in the beginning of 1898, when the English professor went on furlough, Aurobindo was appointed acting professor of English literature.[28]

Professor Ghose

Aurobindo taught at Baroda College from 1898 to 1901 and again from 1905 to 1906. His main responsibility was to prepare undergraduate students for the Bombay University examinations. He liked the work but not the environment. In outward appearance, India's degree-granting universities were as British as their British organizers could make them; in other words, they were cheap imitations of Cambridge and Oxford. Instructors were obliged to follow syllabi that mimicked those of their exemplars. "British art, British philosophy, British text books!" lamented a visiting member of parliament when he was shown around Baroda College. The whole place was "European in everything except in the insufferable heat of the atmosphere"[29]—and the lack of educational depth and rigor. Aurobindo, who had experienced the British system at its best, agreed that the mechanical routine of the Indian version served only "to dull and impoverish and tie up" the students' minds.[30] Based on a curriculum that had little relevance to their lives, taught in a language few really understood, it turned even the brightest into parrots. And in Baroda, a

provincial backwater, the students were not especially bright. Despite his affection for them, he had to admit that they had "no brains" and "did not know
English at all."[31]

Several of Aurobindo's students left accounts of their classroom experiences that permit the reconstruction of a typical course. Aurobindo began with
a set of introductory lectures dealing with the background of the writers or
period assigned. Two such lectures, on Gray and other poets of the eighteenth
century, survive in one of his notebooks.[32] He did not like the poetry of this
period, but he treated it fairly and in depth, demonstrating a detailed knowledge even of minor writers, such as Akenside and Crabbe. After completing
his introductory talks, he took up the assigned texts. In the lower classes he
had to read directly from the books, "stopping when necessary to explain the
meaning of difficult and obscure sentences," as a student recalled. Aurobindo's
own recollection was of "giving notes on everything except prepositions and
conjunctions." With more advanced students, he could escape from this slav-
ery to the texts. Without opening the book, without the aid of notes, he spoke
on the writer under study for as long as an hour and a half. Horrified at first
that the students used "to take down everything verbatim and mug it up,"
he eventually resigned himself to the idea, and began the day's dictation by
having a student read out the last lines of the previous day's lecture. Leaning
back against the table, his thumb and index finger closed, his eyes down, or
perhaps gazing across the room, he spoke as if in trance, without rhetorical
flourishes, simply and to the point. The students sat silently, "spellbound" by
their professor's eloquence. The professor himself would have been happier
if one or two had emerged from their stupor to be more active in class. Only
a few could use the lectures as he intended, as starting points for their own
investigations. The others were interested only in passing their exams. Once a
group of students told him that his lectures were not in agreement with notes
that they had obtained, at some expense, from Bombay. He replied that he had
not read the notes, but that "in any case, they are mostly rubbish." He knew
the importance of examinations, however, and at the end of the term, he gave
special lectures that the students greatly appreciated. These lectures became so
well known that undergraduates from other colleges took the train to Baroda
just to hear the Cambridge-educated professor speak.[33]

Aurobindo encouraged his students to think about what they read and to
put their ideas down on paper. "Correct composition leads to correct thinking," he used to say. When a young friend asked him whether reading Macau-
lay would help his writing style, Aurobindo replied: "You may read any good
author, but you should think for yourself." An imitation, even of a good model,

was still "a copy to be derided by the world." He assigned little homework but asked the students to write compositions in class, which he corrected himself, sometimes making such comments as "How have you come to the College?"[34] He regretted that Indian university life did not extend beyond the classroom, and did what he could to help the students in their extracurricular activities. He contributed a few pieces to the college magazine, and was always ready to help aspiring writers. On occasion he presided over the meetings of the debating society. On the podium, as in the classroom, he avoided gestures and rhetorical effects. Words flowed from him "with natural ease," and his voice was melodious and soft.[35]

DURING HIS YEARS at the college, Aurobindo passed his autumn vacations in Bengal. He was always welcome in the Calcutta house of his aunt Lilavati and her husband Krishna Kumar Mitra, a journalist and Brahmo leader. But he preferred it when the family gathered at his grandfather Rajnarain's place in Deoghar. It was cool in the hills and, after the monsoon, the scenery was fresh and luxuriant. Everyone was in high spirits, especially the children. Once his cousin Basanti was on hand to watch Auro-dada (big brother Auro) unpack. The girl wondered "how many lovely expensive coats and suits and different sorts of luxurious things there must be in those boxes." When he opened them, she "gaped in surprise: just a few ordinary clothes and then—books and more books! My God," she thought, "is Auro-dada *so* fond of reading?" Everyone wanted to have fun during the holidays. Was he going to pass his time reading books, and enjoy doing it too? She was relieved to find that "Auro-dada's great love of reading did not prevent him from taking part in our talk and laughter."[36] Barin, "still a stranger" to his older brother, tried to "tease him out of his books and day-dreams" and sometimes succeeded. Rising from his desk, Aurobindo would chase him around the room, "pretending [an] anger he never felt." With the young people his talk was generally light and humorous, though sometimes he spoke seriously about India, "her past glories and present degradation and possible deliverance"—a dream Barin found "too big for my young mind to grasp."[37]

ALTHOUGH AUROBINDO'S STUDENTS and colleagues generally admired him, he was never really popular. In company he was quiet, particularly regarding himself. He summed up his attitude in a very British saying: "The less one says about oneself the better." On account of his reticence, many people found him shy. It did not follow that he was stiff. Talking with friends, he sometimes broke out in uproarious laughter. Usually, however, his laugh was "like a child's, simple, liquid and soft."[38]

His closest friends were Madhavrao Jadhav, a young officer in the Baroda army, and K. G. Deshpande, the Bombay journalist he had known since his Cambridge days. The three of them were around the same age and had similar political opinions. Madhavrao introduced Aurobindo to his elder brother Khaserao, a high officer of the state who at the time was posted in a different district. Khaserao was having a house built in the Dandia Bazar area of Baroda. When it was finished, Madhavrao and his family moved in. Aurobindo stayed with them on and off during his years at the college.[39]

It was to Khaserao's house that Aurobindo came after the *puja* holidays in 1898. With him was Dinendrakumar Ray, a Bengali writer whom Aurobindo had asked to come and help him learn the language. Dinendrakumar had been apprehensive before meeting his new employer. He pictured a well-built young man "dressed head to toe in English clothing." As befitted an "England-returned" scholar, he would be rude of speech, arrogant of eye, and haughty of demeanor. When they finally met, he could not have been more surprised:

> On his feet old-fashioned slippers with the toes turned up, his clothes of coarse Ahmedabad cotton, on his back a tight waistcoat, around his waist a dhoti with the tail hanging loose, on his head a long flowing mass of hair hanging down to his shoulders, on his face tiny pock-marks, in his eyes a gentle dreamy look—who would have thought that this thin dark-skinned young man was Sriman Aurobindo Ghose?[40]

Aurobindo did not impress at first sight. He was short, around five feet, four inches, and thin, around 113 pounds.[41] His complexion was on the dark side, and the pock-marks, from a case of smallpox, gave a rough look to his otherwise boyish face. Dinendrakumar saw in the "firm set" of his lips the mark of an "inflexible will." Most people were struck rather by the mildness of Aurobindo's expression, though this "slight and unobtrusive figure" had about him a gravity that few failed to notice.[42]

Aurobindo cared little about clothing and never dressed for effect. At home he wore a white undershirt and dhoti; at the college, white drill suits and a turban or cap. Suits also were de rigueur at the Gaekwar's palace. Aurobindo generally complied, though he thought European clothing "hideous." He moved around Baroda in an old ramshackle carriage drawn by a big, plodding nag. Both the carriage, with its purple window panes, and the horse, more asinine than equine, were sufficiently odd to attract attention. Indeed, thought Dinendrakumar, almost everything about Aurobindo was a trifle odd.[43]

In Dinendrakumar's laudatory but not hagiographic memoirs, which have the advantage of having been written only a decade after the events they describe, he often referred to Aurobindo's generosity. Once, seeing that Aurobindo was filling out a money order form, Dinendrakumar asked if he too could send something home. Aurobindo opened the box where he kept his money and, finding there was just a little, gave it all to Dinendrakumar. His friend protested: "What is this? You were just making out a money order so that you could send something home. Send it. I'll send mine later." Aurobindo told him to go ahead.[44] Despite his simple mode of living, he never seemed to have a *pie* left over at the end of the month. This was due in part to his habit of sending much of his salary to his father's mother in Benares and his mother and sister in Deoghar. Benoybhusan and Manmohan, both of whom earned more, contributed less. When Manmohan stopped sending his small contributions, Aurobindo sent more. He used to leave his quarterly salary, a thousand rupees in coins, on his desk and use it "till it was consumed." Rajaram Patkar, the younger brother of K. G. Deshpande's wife, asked him why he left so much money in the open without even keeping an account. Aurobindo laughed and told him, "Well, it is a proof that we are living in the midst of honest and good people."[45]

Rajaram and Dinendrakumar were both amazed by Aurobindo's indifference to food. He consumed without comment whatever was placed before him, even if the cooking was so bad that Dinendrakumar could hardly touch his plate. Aurobindo sometimes got so absorbed in what he was doing that he forgot his meals altogether. Rajaram was on hand one evening when a servant brought Aurobindo's dinner and announced, "*Sab, khanna rakha hai*" (Sir, dinner is served). Aurobindo muttered "yes" without lifting his eyes from his book. An hour later the servant returned to find the meal untouched. He appealed to Rajaram, who timidly pointed out that the food was waiting. Aurobindo looked up, smiled at the boy, went to the table, finished the cold food, and returned to his reading.[46]

Dinendrakumar attributed Aurobindo's good health to his parsimonious eating habits and his leading a "regulated life." He governed his life by the clock, frequently consulting a cheap watch that he carried in his pocket. His friends were struck by his indifference to physical discomfort. He never complained about the heat of Baroda's summers or the chill of its winters. Only on the coldest mornings did he throw a shawl over his shoulders; only on the coldest nights did he sleep under a cotton blanket. His bed, a thin mattress on a cast-iron frame, was one that "even a clerk would have thought it a disgrace to lie down on."[47]

AUROBINDO READ ENORMOUSLY during his years in the college. Every month, sometimes every week, he placed orders with Bombay and Calcutta booksellers. His purchases "did not come by book post but by railway parcel, in enormous packing cases." Aurobindo used to finish the books "in eight or ten days and then placed an order for more." Most of the books he bought were works of literature. Dinendrakumar saw "collections of all the English poets from Chaucer to Swinburne" on his shelves, and "innumerable English novels" heaped up "in corners of the room, in cupboards, and in steel trunks." Like most heavy readers, Aurobindo had a number of books going at the same time. In the first week of January 1901, for example, he was reading two Sanskrit classics—Kalidasa's *Raghuvansa* and the *Hitopadesha*—Gustav Freytag's play *Die Journalisten*, and Tennyson's *Idylls of the King*, the assigned reading for his intermediate arts students. He read with great concentration, as Dinendrakumar relates:

> Sitting in a chair before a table, undisturbed by the terrible biting of the mosquitoes, Aurobindo read at night until one o'clock by the light of a "jewel lamp." I saw him sitting there for hours at a stretch, his eyes glued to the page, his attitude unchanging, like an ascetic rapt in contemplation, oblivious of the world. I don't think he would have noticed if the house caught fire.[48]

Though he lived a thousand miles from Bengal, Aurobindo was anxious to improve his knowledge of Bengali. He could read fairly well, but his speech was still halting, and he had trouble writing an ordinary letter. He worked with Dinendrakumar diligently but haphazardly, sometimes applying himself for several days in a row, then letting a week pass by without doing any work at all. Following his own advice to enter the spirit of a language by means of writing, he passed at a stride from prose drills to an epic in verse. Barin was amazed to see him "scribbling away" at his creation; Manmohan castigated him for misdirecting his energies.[49] Undeterred, he worked on the poem for several months before dropping it entirely. He knew he could not succeed as a Bengali writer. Commenting in 1894 on Bankim's and Madhusudan's early efforts in English, he observed: "The language which a man speaks and which he has never learned, is the language of which he has the nearest sense and in which he expresses himself with the greatest fulness, subtlety and power. . . . To be original in an acquired tongue is hardly feasible."[50] However much he wished to identify himself as an Indian and a Bengali, his natural language was English, and he belonged, willy-nilly, to the English literary world.

During this period, Aurobindo lived the life of a writer. Reading or writing till after midnight, he got up late in the morning and resumed where he had left off, after a cup of tea. Before taking up his pen, he smoked and thought for a while. Once he began, he wrote slowly but steadily, rarely stopping to strike anything out. If someone spoke to him while he was writing, he was disturbed but never let the other person know. After a bath at ten, he went over what he had written, sometimes changing a word or two. On mornings when his writing went well, he went to the office in a particularly cheerful mood.[51]

Little survives of what Aurobindo wrote at this time, suggesting that much of it was thrown away. Perhaps a half-dozen surviving poems can be assigned to the first six years in Baroda. In these, Indian color and symbolism enliven conventional nature imagery and sentiment. In 1898 he put together a collection of the poems he wished to preserve from his first decade of writing. *Songs to Myrtilla*, printed privately in Baroda, contains twenty-one pieces. About a third are on political and literary heroes: Parnell, Goethe, Madhusudan, Bankim; most of the rest are on love. These unremarkable subjects are treated in an unremarkable way; the verse, always competent, rarely breaks out into a memorable phrase. Manmohan, to whom the volume was dedicated, gave it a balanced assessment in a letter to Rabindranath Tagore. Aurobindo, he wrote, "is possessed of considerable powers of language and a real literary gift,—but is lacking in stuff and matter, perhaps in warmth of temperament. But those pieces on Parnell, consisting of fine philosophic reflection, show, I think, that he might do great things."[52] Few people in London would have agreed that the book showed promise. The writers who began to attract attention in the 1890s, among them Manmohan's friends Laurence Binyon and Stephen Phillips and his acquaintances Lionel Johnson and Ernest Dowson, had succeeded in transmuting their classical influences into authentic English utterance. Even Manmohan was writing verse that Yeats could admire. Aurobindo had yet to find his voice.

After publishing *Songs to Myrtilla*, Aurobindo worked on three narrative poems, all of them based on Eastern sources. *Urvasie*, the first and longest, recounts the story of King Pururavas and the heavenly damsel Urvasi. Written in the late Victorian style of Tennyson and Arnold, it contains little of lasting interest. He had it printed sometime around the turn of the century, but soon "got disgusted with it and rejected it."[53] In January 1899 he began another blank-verse narrative, this one based on Arabian folklore. Among the most cherished books in his library was a twelve-volume edition of the Richard Burton translation of the *Thousand and One Nights*.[54] Borrowing from the *Nights* the scene (the desert, Baghdad), some names (Alnuman, Nourredin), and a dose of mystery and magic, he conceived a narrative in twelve cantos, with prologue and epilogue, to be entitled *Khaled of the Sea*. Beginning enthusiastically, he wrote fifteen pages in two months, but then abandoned the project. For a while he toyed with a variety of themes: a trilogy on the life of Nero, a play set in Britain. Then one day in June 1899, while reading the *Mahabharata*, he came across the episode of Ruru and Pramadvara. He thought, "Here's a subject," and before the month was over, he completed a compact narrative, *Love and Death*. The poem poured out "in a white heat of inspiration during 14 days of continuous writing," he later remarked, adding "in the mornings, of course, for I had to attend office the rest of the day and saw friends in the evening."[55] The second part of this sentence is as remarkable as the first. All writers long for that unimpeded flow called inspiration, but those fortunate enough to experience it often find it difficult to integrate it with the rest of their lives. It says something of the solidity of Aurobindo's nature that he could write "in a white heat" between eight and ten in the morning, then take a bath and go to work and, after returning home, pass the evening in the usual way, confident that the flow would return the next morning.

To Aurobindo, inspiration was not a nebulous term for an unusual fluency in writing. It was a specific sort of energy that was behind all genuine poetry. Three years after writing *Love and Death*, he described the "main features" of inspiration in an essay on Kalidasa:

There is a sudden exaltation, a glow, an excitement and a fiery and rapid activity of all the faculties; every cell of the body & of the brain feeling a commotion and working in excited unison under the law of something which is not themselves; the mind becomes illuminated as with a rush of light and grows like a crowded and surging thoroughfare in some brilliantly lighted city, thought treading on the heels of thought faster than the tongue can express or the hand write or the memory record them. And yet while the organs of sense remain overpowered and inactive, the main organs of action may be working with abnormal rapidity, not only the speech and the hand but sometimes even the feet, so that often the writer cannot remain still, but has to walk up and down swiftly or if he sits down, is subject to an involuntary mechanical movement of the limbs.

One can imagine him swinging his legs as he wrote. Such mechanisms, he said, were a sign of imperfect assimilation. Once mastered, inspiration "ceases to be fortuitous and occasional, and becomes more and more within the will of the man and, subject to the necessarily long intervals of repose & recreation, almost a habitually recurring state." But before reaching this stage of assured possession, the poet must pass through a process of "subjecting the personality of the body to the personality of the spirit." This was not without its dangers. If the physical instrument was flawed, the result might be nervous disorientation or insanity. Even at best, the process was "seldom really over before the age of 30"—precisely Aurobindo's age when this posthumously published, obviously autobiographical passage was written.[56]

Dedicating *Love and Death* to Manmohan, Aurobindo spoke of it as "the first considerable effort of my powers."[57] It certainly was the poem in which he found himself, and this meant, in part, freeing himself from his indebtedness to his brother. Other literary influences remained: Stephen Phillips's blank verse narratives, Arnold's *Sohrab and Rustum*, Keats's *Hyperion*.[58] It is against such poems that *Love and Death* must be judged. At its best, it bears comparison with them:

> He down the gulf where the loud waves collapsed
> Descending, saw with floating hair arise
> The daughters of the sea in pale green light,
> A million mystic breasts suddenly bare,
> And came beneath the flood and stunned beheld
> A mute stupendous march of waters race
> To reach some viewless pit beneath the world.[59]

Although certain of the quality of *Love and Death*, Aurobindo was in no special hurry to have it published. Twenty years passed before it finally appeared in print. By then the shock of World War I and the beginnings of literary modernism had so transformed the poetic landscape that a late Victorian blank-verse narrative had no hope of attracting favorable notice.

DURING THE YEARS that Aurobindo taught at the college, the Gaekwar often called him for work. Dinendrakumar was impressed by the style of the summons. An armed Turkish horseman would ride up to the house, dismount, and present the assistant professor of English with a letter from the Gaekwar's secretary, saying something like "Would it be possible for you to meet the

Maharaja at such and such a time?" or "The Maharaja would be highly pleased if you would join him for dinner." As a rule, such invitations could not be refused. Aurobindo drove to the palace, joined the ruler at his table, and stayed on to write letters. Sometimes, however, he told the Gaekwar that he was too busy to come. This astounded Dinendrakumar. "How many noblemen cherished for months on end the vain hope of obtaining a single interview with the Maharaja," he thought, "while this ordinary 'school master' regarded his duty as more important than a visit to the Maharaja's palace." [60]

Aurobindo still did not have a permanent post at the college. In September 1900, the principal asked the Gaekwar to give him one. The ruler, then in Europe, refused to be pinned down. He sent his tentative assent, but added that he might reconsider after his return to Baroda. [61] A short while later he wrote a letter from London saying that he had big plans for Mr. Ghose: He needed the professor's help to write his memoirs and to compile a report enumerating the accomplishments of the first twenty years of his reign. [62] Aurobindo was permitted to teach during the spring term of 1901, but in April was transferred from the college to the revenue commissioner's office. "As a special case," he was allowed to take the vacation he would have been entitled to as a professor. [63] During this break, he got married in Calcutta.

Domestic Virtues

Aurobindo's closest friends were married, as were his older brothers. Like all single men in India, as he approached the age of thirty, he came under increasing pressure to find a wife. Without this pressure, thought Rajaram Patkar, he would never have turned his mind in this direction. But Dinendrakumar Ray, who knew Aurobindo better, was aware that he was "eager to get married" at this time. And once he decided to take the step, "he deliberately went about seeking a bride for himself." [64] One thing was certain: the girl would be Bengali. Aurobindo was convinced, on somewhat scanty evidence, that the women of his home province were "the tenderest, purest & most gracious & loving in the whole world." [65] On one of his trips to Bengal, he had developed a liking for the daughter of one of his associates, a barrister of Calcutta. But the man gave his daughter to someone else, and Aurobindo was obliged to place an advertisement in the newspapers. [66] This came out apparently in the first half of 1900. In July, right in the middle of summer term, he took privilege leave "to go to Calcutta on urgent private business which will not admit of delay." [67]—presumably the selection of his bride. The advertisement had elicited fifty replies. In accordance with Bengali custom, he was taken to the houses of prospective fathers-in-law and given *kanya dekha,* a glimpse of the girl. He saw many candidates without finding what he was looking for. Finally, he was shown Mrinalini, the daughter of Bhupalchandra Bose, and chose her at once.

Mrinalini was thought pretty. Her skin was fair with an attractive rosy tinge. Round features were framed by a mass of thick black curls. But it was her "sweet innocence and childlike simplicity" that Aurobindo liked about her most. Like her husband-to-be, she was quiet and shy.[68] All of fourteen when she was married, she was somewhat old for a Bengali bride; turn-of-the-century fathers were caught between the legal requirements of the Age of Consent Bill and the social reality that it was "considered a disgrace to have an unmarried daughter over 14 years."[69] Meanwhile, Aurobindo was somewhat old for a first-time groom. At twenty-eight, he was twice Mrinalini's age when they were married.

The wedding took place in a house on Baithak Khana Road, in north Calcutta, on April 29, 1901.[70] As Aurobindo insisted, the ceremony was performed according to Hindu rites. Although he was the grandson of one of the principal leaders of the Brahmo movement, he had never admired the organization, which he regarded as a "rehash of that pale & consumptive shadow, English Theism."[71] And though he was not a practicing Hindu, he still believed that Hinduism represented his country's authentic cultural tradition. But he took the demands of Hindu orthodoxy rather lightly. As one who had "crossed the black waters," he was told he would have to perform the rite of *prayaschitta* before he could marry. This involved eating cow-dung or at least having his hair shaved off. He refused to do either. There was a deadlock until someone found "an obliging Brahmin priest" who "satisfied all the requirements of the Shastra for a monetary consideration."[72]

After the ceremony, the newlyweds went to Deoghar, where they spent a month with Aurobindo's relatives. Then, at the end of May, they and Aurobindo's sister Sarojini went to Nainital, a resort in the Himalayas where the Gaekwar was passing the summer. A few weeks earlier the ruler had given Aurobindo a bonus. Now he welcomed him, his wife, and his sister to a bungalow overlooking the lake that gives Nainital its name. Aurobindo and the two young women stayed for about a month. It is often cloudy in Nainital during the summer, and the honeymooners may have been denied a glimpse of the peaks of Trishul and Nanda Devi from Snow View, but they doubtless enjoyed strolling by the lake and wandering through the town's bazaar. Aurobindo spent money freely, acquiring in a week a coal stove, an ivory paper knife, two ivory pens, a silver pen, some "curiosities" (souvenirs), and other necessities and extravagances. An account he kept at this time shows that he was not always as indifferent to money matters as it sometimes appeared to his friends. Besides keeping a record of cash on hand and expenditures, he jotted down the denominations, issuing banks, and serial numbers of his banknotes.[73]

Sometime during their stay in Nainital, Aurobindo and Mrinalini stepped into a photographic studio to have their picture taken. The result shows the young woman in an embroidered sari and jewels seated rather uncomfortably on a bench. Her husband, natty in tweeds, perches beside her. Despite his protective arm, the two do not seem at ease with one another. Mrinalini looks somewhat coolly to the left, Aurobindo to the right. It must have taken them a good amount of time to get to know each other. She spoke little English, his Bengali was far from perfect, and it is hard to imagine what the Cambridge-educated scholar and the girl, who, as her father put it, "evinced no exceptional abilities or tendencies," found to talk about.[74] Aurobindo clearly was not looking for intellectual companionship when he chose her. What then was he looking for?

Four or five years after his marriage, in a commentary on one of the Upanishads, Aurobindo has his spokesman, "the Guru," describe the scale of human love:

> If sensual gratification were all, then it is obvious that I should have no reason to prefer one woman over another and after the brute gratification liking would cease; I have seen this brute impulse given the name of love; perhaps I myself used to give it that name when the protoplasmic animal predominated in me. If emotional gratification were all, then I might indeed cling for a time to the woman who had pleased my body, but only so long as she gave me emotional pleasure, by her obedience, her sympathy with my likes & dislikes, her pleasant speech, her admiration or her answering love. But the moment these cease, my liking also will begin to fade away. This sort of liking too is persistently given the great name and celebrated in poetry & romance. Then if aesthetic gratification were all, my liking for a woman of great beauty or great charm might well outlast the loss of all emotional gratification, but when the wrinkles began to trace the writing of age on her face or when accident marred her beauty, my liking would fade or vanish since the effect would lose the nutrition of present cause. Intellectual gratification seldom enters into the love of a man for a woman; even if it did so, more frequently the intellectual gratification to be derived from a single mind is soon exhausted in daylong and nightlong

companionship. Whence then comes that love which is greater than life and stronger than death, which survives the loss of beauty and the loss of charm, which defies the utmost pain & scorn the object of love can deal out to it, which often pours out from a great & high intellect on one infinitely below it?[75]

The usual desire for gratification, as Aurobindo has the guru call it, was presumably a factor in his decision to get married, but it does not seem to have been an important one. His later writings show that his knowledge of human sexuality was more than academic, but the act seems to have held few charms for him.[76] Consummation may have been delayed because of Mrinalini's youth, and his own stoicism, partly innate and partly learned from philosophers such as Epictetus, would have helped him to keep his sexual tendencies in check.

Aurobindo, Mrinalini, and Sarojini were back in Baroda by the beginning of July 1900. Before going on leave, Aurobindo had rented a house and asked Madhavrao to furnish it. Aurobindo and the two young women moved into the new place on his return. Rajaram Patkar found Sarojini cultured and dignified, Mrinalini childish and spoiled. Aurobindo passed part of his evenings with them. Beyond this, "there was no change in his former daily routine." He continued to meet Madhavrao and Deshpande, but was really, thought Rajaram, "more at ease when left to himself, than in the company of relations & friends."[77] Similarly, Barin Ghose wrote that Aurobindo's "inner detachment and natural quietude of spirit was so complete that it acted as an inhibition and kept suppressed all his feelings and sentiments which go towards the make-up of a family-man or a genial and loveable social character."[78] Aurobindo would have laughed at his brother's jargon-filled account, but he wrote something similar in a letter to his father-in-law: "I am afraid I shall never be good for much in the way of domestic virtues. I have tried, very ineffectively, to do some part of my duty as a son, a brother and a husband, but there is something too strong in me which forces me to subordinate everything else to it."[79]

ONCE HE HAD RETIRED to his room, Aurobindo remained there for hours, and "not even the simple and childlike charms of his wife could drag him away from his studies."[80] In the years after writing *Love and Death*, he seems to have given most of his time to translation and literary criticism. From around 1900 to 1902, his main interest was Sanskrit epic literature. For years he had been annoyed by the works of Orientalists who regarded all forms of Indian literature as inferior to their European counterparts, or even copies of

European models. Indian scholars followed the Western Orientalists' lead, as Aurobindo noted with displeasure while reading a September 1901 article in the *Indian Review* on the date of the *Mahabharata* war. Making this piece the starting point for his own consideration of the question, Aurobindo insisted that it was "not from European scholars that we must expect a solution of the Mahabharata problem." Western scholars, arguing from Homer, were trying to reduce Vyasa's masterpiece to an *Iliad*-like epic less than a tenth of its actual length, along the way informing educated Indians that their national poem was "a mass of old wives' stories without a spark of poetry or imagination."[81] Such views offended his critical sense and his sense of national pride. As alive to Homer's greatness as any English or German scholar, he still considered Vyasa a poet whose vigor had no equal in world literature. Moreover, the *Mahabharata* held the key to classical India, a culture with values that ought to be affirmed:

> There are signs that if Hinduism is to last and we are not to plunge into the vortex of scientific atheism and the breakdown of moral ideals which is engulfing Europe, it must survive as the religion for which Vedanta, Sankhya & Yoga combined to lay the foundations, which Srikrishna announced & which Vyasa formulated.[82]

This passage is one of the first signs that Aurobindo had developed an interest in the religion of his ancestors. Yet he made it clear, in a passage written around this time, that "when I speak of Hinduism I do not refer to the ignorant & customary Hinduism of today . . . but the purer form [of Vedanta] which under the pressure of Science is now reasserting its empire over the Hindu mind."[83] This purer form of Hinduism was for him embodied in the *Bhagavad Gita*. He began a translation of the *Gita* at this time, in which he brought out its emphasis on selfless service: "Not by refraining from works shall a man taste actionlessness and not by mere renouncing of the world shall he reach perfection. . . . Do thou works that the law demands of thee, for action is mightier than inaction."[84]

After 1902, the focus of Aurobindo's studies shifted to Kalidasa, the master of classical Sanskrit poetry. He felt that Kalidasa compared "unfavourably with the inexhaustible flexibility of Valmekie [the author of the *Ramayana*] and the nervous ease of Vyasa" in epic poetry. But in the "more complicated and grandiose metres," Kalidasa was peerless. His *Meghaduta* or *Cloud Messenger* was "the most marvellously perfect descriptive and elegiac poem in the world's literature."[85] Delighted by the "perfection of the harmony" of its verse and the "pathos and passion" of the story, Aurobindo translated it into English verse.[86] Around the same time, he completed a verse translation of one of Kalidasa's dramas, the *Vikramorvasiya*. Fascinated by the psychological suggestiveness of the legend on which it is based, he wrote an essay on the characters of the play. This was intended for a full-length study of Kalidasa and his works, which grew to more than a hundred pages before he set it aside. He did, however, publish one of the chapters in the *Indian Review* in 1902. Discounting his two self-published volumes of verse, this was his first appearance in print since 1894. He had by this time filled at least a dozen notebooks with fair copies of prose and poetic works, many of them ready for publication. He chose not to submit them, either because he thought them below his critical standards, or perhaps above the level of Indian reviews and publishing houses.

DURING THE EARLY YEARS of his reign, Sayajirao Gaekwar was considered the most enlightened of India's native rulers. Indian journalists and public speakers loved to recite his Western-inspired reforms: a program in compulsory primary education, laws banning infant marriage and legalizing widow-remarriage, reform schools, a state bank. Although not entirely undeserved, the Gaekwar's reputation was inflated. If he set aside 4 1/2 pence a year for every student in his realm—more than was set aside in British India—he also allotted a tenth of the state's revenue to his so-called privy purse, giving himself £100,000 a year, then an unimaginable sum, to spend on himself and his family. Besides his three Baroda palaces, he owned extensive properties elsewhere in India and was always looking for more. During one three-month period he kept Aurobindo busy with correspondence concerning the purchase and remodeling of a mansion in Bombay and the design of a dream house in Ooty. In the same three-month period he turned down proposals from state officials to widen Baroda's principal bridge, send three students to Europe, and build a new high school, all on the grounds that the state's finances were in a precarious condition.

Between 1901 and 1904 Aurobindo worked closely with this well-intentioned, self-indulgent man, his duties changing according to the Gaekwar's pleasure. One of his first assignments after returning to Baroda in July 1901 was to see to the education of the ruler's children while their regular tutor was on leave. He found them all dull except for the princess Indira, later the Maharani of Cooch Behar. For their part, the royal children found Aurobindo "too immersed in thoughts and idealistic dreamings really to pay much attention to them." As a result they often played truant. Aurobindo also gave some lessons to the Gaekwar himself, helping him improve his English grammar "by giving exact and minute rules for each construction."[87]

In 1900 or 1901, the Gaekwar asked Aurobindo to compile a report on the administration of the state since his accession. This exercise in self-promotion was to include the "memoirs of his life and of his reign." Aurobindo gathered some material and did a bit of writing, but never completed this project.[88] The ruler found other ways to keep him busy. Whenever there was "an important letter, order, dispatch, correspondence with the British Government or other document" that needed careful phrasing in English, the task fell to Mr. Ghose. One of the longest if not the most interesting assignments he was given was to compile a report on trade in the Baroda state. Given four fat volumes of data in "the vernacular"—Gujarati, Marathi, or both—he was asked to prepare a summary, with recommendations, in English. The result, which runs to seventy-two printed pages, was issued in 1902. Aurobindo's general introduction begins with this warning: "Trade throughout the [Baroda] Raj is in a state of depression and decline. The great industries that once flourished, such as weaving, dyeing, sharafi [jewelry-making] &c. are entirely broken and though a number of small retail trades have sprung up, the balance is greatly on the side of decline." The primary cause of this situation was "European competition." Industrialization had destroyed the market for local products, forcing men to give up their ancestral professions. Money was drained from the state by purchases from Europe and British India and the employment of officials and contractors from the same places.[89] This was as far as he could go in criticizing the British Raj, as the report could be read by British officials. His practical suggestions were confined to ways that the government of Baroda could improve education, support local industries, and stimulate agriculture. The report was circulated for several months, but little or nothing was done to implement his suggestions.

Aurobindo seems to have finished the trade report by April 1902, when he took leave and departed for Bengal. In all likelihood, Mrinalini and Sarojini were with him. "Unfamiliar surroundings, strange faces and an unintelligible tongue or rather two or three unintelligible tongues" made Baroda "intolerable" to them, as he wrote to his uncle Jogen. Sarojini went back to Deoghar while Mrinalini returned to her parents' place in Assam.[90] The separation between husband and wife was meant to be brief, but it lasted at least a year and a half, perhaps twice as long as that.

Revolution and Recreation

Aurobindo spent most of May 1902 in Bengal. His main reason for going was to look in on a revolutionary group, actually a physical culture club with revolutionary pretensions, that had been started a few months earlier. His involvement with this organization was his first overt political move since he abandoned *New Lamps for Old* eight years earlier. In the intervening years, his activities were confined to exchanging ideas with Deshpande and the Jadhavs; he also, as he later wrote, "studied the conditions in the country."[91] What he saw was not encouraging. With few exceptions, people took the perpetuity of British rule for granted. The lower classes, whom Aurobindo had championed in *New Lamps for Old,* remained "sunk in ignorance and overwhelmed with distress," too preoccupied with survival to care who was running the country. The middle classes were still scrambling for the scraps that fell from the government's table. It no doubt rankled that the rulers were foreigners who were contemptuous of the cultures of those they ruled. But such contempt did not prevent people from living their lives as they chose, worshipping in temples, mosques, and gurdwaras, educating and marrying off their children, and looking forward to a relatively secure old age.

For those who had the time, money, and ambition, the Indian National Congress was a means to petition the government for more and better scraps: enlarging advisory councils, holding ICS examinations in India, attending to grievances major and minor. The government ignored all such petitions, but the act of presenting them gave the English-educated elite the illusion that they were taking part in great affairs. The Congress also provided a field for self-assertion and peer competition. Local grandees from Vidarbha, advocates from Vellore, and journalists from Ludhiana could aspire to be included in the counsels of the men who had dominated the organization since its founding. This oligarchy was in permanent control of the subjects committee, which set the agenda for national meetings. Rank-and-file delegates could in theory propose resolutions, but anyone trying to do so without the blessings of the committee would quickly be called to order. The only significant debate in the Congress's first twenty years was over a nonpolitical issue: whether a conference dealing with social reform should be held just after a meeting in the same venue. In 1895 a group of so-called extremists led by Bal Gangadhar Tilak, a journalist and activist from Poona, insisted that the social conference be held in a different place. From then on, the practice of linking the meetings was abandoned.

An honors graduate of Bombay University, Tilak could more than hold his own with the metropolitan elite, but he also could speak to the masses. At a time when the circulation of English newspapers was measured in the hundreds, the *Kesari*, Tilak's Marathi daily, was read by tens of thousands. In 1894 he mobilized his base by transforming the yearly Ganapati *puja*, a domestic ceremony in honor of the elephant-headed god, into a public festival or *utsav*. The next year he launched a second festival, this one commemorating the

Maratha general Shivaji. Both *utsavs* had a covert political purpose. By giving the Hindus of Maharashtra occasions to celebrate their history and traditions, the festivals helped them affirm their cultural and political identity.

Maharashtra was one of the last parts of India to fall to the British, and the people of the region still felt a strong resentment against their foreign rulers. In 1896 two brothers of Poona, Damodar and Balkrishna Chapekar, shot and killed W. C. Rand, the chairman of the Poona plague commission. Though motivated largely by religious fanaticism, the Chapekars did have a crude sort of political awareness. "Efforts not backed by physical force are doomed to failure," Damodar wrote in his prison journal, "the demands of the National Congress have proved futile for this reason."[92] The Chapekars may have gotten their political ideas and their hatred of the Poona plague commission from the pages of Tilak's *Kesari*. So at least thought the government of Bombay, which put Tilak on trial for sedition in 1897. Convicted, he was sentenced to eighteen months of rigorous imprisonment. By the time of his release in September 1898, he was seen as a national hero.

Aurobindo's friend K. G. Deshpande had been a member of Tilak's defense team in 1897; he also had served as editor of *Indu Prakash*. Deshpande's experience brought a touch of practicality to the otherwise theoretical discussions between him, Aurobindo, and the Jadhavs. The four agreed that the British had no right to rule India. Knowing that the colonizers would not leave unless their position became untenable, they spoke of the need for active resistance, even armed rebellion. But they knew that India was not yet ready for this. Aurobindo's allusions to revolution in *New Lamps for Old* had fallen on deaf ears, and may have helped to get the series suppressed.

As the nineteenth century moved towards its close, the British Empire seemed secure throughout the world. The news that the Boers had resisted British encroachment in the Transvaal was greeted by many, Aurobindo among them, with amazement and delight. In a poem "written during the progress of the Boer War," that is, between 1899 and 1902, he congratulated the poorly armed Dutch farmers for defying "the huge colossus who bestrides the earth."[93] Passing in silence over the Boers' own racism, he concluded that destiny had chosen them because they were ready to die for what they believed in. India too could defy imperial Britain if the men of the country could develop the same fighting spirit. But for this to happen, a radical change was needed in the Indian mentality. Pondering over how to bring this about, Aurobindo conceived a three-part program. First, there would be "a secret revolutionary propaganda and organisation of which the central object was the preparation of an armed insurrection." Along with this would come "public propaganda intended to convert the whole nation to the ideal of independence which was regarded ... by the vast majority of Indians as unpractical and impossible, an almost insane chimera." Finally, there would be an "organisation of the people to carry on a public and united opposition and undermining of the foreign rule through an increasing non-co-operation and passive resistance."[94] A bold plan—but how was it to be executed? The organization needed an organizer. Well endowed with the skills of the strategist and propagandist, Aurobindo lacked the push and promotional flair that are needed for grassroots work. Happily, a man with just these abilities, and political ideas that matched Aurobindo's, turned up in Baroda in 1899.[95]

Growing up in Bengal in the 1880s, Jatindranath Banerji dreamed of becoming a soldier, but as a member of what the British labeled a "nonmartial race," he was ineligible to join the Indian army. Putting on the robe of a *sannyasi,* he wandered around northern India, looking for ways to get military training. When he reached Baroda, he met Aurobindo and Madhavrao Jadhav, and Madhavrao got him admitted to the Baroda army. For two or three years Jatin trained to be a soldier and talked with Aurobindo and his friends about the coming revolution. In 1901 or 1902 they decided it was time for Jatin to return to Bengal. Once settled in Calcutta he would set up an *akhara,* or gymnasium, and look around for men he could train. No one expected quick results; the young men of Bengal were famous for their studiousness, docility, and faint-heartedness. Aurobindo thought the program "might occupy a period of 30 years before fruition could become possible."[96] Jatin, younger and more impulsive, had a shorter time frame in mind.

In the years since Jatin had left Bengal, a number of believers in the gospel of physical force had been active in Calcutta. One of them was Sarala Devi Ghosal, a granddaughter of Devendranath Tagore, who was encouraging young men to learn to use of the *lathi,* or bamboo staff. Another was Sister Nivedita, originally Margaret Elizabeth Noble, an Irish disciple of Swami Vivekananda, who was preaching her guru's doctrine of "national man-making" to the youth of the city. Nivedita was in touch with the Russian anarchist Peter Kropotkin and the nationalistic Japanese writer Okakura Kakuzo. Okakura came to Calcutta in 1901 and at a gathering of the town's elite announced: "You are such an educated race. Why do you let a handful of Englishmen tread you down? Do everything you can to achieve freedom, openly as well as secretly. Japan will assist you."[97] One of those present at Okakura's talk was a Calcutta High Court barrister named Pramathanath Mitra. An admirer of European secret societies and an expert in the *lathi,* Mitra was chosen as commander-in-chief of a society to be formed in response to Okakura's challenge.

For a while it went no further than that. Then, sometime in the early part of 1902—the dates and exact sequence of events cannot now be established—a man named Satish Chandra Bose came to Mitra with a proposal. Satish had been inspired by Nivedita to start a physical culture group, which was called, after a book by Bankim Chandra Chatterjee, the Anushilan Samiti, or Cultural Society. Friends told him that Mitra might be willing to put his weight behind the organization. The barrister was delighted when Satish came calling, and accepted his offer to become head of the *samiti*.

All of this happened around the time that Jatin Banerji was setting up his gymnasium in Calcutta. Aurobindo had given him a letter of introduction to Sarala Devi. Jatin met her, Pramathanath Mitra, and others interested in physical culture. Mitra suggested that Jatin and Satish join forces. The two agreed, and in March 1902 a new, expanded Anushilan Samiti was founded. Aurobindo came to Bengal six weeks later. Nothing is known about his activities during the month he was away from Baroda, but it may be assumed that he spent much of his time in Calcutta, and that he spoke with Jatin and probably Mitra as well.

Not long after Aurobindo's visit, Jatin toured the districts. One of his stops was Midnapore, where he got in touch with Jnanendranath and Satyendranath Bose, members of an existing secret society founded apparently by their cousin Jogendranath Bose—Aurobindo's uncle Jogen. The two brothers and their friend Hemchandra Das were thrilled by Jatin's claim that he had been sent by a revolutionary society to start branches in Bengal. He told the same story when he passed through the town of Arbelia: the movement in western India was already well advanced, and Aurobindo Ghose, a Bengali living in Baroda, was one of its leaders. It was Jatin's mission to prepare Bengal for the great upheaval that was to come.

WHILE JATIN GOT ON with his recruitment and training, Aurobindo went back to his work with the Gaekwar. A few weeks after his return to Baroda, his employer called him to Lonavla, a hill resort between Bombay and Poona, and asked him to draw up a document of some sort. Aurobindo wrote it, but, as he explained to Mrinalini in a letter of June 25, 1902, the Gaekwar balked at sending it. Shortly thereafter, "another very big and secret work came up. I had to take care of it. The Worm was very pleased with my work and promised to give me a raise. Who knows whether he will or not? The Worm's promises don't count for much. But he may give it. To all appearances, it looks like the day of the Worm's downfall is not far off. All the signs are bad."[98]

One would like to know what Aurobindo was referring to in this mysterious letter to his wife. The Worm (in Bengali, *kencho*) is obviously the Gaekwar; but what was the document (*prabandha*) that Aurobindo wrote for him, and why did the Gaekwar refuse to issue it? And what was the "very big and secret work"? Years later, Aurobindo wrote that the Gaekwar at least toyed with the idea of making Baroda a center of power around which nationalist and even revolutionary forces could coalesce. In the end he proved too cautious and self-absorbed to take such a dangerous step, but between 1902 and 1904, when Aurobindo worked most closely with him, he seems to have taken some chances.

Aurobindo returned to Baroda from Lonavla at the end of June 1902. The Gaekwar kept him busy, so much so that he fell ill from overwork. It was, as he wrote in a hilarious letter to his uncle, a peculiar malady that allowed him to do as much "kasrat [exercise] and croquet and walking and rushing about" as he pleased, but turned him into an invalid if he did an hour's work. Trying to recover from this illness, he went on two trips with fellow members of the Baroda Cricket Club. First, they watched the Baroda team receive "a jolly good beating" in Ahmedabad, which they celebrated with "a gorgeous dinner in the refreshment room." The waiters brought toast. The men picked two racks clean. The waiters "gave up the toast as a bad job, and brought in two great plates with a mountain of bread on it as large as Nandanpahad. After a short while we were howling for more. This time there was a wild-eyed consultation of waiters and after some minutes they reappeared with large trays of bread carried in both hands." This proved satisfactory. A short while later, Aurobindo and "some dozen rowdies, not to say Hooligans, of our club"—among them several of the highest officers of the state—"went down to Ajwa [a picnic spot near a reservoir] and behaved in such a manner that it is a wonder we were not arrested and locked up." He continues:

> On the way my horse broke down and the four of us had to get down and walk three miles in the heat. At the first village we met a cart coming back from Ajwa and in spite of the carters' protests, seized it, turned the bullocks round and started them back—of course with ourselves in the cart. The bullocks at first thought they were going to do the journey at their usual comfortable two miles an hour, but we convinced them of their error with the ends of our umbrellas and they ran. I don't believe bullocks have ever run so fast since the world began. The way the cart jolted, was a wonder; I know the internal arrangements of my stomach were turned upside down at least 300 times a minute. When we got to Ajwa we had to wait an hour for dinner; as a result I was again able to eat ten times my usual

allowance. As for the behaviour of those trusted pillars of the Baroda Raj at Ajwa, a veil had better be drawn over it; I believe I was the only quiet and decent person in the company.[99]

Aurobindo clearly was less restrained with his cronies than with his students, colleagues, and wife. But he kept something of his reserve even when out having fun. His remark about remaining a gentleman while everyone else was behaving badly was certainly ironic, but it suggests an inner distance between him and his friends that probably neither party ever crossed.

Back in Baroda by August 15, his thirtieth birthday, Aurobindo learned that the Gaekwar had given him the promised raise, a generous ninety rupees a month, making his salary 450 rupees. The ruler also dictated a certificate that read in part: "His Highness is pleased to note that he has found Mr. Ghose a very useful and capable young man. With a little more of regularity and punctual habits he can be of much greater help; and it is hoped that Mr. Ghose will be careful in future not to injure his own interests by any lack of these useful qualities." Aurobindo was "a man of great powers and every use should be made of his talents."[100]

Informing his uncle Jogen of the raise, Aurobindo noted wryly: "Rs 250 promotion after ten years' service does not look very much, but it is better than nothing. At that rate I shall get Rs 700 in 1912 and be drawing about Rs 1000 when I am ready to retire from Baroda either to Bengal or a better world." Giving the news to Mrinalini, he added that the Gaekwar showed "his intention of taking the value of the Rs 90 out of me by burdening me with overwork, so I don't feel very grateful to him." He hoped to return to the college, if only because it would permit him to spend his vacations in Bengal, but he feared that the Gaekwar's suggestion that the dewan use him "for writing Annual Reports etc." meant that his employer did "not want me to get my vacations" at all.[101]

Aurobindo also informed Mrinalini of Baroda's continuing misfortunes. The monsoon had failed and famine threatened. The Ajwa reservoir was almost dry and the danger of cholera acute. As a result, he told her, it would "be impossible" for her "to come to Baroda just now."[102] Even in Assam she would feel a reflection of the problems he was facing. Baroda's treasury, dependent upon agricultural revenue, was almost empty. Officials had been told that if the situation did not improve, they would all be put on half pay. Such a cut would more than cancel out his raise. Since his marriage, he had just been getting by on 360 rupees. Each month he had to send 80 rupees to support his grandmother, mother, and sister, and contribute 90 to his household expenses. If his new pay was halved, he would have no reserves; if the state went bankrupt, he could not even take refuge with his father-in-law, for "then who would send money to [his mother and grandmother in] Deoghur and Benares?"[103]

Aurobindo wrote three letters to Mrinalini between late June and mid-August 1902 and awaited her replies with some anxiety. When he learned that she had caught a cold, he advised her to keep warm, sent her extra money for medicine, and tried to persuade her to go to Deoghar.[104] She preferred to stay with her parents. This was a rather unconventional arrangement. Once a Bengali girl "goes to her father-in-law's house," that is, leaves her family and joins her husband's, she does not usually go back except for occasional visits or to give birth to children. But Mrinalini was young, her husband far away, and his paternal relatives out of the picture. For the moment there was little dishonor in her living with her parents. Still, Aurobindo would have been happier if she were staying with Jogen, Sarojini, and the rest. He wrote to her in August: "I should like you to spend some time in Deoghur, if you do not mind, Assam somehow seems terribly far off; and besides I should like you to form a closer intimacy with my relatives, at least those among them whom I especially love."[105]

Mrinalini remained in Assam while Aurobindo toiled in Baroda. At the end of August, the dewan ordered him to compile a report on the administration of the state for the year 1901–1902.[106] Such reports, meant to satisfy a requirement of the British government, were a mixture of public relations release and cooked-up statistics. Unenthusiastic from the start, Aurobindo did nothing for a year. When reminders from the British political agent piled up, he tried to pass the buck back to the dewan. In the end, the report of 1901–1902 was not published until 1904.[107] There were no further attempts to use his "great powers" in this way. Aurobindo was more agreeable to requests to write speeches for the Gaekwar, but he often found it hard to make changes that others suggested. Once the Gaekwar asked him to make a proposed speech "a little simpler and less learned." "I can't do it," Aurobindo replied, adding, with a gesture towards a colleague, "Let him do it for you." There was silence until Aurobindo spoke again: "Do you really believe that by simplifying the language of the speech a little you will make people think it was written by you? Whether they are good or bad, people know that the speeches of Indian princes are always written by others. . . . This draft is all right as it is." The Gaekwar agreed, and delivered the speech as Aurobindo wrote it.[108]

IN OCTOBER 1902 Sister Nivedita visited Baroda. It had been a difficult year for her. Her master Vivekananda had died on July 4; two weeks later she severed her connection with the monastic order he had founded. Although still dedicated to spiritual practice, she felt driven to throw herself into politics. Not wishing to embarrass the order, she asked for and received her "complete personal freedom."[109] That September she toured western India to spread her ideas and raise funds through public lectures and private meetings with men like the Gaekwar. She arrived in Baroda on October 20. Aurobindo received her at the station. This was their first meeting. He had read and admired her book *Kali the Mother* and heard her name in connection with the Anushilan Samiti. She had been told by friends that Mr. Ghose of Baroda "believed in strength and was a worshipper of Kali"—in other words, that he believed in revolution.[110] The two got along very well, but Nivedita's meeting with the Gaekwar was a failure. At one point he said something that raised her hopes, but in the end he told her that if he had anything more to say, he would do so through Mr. Ghose. He never did, and Nivedita went away disappointed.[111]

A month or so later, Aurobindo's brother Barin turned up in Baroda. Now twenty-two, he had spent the last four years kicking around Bihar and Bengal. After finishing high school, he entered Patna College, but dropped out six months later. For a while he stayed with Manmohan in Dacca and Benoy-bhusan in Cooch Behar. Wearing out his welcome with both brothers, he went back to Patna and opened up a shop, which soon failed. At this point, he decided to visit Aurobindo. Without informing him in advance, he caught a cross-country train and two days later arrived in Baroda, ready for an indefinite stay.

Barin kept himself busy doing something of everything and nothing in particular. He read, he wrote poetry, he played the *esraj*, he puttered around the garden. Aurobindo gave him books: Edmund Burke's *Reflections on the Revolution in France*, M.G. Ranade's *Rise of the Maratha Power*, William Digby's "*Prosperous*" *British India*. In the evenings, when Aurobindo and his friends got together, Barin participated in their increasingly businesslike discussions. He learned that they were in contact with a secret society that was rumored to have existed since the Revolt of 1857 and to have had something to do with the W. C. Rand murder. It was steered, Aurobindo told him, by a "Council of Five" that had some "Mahratta politicians as its members."[112] It is not known for sure who these politicians were, but one may assume that they included Tilak and his associate G. S. Khaparde. The Council had made Aurobindo the head of their Gujarat circle, which at the time consisted of no one but him and his friends.

In December, Aurobindo brought Barin with him when he went to Bombay to talk revolution with G.D. Madgavkar, a sympathetic ICS officer. The principal order of business was a proposal to send Madhavrao Jadhav to Japan for military training. Madgavkar said he would contribute 1,000 rupees toward his expenses. The men also discussed the forthcoming session of the Indian National Congress, which was to be held that year in Ahmedabad. A week before the session, the town hosted an industrial exhibition, at which the Gaekwar was principal speaker. His address was the most remarkable piece of work that Aurobindo ever wrote for him.[113] The Gaekwar began by contrasting the disease, famine, and poverty of India and the energy, efficiency, and prosperity of Europe. The disparity was caused partly by a deficiency of original thinking and leadership, partly by a lack of scientific knowledge. But more fundamentally, India's condition was "the result of acquisition of political power by the East India Company and the absorption of India in the growing British Empire." For India to return to its proper place in the world, a social revolution was needed, a "great national movement in which each man will work for the nation and not for himself or for his caste." The speaker did not disguise the difficulty of what he was suggesting: "Understand what this means. It means action.... Until you realize that the ultimate remedy lies in your own hands and that you have to carry it out by yourselves, no external reform can help you." He concluded by declaring war against the " 'ancient régime' of custom and prejudice" in order to establish "a national art and a national literature and a flourishing commerce" and eventually "a national government."[114]

The Gaekwar delivered this speech to general acclaim on December 15, 1902. Ten days later, the eighteenth session of the Indian National Congress began. None of the speakers came close to the Gaekwar for boldness and political astuteness. The chairman of the Reception Committee proclaimed that the idea underlying the Congress's actions was "that it is for our benefit that the British power should continue to be supreme in our land." He was followed by Surendranath Banerjea, the president of the session, who thundered out: "We plead for the permanence of British rule in India."[115] No doubt both statements were meant to soften the impact of the speakers' timid requests for administrative reform. But the contrast between their cringing and the Gaekwar's forthrightness is striking.

Aurobindo was present at the Ahmedabad Conference and Congress. It was the first time he attended a session of the body he had excoriated in print a decade earlier. His main reason for coming, other than to accompany the Gaekwar, was to contact advanced nationalist politicians, in particular B.G. Tilak. When the two were introduced, Tilak took him outside "and talked to him for an hour in the grounds expressing his contempt for the Reformist movement and explaining his own line of action in Maharashtra." Aurobindo left the conference convinced that Tilak was "the one possible leader for a revolutionary party."[116]

Indian journalists considered the Congress a success. Some even claimed that it marked a general renewal of interest in the Congress movement. Aurobindo was not so sanguine. To a "trained political observer," he wrote in one of his notebooks, it was obvious that the Congress was a spent force. The wave of enthusiasm that marked its beginnings had "dashed itself against the hard facts of human nature," and now throughout the country there was only "the languor, the weakness, the tendency to break up & discohere of the retiring wave." But he found some room for hope. "Behind & under cover of this failure & falling back there has been slowly & silently gathering another & vaster wave the first voices of which are now being heard." Those who were destined "to mount on the rising slope" of the new wave had to study the reasons for earlier failures. The Congress, Aurobindo repeated, "broke itself on the hard facts of human nature."[117] There he stopped, but it is possible to complete his thought. Britain would never hand over a valuable possession without a fight. Unless compelled by widespread agitation, it would never let the people of India play a serious role in their country's administration. The Congress had failed because it did not take these facts into consideration. What had to be done was to radicalize the Congress and mobilize the populace.

Secretary to the Crown

In the beginning of 1903, just after the Ahmedabad Congress, Aurobindo sent Barin to Calcutta to help Jatin Banerji in the work of revolutionary recruitment and organization. Before dispatching him on his mission, he initiated his brother into the secret society. The ceremony was solemn and a bit theatrical. Holding a sword in one hand and a copy of the *Bhagavad Gita* in the other, Barin swore that he would fight to the death for the freedom of India.[118]

When he reached Calcutta, Barin went to the society's headquarters and introduced himself to Jatin. He was impressed, like most people, by the former soldier's physique, bearing, and self-confidence. Jatin's first impressions of Barin are unlikely to have been as favorable. The thin, dreamy, bespectacled youth was not the sort of material he was looking for. But Barin did have an infectious enthusiasm for the cause. One day, while Barin was sitting around at headquarters, a man named Abinash Bhattacharya arrived and asked for information. Barin explained that Jatin was out, made a bit of small talk, and then suddenly cried out: "Brother, if it makes your heart ache to see India in bondage, don't waste any time, join us today, this very moment!" Over-whelmed, Abinash grabbed Barin's hand and answered: "Right, brother! From now on I'm with you."[119] With Barin and Abinash spreading the word and Jatin breaking in the recruits, the society slowly began to take shape.

Back in Baroda, Aurobindo was anxious to see how the activities of society were developing, but he found it hard to get away. The Gaekwar needed his help. Three years earlier, George Nathaniel Curzon, the viceroy and gover-nor general, had issued a circular requiring rulers of native states to obtain permission from the government before going abroad. The Gaekwar applied for permission in 1902 and was refused. He found this unbearable. "We are supposed to be chiefs," he complained, "but we are treated worse than paid servants."[120] In February 1903 he decided to try again, giving to Aurobindo the task of writing the letter to the government. Aurobindo used a great deal of tact to convey the Gaekwar's dispute. What made the Curzon circular so vexatious was the effect it "was calculated to produce on his status and dignity as a Ruler."[121] Aurobindo submitted his draft to his superiors on February 14. He wanted to leave Baroda immediately, but was obliged to wait another week while his leave application was being approved.

When he reached Calcutta, he was happy to discover that the society's recruitment and training were making brisk progress. He met some of the recruits and had discussions with Pramathanath Mitra, whom he initiated into the secret society. The two agreed on the overall line of approach: es-tablish *samitis* throughout the province, provide training in physical culture, and, when the time was right, introduce revolutionary ideas.[122] Before Au-robindo left Bengal, he and Barin went to Midnapore to inspect the local *samiti*. His uncle Jogen, who had grown up in the town, joined them from Deoghar to show them what the local recruits were doing. One of these, Hemchandra Das, accompanied the brothers when they went to a ravine for target practice. "When I saw the way [Aurobindo] and Barin held and aimed the rifle," Hem later recalled, "I realized that this was the first time they had handled one."[123]

There is no record of a meeting between Aurobindo and Mrinalini during his trip to eastern India, but it is likely that he made a point of seeing her in Deoghar or elsewhere. She remained with his relatives when he returned to Baroda, where conditions were still alarming. Plague had broken out again, more virulent than ever, and insufficient rainfall augured famine. Aurobindo thought it would be better for Mrinalini to stay in Bihar. Judging from a let-ter to her from her mother, Mrinalini felt lonely and unhappy. "Keep writing to Aurobindo," her mother said. "In that way you will be doing your duty. He will do whatever he decides to do. That is not your affair. Be always happy. Happiness, sadness—all is in God's hand. No man can interfere with that. Rely always on God."[124] This time-hallowed advice from a Hindu mother to a Hindu daughter may have helped Mrinalini bear her isolation from her husband, family, and friends.

WHEN AUROBINDO GOT BACK to Baroda, he resumed his duties at the palace and also did a bit of part-time teaching. He would have liked to teach more, but the Gaekwar had other ideas. Unable to go to Europe, the ruler decided to pass the summer in Kashmir. Toward the middle of May, already en route, he summoned Aurobindo to serve as his private secretary. Aurobindo caught up with the Gaekwar's party in Srinagar two weeks later. He was impressed, like most visitors, by the charm of Kashmir. When free, he enjoyed an "ideal life dawdling along in the midst of a supreme beauty." But unfortunately "there was the over-industrious Gaekwar to cut short the Paradise! His idea of Paradise was going through administrative papers" and making Aurobindo and others "write speeches for which he got all the credit."[125]

When he had some time to himself, Aurobindo wrote poetry and read Sanskrit literature. Over the past couple of years, the focus of his studies had shifted from Kalidasa to the Upanishads. He read the texts along with the commentaries of Gaudapada and Shankaracharya, with the aid of Paul Deussen's *System of the Vedanta* and other European works.[126] The Western scholars annoyed him, and even Shankaracharya seemed to him to miss the point. Aurobindo had no interest in "what philosophic Hinduism took [the Upanishads] to mean"; what he wanted to discover was "what the Upanishads"—the texts, not the commentaries—"really do mean" in themselves. In the end, he came to believe that their deeper meaning could only be grasped by one who had undergone an "elaborate training" in yoga. He recently had learned a bit about yoga from Deshpande, who had been practicing for a year or two. But his friend made it seem as if yoga required one to renounce action. However interested Aurobindo may have been, he "refused to take it up, because it seemed to him a retreat from life."[127]

Nevertheless, he was prone to experiences that he later understood were yogic in nature. Two of them had come years earlier: the peace he felt when he disembarked in Bombay in 1893, and a vision of a great Being "surging up from within when in danger of a carriage accident" a few months later.[128] More recently, while visiting a shrine to Bhawani, a form of the mother-goddess, in Poona,

The Soul of all that lives, calm, pure, alone,
Revealed its boundless self mystic and bare.[129]

Aurobindo wrote these lines four decades after the event. It is impossible to say how this or the earlier experiences struck him when they occurred. Curiously, he "did not associate them at that time with Yoga."[130] Though they apparently were powerful, he did not mention them in his contemporary writings, and does not seem to have spoken with his friends about them. The same is true of an experience he had in Kashmir in 1903. Srinagar is dominated by a rocky monolith called the Takht-i-Sulaiman, or the Seat of Solomon. On its top is a temple said to have been visited by Shankaracharya himself. Walking along a narrow path near the temple, with a "formless solitude" all around, it seemed to Aurobindo as if

All had become one strange Unnameable,
An unborn sole Reality world-nude,
Topless and fathomless, for ever still.[131]

This was, he later understood, a glimpse of the Absolute, the *brahman*. Such experiences are the basis of Adwaita Vedanta, the philosophy that holds the world to be *maya*, illusion. Striking as it was, however, his experience did not push him in the direction of Adwaita, nor did it impel him to turn his back on life.

THE GAEKWAR AND HIS ENTOURAGE remained in Srinagar until June 7, 1903, when they departed for Achabal. After a week of sightseeing—Achabal is famous for its gardens laid out by the Mughal empress Nur Jahan—the royal party proceeded to Gulmarg, the resort of choice for the region's Indian and British elite. For almost two months the Gaekwar and his family joined this beau monde in its round of luxurious amusements. It was an excellent time to be out of Baroda. Plague mortality reached an all-time high, and the monsoon again was delayed. The Gaekwar busied Aurobindo with writing letter after letter about administrative matters, questions of social reform, a new house in Bombay, a new house in Ooty, alterations to Luxmivilas Palace, buying three elephants, Prince Jaisinghrao's expenses at Oxford, selling the family's famous shawl made of seed pearls ("as an Indian curiosity say in America"),[132] and dozens of other matters serious and trivial. This went on until September, when the Gaekwar returned to Baroda. Aurobindo went back separately. There had been much friction between him and his employer during the trip, and the experiment of his working as the ruler's private secretary was deemed a failure.

Nothing is known about the nature of Aurobindo's service between September 1903 and May 1904. He undoubtedly was doing some sort of work for the Gaekwar, but no record of it survives. A February file mentions that he was then on leave. Years later he remarked that "a great part of the last years [at Baroda] was spent on leave in silent political activity, for he was debarred from public action by his position at Baroda."[133] At one point, perhaps during this undocumented period, he traveled to central India to meet members of an Indian regiment who had expressed some interest in the goals of the secret society. He spoke with some of the sub-officers and men, but the trip had no long-term results.[134] On another occasion (possibly again during the undocumented months), he toured eastern Bengal with Debavrata Bose, an intelligent young man who had joined Jatin's society. Debavrata was an excellent speaker in Bengali, but if he said anything that suggested sedition, his listeners took to their heels. Aurobindo could feel "a black weight of darkness" hanging over the country, a pervasive mood of "apathy and despair." He had gone on the tour to "find out the general attitude of the country and the possibilities of the revolutionary movement." As he inspected the *samitis* and met with the "leading men," he asked himself: "*These are the people who will do it?*" It became obvious to him "that secret action or preparation by itself was not likely to be effective if there were not also a wide public movement which would create a universal patriotic fervour and popularise the idea of independence as the ideal and aim of Indian politics."[135]

With one exception, any stirrings of revolt in the country at that time were momentary ripples on the tranquil sea of the Pax Britannica. The exception came from an unexpected quarter. Toward the end of 1903, the government of Bengal announced its intention to transfer the eastern districts of the province to Assam for reasons of administrative efficiency. Bengal was almost as large as France and much more populous, and there had long been calls to divide the province into more manageable units. As the plan developed, British bureaucrats observed that there would be political advantages to drawing the borderline through the heartland of the region. "I believe that Dacca and Mymensingh [two districts of eastern Bengal] would give far less trouble if they were under Assam,"[136] wrote Andrew Fraser, the incoming lieutenant-governor of Bengal. Other officials agreed, and on December 3 the government announced its plan to transfer those districts, along with the entire division of Chittagong, to Assam.

There was an immediate outcry in the affected districts of Bengal, generally for the wrong reasons. Bengalis objected to being lumped together with the

Assamese, whom they considered their inferiors. Such an attitude, Aurobindo noted in an article, was just playing into the hands of the British. "It should plainly be the policy of the national movement to ignore points of division and to emphasise old and create new points of contact and union." The claimed benefits of the administrative restructuring were just a sop. The people of Bengal needed to be aware "that this measure is no mere administrative proposal but a blow straight at the heart of the nation."[137] Aurobindo never completed or published the piece, but he did bring out an anti-partition pamphlet called *No Compromise*. Barin had it printed in Calcutta secretly and at night, because no registered printer would touch it. Abinash took a copy to Surendranath Banerjea, the leader of the anti-partition movement. "Who has written such English?" Banerjea is supposed to have cried. "No Bengali could do it." Abinash told him about Aurobindo and their revolutionary plans. Seeing that a party of physical force might end up strengthening his hand, Banerjea gave Abinash his blessings but told him to keep his distance.[138]

Barin had been fairly active since he joined the secret society in the beginning of 1903. He had attempted to open centers in different parts of Bengal, and succeeded in Chandernagore, Mymensingh, and other towns where there were groups that could be converted to the revolutionary gospel. In Calcutta, he hung out in College Square and harangued disaffected students. Other recruiters, among them Debavrata Bose and Bhupendranath Dutt, did grassroots work in the metropolis and in the districts. A trickle of young men began showing up at the society's new headquarters on Grey Street. Still, the group's progress was slow. The leaders made up for this by talking big. When Hemchandra Das visited headquarters, Barin and others regaled him with tales of their spread throughout the province. Hem believed these accounts as little as they believed the ones he told in his turn. Taking a look around him at Grey Street, he saw little to get excited about. After two years, the much-vaunted secret society consisted of "one horse, one bicycle . . . and a dozen or so leaders, great and small."[139] The lack of direction and organization opened the way to friction and fragmentation.

One of the society's early conflicts was over an ideological question: the role of physical violence in its activities. To Sarala Devi, the purpose of martial arts training was to develop physical strength and manly attitudes. To Jatin, Barin, and Aurobindo, it was a step toward establishing militias for guerrilla warfare. Sarala Devi broke with the society over this issue. More serious ruptures were caused by pettier problems. Jatin and Barin did not get along personally. Jatin was a natural leader, a good drill master, and (according to his critics) a martinet. Barin was easygoing, undisciplined, and unwilling to take orders from anyone but Aurobindo. When Barin and Jatin disagreed, Barin wrote a letter to his brother. Aurobindo wrote back telling him to work things out himself. The next time Aurobindo came to Calcutta, he rebuked Barin for picking a quarrel and brought about a truce. It proved to be short lived. "The breach was healed," Barin noted, "only to gape wider as soon as his back was turned."[140]

AUROBINDO RESUMED HIS regular work with the Gaekwar in June 1904, this time with the title *huzur kamdar*. This is simply the Marathi equivalent of "private secretary" (the phrase means "secretary to the crown"), and his duties were the same as when he held the more prestigious post. Whenever an important document had to be written in English—about hiring a new principal for the college, restructuring the revenue department, or reorganizing the Baroda army—the Gaekwar summoned Mr. Ghose. This went on until August, when the ruler received a letter from the minister of education asking if Aurobindo could come back to the college. The incoming British principal wanted an Oxford graduate to work as professor of English. In this connection the minister noted: "In the interests of the College I may also remark that Mr. Ghose had acquired a reputation in the College when he was Professor of English, about 4 years back. If his services could be wholly spared to the College, he may be advantageously entrusted with the work that I have chalked out above for a new Oxford man."[141] When the proposal reached the Gaekwar, he discussed it with Aurobindo, who expressed his willingness to return to the college. The Gaekwar was looking forward to a long stay abroad—he had finally obtained the government's permission to go—and saw no reason to keep Aurobindo as *huzur kamdar* during his absence. On September 6 he signed an order assigning him to the college. At the same time he raised his salary to 550 rupees per month. Since this was more than the other professors received, he appointed Aurobindo to the ornamental position of vice principal.

BEFORE BEGINNING WORK at the college, Aurobindo took leave and went to Bengal. The main purpose of his visit was to settle the wrangling between Barin and Jatin, which had split the *samiti*. The breach came, ostensibly, over a personal matter. Jatin was living with a woman of unknown antecedents. He insisted that she was a relative; the others did not believe him. But even if the relationship was legitimate, it broke the rules of the *samiti*, which required all members to abandon personal attachments for the sake of the motherland. Aurobindo ignored the accusations and tried to get to the bottom of the conflict. At first he seemed to have some success, but when the autumn holiday season approached, he and Barin went to Deoghar to be with their family. While they were there, letters arrived with fresh complaints against Jatin. Fed up, Aurobindo told Barin: "I can see that nothing will ever come of Bengal." When he went to Baroda after the holidays, Barin was with him.[142]

Principal Ghose

Aurobindo was back at work in Baroda by the end of October. For a while the pace was leisurely. The Gaekwar was planning his foreign trip and looking ahead to December, when he would be chief speaker at the National Social Conference in Bombay. Mr. A. B. Clarke, the new principal, was learning the ropes before the college reopened in January. Clarke was planning to spend most of his first year on furlough in England. During his absence, Vice Principal Ghose would take his place.

At the end of 1904 or the beginning of 1905, Mrinalini came to Baroda and stayed with her husband for the first time in three years. They kept mostly to themselves, a neighbor recalled.[143] At one point, the couple stayed in Khaserao Jadhav's house along with the Jadhav brothers and their families. Barin also became a member of the household. The men passed the evenings together, joined occasionally by their wives and children. Mrinalini rarely went with the other women when they breached the male stronghold. She remained so shy that she never once spoke to Barin in all the time he stayed with them.[144]

Barin kept himself busy digging in the garden, playing the *esraj,* and writing poetry. With nothing much happening in Bengal, it looked as though he might be staying in Baroda for a while. If he stayed, he would have to find a job. In December, Aurobindo asked the Gaekwar if there was an opening for his brother in the state service. The Gaekwar asked to be reminded about the subject before he left for Europe.[145] Then Barin disappeared into the jungles of central India. He had decided that what the country needed was a society guided by a holy man, modeled after the political *sannyasis* in Bankim Chandra's novel *Anandamath.* The headquarters of the group would be a temple at the source of the sacred river Narmada. Barin took it upon himself to find the holy man and the site for the temple. Aurobindo thought the idea had possibilities. Besides, he knew better than to try to interfere when Barin had a new idea in his head.

THE SPLIT BETWEEN Barin and Jatin, and Jatin's subsequent departure from Calcutta, marked the end of the Bengal secret society. The groups in Calcutta that survived acted alone and without vigor. The revolutionary council had all but ceased to exist. If its members ever met, they were more likely to talk about East Asia than East Bengal. When the Russo-Japanese war broke out in February 1904, there was a flurry of meetings in Calcutta and pan-Asian sentiment soared. But no one expected the Japanese—"a race of dwarfs fed chiefly on rice," as one Indian journalist put it—to succeed in their struggle against a European power.[146] Japan's attack on Port Arthur, followed by its victories in Korea and Manchuria, seemed to hopeful minds in Asia to mark the beginning of a new balance of power in the world.

With the siege of Port Arthur as background, the twentieth annual session of the Indian National Congress was held in Bombay at the end of December. Aurobindo was among those present. His father's friend Sir Henry Cotton presided, insisting that "it would be easy" for the government of Bengal "to devise a scheme [of partition] which would not receive the unanimous disapproval of the affected population."[147] He was lustily cheered for these pronouncements, after which the passive assembly approved the usual spineless resolutions. Aurobindo probably was also present when the Indian Social Conference opened on December 30, and he may have drafted parts of the speech that the Gaekwar delivered on the occasion, notably the following passage about the work that India's wandering *sannyasis* might do for the country: "Asceticism is evil unless it be a humane asceticism, one not divorced from philanthropy. He who surrenders life to help his fellows is a saint, but not he who becomes a beggar to avoid labour or responsibility, or retires to a jungle to save what Kingsley would have called 'his own dirty soul.'"[148]

IN JANUARY 1905 Aurobindo resumed teaching at the college after a gap of almost four years. Dressed neatly in a white suit and turban, he arrived daily at around eleven o'clock, entered his classroom, and began lecturing immediately. With one hand on the table, "he would keep his eyes down and speak as if in half meditation." The assigned text for that year's intermediate examination was Edmund Burke's *Reflections on the Revolution in France*. As a republican and admirer of Napoleon, Aurobindo disagreed with many of Burke's views, but he presented them so lucidly that "there was no need of questions and answers," as a student recalled. This was just as well, for Aurobindo neither asked nor answered questions in class, though he was always ready for consultation afterward. Scorning the usual Indian method of following the text sentence by sentence, he preferred to "throw light on the subject in an all-round way." Several of the students feared that they were not getting what they needed to pass their examinations, but even a dull student recalled that "as his method of teaching consisted in going to the roots, one could never forget what he taught, even though the whole text was not completed." Brighter students were stimulated by his "broad, overall and penetrating view of the subject." Pondering over his exposition, they made use of his suggestions to chart their own course of supplementary reading.[149]

Along with his teaching duties, Aurobindo served as head of the college union, contributed to the *Baroda College Miscellany,* and was director of the state's public library. On top of all this, on March 3 he was appointed acting principal. Until Clarke returned in November, he would be responsible for the administration of the college and its associated high school. For this he received an allowance of 160 rupees, making his monthly salary 710 rupees. This was a healthy sum, though less than the younger Clarke's starting salary of 800 rupees. His tasks as principal were varied: hiring peons, placing professors, ordering supplies, watching the budget, writing official letters and reports. These administrative duties continued even after the end of the term in April.

DURING THE MID-YEAR BREAK, Aurobindo had plenty of time to read and write. Crates of books from Calcutta and Bombay continued to arrive at his door. Unpacked in his presence, they were carried to a room that already was filled to overflowing. Years later, Barin could still recall the scene: "a table, a sofa, a number of chairs, all heaped pell-mell with books and a revolving book-case groaning under their weight—all thinly covered with dust; a quiet small unassuming man buried there for hours in a trance of thought and very often writing page after page of poetry."[150] Aurobindo's reading was as eclectic and polylingual as ever. A program of study jotted down at this time included Johann Wolfgang von Goethe's *Iphigenia in Tauris* and three other German plays; Molière, Ernest Renan, and Octave Feuillet's *Roman d'un jeune homme pauvre*; several Sanskrit dramas; and the Taittiriya, Aitareya, and Chhandogya Upanishads.[151] His writing, still wide-ranging, increasingly focused on Sanskrit scriptures. After completing a translation of eight short Upanishads, he tried his hand at a commentary in dialogue form, taking as his text the briefest and pithiest of them all, the Isha Upanishad. Presenting the essence of Vedanta in eighteen verses, the Isha has attracted generations of commentators, among them the great Shankaracharya. But as Aurobindo read and pondered over the text, he noticed ideas that the commentators had missed or explained away. One verse lays great stress on action: "Do your deeds in this world and wish to live a hundred years." Commentators of the school that sees the world as illusion, *maya,* glossed over the obvious meaning; to them, action was a temporary expedient, as life's purpose was to attain *mukti* or liberation by means of renunciation. Aurobindo took the passage to mean exactly what it says. In a dialogic commentary, Aurobindo has a Guru tell a Student that the true purpose of renunciation is to gain divine power to "pour it in a stream over the world." True *sannyasis* were "the most mighty in God to do the work of God."[152]

The language of Aurobindo's dialogue is heavy and pedantic, the characters shallow and unconvincing, but the work shows evidence of much original thought. Aurobindo had begun his study of the Upanishads with the widely held idea that they "declare the phenomenal world to be unreal." His reading convinced him that this was not their original intent. *Maya,* he insisted, did not mean "illusion" but "the principle of phenomenal existence," that is, the power by which the phenomenal world is created. Only such a conception could account for "*both* the truth of sheer transcendent Absoluteness of the Brahman and the palpable, imperative existence of the phenomenal Universe." Having written this, he added, in a prescient footnote: "Of course I am not prepared, in these limits, to develop the final argument; that would imply a detailed examination of all metaphysical systems, which would be in itself the labour of a lifetime."[153]

At the same time that he was launching his career as a textual scholar, Aurobindo was also writing imaginative literature. A few years earlier, he had begun a play in verse on the Elizabethan model, but gave up after a single act. Sometime around 1905 he tried again, this time with considerable success. *The Viziers of Bassora* is based on the Tale of Nur al-Din Ali and the Damsel Anis al-Jalis, an episode of the *Arabian Nights*—but was it just coincidence that Bassora echoes Baroda, or that the principal problem in the court of Alzayni, as in the Baroda administration, was that the king had two ministers? In the Baroda of fact, the conflict between the dewan and the councilor led to bureaucratic gridlock. In the Bassora of fiction, the jealousy of the evil Almuene towards the noble Alfazzal results in a tangle that only Haroun al Rasheed can resolve. Such parallels cannot be pushed too far, however, as Aurobindo's comedy follows the original story fairly closely. Alfazzal purchases Anice, a Persian slave-girl of surpassing beauty, for the use of Alzayni, the king of Bassora. Before Alfazzal can hand Anice over, she is seduced by Nureddene, Alfazzal's handsome but spendthrift son. Nureddene and Anice live together in happiness until his prodigality reduces them to penury. At Anice's request, Nureddene tries to sell her to one of his friends; but Almuene almost succeeds in buying her for his hideous son Fareed. Nureddene and Anice flee to Baghdad, where they charm first the gardener of Haroun al Rasheed, then the fabled Caliph himself. Haroun sends Nureddene to Bassora with a letter ordering Alzayni to make Nureddene king in his place. Almuene protests and Nureddene is cast into prison. He is about to be executed when Haroun's cavalry arrives. Nureddene becomes king of Bassora and lives happily with his faithful Anice. The underlying plot of this wonder tale is one that Aurobindo returned to repeatedly in his dramatic writing: a beautiful young woman, noble but in bondage, and a handsome young hero, sensitive yet strong, fall irretrievably in love. The hero must battle entrenched inferiors to gain his birthright. In this struggle the heroine, womanly yet resourceful, is his chief helper. In the outer world of action, Aurobindo never sought help from anyone. In the imaginative world of his dramas, his protagonist was never without a partner.

SINCE THE COLLAPSE of the Calcutta *samiti*, Aurobindo and his friends had begun to look elsewhere to fulfill their revolutionary dreams. Japan's victory over Russia made many in India think that the island nation was a model to be emulated, or even an ally in their struggle against the British. But India's interest in Japan was not reciprocated. No Japanese military academy was willing to accept Madhavrao as a student. B. G. Tilak tried to induce the Russian ambassador to get Madhavrao admitted to an academy in Russia; when this attempt failed, Tilak, Aurobindo, and others put together enough money to pay for Madhavrao's passage to Europe. Once there, he managed to enroll himself in a Swiss military academy in Bern.

Summer 1905 was a dull period for the revolutionaries of Baroda. They continued to meet in the evenings to talk about politics or anything else that came up. When they had nothing better to do, they amused themselves by holding séances. Table rapping and other forms of spirit communication were all the rage in the West, and the craze had spread to India too. Aurobindo and his friends tried their hands at automatic writing and were intrigued by the results. Barin turned out to be an unusually good medium, producing what Aurobindo called "some very extraordinary automatic writing . . . in a very brilliant and beautiful English style." These communications included a number of statements that "proved to be true although unknown to the persons concerned or anyone else present."[154] This justified further experimentation. Shortly before Madhavrao left for Europe, he, Aurobindo, Barin, and Deshpande held séances for three days running. They contacted the spirit of the great yogi Ramakrishna Paramhansa and asked him what they should do to improve their country. "*Mandir karo*"—make a temple— the spirit replied. When the men emerged from their room, they informed Rajaram Patkar that "a message from the Goddess has been received." They would build a temple and start an institution to spread the gospel of selfless service to the motherland.[155]

Aurobindo's attitude toward the spirit communications was one of cautious interest. He continued his experiments over the next ten years, eventually concluding that while

> there are sometimes phenomena which point to the intervention of beings of another plane, not always or often of a high order, the mass of such writings comes from a dramatising element in the subconscious mind; sometimes a brilliant vein in the subliminal [mind] is struck and then predictions of the future and statements of things known in the present and past come up, but otherwise these writings have not a great value.[156]

He always considered the 1905 communication from Ramakrishna to be among the most interesting he ever received. But he was inclined, especially later, to interpret the command to build a temple in metaphorical rather than physical terms: one should make oneself a living temple of the spirit. At the time a more concrete interpretation won out.

Some thirty miles from Baroda, on the banks of the Narmada, lies the pilgrimage center of Chandod. More than once, Aurobindo, Barin, Deshpande, and another friend named A.B. Devdhar visited this minor Benares to meet with *sadhus*. When the order to build a temple was received, Deshpande, who was assistant collector of the district, decided to start a school that would combine Sanskrit learning with a modern national education. On March 17, 1905 Deshpande opened the Ganganath Bharatiya Vidyalaya (Ganganath Indian School) near Chandod. Barin, meanwhile, was eager to get started with his order of political *sannyasis*. He persuaded Aurobindo to write something to stir up interest. The result, a twenty-page pamphlet called *Bhawani Mandir*, was printed shortly before August 1905. "A temple is to be erected and consecrated to Bhawani, the Mother, among the hills," the pamphlet begins. "To all the children of the Mother, the call is set forth to help in the sacred work." To answer the question "Who is Bhawani?" Aurobindo drew on Indian metaphysics and European science to draw a picture of "the Infinite Energy, which streams forth from the Eternal and sets the wheel to work." Manifest in other eras as love, knowledge, renunciation, or pity, the creative energy was in this age "the mother of Strength," pure *shakti*. By tapping this universal energy, Europe and Japan had become great, "but in India the breath moves slowly." The *shakti* latent in the millions that made up the nation had to be awakened. Having sketched the metaphysical foundations of his nationalism, Aurobindo turned to practical matters. Three things needed to be done. First, a temple had to be built "far from the contamination of modern cities" where the mother of strength could be adored. Secondly, an order of renunciates practicing the yoga of action had to be founded. These monks would "go forth and carry the flame" of Bhawani "to every nook and corner of our land." Such work would gain strength by being based on the spiritual knowledge of Vedanta. To obtain such knowledge was the real need of the hour.[157]

Writing this pamphlet was Aurobindo's primary contribution to the Bhawani Mandir scheme. He also thought of issuing a series of books for the renunciates to use, to be called the *Bhawani-grantha-mala* or Garland of Books for Bhawani. His commentary on the Isha Upanishad was to be the first of these, but he never completed it. Barin continued to talk about erecting a temple to Bhawani in the central Indian highlands. Aurobindo showed little interest in this side of the project, though once, he, Deshpande, and Barin went to Thane, near Bombay, to present the idea to Charu Chandra Dutt, a Bengali ICS man whom Aurobindo had met a short while earlier. Nothing much came of this or other discussions on the subject. Eventually, Aurobindo later recalled, "the whole thing fizzled out."[158]

IN JUNE 1905 the Government of India accepted the proposal to partition Bengal, creating a new province, Eastern Bengal and Assam, that would incorporate half of the Bengali-speaking districts of the undivided province. The announcement came as a shock, as the talks leading up to the final decision had been held in secret. Government documents reveal that as the idea took shape, political factors became more important than administrative ones. "It is not altogether easy to reply in a dispatch which is sure to be published," one official wrote, "without disclosing the fact that in this scheme" of partition, "one of our main objects is to split up and thereby weaken a solid body of opponents to our rule."[159] The "opponents" were educated Bengali-speaking Hindus, the most politically conscious group in India. After partition, they would be outnumbered in the remnants of Bengal by non-Bengalis, and in East Bengal by Bengali-speaking Muslims. Lord Curzon focused his attention on the latter group in his attempt to win support for the plan. In the new province "the Mohomedans of Eastern Bengal" would regain "a unity which they have not enjoyed since the days of the old Musalman Viceroys and Kings," he said.[160] The East Bengal Muslims, originally as opposed as the Hindus to the proposal, were swayed by Curzon's blandishments.

When the decision to partition the province was reported in the newspapers, it touched off an unprecedented reaction. Exaggerating only a little, the *Sanjivani* declared that the news had "driven the Bengali public completely out of their senses." The paper's editor, Krishna Kumar Mitra (Aurobindo's maternal uncle), wrote that Lord Curzon "will soon feel the effect of this act of his. The Bengalis will never remain silent." Until the partition order was rescinded, he wrote, "the use of articles of foreign make would be regarded as the greatest sin."[161] The response was immediate. At dozens of meetings, thousands of people vowed to stop buying salt, sugar, cloth, or anything else made in Britain. Instead, they would buy only *swadeshi* (indigenous) products.

Most of the momentum behind the *swadeshi* movement came from East Bengal, most of the direction from Calcutta. On August 7 an enormous meeting was held at the capital's town hall to endorse a resolution already passed at district meetings to avoid buying anything manufactured in England. Boycotting British goods meant paying more for inferior replacements. Despite this, the resolution was taken up with surprising unanimity. Students marched in the streets, chanting slogans and singing. The opening words of a song by Bankim Chandra, "Bande Mataram!" (Salutations to the Mother!), became the movement's war cry. For a while the Bengali people were caught up in the sort of enthusiasm that often is felt in the early stages of revolutions. Ordinary men, women, and children were filled with the desire to cooperate, serve, and sacrifice themselves for the motherland.

This, of course, was not all there was to it. Along with feelings of self-sacrifice and solidarity came a surge of hatred, frustration, and rage, directed not only against the government, but also anyone who went against the dictates of the crowd. Bengalis attempting to buy British products were first requested, then pressured to desist. The use of violence, psychological and physical, was not far behind. It soon became apparent that the movement was sustained primarily by a single social group: educated, middle-class, Bengali-speaking Hindus, whose interests would be hurt by partition. The peasantry, mostly uneducated Muslims and lower-caste Hindus, would be largely unaffected by the administrative restructuring, but would have to sacrifice the most to keep the movement alive. A laborer earning fifteen or twenty rupees a month was scarcely in a position to pay double for inferior cloth. Such considerations have prompted some historians to view the *swadeshi* movement as an attempt by the Hindu middle class to make the populace serve their political and economic interests. There is something to be said for such theories, but they do not give the whole story. Ideas and emotions play an enormous role in bringing about political and social change. In August 1905 the Bengali people threw themselves into a movement that benefited few directly but caused many to sacrifice their comfort, their prospects, and even their lives. It was the idea embodied in the cry "Bande Mataram!" much more than economic self-interest that made the *swadeshi* movement possible. And it was the *swadeshi* movement that gave Indian nationalism its teeth.

WHILE BENGAL WAS SEETHING with the first stirrings of the *swadeshi*-boycott movement, Aurobindo was sitting in Baroda, teaching Burke, Scott, and Tennyson and writing office memos and reports. In the midst of these routine activities, he began the practice of yoga. Since his first exposure to this system of spiritual discipline, he had had many occasions to reflect on the possibilities of inner development that it promised. His study of the Upanishads had convinced him that the goal of life was the attainment of union (yoga) with *brahman*, the Absolute. The Upanishads offered techniques through which this union could be achieved. He did not doubt the efficacy of the methods, but he was slow to take them up because he believed at the time that they required abandoning life and action.

Aurobindo's interest in yoga was whetted by what he had read and seen over the past few years. The books of Vivekananda and his master Ramakrishna made a strong impression on him. He saw the latter as a modern representative of a tradition of spiritual experience going back to the Upanishads and earlier. He also became aware of a parallel tradition that emphasized the attainment of extraordinary powers. Seeking the truth behind the so-called occult sciences, he met a man who could tell him exactly what he was thinking.[162] He saw a *sannyasi* cure Barin of a serious fever by taking a glass of water, slicing through the contents with a knife while repeating a mantra, and giving it to the young man to drink. Two cases of cure by means of prayer were reported to him by Madhavrao and by his Deoghar relatives: both times the family prayed together after the doctor had given up, and the patient recovered miraculously.[163]

Nothing miraculous had ever happened to Aurobindo. The closest he had come to it was seeing images and hearing sounds with no apparent physical cause. He spoke about the images with a friend, who told him they were just after-images. Aurobindo listened to his account, and then asked whether "after-images remained before the eyes for two minutes at a time." "No," his friend replied, "only for a few seconds." Could one, Aurobindo continued, "get after-images of things not around one or even not existing upon this earth"? Again, his friend replied in the negative. In this and other cases it seemed to Aurobindo that "so-called scientific explanations break down as soon as you pull them out of their cloudland of mental theory and face them with the actual phenomena they pretend to decipher." Later he found descriptions in the Upanishads of the kind of sights and sounds he was experiencing. This encouraged him to pursue his investigations further. He found that, despite his European education, which included a "period of agnostic denial," he did not feel obliged to "take the attitude of doubt and disbelief which was for so long fashionable in Europe." Experiences and powers that seemed to go beyond the established bounds of science always seemed to him "perfectly natural and credible. Consciousness in its very nature could not be limited by the ordinary physical human-animal consciousness, it must have other ranges."[164]

Around this time, Aurobindo met a leader of the *naga sadhus,* a sect of Hindu ascetics famous for their martial training. Learning that Aurobindo and his friends wanted to drive the British from India, the *sadhu* gave him a *stotra*—a hymn or spell—that he said would help. Aurobindo repeated it without result.[165] The *sadhu* also advised him to make an image of Bagala, a form of the Mother Goddess, and have a brahmin chant the goddess's name a million times while standing in water on one leg. This also had no result; but Aurobindo continued his investigations. He was always ready to listen, but retained his critical perspective. Writing about *sannyasis,* for instance, he noted: "The saffron robe nowadays covers a great deal of selfishness, a great deal of idleness, a great deal of hypocrisy." The trademark of the genuine *sannyasi* was not the saffron robe or "the talk and the outward action" but "the thirst for the Eternal." To find out if this was present, one had to "look in the eyes, watch the slighter, less observed habits, wait for the light on the face."[166] Sometime in 1905 Aurobindo met someone who passed this test.

Deshpande had become acquainted with a swami named Brahmananda, who lived on the banks of the Narmada near Chandod. He was a venerable figure, immeasurably old: two, perhaps three hundred years, people said, and at any rate a generation older than the oldest man in town. Through a combination of *rajayoga* meditation and *hathayoga* exercises, he had preserved his health and vitality, remaining "a man of magnificent physique showing no signs of old age except white beard and hair, extremely tall, robust, able to walk any number of miles a day and tiring out his younger disciples," with "a great head and magnificent face that seemed to belong to men of more ancient times."[167] Aurobindo observed this when he visited Brahmananda with Deshpande and Devdhar, who was one of the swami's disciples. Aurobindo was "greatly impressed" by what he saw and returned more than once. On his last visit, something unusual happened. Brahmananda generally sat with closed or half-closed eyes as his visitors bowed before him to receive his blessings. When Aurobindo's turn came, the swami looked at him with a full gaze. Aurobindo looked back and was struck by the beauty of the old man's eyes, the most remarkable he had ever seen. He later said (as reported by Barin) that the effect was "simply electric or magnetic. A great power of peace and sense of awakening entered [Aurobindo's] soul and wrought an ineffable change." As usual with Barin's accounts, the exaggerated language strains credulity, but there is no doubt that Aurobindo was convinced that Brahmananda had attained an elevated state of consciousness by means of yoga.[168]

On one of their trips to Chandod, Aurobindo and his friends visited the nearby temple town of Karnali. Leaving their boat at the landing, they climbed the stone steps leading from the banks of the Narmada and entered the temple complex. Aurobindo was drawn to the shrine of Kali, the terrible form of the mother goddess, who is especially venerated in Bengal. To the eye of the profane, the Kali image at Karnali is not terribly prepossessing; it is a rough-carved stone smeared with color and covered with gaudy clothes and jewels. But as Aurobindo looked he saw

A living Presence deathless and divine,
A Form that harboured all infinity.[169]

This was the fifth such experience that had come to him. All of the experiences involved striking, if transient, changes in his ordinary state of consciousness, but they had little effect on his outer mode of life. A single experience of the sort Aurobindo had is often enough to impel an Indian man to leave wife, family, and home and begin wandering from place to place, or pass months in meditation. Aurobindo simply returned to his work, not telling anyone what had happened, not even noting down his impressions.

Despite all of the documentation that exists—Aurobindo's letters and other writings, the reminiscences of his friends, his own retrospective accounts—we know very little about what was going on in his mind at this time. Outwardly he was a popular teacher, a competent administrator, an easygoing friend, a dutiful if distant husband. As a writer, he was confident and productive; as a scholar, industrious and painstaking. Like many of his contemporaries, he was interested in improving the lot of his country. What marked him out from many others was his conviction that the first step to social and economic progress was radical political change. So strong was this belief that his other growing interest—to achieve the self-knowledge and self-mastery spoken of in the Upanishads—had to be secondary to it.

But by August 1905 Aurobindo had concluded that the pursuit of inner mastery and the pursuit of political freedom were not incompatible. He had heard that spiritual knowledge gives power, and observed enough to feel that it was not an idle claim. Great figures, from the sages of the Upanishads to living *sannyasis,* had gained and harnessed spiritual power. Such men, he thought, "could not have been after a chimera, and if there was such a more-than-human power why not get it and use it for action."[170]

Thus, toward the beginning of August 1905, Aurobindo began to practice yoga. His friend Devdhar knew something about *pranayama,* or breath-control. He showed Aurobindo how to do it, breathing in and out in a fixed rhythm, paying special attention to the retention of the breath. Aurobindo at once felt results, striking though not particularly spiritual. His health improved. His skin, dark and pockmarked, became lighter and smoother. He could taste an unusual sweetness in his saliva, feel a sort of electricity around his body. His energy, physical as well as mental, increased greatly. His poetic output increased. He saw more frequently, and with more intensity, the visual phenomena he had begun to see earlier.[171] By the end of August, when he wrote a letter to Mrinalini, he could report to her not only that he had started to practice the way of the Vedantic sages, but that, within a month, he had experienced some of the signs of which they spoke.

It is not known how long Mrinalini had been living in eastern India before she received Aurobindo's letter. Her second stay in Baroda seems to have lasted no more than a year. At home, she again became fretful, in part over family matters and money, but also about her husband and her relationship with him. She was now eighteen, old enough to articulate her needs and for him to speak freely to her. His letter of August 30, 1905 to her is one of the most revealing personal documents he ever wrote. *Priyatama Mrinalini* (Dearest Mrinalini), he began:

> I think you have understood by now that the man with whose fate yours is linked is a man of a very unusual kind. My field of action, purpose of life and mental attitude are not the same as those of people of today in this country. I am in every respect different from them and out of the

ordinary. Perhaps you know what ordinary men say of an extraordinary view, an extraordinary endeavor, an extraordinary ambition. [The Bengali adjective is *asadharan*, "uncommon, out of the ordinary."] To them it is madness; but if the madman is successful in his work, he is no longer called a madman but a great genius. But how many are successful in their life's endeavor? Among a thousand men there are five or six who are out of the ordinary and out of those five or six, one perhaps is successful. Far from being a success, I have not even fully entered the field of action. There is nothing for you to do but consider me mad.

Mrinalini had two choices. Either she could dismiss her husband as a madman as did the rest of the world, or "try to be the mad wife of this madman, like the queen of the blind king [in the *Mahabharata*] who became a blind woman by putting a bandage across her eyes." Continuing the madman metaphor, he went on:

I have three madnesses. The first one is this. I firmly believe that the accomplishments, genius, higher studies and learning, and wealth that God has given me belong to Him. I have a right to spend for my own purposes only what is needed for the maintenance of the family and is otherwise absolutely essential. The rest must be returned to God. . . . I have realised that I have been acting all this time like an animal and a thief. Having realised this, I am filled with remorse and am disgusted with myself.

His second madness had seized hold of him "only recently": he was resolved to "have the direct vision of God." For most people being religious meant making a show of public piety. This did not interest him in the least. "If God exists, there must be some way to experience His existence, to meet Him face to face. However arduous this path is, I have made up my mind to follow it." If she wished, she could join him on this path. He certainly would not compel her, but if she wanted, he would write more about it to her. Then there was his third madness:

While others look upon their country as an inert piece of matter—a few meadows and fields, forests and hills and rivers—I look upon Her as the Mother. What would a son do if a demon sat on his mother's breast and started sucking her blood? Would he quietly sit down to his dinner, amuse himself with his wife and children, or would he rush out to deliver his mother? I know I have the strength to deliver this fallen race. It is not physical strength—I am not going to fight with sword or gun—but it is the strength of knowledge. This feeling is not new in me, it is not of today. I was born with it, it is in my very marrow. God sent me to earth to accomplish this great mission.

He had already brought hundreds of people into the movement. He would yet "bring thousands of others onto that same path. I do not say that the work will be accomplished during my lifetime, but it certainly will be done."

What, then, was Mrinalini to do? "The wife is the strength [*shakti*] of her husband," he told her. "Will you diminish the strength of your husband by indifference or redouble it by your sympathy and encouragement?" If she could do the latter, he would give her his strength in return, and this giving would "not diminish my strength but increase it."[172]

He went on to explain that she should not reveal what he had written to anyone—it was for her alone—but she should think quietly about what he had written. Her immediate reaction can be gauged from the notations she made in the margins of his letter. Where he suggested that she should become his "mad" wife, she wrote: "a very sweet word." Where he said that he had resolved to stop living "like an animal and a thief," she wrote "admirable! admirable!! life!!"[173] While she certainly sympathized with her husband's ambitions, Mrinalini still wanted a secure domestic existence, and he was increasingly unable to give her one. Instead, he suggested that she accept his ambitions as her own, encouraging and helping him in his work. Using the time-honored formulas of traditional Hinduism, he asked her to accept him as her guru, her god. But there was another side to the Hindu conception of woman, one current especially in Mother goddess–worshipping Bengal: the idea that the wife is her husband's *shakti*, or power. At the same time that he asked his wife to follow him, he also asked for her counsel and support.

Mrinalini's difficulties in following her husband were not due to any proto-feminist rejection of male dominance. Such an idea would never have occurred to her. She was happy to accept the role of a submissive wife, but she wanted the script to be one she could understand, one that followed the conventions of nineteenth-century middle-class life. The conventions required that her husband earn enough to maintain her decently and to fulfill his other responsibilities toward her. She could not understand his desire to use his money for "good works" when he neglected to send her enough to live in comfort, obliging her to look elsewhere for support.

It is hard to determine what Mrinalini made of her "extraordinary" husband. She certainly never considered him literally "mad," but she must have had trouble understanding him. For his part, he certainly considered himself to be out of the ordinary. His poetic inspiration and political vocation set him apart from those around him. The result was a sense of personal isolation that he probably did not expect his wife to assuage. He had come to realize that the void could only be filled by the "direct vision of God."

Taking Leave

Throughout the summer of 1905, Aurobindo taught classes in English literature and fulfilled his administrative duties. While the boycott movement picked up momentum and the Russo-Japanese war wound down, he lectured his junior students on Walter Scott's *Rokeby*, his intermediate class on Edmund Burke's *Reflections on the Revolution in France,* and the B.A. men on modern poets, such as Byron. A variety of paperwork landed on his desk. Asked his opinion of a proposed teacher certification exam, he wrote that the state should forgo this "up-to-date American machine" and develop its own training program. When a respected, underpaid clerk applied for a raise, he sent a proposal to the dewan with recommendations from himself and others, only to have it returned on account of procedural irregularities.[174]

The college term finished at the end of September and two weeks of examinations began. Aurobindo continued his work in the principal's office and also took part in public activities. The *swadeshi* movement had reached western India, and he and his friends started an association to promote indigenous products. On September 24 he attended a *swadeshi* meeting in Baroda, speaking in favor of one of the resolutions. This was his first appearance at a political meeting.

Aurobindo's various projects obliged him to spend a lot of money. Explaining his lack of funds in a letter to Mrinalini, he said that he had to help to maintain Madhavrao in Europe and also "to carry on another movement which requires unlimited money," a reference, perhaps, to his attempts to start the revolutionary movement again.[175] Mrinalini tended to let off steam in long emotional letters. He took this in stride and did not rebuke her for it. She was in fact causing him less anxiety than was Barin. In a second letter to Mrinalini, he wrote that his younger brother was "in an exceedingly bad state of health," yet despite his lingering fever, "he still goes out in the service of his country"—only to fall sick again and return to Baroda.[176]

Aurobindo broke off his second letter with the comment that it was time for his "evening practice." He continued to do *pranayama* in the mornings and evenings, for a total of six hours a day. The resulting lightness and physical purification he felt increased when he became a vegetarian. At dinner he took only bananas and milk, then passed the rest of the evening alone. Rajaram Patkar often found him sitting "in a contemplative mood." "Serene and calm," he had "the gravity of a man of ripe old age."[177] As far as Rajaram could see, Aurobindo was reading less; his manuscripts show that he was writing more. His notebooks are filled with drafts of ambitious works, most of which were left incomplete. Around this time he began a commentary on the Isha Upanishad that he called *The Karmayogin*. The title gives the clue to his interpretation. A *karmayogin* is one who follows the way of works, doing action (*karma*) to attain perfection. "Whatever others may do," Aurobindo wrote, "the Karmayogin must not remove himself from the field of action and give up work in the world." It followed that someone who felt called to do patriotic action could carry it out "calmly and without desire, seeking only through his life and actions to get nearer to Him who is the Lord of life and master of all actions."[178]

ON OCTOBER 16, 1905 the partition of Bengal went into effect. Throughout Bengal and the new province of Eastern Bengal and Assam the day was observed as one of mourning. At the suggestion of the poet Rabindranath Tagore, people tied *rakhi* threads around each other's wrists to symbolize the unbreakable bond between East and West. In Calcutta a great throng gathered together to lay the foundation stone of a Federation Hall that would embody this ideal in stone.

While the elite of Calcutta were participating in ceremonies, the Hindus of Eastern Bengal were organizing grassroots resistance. In the new capital of Dacca, they refused to give the incoming lieutenant-governor, an undistinguished bureaucrat named Bampfylde Fuller, the treatment that British potentates expected as their due. When Fuller arrived to take up his post, only a few hundred people came to greet him. The spirit of defiance spread throughout the province. When the boycott was not observed voluntarily, it was enforced by Hindu "volunteers." This sometimes led to clashes with people, many of them Muslims, who were not inclined to make a sacrifice for an abstraction that did not mean much to them. As the situation spun out of control, Fuller asked the viceroy to grant him extraordinary powers. The Viceroy complied, and Fuller began to rule his province by ordinance. Public assemblies and processions were banned. The cry "Bande Mataram" was outlawed. Non-Bengali policemen were billeted in towns where the boycott was being enforced. Soon, newspapers carried reports that these punitive police were attacking innocent men and raping women.

Barisal, East Bengal was one of the flashpoints of the movement. On November 7, Aswini Kumar Dutt and other local leaders issued a circular urging people to buy locally produced goods instead of imported ones. Fuller denounced this perfectly legal circular as sedition. Proceeding to Barisal, he arrayed punitive police on the banks of the river and summoned Dutt and his associates to his barge, demanding that they withdraw their circular. Apprehensive that their arrest might spark a riot, Dutt and the others agreed to reconsider. A few days later they withdrew the circular because, they said, it contained "expressions that may tend to lead people to commit breaches of peace." Newspaper reports published that November made it seem as though Dutt had collapsed in the face of Fuller's threats.[179] When Aurobindo saw one such report, he was furious. "No Bengali can read the account of the interview between Mʳ Fuller and the Barisal leaders, without a blush of shame for himself and his nation," he wrote. Fuller had insulted "men of culture, worth and dignity." What ought they

> have done in reply? Surely they should have repelled the insults with a calm and simple dignity, or if that would not serve, with a self-assertion as haughty, if less violent than the self-assertion of the unmannerly official before them, and to the demand for the withdrawal of their appeal they should have returned a plain and quiet negative. And if as a result Mʳ Fuller were immediately to send them to the prison, or the whipping-post, or the gallows itself, what difference would that make to their duty as public men & national leaders?

This is the earliest surviving written expression of his uncompromising sense of national duty. More pragmatic was his strategy of response:

> Let the authorities remember this, that when a Government breaks the Law, by their very act the people are absolved from the obligation of obeying the Law. But let the people on their side so long as they are permitted to do so abstain from aggressive violence, let them study carefully to put their oppressors always in the wrong; but from no legitimate kind of passive resistance should they shrink.[180]

This passage gives the earliest hint of Aurobindo's interest in a technique that would become India's foremost means of resistance. In substance and in tone, his article was ahead of what was appearing in the most advanced newspapers. But he did not publish it. The piece remained in his notebook along with incomplete articles on Vedantic interpretation and English literature.

Much of the driving power of the *swadeshi* movement came from student volunteers who picketed shops where foreign products were sold. The government decided to put a stop to this. On October 22, a circular was published over the name of R.W. Carlyle that prohibited students from attending political rallies. A second circular threatened heads of schools and colleges with the withdrawal of grants in aid if their students participated in the boycott movement. Bengalis of every shade of opinion opposed these arbitrary decrees. For a decade or more, Bengali intellectuals had been talking about national education. People decided it was time to give form to the idea. National schools and colleges would be established to replace British institutions. Subodh Chandra Mallik, the young heir to a shipbuilding fortune, pledged 100,000 rupees to the cause. He and Aurobindo had met the year before and found that they had a lot in common. As talks on the national college continued, Mallik let it be known that his donation would be tied to the privilege of naming the institution's first principal.[181]

Aurobindo was ready to leave Baroda. Mallik's offer of the principalship of the national college was all that he needed to start making plans. At the end of November, he took unofficial leave and went to Calcutta to test the waters. Staying in the Mallik house, he contacted a group of Bengali intellectuals who called themselves "the new party." Their leader was Bipinchandra Pal. A former Brahmo preacher and long-time Congressman, Pal had remained for years in the shadow of Surendranath Banerjea. But after the *swadeshi* movement started, he emerged as a proponent of boycott as a political weapon. To him were attracted men of the younger generation—Surendranath Haldar, Chittaranjan Das, Hemendra Prasad Ghose—who were fed up with the Banerjea coterie. One evening that December, while Pal, Haldar, and Das were holding forth on the need for a new English newspaper, the journalist Suresh Chandra Deb noticed "a retiring figure sitting quietly in a chair, whose name I later came to know was Aurobindo Ghose." As the discussion turned to the resolutions to be passed at the Congress, Aurobindo "remained a silent listener," content to watch from the sidelines.[182]

The chief topics of discussion by the new as well as the old schools of politics were the national education movement and the upcoming annual session of the Indian National Congress. That December, a committee of education experts was formed to draw up a plan for a national council of education. They were asked to submit their report early in 1906. The Congress session, which would be held in Benares at the end of December, was shaping up to be the most significant since the founding of the organization twenty years earlier. The more advanced leaders of the West and North—Tilak of Poona, G.S. Khaparde of Vidarbha, Lala Lajpat Rai of Punjab—took hold of the boycott to promote the more aggressive nationalism they favored. The Bombay caucus that still controlled the Congress had been able, so far, to stifle this approach; but it was becoming more and more difficult to dampen the enthusiasm that was emanating from Bengal.

Aurobindo probably was present at the Benares Congress, though he is not mentioned in any of the accounts of those who wrote about the watershed session. At the plenary meeting on December 27, delegates and visitors listened to the presidential speech of G.K. Gokhale, a leader of Poona, whom Aurobindo considered a political nullity. Gokhale had just returned from a three-month trip to England, where he had called for eventual colonial self-government, and offered a measured defense of the boycott. In Benares he took up the same themes, winning the grudging approval even of G.S. Khaparde, who noted that Gokhale's speech "was not quite in the Ultra Moderate style." But that evening, when the subjects committee met to frame the resolutions, Gokhale showed himself to be very much the autocrat. He "did not count votes and decided matters on his impressions." The two bones of contention were a resolution welcoming the Prince of Wales to India and another endorsing the boycott. The first carried in committee, but Tilak, Khaparde, and Lajpat Rai threatened to oppose it in the open session. The next morning, Gokhale cut a deal with them. Tilak's party could walk out when the welcoming resolution was passed; in exchange, the old guard would support the boycott resolution. This they did, but not before they had amended it in their favor. Still, Khaparde could crow after the session was over, "the so-called Moderates have lost all along the line. Wacha, Satalwad and others [from Bombay] who came with a mandate from Sir Pherozsha Mehta, could not make an impression." Tilak too thought that "the new party of young men asserted itself better this time, though we did not get all we wanted." Still, it seemed to him "that our progressive principles would soon be recognised & acted upon" by the Congress.[183]

BACK IN BARODA by the beginning of 1906, Aurobindo was waiting for the moment when he could resign. Principal Clarke was supposed to return in January but he kept delaying his return, and Aurobindo had to resume his duties. "The College started at 11.00 a.m.," recalled Sanker Balwant Didmishe, "but Sri Arvind Babu came exactly at 11.30, went straight to his room and began teaching." Didmishe's "Junior B.A. with voluntary English Literature" class met in the principal's office. Following his habit, Aurobindo asked one of the young men to read the last few lines from their previous day's notes, then continued his dictation, not even glancing at the notes he had written eight years earlier. Gazing absently at the opposite wall, he spoke for an hour and a half on Pope, Dryden, Goldsmith, and other writers he did not admire.[184] Later, in the same office, he dispatched the usual load of business—letters, applications, memos, accounts—before driving home in the evening.

In the office and the classroom, Aurobindo was always dressed in the same way: white suit, black tie, North Indian turban. Yet behind his conventional appearance there was something out of the ordinary. "His mind seemed to be in a ferment," one student remembered, "he had the eyes of a mystic." (This echoes the appraisal of matter-of-fact Englishman Principal Clarke. "So you met Aurobindo Ghosh," he asked a fellow Oxbridge graduate. "Did you notice his eyes? There is mystic fire and light in them. They penetrate into the beyond."[185]) To many of his students, Aurobindo was "a figure enveloped in mystery." According to Kanaiyalal Munshi, "he was reputed to be a poet, a master of many languages and in touch with Russian nihilists." Munshi got up the nerve to speak with him only once. "How can nationalism be developed?" he asked. Aurobindo "pointed to a wall-map of India and said something to this effect":

> Look at that map. Learn to find in it the portrait of Bharatmata [Mother India]. The cities, mountains, rivers and forests are the materials which go to make up Her body. The people inhabiting the country are the cells which go to make up Her living tissues. Our literature is Her memory and speech. The spirit of Her culture is Her soul. The happiness and freedom of Her children is Her salvation. Behold Bharat as a living Mother, meditate upon Her and worship Her in the nine-fold way of Bhakti.

Munshi was disappointed. He was hoping for a list of books to study. Aurobindo suggested he try something by Swami Vivekananda.[186]

On February 1, 1906, with Clarke scheduled to return the next day, Aurobindo applied for two months' leave to commence on Monday, February 19. This would take him through mid-April, when the college vacations began. If all went according to plan, he would have more than four months in Calcutta and return only to terminate his service. His application was approved quickly by the education minister and accountant general, but ran into trouble when it reached the dewan's office. For no particular reason, the chief bureaucrat of the realm delayed signing the document until the last day of February. "I have lost ten days for nothing," Aurobindo complained in a letter to his wife.

Despite the frustrating circumstances, Aurobindo made good use of his time. On January 31 he begun to write a tragedy in verse called *Rodogune*. He completed it two weeks later, and then spent parts of the ten "lost" days making a fair copy. The play is based on one of the same name by Pierre Corneille, the prime mover of classical French theatre. Corneille's plot turns on the scheming of Cleopatra of Syria, who murders her husband and one of her sons before drinking the poison that she had prepared for her other son. The only admirable character in the tragedy is the Parthian princess Rodogune. Imprisoned by Cleopatra and promised to the eldest of her sons, she announces that she will marry the brother who has the audacity to kill his mother. In Aurobindo's play, Rodogune has a more passive role as the root of the conflict between the twin brothers Antiochus and Timocles. Upon the death of her second husband, Cleopatra summons her sons from exile. She must declare which is the first-born, for he will ascend the throne and take Rodogune as his wife. When the brothers arrive, Timocles bubbles over with affection while Antiochus is cold and aloof. Cleopatra says, falsely, that Timocles is the eldest. Rodogune refuses to accept him, for she has fallen in love with Antiochus. "When he looked on me," she confesses to a friend, "I felt at last I was a slave-girl / And loved the thought."[187] Timocles is driven mad by jealousy and eventually kills his brother. Owing to their conflict, Syria is "riven asunder" and laid open to attack by foreign foes.

A tragedy in verse on the Shakespearean model now seems to be such a throwback that it is hard to evaluate *Rodogune* as literature. Viewed as drama, it is original and well-plotted, owing little to Corneille except the basic story. Viewed as poetry, it can hold its own against contemporary plays in verse by Stephen Phillips and Laurence Binyon. Its primary defect is its flat, allegorical characters. Antiochus never says an ignoble word or does an ignoble deed. Timocles comes across as a comic buffoon, not a tragic figure, while Rodogune is too colorless to inspire either devotion or jealousy. But the characters' flatness makes it easier for the author to bring out the conflict at the heart of the drama: the life of pleasure versus the life of action. Antiochus, marked for kingship, is fated to yearn for Rodogune's beauty. Light-hearted Timocles becomes a monster when he aspires for the throne and the captive princess. Strife seems inevitable, though as the action reaches its climax, the author puts a third possibility in the mouth of an Eremite who appears in the desert just as Antiochus declares: "I thirst for mightier things / Than earth has." "Seek them in thyself," the Eremite answers; it is in the soul that the real battles are fought and the real empire is won. But the Eremite knows that Antiochus is doomed to return to Antioch and defeat, for "that sudden disappointment," will turn him to his "true crown."[188] This is the doctrine of *karmayoga*—renouncing desire but embracing action—given a tragic turn under the influence of Greek drama. The scene in which Antiochus meets his end was the last one Aurobindo wrote. Three weeks later, he threw himself into the struggle against British colonialism, foreseeing perhaps a similar end but certain of his calling.

As March approached, Aurobindo readied himself for his departure. His young friend Rajaram Patkar found him in high spirits. When Rajaram asked why, Aurobindo replied that the time for serving his country had come. "My prayer is answered and I will be leaving Baroda very soon."[189] On February 28, he accepted an invitation to visit a photographic studio run by some former students. It was apparently at this time that he sat for photographs with one of his classes. Sporting a three-piece suit, a tie, and a turban, with a watch in his pocket and a cane in his hand, he looks very much the prosperous middle-class professional—but the eyes are those of a poet.[190]

On March 2, just before boarding the train, Aurobindo dashed off a letter to Mrinalini. He would reach Calcutta on the fifth, but he would not be staying with his aunt and uncle. He needed a place where he could do his *pranayama* in peace. If he got a chance, he would go to Assam and bring Mrinalini down to Calcutta. But she should not count on this. Once he reached Bengal, he would have a thousand things to do.[191]

PART THREE: *Revolutionary*

I am an idealist to the marrow, and could only be useful when there is something drastic to be done, a radical or revolutionary line to be taken (I do not mean revolutionary by violence), a movement with an ideal aim and direct method to be inspired and organised.

4. Into the Fray

Calcutta, 1906–1908

I entered into political action and continued it from 1903 to 1910 with one aim and one alone, to get into the mind of the people a settled will for freedom and the necessity of a struggle to achieve it in place of the futile ambling Congress methods till then in vogue.

A Negligible Factor

Aurobindo was in Calcutta on March 11, 1906 when the report of the educational experts' committee set up the previous December was considered. After some deliberation, the assembled educators, professionals, landowners, and other leading citizens resolved to establish the National Council of Education. Aurobindo was one of its ninety-two founding members. The other ninety-one knew him as an England-educated Bengali who had been working in Gujarat as a professor in the Gaekwar's college. Most also were aware that he was the designated principal of the college that they were going to establish. Even so he remained an outsider. Looking back three years later on Aurobindo's entry into the public life of Bengal, his colleague Jitendra Lal Bannerji recalled that he was looked on then as "an obscure school-master in a far-off province of India—one who had apparently failed in life and had retired into oblivion—a man unknown, unheard-of." To call the professor from Baroda a failure was to exaggerate his insignificance, but not by much. He had done little in thirty-three years to make a name for himself. Since his return from England in 1893, he had risen from trainee to secretary to the Gaekwar and vice principal of Baroda College. He might have looked forward to a ministerial post in ten or twenty years, but his interests lay elsewhere, in literature and revolutionary politics. In these fields he had taken some preliminary steps, but little more. As a writer he had achieved fluidity, had begun to find his voice, and was on the trail of the themes that would carry him into mature expression, but he had produced comparatively little and published less. As an organizer, he had helped to found a revolutionary group in 1902, but little remained of the organization, and the revolutionary impetus had passed from Calcutta to Dacca. Overall, "in the stirring and slow-heaving political atmosphere of the time," Aurobindo was, in Jitendra Lal's summing up, "an altogether negligible factor."[1]

During the first four months of 1906 Aurobindo put a good deal of energy into the business of the National Council of Education. The National College would be opening later that year. Throughout April and May, meetings were held, minutes written, schedules set, prospectuses issued. Aurobindo's name appears on many of these documents. The organizers were always happy for a chance to announce that "Mr Aravinda Ghose. B.A. (Cantab.)" was a member of the faculty. That he had no degree, Cantabrigian or other, was not allowed to spoil his English cachet.

While Aurobindo was engaged in his administrative grind, he was also trying to find ways "to popularise the idea of violent revolt."[2] So far the only vehicles for this kind of thing were fugitive pamphlets and a Bengali newspaper, *Sandhya*. When Barin came to Calcutta, he brought the text of *Bhawani Mandir* and had it printed secretly. But Aurobindo's ideas were too cerebral to excite potential revolutionaries. To reach them, a new sort of newspaper was needed, and Barin and Aurobindo decided to start one. The first issue of *Jugantar*, or The New Era, came out in the middle of March. Two weeks later, Aurobindo published an essay in which he set forth *Jugantar*'s political ideal. In brief, the aim was liberation; the means, revolution. The Congress wanted "to reduce the proportion of iron" and increase "the proportions of gold and silver" in India's chains of servitude, but this would never work. The time had come to "break the golden chain" that attached India to England. "We must find the right way," Aurobindo concluded, "to attain our objective in accordance with our national temperament and the conditions of the country."[3] "Our Political Ideal" was Aurobindo's first published Bengali article, and it shows some mastery of the language, though it needed touching up and like all of his Bengali writings was filled with uncolloquial expressions. Happy as he was to be writing in the language of his province, he was under no illusion that he could be a regular contributor to a Bengali newspaper. He left the writing of *Jugantar* to Barin and Debavrata Bose. They and their colleagues turned it into an influential newspaper that combined emotionally affecting language, solid thought, and daring suggestions.

AUROBINDO HAD NEVER liked the Indian National Congress, but he could see that it was the only public body in the country that had a chance of becoming a nationalist force. The Bengal provincial conference of the Congress was scheduled to be held in Barisal in the beginning of April. Aurobindo decided to attend. On April 12 he joined hundreds of others on the train from Calcutta to Khulna, and in the evening boarded the Khulna–Barisal steamer. It arrived the next day, around the same time as the southbound steamer from Narayanganj. Delegates on both boats cried out the forbidden mantra, "Bande Mataram." Mr. F. E. Kemp, the local superintendent of police, asked veteran leader Surendranath Banerjea to pledge not to organize processions or to violate the ordinance against crying "Bande Mataram." After consulting with others, Banerjea declined to bind himself. The next day, five thousand men assembled to hear a speech by conference president Abdul Rasul, a barrister and token Muslim Congressman. Then, to test the legality of the government's orders, they formed a procession to escort the president to the meeting place. Loud cries of "Bande Mataram" rang out as the marchers neared a detachment of police armed with *lathis* and guns. Kemp let Rasul and the older delegates, Aurobindo among them, pass. Then he ordered his men to break up the procession. *Lathis* raised, policemen went after the younger volunteers, who were marching behind the delegates in ranks of four. The volunteers continued to shout "Bande Mataram" as the sticks came down on their heads. Several were badly injured.

The delegates rushed back to stop the carnage. Banerjea told Kemp that he alone was responsible, and challenged the superintendent to arrest him. Kemp promptly complied, ignoring Motilal Ghosh and others who were clamoring to join Banerjea in his politically astute martyrdom. Taken to the magistrate, Banerjea was tried and fined 200 rupees for the procession and 200 rupees for contempt. Great excitement prevailed. "This is the end, the beginning of the end of the British rule in India," declared Bhupendranath Bose. Looking on from the sidelines, Aurobindo "was unperturbed" but satisfied by this turn of events.[4]

That night the leaders decided to reconvene the conference the following day. At eleven o'clock in the morning, six thousand delegates and observers listened to speeches and passed a few resolutions. At two o'clock, Kemp appeared and presented an order banning further proceedings. Everyone quietly dispersed. Aurobindo wrote later that this was done "not from respect for executive authority but purely for reasons of political strategy," but it is unlikely that he supported the pullback. He was glad, however, that "immediately afterwards the right of public meeting was asserted in defiance of executive ukase by the Moderate leaders near Barisal."[5] At the same time he and others were asserting this same right in the East Bengal hinterland. Bipinchandra Pal had been invited to visit a number of towns in the region. He took Aurobindo and Subodh Mallik along. Aurobindo was pleased by what he saw. A few years earlier, when he toured the same area, it seemed to him that there was "a hell of black death" all around. Now the mood was one of "high exalta- tions and self-forgetfulness."[6] Pal gave dozens of speeches, the effect of which could still be measured a decade later. As villagers and townsmen listened to him, they could see in the background "a silent distant figure lost in his own thoughts, speaking the fewest of words, observing the effect of the language in which Bipin Chandra Pal clothed the present degradation and the future ennobling of his people." When the people asked to hear Aurobindo speak, Pal replied: "Try to assimilate what I am telling you. When he speaks, he will speak only fire."[7]

Aurobindo's reticence was only partly due to his temperament. He was incapable of addressing a meeting in Bengali, and had trouble understanding the East Bengal dialects. Still, he took part in closed-door discussions with local politicians.[8] Among the members of the new party, he stood out as the most uncompromising. On their way to Brahmanbaria, Pal heard that the lo- cal magistrate had passed an order prohibiting meetings. It might be better, he suggested, to go to a place they were not expected and hold the meeting there. Aurobindo did not agree: "We are going to Brahmanbaria and nowhere else," he said.[9] They went, Pal spoke, and the police did not interfere. Though he remained mostly in the background during the six-week tour, Aurobindo's presence was noticed by the *Bengalee*, an English newspaper of Calcutta, and by the British police. His name began to appear in reports of the Criminal Investigation Department (CID). Whether he liked it or not, his political career had begun.[10]

BACK IN CALCUTTA by the end of May, Aurobindo was at the meeting that approved the memorandum of association of the National Council of Education. He and seven others signed this historic document; he used the Bengalicized spelling "Aurobindo Ghose," which afterwards became his nor- mal way of signing. The principal objects of the association were set forth in the memorandum's second paragraph:

To impart and promote the imparting of Education—Literary and Sci- entific, as well as Technical and Professional—on National lines and ex- clusively under National control—not in opposition to, but standing apart from, the existing systems of Primary, Secondary and Collegiate Educa- tion—attaching special importance to a knowledge of the Country, its Lit- erature, History and Philosophy, and designed to incorporate with the best

Oriental ideals of life and thought, the best assimilable ideals of the West and to inspire students with a genuine love for, and a real desire to serve, the country.[11]

The phrase "not in opposition to, but standing apart from" was inserted by the council's moderate members and represented a retreat from the movement's original purpose. What had begun as an act of defiance in the face of colonial interference was being transformed into an Indianized adjunct to the British educational system.

But if moderation was on the upswing in education, it had temporarily lost ground in politics. The Barisal events rekindled the boycott movement. Protest meetings were held in every part of Bengal and in places as far away as Delhi. In Maharashtra, Tilak promoted boycott to advance the aggressive nationalism he had long been trying to develop. That May, he accepted an invitation to celebrate the Shivaji festival in Calcutta, and thousands flocked to hear him speak. He and Aurobindo met once or twice at this time. Aurobindo told him about recent political developments, and perhaps also of his hopes to renew revolutionary activities. He continued to think of Tilak as the best man to coordinate the activities of the advanced groups within the Congress. The 1906 session was going to be held in Calcutta. Aurobindo and others put Tilak's name forward as the host city's choice for president.

Aurobindo's leave from Baroda College was due to end in the second week of June. He already had sent a telegram to Principal Clarke applying for a year's leave without pay, but he had to report in Baroda by the eleventh if he wanted his last two months' salary—money he could not do without in his present circumstances. On June 8 he boarded the train for Bombay. Before leaving he wrote his father-in-law explaining why he had not been able to go to Shillong to visit Mrinalini. This was the letter in which he acknowledged that he had been remiss in "domestic virtues" and spoke of "something too strong" in him that compelled him to sacrifice conjugal happiness to it.[12]

Aurobindo reached Baroda by June 11. A week later he had the signatures of the Baroda state council on his leave application. Four months earlier, while waiting for a leave to be approved, he had written the tragedy *Rodogune*. This time he wrote another drama, *Perseus the Deliverer.* Set, like *Rodogune,* in Syria, *Perseus* is based not on history but mythology: the story of Perseus and Andromeda as told by Ovid and other classical writers. Aurobindo took from his predecessors only the skeleton of the story. Perseus, the son of Zeus and

Danaë, finds Andromeda chained to a rock as a sacrifice to Poseidon. He slays the monster sent to devour her, turns her suitor Phineus to stone, and marries her. Aurobindo turned the story into a Shakespearean romance, complete with clowns, soubrette, soldiers, monsters, royalty, and hoi polloi. Even more than *Rodogune*, *Perseus* belongs in style and conception to a bygone era. Chained to the rock, Andromeda muses:

> I will not die! I am too young,
> And life was recently so beautiful.
> It is too hard, too hard a fate to bear.[13]

In the face of such passages, it is easy to dismiss *Perseus* as intolerably mawkish. But the play is not without psychological interest. Perseus reaches the beach just as Andromeda, "stripped of all but a single light robe," is about to be devoured by a monster with eyes "hideous with brutish longing."[14] Perseus sweeps down, slays the monster, and carries off the girl. This incident, the highlight of the Perseus-Andromeda legend, is also an instance of the central situation in all of Aurobindo's plays: A beautiful, self-reliant heroine is lifted from bondage by a strong, handsome hero.

Aurobindo promised the text of *Perseus* to his friend K.G. Deshpande, who was planning to bring out an English journal from Baroda. The two spent a good amount of time together during Aurobindo's visit. At one point, they went together to Chandod, where they looked in on Deshpande's new national school and met Swami Keshavananda, the successor of Swami Brahmananda. A pedantic practitioner of *hathayoga*, Keshavananda was by no means as impressive as his master. Still, Aurobindo and Deshpande passed the day with him discussing spiritual matters.

Bande Mataram

On his return to Calcutta, Aurobindo resumed work at the National Council of Education. On July 24, he was named a lecturer in the National College. He would hold this position along with that of principal; but the duties of the principal were watered down. He would be in charge of "all matters relating to study," while "all questions of Executive management" would be handled by the superintendent, Satischandra Mukherjee.[15] The outsider from Gujarat carried too little weight to be given control of a project that prominent lawyers such as Ashutosh Chowdhuri and Rashbehari Ghose had a stake in.

Chowdhuri and Ghose were both associated with the old school of Congress politics. Its leader was Surendranath Banerjea; its bête noire was Bipinchandra Pal, whose radical group was gaining in strength and influence. Around the same time, two parallel blocs emerged in Western India: those looking to established leaders Pherozshah Mehta and G. K. Gokhale on the one hand, and those favoring Tilak on the other. Neither of these factions had official names, but by the middle of the year they generally were known by the labels they applied to each other: Moderates and Extremists.

The emergence of Extremism had the old-line Moderates worried. "Do they mean to establish a 'swarajya' [self-governed state] ... with the help of a few foolish, misguided young boys playing lathis?" wondered G.N. Madholkar, the Moderate leader of Vidarbha. "I feel that our work will be retarded,— possibly all the results secured till now nullified, by the insane propaganda launched by the extremists since last year." He agreed that Indians had to obtain "a larger share in the direction of their own affairs," but he insisted that "the existence and maintenance of the British Government is a *sine qua non*." The Extremists rejected all of this. It was time, wrote Madholkar's rival G.S. Khaparde, for the Congress to replace its "begging petitions" with a policy of self-help.[16] The Moderates still hoped that the Government of India would listen to their meekly worded prayers. They were overjoyed when the newly elected Liberal government in England appointed John Morley as secretary of state for India. Friend and biographer of Gladstone, longtime supporter of Home Rule for Ireland, Morley appeared to be the perfect choice for Indians eager for reform. He soon disappointed his admirers. Speaking about the partition of Bengal, he said that while it was "undoubtedly an administrative operation which went wholly and decisively against the wishes of most of the people concerned," it was and would remain "a settled fact."[17]

Morley wanted to introduce a modest set of reforms, but he had to deal with powerful interests in London and Calcutta. These were personified by Gilbert John, Fourth Earl of Minto, the new Viceroy of India. Appointed by the outgoing Conservatives, famous chiefly for riding his own horse in the Epsom Derby, Minto was the image of the aristocratic imperialist. And it was he, not Morley, who would decide what reforms got through. Moderates like Gokhale tried to convince Minto's government that the changes they were pushing for were reasonable and just; at the same time, they had to undermine the activities of the radicals. If Tilak and Pal continued to make their demands, they might scare off reform for another generation.

The growing rift between the Moderates and Extremists made it difficult to conduct Congress business. The next national session was scheduled to be held in Calcutta at the end of December. The local organization had to choose a reception committee, which would nominate the president. The two parties could not agree on the composition of the committee. Warnings came from Bombay, home of the Mehta-Gokhale cabal that had hitherto controlled the organization, that if Calcutta could not host the Congress, it would be moved to another locale. More meetings were held. Neither side gave ground. The debate spilled over into the columns of the newspapers. Here the Extremists were at a disadvantage, because they had no English-language organ. Lack of funds had always prevented them from starting one, but toward the beginning of August, Pal decided to launch a paper and worry about finances later. Getting a small advance from Haridas Haldar, he registered a new newspaper to be called, provocatively, *Bande Mataram.* Now all he needed was writers. On the evening of August 5, he went to Subodh Mallik's place and asked Aurobindo to contribute some articles. Aurobindo was surprised—he had not been in on the planning—but he readily agreed. The next day, Pal left on a tour of East Bengal, the first issue of the paper barely dry in his hands. A contribution by Aurobindo—"John Morley: Three Phases"—appeared in the second or third issue. It was the first of hundreds of articles he would write for *Bande Mataram* over the next two years.[18]

THE ORGANIZERS OF the National Council of Education had decided that the National College would open on August 15, the thirty-fourth birthday of its first principal. A handful of students came forward to enroll themselves. One of them was Balai Debsharma. Asked if he wanted to meet Principal Ghose, he went to the office and saw "a young man of placid appearance" sitting at the desk. Like many others, Balai was struck by Aurobindo's eyes, "which seemed withdrawn from the outer world and concentrated on the inner spaces of his consciousness." Aurobindo gave a talk to the students that day, but not about education. A short while earlier, a Calcutta University student had fallen from the verandah of a university building and lay unconscious in the road. A crowd of people gathered, but all they could do was wring their hands. A passing Englishman saw the boy, put him in his car, and drove directly to the hospital. Recounting the incident, Aurobindo said that the Englishman's action was an example of the practical ability that had given Europe the mastery of the world. Modern India had to develop this practicality and combine it with its innate spiritual sense.[19]

During August and September, Aurobindo gave much of his attention to administrative matters. Committees were formed, resolutions passed, syllabi written, and appointments made. At one point he wrote some notes on teaching that were read out at a professors' meeting. He also helped to write the history examinations for the fifth and seventh standards. The questions—on Greek, Roman, English, and Indian history—were rather conventional: "What were the main causes which led to the decline of the Republic and the establishment of the Empire?" "When and in what form did England's connexion with India begin, and what is the nature of that connexion now?"[20] (Rather astonishingly, this question was later cited in an investigation by the CID.) But for the most part, his duties consisted of giving lectures in English and history. They were not well attended; during 1906 only seventeen students were taking college-level courses.

Aurobindo's pay as principal and professor was 150 rupees a month. This was 400 rupees less than his salary at Baroda, not counting his acting allowance. A year or two later, when he became nationally known, it was trumpeted abroad that he had given up the princely salary of 700, 750, or 800 rupees in exchange for a paltry 150 rupees. He had nothing to do with these exaggerated reports, and seems to have taken his reduced circumstances in stride. He did, however, have to cut back on his expenses. No longer could he order huge parcels full of books. He also delayed bringing Mrinalini down from Shillong to join him.

For most of 1906 Aurobindo stayed in the Mallik mansion in Wellington Square. Returning home in the evenings after giving his lectures, he would join an impromptu soirée that included many of the most brilliant minds in Calcutta. Seated quietly to one side, often engrossed in a book, he commanded attention on the rare occasions that he spoke. In such company, he generally used English. If he spoke in Bengali, "the foreign accent and a lisping sound made it pleasant to the ear." When the conversation was light, his remarks were punctuated with an agreeable "tinkling laughter." When it turned to current events, his voice took on the firmness of informed conviction. Occasionally, his brother Manmohan dropped by to insist that Aurobindo, a born poet, should not waste his energy on politics. Aurobindo laughed, and soon he and Manmohan were engrossed in talk of Homer or Simonides.[21]

AUROBINDO CONTINUED TO WRITE for *Bande Mataram* after Pal returned from his tour. Hemendra Prasad Ghose and Shyamsundar Chakravarty joined the paper as managing editors. Hemendra Prasad found the work hard going, "and the utter want of organization in the office makes it harder still." During August and September, the Extremists held several meetings to decide the future of the party and of *Bande Mataram*. Aurobindo said that they should take up the paper as their organ and directly attack the Moderates and the British. Forging an alliance with Tilak's group in Poona, they should act as a national party. Electing Tilak as president of the 1906 session would be the first clash in a contest "for the control of the Congress and of public opinion and action in the country."[22] The basics of his program were accepted, and *Bande Mataram* became the most powerful voice of Extremism in India. Its editorials, contributed anonymously by Aurobindo, Pal, Chakravarty, and others, set a new standard for English journalism in India. The writers put the Moderates on the defensive by insisting that the "mendicant policy" was ineffective: "We do not care to deny that in small matters petitioning may bring us a trivial concession here or a slight abatement of oppression there. . . . But nothing important, nothing lasting, nothing affecting the vital questions which most closely concern us, can be hoped for from mere mendicancy."[23] When the Moderates cried that the Extremists were weakening the Congress by harping on points of difference rather than forming a common front against the British, Aurobindo demurred:

> The old leaders are now telling the country that there is no need of a conflict as their ideals are identical with those of the new party, and it is only the latter who are heating themselves into a passion about nothing. . . . But yesterday we learned that Babu Bhupendranath Bose insists on our working in association with the Government and not in opposition! This is emphatically not the ideal of the new party, for we are opposed to any accommodation with the Government which precedes or dispenses with the concession of effective self-government to the Indian people.[24]

Pal had made the same point the previous week. The Moderates and their British friends, he wrote, wanted "to make the Government of India popular, without ceasing in any sense to be essentially British. We desire to make it autonomous and absolutely free of British control." The *Times* of London found this sufficiently astonishing to quote as an example of the dangerously radical tone that Bengali politicians were taking.[25]

Bande Mataram's editorials altered the course of Indian politics, but the paper remained mired in disorganization and debt. Aurobindo proposed reorganizing it as a joint-stock company, and his plan was accepted in principle. A more divisive question was whether Pal should continue as editor. More than half of those concerned would have been happier with Aurobindo at the helm. A shareholders' meeting was held in the second week of October, at which it was decided that Pal and Aurobindo would be joint editors. Pal was given a salary of 100 rupees a month; Aurobindo agreed to go without pay. A day or two later Bande Mataram Printing and Publishing was registered as a limited company.

On October 17 publication was halted while the paper was being reorganized. When it reappeared on October 23, the notice on the front page stating that Pal was editor-in-chief was gone. Fuming, Pal refused to come to the office. Hemendra Prasad Ghose did not regret his departure. "People were making use of his 'past' to cry the paper down," he wrote, referring to an earlier incident in which Pal had been accused of misuse of funds.[26] Despite the internal friction, plans to revamp the newspaper's format went ahead. On November 1 the first issue of an enlarged and redesigned *Bande Mataram* appeared. Despite a cyclonic rainstorm that kept people home, the entire print run of 1,500 copies quickly sold out.

THE RAIN CONTINUED. Reports came in of catastrophic floods and widespread suffering. There was a wave of influenza in the capital, and on November 4 Aurobindo came down with a fever. Shifted to his father-in-law's house in Mott's Lane, his condition did not improve. Confined to bed, he was unable to work, and on November 14, he took sick leave from the college. Years later he explained that his illness was due to irregularity in the practice of *pranayama*. During his last two years in Baroda, he had practiced for as many as six hours a day, and his body had become accustomed to the heightened flow of energy that *pranayama* gives. When he settled in Calcutta, the ceaseless round of meetings and lectures made it impossible for him to continue. Abruptly stopping the exercises knocked his system off balance, and left him open to the disease. He remained "dangerously ill" for a number of weeks.[27]

During his absence, Subodh Mallik and his allies forced Pal out of *Bande Mataram*. When Aurobindo returned to the office, it was understood that he was in charge. He was not altogether happy about Pal's exit. While "not a man of action or capable of political leadership," Pal was, Aurobindo thought, "perhaps the best and most original political thinker in the country, an excellent writer and a magnificent orator." Pal reciprocated the sentiments contained in this retrospective passage in an article of 1909: "The hand of the master [Aurobindo] was in it, from the very beginning," and this raised *Bande Mataram* to a level "unsurpassed by any journal in the country."[28] These tributes show the personal regard that the two men had for one another, but they mask the issues that divided them and their supporters. During the struggle to decide who the editor of the paper would be, Aurobindo remained for the most part in the background. But, as he was frank enough to admit later, "I used to practise what you may call voluntary self-effacement or self-denial and I liked to keep myself behind. . . . But I can't say that I was more modest within than others."[29] On important questions his mind was firm if not inflexible. On the key points at issue in the *Bande Mataram* conflict—the need for direct criticism of the Moderates and for revolutionary propaganda—he was certain that he was right and Pal wrong. Once Pal had left the paper and it fell to Aurobindo to draft a new scheme of management, he did not hesitate to assign himself full powers, with the ability to make final decisions.[30]

His "voluntary self-effacement" was put to the test on December 12 when an officious secretary printed his name as editor-in-chief where Pal's name used to be. Aurobindo was furious when he saw it. It gave him publicity he did not want, and also ran counter to an earlier decision that the editor of the paper would not be named. He spoke to the secretary "pretty harshly" about it. Hemendra Prasad, who witnessed the outburst, thought that Aurobindo was more than just harsh. "Well if you take the clothes away there remains little to distinguish one human radish from another," he noted in a Shakespearean allusion. A day later, he was more explicit: "Babu Aurobindo Ghose is an extremely strange man. And I suspect a tinge of lunacy is not absent in him. His mother is a lunatic. And it is not at all strange"—not strange, that is, that the madness in Aurobindo's family might express itself in him as an intensity that exceeded the norm.[31] But the explosion of December 12 was exceptional. Throughout his life, Aurobindo was noted for his freedom from anger. People who saw him at the office were impressed by his quiet, retiring nature and his ability to concentrate even amid the bustle of a big-city newspaper. Occasionally, however, his associates felt his wrath. "He hated indiscipline," recalled one *Bande Mataram* writer, and "did not like others to cross him." When annoyed he kept quiet; when angry "his lips trembled a little."[32]

Four days after the incident in the office, Aurobindo left Calcutta for Deoghar. His health was still precarious, and the Congress session less than two weeks away. He hoped that a week in the bracing air of the hills would help him recover his strength.

THE PROBLEM OF CHOOSING the president of the Congress session had been solved in an underhanded way. Fearful that the Extremists might succeed in electing Tilak, the Moderates asked the venerable Dadabhai Naoroji to accept the nomination. No one could oppose the Grand Old Man of Indian Politics, and when Naoroji assented, the matter was closed. The Bengal Congress still had to form its executive committee, however. The Moderates tried to gain the advantage by changing the date of a crucial meeting, but the Extremists still managed to get five men—Pal, Aurobindo, Subodh Mallik, Chittaranjan Das, and Rajat Rai—appointed to the committee.[33] The two parties then had to agree on the issues to be considered by the Congress. The Extremists had already hammered out a program of political autonomy, boycott, *swadeshi,* and national education. The Moderates supported boycott and *swadeshi* fully, national education with reservations, and autonomy not at all. Unable to force their program through, the Extremists took it to the public. On December 23, visiting leaders Lajpat Rai and Tilak addressed a mammoth demonstration in Calcutta's Beadon Square. Pal convened a meeting of party leaders the next day. They decided that if the subjects committee turned down their proposals, they would move amendments in the Congress assembly.

It was then that Aurobindo returned from Deoghar. By this time it was an open secret that the principal from Baroda was the de facto editor of *Bande Mataram.* People streamed in from everywhere to meet him. Tilak was among the callers. A day or two later, Aurobindo lauded the Poona leader in a *Bande Mataram* editorial. Dadabhai Naoroji, the elected president, was "the man of the past." Tilak was the "man of the future." He was, Aurobindo wrote, "preeminently the man who acts, and action is to be the note of our future political energies." Naoroji, greater than "any other of our older politicians dead or living," yet remained "the man who remonstrates," for "remonstrance, not action, was the note of our political energies of the past." In his landmark economic studies, Naoroji had demonstrated that India's poverty was the result of British rule. But he had not taken the further step of insisting that "the effect could only be cured by removal of the cause, in other words, by the substitution of autonomy in place of a British or British-controlled government." This was left for the Extremists to do.[34]

The Congress began on December 26 with its usual pomp. Naoroji's opening address was a disappointment to the Extremists. But the real action, as always, took place in the closed meetings of the subjects committee. This suited Aurobindo, who was a committee member for the first time. His party decided to use its local advantage to force the adoption of its program. The Moderates opposed them bitterly. Pherozshah Mehta rose to lecture the Extremists, but was shouted down. Madan Mohan Malaviya "made quite an exhibition of himself" (as Khaparde observed), while G.K. Gokhale "walked about and talked like a woman with a complaint."[35] To postpone the conflict, "noncontentious" issues were taken up with first. But finally it was time to decide upon the phrasing of the *swadeshi* and boycott resolutions. The Moderates insisted that the boycott be limited to Bengal and linked to the specific grievance of the province's partition. Pal, on behalf of the Extremists, called for a universal political and economic boycott. An informal poll was taken. The chairman ruled that the Moderates had the majority. There was a "heated discussion," after which most of the Extremists walked out. Tilak, a seasoned tactician, remained behind. After sitting through the meeting, he met with the other Extremists. They agreed to accept the Moderates' wording so long as the phrase "even at some sacrifice" was tacked on to the resolution endorsing the purchase of *swadeshi* goods. Tilak then met with the Moderates and pushed through the compromise over Mehta's objection. "You would not and could not have treated me like this in Bombay," Mehta muttered to his rival. In the general assembly, the modified resolutions were proposed, seconded, and passed. Caught up in the enthusiasm, Naoroji declared in his closing speech that the aim of the Congress was to secure *swaraj* or colonial self-government. This watered down the force of a word that to the Extremists meant complete autonomy, but it was still the most daring phrase ever spoken from the podium by a Congress president.[36]

The Extremists were generally happy with the results of the session. "We were able to carry out 3/4 of our programme," wrote Tilak to an associate.[37] In fact, the Moderates had their way on most issues, but people were beginning to feel that "the Extremists are in the ascendant," as Moderate Motilal Nehru wrote his son Jawaharlal. In England, the Tory press exploded with jingoistic rhetoric: "We have won India by the sword," proclaimed a writer in the *Times*, "and it is well for the small and highly-educated classes, which are alone represented by the Congress, that the British sword stands between them and their native enemies. That is the fundamental fact in the whole situation which makes all claims for full self government in India absurd."[38]

Summing up the results of the Congress in a *Bande Mataram* article, Aurobindo calculated the gains and losses from the points of view of the British and Indian parties. The Conservatives could not "conceal their rage and disappointment"; the Liberals, generally pleased, were upset by the demand for self-government. The Moderates were relieved that "no strongly worded resolutions have been passed," but they had to worry about their ability to control the Congress in the future. As for the Extremists, Aurobindo at least was less than fully satisfied: "No strongly worded resolutions have been passed and we are glad that none have been passed, for we believe in strong action and not in strong words."[39]

As far as it went, Aurobindo's article was an insightful summary of the political situation at the end of 1906. But it missed out completely on one crucial factor. In October, Lord Minto received a deputation of influential Muslims. After hearing them out, he said, in a prepared statement: "You justly claim that your position should be estimated not merely on your numerical strength but in respect of the political importance of your community and the service it has rendered to the Empire." In this Minto was "entirely in accord with you."[40] Faced with growing opposition from upper-class Hindus, the British were in need of "native" allies. One third of India's population was Muslim. Lagging behind the Hindus in education and employment, the Muslims had come to believe that it was in their interest to establish a bloc to offset Hindu influence. In December 1906, two months after the Muslim deputation, the first meeting of the All-India Muslim League was held. Its stated aims were "to protect the cause and advance the interests of our co-religionalists throughout the country" and "to controvert the growing influence of the so-called Indian National Congress."[41] This declaration marked the beginning of sectarian politics in India.

Before the deputation, Pal and other congressmen, Extremist and Moderate, had made half-hearted attempts to woo Muslims. Calls for the two communities to stand together against their common adversary were routine, yet the gap between them grew. In the wake of the deputation, the *Jugantar* took a threatening stance: "Musalmans, be warned! . . . The Hindus are certain to be independent. Will the Musalmans allow themselves to be without that nectar?"[42] Aurobindo's own response to the problem was to ignore it. The one thing necessary was to popularize the gospel of national autonomy. To achieve this, the Extremists had first to outmaneuver the Moderates and capture the Congress. He believed that as the movement progressed, the Muslims would see that their interests were identical to the Hindus'. It soon would become impossible for anyone to maintain this complacent attitude.

Three months after the Congress, Hindu–Muslim rioting broke out in East Bengal. The police were slow to answer Hindu calls for help, and the situation got out of control. Considering the riots in *Bande Mataram,* Aurobindo blamed the British. The Muslims had not planned the attacks, but had been goaded by the government. The Hindus retaliated only after "serious and even unbearable provocation." The violence was regrettable, but at least it showed that Hindus were developing "the habit of rising immediately and boldly to the height of even the greatest emergency."[43] A hundred years later, the East Bengal riots are remembered not as occasions of Hindu self-assertion, but as early examples of the communal violence—to use a term that had not yet been invented—that continues to the present day. Aurobindo and other Extremists are sometimes accused by liberal and left-wing historians of preparing the way for communalism by giving a Hindu slant to the movement. Similarly, the British charged in 1907 that the *swadeshi* movement was "an essentially Hindu movement." Aurobindo gave the lie to this. The movement, he wrote, was not based on any religion, but was itself a "national religion" in which service to the motherland was "espoused with religious fervour and enthusiasm." Concentrated on the anti-British struggle, he regarded other questions as secondary matters. To deal with economic, social, or moral concerns before independence was realized was "the height of ignorance and futility."[44] He could not anticipate in 1907 that the social problem of communalism would bring about the partition of the country forty years later.

Passive and Active Resistance

Aurobindo's health did not improve. A friend who visited him early in January found him recumbent in a room with few amenities: a wooden bedstead without a mattress, a chair, a small cupboard, a steel trunk. Mrinalini came bringing food and medicine.[45] When his fever persisted, he decided to return to Deoghar. Extending his leave from the college and making arrangements for the running of *Bande Mataram*, he left the city in the second week of January.[46] He stayed away for almost three months.

At first he did nothing in particular; then he began to write a play. Between January 28 and February 4 he completed two and a half acts of a dramatic romance based on the story of Bappa Rawal, the eighth-century Rajput hero. This incomplete work has all of the components of his finished plays: a hero deprived of his birthright, powerful enemies he must defeat, and a beautiful spirited girl who becomes his captive. If one wished to search the plot for biographical traces, one could see Bappa as the leader of a group of upstart rebels, whose watchword—"Dare greatly and thou shalt be great"[47]—could almost have graced a *Bande Mataram* editorial. Ichalgurh, the would-be savior of Comol Cumary, looks rather like an old-time Moderate. Wounded by Bappa, he cries out in admiration: "Young hero who in thy first battle o'erbear'st / Maturer victors!"[48] Comol is not only the key to the kingdom, but also the ideal woman whom Bappa (like Antiochus and Perseus) had been longing to meet.

As Aurobindo's strength returned, he began to write short pieces for *Bande Mataram*. In a "By the Way" column published on February 28, he archly explained his absence from the capital: "Seeing the Extremists fare very well at the last Congress I thought I had some claim to a well-earned repose. When all India kindly took to my views and fought for them in the National Assembly I thought I could suspend my activity for a time." This was a prelude to some light-hearted digs at Gokhale. But he did not avoid direct criticism:

> To include India in a federation of colonies and the motherland is mad-
> ness without method. The patriotism that wishes the country to lose itself
> within an Empire which justifies its name by its conquest—the colonies
> being no portion of the Empire in its strict sense—is also madness without
> method. But to talk of absolute independence and autonomy—though this
> be madness, yet there is method in it.[49]

This may have been the first time that he or any Indian politician had used the word "independence" in a published article. From this point on, it became a primary theme of his writing.

Before returning from Deoghar, Aurobindo began a series of essays on the ideal of self-government and the means by which it could be attained. It was called *The Doctrine of Passive Resistance*. There were three possible strategies for achieving independence, Aurobindo wrote: petitioning, self-development, and organized resistance. Petitioning, the Moderates' method, could never succeed. No subject nation had ever been freed on request. Self-development was nec-essary, but if it was not supported by organized political strength, the nation would sink back into "weakness, helplessness and despondency," for

> Political freedom is the life-breath of a nation; to attempt social reform,
> educational reform, industrial expansion, the moral improvement of the
> race without aiming first and foremost at political freedom, is the very
> height of ignorance and futility.... The primary requisite for national
> progress, national reform, is the free habit of free and healthy national
> thought and action which is impossible in a state of servitude.[50]

It was not in Britain's interest to let Indian self-development go too far. Therefore, Aurobindo concluded, "we shall have to fall back on the third pol-icy of organized resistance, and have only to decide what form the resistance should take, passive or active."[51]

Resistance could have one of two aims: establishing a new form of govern-ment or removing the more objectionable features of the old. The second was only possible when the government was "indigenous and all classes have a recognised place in the political scheme of the State." Where the ruling class was a "despotic oligarchy," as in Russia or India, it was necessary to insist on "a free national Government unhampered even in the least degree by foreign control." Resistance to the oligarchy could take three forms. It could "attempt to make administration under existing conditions impossible by an organised aggressive resistance," as the Irish had tried under Parnell. It could follow the Russian example, engaging in "an untiring and implacable campaign of assassination and a confused welter of riots, strikes and agrarian risings all over the country." Finally there was the "old time-honoured method" of "armed revolt." Aurobindo thought that each of these methods had its place. He personally preferred the third, but he could not, of course, announce this in the pages of *Bande Mataram*. Instead he wrote: "The present circumstances in India seem to point to passive resistance as our most natural and suitable weapon," adding immediately and with surprising frankness: "We would not for a moment be understood to base this conclusion upon any condemnation of other methods as in all circumstances criminal and unjustifiable." Because liberty is the life-breath of a nation, "when the life is attacked . . . every means of self-preservation becomes right and justifiable."[52]

The Extremists of Bengal offered boycott as their primary means of passive resistance. In South Africa, Mohandas K. Gandhi had launched a similar movement, which he called *satyagraha*. Aurobindo made it clear that the Extremists' passive resistance differed from Gandhi's in one important respect. It was an article of faith for Gandhi that violence had to be avoided in all circumstances. Aurobindo did not agree. As he wrote in the sixth article of his series:

> To submit to illegal and violent methods of coercion, to accept outrage and hooliganism as part of the legal procedure of the country is to be guilty of cowardice, and, by dwarfing national manhood, to sin against the divinity within ourselves and the divinity in our motherland. The moment coercion of this kind is attempted, passive resistance ceases and active resistance becomes a duty.[53]

This makes it seem as if he regarded active resistance a last resort, but such was not the case. From as early as 1893, he had looked on revolution as the most effective means of achieving political freedom. From the beginning of 1906, when he settled in Bengal, he had given most of his attention to the public movement; but he never gave up hope that an organized movement of militant revolt would help drive the British from India.

THE *SAMITIS* THAT Aurobindo and his friends had started in 1902 were meant to become the nucleus of a disciplined guerrilla force. He believed that in a country as large as India, "even a guerrilla warfare accompanied by general resistance and revolt" would eventually—he was thinking in terms of two or three decades—make it impossible for the British to govern. Faced with a spirited resistance, "they would in the end try to arrive at an accommodation," or even "grant independence rather than have it forcefully wrested from them."[54] For this plan to work, the cadres had to be content with a long, slow development. This did not suit the Bengali temperament. "Bengalis are too emotional," Aurobindo remarked once in this connection. They "want quick results." In 1906 they wanted assassinations, but Aurobindo did not think that killing officials would be much help. "It was never my idea," he wrote years later, "that by throwing a few bombs we could overthrow the British Government." But he never stood in the way of those who plotted assassination. Asked why in 1938, he replied: "It is not wise to check things when they have taken a strong shape, for something good may come out of them." At the least, he reasoned, such attempts would help to popularize the revolutionaries' ideals. Learning "to kill and get killed," the revolutionaries would inspire others with their fighting spirit.[55]

Once Aurobindo began his career as a journalist and politician, the reins of the revolutionary movement passed from him to his brother Barin. Returning to Calcutta in the beginning of 1906, Barin contacted Hemchandra Das and others who were eager for revolutionary action. In June, he and Hem went to East Bengal to assassinate Bampfylde Fuller. They journeyed from one corner of the province to the other trying to find a place for the job. Soon they had spent all of their money and Barin sent Hem back to ask Aurobindo for advice. Aurobindo gave him what little money he had, then—according to Hem—suggested that they look for someone to rob. Hem was not surprised: the leaders of the *samiti* already had decided that robbery was a legitimate way for revolutionaries to raise money. Hem returned to East Bengal where he and Barin, helped out by a new recruit named Narendranath Goswami, tried to rob the house of a reputedly rich woman near Rangpur. After their failure, Hem and another recruit named Prafulla Chaki went to Naihati Junction, where they planned to board Fuller's train and shoot him. Luckily for them, the train did not arrive. Downcast, they returned to Calcutta and told Aurobindo the story. "He listened to it calmly," Hem later recalled, "and told us to go home."[56]

Depressed by these setbacks, Hem and Barin concluded that India was not ready for revolutionary action. They reacted in different ways. Barin fell back on his old idea of setting up an ashram where political *sannyasis* could be trained. Hem decided that what was needed was technical know-how, and he went to Europe to get it. Arriving in Marseille toward the end of 1906, he spent a few months trying to get in contact with revolutionaries, or people who knew revolutionaries, in Switzerland, France, and England. Finally he found a backer to support him while he studied chemistry in Paris. The French capital was then home to hundreds of revolutionaries of every sort. Most notorious were the anarchists of the individualistic school, who succeeded in assassinating six heads of state and dozens of minor figures between 1878 and 1912. In France, individual anarchism had been on the decline since 1894, when the so-called dynamite era ended, but a few die-hard believers in "propaganda of the deed" still flourished. Among them was Joseph Albert, known as Libertad. Someone introduced this man to Hem and his friend Pandurang Bapat in July 1907.[57] Libertad took the young Indians to meetings of socialists, communists, syndicalists, anarchists, and others. They had no interest in these competing doctrines; what they wanted was practical training. Finally, with the help of a female anarchist, apparently Emma Goldman, they were admitted to a party headed by a mysterious Russian known as Ph.D. During the latter part of 1907, the two Indians studied history, geography, economics, socialism, communism, and finally, the subjects they had come to learn: explosive chemistry and revolutionary organization.[58]

While Hem was mastering the technology of terrorism in Paris, Barin was setting up a training center in the suburbs of Calcutta. The children of Dr. K.D. Ghose owned a property in Maniktala, just north of the city. "The Garden," as the place was known, consisted of two acres of land, a dilapidated house and a couple of ponds. As a site for a temple to Bhawani it was less romantic than the source of the Narmada, but it was close to the city and at the same time comparatively secluded. Toward the beginning of 1907 Barin and some young recruits began to live intermittently at the Garden. Simultaneously, Barin and his editorial colleagues decided to preach revolution in the columns of the *Jugantar*. In a three-part series called *Principles of Revolution,* the anonymous writer considered the ways of molding opinion (newspapers, songs, literature, theatre, secret meetings), obtaining weapons (manufacture, smuggling, theft), and collecting funds (donations, robbery). Other articles hinted at how the principles were to be applied: "The number of Englishmen in the entire country is not more than a lakh and a half [150,000]," one article pointed out. "And what is the number of English officials in each district? With a firm resolve you can bring English rule to an end in a single day."[59]

AUROBINDO RETURNED TO Calcutta from Deoghar in April 1907. The demand for *Bande Mataram* was growing, but its finances remained precarious. To improve the cash flow and take the message to other provinces, he and his colleagues launched a Sunday edition that contained editorials and news from the preceding week along with some original pieces. Between June and October, *Perseus the Deliverer* shared space with articles criticizing the secretary of state, the government of Bengal, and the Moderate party.

Aurobindo's colleagues at the office began calling him the Chief. He certainly was in charge, but he led by suggestion rather than command. Most people found him reserved and unassuming, but one colleague noted that he "had a will of his own on which he broke many opponents." On the job, Hemendra Prasad recalled, Aurobindo was always "sensitive of the susceptibilities of his fellow workers." Once he waited for an hour to get Hemendra's permission to change a single word in one of his articles. When his mood was light, people were "captivated by his simple childlike laughter and behaviour," but even those who knew him well had to screw up their courage to approach him.[60]

Aurobindo was living again in the Mallik mansion, where he did most of his *Bande Mataram* writing. People were amazed at his ability to concentrate in the midst of noise and distractions. Arthur Roy once watched him write an article "while he turned half round to us and was engaged in lively discussion." When he finished the piece, "he just gathered the sheets together" and without looking them over, "sent them down to the press as the editorial for the next day." Sometimes someone came from the office to pick up his piece. If he had not finished when the man arrived, he asked him to wait. "Sometimes looking at the paper, sometimes not glancing at it, he would write. The pen or pencil did not stop at all. After writing a few pages he would say, 'do you think that will do?'" If the answer was yes, he would turn to other things. If not, he would go over to the news desk and "look over the telegram sheets and write a 'para' or two, as the mood was on."[61]

People who met Aurobindo at work were surprised by his unprepossessing appearance. When Upendranath Banerjee first came to the office, he was astounded to learn that this "thin, dark, disease-stricken" man was the redoubtable Aurobindo Ghose. The one thing that struck him was Aurobindo's "wonderful, indescribable" eyes. Another *Bande Mataram* staffer recalled that Aurobindo's dress "was one of the plainest: an ordinary coat buttoned up to the neck and a common dhoti. It seemed nobody cared to clothe him properly, while he was himself too preoccupied to give attention to it. He seemed oblivious of his body even." Most people found him distant, as Abinash Bhattacharya, a member of Barin's *samiti*, relates:

> He was always meditating deeply about something. When he looked at one, he seemed not to view one, as if mentally he was soaring far, far

away. I found him always sitting in the same posture with a pen in his hand, deeply immersed in thought. That he had few words for others was not due to any inherent pride or superciliousness. It was probably in his nature.[62]

His appearance might have improved if Mrinalini had been staying with him. In her absence, Abinash became "the chief's housewife." He found Aurobindo an undemanding charge. Whatever food was placed before him, he ate; whatever clothing was laid out for him, he put on. If his shoes had holes in them, he either did not notice or did not care.[63] When Aurobindo ran out of money—which was often, because he rarely took his *Bande Mataram* salary—Abinash or Shyamsundar Chakravarty had to go to the office to ask Hemendra Prasad for "a few rupees . . . to purchase rice for Aurobindo's house." The Chief, they said, was "either practising 'yoga' or immersed in writing for the 'Bande Mataram,' and they would not worry him."[64]

Aurobindo's *Doctrine of Passive Resistance* ran from April 11 to April 23. Three days later, he published the first of another series of articles entitled *Shall India be Free?* He got to the point right off:

> Liberty is the first requisite for the sound health and vigorous life of a nation. A foreign domination is in itself an unnatural condition, and if permitted, must bring about other unhealthy and unnatural conditions in the subject people which will lead to fatal decay and disorganisation. Foreign rule cannot build up a nation,—only the resistance to foreign rule can weld the discordant elements of a people into an indivisible unity. . . .
>
> These considerations are not abstract ideas, but the undeniable teaching of history which is the record of the world's experience. Nationalism [i.e., the Extremist Party] takes its stand upon this experience and calls upon the people of India not to allow themselves to fall into the acquiescence in subjection which is the death-sleep of nations, but to make that use of the alien domination which Nature intended,—to struggle against it and throw it off for unity, for self-realisation as an independent national organism.[65]

Aurobindo contrasted the standpoint of the Extremists with those of the other two Congress factions: the Loyalists, who regarded "the rule of the British bureaucracy as a dispensation of Providence," and the Moderates, "a hybrid species, emotionally Nationalist, intellectually Loyalist."[66] Their belief that India would be helped by increased native participation in the government was fundamentally flawed. "National independence is absolutely necessary to national growth," he wrote; "there can be no national development without national liberty."[67] A century later, it is easy to underestimate how radical this sort of thinking was. The British Empire was at its apogee, the imperial system the basis of the international order. The most sympathetic friends of India in England did not envisage the country's freedom within their lifetimes. Few in India even thought about the problem; those who did hoped at best for more responsible posts for Indians. Pal's call for "national autonomy" or Tilak's cry that "Swarajya is my birthright and I will have it!" were revelations. It was left to Aurobindo to insist unambiguously on "absolute independence" and to construct a consistent policy on that basis.

More than any other newspaper of the day, a contemporary wrote, *Bande Mataram*

> gave vent to what was boiling in men's hearts. It said things which others did not, could not or dared not articulate. It campaigned for the freedom of India, freedom from the hands of the British. To utter such things was rank sedition in those days, but somehow it touched the hearts of a people lulled into slavery for so long.[68]

Its forthright articles won it unprecedented popularity and influence. "No newspaper that we know of has ever evoked such passionate personal enthusiasm as the 'Bande Mataram' did during its short tenure of life," Jitendra Lal Bannerji recalled.[69] The memoirs of many who later became prominent in the movement show that the praise was not hyperbole. Aurobindo's editorials inspired Kakasaheb Kalelkar in Gujarat, R.R. Diwakar in Karnataka, Hasrat Mohani in the North, R.K. Shanmugham Chetty in the South, along with hundreds of others. The paper's influence was commented on by Gandhi in South Africa and felt by Nehru in England. Throughout Europe it helped radicalize the expatriate Indian community, converting Shamaji Krishnavarma and Bhikhaiji Cama from nonviolence to revolution.

Bande Mataram was also read by the British. After going through *The Doctrine of Passive Resistance*, the director of criminal intelligence noted that the articles were "very well written and the tone is wonderfully restrained for Bengali lucubrations." He thought the movement needed "to be watched for it might develop into dangerous proportions under favourable circumstances."[70] Meanwhile, Bipin Pal crowed that "long extracts" from *Bande Mataram* were being "reproduced, week after week, even in the exclusive columns of the 'Times' in London."[71] Although flattered by the attentions of the British press, Aurobindo never addressed a British audience; that would have been a form of the mendicant policy he deplored. Neither did he base "his case for freedom on racial hatred or charges of tyranny or misgovernment" like *Sandhya* or *Jugantar*. The basis of his claim was simply "the inalienable right of the nation to independence." His stand, consistently repeated in the paper, was that "even good [foreign] government could not take the place of national government—independence."[72]

The activist politics that had begun in Bengal were now spreading across the country. In plague-stricken Punjab, the farmers became restive when the local government raised water rates and revenue assessments. Riots broke out in Lahore and Rawalpindi, and there were reports of disaffection among Sikh soldiers. Painting an exaggerated picture of the danger, the governor of Punjab called for the deportation of Lala Lajpat Rai, the Punjab Congress leader, and Ajit Singh, an agrarian agitator. On May 9, Rai was taken into custody and deported to Burma without trial. A telegraphic report of his seizure reached Calcutta the same night, and a subeditor brought it to Subodh Mallik's house. Angry at first for being roused from his sleep, Aurobindo went through the telegram, asked for paper and pencil, and wrote:

> The sympathetic administration of Mr. Morley has for the present attained its records;—but for the present only. Lala Lajpat Rai has been deported out of British India. The fact is its own comment. The telegram goes on to say that indignation meetings have been forbidden for four days. Indignation meetings? The hour for speeches and fine writing is past. The bureaucracy has thrown down the gauntlet. We take it up. Men of the Punjab! Race of the lion! Show these men who would stamp you into the dust that for one Lajpat they have taken away, a hundred Lajpats will arise in his place. Let them hear a hundred times louder your war-cry—*Jai Hindusthan!*[73]

At the same time that the government was jailing Extremists, it was building bridges with the Moderates. In exchange for toning down the nationalist movement, Moderate leaders would be rewarded with seats in the reorganized legislative councils that were a principal feature of a package of reforms that the secretary of state and viceroy were working on. Before the public unveiling of the Morley-Minto Reforms, the Viceroy had tête-à-têtes with Gokhale, Banerjea, and others. Gokhale, according to Minto's secretary, expressed "apprehension about the rising generation"; Banerjea, according to Minto himself, sat "on my sofa with his Mahommedan opponents, asking for my assistance to moderate the evil passions of the Bengali and inveighing against the extravagances of Bipin Chandra Pal."[74] At that moment Pal was bringing regions yet untouched by the new spirit—Orissa, coastal Andhra, Madras—into the mainstream of the nationalist movement. The governor of Madras pressed Minto to deport Pal, and only Morley's veto kept Pal from sharing Lajpat Rai's fate. In May public assemblies were banned in Punjab and eastern Bengal, and a circular was issued in western Bengal to curb student participation in the movement. Calcutta, meanwhile, was rife with rumors that *Jugantar* and *Bande Mataram* would be charged with sedition. On June 8 these newspapers, along with *Sandhya*, were warned that they were liable to prosecution unless they moderated their tone. This was not an empty threat. Earlier in the year, editors in Bombay and Punjab had been convicted of sedition and sentenced to a year or more of prison.

The *Jugantar* editors treated the government's warning as a "big pretentious joke." In the next issue, they called the British Empire "a huge sham" that "a slight pull or little push" would "bring crashing down."[75] Aurobindo and colleagues were a little more circumspect, but did not stop criticizing the government. Commenting on Morley's "sickening cant" on the subject of free speech, Aurobindo wrote: "The freedom of a subject race is only the freedom to starve and die, all the rest of its existence being on sufferance from those who govern."[76]

On July 1 the police raided *Jugantar's* office, demanding to know the name of the editor. Bhupendranath Dutt said that he was in charge. The police noted this down and departed with a load of documents. Four days later they arrested Bhupen and charged him with sedition. During a night spent in jail, he reconsidered the matter and "sent to the commissioner of police a petition to the effect that he was young and inexperienced . . . and had been misled by the swadeshi agitators." Aurobindo was outraged when he heard of this. Years later he noted privately that Bhupen had "declared himself the editor, although that was quite untrue," in a simple "spirit of bravado." If he backed down now, Aurobindo thought, the party would be disgraced. Fortunately, things were not beyond salvation. He urged Bhupen to take responsibility for the paper and the allegedly seditious articles. He should stand trial, but refuse to defend himself. Bhupen agreed, and three weeks later, instead of presenting his defense, he read a statement written by Aurobindo, which read:

> I am solely responsible for all the articles in question. I have done what I
> have considered in good faith to be my duty by my country. I do not wish
> the prosecution to be put to the trouble and expense of proving what I

have no intention to deny. I do not wish to make any other statement or to take any further action in the trial.

This caused an immediate sensation. Bhupen's stance, declared the *Indian Empire*, was "bold and unequivocal" and "without a parallel in the country." It was the first instance of noncooperation with the courts of British India, a tactic that Gandhi and his followers would later perfect. On July 24, Bhupen was sentenced to one year's rigorous imprisonment. He went to jail a hero, and the prestige of *Jugantar* soared.[77]

It was the policy of *Bande Mataram* that the editors would be shielded from prosecution. There was thus no declared editor-in-chief. The declared printer, required by the law, was a man prepared to go to jail while others continued the work. Certain now that the police were about to arrive, the staff of *Bande Mataram* made sure that no evidence about the editors would be found in the office. All references to Aurobindo in the account books and correspondence were "erased by the knife."[78]

On July 30, a squad of policemen descended on the *Bande Mataram* office. Shyamsundar Chakravarty was on duty. The superintendent demanded his name. Shyamsundar asked to see the warrant. Noting that it sanctioned search and not arrest, he made no further comment. The squad spent several hours in the office, and carried off piles of documents. Over the next two weeks, police officials went through what was seized, looking for proof that Aurobindo was the editor. They held a warrant for his arrest, but they did not want to serve it until they were sure of his involvement. What they found was disappointing, but they had to act before the warrant expired. On August 16 a detective went to the office and told the manager that he had a warrant for Aurobindo's arrest. That evening Aurobindo was dining at the home of Byomkesh Chakravarty, a barrister. They decided that he should surrender. He went to the local station, where he was arrested and released on payment of two sureties of 2,500 rupees each. The next day he reported to Calcutta's commissioner of police, who ordered him to appear before the chief presidency magistrate on August 26.[79]

Center Stage

On the morning of August 18, 1907, Aurobindo woke to find himself a celebrity. His case was discussed in every Calcutta newspaper and many in other parts of the country. The *Madras Standard*, a daily that he had criticized in *Bande Mataram*, devoted half a column to his case:

Perhaps, very few outside Bengal have heard of Mr. Arabinda Ghose. . . . No English or Anglo-Indian paper, so far as we are aware, has failed to recognize the singular literary ability and originality of the leading articles in *Bande Mataram,* but many people attributed their authorship to Mr. Bepin Chandra Pal, not knowing who exactly was the power behind the paper. In his telegram published elsewhere, our Calcutta correspondent speaks thus of Mr. Arabinda Ghose:—"I have not the honour of knowing Mr. Ghose personally, but from all accounts, he was a thoroughly sincere man. Of his abilities of a writer and organizer, it would be impertinence to speak. Whatever errors of indiscretion he may have been guilty of, his independence and uprightness are acknowledged by all hands."[80]

A writer for the *Indian Patriot* was even more lavish in his praise, and added some personal observations:

Mr. Aravinda Ghose is no notoriety hunter, is no demagogue who wants to become prominent by courting conviction for sedition. A man of very fine culture, his is a loveable nature; merry, sparkling with wit and humour, ready in refined repartee, he is one of those men to be in whose company is a joy and behind whose exterior is a steadily glowing fire of unseen devotion to a cause.[81]

Another article published later in the same paper bordered on the hagiographic: "Thy courage shall live to inspire thy race. Thou shalt live not only in marble and gold but in poet's song which is more enduring."[82] The perpetrator of this effusion was apparently unaware that the greatest Indian poet of the day had already composed a tribute to Aurobindo. On August 24, Rabindranath Tagore wrote (in Bengali) the now famous lines:

Rabindranath, O Aurobindo, bows to thee!
O friend, my country's friend, O voice incarnate, free,
Of India's soul! . . .
The king's a shadow,—punishment is but a breath;
Where is the tyranny of wrong, and where is death?[83]

Aurobindo had resigned from the National College when his arrest seemed imminent. The administration was content, but the students and teachers met to express their "sympathy in [his] present troubles" and invited him to the college to be fêted and photographed. On August 23 he went to Bowbazar Street, where he received the treatment that public figures in India have to get used to: a ceremonial welcome, garlanding, photo opportunity, food, more food, and a command to speak. His response that day was unusually personal:

> In the meeting you held yesterday I see that you expressed sympathy with me in what you call my present troubles. I don't know whether I should call them troubles at all, for the experience that I am going to undergo was long foreseen as inevitable in the discharge of the mission that I have taken up from my childhood, and I am approaching it without regret. . . .
>
> The only piece of advice that I can give you now is—carry out the work, the mission, for which this college was created. . . . What we want here is not merely to give you a little information, not merely to open to you careers for earning a livelihood, but to build up sons for the Motherland to work and to suffer for her. . . . Work that she may prosper. Suffer that she may rejoice. All is contained in that one single advice.[84]

At this point, he seemed to be resigned to a term in prison. In the face of that prospect he was, Hemendra Prasad observed, "wonderfully composed." Most people assumed that he would refuse to defend himself, but he had no intention of following the example he had created for Bhupen Dutt. If the government was going to take him out of action, it would have to convict him. To do this, it would have to prove that *Bande Mataram* had published sedition, and that he, as editor, was responsible. A crime carrying a maximum penalty of transportation for life, sedition was defined as the dissemination of ideas "calculated to bring the Government into hatred and contempt."[85] Aurobindo's articles were certainly critical of the Raj, but they were too carefully worded for the government to base its case on them. Instead it chose to prosecute Aurobindo, the manager, and the printer for publishing translations of articles that had figured in the *Jugantar* trial and a supposed letter to the editor that contained passages such as this: "Mr. Morley thinks we cannot govern ourselves if the English walk out of the country; this of course they shall never do; but if we expel them by force we shall then be able to govern ourselves because the fact of our success in expelling them will have demonstrated our capacity for self-government."[86]

The case was taken up by Douglas H. Kingsford, the chief presidency magistrate, on August 26. Wanting to establish that Aurobindo was the editor of the paper, the prosecution called Bipinchandra Pal. Pal refused to take the oath and declined to give evidence. Called again three days later he repeated his performance, and was charged with contempt of court. Tried before a junior magistrate, he was convicted and sentenced to six months of simple imprisonment. Shyamsundar Chakravarty also was called; he said that the paper had no editor. Aurobindo himself signed a statement containing the patently false assertion: "I am not now and never have been the editor of the Bande Mataram paper and have never edited the same."[87] The only witness that the state could induce to give evidence against Aurobindo (for a rumored 300 rupees) was a dismissed former proofreader named Anukul Mukherjee. This man had a rather poor idea of what an editor did, and his testimony was invalidated on cross examination.

The trial dragged on through most of September. On September 23, Kingsford delivered his judgment. He ruled that the letter to the editor was seditious, as was the republication of the *Jugantar* articles, but he convicted only the printer, whose liability was statutory. Regarding Aurobindo's connection to *Bande Mataram,* the magistrate found the evidence inconclusive. In acquitting him, he noted that Aurobindo was "a man of exceptionally good attainments who was interested in the promotion of this paper and had differentiated himself from the ordinary staff by refusing to take any fixed salary for his labour."[88]

A few hours after Aurobindo's acquittal, another sedition case was heard. Brahmabandhav Upadhyaya, the editor of *Sandhya,* took full responsibility for the paper's content but refused to take part in the trial, because, he said, "I do not believe that . . . I am in any way accountable to the alien people who happen to rule over us." "This eclipses all previous performances," noted Hemendra Prasad, who had written a few days earlier that opinion was divided over Aurobindo's "having entered into defence after having made Bhupendra of *Jugantar* do what he did."[89] Aurobindo explained his course of action in a September 26 editorial. He noted that the editor of the *Statesman* had written that none of "the great English political writers" had ever "endeavoured to evade the law by raising technical difficulties as to his share of responsibility." Aurobindo answered: "In England a publicist or propagandist has always had the advantage of being tried by a jury of his own peers and in all but rare cases enjoyed every reasonable chance of a fair trial but the reverse is the case in countries circumstanced as India is today." A nationalist editor

owes no moral obligation of quixotic candour to antagonists who themselves recognise no moral obligation in their struggle with him. Whatever he owes, is to his people and the mission he has to discharge. . . . The primary object of the Nationalist organs must be to keep up their propaganda until it is rendered physically impossible by the growing severity of bureaucratic enactments. Bhupendranath and Basanta [another *Jugantar* editor] deliberately exposed themselves to the worst effects of bureaucratic wrath in order to give an example to the country of heroic self-sacrifice and a living demonstration of the spirit of Swarajism; but they did it in the full confidence that the *Jugantar* would continue undaunted and unchanged in the course it conceived to be its duty to the nation.[90]

The general satisfaction at Aurobindo's acquittal—there were celebrations in every part of the country—shows that people did not condemn him for his action.

Among the politicians of the day, Aurobindo was regarded as a model of disinterestedness, and nothing in the biographical record belies this perception. Unlike Surendranath Banerjea and Bipinchandra Pal, he was never accused of profiting from his leadership, and he did not pursue position or fame. But there was a personal side to his action, as he himself acknowledged. He had a fighter's temperament and took a visceral pleasure in the rough and tumble of political action.[91] His unwillingness to compromise was his strength as well as his weakness. He was—as he wrote in a letter of 1920—the right person to call on "when there is something drastic to be done, a radical or revolutionary line to be taken."[92] In the give-and-take of day-to-day politics he was less effective. He approved of but could not follow Tilak's advice that a politician should be ready to accept half a loaf, and then demand the rest. Contemporaries and historians questioned his right to be called an effective politician. Certainly he was not a great builder or steady worker. But his radical interventions opened up paths that others could hardly imagine.

AUROBINDO WAS ALWAYS most comfortable when working "behind the scenes."[93] When the *Bande Mataram* trial ended, he would have liked to resume his backstage position; but owing to the imprisonment of Pal, he was obliged to come forward and lead the party.[94] As the annual session of the Congress approached, party positions became more and more polarized. The Extremists wanted to extend their gains, the Moderates to recover their lost ground. As in 1906, the most contentious issue was selecting the session's president. The Extremists again promoted Tilak; the Moderates were determined to block him. The session was scheduled to be held in Nagpur, which the Moderates thought a safe site. But local Extremists managed to intimidate the Moderate reception committee chairman, who feared Tilak might be elected.

Panic-stricken, he wrote Mehta and Gokhale suggesting that they move the session to another venue.

Unaware of the details of the developments in Nagpur, Aurobindo wrote in *Bande Mataram* on local, national and international affairs. He also helped to reorganize the newspaper's office, which had been thrown into chaos by the trial. Adding to his workload, he began receiving letters from people known and unknown containing praise, advice, requests for interviews, requests for employment, and so forth. Other people came knocking at his door. Embarrassed about the trouble that the visitors caused the Malliks, he asked Abinash to look for another place for him to live.

Aurobindo also was thinking about moving because he wanted Mrinalini and Sarojini to come and stay with him. He had no wish to start a family, though people urged him to do so; but he did feel duty-bound to support his wife and sister, even though he had hardly enough money to support himself. Since his resignation from the college, his only income was his 50-rupee salary from *Bande Mataram*, which he refused to accept as long as the paper was in the red. Early in October Abinash found a place at 19–3 Choku Khansama's Lane, and Aurobindo, Mrinalini, Sarojini, and Abinash moved in. Two weeks later, on October 24, Aurobindo and his wife and sister left for Deoghar. The *puja* holidays were approaching, and he hoped that a stay in the hills would help him get over the ill health that had been dogging him for more than a year.

Aurobindo spent five or six weeks in Deoghar. Visiting from Calcutta were his mother's sister Lilavati and her husband Krishna Kumar Mitra, along with the usual assortment of aunts, uncles, nieces, and nephews. Before leaving Calcutta, he had instructed the *Bande Mataram* staff to send the newspapers. When not occupied with his relatives, he wrote political commentary. All eyes were fixed on Nagpur, where the deadlock continued. Eventually, the Moderates, who were in communication with Gokhale and Mehta, not to mention the British chief commissioner, announced that they could not host the session. On November 10 the Congress Central Standing Committee met in the house of Pherozshah Mehta in Bombay and chose a new venue, the thoroughly Moderate city of Surat. Aurobindo was incensed:

A meeting is announced not at Nagpur . . . but in Bombay and at Sir Pherozshah Mehta's bungalow, as if the Committee and the Congress itself were Sir Pherozshah's personal moveable property; and . . . the moderate majority records a predetermined decision to transfer Sir Pherozshah's moveable property to Surat at a safe distance from Bengal where the Loyalist position is as yet unbreached and there is no time for the Nationalists to instruct public opinion before the holding of the session.[95]

As his party's fortunes declined, he foresaw the coming of a period of "inevitable repression," which would be followed, just as inevitably, by the triumph of the Extremist idea:

> The enemies of the idea have sworn to give it short shrift. They promulgate an ordinance to the effect that it shall not dare to live, and pass a law that it shall be dumb on pain of imprisonment and death, and add a bye-law that whoever has power and authority in any part of the land shall seek out the first-born and the young children of the idea and put them to the sword. . . . But in spite of all and largely because of all the prosecution, denunciation and disparagement the idea gathers strength and increases . . . For the idea is God's deputy and life and death, victory and defeat, joy and suffering have become its servants and cannot help ministering to its divine purpose.[96]

The ordinance that Aurobindo referred to in this apocalyptic passage was the Seditious Meetings Act of November 1907, which permitted local governments to prohibit public meetings in areas that had been placed under an official ban. This, along with continued prosecutions of nationalist newspapers, was the bureaucracy's way of dealing with violence and unrest. In August and September, roughnecks assaulted Europeans in northern Bengal, and a mob attacked a police detachment in Mymensingh. In October, police attempts to break up a meeting in Calcutta were followed by two days of rioting during which "wild unrest" prevailed. Several citizens were killed; a European constable had his hand cut off. It was, thought Hemendra Prasad, "the first explosion of the powder magazine."[97]

Bengali youths no longer feared arrest. In September, on the opening day of the *Bande Mataram* trial, students gathered outside the courthouse shouting "Bande Mataram" and the names of Pal and Aurobindo. Policemen were sent to break up the demonstration. One European sergeant, wielding his stick with special gusto, hit a fifteen-year-old boy named Sushil Sen. Sushil retaliated with his umbrella and with his fists. Overpowered and arrested, he was tried the next day and awarded fifteen stripes—lashes on the buttocks with a rattan cane—by Magistrate Kingsford. The boy received this punishment stoically and was proclaimed a hero. Shortly afterwards he joined Barin Ghose's *samiti*.

THE YEAR 1907 had been a good one for revolutionary recruitment. *Jugantar*'s notoriety and continued boldness brought dozens of young men to the office door. Quickly taken into confidence, the newcomers were told that a secret society was forming that would drive the British from India. Those who wanted to know more were introduced to the leaders. If the initiates seemed to be good prospects, they were taken to the Garden and shown around. As the Maniktala ashram took shape, Barin decided to cut his connection with *Jugantar,* as the paper was attracting too much attention. Police searches and surveillance at the *Jugantar* office had become routine.

By the middle of the year, Barin had gathered about a dozen apprentice revolutionaries. All were young—most were between fifteen and twenty years old—all were more or less educated, and all were Hindu. Invariably from the "respectable" (*bhadralok*) classes and for the most part well brought up, they had a tendency to wildness and indiscipline. Neither school nor the boycott movement attracted them. To earn their spurs, they were ready to deliver a pistol across the province or to turn a heap of chemicals into a bomb. Some of the boys started living at the Garden, others visited from time to time. A few took part in actions. That summer, several members of the group tried to rob a rich moneylender near Burdwan. A month or two later, Aurobindo's associate Charu Chandra Dutt plotted to kill Sir Andrew Fraser, the lieutenant-governor of Bengal, in Darjeeling. Dutt's accomplice in this attempt was Prafulla Chaki, the young man who had accompanied Hem Das to Naihati Junction the previous year. The Darjeeling attempt failed, as had all previous attempts. Not long afterward, Aurobindo wrote during an automatic writing session:

> Bengalees are a timid race but they are very desirous of being brave—Many make attempts, but few can succeed—You do a lot of work but not properly. Because you do not see to the execution....
>
> Sudhir will be a good man for the next attempt. Prafulla has lost confidence in himself. Because he could not do it—Many will try but fail....
>
> Yes, make a good attempt—No—You will not be overbourne with the small charge of the stuff—Barin makes mistakes—Be more selfreliant.[98]

Years later Aurobindo said that he did not know the men in Barin's group until he met them in jail. This is broadly true, though certainly he knew some of the older men, such as Upendranath Banerjee and Hemchandra Das, and had contact with a few members of the younger generation, such as

Abinash Bhattacharya, Satyen Bose, Sudhir Sarkar, Sailen Bose, and perhaps also Prafulla Chaki. But there is no reason to doubt the gist of what he said later about the revolutionaries' actions:

> It was all Barin's work. I never knew who these boys were and never saw them. . . . It is true that Barin used to consult me or Mullick for any advice. But the whole movement was in his hands. I had no time for it. I was busy with Congress politics and *Bande Mataram*. My part in it was most undramatic.[99]

What is unclear is the amount of detail that Barin reported and the exact nature of the advice that Aurobindo gave in return. Not knowing this, it is impossible to say whether Aurobindo was aware that while he was vacationing in Deoghar, Barin twice tried to blow up the lieutenant-governor's train.

Barin and his friends had been experimenting with bombs since 1906. Their early efforts, using the ingredients of safety matches, were only good for impressing potential donors. They made a technological leap when they were joined by Ullaskar Dutt, a dropout from Howrah who had taught himself chemistry after reading about the coming revolution in *Jugantar*. By October he was ready to make a bomb powerful enough to destroy a train. The group acquired some dynamite from a friend whose father owned a mine. Ullaskar loaded it into an iron cylinder and attached a detonator of his own manufacture. Learning that Fraser was planning to travel north from Calcutta on November 5, they went to a suitable spot on the railroad line to place the bomb, but the train rushed by before they could do so. Undeterred, they tried again ten days later when Fraser was scheduled to return. This time they laid the bomb in time, but the train did not come.

Disappointed but still determined to kill Bengal's highest official, Barin and Ullaskar planned their next attempt in advance. The newspapers had reported that Fraser would return to Calcutta from the south in the first week of December. While Ullaskar was working on his biggest bomb yet, Prafulla Chaki and Bibhutibhusan Sarkar went to Narayangarh, near Midnapore, to dig a hole beneath the rails. After finishing the spade work, they returned to Calcutta and, on December 3, came back with Barin and the bomb. Placing it in the hole and setting the fuse, they waited for the train. It did not come. Prafulla and Bibhutibhusan dug up the bomb while Barin hurried back to Calcutta. He returned with a newspaper that said that Fraser would depart on the night of December 5. Going back to their hole, they again placed the bomb and then sat down to a meal of sweetmeats. Barin walked back to Narayangarh to catch the last regular train to Calcutta. When it passed the spot where Bibhuti and Prafulla were waiting, they set the fuse and started for home. A few hours later Fuller's special train passed over the bomb. It exploded deafeningly. The engine heaved upward, but the train did not derail. Climbing down, the lieutenant-governor surveyed the damage and ordered an investigation.

AUROBINDO HAD RETURNED to Calcutta from Deoghar a few days earlier. The month before the start of the Congress promised to be hectic. When the Mehta–Gokhale cabal moved the session to Surat and chose Calcutta Moderate Rashbehari Ghose as their president, Aurobindo and others favored seceding and forming their own organization. Tilak preferred to work within the Congress, but he suggested that the Extremists hold conferences before and after the session. Aurobindo went along with this. He wrote in *Bande Mataram* that the Extremists had "no desire to break the Congress or to part company with our less forward countrymen." On the other hand, the Extremists had "our path to follow and our work to do, and if you [Moderates] will not allow us a place in the assembly you call National, we will make one for ourselves out of it and around it."[100]

Aurobindo's words were intended mainly for Surendranath Banerjea, the leader of the Calcutta Moderates. The struggle between Banerjea and Aurobindo for control of the Bengal Congress would come to a head at the Midnapore district conference on December 7. Aurobindo planned to attend. Just before leaving Calcutta, he wrote a letter to his wife. "Here I do not have a minute to spare," he told her. "I am in charge of the writing; I am in charge of the Congress work; I have to settle the *Bande Mataram* affair. I am finding it difficult to cope with it all." It was, in sum, "a time of great anxiety for me. There are pulls from every side that are enough to drive one mad."[101] Among these pulls were those caused by Barin and the other revolutionaries. The news of the attempt on Fraser was not generally known, but Barin had returned to Calcutta that morning, had met Aurobindo, and presumably had told him about the bomb. As burdened and anxious as Aurobindo was, he took a moment to console Mrinalini, who was unhappy about having to stay in Deoghar: "If at this time you also get restless, it can only increase my worry and anxiety. But if you could write encouraging and comforting letters, that would give me great strength. I should then be able to overcome all fears and dangers with a cheerful heart."[102]

In Midnapore, before the conference, Aurobindo met with his cousin Satyendranath Bose, who was captain of the conference volunteers and leader of the local revolutionaries. Satyen briefed him on the situation. The Moderates were in the majority, but the Extremists had plenty of enthusiasm. Satyen had demanded an undertaking from the president-elect, a cautious Moderate named K.B. Dutt, that he would speak on *swaraj*, or full autonomy. Dutt refused. He demanded that Satyen rein in his volunteers. Satyen refused. When the conference began, the volunteers were marshaled strong, with turbans on their heads, badges on their chests, and *lathis* in their hands. On the platform sat the British magistrate and police superintendent, whom the organizers hoped would overawe the Extremists. Once the preliminaries were over, Banerjea proposed Dutt to the chair. The motion carried and Dutt began his speech. An Extremist stood and demanded that he speak about *swaraj*. Dutt continued to read his prepared text. The volunteers began to wave their *lathis* and create an uproar. When the tumult became too loud for Dutt to continue, he went to Aurobindo and pleaded with him to calm the young men down. Aurobindo gave no answer and the turmoil continued. Eventually the Moderates moved to a different hall to pass their resolutions.[103]

Aurobindo was satisfied with what happened at the conference. When he returned to Calcutta, he wrote in *Bande Mataram:* "Midnapore has taken the initiative in giving Nationalism [that is, the Extremist Party] an organised shape and form."[104] He would have been happy for the party to continue on its own, but he had promised to bring the Bengal Extremists to Surat. On December 11, 14, and 15, he was present at pre-Congress meetings in various Calcutta squares. On December 14, pressed by the people to speak, he said a few words in English, his maiden political speech. The next day the crowd called out for him again, and he had to take the floor. "I have made it a rule not to speak in public," he began, because his early departure for England had kept him from mastering his mother tongue, "and rather than address you, my countrymen, in a language which is not mine and which is not yours, I kept silent." He then explained the position of the Extremists.[105]

On December 20, he took time off from his political work to attend a meeting of the executive committee of the National Council of Education. Later that evening, while he was working at the Mallik mansion, the butler told him that there was someone at the door for him. Aurobindo went downstairs and shook hands with Henry Nevinson, a correspondent for the *Manchester Guardian*. As they sat down to speak, Nevinson's experienced eyes searched the man before him for clues to his character: "He was a youngish man, I should think still under thirty. [He was thirty-five.] Intent dark eyes looked out from his thin, clear-cut face with a gravity that seemed immovable, but the figure and bearing were those of an English graduate." Himself a graduate of Oxford and interested in radical causes—he had covered the 1905–1906 revolution in Russia and was a personal friend of Kropotkin's—Nevinson found much to admire in Aurobindo's politics: "His purpose, as he explained it to me, was the Irish policy of Sinn Fein—a universal Swadeshi, not limited to goods but including every phase of life. His Nationalists would let the Government go its own way and take no notice of it at all." The Extremists "proposed to work on the three lines of a national education, independent of Government but including the methods of European science; a national industry, with boycott of all foreign goods except the few things India could not produce; and the encouragement of private arbitration, in place of the law-courts, for the settlement of disputes." But behind these simple means a deeper spirit was at work. As Nevinson related, "Arabindo Ghose had already, I think, formed the project of developing out of the Congress, or in place of the Congress, a nationalist and democratic body that would prepare the country for self-government." Nevinson found in Aurobindo's words "a religious tone, a spiritual elevation," very different from "the shrewd political judgment of Poona Extremists":

> In an age of supernatural religion Arabindo would have become what the irreligious mean by a fanatic. He was possessed by that concentrated vision, that limited and absorbing devotion. Like a horse in blinkers, he ran straight, regardless of everything except the narrow bit of road in front. But at the end of that road he saw a vision more inspiring and spiritual than any fanatic saw who rushed on death with Paradise in sight. Nationalism to him was far more than a political object or a means of material improvement. To him it was surrounded by a mist of glory, the halo that mediaeval saints beheld gleaming around the head of martyrs. Grave with intensity, careless of fate or opinion, and one of the most silent men I have known, he was of the stuff that dreamers are made of, but dreamers who will act their dream, indifferent to the means.[106]

The next day, Aurobindo and the other Bengal delegates left for Surat. Recalling the journey years later, Barin wrote:

> Aurobindo the new idol of the nation was hardly known then by his face and at every small and big station a frantic crowd rushed about . . . looking for him in the first and second class carriages, while all the while Aurobindo sat unobserved in a third class compartment. By the time this fact became known and he was found out, the train was about to start.

The secretary of the Bengal Moderates, who was traveling first class, "tried again and again" to invite Aurobindo into his carriage "and keep him there to save his face." At places where longer stops were arranged, Aurobindo disembarked and delivered impromptu speeches. "Small in stature and slender in build, this quiet unobtrusive man was often lost in the crowd of his own admirers. When he rose to speak his voice was hardly audible except to those nearest to him,—that thin and almost girlish voice which in measured cadence gave vent to truths ringing with strength and beauty." As soon as they reached Bombay, they were taken to the beach to attend a meeting. "We could hardly walk to the place through the living streams converging through the streets and lanes towards the chosen spot, automatically stopping all vehicular traffic for a time." To Barin, the ecstatic throng represented "the awakening of the whole nation from its age-long sleep and inertia into conscious life."[107]

Aurobindo and his companions reached Surat on December 24. For the first time, the two parties were staying in separate camps. The Moderates had set themselves up near the pavilion. Barin was repelled by the fashionably European atmosphere: the pompous decorations, luxurious tents, inaccessible leaders, and servants rushing here and there. The Extremists in contrast were crammed into *dharmasalas* and houses near the center of town. Aurobindo and Tilak did their work in an open room while "streams of people flowed up the staircase" to catch a glimpse of them.[108] Tilak brought Aurobindo up to date. The Moderates were planning to use their local strength to recoup their losses of the previous year. The Congress reception committee, under Gokhale's instructions, had refused to release the draft resolutions. People said that the Moderate drafts were retrograde. Tilak made it clear that he did not want the Congress to split, but he was determined to prevent any backpedaling.

In the afternoon, the Extremists held the first of their planned party conferences. Tilak's lieutenant Khaparde proposed Aurobindo to the chair. In a brief statement, Aurobindo said that the purpose of the meetings was to transform the Congress from "a body for the concentration of opinion to a body for the concentration of work." He then asked Tilak to take the floor. The Poona leader explained the party's program and said that they would try to impose it on the Congress. Specifically, they would ask Rashbehari Ghose to step down in favor of Lala Lajpat Rai, who had recently returned from deportation; push for advanced resolutions on *swaraj, swadeshi,* and national education; and propose amendments to any resolution that did not satisfy them. Aurobindo closed the meeting by saying that, while he had favored seceding from the Congress, he would never do so if it meant breaking with Tilak.[109]

The next morning, Tilak went to the Moderates' camp. Mehta and Gokhale received him haughtily, but he persisted in his attempts to create a compromise. Later in the day, he went to the station to receive Lajpat Rai. The Punjab leader was given a tremendous welcome, but he disappointed his allies by saying that he would not accept the presidential nomination. Assuming the mantle of peacemaker, he conferred with members of both parties. To Aurobindo he suggested that "as a teacher his role was above party strife." Aurobindo replied: "You cannot fill the cup till you have emptied it," pouring the contents of an imaginary cup on the floor.[110]

To avoid problems at the session, which would open the next day, Rai proposed setting up a committee consisting of five members from each party. The Extremists agreed, selecting Tilak, Aurobindo, and three others as their representatives. Rai took his proposal to Gokhale, who turned him down, confident that his party was stronger. In the evening, the Extremists held another conference; Aurobindo again was the chair. "That night," Nevinson reported, "few slept. Backwards and forwards, from tent to tent and house to house, the leaders passed, discussing, consulting, deliberating, full of uncertainty and apprehension. Morning found them still apprehensive and uncertain." In a last-minute attempt to avoid conflict, Tilak, Aurobindo, and other Extremists spoke with Surendranath Banerjea. They said that they would drop their opposition to the president if the Moderates made a "graceful allusion" to "the desire of the public to have Lajpat Rai in the Chair," and promised not to renege on the Calcutta resolutions. Banerjea did not object, but said that he needed to get the approval of the reception committee. The committee chairman, a local solicitor named Tribhovandas Malvi, refused to meet anyone.[111]

The session began that afternoon. Every one of the ten thousand seats in the pavilion was taken. There were 1,600 delegates, of whom, in Nevinson's estimation, 500 "might be called Extremists of one kind or another." Still waiting for a copy of the resolutions, Tilak and Khaparde tried to meet with Malvi, who again refused to see them. Only when the chairman had begun his welcoming speech did Tilak received the draft. He was stunned. All of the Calcutta resolutions were going to be changed.[112] Malvi was followed by another local leader, who proposed Rashbehari Ghose to the chair. Surendranath Banerjea rose to second the motion. The great orator, master of a hundred meetings, said hardly a dozen words before chaos broke out. "Remember Midnapore!" cried the Bengali Extremists. "Remember Nagpur!" echoed the Maharashtrians. Soon all ten thousand were shouting. Banerjea climbed on a table to continue his speech, but was not heard. The tumult gave no sign of abating and the session was suspended.[113]

That evening many attempts were made to patch things up. Banerjea invited the Bengali delegates to his tent. Aurobindo went with the younger Extremists. Banerjea scolded them for weakening the united Bengal front, and offered them a compromise agreement. It passed unsigned from one hand to another until Satyen Bose tore it up. As the Extremists followed their leader as he walked out of the room, one of Banerjea's lieutenants raised his fist and shouted: "Aurobindo, go eat Tilak's shit!"[114]

The next morning tempers were still frayed, but most of the delegates wanted to see the session through. By one o'clock the pavilion was filled to overflowing. Aurobindo sat in the front surrounded by a dozen young Bengalis. Near him was Tilak, who declined to take his place on the platform. When the dignitaries had taken their seats, Tilak sent a note to the reception committee chairman saying that he would move an amendment after the seconding of the presidential nomination. Banerjea was allowed to conclude his interrupted speech. Motilal Nehru added a few words, and Malvi declared Rashbehari Ghose elected. Tilak rose to move his amendment. Rashbehari began his speech. Tilak protested, but was shouted down. Tilak stood his ground even when a group of paid hooligans rushed for him. Maharashtrian Extremists mounted a counterattack. A Mahratta shoe flew through the air, rebounding off Banerjea and striking Mehta. Pandemonium broke loose. Aurobindo, surrounded by his guard of Bengalis, watched calmly as chairs were thrown and heads broken. At one point Satyen Bose rushed up to him and said, "I have a pistol with me, shall I shoot Suren Banerjea?" "For Heavens sake, don't do that!" Aurobindo replied. Soon Satyen, Barin, and the other young men found a way to escort him out of the pavilion. As he walked through the doorway, a Moderate supporter spat on him from above.[115]

That evening and night, despite the general ill feeling, mediators tried to continue the session. But the acrimony had become too acute. The next day, the Moderates held a separate convention in the pavilion under police guard. No one could enter without signing the Moderate declaration, or "creed." When he heard of this move, Tilak suggested that the Extremists sign the creed, swamp the convention, and regain control of the Congress. Aurobindo argued against this. It would mean submission to autocrats, he said. Tilak conceded the point, which was largely academic, as Extremists who tried to sign were turned away.[116] That evening the Extremists held their own closed meeting. Aurobindo, "with his grave and desperately immovable face" (as Nevinson described it) "took the Chair, and sat unmoved, with far-off eyes, as one who gazes at futurity." Tilak rose and spoke for ninety minutes about what had happened and what their next steps must be.

A national committee was appointed to keep watch over events. Aurobindo was named its president.[117]

The following day the last of the Extremists' conferences was held. As usual Aurobindo presided and Tilak was the principal speaker. This time they dealt mostly with practical matters of promotional strategy and party organization.[118] Most of the Extremists planned to leave Surat after the meeting, but Tilak remained behind to draft a reply to a press release that the Moderates had issued. Aurobindo stayed behind as well, and on December 30 added his signature to Tilak's statement. In it, the Extremists blamed the split on the Moderates, in particular for not providing them with copies of the draft resolutions, for reneging on the Calcutta resolutions, and for not letting Tilak move his amendment. At the time, however, few people were convinced by Tilak's arguments. Most blamed the split on him, even though he unquestionably wanted the Congress to remain intact. It was Aurobindo and the younger men from Bengal and Maharashtra who wanted to break with the Moderates. Sometime before the final melee, a group of Maharashtrians learned that the Moderates planned to reorganize the Congress so that they would hold the majority for years to come. Determined to prevent this, the Maharashtrians asked Aurobindo if they should break up the Congress. He told them, "You must either swamp it or break it." It was men from Maharashtra who led the charge to the platform. Years later Aurobindo observed in a letter that his advice was, in effect, "the order that led to the breaking of the Congress." This gives too much importance to a single factor in a complex chain of events. The differences that brought about the split had been building for months. Even without Aurobindo's "order," Tilak's stance and the attack against him would have led to a free-for-all. However, it is true that Aurobindo was the main Extremist in favor of secession, and the elements in the party that supported this course gravitated to him. In the same letter, Aurobindo noted that his refusal to join the Moderate convention was the other "decisive" occurrence at Surat. But he conceded elsewhere that the Moderates would not have let the Extremists join in any event.[119] In attempting to keep the Congress whole, Tilak had to struggle against both Moderate obduracy and Aurobindo's intransigence.

The split between the Moderates and the Extremists was not the only parting of the ways at Surat. On December 27, the day of the riot in the pavilion, Barin tried to arrange a conference of revolutionaries from all parts of India. He sent a note to Aurobindo, asking him to persuade his friends to come. "Dear Brother," he began, "now is the time. We must have *sweets* all over India readymade for imergencies [*sic*]." "Sweets" was Barin's code word for bombs. Aurobindo stuffed this compromising note into his pocket, but did not attend the conference. Neither did Tilak, nor any other Maharashtrian. Barin concluded that "we had to walk our lone path and somehow convince and initiate the whole of Congress-minded India into this new creed of violent and armed revolution."[120]

Barin's plans included finding a spiritual guide to lead his proposed band of revolutionary *sannyasis*. During an earlier trip to western India, he had met a Maharashtrian yogi named Vishnu Bhaskar Lele. When the two men meditated together, Lele opened Barin to his "first glimpse of spiritual awakening." Barin was sufficiently impressed to recommend Lele to his brother. Aurobindo had been wanting to consult with a yogi for some time. His inner progress had stopped amid the helter-skelter life he had been leading. He told Barin that he would be happy to meet Lele, Barin sent the yogi Aurobindo's address in Baroda, where he would be going next.[121]

Silence and Action

Aurobindo left Surat on the morning of the last day of 1907. When he and Barin reached Baroda, they were met by an excited crowd of old friends and acquaintances and hundreds of unknown admirers. Waving flags and shouting slogans, the crowd followed his carriage as it proceeded from the station to Khaserao Jadhav's house. Along the way a group of Baroda College students unyoked the horses and pulled the carriage themselves.[122]

Moments after Aurobindo's arrival, Vishnu Bhaskar Lele knocked at the door. The yogi was a man in his late thirties, a year or two older than Aurobindo. He worked as a government clerk and looked it: stocky frame, nondescript face, thick nose, rustic dress, unrefined speech. But Aurobindo saw in his eyes both childlike devotion and latent power, and he had no qualms about putting himself in his hands. He told Lele that he had taken up yoga three years earlier, beginning with *pranayama*. For a while he had obtained some interesting results: great energy, visual phenomena, fluency in writing poetry. Then he got involved in politics. His *pranayama* became irregular and he fell ill. Since then he had been "doing nothing and did not know what to do or where to turn." He wanted to resume his practice but was unwilling to give up his work. Rather, he hoped that yoga would give him the strength to do it better. Lele replied, unexpectedly, that yoga would be easy for Aurobindo, as he was a poet. There was no need to give up his work, but it would be better if he could take a few days off.[123] Aurobindo agreed, but time off was going to be hard to arrange.

Dozens of friends were looking forward to meeting him. Hordes of people were camped on the lawn waiting for a glimpse of the famous leader. He had speeches to deliver in Baroda, Bombay, and Poona, and much work and an impatient wife in Bengal. Apparently (the sequence of events is uncertain) he decided to take care of his most pressing engagements in Baroda before going off with Lele. Over the course of a few days, he delivered two or three speeches and spoke with a number of individuals about politics and revolution. When he was free, his friends spirited him away to a house in the middle of town that was owned by a friend of Lele's. Here, in a room on the top floor, teacher and student sat down together.

Lele asked Aurobindo to meditate. "Do not think," he said, "look only at your mind; you will see thoughts *coming into it*; before they can enter throw these away from your mind till your mind is capable of complete silence." Aurobindo had never heard of such an idea, but he followed his teacher's instructions. "In a moment" his mind became quiet "as a windless air on a high mountain summit." Then, to his astonishment, he saw that what Lele said was true: His thoughts were not arising from within but "coming in a concrete way from outside." As the intruders approached, "before they could enter and take hold of the brain," he pushed them back—not by a "forcible rejection," but by a sort of conscious detachment. In three days, "really in one," his mind "became full of an eternal silence."[124]

Lele wanted Aurobindo to silence his mind so that he could establish a relationship with a personal godhead and learn to follow its guidance. He told his student that a voice would arise in the silence. None did. Nothing at all came out of that "absolute stillness," which had blotted out "all mental, emotional and other inner activities." Outwardly, the "movements of the ordinary life" continued, but they "were carried on by some habitual activity of Prakriti [nature] alone which was not felt as belonging to oneself." There was no sense of individuality. All that remained was an ineffable something, a formless reality or *brahman* or "That," but "what realised that Reality" was not an individual but "a nameless consciousness which was not other than That."[125]

Grave difficulties attend any attempt to describe this state. After writing the last sentence in 1946, Aurobindo added: "Mark that I did not think these things, there were no thoughts and concepts nor did they present themselves like that to any Me; it simply just was so or was self-apparently so." Elsewhere he tried to explain the experience in phenomenological terms:

There was no ego, no real world—only when one looked through the immobile senses, something perceived or bore upon its sheer silence a world of empty forms, materialised shadows without true substance. There was no One or many even, only just absolutely That, featureless, relationless, sheer, indescribable, unthinkable, absolute, yet supremely real and solely real. This was no mental realisation nor something glimpsed somewhere above,—no abstraction,—it was positive, the only positive reality,—although not a spatial physical world, pervading, occupying or rather flooding and drowning this semblance of a physical world, leaving no room or space for any reality but itself, allowing nothing else to seem at all actual, positive or substantial. I cannot say there was anything exhilarating or rapturous in the experience . . . but what it brought was an inexpressible Peace, a stupendous silence, an infinity of release and freedom.[126]

It was, in a word, *nirvana*, in the Vedantic rather than the Buddhist sense: a "blowing out" or extinction of world and personality. Perception remained, but it was accompanied by an overwhelming sense of the unreality of the things perceived. The world was seen as a vast *maya* or illusion. It was precisely the experience that Aurobindo did not want from yoga. He had always rejected *mayavada*, the school of Vedanta that holds that the world is an illusion. Now he found himself plunged in the experience that *mayavada* is based on, and it was so strong he could not have gotten out of it even if he had tried.

Lele too had hoped for something different for his student. The inner divinity whose voice he wanted Aurobindo to hear is poles apart from the impersonal Absolute that his student had become absorbed in. But Lele knew better than to try to interfere. He prayed for Aurobindo to emerge from the experience or else to pass on to something beyond it. In the meantime, he watched as Aurobindo let the experience "have its full play and produce its full experimental consequences."[127]

This experience of the silent *brahman* coming at the peak of Aurobindo's political career was the most dramatic turning-point in his life. He had arrived in Baroda as a leader of a movement that involved the lives and energies of thousands of people. Its demand—independence from the world's dominant imperial power—had enormous potential consequences. As a journalist and organizer, Aurobindo's authority was exceeded only by Tilak's; as an inspiration to the revolutionaries, his influence was unrivalled. And for politicians as well as revolutionaries, it was a moment of crisis. The terrorists had struck in Narayangarh and the police were on their trail. The Congress had split and the Extremists were in danger of being shut out from the organization. It would thus be safe to say that when Aurobindo left Surat, he had a number of things on his mind. Now, by his own account, his mind was "full of an eternal silence." Aurobindo's experience of the passive *brahman* "remained unimpaired for several months"—indeed, he later explained, it remained with him for years, so that he could write in 1936 that it was "there now though in fusion with other realisations."[128]

How does a biographer deal with such statements? Up to this point, it has been possible to satisfy the insistence of critical readers for objective verification. But when one writes about subjective experiences, this sort of verification is not possible. "One cannot criticize the vision of a mystic," the philosopher William James once observed, "one can but pass it by, or else accept it as having some amount of evidential weight."[129] To pass by Aurobindo's spiritual experiences would be to ignore the most significant part of his life. This biographer therefore will make use of Aurobindo's accounts of his experiences, trying to square them when possible with other sorts of evidence, but not treating them as data for psychological or sociological analysis.

AUROBINDO REMAINED ALONE with Lele for a week or more. During this period, Barin reported, "batches of young men traversed the town in search of their newly-found leader who had so suddenly and mysteriously disappeared from among them, upsetting all their crowded programmes and arrangements."[130] Eventually Aurobindo had to emerge. After finishing his business in Baroda, he, Barin, and Lele took the train to Bombay. There Barin departed for Calcutta, while Aurobindo and Lele went on to Poona. Reaching the city on January 11, 1908, Aurobindo spent a few days with Tilak and other friends. There were *pan supari* parties, visits to local institutions, and at least one meeting with aspiring revolutionaries. On the evening of January 13, Aurobindo spoke at Tilak's residence before an audience of some four thousand. He began by avowing that he was no speaker—"My weapon is the pen and not the tongue"—and then gave an account of the movement in Bengal. He concluded that if people in all parts of India began to work together, the country would soon attain "greatness, prosperity and freedom."[131]

Aurobindo was back in Bombay by January 15. That evening he gave another lecture to an audience numbering five thousand. After that, he had a few days' respite. He stayed in a *chawl* or tenement building on Grant Road—an unlovely part of an unlovely town. The walls of the room were blackened by cooking fires. The air was thick with smoke. Aurobindo was untroubled. Looking without, as he wrote years later in a sonnet called "Nirvana," he saw nothing but *maya*:

The city, a shadow picture without tone,
Floats, quivers unreal; forms without relief
Flow, a cinema's vacant shapes, like a reef
Floundering in shoreless gulfs the world is done.

Looking within, he found no residue of personality:

The mind from thought released, the heart from grief
Grow inexistent now beyond belief;
There is no I, no Nature, known-unknown.

All that remained was a "Peace, stupendous, featureless, still," within which "what once was I" had become "a silent unnamed emptiness" ready to "fade in the Unknowable" or else to pour itself out into the sea of life and action.[132]

Many people came to see him in his Grant Road *chawl*. He spoke with them, sometimes went out with them to meetings, but remained absorbed in his experience. His mental and physical activities, he later explained, "proceeded on the surface" without disturbing the inner silence. But on January 19, before going to give a speech, he found that "there was no activity on the surface"—his mind was a perfect blank. He asked Lele, "How am I going to speak? Not a single thought is coming to me." Lele told him to pray. Aurobindo said he did not feel like praying (he had never been the praying sort). Lele said it did not matter; he and others would do the praying. Aurobindo should go, "make *namaskara* to the audience and wait and speech would come to him from some other source than the mind." Aurobindo agreed and went to the hall. Friends found him withdrawn, apparently "dazed." When they spoke, "he took refuge in silence." Someone handed him a copy of *Bande Mataram*. His eyes fell on two headlines: THE 'YUGANTAR TRIAL', JUDGMENT DELIVERED and ANOTHER NEWSPAPER PROSECUTION, THE 'NABASAKTI' OFFICE SACKED. These remained in his mind as he went to face the audience. As instructed, he made *namaskara*, called for inspiration, and waited.[133] Just as Lele said, words came out of the silence: crisp phrases quite different from his usual discursive style:

You call yourself Nationalists. What is Nationalism? Nationalism is not a mere political programme; Nationalism is a religion that has come from God; Nationalism is a creed in which you shall have to live. . . .

It is not by any mere political programme, not by National Education alone, not by Swadeshi alone, not by Boycott alone, that this country can be saved. . . . They are merely particular concrete lines upon which the spirit of God is working in a nation; but they are not in themselves the one thing needful.

What is the one thing needful.... [Those behind the movement in Bengal] have had one over-mastering idea, one idea which nothing can shake, and this was the idea that there is a great power at work to help India, and that we are doing what it bids us.... God is doing everything. We are not doing anything.... Faith then is what we have in Bengal....

Another thing, which is only another name for faith, is selflessness.... This is the second aspect of our religion, and is the absolute denial of the idea of one's separate self, and the finding of one's higher eternal Self in the three hundred millions of people in whom God Himself lives....

The third thing, which is again another name for faith and selflessness is courage.... If you do not have the divine strength of faith and unselfishness, you will not be able to escape from other attachments, you will not like to bear affliction simply for the sake of a change by which you will not profit. How can courage come from such a source? But when you have a higher idea, when you have realised that you have nothing, that you are nothing and that the three hundred millions of people of this country are God in the nation ... you will then realise that it is something immortal, that the idea for which you are working is something immortal and that it is an immortal Power which is working in you.

The three things that Aurobindo spoke of—faith, selflessness, and courage—were the qualities that nationalists should cultivate "so that everything you do may be not your own doing, but the doing of that Truth within you." What they were called on to do was not to carry out a "mere political uprising," but to "shape the life of this great nation so that it may be fit to reveal" that truth.[134]

Aurobindo's speech of January 19, 1908 is one of his most quoted political utterances. Admirers cite it as an expression of enlightened politics based on the ancient greatness of Hinduism. Detractors regard it as a dangerous mixture of religion and nationalism. Both are reading into it things that are not there. Apart from a few literary references, Aurobindo did not allude to Hinduism. The "religion" he referred to was the "religion of Nationalism," the sacrifice of all one is and has to the nation "in a religious spirit," that is, with faith, unselfishness, and courage. The "Nationalism" he referred to was the program of the Nationalist (Extremist) party. He specifically excluded nationalism in its normal political sense. The speech, to be sure, is shot through with religion, but not religion as the term is ordinarily understood. Aurobindo was stating his own credo of dedication and self-sacrifice for the sake of the nation. Nothing else he ever said or wrote goes farther in explaining the fearlessness, if not the rashness, with which he pursued his political aims.

Aurobindo remained in Bombay until January 24. Before leaving the city, he went to Lele to ask for guidance. Lele began to give him detailed instructions—to meditate at a fixed time, and so forth—then stopped and asked him if "he could surrender himself entirely to the Inner Guide within him and move as it moved him." Aurobindo told Lele he could. Lele replied that in that case, he had no further need of instruction.[135] This ability to hear and be guided by an inner voice was one of three things that Aurobindo got from Lele. The others were the ability to silence the mind and open to the *brahman* experience and the ability to speak, and later to write, by opening to an inner inspiration. He always was grateful to Lele for showing him the way to developing these inner abilities. But he did not need his guidance any longer. The two would meet again in Calcutta, but not as guru and disciple.

AUROBINDO WANTED TO RETURN directly to Bengal, but his friends in Maharashtra would not hear of it. On the way he stopped in Nashik, Dhule, Amravati, and Nagpur, delivering nine speeches in as many days. The pattern of his visits was always the same: a ceremonial reception at the station, with garlanding, songs, and welcoming speeches; a procession with his carriage drawn by local schoolboys; then, a stay in the house of a local sympathizer. In the evening, and perhaps also the next morning, he would be taken to a open space or theater, where he would speak in English to a crowd of thousands, most of whom could not understand him. Wherever he was taken, he was treated like visiting royalty. But he seems to have kept his perspective. In the beginning of February, he wrote in *Bande Mataram:*

> These are times of revolution when tomorrow casts aside the fame, popularity and pomp of today. The man whose carriage is today dragged through great cities by shouting thousands amid cries of "Bande Mataram" and showers of garlands, will tomorrow be disregarded, perhaps hissed and forbidden to speak. . . . Men who are now acclaimed as Extremists, leaders of the forward movement, preachers of Nationalism, and embodiments of the popular feeling will tomorrow find themselves left behind, cast aside, a living monument of the vanity of personal ambition.[136]

Aurobindo had delivered his first political speech in December 1907. In January and February 1908 he gave at least fifteen. For the most part, he was well received. "He does not have a loud voice," a Nagpur resident recalled. "But when he started speaking slowly in distinctive tones, we all felt a kind of rhythm creeping over the vast concourse and when the lecture was over, we woke up as from an enchantment." Most Nationalist speakers had a much more vehement style. His collaborator Shyamsundar Chakravarty used to move about on the platform, crying and "gesticulating violently, like a mad man, while giving vent to his stray feelings." Aurobindo rose without fanfare "and standing like a quiet statue of Buddha" spoke "in his terse forceful style and simple and dignified English," giving his thoughts "beautifully mould-ed and controlled expression" and carrying "the whole audience with him." "Without making any effort at oratory," another listener recalled, Aurobindo managed to hold the audience with his "impassioned eloquence"—this despite his being far from impressive as a speaker: short, thin, with a drawn and angu-lar face and a voice high-pitched to the point of shrillness.[137]

AUROBINDO REACHED CALCUTTA on February 3, almost a month after the date he had given to his wife before his departure. He found an agitated letter from her. She complained of being abandoned in Deoghar, and demanded to be taken to Calcutta as soon as possible. Once there, she would certainly not stay with her father's friend Girish Bose. "You have married," she reminded her husband. "This being the case, why should my father look after me, not to mention Girish Babu? If you are able to provide for me, well and good. If not, let me die of starvation. One thing more, henceforth you must not take one single penny from my father." To do so was shameful, but Aurobindo did "not feel insulted even when abused." He must obtain some money in a dignified way and send it to her as quickly as possible. Not only she but Aurobindo's mother depended on it. After continuing in this vein for a number of pages, she begged him for a reply—"only a few lines. Will you please oblige me by writing these few lines?"[138]

Two weeks later, Aurobindo answered her. His letter shows better than any retrospective account the effects of his January experiences:

I was to have come on January 8, but could not. This did not happen of my own accord. I had to go where God took me. This time I did not go for my own work; it was for His work that I went. The state of my mind has undergone a change. But of this I shall not speak in this letter. Come here, and I shall tell you what is to be told. But there is something that has to be said at once. From now on I am no longer the master of my own will. Like a puppet I must go wherever God takes me; like a puppet I do whatever he makes me do. . . . From now on you will have to understand that all I do does not depend upon my will, but is done at the command of God. When you come here, you will understand the meaning of my words. I hope that God will show you the Light he has shown me in his infinite Grace. But that depends on His Will. If you wish to share my life and ideal you must strive to your utmost so that, on the strength of your ardent desire, He may in his Grace reveal the path to you also. Do not let anyone see this letter, for what I have said is extremely secret. I have not spoken about this to anyone but you; I am forbidden to do so.[139]

The prohibition was an inward one. Despite the enormous changes he had passed through since December, he spoke about them to no one.

Revolution, Bare and Grim

Aurobindo arrived in Calcutta on February 4 or 5. Lacking a house, he went to stay with Subodh Mallik at Wellington Square. Almost immediately he began to write for *Bande Mataram*. He recalled later that everything he wrote "got itself done without any thought entering my mind or the silence being in the least disturbed or diminished." But there was no noticeable diminution in the force or relevance of his output. Indeed, a colleague thought, his articles had a new "this-worldly colour."[140]

During his absence, *Bande Mataram* had fallen into administrative and financial chaos. The paper was running a deficit of 300 rupees a month, the editorial staff was quarrelling, and Hemendra Prasad Ghose had quit. On February 8 Aurobindo called a meeting of the *Bande Mataram* company. Later the same day, he went to a meeting of the executive committee of the National Council of Education. The following term, he would be lecturing in the college on history, political science, English, French, and German. But this teaching, and solving *Bande Mataram*'s problems, would have to wait until he and others got back from the Bengal Provincial Conference, held in Pabna, East Bengal on February 11 and 12. This was the first meeting of the Bengal Congress since the abortive national session. The outcome would be extremely important. If the Moderates and Extremists could not reconcile their differences, the movement would be weakened to such an extent that the government might move against it. Recognizing this, the two parties tried to work out a modus vivendi. The Extremists, strong in the Pabna region, had nominated the radical Aswini Kumar Dutt as president. The Moderates told them that they would not attend if Dutt was elected. As a compromise the poet Rabindranath Tagore, universally respected and above party politics, was asked to preside. To Aurobindo fell the honor of seconding the motion to call Tagore to the chair. He "said that the president was a national poet and had done much to inculcate the new idea," infusing "a new spirit in the country."[141]

The subjects committee met on the evening of February 11 and the following morning. Most of the draft resolutions were accepted without debate. When the contentious issue of *swaraj* was reached, there were heated discussions about what sort of self-government was to be demanded. The Extremists wanted to go beyond the 1906 resolution by asking for complete independence. The Moderates were not prepared to go so far, and threatened to walk out. Finally, a compromise was reached. Aurobindo later explained that the Extremists agreed to it because they "did not wish to alienate" an "influential minority"—that is, the Moderate Party.[142] There was more than a little bravado in this statement, though at Pabna one could feel that Extremism was on the rise. In his concluding address, Tagore spoke on *swaraj*, and in Aurobindo's telling,

> out of the gladness of his heart there burst from him a flood of inspiring eloquence which made the whole audience astir with feelings of impassioned aspiration. Swaraj was the theme of his eloquence and to anyone listening carefully, it was evident that Swaraj unlimited and without reservation, was the idea enthroned in the heart of the poet.[143]

Back in Calcutta, Aurobindo moved into a new house at 23 Scott's Lane. Mrinalini joined him there a few weeks later. His routine now included an hour or two of yogic practices in the morning. When not otherwise occupied, he passed much of his time in meditation. When visitors called, he spoke for as long as they stayed, then lapsed back into silence. Friends like Charu Chandra Dutt found him "listless and absent-minded."[144] Yet he remained an effective writer and administrator. Once Shyamsundar Chakravarty rushed over to Scott's Lane to see if Aurobindo's editorial was ready. Aurobindo had written nothing. As Shyamsundar watched, he took some packing paper from his desk and started to write. Fifteen minutes later, he handed the piece over. He had not paused once to think, strike out, or revise.

Sometime during this period, Aurobindo drafted a scheme to reorganize the *Bande Mataram* Company. He would be managing director, assisted by a five-member managing committee. The success of the company depended on the sale of shares to the public. Aurobindo wrote a note assuring potential investors that the *Bande Mataram* was no longer only "a patriotic undertaking which deserved support" but a successful concern, the promoters of which were "in a position to approach the public with an offer of shares on which a dividend for the next year is practically assured." He, Hemendra Prasad, and Shyamsundar spent a number of mornings peddling these sure-fire investments from door to door.[145]

TOWARD THE END OF FEBRUARY, Vishnu Bhaskar Lele came to Calcutta. When he met Aurobindo, he asked if he was meditating regularly. Aurobindo replied in the negative, not adding that he was, in effect, meditating all the time. Lele had come at the invitation of Barin Ghose, who still was looking for a guru for his Maniktala ashram. Lele quickly discovered what kind of yoga the young men were practicing. He told them that they were on the wrong path; India would achieve its freedom, but not through violence. What was needed was men with purified hearts who were ready to carry out God's will. Barin and the others laughed at this. Nothing was ever going to happen, they argued, unless someone showed the British the door. Lele repeated his warning. "You mean they're going to make us dance at the end of a rope?" the young men asked. "What will happen will be much worse," the guru replied.[146]

After their near success in derailing the lieutenant-governor's train, Barin and his friends had continued to plan new actions. At this time, Hemchandra Das returned from Europe with a trunk full of up-to-date technical literature, the most important item of which was a seventy-page manual on bomb-making, translated from the Russian. Hem had not intended to join forces with Barin, but after a talk with Aurobindo, agreed to cooperate. With Fraser on the alert, a new target was needed. The obvious choice was Douglas Kingsford, chief presidency magistrate of Calcutta, who had ordered the whipping of Sushil Sen and sentenced Bhupen Dutt and other Extremist editors to rigorous imprisonment. Kingsford also had acquitted Aurobindo, but this was the exception. Hem decided to make a package bomb and have it delivered to the magistrate's door. Filling a tin of Cadbury's cocoa with a pound of picric acid, he placed it and three detonators in a hollowed-out copy of Herbert Broom's *Commentaries on the Common Law*. A spring device would set the bomb off as soon as the book was opened. Hem wrapped the bomb in brown paper and gave it to Paresh Mallick, a member of Barin's group. Dressed as a delivery boy, Paresh handed it to Kingsford's servant, who gave it to his master. Too busy to examine the package, Kingsford put it on a shelf and went back to work. The bomb, it later was discovered, was very well made. Had the magistrate opened it, he would certainly have been blown to pieces.[147]

Ullaskar Dutt, Barin's explosives expert, also had been busy. In January or February, he, Barin, and some others had gone to Deoghar. There Ullaskar succeeded in charging a shell with picric acid, and he and others went to an isolated spot to try it out. One of the group, Prafulla Chakravarty, was given the honor of throwing the bomb. It worked beautifully, but Prafulla and Ullaskar did not take cover quickly enough. Prafulla was killed on the spot, Ullaskar seriously wounded.

One of the reasons that Barin had gone to Deoghar was to get out of range of the Calcutta police. His fears that they were closing in were justified. In the course of its investigation of the Narayangarh train bombing, the CID had got word of a mysterious garden near the capital, and penetrated the Midnapore *samiti*. Satyen Bose, the leader of that group, provided the infiltrator with a good deal of information, including the names of Aurobindo and Barin. Soon the government of Bengal and the Calcutta police had a fair idea of what the revolutionaries were doing. The government advised F.L. Halliday, the capital's commissioner of police, "to take no action in Calcutta as it was feared that the conspirators might take alarm and re-form at another centre which would not be known, and would therefore presumably be the more dangerous." Halliday agreed, but assigned men to watch the Garden and several houses in the city.[148]

One of these places was Aurobindo's residence at 23 Scott's Lane. Two members of the society—Abinash Bhattacharya and Sailen Bose—lived downstairs. Barin and others used their rooms for meetings. Barin occasionally referred matters to his elder brother. On April 5, Barin asked Aurobindo what he thought of his plan to assassinate Léon Tardival, the mayor of the French enclave of Chandernagore. "Why do you want to do this?" Aurobindo asked. "He broke up a swadeshi meeting and oppressed the local people," Barin replied. "So he ought to be killed? How many people will you kill in that way? I cannot give my consent. Nothing will come of it." Barin disagreed: "If this isn't done, these oppressors will never learn the lesson we have to teach them." Seeing that his brother had made up his mind, Aurobindo concluded: "Very well. If that's what you think, go ahead and do it." Barin then went down and told the men who were waiting: "*Sejda* [elder brother] agrees."[149]

Five days later, Barin, Indubhusan Roy, and Narendranath Goswami went to Chandernagore. One of them was carrying a bomb disguised as a carriage lantern. On the evening of April 11, Barin passed the bomb to Indubhusan, who threw it through a grating into the room where the mayor was dining with his wife. The detonator exploded, but not the charge. For the fifth time, an attempt to assassinate a government official with a bomb had failed.[150]

Aurobindo knew that Barin was acting recklessly and occasionally asked him to be more careful, but he never stood in his brother's way. Great sacrifices were necessary if India was to be free. Many would die, but death was nothing to fear. In a piece published in *Bande Mataram* on April 11—coincidentally the day of the Chandernagore bombing—he wrote: "Self-abandonment is the demand made upon us" by the motherland. "She asks of us, 'How many will live for me? How many will die for me?' and awaits our answer."[151]

BIPINCHANDRA PAL'S PRISON SENTENCE ended on March 9. The next day, he arrived in Calcutta and was received by tens of thousands. Aurobindo was quick to promote him as the spokesman of the Bengal Extremists. He was hoping to resume his position "behind the scenes," but for the moment his presence in front was necessary. During the first two weeks of April, he addressed seven political meetings. His tone was often apocalyptic. On April 3, he said, according to a police stenographer, "There is no longer time for speaking or writing [about] the Motherland." Now it was "the time when the brain is to be prepared for devising plans, the body for working hard and the hand for fighting out the country's cause."[152] Two weeks later, he left Calcutta to attend a conference in East Bengal, where he spoke on the importance of village associations. Since the British took over, he said, "we look to a foreign source for everything." As a result, the old "habit of mutual assistance, this sense of mutual duty has disappeared. Every man is for himself and if anything is to be done for our brothers, there is the government to do it and it is no concern of ours." This habit of relying on the British had helped "set Hindu and Mahomedan at variance." The results were riots such as those that had shaken the region the previous year. The answer to such problems was a return to the sense of mutual affection between the groups, and this could come about only by the growth of local associations.[153] On April 21, he returned to Calcutta, where he delivered a speech on the Congress crisis. A few days earlier the Moderates had held a national conference in Allahabad. The outcome was as the Extremists had feared. The so-called creed drafted at Surat was made official. The aim of the Congress would be colonial self-government, not independence, achieved by "constitutional means,"—in other words, there would be no boycott outside of Bengal. Finally, Congress meetings would be held in an "orderly manner," in obedience to the Mehta-Gokhale cabal. Not all of those present favored the retrograde movement. Lajpat Rai declared "that none of us had the right to exclude from the deliberations of the Congress anybody who pitched his ideal so high as the complete independence of his mother country." He believed "that no assembly in India could be called national which precluded by virtue of his creed a man of purity and of the absolute disinterestedness and high patriotism of the nation as Aurobindo Ghose."[154] Rai's Moderate friends did not agree, and the Congress returned to its decorous inutility.

Writing in *Bande Mataram* on April 23 under the heading "The Wheat and the Chaff," Aurobindo declared that "the day of compromises is past." The issue had been drawn in terms "frank, clear and unmistakable." It was a choice between "the lovers of freedom and the lovers of servitude," between "the politicians and the martyrs, between the advocates of a contradiction and the preachers of the unadorned Truth." This polarization, he said, "will bring the strength of Nationalism, the sincerity of its followers and the validity of its principles to the fiercest test that any cause can undergo." What the motherland needed was "hard clear steel for her sword, hard massive granite for her fortress, wood that will not break for the handle of her bow, tough substance and true for the axle of her chariot."[155] Back at the *Bande Mataram* office, the battle was being fought not with chariots and swords, but checkbooks and ledgers. New metal types were needed, but there was not enough money to pay for them. A sympathetic lawyer gave them 2,000 rupees. Subodh Mallik promised to stand guarantee for the balance, but reneged. Most of April 24 was passed in negotiations on these and related matters, but Aurobindo also managed to write a *Bande Mataram* editorial in which he set forth "The One Thing Needful." This was, of course, independence. "No political change can work itself out until the forces of change have taken possession of the government.... The possession of the Government by the people is therefore the first condition of Indian regeneration. Until this is attained, nothing else can be attained."[156]

EVERYONE ON THE *Bande Mataram* staff knew that the loiterers outside of the office were in the pay of the CID, as were the men who trailed Barin through north Calcutta. On April 24, detectives followed him from the Garden to 23 Scott's Lane, and the next day to Hem Das's workshop at 15 Gopi Mohan Dutt Lane. From Hem's, Barin went to 48 Grey Street, the office of the Bengali daily *Nabashakti*. Aurobindo had agreed to take up the editing of that paper, and was planning to move to 48 Grey Street with Mrinalini and Sarojini.

Barin was preoccupied with an action planned for the next few days in a place three hundred miles distant. The government, fearing for the safety of Douglas Kingsford, had promoted him to district judge and posted him in

Muzaffarpur, in northern Bihar. In March, Kingsford had packed his furniture, papers and library, which included the still unopened book-bomb, and moved to the remote provincial town. Barin was still obsessed with the idea of killing him, however, and claimed he had his brother's consent for the job. In the beginning of April, he sent two of his men on a reconnaissance mission to Muzaffarpur. When they returned, he took one of them, Prafulla Chaki, to Hem Das's lab. Hem gave Barin and Prafulla a fist-sized bomb filled with six ounces of dynamite, a detonator, and a black powder fuse. A few days later, Prafulla and a new man named Khudiram Bose took the train to Muzaffarpur. The police there were on the alert. A few days earlier, Commissioner Halliday had heard a rumor that an attempt was going to be made on Kingsford's life. He passed this along to Muzaffarpur's superintendent of police, who informed Kingsford, who dismissed the whole thing. Nevertheless, the superintendent assigned four men to watch the judge's house and to follow him wherever he went.

Meanwhile, Aurobindo was busy. *Bande Mataram* was about to come out in a redesigned format, and the *Nabashakti* was set to appear. On April 28, he and his household shifted from Scott's Lane to 48 Grey Street. The same day he found time to write an article on the "new conditions." Up until then, there had been "a general shrinking from the full danger of the struggle, a wish to try by how few sacrifices the work can be accomplished and at how cheap a cost the priceless boon of liberty can be purchased." But "a fresh stage is at hand in which this reluctance can no longer be indulged. . . . The destruction of the Congress, begun at Surat and completed at Allahabad, is the prelude for the outburst of the storm that has long been brewing." The preparatory stage of the movement was over. "Revolution, bare and grim, is preparing the battle-field, mowing down the centres of order which were evolving a new cosmos and building up the materials of a gigantic downfall and a mighty new-creation. We could have wished it otherwise, but God's will be done."[157]

The day the article appeared in Calcutta, Prafulla and Khudiram surveyed the Muzaffarpur park. The British club where Kingsford went after work was across the road. A constable noticed the Bengali strangers, and when they returned the next day, he asked them who they were. Just schoolboys, they replied in their unconvincing Hindi. "Move on," he said. "The *sahebs* pass by this road." The boys moved away, then doubled back, hid in a thicket, took out their bomb, and waited. In the club, Kingsford was enjoying a game of bridge with his wife and the wife and daughter of a barrister named Pringle Kennedy. The foursome finished their last rubber around 8:30. Bidding the Kingsfords good-bye, the two Kennedy women got into their carriage and started for home. The judge and his wife, traveling in an almost identical carriage, were right behind them. As the Kennedys passed the trees where Khudiram and Prafulla were waiting, Khudiram ran up and threw the bomb through the carriage window. It exploded. Both women were fatally wounded.[158]

In the ensuing confusion, the young men got away and left town separately. Both decided to return to Calcutta by rail. Khudiram marched through the night, reaching the station at Waini the next morning. Two constables saw him, questioned him, and pursued him when he bolted. He was caught and taken back to Muzaffarpur, where he confessed to throwing the bomb. Prafulla meanwhile had boarded a southbound train, where he struck up a conversation with another Bengali. This man, Nandalal Bannerjee, an off-duty sub-inspector, guessed correctly that Prafulla had something to do with the previous day's murders, and at a stop he wired for instructions. The next morning, at another station, he got his reply: "Arrest and bring the man here." Turning to Prafulla, he told him he was under arrest. Prafulla sprinted down the platform. Finding himself cornered, he took out his revolver, fired wildly at his pursuers, then shoved the barrel into his mouth and pulled the trigger.[159]

On the morning of May 1, the government of Bengal, the CID, and the Calcutta town police received news of the Muzaffarpur bombing. Lieutenant-Governor Fraser's first thought was to eliminate the leaders of the gang that had tried to kill him and Kingsford. Afraid that the evidence would be insufficient to convict them of a crime, he wired the government of India for permission to deport five men: Aurobindo Ghose, Barin Ghose, Satyendranath Bose, Abinash Bhattacharya, and Hemchandra Das. Detained without arrest and held without trial, they could be sent to a prison outside Bengal and kept for an unspecified period. Unaware of this plan, the Calcutta police went through the usual legal procedures: Commissioner Halliday and a CID inspector visited a magistrate and lodged a complaint against "Arabindo's gang of outlaws." The magistrate gave them warrants to search eight places in the city and Maniktala. At seven o'clock, there was a meeting of provincial and town police in Halliday's residence. All of Calcutta's police superintendents, along with dozens of inspectors and sub-inspectors and more than a hundred constables, were mustered.

Aurobindo passed most of the day at the *Bande Mataram* office. At some point, Shyamsundar handed him a telegram with a report of the Muzaffarpur bombing. Later, in the British-run *Empire*, he read: BOMB OUTRAGE IN BEHAR. EUROPEAN LADIES KILLED. ATTEMPT TO ASSASSINATE MR. KINGSFORD. The story went on to say that Commissioner Halliday had confirmed the facts "but was reticent as to particulars." The reporter added, however, that "the perpetrators are believed to be well-known." Aurobindo took special note of that sentence.[160] When he returned to Grey Street, he made sure that the material that had been stored there was taken away. He also told Barin to get rid of the arms and explosives at the Garden.[161] This was easier said than done. Barin had more than a dozen firearms, along with boxes of ammunition, bombs in various stages of preparation, tools, chemicals, books on explosives, and piles and piles of papers, many of them extremely incriminating. Barin knew he could not keep the arms, but could not bring himself to destroy them. Instead he and others dug a few shallow pits and hid them. By the time they finished it was late. They gathered up some of the papers and burned them, rolled out their mats, and fell asleep.

Aurobindo spent the evening working at Grey Street. The place had been occupied just three days earlier, and his room was all but bare: two cupboards, a safe, a couple of boxes, a straw mat. On a shelf of the cupboard was an article entitled "The Morality of Boycott," an answer to a charge by Rabindranath Tagore that the boycott was an act of hate.

> A certain class of minds shrink from aggressiveness as if it were a sin. Their temperament forbids them to feel the delight of battle and they look on what they cannot understand as something monstrous and sinful. "Heal hate by love, drive out injustice by justice, slay sin by righteousness" is their cry. . . . The Gita is the best answer to those who shrink from battle as a sin and aggression as a lowering of morality. . . .
>
> Another question is the use of violence in the furtherance of boycott. This is, in our view, purely a matter of policy and expediency. An act of violence brings us into conflict with the law and may be inexpedient for a race circumstanced like ours. But the moral question does not arise.[162]

Finishing his work, he lay down beside his wife, closed his eyes and went to sleep.

5. In Jail and After

Bengal, 1908–1910

I have spoken of spending a year in prison. It would have been better to say spending a year as a forest recluse, as a dweller in an ashram.... The only result of the unfriendly attention of the British government was that I found God.

A Rude Awakening

On the morning of May 2, 1908 Aurobindo woke to the sound of his sister screaming. As he opened his eyes, Sarojini rushed into the room followed closely by a man with a revolver. In a moment, a second armed man appeared. "Are you Aurobindo Ghose?" he asked. Aurobindo replied in the affirmative. "Arrest him!" the man cried to the constables who followed him into the room. To Aurobindo he then directed "an extremely objectionable expression." Aurobindo protested, and there was a brief and angry exchange.[1] Mrinalini, mute with embarrassment and fear, rushed out of the room with Sarojini.

Aurobindo asked his captor, Superintendent John Creagan, to let him see his warrant. Creagan handed over a piece of paper, which read:

> WHEREAS ... it has been made to appear to me that the production of *bombs, materials for preparation of bombs, arms & ammunition and correspondences* essential to the enquiry now being made or about to be made into the said offence or suspected offence; This is to authorize and require you to search for the said *bombs &c* in the *Navashakti office Grey Street.*[2]

It was a search warrant, not an arrest warrant. Nevertheless Aurobindo signed it in the manner of an office memorandum:

Seen.

5.55 am. Aurobindo Ghose

2.5.08

At an order from Creagan, handcuffs were placed around Aurobindo's wrists and a rope tied around his waist. Soon Abinash Bhattacharya and Sailen Bose, similarly trussed up, were shoved into the room. By now policemen were swarming through the house; two superintendents, three inspectors, two sub-inspectors, six sergeants, and twenty-five or thirty constables had been sent.[3] While this detachment secured the building, Creagan and others began their search, which lasted for five and a half hours. Hundreds of documents were removed from the trunks and cupboards: Aurobindo's correspondence with Mrinalini, notebooks filled with unpublished writings, letters from Tilak and other associates, articles such as "The Morality of Boycott," printed matter, cuttings, photographs, account books, and more. All was pawed through, initialed, numbered, and set aside for removal. During this process, Aurobindo said nothing: no objections, no explanations. If he was asked to produce a key, he did so; otherwise he remained completely silent.

Creagan soon realized that his pickings were pretty slim. There were no bombs, no explosives, no material for making bombs. The most noteworthy item was the letter Barin had written at Surat, informing his brother that it was time for "*sweets* all over India." The superintendent had to hope that more compromising passages would turn up when they sifted through the material back at headquarters. Aurobindo, presumably, was making similar calculations himself. If his own house was clean, what other places were being searched and with what result? He had no idea of what was happening in the other parts of the city, as his lawyer had been refused permission to see him. If he had known, he would have had reason to feel uneasy. Seven other search parties had been dispatched along with Creagan's. Six had gone to north Calcutta, with mixed results. There was nothing at Aurobindo's old house at 23 Scott's Lane, but in a house on Harrison Road police discovered containers full of chemicals, bombs, and explosives, which Ullaskar had left in the care of some friends a few days earlier. The friends, who knew nothing about the contents, were arrested. At Hem Das's house, the police found documents and materials that showed his interest in making bombs. He and two of his associates were hauled away. But the findings in Calcutta were overshadowed by those in the Maniktala Garden, where a party under the command of a single European inspector arrested Barin and fourteen others. Moved by a romantic idea of self-sacrifice, Barin offered to make a statement even before the search had begun. He imagined that if he and a few others took full responsibility, most of the younger boys, and Aurobindo as well, might get off. As it was, no one could be found at that hour to take down a confession, but Barin still proved very helpful. In the garden, he showed the police where the guns and chemicals were buried. In the house, the searchers found hundreds of documents that had escaped the fire, including a copy of the Paris explosives manual and some operational notes in Barin's hand in which the initials "A.G." figured prominently.

CREAGAN AND HIS ASSISTANTS finished their search of Grey Street at around 11:30 in the morning. Aurobindo, Abinash, and Sailen were then escorted to a waiting paddy wagon. On their way, they crossed Aurobindo's uncle Krishna Kumar Mitra and Moderate politician Bhupendranath Bose. These men asked the police what the three detainees were being charged with. A detective mentioned the section of the penal code that dealt with murder.[4]

The three were taken to the local police station, where they were allowed a quick meal and bath. Their next destination was the police headquarters at Lal Bazar, where they were put in separate cells. Officers tried to induce them to confess, saying that Barin already had done so. Aurobindo did not believe that his brother could have been so stupid. After a few hours, the three were taken to the office of the detective police on Royd Street, where they spent the night.

From the moment of his arrest, though outwardly calm, Aurobindo was troubled within. "I was shaken in faith for a while," he later admitted, "for I could not look into the heart of His intention. Therefore I faltered for a moment and cried out in my heart to Him, 'What is this that has happened to me? I believed that I had a mission to work for the people of my country and until that work was done, I should have Thy protection. Why then am I here and on such a charge?'" In the lock-up at Royd Street, he waited for an answer. None came.

The next morning, Aurobindo and his two companions were taken back to Lal Bazar, where they were brought before Commissioner Halliday. "Are you not ashamed of taking part in this dreadful crime?" the Englishman asked Aurobindo. "What right have you to assume that I had any share in it?" Aurobindo replied. "I don't assume. I know," said Halliday. "I don't know what you imagine you know," Aurobindo concluded. "I deny all connection." When Halliday learned that Aurobindo was in contact with younger, less experienced prisoners, he had him put in a separate cell.[5]

Although the police were frustrated in their attempts to get confessions from Aurobindo and the other Calcutta prisoners, they had gratifying success with Barin and others who had been picked up in Maniktala. Barin, Upendranath, and Ullaskar decided that they, along with Bibhutibhusan Sarkar and Indubhusan Roy, would take responsibility for everything. Bibhuti and Indu, certain they would be hanged in any event, agreed. After writing out statements in which they implicated themselves, the five were taken before a magistrate in Alipore, the Calcutta suburb that was the headquarters of the district in which the Garden lay. Here they repeated their confessions orally.

On the afternoon of May 5, Aurobindo and the others arrested in Calcutta were taken to the court of the chief presidency magistrate. Here Aurobindo was allowed to speak with his lawyers and one of his relatives. "According to the police, a number of suspicious documents have been found in your house," a lawyer told him. "Were there really any such things there?" Aurobindo said, "I can say without any hesitation that there were none; it is quite impossible." Turning to his relative, he added, "Tell everyone at home not to worry. My innocence will be vindicated."[6] His confidence was not feigned. Since his arrest, he had been asking his inner guide in anguish why he was there. At Royd Street and Lal Bazar he had meditated and prayed, but remained uneasy. Finally, on the morning of May 5, he heard an answer: "Wait and see." At that moment, he regained his calm.[7]

The chief presidency magistrate transferred the cases of Aurobindo and the other Calcutta prisoners to the magistrate's court in Alipore. That way all of the men arrested at the Garden and in Calcutta could be tried together. As Aurobindo, Abinash, and others were led from the courtroom to the police van, Abinash's brother gave them a newspaper with a report of the confessions of Barin, Upendranath and the rest. "Has Barin gone off his head?" Aurobindo wondered.[8]

DRIVING THROUGH CALCUTTA and into the southern suburbs, the Black Maria pulled up at the gate of Alipore Jail. Aurobindo was taken to a block of solitary cells and locked into cell number six. His new accommodations were a cubicle nine feet long and five feet wide. The walls had no windows or other openings. Air and light could enter only through a barred metal door in the front. On the other side of the bars was a tiny walled courtyard. A wooden door leading from this to the main jail yard was closed. The furnishings in the cell consisted of two coarse blankets, some utensils, and two baskets that did duty for latrines.[9]

Aurobindo sat on the blankets to survey his new domain. Everything seemed so new and different that he was actually cheerful. Even the sight of his dinner—"coarse rice, spiced with husk, pebbles, insects, hair and so forth"—did nothing to dampen his humor. He went to bed early and slept well, though each time the guards were changed, he was awakened by the new man's shouting, which continued until Aurobindo proved that he was still alive.

A bell rang at 4:30 the next morning to summon the convicts to their labors. Aurobindo got up as well. At five o'clock, the door of his cell was opened and he was allowed into his little enclosed courtyard to wash. Soon he had his first glimpse of the staple of the prison diet, *lafsi*, or rice gruel. For the moment, a glimpse was enough. At 10:30 he took a bath and gave his clothes to be washed. Lunch, more *lafsi*, was served at eleven o'clock. To avoid the proximity of the privy basket, he ate in the courtyard. Locked back in the cell, he was happy to find that the courtyard door was left open, allowing him to peer into the jail yard. A tree by the wall had astonishing foliage. The passing of the guard became a regular visit from a friend. At five o'clock there was a final serving of gruel, after which the outer door was closed. An hour or two later, when the last of the daylight faded, he rolled up one of his blankets for a pillow, stretched out on the other, and went to sleep.

The next ten days were outwardly much like the first. Aurobindo learned that *lafsi* had three incarnations, which he named, in Upanishadic language, *prajna*, *hiranyagarbha*, and *virat*. *Prajna* was ordinary gruel; *hiranyagarbha* was rendered yellowish by a slight mixture of dal; *virat* was sweetened with a dash of molasses The only other item on the menu was boiled greens. The meals were served in a little tin bowl that also had to be used for drinking, gargling, bathing, washing, and as a toilet mug. (A good way to get over the sense of disgust, Aurobindo thought.) This versatile vessel and a matching plate were Aurobindo's "solitary treasures," and he took care to make them shine.[10]

Aurobindo's ironic reflections on his dismal surroundings could not keep him entertained for long. A week earlier he had been in charge of a household, a newspaper, and a political movement. There were speeches to be delivered and battles to be fought with the Moderates and the government of India. When not otherwise occupied, he could have spoken with friends and family, gone for a walk, read, or meditated. Instead, he was penned up in a cage hardly suitable for an animal. There was nothing to do, no one to talk to, nothing to write with, nothing to read. He could meditate, of course, but he soon discovered that it was one thing to meditate at home in self-imposed solitude and another to do so in solitary confinement. He could manage for an hour or so, but when he tried to continue, his mind was pulled in a thousand different directions, or else became inert. For several days he suffered "intense mental agony." Soon his thoughts became so wild and unregulated that he wondered whether he was going insane. In desperation he called on the divine for help. In a moment his mind was flooded with coolness, his heart with happiness. From this point on, he found jail life bearable. He still had his moments of doubt and disquiet, not to mention physical discomfort, but he always was able to regain his poise and could meditate for as long as he liked. Looking back later, he realized that even when he believed himself close to insanity, a part of his consciousness remained detached, observing the mind without being caught up in its movements. From this, he learned to take his stand in the "witness consciousness" even when his outer mind was in torment. He also learned, perhaps for the first time in his life, about the efficacy of prayer. He realized that yoga was as much a matter of faith as of unaided human effort.

Sitting in his cell, Aurobindo remembered that a few weeks before his arrest, he had received an inner prompting to draw back temporarily from politics. He had ignored the feeling then. In the solitude and silence of Alipore Jail, he again heard his guide: "The bonds you had not strength to break, I have broken for you, because it is not my will nor was it ever my intention that that should continue. I have another thing for you to do and it is for that I have brought you here, to teach you what you could not learn for yourself and to train you for my work."[11]

Aurobindo's training then began. Ten days into his imprisonment, he was allowed to write home for clothing and, more important, for books. He asked for the *Gita* and the Upanishads, books he knew well but rediscovered at Alipore:

> I was able not only to understand intellectually but to realise what Srikrishna demanded of Arjuna [in the *Gita*] and what He demands of those who aspire to do His work, to be free from repulsion and desire, to do work for Him without the demand for fruit, to renounce self-will and become a passive and faithful instrument in His hands, to have an equal heart for high and low, friend and opponent, success and failure, yet not to do His work negligently.[12]

A short while later, he was allowed two walks in the yard outside his cell each day. "I enjoyed these periods very much," he later recalled:

> On one side was the jail workshop, on the other side the cowshed; these were the two limits of my free domain. Strolling back and forth—from the workshop to the cowshed, from the cowshed to the workshop—I would

recite the profound, inspiring and inexhaustibly strength-giving words of the Upanishads. Or else, watching the movements and activities of the prisoners, I would try to realise the fundamental truth that the Lord dwells in all. Repeating silently in my mind the words, *sarvam khalvidam brahma,* "All this is verily the Eternal," I would project that realisation on everything in existence—trees and houses and walls, man and beast and bird, metal and earth. As I did this, I would get into a state in which the prison no longer appeared to be a prison at all. It was as if this high rampart, this iron grating, these high walls, this sunlit tree with its bluish leaves and these ordinary material things were no longer inert objects, but as if alive with an all-pervading consciousness.[13]

ON MAY 18 Aurobindo and more than two dozen others were summoned from their cells and, under heavy guard, packed into vans and driven to the Alipore magistrate's court. As soon as the doors of the van were closed, the young men exploded in a cacophony of talk, songs, jokes, and laughter. Aurobindo sat through it unmoved. Having learned to appreciate his solitude, he had to make an effort to remain detached in the midst of their boisterousness.

At the court complex, the prisoners were met by a throng of supporters kept at bay by a squad of mounted policemen. Thirty constables, armed with swords and rifles fitted with bayonets, stood guard. As the prisoners were made to stand in rows, the onlookers were struck by their untroubled faces. It seemed, wrote a reporter for the *Empire,* "that not a soul of the gang had a care in the world." All of them were barefoot except Aurobindo; when he noticed this disparity, he left his own slippers behind. After roll call, he and the others were marched to the courtroom for the first day of the preliminary hearing of *Emperor vs. Arabindo Ghose and Others,* otherwise known as the Alipore Bomb Trial.[14]

The previous day, the police had filed a first information report and the government had given its sanction. The state accused the prisoners of "organising a band for the purpose of waging war against the Government by means of criminal force," charging each, among other things, with conspiracy to "wage war against the king," the Indian equivalent of high treason.

It seemed certain that those who had confessed would be convicted. The prosecution's problem was to implicate those who had not made statements and against whom the evidence was weak. Of the dozen who fell into this category, Aurobindo was by far the most important. A few days earlier, Lieutenant-Governor Fraser had told the chief secretary of the Government of Bengal to study the evidence against Aurobindo, determine the likelihood of a conviction, and send a report to the Government of India. In his report, the chief secretary conceded that the evidence was "not such as would constitute clear legal proof" that Aurobindo was a member of the secret society. Still, the Government of Bengal "had no doubt whatsoever" that he was "the master mind at the back of the whole extremist campaign in Bengal." In addition to being a "fluent and impressive writer," he was an "organiser of great ability and ingenuity." It would count for nothing if the others were convicted but Aurobindo was set free. He would "waste no time in starting a fresh conspiracy." Therefore, "in the interest of peace and good government," the Government of Bengal asked the Government of India to deport him.[15]

Fraser followed up the report with a personal letter to the viceroy, in which he demanded Aurobindo's deportation in the strongest terms. The man, Fraser wrote, was

> able, cunning, fanatical: these qualities have the vigour in him which they not infrequently have in the man who is not quite sane. He is the leader. He is regarded and spoken of by all as the disciples regard a great Master. He has been in the forefront of all, advising seditious writing and authorising murder. But he has kept himself, like a careful and valued General, out of sight of "the enemy". We cannot get evidence against him such as would secure his conviction in a Court. But we have been fortunate enough to get papers which show his connection with the conspiracy, and information as to his action, quite sufficient to convince the reasonable mind and justify deportation.
>
> I certainly hope no sentiment will be allowed to prevent this.[16]

The sentiment Fraser referred to was the traditional British belief that prisoners are entitled to habeas corpus and an impartial trial. When Lajpat Rai and Ajit Singh were deported in 1907, Englishmen with no special sympathy for India protested in the press and Parliament. The Government of India did not want to face this sort of criticism again. Refusing Fraser's request, Minto's secretary noted that "in matters such as this we must rely on the police . . . and I believe that in this particular case, when once the easy solution by deportation is banished, the police may be able to secure a conviction under the ordinary law." Disappointed, the Bengal government instructed the inspector general of police to follow every clue that connected Aurobindo with the conspiracy and to make "every effort to procure a conviction in court."[17]

The government hired Eardley Norton, the leading barrister of Madras, to head the prosecution. It was rumored that his pay was the staggering sum of 1,000 rupees a day. Several members of the Calcutta detective police were assigned full time to the case, sifting through the piles of evidence to piece together an account of the events leading up to the Muzaffarpur murders. Norton was to do the rest.

Aurobindo took scant interest in the proceedings of the hearing. He concentrated on his inner life when he could, but he sometimes found it hard to avoid being distracted by the flood of sights and sounds. When he could do nothing else, he looked on with amusement as Norton wove the evidence into a grand historical drama:

> Just as Holinshed, Hall and Plutarch gathered the materials for Shakespeare's historical plays, so the police had collected the material for this drama of a case. Mr. Norton was its Shakespeare. I noticed one difference between Shakespeare and Norton, however. Shakespeare occasionally would leave out some part of the material that had been collected; but Mr. Norton never left out one jot of what he received. . . . By adding plentiful amounts of suggestion, inference and hypothesis from his own imagination, he managed to create such a wonderful plot that Shakespeare and Defoe and the other great poets and novelists would have acknowledged defeat at the hands of this great master. . . . It gave me great pleasure to find that Mr. Norton chose to make me the protagonist of his drama.[18]

The main member of Norton's audience was Leonard Birley, ICS, the additional district magistrate of Alipore. Aroused by the importance of the case, Birley asked the government to assign it to him and began to take evidence even before the complaint had been lodged. He was willing to examine every witness that the prosecution summoned and to record all evidence placed before him. As a result, he heard the testimony of 222 witnesses and accepted 2,000 material and documentary exhibits. As the mass of evidence mounted, the prisoners had good reason to feel anxious. For the most part, however, they treated the proceedings as a farce. In the dock they read, chatted, or laughed, mocking the witnesses' bad English and the magistrate's bad Bengali. The only way Birley could make them quiet down was to threaten the ultimate punishment, no lunch.

As the hearing progressed, Aurobindo could draw back from the commotion in the courtroom, becoming absorbed in his inner experience. At all times, he felt the presence of his guide:

He said to me, "When you were cast into jail, did not your heart fail and did you not cry out to me, where is Thy protection? Look now at the Magistrate, look now at the Prosecuting Counsel." I looked and it was not the Magistrate whom I saw, it was Vasudeva [Krishna], it was Narayana [Krishna] who was sitting there on the bench. I looked at the Prosecuting Counsel and it was not the Counsel for the prosecution that I saw; it was Srikrishna who sat there, it was my Lover and Friend who sat there and smiled.[19]

THE HEARING CONTINUED, with frequent adjournments, into June. After each session, the prisoners were escorted to police vans and driven back to the jail. At first, they were met by a platoon of armed sergeants who took them to their cells. But eventually the police relaxed their guard, letting the prisoners stroll back on their own like schoolboys returning from an outing. Meetings with family and friends were permitted, and the interview periods became theatrical events, with much wailing and embracing through the bars. Starting in the second week of June, prisoners were allowed gifts of fruit, which greatly improved their diets. Then, on June 13, all of the prisoners were transferred from their cells to a single spacious ward consisting of one large room and two connected wings. Everyone but Aurobindo greeted this move with delight. The young men arranged themselves according to their interests. Those given to amusements took over the central room, while the intellectuals and the contemplatives settled down in the wings. Aurobindo chose a corner of the contemplatives' wing, but found it difficult to concentrate amid the activity in the other parts of the ward.

From time to time, Aurobindo chatted with those he already knew, such as Abinash and Barin. He also found a hanger-on in Narendranath Goswami, a young man who had taken part in a few of the actions. Aurobindo found him "an interesting psychological study." A landowner's son, Naren was unaccustomed to privation and discomfort. While the others were resigned to imprisonment or worse, he was resolved to get out by any means possible. His father, he said, knew all about the law and could hire lawyers and buy witnesses. There was also the possibility of enlisting the help of the police. Soon Naren was conferring not only with his father, but also one of the detectives. After such meetings, he became inquisitive, asking the others about the country-wide conspiracy that the police were sure existed.[20]

One day, Naren told Aurobindo that the police had asked him to turn King's evidence in exchange for pardon. "What did you tell them?" Aurobindo inquired. Naren said he had not told them anything. But three days later, Naren complained that the police were still asking him questions. Aurobindo suggested that Naren tell them that Sir Andrew Fraser was the head of the conspiracy. "I did something like that," Naren replied. "I told them that Surendranath Banerjea was our head and that once I showed him a bomb." "What made you say that?" Aurobindo asked. Naren continued: "I'm not going to stop till I've really screwed the bastards." If he kept on feeding them false information, Naren thought, "the case might fizzle out." Aurobindo told him to stop playing games. It appeared to him that the young man was wavering. Naren seemed to believe that he could help the others by misleading the police, but he clearly was tempted by their offers of pardon.[21]

In Courtroom and Jail

On June 20 five more bomb trial prisoners arrived in Alipore. There were now too many for all of them to stay in the three-room ward where Aurobindo and the others had been staying. Still wishing to keep the revolutionaries apart from the other prisoners, the authorities moved them all to a single large room known as Ward 23. Aurobindo found a place in a corner and tried to continue his meditation and reading, but it was increasingly difficult to do so with so many running around, finding novel ways to keep themselves amused. The only one not sharing in the fun was Narendranath Goswami. The others had stopped talking to him, and soon found an excuse to give him a beating.

On June 22 the hearing was resumed after a week's recess. The next morning, Norton rose and told the magistrate that Narendranath Goswami had agreed to turn King's evidence. Asked by the magistrate if he would tell the whole truth, Naren replied in the affirmative. Pardoned, he began his testimony.[22] He said that he had joined the secret society in 1906. He learned that its leaders were Jatindranath Banerji and Aurobindo Ghose. He pointed Aurobindo out when asked to identify him. For the next several hours, Naren gave a detailed account of the early activities of the society. His testimony continued the next day, and the next, into the month of July. He named the names not only of people in the courtroom, but also of several who had not been arrested. These men were picked up and brought to Alipore jail. All those arrested after May, the so-called "second batch," had to wait in jail until the magistrate finished hearing the cases of Barin, Aurobindo and the thirty-one others in the first batch.

From the time of the first arrests in May, the Indian and foreign press had given much excited coverage to the trial. The *Times* (London) published a number of reports, one of them outlining the "brilliant career" of the principal culprit. [23] Back home, Indian papers printed column after column on what they called the Great Calcutta Sensation. People were shocked by the violence and deaths, but proud of the daring and initiative of Barin's group. Their deeds were "a glorious vindication of Bengalee character," wrote the editor of the *Indian World*. They showed "not only a striking amount of boldness and determination, but also a certain degree of heroism which constitutes the real essence of patriotism."[24] Meanwhile the British community was crying for blood: "What would a thousand executions of such miscreants weigh against one good and virtuous life?" asked the *Eastern Bengal and Assam Era*. The paper *Asian* suggested that lynching was the right way to deal with the prisoners. The government should initiate house-to-house searches, suppress every "seditious native rag of a newspaper," and deport the leaders without trial. To Kingsford the paper offered this advice:

> We recommend to his notice a Mauser pistol, with the nickel filed off the nose of the bullets or a Colt's Automatic which carries a heavy soft bullet and is a hard hitting and punishing weapon. We hope Mr Kingsford will be able to secure a big bag and we envy him the opportunity. He will be more than justified in letting daylight into every strange native approaching his house or his person.[25]

Lord Minto dismissed such reactions as "hysterical" but noted privately: "It is impossible to treat the present situation too seriously. We are face to face with imminent danger from a conspiracy which in any country might bring about pitiable results, but in India is a hundredfold more dangerous than elsewhere."[26]

In fact the arrests had destroyed the Calcutta secret society, though for a couple of weeks there was a run of copycat bombings in the city. This encouraged antiterrorist rhetoric in the Indian press. When Aurobindo heard about these articles, he got hold of pencil and paper and wrote a series of essays on the message, morality, psychology, and policy of the bomb. These were smuggled out of jail but never printed. Hem Das also produced some revolutionary literature: a pamphlet with instructions for making picric acid bombs, complete with formulas and explanatory diagrams. This was smuggled out, set in type, smuggled back in for proof correction, and finally printed and circulated. All of the smuggling in and out took place during interviews with visitors, which were conducted with remarkable laxity. The staff was so impressed by the good behavior of the prisoners that it barely searched them or those who came to see them. It was easy to conceal objects in the folds of dhotis and saris and to pass them from one person to another while they were embracing through the bars. Once the prisoners discovered that they could send and receive messages, they decided to try heavier items, such as tins of tobacco and opium—much in demand by convicts and warders—and finally guns and ammunition.

The purpose of the guns was to stage a jailbreak. Barin, never at a loss for quixotic ideas, had planned one down to the details. Friends outside would get hold of a motor car, some weapons, and one or two bombs. They would smuggle in six or seven revolvers, wax to take impressions of the keys, and acid to throw on the guards. One day, four of the prisoners would pull out their revolvers, shoot their way to the walls, scale them with ladders made from blankets, rush to the waiting car, and be driven away. Once free, they would take refuge in Sundarbans (like Bankim's heroine Devi Chaudhurani), Kaimurgiri (the proposed site of Bhawani Mandir), Afghanistan, or somewhere else. From there they would assemble a liberation army to lead the masses to victory. As persuasive as ever, Barin sold his idea to a number of the other prisoners and also to a revolutionary group in Chandernagore. Before carrying out the plan, however, he sent someone to inform his brother. Aurobindo heard the messenger out, then replied: "I mean to stand trial."[27]

On August 13 the magistrate examined the prisoners of the first batch. "I do not wish to make any statement here," Aurobindo told him. Most of the others followed his example. Those who had confessed denied the veracity of their statements and refused to answer questions. The following day, two lawyers for the defense applied to cross-examine Narendranath Goswami. After some consideration, doubtless influenced by the government's demand for speed, Birley rejected the application. On August 15, after witness number 222 had been examined, the defense again submitted its application. Using the discretion the government had granted him that morning, Birley rejected it, saying he "did not want it to last forever."[28]

The prisoners were particularly jolly that day. An *Empire* reporter asked them why. "Ask Aurobindo," they said. Turning to him, the reporter noticed that his face, "hitherto grave and prepossessed, had been metamorphosised into one of sprightliness and sunniness." Questioned about the prisoners' changed mood, Aurobindo said it was due in part to him. "Today is my birthday"—he had turned thirty-six—"and we are celebrating it as best we can under the circumstances." The anniversary of his birth, he went on, was often a special day for him. In 1906 it had marked the opening of the Bengal National College. In 1907 it came at the time of his arrest in the *Bande Mataram* sedition case. And this day, "the Magistrate has given a definite assurance that he will commit on the evidence given in this, a case not of sedition but revolution," and also that he would charge Barin with abetment of murder. Altogether "a remarkable string of coincidences." After speaking a while about the tediousness of the hearing, Aurobindo concluded: "You can add to these coincidences the fact that I shall be very probably coming back from the [penal colony in the] Andamans on my birthday next year."[29]

The first batch of prisoners made its last appearance before the magistrate on August 19. Birley committed thirty-one of them to be tried at the Alipore Sessions Court on charges of waging war against the king. He noted that the evidence against Aurobindo—in particular the "sweets letter" and the testimony of Narendranath Goswami—showed that he supported the aims of the secret society, was connected with some of its members, and was consulted by them on important occasions. There was thus a prima facie case against him for conspiring to wage war. If convicted of this charge, he might spend the rest of his life in the Andamans.

The prisoners returned to Ward 23 to await the outcome of the hearing against the second batch. During this period, a wet and blustery time, Aurobindo fell ill with fever. The doctor prevailed upon him to spend a few days in the hospital where he could be given special food. Aurobindo agreed, but after a day or two asked to be sent back to the ward. There he again became feverish, and again was sent to the hospital. On August 30 his sister and two others visited him, Barin, and their cousin Satyen Bose. Barin also had a visit from Srishchandra Ghose, a revolutionary from Chandernagore. Srish gave him a bundle of clothing that concealed a .38 caliber revolver. Barin took the gun to the ward and gave it to Kanailal Dutt, who gave it to Satyen Bose. A week or so earlier, Kanailal had given Satyen a .45 caliber horse pistol. Satyen said it was too big; hence the second delivery. As he took the new pistol from Kanai, Satyen told him that he was planning to shoot Narendranath Goswami. He had heard that the approver planned to implicate more people. Satyen and Hem Das had decided that silencing Naren was more important than Barin's jailbreak. Kanai agreed and told Satyen to count him in.

Satyen had already laid plans. On August 29 he had sent a message to Naren, who since his pardon had been staying in the European ward. Satyen said he wanted to meet him. Disregarding a warning from the jailer, Naren went to the hospital, where Satyen told him that he wanted to turn King's evidence. Could Naren speak to the authorities? Naren agreed. The next day, he returned and told Satyen that the authorities were well disposed.[30]

Aurobindo had by now returned to Ward 23. On the morning of August 31, still weak from his fever, he decided not to go to the yard for exercise. While the others were gone, he enjoyed a rare moment of quiet. Then he heard some shouting. A convict was running around, screaming: "They bumped off Naren Goswami! They bumped off Naren Goswami!"[31] The prisoners in the yard were herded back into the ward and he learned the outlines of the story from them.

At around 6:30 in the morning, Satyen sent for Naren. Naren came half an hour later in the company of a convict-warder named Higgins. Naren sent Higgins ahead to fetch Satyen, but Satyen emerged along with Kanai before the Briton could reach the ward. Leaving Higgins in the dispensary, the three Bengalis went to the veranda to speak. After a bit of conversation, Kanai and Satyen pulled out their guns. One of them fired as Naren fled, crying, "For God's sake, Mr. Higgins, save me!" Trapped in a corner, shivering with fear, he watched as Higgins grappled with Kanai. In the confusion, Higgins was shot through the wrist while Naren took a bullet to the thigh. The two wounded men stumbled down the stairs. Kanai and Satyen pursued them, but Naren and Higgins managed to reach the jail office. The jailor and others came out just as Kanai and Satyen appeared. "Get out of the way or I'll shoot you all," Kanai cried. A prisoner made a dive for Satyen while Kanai aimed and fired. The bullet hit Naren squarely, piercing his spine and sending him flying into the drain. Kanai and Satyen submitted to capture after emptying their cylinders into Naren's dying body.[32]

After the assassins had been locked up and Naren declared dead, the jail officials searched the bomb case prisoners in Ward 23. The prisoners were deprived of everything but the clothes they were wearing. A few days later, they all were placed in solitary confinement. A squad of Gordon Highlanders stood sentry over them night and day. Sick prisoners had to remain in their cells. This draconian regime lasted more than six weeks, as the hearing against the second batch continued.

ALONE IN HIS CELL, Aurobindo passed his days in meditation and other yogic practices. Speaking later about this stage of his *sadhana* or practice of yoga, he gave few details: "What happened to me during this period I am not impelled to say, but only this that day after day, He showed me His wonders."[33] It was a tumultuous time in his inner life. For ten days, "brilliant visions and fine experiences," then "there suddenly came a blow from above and the whole thing was smashed. Again there was a period of similar bright visions, followed by another smashing blow." At length he learned "that all that presents itself in brilliant colours is not the highest Truth." Throughout these experiences, his critical mind remained alert, and as a result, "he took them all with reservations."[34] This was especially important during the brief but intense moments when he was overcome by visions of suffering or invaded by thoughts of hatred. He also had "vivid" and "gigantic" visions that he recognized later as foreshadowings of World War I. The disquieting thoughts and images continued until his mind stopped reacting to them. Critical detachment also was needed when he had visions of the opposite sort, scenes of unearthly beauty that seemed to belong to an inner paradise.

At one point he experienced such a flood of inner vitality that he felt no need to eat, and as the food he was given was repulsive in any case, he decided to throw it in his privy basket. This went on for a number of days until he decided to experiment with fasting. After losing ten pounds in as many days, he began to eat again. During the same period he slept one night out of three, not with the idea of conquering sleep, but simply because the pressure of his *sadhana* was so strong.

The flow of experiences had other effects on his body. He found that painful contacts—ant bites, for instance—could be felt as *ananda*, or bliss, and that heat and cold seemed to resolve themselves into different workings of *ananda*. At one point, he found his body had developed "a certain subtlety" that allowed him to throw off all fatigue. He recognized this as the power of *anima* that is mentioned in the *Yoga Sutras*. *Anima* is supposed to be related to another power called *utthapana*, normally translated as "levitation." Aurobindo wondered if *utthapana* really existed; no sooner had he asked himself than he found his body raised into a posture he never could have assumed on his own. Later he found that he could keep his arms raised for long periods without muscular exertion.

When he heard that the trial was about to resume, he was almost sorry that he would have to rejoin the others. They meanwhile had been hearing strange stories about him. He did not eat, did not sleep, sat in weird postures, held his arms in the air. They wondered if he had lost his balance. Their fears were put to rest when they saw him. Standing with his dhoti tucked up like a workman's, a shawl thrown carelessly over his shoulders, he looked strange, to be sure, but not mad. And his face was that of an untroubled child.[35]

The High Court of History

Early in the morning of October 19, 1908 the court complex at Alipore was surrounded by constables. Special precautions, "such as had never been known to be taken in any previous case," made it difficult for reporters to watch the arrival of the bomb case prisoners. The vans pulled up; the prisoners had their handcuffs removed and they were herded into the courtroom and packed into a dock that had been enlarged to accommodate them all. Reporters were struck by their "pale and emaciated" appearance. Aurobindo in particular "looked like the ghost of his formerly lean self."[36]

At 11:20 everyone stood as Charles Porten Beachcroft, the additional sessions judge of the 24 Parganas District, mounted the bench. Looking down, he could recognize one of the prisoners. Nineteen years earlier, Beachcroft and Aurobindo had passed the ICS entrance examination together. Both did well in Greek, Beachcroft standing second to Aurobindo's first. Over the next two years, as students in neighboring colleges, they had met from time to time, particularly in Bengali class, where Beachcroft, ironically, did better than Aurobindo did. They lost touch with one another after leaving for India. While Beachcroft climbed the ranks of the Bengal Civil Service, Aurobindo labored in the relative obscurity of Baroda, only to emerge in 1907 as the principal antigovernment spokesman in Bengal.

A total of fifteen barristers, pleaders, and vakils appeared for the accused. Byomkesh Chakravarty, who was representing Aurobindo, began by raising objections about the conduct of the hearing. This occupied everyone until lunch. After the court rose, the prisoners were allowed to visit the latrine. On the way they walked past a Kinetograph cameraman, who had obtained, on false pretenses, permission to make "life-motion portraits" of them. The film was later confiscated and has been lost.[37] Back in court, doubtless excited by the experience, the prisoners listened as Chakravarty spent the rest of the day raising further objections about the charges. This continued through most of the next morning. Beachcroft eventually ruled that the charges were in order, but to clarify them he reframed them. All of the accused were charged with waging war against the king, with conspiring and making preparations to commit the crime, and with abetting others to do so. The first charge, if proven, carried the penalty of death; the others, long terms of imprisonment. All of the prisoners pleaded not guilty to the charges. The government then opened its case. Summing up in a report published in the *Times* two days later, a Reuters correspondent wrote:

> Mr. Arabindo Ghose and a number of other Bengalis arrested at the time of the great bomb discoveries in the suburbs of Calcutta are being tried at the Alipore sessions for conspiracy to overthrow the government. . . .
>
> Mr. Eardley Norton . . . in opening the case for the prosecution said that the evidence would prove that Mr. Arabindo Ghose was the head and

front of the conspiracy. His speech is expected to last several days, and the trial may last some weeks.[38]

The trial in fact lasted six months. After Norton had outlined the government's case, the prosecution put in its evidence, a total of 1,500 documents and material objects. The defense added 54. Most of the witnesses who deposed in the lower court were asked to repeat their performances. One was not alive to do so. When Norton tried to enter the testimony of Narendranath Goswami, the defense objected. Two days later, Beachcroft ruled that Birley had violated the law by refusing to allow the defense to cross-examine the witness on August 15. As a result, Beachcroft concluded, Goswami's testimony was invalid. This changed the whole complexion of the case.[39]

Byomkesh Chakravarty represented Aurobindo for less than a month. As a leading Calcutta barrister he demanded huge fees, and Aurobindo's defense fund, insufficient even for him, had to be used for others as well. When Chakravarty pulled out, Aurobindo's uncle Krishna Kumar Mitra, who was coordinating the defense, was at a loss. In desperation he rushed to a junior lawyer, Chittaranjan Das, and begged him to take it up. Das agreed, and threw himself heart and soul into the trial. The prosecution thought it would be easy to show that Barin, Ullaskar, Upendranath, and others had taken part in revolutionary activities. Their confessions, though withdrawn, could still be used as evidence. And then there were the rifles, revolvers, chemicals, and bombs. Norton's primary problem, however, was to prove that Aurobindo was involved in a conspiracy to wage war against the king. The documents that the prosecution put in as evidence were meant to establish this. *Bande Mataram* and *Jugantar* were the voices of the conspiracy, publishing the conspirators' aim of creating an independent Indian state. Correspondence and other documents found in Aurobindo's possession proved that he was in contact with members of the secret society. His own brother, Barin, was its head. It was evident, Norton urged, that Aurobindo was "the guiding spirit of the whole gang."[40] As the trial dragged on, it grew obvious to everyone that the government was turning a conspiracy case into the pursuit of a single individual.

Meanwhile, the defense intended to show that there was no conspiracy at all. The attempts to assassinate government officials were meant to repay private grudges, not to topple the government. Aurobindo certainly had written and spoken in favor of independence, but no Englishman could condemn this. What Aurobindo did, he did as a politician and philosopher, but not as a revolutionary. As for the so-called proofs of his client's culpability, Das pointed out that "where the prosecution associated Aurobindo with the conspiracy there we find some sort of difficulty with the evidence." The implication was that many of the apparently incriminating documents had been forged by the police.[41]

Aurobindo paid little attention to the arguments being advanced for his benefit. Before Das took up his defense, Aurobindo had written some instructions for Chakravarty informing him "what was false in the evidence" against him "and on what points the witnesses might be cross-examined." He continued this after Das's arrival, but then he heard his inner guide: "This is the man who will save you from the snares put around your feet. Put aside those papers. It is not you who will instruct him. I will instruct him."[42] From that point onward he took no interest in the case. If he had to write something for Das, he did so mechanically or let Abinash answer for him.

Owing to the length of the proceedings, the prisoners were allowed to sit on benches in the dock. This kindness was offset by other, less thoughtful arrangements. One morning in October, they found that the dock had been surrounded by a framework of iron mesh netting. A policeman opened a gate to let them in and locked it behind them. Throughout the proceedings, an armed constable sat by the entrance. Other guards were placed in various parts of the room, and Norton kept a loaded revolver on his desk. On their way to and from the court, the prisoners were handcuffed two by two and fastened to a chain in the van. All the way, they sang and joked and laughed. In the dock they seated themselves according to their convictions. Those interested in spirituality clustered around Aurobindo. The hardcore revolutionaries found a leader in Hem Das. The two groups exchanged criticisms that were sometimes rather bitter. When their voices became too loud, the judge demanded silence. At one point he asked Aurobindo to intervene. Aurobindo answered that as far as he was concerned the others could do as they liked. As a rule, he sat alone, sometimes listening to the speeches but more often absorbed in meditation. Some concluded that he was morose if not depressed. By his own retrospective account, he was enjoying the bliss of cosmic consciousness. The vision of God in all became his normal state.

PROPERLY SPEAKING, Aurobindo's practice of yoga had begun in January 1908 with the experience of the "silent, spaceless and timeless Brahman," which he had while meditating with Lele in Baroda. This was followed five months later by the experience of the active *brahman*, "as all beings and all that is." The first carried the sense of the unreality of the world and its objects; the second brought the awareness that the Divine was present in all things. As his meditations continued, he found that the realizations of the passive and the active brahman, with the perception of the universe corresponding to each, could alternate, then coexist, then fuse.[43] The uniting of the two in "the supreme Reality with the static and dynamic Brahman as its two aspects," would be, when attained, his third major realization. But for the fusion to take place, his governing power of consciousness had to be something higher than the ordinary mind. Faced with this problem, he heard a voice within that he took to be that of Swami Vivekananda. The voice said "certain things about the processes of the higher truth consciousness," in particular the workings of the level of consciousness that Aurobindo later called the intuitive mind. This was something completely new to him. After two or three weeks, the voice fell silent, having "finished all it had to say on that subject." When Aurobindo began to apply what he had learned, he found that it was "precise even in the minutest details."[44]

Aurobindo heard "all sorts of voices" while meditating in jail, but he was careful not to follow them all. An inner discrimination helped him distinguish helpful from unhelpful or even deceptive influences. The voice of Vivekananda seemed to him worth heeding because it offered verifiable knowledge and seemed to come from a trustworthy source; the sense of Vivekananda's presence carried conviction. He might still have doubted what he heard, for "one can always doubt"; on the other hand "one can't get very far like that." So he went forward, cautiously, and discovered that the voice had not misled him. Years later he wondered whether its source was actually the spirit of Vivekananda. It might, he thought, have been "a part of my own mind separating and taking [another] form." In any case, what the voice told him proved to be very valuable.[45]

Since his meeting with Lele, Aurobindo had "accepted the rule of following the inner guidance implicitly and moving only as I was moved by the Divine." The development he underwent during his stay in Alipore turned this rule "into an absolute law of the being."[46] But he still had to differentiate between useful guidance and misleading indications. Some "voices" are simply "movements of one's nature that take upon themselves a voice." Others are "suggestions from outside" presenting themselves as authoritative sources of guidance.[47] The most authoritative kinds of voice were those that Aurobindo called *adesha*s—commands coming, or seeming to come, directly from the Divine. But even here, he learned, "distinctions have to be made. The Divine speaks to us in many ways and it is not always the imperative adesh that comes. When it does, it is clear and irresistible, the mind has to obey and there is no question possible."[48] During his stay in Alipore, Aurobindo received such an *adesh*. It brought him two messages. The first was that he was certain to be released, for he had special work to do for the Indian nation. The second was that this work was at root spiritual: God was giving India freedom "for the service of the world."[49]

THROUGHOUT NOVEMBER AND DECEMBER, Aurobindo's life went on in the limited compass of courtroom and jail. He remained in solitary confinement, changing cells every week or so. But the strictness instituted after Narendranath's murder was gradually relaxed. The prisoners were allowed to exercise, then to eat outside their cells, and finally to take baths and wash their clothes in the yard. They were, of course, carefully watched by the warders as well as the Gordon Highlanders. One, a Scot that the prisoners dubbed Ruffian, had taken an interest in Aurobindo. Once he called into his cell, "Abrindo must now be brooding over his good old Cambridge days." Aurobindo said nothing and the hectoring continued: "Abrindo, you are caught at last, you are caught at last." This went on until Aurobindo replied: "And yet I will escape, and yet I will escape." On another occasion, Ruffian gave Aurobindo a shove as he was exercising in the yard. Aurobindo turned, looked at the man sternly and said: "Remember, I am a gentleman." "I also am a gentleman," Ruffian stammered as he ran off to report that Aurobindo had given him an "insubordinate look." The young men became agitated until the superintendent asked them to bear their crosses like good Christians.[50]

The case, adjourned for a week for Christmas holidays, resumed on January 2, 1909. Day after day, witnesses were examined and cross-examined. Then, on February 26, the judge began to record the accused persons' statements. Most refused to tell him anything. Asked why, seventeen-year-old Sushil Sen explained: "Anything I say might be twisted into law." When Aurobindo's turn came, he made no oral statement but submitted a written text that his lawyers had drawn up, explaining away some damaging written remarks and undercutting evidence that seemed to connect him with the other accused. When he mounted the stand, reporters were struck by his sickly appearance. He "looked awfully anaemic," one wrote, "and seemed so weak that he was hardly able to speak audibly."[51]

Around this time, the police discovered that a piece of the cage surrounding the dock had been cut off. The next day, the prisoners' handcuffs were not removed when they were led into the courtroom. While they sat in the dock, they were shackled to a chain passed through their handcuffs. The defense protested this unprecedented arrangement; the judge replied that he could not interfere.[52] The newspapers reported the chaining and before long a question was raised in the British Parliament. Embarrassed, the Government of India asked the Government of Bengal whether there had been "reasonable expectation of violence or rescue."[53] Bengal's chief secretary replied in the affirmative, and given what was happening in the province, one can hardly blame him. On November 7, a man attempted to shoot Andrew Fraser at a public meeting. Two days later, Nandalal Bannerjee, the policeman who had arrested Prafulla Chaki near Muzaffarpur, was gunned down in a north Calcutta street. Four days after that, the informer in another case was murdered and decapitated in Dacca. Shaken by these developments, the Government of Bengal rounded up nine nationalist leaders—Aurobindo's uncle Krishna Kumar Mitra, his *Bande Mataram* associates Shyamsundar Chakravarty and Subodh Mallik, Extremist organizers Aswini Kumar Dutt and Manoranjan Guha Thakurta, and four others—and deported them to various places in north India and Burma. Neither this nor other repressive measures slowed the spread of terrorism, which soon appeared in Alipore. On February 10, 1910 a man named Charu Bose entered the Alipore magistrate's court where the public prosecutor, Ashutosh Biswas, was conducting another case. As Ashutosh left the courtroom, Charu ran up and shot him at point blank range. A few minutes later an orderly came to Beachcroft's courtroom and announced that Ashutosh was dead. Shaken, Beachcroft adjourned his court for the day.

On March 4 the prosecution closed its case and Norton began his argument. It took him fourteen sessions, stretching over three weeks, to say what he had to say about the conspiracy and its leader. The first defense lawyer took his turn on March 20. Three days later Das began his argument on behalf of Aurobindo. He took a week to complete it. On the last day, he summed up his client's case in the first person:

> The whole of my case before you is this. If it is suggested that I preached the ideal of freedom to my country, which is against the law, I plead guilty to the charge. If that is the law here, I say that I have done that and I request you to convict me. . . . If that is my charge you can chain me, imprison me, but you will never get out of me a denial of that charge.

Reverting to his own voice, Das concluded:

> My appeal to you therefore is that a man like this who is being charged with the offences imputed to him stands not only before the bar in this Court but stands before the bar of the High Court of History and my appeal to you is that long after this controversy is hushed in silence, long after this turmoil, this agitation ceases, long after he is dead and gone, he will be looked

upon as the poet of patriotism, as the prophet of nationalism and the lover of humanity. Long after he is dead and gone his words will be echoed and re-echoed not only in India, but across distant seas and lands.[54]

The defense arguments continued until the middle of April. The judge then heard the opinions of the assessors, and announced he would take a month to write his judgment.

ON MAY 5, 1909 Aurobindo completed one year as a prisoner in Alipore jail. The next morning he and the others were told that judgment would be delivered that day. The government ordered special arrangements to be made. "Five hundred men comprising the Bengal armed and military police ... were patrolling the many roads and by-lanes leading from the jail to the Court." The vans from the jail, escorted by a detachment of Gordon Highlanders, arrived at the court at ten o'clock. The prisoners were released from their shackles and led, under guard, to the dock. There they waited a half-hour until the judge appeared. As he mounted the bench, a "sudden hush fell upon the court and the prisoners pressed eagerly to the front of the netted dock." Beachcroft delivered no speech, but, "with a perceptible tremor in his voice," read out the list of those he had found guilty:

I convict Barindra Kumar Ghose and Ullaskar Dutt under sections 121, 121A and 122 of the Indian Penal Code and sentence them to be hanged by the neck until they are dead—all their property to be forfeited. They will have one week in which to appeal.

I convict Upendranath Banarjee, Bibhuti Bhusan Sircar, Rishi Case Kanji Lal, Birendra Chandra Sen, Sudhir Kumar Ghose [Sarkar], Indra Nath Nandy, Abinash Chunder Bhattacharjee, Sailendra Nath Bose and Hem Chunder Dass under the same sections and sentence them to transportation for life—all their property to be forfeited.

The judge convicted eight other prisoners under various sections and sentenced them to various terms of imprisonment. Those whose names he did not mention—Aurobindo and sixteen others—were acquitted.[55]

"The sentences were received in silence," noted police official F. C. Daly, "that is, silence compared to the turmoil that there has usually been in the Dock." Aurobindo "as usual, looked stoically indifferent, but seemed well pleased with himself when he was allowed to walk out and leave the Court."[56]

THE JUDGMENT, all 354 pages of it, was released later the same day. Beachcroft wrote that there had been a conspiracy that led to several acts of violence. The men who planned these acts were awarded the penalty of death; those who carried them out received transportation for life; those who had some connection with those who carried them out received a longer or shorter term of imprisonment.

The judge devoted a page or two to most of the accused. To Aurobindo he devoted fifty. Before beginning his analysis, he observed, in a rueful aside: "He is the accused, whom more than any other the prosecution are anxious to have convicted and but for his presence in the dock there is no doubt that the case would have been finished long ago." The evidence against Aurobindo consisted almost entirely of documents: letters, published writings, transcriptions of speeches, and documents written by others in which he was mentioned. The prosecution maintained that his published writings and speeches proved that Aurobindo favored independence. His unpublished writings and letters, along with certain other documents, showed that he supported the use of violence to achieve this aim. Other evidence, including the testimony of the shadowing detectives, showed that he was in contact with those who committed violent acts. The defense conceded that Aurobindo favored independence, but insisted that he based his claim on his belief that national freedom was a prerequisite to individual salvation. A related belief made him an opponent of violent methods.

Beachcroft analyzed the evidence in great detail. Aurobindo's letters, particularly those to his wife, contained expressions that were suspicious if one began with the idea that Aurobindo was a conspirator. Otherwise, they were "capable of an innocent explanation." His speeches espousing the idea of freedom and self-help helped the defense more than the prosecution. "The Morality of Boycott" and another incomplete essay seemed to suggest that Aurobindo did not oppose the use of violence, but it was "a point in Arabinda's favour" that he did not publish them.[57] In the end there were just two pieces of evidence that threw real doubt on Aurobindo's innocence: the "sweets letter," in which Barin informed his brother that it was the time for "*sweets* all over India readymade for imergencies"; and the "scribblings," which mentioned known revolutionaries and "the small charge of the stuff." In regard to the letter, the judge conceded that "sweets" may well have been a code word for bombs, but he also found that it was "of so suspicious a character that I hesitate to accept it." As for the "scribblings," they were certainly a "difficult point." But when he took all the evidence together, Beachcroft had to conclude that it fell short "of such proof that would justify me in finding him guilty of so serious a charge."[58]

In so ruling Beachcroft upheld the highest traditions of British jurisprudence. He also allowed a man who was guilty as charged to go free. There certainly had been a conspiracy to deprive the king of the sovereignty of British India and Aurobindo certainly was part of it. Another judge might easily have convicted him. As F.C. Daly later observed, "It is hard to see how on the evidence laid before the Court the Judge could have believed that Aurobindo had no guilty knowledge of what was going on and that it did not have his tacit approval, if not enthusiastic encouragement." Daly's own analysis, published in a secret report of 1911, was remarkably accurate:

> Though Arabindo may be regarded as a man too clever and foreseeing to believe that success would attend a little effort of this kind of revolution, he possibly believed that an open demonstration of murder by bombs and an exhibition of the audacity to which Bengali youths had been brought to by the new system of training, would have a stimulating effect on the spirits of others and would excite the minds of the young men throughout India and develop in them a spirit of reckless daring that would be of great use in the big venture which he possibly had in his mind's eye and for which he intended to wait a suitable opportunity, such as the embarrassment of England in a big foreign war.[59]

So astonishing was Aurobindo's release that some have suggested that Beachcroft acquitted him out of old-boy favoritism. There is no reason to believe this, though it must be admitted that the judge found "innocent explanations" for documents that others might have found damaging and "hesitated to accept" such incriminating pieces of evidence as the "sweets letter" and the "scribblings." Both of these documents were exactly what the prosecution claimed them to be: proof that Aurobindo was aware of the activities of Barin's group. Aurobindo owed his escape in part to the clumsiness of the police in filing the documents, but more to a run of good luck that began when he told Barin to get rid of the guns that had been stored in the Grey Street house and ended when an attorney for the defense, for no particular reason, applied to cross-examine Narendranath Goswami in the magistrate's court and was refused permission to do so. Had Narendranath's testimony been accepted, it is all but certain that Aurobindo would have been sentenced to a long term of transportation to the Andamans.

Karmayogin

From the court, Aurobindo went to the house of his lawyer, Chittaranjan Das. He was then driven to 6 College Square, the north Calcutta residence of his uncle Krishna Kumar Mitra. Krishna Kumar, one of the nine deportees, was still in detention in Agra. His family, as their friend Sister Nivedita reported, was "utterly smitten down by his removal."[60] Aurobindo stayed with the Mitras for the next ten months, becoming the head of a household that included his aunt Lilavati and his cousins Kumudini, Basanti, and Sukumar. It did not include Mrinalini, who stayed in the Calcutta home of her father's friend Girish Bose.

Aurobindo remained at home through most of the month of May, receiving hundreds of visitors who came to College Square to meet him. "Bengalis and Punjabis, old or young, rich or poor, even the lame and the cripple amongst the street beggars—whoever are coming to him he is receiving and answering questions of one and all, quite freely and with his usual simplicity of manners," wrote a newspaper reporter.[61] Among the callers were the poet Rabindranath Tagore, professors Jitendra Lal Bannerji and Jyotish Ghosh, and old associates Pramathanath Mitra, Gispati Kabyatirtha, Surendranath Haldar, and Bejoy Chandra Chatterji.[62] Bejoy, a former *Bande Mataram* editor, told him about the paper's demise. The staff had carried on after Aurobindo's arrest, but by October 1908 they had run out of money. Wishing to go down in a blaze of glory, Bejoy wrote an article that the police could not ignore. The paper quickly was shut down and its press confiscated.[63]

If *Bande Mataram* had been alive, it is likely that Aurobindo would have begun to write for it again. As it was, he stayed at home, practicing yoga, reading, writing in his notebooks, and reflecting on the political situation. From newspaper reports and talks with friends he pieced together a picture of what was happening in the country. In brief, the years 1908 and 1909 had been a disaster for the Extremists and for Indian nationalism in general. The government had enacted a number of repressive laws. The Explosive Substances Act was followed by the Newspapers (Incitement to Offences) Act of 1908, which allowed magistrates to order the forfeiture of presses that printed "incitement to murder" or other forms of violence.[64] It was under this act that *Bande Mataram* and *Jugantar* met their end. But the most important victim of the new legislation was Bal Gangadhar Tilak. Arrested for an article in which he wrote that the rise of terrorism was due to "the exasperation produced by the autocratic exercise of power by the unrestrained and powerful white official class," he was charged with sedition, tried, found guilty, and sentenced to six years imprisonment in Mandalay.[65] The summary deportation of the nine Bengali leaders followed in December. Along the way, the government passed the Criminal Law Amendment Act, which authorized nonjury prosecutions and permitted magistrates to proscribe meetings and associations. As a result, in January the Dacca Anushilan and a half-dozen other *samitis* were banned—and went underground.

The cumulative effect of the new measures was to destroy the Extremist party. Leaders who had not been deported or imprisoned—Bipinchandra Pal, Lajpat Rai, G.S. Khaparde—exiled themselves to the comparative safety of England. The few Extremists who were still at large were shut out from the Indian National Congress. At the same time, the government was drawing closer to the Moderates. G.K. Gokhale was in the viceroy's good graces; Rashbehari Ghose became his cat's-paw. Elected president of the Moderates-only Congress, Rashbehari met with Lord Minto, who convinced him to run the Congress "in conformity with ideas as to which he and I might agree." At the 1908 national session, Rashbehari proclaimed from the presidential chair, "When in the fullness of time the people have outgrown the present system of administration" they might hope for "the extension to India of the colonial form of self-government"—though, as he reminded his listeners, "this ideal can only be realised in the distant future."[66]

The same month that Rashbehari uttered his rousing bromides, John Morley announced the proposed reforms of Indian councils and legislatures that he and Minto had been working on. In the months that followed, even the most moderate Moderates realized that the reforms were shams, but they kept their disappointment to themselves. After all, they would fill the posts that the reforms created. The Extremists and revolutionaries who had always condemned the proposals found to their surprise that they were being given credit for them. "It is common talk in Calcutta," noted an official in May 1909, "that the Council reforms and the appointment of the Hon'ble Mr Sinha [to the viceroy's council] were the direct result of the conspiracy. It is said that the Congress begged for twenty years and got nothing, but one year of bombs has brought all this reform."[67] Such talk was exaggerated. The reforms were conceived in 1906, two years before the bombings. But it cannot be denied that the terrorists pushed Morley to demand substantial changes. Three months after Muzaffarpur, Minto was still thinking about a powerless council of notables. Morley lashed out: "*India can't wait! . . .* It [the reform scheme] will have to be extended immensely."[68]

This, in sum, was the political position at the time of Aurobindo's release.

Surveying the ruins, he could see that the movement had to be kept from laps-
ing, and he could find no one but himself to do it. After his experiences in jail,
he felt a strong push to devote himself to yoga, but it did not seem possible for
him to give up either politics or journalism. Turning down an offer to write
for the *Bengalee*, he decided to bring out his own weekly newspaper, in which
he would discuss not only "national religion" but also literature, philosophy, art,
and other subjects.

TOWARD THE END OF MAY, Aurobindo agreed to give a speech in Uttarpara, his first public appearance since his acquittal. Arriving in the town in the
evening of May 30, he was received with cries of "Bande Mataram," garlanded,
given refreshments, and escorted to the library where the meeting was being
held. As he sat before the six hundred people who filled the library's courtyard,
"there came into my mind [as he later told his audience] a word that I have to
speak to you, a word that I have to speak to the whole of the Indian Nation."
This "word" was something he spoke "under an impulse and compulsion": the
story of his arrest and trial, his experience of the presence of the Divine, and
his *adesh* or command to tell the people of India that "it is for the world and
not for themselves that they arise."

Aurobindo had been invited to Uttarpara by the local Society for the Protection of Religion (*dharma rakshini sabha*). In the course of his speech he
referred often to Hinduism, which he identified with the *sanatana dharma*, the
eternal law of being. But he concluded with a question:

> What is the Hindu religion? What is this religion that we call Sanatana,
> eternal? It is the Hindu religion only because the Hindu nation has kept
> it, because in this peninsula it grew up in the seclusion of the sea and the
> Himalayas, because in this sacred and ancient land it was given as a charge
> to the Aryan race to preserve through the ages. But it is not circumscribed
> by the confines of a single country, it does not belong peculiarly and for
> ever to a bounded part of the world.

What was eternal was the inner core of Hinduism, not its outward forms
and practices. "A narrow religion, a sectarian religion, an exclusive religion can
only live for a limited time and a limited purpose," but the eternal religion
would live forever because it was based on the realization that God "is in all
men and all things." A year and a half earlier, he reminded his audience, he
had said "nationalism is not politics but a religion." Now he put the same thing

in a different way: "The Sanatan Dharma"—no limited creed but the eternal religion itself—"that is nationalism." This was the message he had been given to speak, and having said it, he sat down.[69]

The Uttarpara Speech has been printed and cited innumerable times since its delivery, mostly because it was the first and last occasion that Aurobindo spoke of his spiritual experiences in public. As such, it is an important document for scholars of mysticism. But historians, political scientists, and politicians also discuss the speech. Left-wing critics hold it up as proof that Aurobindo's nationalism was Hindu at its core, and suggest that this bias encouraged the growth of communalism, which made the partition of the country inevitable. Right-wing enthusiasts regard the speech as an inspired expression of the imperishable Indian spirit, citing passages of the speech out of context to make it seem as if Aurobindo endorsed their programs. These readings are both partial and thus both false; Aurobindo's "universal religion" was not limited to any particular creed. It had been given classic expression in the Upanishads and *Gita,* but it was also at the core of such scriptures as the Bible and the Koran. More important, "its real, most authoritative scripture is in the heart [of every individual] in which the Eternal has His dwelling."[70] The true *sanatana dharma* was not a matter of belief but of spiritual experience and inner communion with the Divine.

Such experience and communion was now the main motive of Aurobindo's life; but he did not believe that it ruled out an active life in the world. Calls to attend meetings poured in, and he accepted many of them. At the same time, he put the finishing touches on the first issue of his new newspaper. Then he departed for Barisal, East Bengal, where he had been invited to attend a conference.

DURING HIS TRIP TO EAST BENGAL, Aurobindo kept an account of his inner experiences in a pocket diary. It begins on June 17, 1909 while he was on his way to Khulna. The next morning, traveling by steamer to Barisal, he experienced an explosion of visual and auditory images and physical and kinesthetic sensations. A blue after-image of the sun yielded to a "pattern of bloodred curves on yellowish background," followed by a "Violet sword" and "Bloodred sword." There was also a voice rising from the *chitta* (basic consciousness) into the brain. His body experienced various forms of physical *ananda* or delight, which made all outward touches pleasurable. He had the sense of being "held & moved, the hold always there, not always noticed." In the midst of all of this he had the "realisation of Vasudeva," and passed into various forms of trance, "brief but very deep in spite of loud noise [the steamboat's engine] at ear." His visions were of everyday beings and things rather than otherworldly objects: his cousin Kumudini, a glass jug, a blue sun, a "bill with rose red letters," other printed matter, the kitten at his uncle's house. He also had a vivid perception of natural forces: "Saw wind very clearly against light clouds under thick dark ones and a pillar of cloudy moisture." As a storm rose, he could see a current of wind blowing "violently from right with whirls, eddies & upward and downward pourings." That afternoon he heard the voice of Sri Krishna: "I come to slay."[71] In the evening, he reached Barisal and was taken to a Kali temple. There he experienced the presence of the goddess.

Throughout his stay in Barisal, he continued to see visions, hear voices and feel unusual sensations. There were also some "prophesies of future" and "suggestions for practical work."[72] Meanwhile he was meeting with people and delivering public speeches. It is clear from the diary that his experiences continued while he was interacting with others. Writing about this period two decades later, he told a correspondent: "As for concentration and perfection of the being and the finding of the inner self, I did as much of it walking in the streets of Calcutta to my work or in duty with men during my work as alone and in solitude."[73]

THE FIRST ISSUE of the *Karmayogin*, Aurobindo's new weekly newspaper, appeared on June 19, 1909. Two essays in it set the tone of the publication. The first, "Ourselves," chalked out the *Karmayogin*'s aim to unite India's political, social, and industrial activities. At the moment, all three were "sluggish, scattered and ineffectual," but he could see, beneath the surface, the beginning of a trend for them "to unite again into one mighty, invincible and grandiose flood. To assist that tendency, to give voice and definiteness to the deeper aspirations now forming obscurely within the national consciousness is the chosen work of the *Karmayogin*."[74] In the second essay, "The Ideal of the Karmayogin," he went further in his effort to close the gap between the spiritual and practical spheres:

> The task we set before ourselves is not mechanical but moral and spiritual. We aim not at the alteration of a form of government but at the building of a nation. Of that task politics is a part, but only a part. We shall devote ourselves not to politics alone, nor to social questions alone, nor to theology or philosophy or literature or science by themselves, but we include all these in one entity which we believe to be all-important, the *dharma*, the

national religion which we also believe to be universal. . . . It is a spiritual revolution we foresee and the material is only its shadow and reflex.[75]

The universal religion Aurobindo referred to here was the *sanatana dharma* about which he had spoken at Uttarpara. This was not, he again emphasized, Hinduism as generally understood, but a religion "which embraces Science and faith, Theism, Christianity, Mahomedanism and Buddhism and yet is none of these." Indian culture was eclectic: it had taken into itself "numerous sources of strength from foreign strains of blood and other types of civilisation." This gave it a special destiny. Once India had recovered its spiritual nature by means of *karmayoga,* it would regain its "social soundness, intellectual pre-eminence, political freedom," and in the end achieve "the mastery of human thought, the hegemony of the world."[76]

Although by no means a chauvinist, Aurobindo was convinced of the essential superiority of Indian culture. A century later, when all forms of essentialism are suspect and national exceptionalism—whether American, Russian, Chinese, Japanese, or other—is subject to well-deserved condemnation, one might wonder whether Indian essentialism and exceptionalism have much to recommend themselves. But this was not the problem in July 1909. India was dominated by an arrogant foreign imperialism, its culture denounced by a colonizer who made no effort to understand it. The first task of peoples so situated, as the philosopher Charles Taylor has written, is "to purge themselves" of the "destructive identity" imposed on them by their oppressors.[77] This is just what Aurobindo was doing when he wrote in the *Karmayogin:*

> Our ideal is that of Swaraj or absolute autonomy free from foreign control. We claim the right of every nation to live its own life by its own energies according to its own nature and ideals. We reject the claim of aliens to force upon us a civilisation inferior to our own or to keep us out of our inheritance on the untenable ground of a superior fitness. . . . We demand the realisation of our corporate existence as a distinct race and nation because that is the only way in which the ultimate brotherhood of humanity can be achieved, not by blotting out individual peoples and effacing outward distinctions, but by removing the internal obstacles to unity, the causes of hatred, malice and misunderstanding.[78]

THE *KARMAYOGIN* WAS A SUCCESS. Each issue quickly sold out, and the publication remained self-supporting throughout its career.[79] Subscribers were enrolled from Madras, Maharashtra, and the North. Bengali, Hindi, and Tamil editions were started, and a Marathi edition planned. Calcutta Extremists such as Suresh Chandra Deb felt that the *Karmayogin* "brought to our thoughts and activities some sort of coherence out of the confusion created by the repression by the government and the safe policy of our elder politicians." But some of the younger men found the new journal "a bitter pill to swallow."[80] They were expecting the same sort of hard-hitting commentary that Aurobindo published in *Bande Mataram*, but in the *Karmayogin* he seemed just as likely to speak about yoga, philosophy, or art as about the political situation. In art criticism he advocated the new "national" school, reproducing articles by Ananda Coomaraswamy and lauding the works of Abanindranath Tagore. His eye for composition was always searching and his comments sometimes provocative, as when he asserted that a painting by a student in the Government School of Art was better than a famous Raphael.[81] But he did not turn his back on political issues such as the Hindu–Muslim problem. In the issue of July 17, 1909 he wrote that there was "absolutely no reason why the electoral question should create bad blood between the two communities." Union could never be achieved "by political adjustments"; it had to be "sought deeper down, in the heart and the mind, for where the causes of disunion are, there the remedies must be sought." Sound psychology, but few Muslims were comforted by his assertion that "our Musulman brother" was as Indian as any Hindu, since "in him too Narayana dwells and to him too our Mother has given a permanent place in her bosom."[82] Only highly cultivated men like Abul Kalam Azad could see the sense behind the Hindu imagery. Azad visited Aurobindo a few times in the *Karmayogin* office and was briefly in contact with one of the revolutionary groups.[83] But most Muslims stayed away from Extremist politics, which appeared to them to be dominated by Hindu interests.

Aurobindo promised "to make it a main part of our work to place Mahomed and Islam in a new light before our readers." He never got around to it. For him Indian politics meant the struggle against the British and the competition with the Moderates for the control of the movement. Over time he gave more and more space to attacks on Britons such as John Morley and Edward Baker and on Moderates such as G. K. Gokhale and Pherozshah Mehta. Baker, the new lieutenant-governor, demanded the cooperation of the people. A natural enough desire "under normal circumstances," Aurobindo wrote, but "the circumstances in India are not normal." A government could expect cooperation only if it "represents the nation or is in the habit of consulting its wishes." But "the Government in India does not represent the nation, and in Bengal at least it has distinctly set itself against its wishes." Still, the government had its allies among the Moderates. In an astonishing speech in Poona, Gokhale declared: "Only madmen outside lunatic asylums could think or talk of independence."[84] This meant, Aurobindo observed, that "Tilak, Chidambaram, Aswini Kumar, Manoranjan, Bipin Chandra, Aurobindo, are madmen outside the lunatic asylum." In Europe "the love of independence may be a virtue," but in India it was "crime and lunacy." After Gokhale's sellout, the Extremists could no longer look on him "as a brother with whom we had our own private differences." He was a traitor and true nationalists could have nothing to do with him.[85]

On the platform Aurobindo was even more outspoken. From the middle of June to the middle of July, he delivered speeches in Barisal, Khulna, Howrah, Calcutta, and other places. His theme was always the same: the need to remain firm in spite of repression, to continue the boycott, to persevere with self-help and passive resistance. In a word, the people had to learn how to suffer. "Imprisonment in a righteous cause was not so terrible as it seemed," he told his audience in Calcutta. He had heard that the police were planning to deport him. He "was not a model of courage," he said, but "residence for the best part of a year in a solitary cell had been an experience which took away all the terrors of deportation." In fact, as he had "an unfortunate temper," "intimidation only made him persist in doing his duty more obstinately."[86]

Aurobindo's speeches were much remarked on, and much of the reaction was negative. "We cannot help feeling some concern for a man who possesses such enormous power for good, and employs it for his own harm," wrote the normally friendly *Indian Patriot*.[87] The Uttarpara speech, with its account of spiritual experiences, came in for a good deal of criticism. Shamji Krishnavarma, expatriate editor of the *Indian Sociologist*, sneered that there seemed to be a rash of revelations in the jails of Bengal, what with Aurobindo's vision coming just a year after Bipinchandra Pal's. Sister Nivedita observed in a letter to a friend that Aurobindo "is lecturing widely, and I think unwisely. But he believes himself divinely impelled and therefore not to be arrested. Of course many of us do strange things, because, for reasons known only to ourselves, 'We can no other'—but certainly GOD gives no promise of indemnity!" She summed up that "religious experience and strategy are by no means the same thing, and ought not to be confused."[88] In a later letter, she spoke of Aurobindo as "the Bengali Mazzini," echoing a comparison between him and the Italian revolutionary politician and philosopher that Annie Besant, the president of the Theosophical Society, had drawn earlier. Aurobindo, Besant had written, was "a man of the type of Mazzini, with the difference that he is fanatical, which Mazzini was not." Although "entirely unselfish" and with "no personal axe to grind," Aurobindo was "dangerous because he would use any method which would upset British rule." The editor of the *Modern Review* came to Aurobindo's defense, calling Besant's remarks "unjust, improper and uncalled for" and pointing out that Mazzini also had been called a fanatic because "he did not shrink from employing all the weapons of conspiracy, including even assassination."[89]

AUROBINDO WAS NOT WRONG when he remarked in his Calcutta speech that the British were thinking about deporting him. They were, in fact, examining three different ways to eliminate him: appeal, deportation, and prosecution. On the day of Aurobindo's release from jail, Eardley Norton and F.C. Daly began to scrutinize the judgment to see if there was a case for appeal. Norton believed there was, and urged that the judgment be sent to an outside expert for an opinion. This was done. Two weeks later, the report came back. The referee, E. P. Chapman, thought that the acquittal of Aurobindo was "assailable on several material points," and that if he had tried the case, he probably would have convicted Aurobindo. "*BUT*," he added, "the issue of such a case especially in the form of an appeal against acquittal cannot be otherwise than doubtful." He therefore advised "against an appeal." If the government managed to convict Aurobindo, Chapman thought, "he is then likely to develop into a myth." If it let him keep his freedom, "he may actually be less dangerous," for "in the wear and tear of actual life, his impracticality is certain to disclose itself."[90] Agreeing with Chapman, F.W. Duke, chief secretary of the Government of Bengal, decided not to appeal. A month later, however, after the *Karmayogin* appeared, H.A. Stuart, chief secretary of the Government of India, wrote that so far as he could see there were "no political reasons" for not appealing. In response to this pressure, the Government of Bengal sent Beachcroft's judgment to an expert in Bombay, with whom it remained for almost a month.

Meanwhile the Government of India was examining the two other options. "I would not hesitate to deport Arabindo if he cannot be silenced in any other way," Stuart wrote to his counterpart in Bengal. "If he is allowed to go on he will very soon have the country in a blaze again. We should certainly have deported him last December [along with Krishna Kumar Mitra, Subodh Mallik, et al.] if he had not been in jail then."[91] Lord Minto, the viceroy, agreed, but was hesitant to resort to deportation again. An ordinary prosecution for a crime such as sedition would be much better, he thought. As he wrote to the secretary of state, "Aurobindo is again on the warpath. I only hope he will commit himself sufficiently for us to be able to prosecute."[92] Since he began giving speeches, CID detectives had been noting down every word he spoke. The speeches of June, though "objectionable," contained nothing that amounted to sedition. But the speech in Calcutta, where he said that "imprisonment in a righteous cause was not intolerable," seemed to Baker, the Bengal lieutenant-governor, to cross the line. "Please consult Legal Remembrancer quickly," he wrote to Duke. The legal remembrancer thought that the speech was indictable, but noted that the government could only prosecute if the text was published. Aurobindo did not oblige them. The speech should normally have gone into the *Karmayogin* of July 17, but for some reason it never appeared in print.[93] On July 21, Duke wrote a long report on the Aurobindo problem. His advice regarding sedition was to give Aurobindo "more rope." Regarding deportation, he referred the matter back to his superior. Baker considered it for a day; then, on July 23, told his secretary to inform the viceroy that the Government of Bengal would not propose deportation.[94]

At the bottom of Aurobindo's file, Baker noted that "the whole matter should be kept strictly confidential." If he was afraid of a leak, his fears were not unfounded. During the last week of July, Nivedita visited Aurobindo and informed him that friends in government had informed her that Baker was planning to deport him. She advised him "to leave British India and work from outside so that his work would not be stopped." Aurobindo did not think this was necessary. Instead, he said, he would publish an open letter in which he mentioned the possibility of deportation. This, he thought, would tie the authorities' hands. His letter was published in the *Karmayogin* on July 31. When nobody came to take him away, he believed that his plan had worked, though the decision not to deport him had been made the previous week. His open letter is important primarily as a statement of the Extremists' ideal ("Swaraj or absolute autonomy free from foreign control") and as an outline of the party's immediate program. This he summed up under six headings, the first four of which were a peaceful policy of "self-help and passive resistance"; dealings with the government on the basis of the principle of "No control, no co-operation"; "rapprochement with the Moderate party" when possible; and extension of the boycott movement. Aurobindo's letter was "*the* sensation of the week" (wrote Nivedita to a friend) as the city got ready for the August 7 celebrations marking the fourth anniversary of the boycott.[95]

Departure

The boycott celebrations were unsuccessful. Most shops and businesses remained open, and though the usual procession took place, the turnout was disappointing. At Greer Park, a couple of thousand apathetic men and boys showed up for the speech of Bhupendranath Bose. "A public speaker in England would regard such a gathering as almost an insult," wrote the *Times*'s correspondent, who added: "The remarkable fact was, however, that, dampened as the crowd was" by Bhupendranath's hour-long oration, "it burst into loud cheering when Mr Arabindo Ghose was seen standing" near the speaker's table. "He was unquestionably the hero of the meeting," the correspondent thought. There were cries for Aurobindo to speak. In response he mounted the platform, but Bhupendranath, who had promised the government that he would not let Aurobindo speak, abruptly declared the meeting over, and everyone went home.[96]

"A national festival is the symbol of the national vitality," Aurobindo wrote in the next issue of the *Karmayogin*. "Therefore we regard the holding of the Boycott Day as a national duty."[97] Implicit in this was the recognition that national vitality was at a low ebb. He was especially annoyed that the leadership of the National Council of Education had forbidden students to attend. This, he wrote, was "the crowning act of a policy by which they are betraying the trust reposed in them by the nation, contradicting the very object of the institution and utterly ruining a great and salutary movement." His assessment agreed with that of the lieutenant-governor: "The National Council of Education," Baker wrote to the viceroy, "which was originally an Extremist organisation has been captured by the Moderates."[98]

Aurobindo continued to appear in public, but he commented privately that he wanted to take a break to "look to his health."[99] By this he doubtless meant that he wanted to devote more time to yoga. Meanwhile, he worked incessantly. At the end of August, he launched a new Bengali weekly called *Dharma*, writing most of its longer articles himself. His Bengali, improved by his "immersion course" at Alipore, was competent but far from brilliant. Though generally correct, as his brother later wrote, it contained "mistakes in construction all the same," while the style was "stiff and conventional."[100] Aurobindo wrote on yoga and philosophy, and also commented on political events. It was possible for writers to be more outspoken in Indian languages than in English because it was difficult for the government to prove sedition when it had to use official translations.

THE GOVERNMENT WAS pleased about the general decline of the national movement during 1908 and 1909. The only discordant note in the post-Alipore harmony was Aurobindo. Lieutenant-Governor Baker wrote in July that Aurobindo was "the most disturbing factor at present in the province." He was, commented Baker's counterpart in Eastern Bengal and Assam, a "dangerous character." He was, the viceroy told the secretary of state, "chiefly responsible" for "the evils of the situation." He was, insisted Minto's chief secretary, "a peculiarly dangerous element in Bengal at the moment."[101] How were these officials going to silence this dangerous character? The three methods investigated and rejected in July—appeal, deportation, and prosecution—were all still possible. On August 10, 1909 the opinion of the advocate general of Bombay on the Alipore judgment was received. He said there was a "fair chance of conviction against Arabinda Ghose being obtained on appeal." But he could not affirmatively answer the question of whether the government had a two-to-one chance of winning. Forwarding this opinion to the lieutenant-governor, Duke, the Bengal chief secretary, said he agreed that there should be no appeal "without strong prospects of success," but added that he was "reluctant to give it up in this case, for Arabinda is the most dangerous of our adversaries now at large." Baker considered the matter for two days; then, on August 18, he decided not to appeal. He would have liked to do so, both because he thought Aurobindo was guilty and because Aurobindo was "one of the most dangerous factors in the present situation." But an appeal would simply revive antigovernment feeling. The movement was dying out by itself. Why risk stirring it to life with a case the result of which could not be guaranteed?[102]

The Government of India accepted Baker's decision with some regret. Stuart, the chief secretary, was convinced that there had been a miscarriage of justice at Alipore. He agreed that the success of an appeal was "far from certain," yet stressed that Aurobindo "should not be allowed to escape" because he was a highly dangerous character (over the next few months the term became a regular catchword in officialdom). The idea of appealing should not be dropped, he argued. Let other experts be approached, and let Norton induce the judge of the appeal of the Alipore convicts to say something about the admissibility of the "sweets letter." Norton tried, but the judge rebuked him at once.

Then there were the other two approaches. A sedition prosecution was more attractive than deportation, but Aurobindo, they all knew, was "unlikely to slip" in print. A speech he gave on August 22 was noted down and scrutinized, but it was decided that it was "impossible to prosecute on the basis of a single shorthand report." The *Karmayogin* was still publishing "mischievous

articles," to which were added *Dharma's* "objectionable" productions. Some of
these seemed to cross the line, but nothing Aurobindo wrote went far enough
to satisfy the government that a sedition prosecution was safe.[103] This may
be compared to a Bombay court's sentencing of A.B. Kolhatkar to two and
a half years' imprisonment, three months of which were spent in chains, for
publishing some of Aurobindo's 1908 speeches, which the Alipore court had
considered nonseditious. As for deportation, Minto for one was more than
willing, and suggested as much to the secretary of state in a letter of August 5.
The same day an old India hand named John D. Rees declared in the House
of Commons: "I hope the government will deport this man." Deportation
without trial was, admittedly, autocratic, but "in order to make the people of
the East realise that their rulers had power it was essential to use it autocrati-
cally in grave and critical situations."[104] Despite such pressure, Baker refused
to overturn his earlier decision not to endorse deportation. For the moment,
Aurobindo was safe.

THE 1909 Bengal Provincial Conference was scheduled to be held in the
town of Hooghly on September 4 and 5. Regarding it as an important engagement in the battle between the Moderates and Extremists, Aurobindo used
all of his skills as an organizer to see that his party was well represented. The
Moderates had selected Hooghly as a safe venue, as they controlled the local
reception committee. They made use of this advantage to disqualify a number of Extremist delegates. They even attempted to disqualify Aurobindo, but
failed: He went to Hooghly as the delegate of two towns and two student
bodies. People were surprised that he showed no bitterness toward his rivals.
In Hooghly he spoke with a journalist named Paranjpe, who insisted that it
was time to trounce the Moderates "by any means fair or foul." Aurobindo did
not agree. Surendranath Banerjea and the Moderates had done great work for
the nation, Aurobindo said. The Extremists were standing on their shoulders.
Illicit means were out of the question; but his party would do everything it
could to get its program accepted.[105]

The first order of business after the conference opened was to select the
subjects committee. Surendranath, as leader of the Moderates, wanted to name
ten of the fifteen members. Aurobindo wanted seven, not five, but said he
would settle for six. Surendranath allowed Aurobindo to name six members,
as the Moderates would still have a three-vote advantage. Then came the time
to formulate the resolutions to be passed in the open assembly. The Extremists
had their way with the resolution condemning the reforms, but not with the

all-important boycott resolution. Seeing that his party could not win, but not wanting to force a split, Aurobindo said he would agree to the Moderates' version so long as he was allowed to explain his decision in the open session.[106]

The next day, the resolutions were taken up and passed one by one. When it came time to consider the boycott resolution, Extremists became restive when they saw that the Moderate version had won out. The president of the session, then Surendranath, tried to quiet the tumult and failed. It looked as though the conference would become another Surat. The Extremists were prepared to wreck it if Aurobindo gave the word. Instead, he stood up and raised his arm. The entire assembly fell silent. He explained that he had intended to amend the resolution, but when he saw that such pressure might split the Bengal Congress, he decided to let the Moderates have their way. "At the same time," he added, "we want it to be clearly understood that in taking this course we are not for a moment receding from the policy and line we have taken up."[107] Because the conference was unwilling to endorse their version, the Extremists should leave the pavilion. They did so "in disciplined silence as if a single body."[108] This was the climactic moment of the conference. The Moderates watched in amazement as half of the delegates walked out at the bidding of a thirty-seven-year-old upstart.

A day or two later, Aurobindo and some of his colleagues left for a conference in the distant Surma Valley. At Jalsukia, the site of the conference, he was received with great enthusiasm. During a meeting he observed that in "this remote corner of the eastern region the term 'Moderate' has ceased to be." With no prodding from him, the conference passed resolutions far in advance of those decided on at Hooghly.[109] At the conference's close, he gave a speech on self-help and passive resistance. Few of his listeners could understand his English, but they went away satisfied. Most had come "just to hear him speak and have his *darshan*." Many had heard that he was a practicing yogi, and sought his help in spiritual matters.[110]

After the conference, Aurobindo and some others toured East Bengal by boat. This was the closest he would get to the break from politics he had been hoping for since July. Back in Calcutta, he avoided public appearances; but October 16 was approaching. He was determined that the observance of the anniversary of the partition of Bengal would not fall as flat as the boycott anniversary. Between October 9 and 15, he spoke at three rallies, referring to the manifold problems besetting the movement. The most obvious of these were the government's anti-Extremist diktats. One of them had criminalized the Anushilan *samiti*. Aurobindo said he was shocked by this: "We all know what the Anushilan Samiti is. We know that it is one of those Samitis which has the least to do with politics." This was, of course, untrue. As one of the *samiti*'s founders, he knew perfectly well that its open activities were meant to mask its revolutionary aim. The government knew this too, and had shut the *samiti* down. Aurobindo told his listeners to remain firm:

> Remember the people of England do not understand weakness. . . . They only understand resolution, steadfastness and determination. . . . If only we are true and hold firm, everything in this God-given movement will help towards the goal. . . . Whatever happens let us have faith and courage— faith that looks beyond all momentary obstacles and reverses and sees the goal that God has set before us, and the courage that never flinches for a moment but moves forward calmly, wisely, but strongly and irresistibly to that goal.[111]

It was the same message that he had given in Bombay two years earlier, but in Bombay he was speaking to cheering thousands; here, to a hundred or so dispirited men and boys.

Despite Aurobindo's efforts, the Partition Day observances were unsuccessful. He attended the main meeting at Beadon Square, where he spoke a few words in Bengali. A newspaper photographer took a picture of the occasion. Aurobindo stands in a corner of the square with a small group of men. One of them holds a black umbrella over his head. There is nothing to suggest that anything important is happening. It hardly looks like a public meeting at all.

THE LAST TWO WEEKS of October were occupied by the *puja* holidays. Aurobindo used the break to spend time with family and friends, do some nonjournalistic writing, and meditate. When Suresh Deb called on him at 6 College Square, he was met by Aurobindo's "winsome smile." The young journalist found the Chief more interested in his "new psycho-physical discipline" than in current political developments.[112] It was probably at this time that Aurobindo wrote *The National Value of Art*, a series of essays he began to publish in November. He also worked on some of his poems and a translation of Bankim Chandra Chatterjee's *Anandamath*. By the beginning of November he was back to his normal routine. After passing the afternoon at the *Karmayogin* office, he would walk back to 6 College Square and spend the evening with friends. One day they had an unexpected visitor: Ramsay MacDonald, an M.P. and the leader of the British Labour Party. After a brief talk with Aurobindo, the future prime minister wrote:

I called on one whose name is on every lip as a wild extremist who toys
with bombs and across whose path the shadow of the hangman falls. He
sat under a printed text, "I will go on in the strength of the Lord God"
[*Psalms* 71:16]; he talked of the things which trouble the soul of man. . . .
He was far more of a mystic than of a politician. He saw India seated on a
temple throne. But how it was to arise, what the next step was to be, what
the morrow of independence was to bring—to these he had given little
thought. They were not of the nature of his genius.[113]

MacDonald's visit was only one sign of Aurobindo's growing celebrity.
Others ranged from the banal to the grandiloquent. An advertisement in
Karmayogin featured an endorsement by him of a *swadeshi* self-oiling comb:
"The idea *** is a very ingenious one and has been ingeniously carried out ***
The comb serves its purpose well."[114] In London, Bipin Pal published a profile
of his former colleague. In Calcutta, Jitendra Lal Bannerji published another.
In an effort to explain the "marvellous change" of an "obscure school-master"
into a national political leader, Bannerji proposed to give his readers what was
needed to plumb the "secret of that mysterious personality which has drawn
to itself so much love, hope and reverence." Glowing portraits of Rajnarain
Bose and Dr. K.D. Ghose were followed by a potted biography of Aurobindo
that stressed his intelligence and self-sacrifice. Released from jail after a year's
confinement, he "is like gold, thrice tested in fire." Some called him a visionary
and a dreamer. Jitendra Lal had no quarrel with that: "Yes, Aravinda Ghosh is
a dreamer—but he has dreamed golden dreams for his country and people—
visions of glory and triumph."[115] This article may be said to mark the beginning of the Aurobindo legend, which would assume new forms in the years
to come. But Aurobindo does not seem to have taken Jitendra Lal's article
too seriously. In December he published a letter by a professor named Hiralal
Haldar that scoffed at Jitendra Lal's hero-worshipping tone.[116]

Critics of Aurobindo could be as zealous in detraction as Jitendra Lal was
in praise. Annie Besant again proclaimed him dangerous, even fanatical on
account of "his refusal to work with any Englishmen."[117] Members of government used the same terms to describe the man they were trying to imprison.
Some added that they thought he was slightly off his head: "There is madness
in his family," wrote the viceroy to the secretary of state, "and he probably has
a bee in his bonnet." Minto seems to have picked up this notion from R.C.
Dutt, a onetime friend of Aurobindo's, who had been asked for information
by the political agent of Baroda. "Arabindo's mother was off her mind," Dutt
volunteered, "and Arabindo himself was eccentric."[118] Other Moderates spoke

privately in terms similar to Dutt's. Publicly they charged Aurobindo with being an impractical dreamer, an "impatient idealist."[119] About this epithet Aurobindo wrote:

> The reproach of idealism has always been brought against those who work with their eye on the future by the politicians wise in their own estimation who look only to the present. . . . The whole Asiatic world is moving forward with enormous rapidity. In Persia, in Turkey, in Japan the impatient idealists have by means suited to the conditions of the country effected the freedom and are now building up the dignity and strength of their motherland. . . . Of all the great nations of the world India alone is bidden to wait. . . . Under the circumstances, which is the more unpractical and idealistic, the impatience of the Nationalist or the supine and trustful patience of the President of the Hooghly Conference?[120]

In the *Karmayogin* he wrote on education, art, and society, and continued to comment on the season's political issues: the Alipore appeals, the Hindu–Muslim problem, Asian politics, the British general elections. In the high court, the judges set aside the death sentences of Barin and Ullaskar Dutt, awarding them life transportation instead. Eight other Alipore convicts had their terms of imprisonment reduced; one was acquitted and released. On the fate of the other five, the two judges were divided and referred the cases to a third. Meanwhile the six-month period for the filing of appeals expired, making it impossible for the government to eliminate Aurobindo in that way. Work on a possible appeal of his Alipore acquittal continued right down to the deadline.

Twice in November Aurobindo considered the Hindu–Muslim divide. He made it clear that he rejected separate electorates for Muslims "not because we are opposed to a large Mahomedan influence in popular assemblies when they come but because we will be no party to a distinction which recognises Hindu and Mahomedan as permanently separate political units and thus precludes the growth of a single and indivisible Indian nation." The recently mooted Hindu Sabha was based on the same misconception. "We do not understand Hindu nationalism as a possibility under modern conditions," he wrote. "Under modern conditions India can only exist as a whole."[121]

He devoted much of his energy to trying to unite the two factions of Congress. At Hooghly, a committee had been formed to find ways to do this. It consisted of four Moderates led by Surendranath Banerjea and four Extremists led by Aurobindo. These men met a number of times in November and December. The main issue was the Moderate "creed" and the Congress's rules of procedure. One of the rules, expressly formulated to exclude the Extremists, was that bodies of less than three years' standing could not send delegates to national meetings. Surendranath said that there was nothing to prevent his party from electing Extremist delegates. Jitendra Lal Bannerji and other Extremists found this tempting, but Aurobindo saw it as an attempt "to annex the Extremist party." When it was time for him to speak, he ignored Surendranath's blandishments and Jitendra Lal's reasonings and, with fewer than thirty words, put paid to the negotiations.[122]

"We regret to announce to the country that there is not the least possibility of having a united Congress," he wrote soon afterwards in *Dharma*.[123] The failure of the negotiations, together with the revelation that the reforms were not what the government had promised, seemed to him to mark the end of an era in the national movement. The moment was critical enough for him to write and publish a second open letter in the *Karmayogin*, in which he set forth the position of the Extremists. It was headed "To My Countrymen." Since 1905, the national movement had proceeded through the union of the Moderates and Extremists "on the platform of self-help and passive resistance." At present, it was clear that the Moderates were doomed to isolation. The government had betrayed them; the reforms they had petitioned for were fraudulent. The Extremists had attempted to meet them on equal terms, but "the hand which we held out has been rejected." It was clear that "the future of the nation is in our hands"; the Extremists had to "take up the work God has given us," to be ready "to sacrifice greatly and venture greatly because the mission also is great":

> What is it for which we strive? The perfect self-fulfilment of India and the independence which is the condition of self-fulfilment are our ultimate goal. In the meanwhile such imperfect self-development and such incomplete self-government as are possible in less favourable circumstances, must be attained as a preliminary to the more distant realisation. What we seek is to evolve self-government either through our own institutions or through those provided for us by the law of the land.

But the first need was for the Extremists to establish a national executive with branches throughout the country; eventually the Extremist party would replace the moribund Congress as the focus of nationalist activity in India.[124]

SINCE HIS RELEASE from jail, Aurobindo had had little to do with the revolutionaries. He advised leaders such as Jatindranath Mukherjee when they approached him, but his position as the country's most visible Extremist made more active involvement impossible. After the arrests of 1908 there had been a lull in revolutionary activity, but in 1909 it began to heat up again. In November 1909 an unknown terrorist threw a bomb at Lord Minto in Ahmedabad, but the viceroy escaped without injuries. A month later, members of a Maharashtrian group shot and killed the district magistrate of Nashik. Then, on January 24, 1910, a young Bengali named Birendranath Dutta Gupta shot Calcutta detective Shamsul Alam on the verandah of the Alipore courthouse. Birendranath was captured, but his accomplice Satish Sarkar got away. Satish ran to tell Jatin Mukherjee, who had planned the assassination. Rather rashly, Jatindranath told Satish to go to the *Karmayogin* office to inform Aurobindo. He was, Satish later recalled, "very happy" to hear the news.[125]

Aurobindo's happiness doubtless was genuine, but his feelings about terrorism had changed. Before Alipore he had looked upon actions as steps in the development of an organized militant insurrection. More recently he had grown aware of the "immense difference between Indian conditions in modern times and the historical precedents on which the revolutionists rely." Mechanized armies and well-armed police gave the government an unbeatable advantage.[126] After weighing the benefits of terrorism against the retaliatory damage that the government could inflict, he concluded that such activity was counterproductive. Terrorist acts would force the government to strike "repeated blows" that would paralyze "the hope and the effort to revive the activity of that broader and calmer Nationalism which, recognising modern conditions, still commands the bulk of the nation."[127]

Fresh blows were quick in coming. On February 8 the government passed a new Press Act that obliged press owners to deposit a security that would be seized along with the press itself if objectionable material was published. Consenting to the act, Secretary of State Morley wrote that it was just "a pill for an earthquake."[128] The Government of Bengal was ready to prescribe stronger medicine. The same men who seven months earlier had refused to deport Aurobindo alone now proposed to deport not just him but fifty-two others—practically every significant participant in the movement except the most innocuous Moderates. The Government of India, which earlier had pressed for Aurobindo's removal, could not approve of such a step, but it remained on the lookout for an acceptable way to eliminate its "most dangerous adversary." In the middle of January, H.A. Stuart, chief secretary of the Government of India, asked the Government of Bengal to look into the possibility of prosecuting Aurobindo for "To My Countrymen." A month later the chief secretary of the Government of Bengal informed the Government of India that Bengal would be willing to prosecute "if the connection of Arabinda Ghose with the *Karmayogin* can be definitely established."[129]

Aurobindo knew nothing of the two governments' efforts to deport or imprison him, but he did know that the press act spelled the end of the free expression of political opinion. He therefore announced in the *Karmayogin* that the paper would abstain "from comment on current Indian politics or criticism of Government and its measures until more favourable and normal conditions return." The Extremists were "doubly inhibited, inhibited from below by the paralysing effect of successful or attempted assassinations, inhibited from above by panic-stricken suspicion, panic-stricken repression." But the promoters of repression and revolution would have to settle their conflict on their own; the Extremists would stand aside, "sure that Time will work for us in the future as it has done in the past, and that, if we bear faithfully the burden of the ideal God has laid upon us, our hour may be delayed, but not denied to us forever."[130]

Aurobindo then ceased to write about politics in the *Karmayogin*. Its columns were filled with pieces on art, education, literature, and philosophy, as well as translations of the Upanishads. The philosophical articles take up, in a nonacademic way, some of the classic problems of the discipline: the relation between the individual and the cosmos, the puzzle of free will and fate, the origin and significance of evil. His essays on these subjects are clear and well expressed, though not particularly original. Many of them try to harmonize the Upanishads and late Victorian science by means of evolution. Some of his arguments now seem rather quaint. A seed grows into a certain sort of tree, Aurobindo wrote, because "the tree is the idea involved in the seed."[131] In the light of molecular biology, this is at best a vivid metaphor.

He passed his evenings at the *Karmayogin* office. After work, he sat with a group of young men: Bijoy Nag, Biren Ghose, and Nolini Kanta Gupta, all veterans of the Alipore trial; Suresh Chandra Chakravarty, known as Moni, the younger brother of another revolutionary; his brother-in-law Saurindranath Bose; and a few others. Deciding that his companions ought to be cultivating their minds, he provided them with books such as Thomas Carlyle's *French Revolution*, gave them lessons in Latin and French, and arranged for a tutor to teach them Hindi. He also got the idea of learning a little Tamil and engaged a Malabari pandit for the purpose. His desire to learn a language that was of no use to him in Calcutta seems to have stemmed, at least in part, from his contacts with men from the Madras presidency. In July he had met one of the promoters of the Swadeshi Steam Navigation Company of Tuticorin. A month or so later, he gave an interview to *India*, a Tamil weekly published by one of the company's main promoters, a man named S. Srinivasacharya. Toward the beginning of 1910 Srinivasacharya's brother Parthasarathi came to Calcutta and spoke with Aurobindo about their group's activities. Originally they had brought out *India* from Madras, but after the editor was arrested for sedition in 1908, they had shifted to the French-ruled enclave of Pondicherry.[132]

IN THE BEGINNING of February, the nine deportees were released. On the eleventh, Aurobindo was at the station when his uncle Krishna Kumar Mitra returned from the North. Four days later, he welcomed his old colleague Shyamsundar Chakravarty when his ship from Burma reached Calcutta. Quite possibly the same evening (or at most a day or two later), Aurobindo, Suresh, Biren and some others were sitting at the office when their friend Ramchandra Majumdar burst in. In an agitated voice, he said that Aurobindo was about to be arrested. A relative of his who worked in the police department had told him that a warrant had been issued. (This information was premature. The government was thinking of arresting Aurobindo, but the warrant would not be issued for another six weeks.) The young men began talking about what they would do. Aurobindo said nothing. After a minute, he stood up and announced that he was going to Chandernagore. He, Suresh, Biren and Ramchandra left the office almost immediately. Taking a twisting path through the alleys of north Calcutta, Ramchandra led them to the Hooghly. Seeing a boat at the ghat, he called out: "Hey, do you want a fare?" The boatman came over, and Aurobindo, Suresh and Biren got in. Within minutes they were on their way.[133]

Years later Aurobindo explained that when he heard Ramchandra's warning, he went within and heard a voice—an *adesh*—that said "Go to Chandernagore." He obeyed it without reflection. Had he given it any thought, however, he would have found good reasons to comply. Chandernagore was a French possession, one of five scattered enclaves that made up the French settlements in India. Outside the jurisdiction of the British police, it had become an important center of nationalist activity. For a man with a British warrant against him, it was the best place near Calcutta to go. The *adesh* also came at an opportune moment. Aurobindo had written ten days earlier that he would "refrain from farther political action" until a "more settled state of things supervenes"—something that was unlikely to happen very soon. This period of political paralysis coincided with his own wish to retire from politics and spend more time practicing yoga. In December, he had looked into the possibility of buying land outside Calcutta to found a spiritual ashram.[134]

Nothing came of this idea, but his urge to leave politics remained. It was only his awareness that his party depended on him that kept him in the field. But the return of Shyamsundar and the other deportees meant that the movement would not be leaderless if he left. In addition, the arrival of his uncle Krishna Kumar Mitra meant that his last family duty—looking after his aunt and her children—had come to an end.

This is not to suggest that he thought all this through when he decided to leave Calcutta. By his own account, his "habit in action was not to devise beforehand and plan but to keep a fixed purpose, watch events, prepare forces and act when he felt it to be the right moment."[135] The moment for his departure had come. As he sailed up the Hooghly in his little wooden boat, he probably was not looking further ahead than the next few days.

Chandernagore

At four the next morning the boat landed at the Chandernagore Strand. Aurobindo knew only one person in town, Charuchandra Roy, a high school principal who had founded a revolutionary group. He and Aurobindo had met in jail. Arrested after the testimony of Narendranath Goswami, Charuchandra spent a few months at Alipore before the French government intervened on his behalf. Those months had been the most terrible of his life. Middle-aged, married, with a respectable position in society, he had broken down completely when he found himself locked in a solitary cell. Had he been forced to remain any longer, he was sure he would have gone insane.

Once the boat was tied up at the ghat, Aurobindo sent Biren to find Charuchandra and ask him for shelter. When the young man knocked at his door, Charuchandra was far from pleased. He asked Biren to tell Aurobindo that he could not help. It would be best, he said, for Aurobindo to go to France. This caused some merriment back at the boat. Did the recusant revolutionary expect them to sail their little craft all the way to Marseille? Not knowing what to do, but certain his voice had not misled him, Aurobindo remained in the boat with his two companions. After an hour or so, a stranger approached. "Do you come from Calcutta?" he cried. "Why do you ask?" came the guarded reply. "Is Aurobindo Babu in the boat?" the stranger ventured. "Get into the boat, please," he was told.[136]

The stranger introduced himself as Motilal Roy. He was a member of a revolutionary group that was loosely connected with Charuchandra's. Ten minutes earlier he had been on his way to work when his friend Srishchandra

Ghose, the man who had helped to smuggle pistols into Alipore jail in 1908, had told him that Aurobindo had come to town, but that Charuchandra had refused to receive him. "What a pity the matter should end so discreditably," Srish concluded. Motilal was a fervent admirer of Aurobindo's. Learning that his idol had come to town, he started sprinting for the Strand.[137]

Once the young man had been admitted to the cabin, Aurobindo inquired how he had learned of his predicament. After Motilal explained, Aurobindo asked: "What can you do for me? Would it be convenient for you to shelter me?" Flushed with pride, Motilal blurted out: "Indeed, I have come to receive you. . . . Do not trouble yourself. I will take care of the arrangements personally."[138]

Aurobindo told Biren and Suresh to take the boat back to Calcutta. Once there, they should go to Nivedita, explain what had happened, and ask her to look after the *Karmayogin*.[139] Then he followed Motilal to his house. In an unused storeroom, Motilal spread a carpet on the dust-covered floor. Aurobindo "sat down noiselessly like a marionette." Leaving his guest to himself, Motilal went off to do some errands. When he returned, he found Aurobindo "sitting silently with his eyes fixed in an upward stare." He had, the young man thought, "utterly resigned himself to God. When he talked, words came out of his mouth as if someone else made him speak. If his hand moved, it was controlled as it were by a third agency."[140]

Aurobindo passed that day in Motilal's storeroom. At night he was taken to another man's house, where he spent the next twenty-four hours. When Motilal saw him again, Aurobindo asked if he could take him back to his house. Aurobindo had had to share a room with another person and found this disturbing. Motilal agreed, and readied a room. Here Aurobindo passed the next few days.

All told, Aurobindo spent a month and a half in Chandernagore. For security reasons, Motilal and his friends kept shifting him from house to house. During these weeks, Aurobindo later wrote, he was "entirely engaged in Sadhana." His power of yogic vision developed enormously. Writing appeared in the surrounding "ether." Sometimes this *akasha lipi* brought knowledge of the past, the future, or the remote present. He also saw *rupas*, or forms, that seemed to be significant. Many of them were of ordinary objects, but there was also the occasional deity. Three goddesses appeared that he identified as Ila, Saraswati, and Sarama, Vedic *devatas* who represent "three out of the four faculties of the intuitive reason,—revelation, inspiration and intuition."[141]

Motilal had long been fascinated by yoga and was delighted to find himself in the company of an advanced practitioner. Perhaps out of gratitude for the young man's assistance, Aurobindo set aside his reticence and answered questions. He had spoken about yoga with others before, but had never treated anyone as a disciple. Motilal may have been his first. Before leaving Chandernagore, he gave him one or more *mantras,* the traditional sign of initiation.

Aurobindo remained in contact with people in Calcutta through his cousin Sukumar Mitra, who sent him clothing and other necessities as well as oral and written communications. Aurobindo's absence from Calcutta had by now been noticed, and there was much speculation as to his whereabouts. In response to an imaginative newspaper story, Aurobindo wrote this tongue-in-cheek paragraph, which was published in the *Karmayogin* on March 19:

> We are greatly astonished to learn from the local Press that Sj. Aurobindo Ghose has disappeared from Calcutta and is now interviewing the Mahatmas in Tibet. We are ourselves unaware of this mysterious disappearance. As a matter of fact Sj. Aurobindo is in our midst and, if he is doing any astral business with Kuthumi or any of the other great Rishis, the fact is unknown to his other Koshas ["sheaths"]. Only as he requires perfect solitude and freedom from disturbance for his Sadhan for some time, his address is being kept a strict secret. . . . For similar reasons he is unable to engage in journalistic works, and *Dharma* has been entrusted to other hands.[142]

At the time this was written, Nivedita had edited four issues of the *Karmayogin.* All of them contained pieces by Aurobindo that he had left behind in Calcutta. Nivedita herself contributed articles on religion and politics and kept alive Aurobindo's column, "Passing Thoughts." This helped to create the impression that Aurobindo was still in charge. At one point during his stay in Chandernagore he wrote enough material to fill three issues of the journal: three installments of "Passing Thoughts," three "Conversations of the Dead," three "Epistles from Abroad," three poems, two satirical sketches, and a number of essays on history, art, and yoga. The manuscripts of these writings were sent to Calcutta, but were not published.

Aurobindo's friends in Chandernagore had difficulty sheltering him. Aware that the present arrangement was not viable, they began looking into various alternatives. Then, sometime in March, Aurobindo received another *adesh*: "Go to Pondicherry." Pondicherry, the capital of the French settlements in India, was more than a thousand miles to the south. Between it and Chandernagore lay the entire length of British India. Getting from one place to the other would be a problem. After working out the outlines of a plan, he wrote notes to his cousin Sukumar Mitra and to Suresh Chandra Chakravarty, giving each a mission. Sukumar was to arrange for Aurobindo's passage to Pondicherry, Suresh to go there beforehand and tell the local Extremists of his impending arrival. Sukumar learned that the steamship company Messageries Maritimes offered service to Colombo and France by way of Pondicherry. The next departure, by the *Dupleix,* would be on the morning of April 1. Aware that his house was under surveillance and that he was shadowed wherever he went, Sukumar asked a friend named Nagendrakumar Guharoy to come to his house at College Square. Pointing out two trunks, he told Nagen to take them to his hostel and to return the next day. When Nagen arrived, Sukumar gave him a sum of money and told him to buy two tickets for Colombo on board the *Dupleix* from a travel agent. The second ticket was for Bijoy Nag, the former member of Barin's society, who would be traveling with Aurobindo. Sukumar told Nagen that the passengers' names were Jotindra Nath Mitter and Bankim Chandra Bhowmik. Nagen was to inform the company that one of the passengers was weak from malaria, so that both would board the ship from their boat and not at the wharf. Nagen followed these instructions to the letter.

While Sukumar and Nagen were making the arrangements, Suresh was traveling south on the Madras Mail. The young man, only eighteen years old, had been selected to go to Pondicherry because, unlike most of his friends, he did not have a police record. Feeling silly in brand-new European clothes, he had gone to the station on March 28 and taken his seat in a second-class compartment. It was his first trip out of the province and he was both excited and tense. All he had with him was a small bag, a pulp novel called *Love Made Manifest,* a few rupees, and a letter from Aurobindo addressed to Parthasarathi Iyengar, care of the *India* office, Pondicherry. Suresh arrived in the French city early on the morning of March 31. As soon as it was light, he went in search of the *India* office. Getting directions was not easy, as he knew no Tamil or French and only a little English.

The same morning, Sukumar, Motilal, and others were finalizing their plan to get Aurobindo from Chandernagore to Calcutta.[143] Three boats would be involved: one to ferry him across the river to Agarpara, another to take him downstream to Uttarpara, where the third boat, from Calcutta, would meet him and take him to the wharf. The first two legs of the journey went well, but when Aurobindo and his companions reached Uttarpara, they missed their rendezvous with the third boat. Amarendranath Chatterjee, who had arranged the second boat, decided to take it all the way to Calcutta. Arriving at the wharf and finding no one there, Amar took Aurobindo by carriage to 6 College Square. Sukumar was not at home, so they returned to the wharf and waited.

When Nagen Guharoy, who had hired the third boat, realized that he had missed Amarendranath's boat, he went back to Calcutta. Once there, he hurried to College Square, where he reported to Sukumar. Sukumar told him to go to the *Dupleix* and remove Aurobindo's trunks. While he was doing this, Nagen was told that the passengers had missed the medical examination and would have to go directly to a doctor's house to take it. But they had to hurry; no one could board the ship after eleven o'clock. Nagen returned to College Square. By this time Sukumar had learned that Aurobindo and Bijoy were at the wharf, and he told Nagen to take the trunks and tickets and hurry there. At the wharf, Nagen finally met up with Amarendranath and Aurobindo. He jumped into their carriage and they rushed off to find the doctor. By then the younger men were all rather frazzled; Aurobindo, in contrast, was "absolutely calm."[144]

The doctor lived on Theatre Road, just off Chowringhee Avenue. He saw "Jotindra Nath Mitter" and "Bankim Chandra Bhowmik" at about ten o'clock. While examining the first passenger, the doctor remarked that he had an excellent command of English. Aurobindo replied that he had been educated in England. Within a few minutes the passengers were on their way. An examination at the wharf might not have gone so well. Two policemen were on duty there, and Aurobindo's face was known.

The passengers with their escorts reached the ship just before eleven o'clock. Once safely in the cabin, Amar gave some money to Aurobindo and made *namaskar*. Nagen, more formally, placed his head on Aurobindo's feet. He and Amar then said goodbye. A few hours later, the *Dupleix* weighed anchor and began its journey south.

AT THE TIME OF HIS DEPARTURE, Aurobindo was planning to remain in Pondicherry for a few months, perhaps a year. His purpose in going—as he had written in the *Karmayogin*—was to obtain "perfect solitude and freedom from disturbance for his Sadhan for some time." As he would write to another newspaper, he also needed freedom from disturbance "by political action and pursuit."[145] This meant that he planned to stay underground until the charges against him were disproved. Beyond that, the length of his retirement depended on his *sadhana*. A process had begun that he intended to see through to the end.[146] But by saying that he needed solitude to do yoga "for some time," he implied that he intended to resume his public if not his political activities. As it turned out, he remained in solitude for the rest of his life.

In retrospective accounts, Aurobindo mentioned his *adesh* and the need to concentrate on yoga as the reasons for his withdrawal from politics. But he also remarked that from the end of 1909 he had been pondering the course of the movement, and had decided "that the nation was not yet sufficiently trained to carry out his policy and programme." Two possible alternatives presented themselves to him: a Home Rule movement along Irish lines and a Gandhi-style movement of passive resistance. Whatever their virtues—and both would be used with some success—he knew that he could never lead such movements. That would have meant drawing back from the goal of independence, and it was not in his nature to do this.[147]

Aurobindo wrote later that at the time of his departure he could see that the government would "have to begin trying to meet the national aspiration half-way," and would eventually concede freedom rather than having it wrested away. He therefore felt that the success of the movement was sure.[148] He had to look beyond the obvious to be so assured. The British still controlled the country; the Extremist party was broken and rudderless; the movement as a whole was disorganized and ineffectual. Much work had to be done to turn the promises of 1906 into the fulfillment of 1947. It was thus not unnatural, when he declined to return to the field, that many connected with the movement became disillusioned with him. Jawaharlal Nehru put it mildly when he wrote in 1962, "most of the people of my generation, who were immersed in political aspects of our struggle, did not understand why he did so [retired from politics]."[149] K.M. Munshi, Aurobindo's greatest admirer among Congress politicians, even wondered whether Aurobindo's "flight" was due to the "latent roots" of fear. There is no evidence to support this conjecture. Barin Ghose, who was not above criticizing his brother, wrote that everyone who had met him agreed that "fear is a thing unknown to him." It would have been quite possible, thought Barin, for Aurobindo "to have guided the revolutionary movement from outside British India if he chose, but he was too utterly sincere to do so as he had already felt how the higher light claimed him for its own."[150]

Aurobindo's career in Indian politics lasted just four years, from February 1906 to February 1910. For a year of that time he was a prisoner in Alipore jail; during the first six months he was inactive and unknown. This leaves two and a half years when he played a major role, and even then he remained "behind the scenes" as much as possible. Two and a half years is not a long time, particularly when viewed against the sixty or more years that the freedom movement lasted. Yet Aurobindo is often regarded as one of the protagonists of the movement, one of the founding fathers of the nation. Even those who would dispute his place in the national pantheon concede that he was a highly influential leader and thinker. He was active at the moment when Indian nationalism came of age. Between 1885 and 1905 the Congress accomplished virtually nothing. Aurobindo was among the first to present a reasoned critique of this unproductive body. He soon was silenced, but eleven years later, when the *swadeshi* movement began, he came to Calcutta and helped to turn the Congress into an instrument of political change.

Stock narratives of the freedom movement devote much attention to the clash between the Moderates and Extremists. The importance of this conflict may be overplayed, but it is broadly true that there was no real freedom movement until the Extremists set forth their aims and methods. The primary aim, political independence, was announced by Aurobindo in the columns of *Bande Mataram*. Derided at the time as the dream of a visionary or the ravings of a lunatic, it was adopted as the goal of the Congress in 1929—twenty-three years later—and then accepted by the nation at large.

Chief among the Extremists' methods was passive resistance. Taken up spontaneously at the start of the boycott movement, it was first explained in detail in Aurobindo's *Doctrine of Passive Resistance* and later developed as a strategy of "no control, no co-operation." Twelve years later, in the hands of Gandhi and his colleagues, passive resistance became the movement's primary tool. But there was a difference between passive resistance as preached by Aurobindo and as practiced by Gandhi. Aurobindo regarded it as a valuable strategy for a country in India's position, but he also insisted that a country so positioned had the right to use violence to achieve its aims. Gandhi and his followers abjured violence on principle. They obtained good results by means of nonviolent noncooperation, but it cannot be denied that violence real and threatened did as much as passive resistance to bring the British to the negotiating table. If the government consented to deal with Gandhi, it was because they were obliged to accept him as the lesser of two evils.

At the beginning of the twentieth century, Aurobindo and his colleagues were proud to call themselves nationalists. At the beginning of the twenty-first century, this term has lost most of its glow. Looking back over the last hundred years, it is clear that many of the worst injustices and atrocities have been committed by self-professed nationalists. But it would be wrong to group pre-1947 Indian nationalism with the kind that drove Europe into World War I or encouraged the rise of Benito Mussolini, Adolf Hitler, and Slobodan Milošević. Indian nationalism arose in response to an intolerable situation: domination by foreigners who bled the land of its wealth and regarded those they called natives as members of an inferior race unfit to govern their own country. Indian nationalism had no ambitions outside its borders and no plan to eradicate its minorities; it failed, however, to solve the problem of communalism. Aurobindo regarded religious conflict as a purely social matter, refusing to see it as a vital political issue. He tried, half-heartedly, to bring Muslims into the movement, but he never gave the problem the attention that hindsight shows that it deserved. But could anything said or done in 1907 have changed the outcome forty years later? Probably not. Still, partition and the bloodletting that accompanied it were the movement's principal failings, and Aurobindo and his colleagues have to take their share of the blame.

Aurobindo is remembered more for his ideas than his active leadership. Yet for more than a year, April 1907 to May 1908, he directed the Bengal Extremists, and for a somewhat shorter period, May 1909 to February 1910, he was the most active Extremist strategist and spokesman in the country. During these intervals he proved himself to be an effective leader. Recent scholarship has downplayed the importance of political leadership in the independence movement. The commemorative historiography of the postindependence years has been replaced by a search for the voice of the "subaltern," the neglected lower classes. By and large, this has been a healthy development. A narrow focus on leaders and parties is fine for schoolbooks and rallies, but it misses social and economic issues and underrates the activities of the masses. But subaltern historiography has its weaknesses too, notably its blindness to the power of ideas. Mass movements do not simply happen. The masses have to be aroused and mobilized, and this usually is done by elites—Mirabeau, Mazzini, Lenin, Aurobindo, Gandhi.

Aurobindo's role as a nationalist leader was primarily that of strategist and organizer. His characteristics in this work were intransigence and a preference for behind-the-scenes maneuvers. His intransigence tended to limit his effectiveness. At the Calcutta Congress of 1906, the Extremists got their program across because pragmatists such as Tilak were ready to take over once the idealists had their say. Three years later, when Aurobindo was on his own, his inability to compromise made it impossible for him to reach a settlement with the Moderates just when the parties needed each other to survive.

Englishmen skilled in the ways of parliamentary politics, such as Ramsay MacDonald, could see that Aurobindo, for all his brilliance, did not have the makings of a frontline politician. He was, as a perceptive CID official wrote, "much more a poet and a mystic than a man of action." Many of Aurobindo's nationalist colleagues shared this view. Labor organizer A.C. Banerjea "always thought him more a philosopher than a politician." Charuchandra Roy said similarly: "Sri Aurobindo is a learned man, there is no doubt of it. He is a good man, there is no doubt of it either. But he has never been a practical politician, that is also without any doubt."[151] Aurobindo himself conceded that he was "more fitted for intellectual pursuits like poetry than for politics." But once involved, he used his intellectual powers effectively. His chief aim in entering politics was "to get into the mind of the people a settled will for freedom and the necessity of a struggle to achieve it."[152] He succeeded in infusing this will into the mind of a whole generation.

"Was Aurobindo a man of action?" This question was asked by K.M. Munshi, a seasoned politician, in 1951. He answered it himself: "It is a superficial view which identifies a man of action necessarily with restless hours, ceaseless jostling with men, with public meetings and newspaper headlines. If action implies power to move men, Aurobindo was a great Karmayogi."[153] This may be simply another way of saying that Aurobindo was less a man of action than a man of ideas; but it also acknowledges that ideas change people and people change the course of events.

Aurobindo (seated center) and his family in England, 1879.

Aurobindo in England, circa 1886.

Left: Aurobindo with his wife Mrinalini, 1901.

Below: Aurobindo (seated right) with other officers of the Baroda State, Kashmir, 1903.

Above: Aurobindo with Baroda College
students, 1906.

Right: Aurobindo holding a copy of
Bande Mataram, September 1907.

Nationalist conference in Surat, December 1907. Aurobindo, the conference president, is seated at the table; Bal Gangadhar Tilak is addressing the gathering.

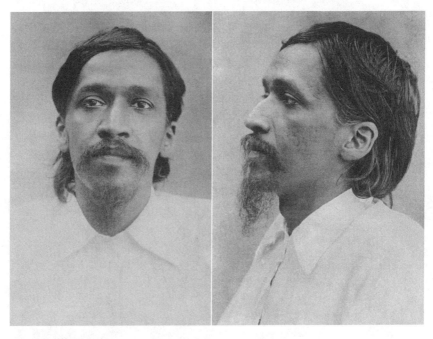

Police photographs of Aurobindo taken while he was a prisoner in Alipore Jail, 1909.

Aurobindo in Pondicherry, circa 1915.

Mirra Richard in Japan, 1916–1920.

Rabindranath Tagore (center), with
Mirra Richard and Paul Richard
(right), and others, Japan, 1917.

Aurobindo in Pondicherry, circa 1915–1918.

Aurobindo with Nolini Kanta Gupta (seated right), Suresh Chandra Chakravarty (standing right), and others, circa 1915–1918.

Above: The house at 9 rue de la Marine ("Library House") during the 1920s.

Right: Sri Aurobindo and the Mother giving darshan, April 24, 1950 (photograph Henri Cartier-Bresson).

Sri Aurobindo in his room in Pondicherry, April 25, 1950 (photograph Henri Cartier-Bresson).

Sri Aurobindo on his deathbed ("*mahasamadhi*"), December 5, 1950 (photograph Vidyavrata Arya).

PART FOUR: *Yogi and Philosopher*

And philosophy! Let me tell you in confidence that I never, never, never was a philosopher—although I have written philosophy which is another story altogether. I knew precious little about philosophy before I did the Yoga and came to Pondicherry—I was a poet and a politician, not a philosopher. How I managed to do it? First, because Richard proposed to me to cooperate in a philosophical review—and as my theory was that a Yogi ought to be able to turn his hand to anything I could not very well refuse: and then he had to go to the war and left me with 64 pages a month of philosophy all to write by my lonely self. Secondly, I had only to write down in the terms of the intellect all that I had observed and come to know in practising yoga daily and the philosophy was there automatically. But that is not being a philosopher!

6. A Laboratory Experiment

Pondicherry, 1910–1915

I am no longer first and foremost a politician, but have definitely commenced another kind of work with a spiritual basis, a work of spiritual, social, cultural and economic reconstruction of an almost revolutionary kind, and am even making or at least supervising a sort of practical or laboratory experiment in that sense which needs all the attention and energy that I can have to spare.

In French India

While Aurobindo and Bijoy were steaming south aboard the *Dupleix,* Suresh was trying to convince the Pondicherry Extremists that Aurobindo was about to arrive. After reaching the town on March 31, 1910 Suresh had gone to the *India* office in search of Parthasarathi Iyengar. Parthasarathi was not there, but his brother, Srinivasacharya, was. He read the letter Suresh had brought and said that he would make the necessary arrangements. In the meantime, Suresh would be his guest. For the next three days, Suresh sat around the house, reminding his host occasionally that Aurobindo's ship was due on April 4. Each time, Srinivasacharya waved him aside with an insouciant "We're looking into it." As far as Suresh could tell, nothing was being done. Finally he insisted on seeing the place they had fixed up for Aurobindo. A young man took him to a run-down neighborhood and showed him a room above a printing establishment. Suresh was stunned but too embarrassed to protest.[1]

As the owner of a newspaper that had been banned in British India, Srinivasacharya was taking no chances. Two years earlier, the registered editor of *India* had been tried for sedition and sentenced to five years' hard labor. Warned that he was next on the list, the actual editor, Subramania Bharati, took refuge in Pondicherry. Srinivasacharya soon joined him there. It did not take long for the CID to find them, and from then on they were kept under surveillance. Though Aurobindo's letter seemed genuine, and Suresh's story convincing, Bharati and Srinivasacharya decided to keep Suresh in the dark.

At the same time they went to a friend of theirs, a businessman named San-kara Chettiar, and asked him if he could take Aurobindo in. Chettiar gave them the top floor of his house to use. Bharati and Srinivasacharya readied the place and also began to make arrangements for a reception. Suresh was horri-fied when he got wind of this. He reminded them that Aurobindo was wanted by the police, and would not be amenable to a public reception. The Tamil men were disappointed, but agreed to drop the plan.[2]

The *Dupleix* had an uneventful voyage along the coast of eastern India. At around two o'clock in the afternoon on April 4, 1910 it cast anchor off Pondi-cherry.[3] Aurobindo and Bijoy went up on deck to scan the launch that was meet-ing the ship. They were relieved when they saw that Suresh was aboard. When the launch reached the *Dupleix*, Suresh clambered up the ladder, followed slow-ly by Srinivasacharya. After brief greetings, they all went to Aurobindo's cabin for tea. Once arrangements had been made to remove the luggage, the four men boarded the launch and in fifteen minutes were standing on French soil. A carriage was waiting for them. Aurobindo and Srinivasacharya got in and set off down the Cours Chabrol. Srinivasacharya explained that a friend had lent them an apartment on the top floor of his house. Aurobindo was hoping for a place of his own, but said he would take a look. When they reached the house and Aurobindo was taken upstairs, he saw that it was as good a hiding place as anyone might desire. When the door at the head of the stairs was closed, the apartment stood on its own. Set back from the facade, it could hardly be seen from below. An air shaft in the wall ran all the way to the ground, permitting the occupant to hear what was happening below and to send and receive things by means of a makeshift dumbwaiter. It seemed to Suresh as if the place had been designed for hiding fugitives. He, Bijoy, and Aurobindo moved in at once. It would be three months before any of them set foot outside.

Aurobindo's first impression of Pondicherry was that "it was absolutely dead."[4] But the colony had had an eventful history. Bought by the French from the Raja of Gingee towards the end of the seventeenth century, it be-came their base in their struggles with the British and the Dutch for control of southern India. The apogee of French influence came around 1750, when Joseph François Dupleix established a protectorate over Arcot and won pock-ets of territory from Rajahmundry to Srirangam. Its nadir came just ten years later, when the British captured Pondicherry and destroyed it. Later restored to the French, the town passed between them and their rivals five times in the next fifty years. Finally, after the Napoleonic wars, Pondicherry, Chand-ernagore, and three other enclaves were reorganized as the Établissements Français dans l'Inde.

The side of town closest to the sea, known as the Ville Blanche, or White Town, contained the governor's palace, administrative buildings, and a number of fine old houses. To visitors from France, the streets evoked the provinces of their youth, or of a vanished epoch. Wandering in the Ville Blanche a decade before Aurobindo's arrival, the novelist Pierre Loti was delighted to find names like "Rue Royale" carved in stone in eighteenth-century letters. But his overall impression was one of torpor and decay. The streets were deserted. The untended fountain and square had an air of "infinite sadness."[5] Across a drainage canal lay the Ville Indienne, or native quarter—less politely, the Ville Noire, or Black Town—an outgrowth of the village that was all the French found when they arrived. More animated than the White Town, it contained shops, bazaars, and temples, along with clusters of brick and mud houses in which several thousand Tamils lived. They went about their business for the most part unconcerned with what the handful of foreigners and creoles in the White Town said or did.

THE DAY AUROBINDO reached Pondicherry, the warrant for his arrest that had been rumored since February was issued. He was charged with sedition for writing and publishing the article "To My Countrymen." Another warrant was issued against the printer of the paper, Manmohan Ghose (no relation), who was arrested. Aurobindo was classed as an absconder when the warrant against him could not be served. For two weeks, rumors of his whereabouts abounded. At one point the police were certain that he had gone to Tibet and looked into the possibility of extraditing him from there. Finally it was reported that he was in Pondicherry. Within a few days his presence was confirmed, but nobody believed that he intended to stay in the sleepy French port for long. Fresh warrants were applied for in Bombay, Madras, and Colombo. It was rumored that he was on his way to Europe. But Aurobindo did not move from Pondicherry. Mindful of the attitude of the French when Charuchandra Roy had been arrested the year before, Secretary of State Morley cabled the viceroy: "No extradition should be asked for."[6]

Morley had learned about the warrant and investigation along with everyone else in London when an article appeared in the *Times* on April 7. Perturbed, he wrote to Minto: "Under what law has the warrant been issued? Does the article contain direct incitement to violence or assassination?"[7] Morley feared repercussions at home. He did not have long to wait. That afternoon, Ramsay MacDonald stood up in the House of Commons and asked if the *Times* report was true. He did not get an answer for three weeks. During the interval Morley pressed the Governments of India and Bengal to withdraw the prosecution. He wanted to know what the authorities thought indictable in an article that, on the face of it, was rather innocuous. He had not been enlightened by April 28, when MacDonald again raised his question. Edwin Montagu, the parliamentary undersecretary for India, tried to brush the matter aside, saying that the government did not have enough information to answer. MacDonald refused to accept this and initiated a debate that lasted for an hour and a half. If the warrant had been issued with evidence behind it, "why had it not been served, and why was Mr. Arabindo Ghose still allowed [to be] at large? It was well known," the Labour M.P. added, that "Mr. Ghose had left public life and become a religious recluse." He had been "tried on an accusation which might have cost him his life, and acquitted. But even after that acquittal it was common report in India that he was actually put on the suspected list and considered for deportation." Quoting at length from Aurobindo's writings, MacDonald noted that they constituted an effective criticism of terrorism. He closed by saying that unless the government administered India "with more generosity, some catholicity of sentiment, and some serious effort to associate with themselves men like Mr. Arabindo Ghose, the future was going to be much darker than it was at present." He was followed by his colleague Keir Hardie, who insisted that the government declare that "the movement [in India] would not be prevented by intimidation of this kind." When Hardie had finished, Montagu answered. As the case would soon be taken up, it was not proper for anyone in Parliament to comment on it. If Aurobindo was acquitted, MacDonald and Hardie could question the government's conduct.[8] A short while later, Aurobindo read a summary of this debate in the *Hindu*, a nationalist newspaper of Madras. This helped shape his course of action. Until judgment was delivered in the *Karmayogin* case, he would remain under cover in Pondicherry.

AUROBINDO KEPT TO HIMSELF in Sankara Chettiar's house. He went to the first floor once a day to take his bath, to the second floor to use the toilet, and to the kitchen to eat. Otherwise he remained in his room except for an occasional stroll on the veranda. To avoid being discovered, he asked Suresh and Bijoy to remain in the house as well.[9] Despite these precautions, detectives identified them not long after their arrival. Thereafter there were always a group of plainclothesmen sitting across the street.[10] One of them reported around this time that Aurobindo seemed "to be in very poor health" and was "greatly reduced." It was rumoured that he was "suffering from some kidney trouble."[11] A year in jail, followed by nine months of hectic activity and six weeks of forced seclusion, had not done his body any good. But for the first time since leaving Baroda, he could lead a regular life in reasonably healthful circumstances.

Aurobindo slept on the floor on a thin mattress. He rose around 5:30, and a half-hour later, was served a cup of tea. At ten o'clock Suresh and Bijoy began to prepare the day's meal, using vegetables brought from the market by Chettiar's servants. The menu never changed: rice, *moong dal,* eggplant, and pumpkin. The meal was served South Indian style, on banana leaves spread on the floor. Aurobindo ate quickly and returned to his room. At four, he had another cup of tea, and before retiring, a small serving of *payas.* As a mark of respect, his tea was sent in a silver tumbler. It never occurred to Chettiar, no tea-drinker himself, that a thin metal vessel was not the best for serving a hot liquid. Twice a day for six months the tea came in the silver tumbler; twice a day Aurobindo drank it without complaint. Anyone else, thought Suresh, would at least have dropped a hint that a porcelain cup was more suitable. Aurobindo simply drank his tea. This silent bearing of discomfort seemed to Suresh to reveal a significant characteristic of Aurobindo's nature:

> Many practice austerity, some willingly, some because they have no choice. But in most cases it is done with a kind of secret suppressed complaint. Or else there is a sense of having performed a sort of penance, an egoistic feeling of self-satisfaction in what one has done. But in Aurobindo's case it was straightforward and natural, without any showing off or desire for praise.[12]

At one point while staying in Chettiar's house, Aurobindo undertook a fast. He had fasted before, for ten days, in Alipore Jail. This time, he fasted for twenty-three. During this period, he maintained his usual activities: *sadhana,* writing, and walking for eight hours a day. He felt no reduction of strength, but lost ten pounds. When he began to eat again, he did not increase gradually, as generally is recommended, but by taking at once his usual amount.[13]

AUROBINDO'S ONLY REGULAR visitors were Srinivasacharya and Bharati. Srinivasacharya, a man of about thirty, had been educated in Pondicherry's Calvé College. Returning to the family home in Triplicane, Madras, he became involved in the nationalist movement. One of his cousins started *India* in 1906 or 1907, and it soon became the most outspoken nationalist newspaper in the city. Its success was due largely to the genius of Bharati, its editor.

Acclaimed a literary prodigy while still a child, he dedicated his pen to the national movement from the time of the partition of Bengal. Many of the poems for which he is famous were published first in *India*.

Bharati and Aurobindo were both intellectual "all-rounders," as Bharati's friend Ramaswami Aiyangar remarked. To listen to their talks was "a sort of variety entertainment. Only the level was very high." Ramaswami was struck that when Aurobindo spoke about revolution, he did not administer an oath of secrecy or anything like that. This was, he thought, "a very remarkable trait in Aurobindo's character. He trusted our honour and sense of patriotism."[14] It also helps to explain how the police found it easy to get information about Aurobindo and his friends.

Ramaswami first came to Chettiar's house at the request of K. V. Ranga-swami Iyengar, a landowner in the Kaveri delta region. Rangaswami admired Aurobindo for his nationalistic writings, but he had another reason for wanting to meet him. His grandfather's guru, a man called Sri Vasudeva, had died some thirty years earlier. Asked by his disciples who they should turn to when he was gone, he replied that "a Yogi from the North would come as a fugitive to the South and practice there an integral Yoga." This yogi would make himself known by three sayings. Aurobindo had come from the North as a fugitive, and practiced an integral (*purna*) yoga. As for the sayings, might they not be the "three madnesses" he had mentioned in one of the letters to his wife, which were published at the time of his trial?[15] Rangaswami Iyengar requested an interview with Aurobindo to confirm his inference. Convinced after the meeting that Aurobindo was the promised yogi from the North, Rangaswami decided to help him. A while earlier, while doing some automatic writing, Aurobindo had received a series of yogic teachings in English. It seemed to him that the spirit who transmitted them might have been that of the reformer Ram Mohun Roy. Be that as it may (it should be remembered that he came to ascribe most such writings to "a dramatising element in the subconscious mind"),[16] the sessions resulted in a nine-chapter book called *Yogic Sadhan*. When Rangaswami heard about the book, he arranged to have it printed. He also, at some point, promised to give Aurobindo some direct financial help.

Two weeks into their stay in Pondicherry, Aurobindo, Bijoy, and Suresh noticed an increase of activity in the normally moribund town. Gangs of drunken men roamed through the streets, shouting, throwing stones, and intimidating anyone who happened to be out. When the newcomers asked what the trouble was, they were told: no trouble, just the French elections. Selected male residents of Pondicherry enjoyed the right to elect a representative to the French Chamber of Deputies. All of the candidates were French, and few had ever laid eyes on the colony. Every four years, two contenders—one for the European and one for the *Hindou* (Indian) party—paid agents in Pondicherry to do what was necessary to get them elected. The agents engaged in massive electoral fraud, hiring bands of local hooligans to make sure the voting went their way. The Indian party had been successful in the last few elections because its mafia was better organized. But in 1910 a faction of the party switched to the other side. The violence was worse than ever, reaching its peak on election day, April 24. When the ballots were counted, the European candidate, a Parisian journalist named Paul Bluysen, was pronounced the winner.[17]

A few days after the election, Srinivasacharya and Bharati paid a routine visit to Aurobindo but made an unusual request. There was a Frenchman who wanted to meet him, they said. His name was Paul Richard. A barrister at the Court of Appeals in Paris, Richard had come to India on the understanding that he would be a candidate, but on his arrival in Bombay, he learned that the ticket had been given to someone else.[18] Undeterred, he continued on to Pondicherry, where he observed the election and met some local politicians. While speaking with Chettiar and Chettiar's friend Zir Naidu, he remarked that he was eager to meet a yogi. Was there anyone in Pondicherry who could help him get in touch with one? Chettiar or Naidu blurted out that a yogi had recently come to Pondicherry, but unfortunately he refused to see anyone. Excited, Richard asked them to arrange a meeting. If the yogi refused to speak with him, he would be satisfied with a glimpse from afar. They said they would do what they could. The next time Srinivasacharya and Bharati went to Chettiar's house, he told them about his conversation with Richard. They said they would talk to Aurobindo about it.[19]

Upstairs in Aurobindo's room, Bharati and Srinivasacharya apologized for their friend's indiscretion. But they asked whether he might not consider meeting the Frenchman. Aurobindo refused outright. He had no intention of satisfying a visitor's curiosity. Bharati and Srinivasacharya persisted. Their position in Pondicherry was insecure, they said. Friendship with a Parisian barrister might be useful for them all. Aurobindo relented. He would see the man once, but not for long.

That evening, the two Tamil men brought Richard to Sankara Chettiar's house and introduced him to Aurobindo. Richard told them about his life. Born in a village near Montpellier in 1874, he had been educated in Marseille and done military service in North Africa. Returning to France, he entered a seminary to prepare for the Protestant ministry. In 1900 he was sent to

Lille, where he served for four years as a clergyman in the French Reformed Church, but then quit the cloth to study law. Two years later, he ran for public office and lost. Moving to Paris, he became a barrister but continued to look for ways to enter politics. At the same time he began to attend meetings of occult and spiritual organizations. Once he traveled to Algeria to meet the head of the Mouvement Cosmique, a group that taught a modernized Kabbalah. In France he became acquainted with Mirra Alfassa, a member of the movement's Paris chapter. Soon the two were living together. With Mirra's help, Richard began to write books on spiritual subjects. Their first production was *L'éthère vivante* (The Living Ether). Toward the beginning of 1910, one of Richard's colleagues suddenly asked: "Would you like to take my place as a candidate for the election in Pondicherry?"[20] Richard jumped at the chance, and soon was on his way to India.

As he spoke with Aurobindo, Richard began to feel that the two of them were destined to work together. Aurobindo, at first distant, eventually warmed to the Frenchman. Their talk became animated. Richard had plenty of ideas, but for the moment he had to return to France. While there, he would speak to people he knew about the plight of the refugees of Pondicherry. The two said good bye and agreed to stay in touch.

DURING HIS SIX-MONTH STAY in Chettiar's house, Aurobindo wrote a good deal, as he had, for the first time since 1907, the leisure to undertake an extended work. In jail he had received a few lines of a poem about the fall of Troy. Unable to write them down, he kept them in memory for more than a year. In April 1910 he resumed work on the poem, a narrative in dactylic hexameters called *Ilion*. He derived its plot from his study of classical sources, but its details came from his inner vision. As he wrote in one passage:

> So they arrived from Zeus, an army led by the death-god.
> So one can see them still who has sight from the gods in the trance-sleep
> Out from the tent emerging on Phrygia's coasts in their armour ...
> Mixed in a glittering rout on the Ocean beaches one sees them,
> Perfect and beautiful figures and fronts, not as now are we mortals
> Marred and crushed by our burden long of thought and of labour;
> Perfect were these as our race bright-imaged was first by the Thinker.[21]

More beautiful than any of the Greeks was the Amazon Penthesilea. Aurobindo's treatment of her appears to have been influenced by Kali or Durga, the terrible forms of the Mother Goddess. Such an archetype seems to have been in his mind, for a month after finishing the first book of *Ilion,* he began work on a play about the attempt of a spirited woman to stab a king to death. *Eric,* set in Norway in the age of the Vikings, features Aurobindo's usual dramatic characters: a handsome contender for a throne and a high born lady in the guise of a serving woman. In the end, King Eric marries the beautiful, dangerous Auslaug, who has given him what he most needed:

> Strength in the nature, wisdom in the mind,
> Love in the heart complete the trinity
> Of glorious manhood.[22]

AUROBINDO LATER EXPLAINED that he came to Pondicherry "with some intention of returning to the political field under more favourable circumstances."[23] He seems to have told Bijoy and Suresh that he would be staying in South India for around three months. Apparently he thought that the *Karmayogin* case would take that long to decide. It took considerably longer. Proceedings against the printer (and Aurobindo in absentia) continued through the month of May. Secretary of State Morley did not hesitate to tell the viceroy that he thought the prosecution was a mistake: "As to the famous Arabindo, my satisfaction is not at all lively. . . . I have always understood that proceedings for sedition were only advised when a conviction was reasonably certain. Is a conviction reasonably certain in this case? I should think decidedly not, and I *hope not.*"[24] Nonplussed by Morley's attitude, Minto tried to defend himself in a letter of May 26: "As to the celebrated Arabindo, I confess, I cannot in the least understand your hope that we shall not get a conviction against him! I can only repeat what I said to you in my letter of April 14th that he is the most dangerous man we have now to reckon with. . . . In the meanwhile Arabindo is in Pondicherry where he seems to have formed some undesirable French connections [the reference presumably is to Paul Richard] and will probably sail for France."[25] Three weeks later, the viceroy had the pleasure of reporting that the *Karmayogin*'s printer had been found guilty of sedition and sentenced to six months' hard labor. After the verdict was handed down, orders were passed declaring Aurobindo a fugitive from justice and attaching his property. The defense began to work on an appeal, which was filed in the middle of August. After considerable delay, the case was put on the schedule of the Calcutta High Court.

Aurobindo certainly could not return to British India before the appeal had been heard. But he had begun to think that he might stay in Pondicherry for a while whatever the outcome. During his last few months in Calcutta, he had felt a strong pressure to devote more of his time to yoga, and his stay in Pondicherry reinforced this feeling. As he meditated and thought at Chettiar's place, "the magnitude of the spiritual work he had taken up appeared to him and he saw that it would need the exclusive concentration of all his energies."[26] He wrote this passage, in the third person, a quarter of a century later. In 1910 he said little to those around him; but at least once, while speaking with Bharati and Srinivasacharya about his vision of a "divine life," he added that "when he had that divine illumination he found within himself something compelling him to break away from his present political life, and at the same time there was some other thing in him which resisted and refused to do so; it was only after a few days' struggle that he gained peace of mind when [he] decided to give it up."[27] A rationalist, Srinivasacharya noted certain circumstances that might have helped Aurobindo arrive at his decision. First there was the meeting with Richard, and the barrister's promise to speak to influential people in France. Second there was Rangaswami Iyengar's interest in Aurobindo. In October the landowner honored his promise, sending 1,000 rupees to cover Aurobindo's expenses for a year.

A short while before this, Mrinalini's cousin Saurin Bose came to Pondicherry. If he brought a message from Mrinalini or her father, nothing is known of it. Saurin decided to join the household, which soon moved to a rented house at 42 rue de Pavillon. The new place was owned by a relative of Sankara Chettiar's named Sundara Chettiar, who let it out for 20 rupees a month. This was a low rent for the property, but Aurobindo could never have afforded it without Rangaswami's money.

A month after he and the three young men moved into Sundara Chettiar's house, Aurobindo wrote a letter to the editor of the *Hindu* announcing his presence in Pondicherry:

> I left British India over a month before proceedings were taken against me and, as I had purposely retired here in order to pursue my Yogic sadhana undisturbed by political action or pursuit and had already severed connection with my political work, I did not feel called upon to surrender on the warrant for sedition, as might have been incumbent on me if I had remained in the political field. I have since lived here as a religious recluse [a phrase borrowed from MacDonald], visited only by a few friends, French and Indian, but my whereabouts have been an open secret, long known to the agents of the Government and widely rumoured in Madras as well as perfectly well-known to every one in Pondicherry. I find myself now

compelled, somewhat against my will, to give my presence here a wider publicity. . . . I wish, at the same time, to make it perfectly clear that I have retired for the time from political activity of any kind and that I will see and correspond with no one in connection with political subjects. I defer all explanation or justification of my action in leaving British India until the High Court in Calcutta shall have pronounced on the culpability or innocence of the writing in the KARMAYOGIN on which I am indicted.[28]

This was published in the *Hindu* on November 8. When Aurobindo opened his copy of the paper, he was surprised to find not only his letter, but a news item reporting that the Calcutta High Court had delivered its judgment in the *Karmayogin* case the previous day. The two judges found "To My Countrymen" not seditious and set aside the printer's conviction. After expressing his pleasure in the judges' decision, the writer of the story went on to speculate that Aurobindo "would probably now return to the field of his public activities" without fear of "the minions of the law."[29] Many others in British India, in particular Aurobindo's associates, must have thought the same thing. They were destined to be disappointed. Aurobindo had already decided to stay in Pondicherry. Even when it became clear that he would not be arrested if he returned to British India, he chose not to return to Bengal. He would remain in Pondicherry for a year or two, until he had finished his *sadhana*.

A Seed Plot

Aurobindo lived in Sundara Chettiar's house for about six months. It was a large, airy place, only three blocks from the sea, and he was "decidedly better off here than [when] he was living in the Black Town," as the British consul reported to the Government of India.[30] A servant helped with the chores. A dog, Yogini, joined the household. Each evening, Suresh, Bijoy, and Saurin walked on the beach. Soon they were joined by Nolini Kanta Gupta, a former revolutionary who had been tried and acquitted at Alipore.

Bharati and Srinivasacharya visited less often, as they lived on the other side of town. But once Aurobindo's presence became public knowledge, he began to receive visits from people he did not know from every part of India. By February the problem had become so acute that he had to write to the *Hindu* "to seek the protection of publicity against attempts that are being made to prejudice my name and reputation even in my retirement in Pondicherry." One visitor who was denied admission to the house started making a scene, telling people that he had the Maniktala bomb formula and was ready to use it. Aurobindo took him for "a dismissed spy trying to storm his way into the kingdom of heaven." More generally, Aurobindo was

> besieged by devotees who insist on seeing me whether I will or not. They have crossed all India to see me—from Karachi's waters, from the rivers of the Punjab, whence do they not come? They only wish to stand at a distance and get mukti by gazing on my face; or they will sit at my feet, live with me wherever I am or follow me to whatever lands. They clamber on to my windows to see me or loiter and write letters from neighboring Police stations. I wish to inform all future pilgrims of the kind that their journey will be in vain and to request those to whom they give reports of myself and my imaginary conversations, to disbelieve entirely whatever they may say.[31]

Aurobindo's unwanted celebrity drove him deeper into seclusion. Most of the time he remained in his room, meditating, writing, and exercising by walking back and forth for hours. He continued to work on *Ilion* and *Eric* and rewrote the drama *Rodogune,* which the Calcutta police had seized when arresting him. Other writings that can be dated to this period are a group of essays on philosophy and yoga, and some curious texts written in Greek, Latin, French, Italian, German, and other languages. These may be related to the philological research he was engrossed in at this time. His study of Tamil led him to a comparative study of that language and Sanskrit, and this launched him into a "far more interesting research": to discover the "true law, origins and, as it were, the embryology of the Aryan tongues."[32] This led him to the Vedas. Despite his familiarity with the Upanishads and the *Gita,* he had only a passing acquaintance with these most ancient of Indian scriptures. When he took them up in Pondicherry, he was surprised to discover a concealed system of psychological meanings that threw light on his yogic experiences. Pursuing this research, he wrote commentaries, translations, and notes on the significance of Vedic root-words and their relationship to those of other languages.

In April 1911, Aurobindo took a two-year lease on a house at 10 rue St. Louis. He still had not abandoned his idea of returning to Bengal when his *sadhana* was finished, but the two-year lease makes it clear that he did not think this would happen anytime soon. A letter he wrote to his father-in-law that July gave Bhupalchandra the idea that Aurobindo "was anxious to return home." But even when Bhupalchandra learned from the British that Aurobindo could return to Bengal "as a perfectly free man," Aurobindo made no move in that direction.[33] Another letter of July, this one written to Paul Richard, makes Aurobindo's reasons clear: "I need some place of refuge in which I can complete my Yoga unassailed and build up other souls around me. It seems to me that Pondicherry is the place appointed by those who are Beyond, but you know how much effort is needed to establish the thing that is purposed upon the material plane."[34]

For Aurobindo to remain in Pondicherry, he needed freedom from interference by the colonial governments and a reliable source of funds. Even after he had learned that he could go to Bengal a "free man," he still believed that the British would harass him and arrest him if they could. He may have been right about this. Bureaucrats in London and Calcutta continued to refer to him as "dangerous." Some wanted him behind bars. But the Earl of Crewe, the new secretary of state for India, thought it would be better if he remained where it was. "Aurobindo, dangerous though I daresay he is in fact, is well known here [in London]," he wrote in a note to the viceroy. He "ought not to have been attacked [in the *Karmayogin* case] without the clearest proof."[35]

By the Summer of 1911 things seemed to be moving towards normalcy. Then William Ashe, the collector of Tirunelvelli, Madras presidency, was shot dead. The assassin, a young man named Vanchi Aiyar, killed himself after the attack. His accomplice fled but was caught, and from him and other sources, the CID learned that Vanchi Aiyar had been coached by V. V. S. Aiyar, a Tamil revolutionary living in Pondicherry. Warrants for complicity in the murder were issued against V. V. S. Aiyar, Srinivasacharya, Bharati, and three others.[36] Aurobindo was not named in the investigation and certainly was not connected with the murder, but he knew that the Ashe case would compromise his position in Pondicherry. An article published in the *Madras Times* in July confirmed his apprehensions. Under the heading "Anarchism in the French Settlements," the writer said:

> The recent tragedy has done a service of no small value to the welfare of this province, by drawing the attention, both of the authorities and the public, to the mischief being wrought by the political refugees in Pondicherry. . . . If our correspondent is correctly informed, there is an organised Party in French India which supports Mr. Arabindo Ghosh and his friends. That party, however, is, evidently, not very strong at present, and we do not doubt that the majority of French Colonials, whether European

or Indian, would accord their support to a measure designed to secure the extradition of Political offenders from French territory.[37]

Aurobindo wrote the letter in which he told Richard that he needed a place where he could complete his yoga "unassailed" a day or two after reading this. He evidently felt that his "place of refuge" was in jeopardy, and asked Richard to do what he could. Sometime later, the Frenchman had good news to report. A letter requesting Aurobindo's extradition had been sent to Paris, where it came to the attention of Mattéo Alfassa, an official in the colonial office, who happened to be the brother of Richard's wife Mirra. Aware of his brother-in-law's friendship with Aurobindo, Alfassa saw to it that letter was not acted on.[38]

In mid-July, Aurobindo wrote a letter to the editor of the *Madras Times,* which declined to publish it. He therefore was obliged to ask the *Hindu* "for the opportunity of reply denied to me in the paper by which I am attacked." The *Times* had said that Aurobindo wore the robe of a *sannyasi* but continued to be an active revolutionary. Aurobindo replied: "It is untrue that I am masquerading or have ever masqueraded as an ascetic; I live as a simple householder practising Yoga without Sannyas just as I have been practising it for the last six years." He then rebutted various assertions made in the *Times* article, including the claim that Pondicherry was "swarming with dangerous people from British India."[39] In a second letter he restated the reasons for his withdrawal to Pondicherry:

> I left British India in order to pursue my practice of Yoga undisturbed either by my old political connections or by the harassment of me which seemed to have become a necessity of life to some police officials. Ceasing to be a political combatant, I could not hold myself bound to pass the better part of my life as an undertrial prisoner disproving charge after charge made on tainted evidence too lightly accepted by prejudiced minds. . . . I have practised an absolute political passivity. I have discountenanced any idea of carrying on propaganda from British India, giving all who consulted me the one advice, "Wait for better times and God's will."[40]

Aurobindo's letters did little to relieve the tension in Pondicherry. In the wake of the Ashe murder, a horde of policemen descended on the town. By the Autumn of 1912 one inspector, nine sub-inspectors, and forty-five men were keeping track of thirty-nine suspects. These were divided into four classes, designated A, B, C, and D. Class A consisted of men believed to be complicit in Ashe's murder: V. V. S. Aiyar, Srinivasacharya, Bharati, and three others. They were to be shadowed closely and arrested if they entered British India. Aurobindo, his four Bengali companions, Ramaswami Aiyangar, and eleven other Tamils comprised Class B. They were to be shadowed wherever they went. The men in the other two classes were simply kept note of.[41] Aurobindo was little affected by the shadowing, as he rarely if ever went out. But the others could not move without someone moving behind them, out of reach but never out of sight.

The British could do little so long as the suspects remained in Pondicherry. At one point it was rumored that the police were plotting to kidnap and carry them across the border. The Class A suspects were the main targets, but Aurobindo's companions were afraid that he too was on the list. They armed themselves with bottles of acid and remained vigilant until they felt that the danger had passed.[42] Another plot—this one not just rumored—involved an attempt to plant false evidence. A man named Mayuresan who had made a decent living supplying information to the British decided to sell his wares to the French. He forged some papers purporting to show that Aiyar and the Bengali refugees were connected with a terrorist plot. This "evidence" was sealed in a jar and thrown into Aiyar's well, where it was meant to be discovered by the French police acting on a tip from Mayuresan. Before this could happen, Aiyar's maidservant noticed the jar. She pointed it out to her employer, who took it to Srinivasacharya and Bharati. The three then went to Aurobindo, who suggested that they report the matter to the French. Srinivasacharya arranged a meeting with the governor, who told them to complain to the police. A short while later, an investigating magistrate was sent to search the houses of Aiyar, Srinivasacharya, Bharati, and Aurobindo. In the course of his search of Aurobindo's place, the magistrate came across some Latin and Greek texts: "*Il sait du latin, il sait du grec!*" he muttered. A man who knew the languages of Horace and Homer could hardly be a threat to the French Republic. Apologizing for the intrusion, he said good bye.[43]

Writing to Motilal Roy in Chandernagore on July 3, 1912 Aurobindo noted that his problems with the government were disappearing, but his monetary difficulties were acute. "The situation just now," he said, "is that we have Rs 1 1/2 or so in hand." Srinivasacharya and Bharati had no money to lend. A messenger sent "to the South"—presumably to Rangaswami Iyengar—had not come back, and in any case, it did not appear as though Rangaswami could supply all the money they needed. Aurobindo therefore had to look for other sources. One of these was Motilal himself, who in 1911 had visited Pondicherry and seen for himself the penury to which Aurobindo and the others had been reduced. Aurobindo did not speak about the problem, but Saurin begged Motilal to send fifty rupees a month. Motilal did what he could, obtaining funds by "any means that came to my hands—from my family expenses, my business-income, my wife's ornaments, by loan."[44] In his letter of 1912 Aurobindo asked him to contact a relative of Bijoy's who had taken an interest in him. He also enclosed a letter to one of his Baroda friends, which he asked Motilal to forward. "If he can give you anything for me," he wrote, "please send it without the least delay. If not, I must ask you to procure for me by will-power or any other power in heaven or on earth Rs. 50 at least as a loan."[45]

AUROBINDO CORRESPONDED REGULARLY with Motilal over the next eight years. A letter he wrote just after his birthday on August 15, 1912 is important for what it says about his *sadhana* and his plans for future work. His birthday, he wrote, was "usually a notable day for me personally either in Sadhana or life." This time it marked a major turning point in his yoga:

> My subjective Sadhana may be said to have received its final seal and something like its consummation by a prolonged realisation and dwelling in Parabrahman for many hours. Since then, egoism is dead for all in me except the Annamaya Atma,—the physical self which awaits one farther realisation before it is entirely liberated from occasional visitings or external touches of the old separated existence.[46]

In Aurobindo's system of yoga, *parabrahman* is the "the supreme Reality with the static and dynamic Brahman as its two aspects." He had realized the static *brahman* first in 1908, while meditating with Lele. The realization of the active *brahman,* or cosmic consciousness, followed a few months later, in Alipore jail. The *parabrahman* realization, he later understood, was the third of the "four great realisations on which his Yoga and his spiritual philosophy are founded." It prepared the way for the final realization, "that of the higher planes of consciousness leading to the Supermind."[47] Of these planes, and the supermind, he was only dimly aware in August 1912. All that he knew at the time was that his "physical self" awaited "one farther realisation before it is entirely liberated from occasional visitings or external touches of the old separated existence."[48]

The realization of *parabrahman* had given him "the essential knowledge or Shakti [power]," Aurobindo explained to Motilal. His future *sadhana* would be "for life, practical knowledge and Shakti . . . established in the same physical self and directed to my work in life." This work would have four parts, as Aurobindo wrote:

> 1. To re-explain the Sanatana Dharma [eternal law of being] to the human intellect in all its parts, from a new standpoint. This work is already beginning, and three parts of it are being clearly worked out. Sri Krishna has shown me the true meaning of the Vedas, not only so, but he has shown me a new Science of Philology showing the process and origins of human speech so that a new Nirukta [Vedic etymology] can be formed and the new interpretation of the Veda based upon it. He has also shown me the meaning of all in the Upanishads that is not understood either by Indians or Europeans. I have therefore to re-explain the whole Vedanta and Veda in such a way that it will be seen how all religion arises out of it and is one everywhere. In this way it will be proved that India is the centre of the religious life of the world and its destined saviour through the Sanatana Dharma.
>
> 2. On the basis of Vedic knowledge, to establish a Yogic Sadhana which will not only liberate the soul, but prepare a perfect humanity and help in the restoration of the Satya Yuga [Age of Truth]. That work has to begin now but it will not be complete till the end of the Kali [Iron Age].
>
> 3. India being the centre, to work for her restoration to her proper place in the world; but this restoration must be effected as a part of the above work and by means of Yoga applied to human means and instruments, not otherwise.
>
> 4. A perfect humanity being intended, society will have to be remodelled so as to be fit to contain that perfection.[49]

Aurobindo's program would keep him busy for the rest of his life. So far he had started on only the first two parts, scholarly writing and the founding of a new yogic *sadhana*. The scholarly work was focused on the Vedas and linguistics. A year or so earlier, he had purchased three ledgers from the Pondicherry bazaar. On the first page of each he wrote a title. The first was "Origines Aryacae. Material for a full philological reconstruction of the old Aryabhasha from which the Indo Aryan and Dravidian languages are all derived." The second was "The Rig-Veda with a Translation and Commentary in English," and the third, "Record of Writings in Different Languages, whether acquired by inspiration, communication or by the writing in the ether."[50] He made considerable progress on the first two projects, but his scholarly mind, then as throughout his life, could not confine itself to three or four lines of research. The ledgers were soon filled with different sorts of writings: translations of and commentaries on the Upanishads, essays on philosophy and yoga, studies of the *Mahabharata* and *Ramayana,* a translation of Kalidasa, passages for *Eric,* and two medium-length poems. This flood of writing soon spilled over into ten or twenty other notebooks.

While producing this extensive body of literature, Aurobindo had "begun but on a very small scale the second part of my work which will consist in making men for the new age by imparting whatever Siddhi [perfection] I get to those who are chosen. From this point of view, our little colony here is a sort of seed plot, a laboratory. The things I work out in it, are then extended outside." The "little colony" was Aurobindo's household, consisting for the moment of himself and four or five others. His work with them was "progressing at last on definite lines and with a certain steadiness, not very rapid, but still definite results are forming."[51] It is not unusual for a man of realization to transmit his discipline to others. What may have been unique in Aurobindo's case was his doing so without letting his "disciples" know what he was doing, or even asking them to follow a spiritual life. The four young men spent their time walking about, playing football, and amusing themselves. According to one detective, they were said to worship Kali, and "their worship apparently permitted unbridled license of which they took the fullest advantage."[52] Though certainly exaggerated, the description suggests a rather bohemian lifestyle. Aurobindo gave some of them lessons in Latin, Italian, and French, the closest he came to giving them anything like *upadesha* or yogic training. Ramaswami Aiyangar, who spent several years in the house, reported later: "I know nothing about his yoga."[53] Aurobindo apparently never brought the subject up.

In speaking of his "colony" to Motilal, Aurobindo clarified that he had no desire to found a religious body. Motilal had mentioned the Ramakrishna Mission, an organization founded by Swami Vivekananda to perpetuate the work of Ramakrishna. Aurobindo had the greatest respect for Ramakrishna and Vivekananda, and he had received spiritual help from both. But he felt that the Mission had fallen into the "error of all 'Churches' and organised religious bodies." By keeping "too much to the forms of Ramakrishna & Vivekananda," the people of the Mission made it impossible to "keep themselves open for new outpourings of their spirit."[54] He was determined to prevent such stultification. His yoga would have no prescribed methods, no fixed forms.

ALTHOUGH AUROBINDO WAS unwilling to receive casual visitors, he made exceptions for friends and friends of friends. Two people who met him in the house in rue St. Louis in 1911 and 1912 left detailed accounts of their visits. In November 1911 Alexandra David-Néel, later famous as the first Caucasian woman to enter Tibet, came at the suggestion of Paul and Mirra Richard. Her impressions of Pondicherry tally with those of Pierre Loti and other French literary tourists: "a dead city that had once been something and remembered it, rigid in its dignity, irreproachably correct, concealing beneath an impeccable coat of whitewash the cracks in the old walls." Aurobindo received her in an upstairs room, bare of all but a table and two chairs. He "was sitting in one of the chairs, his back to a wide-open window. Nothing could be seen through the window, neither building nor tree. The vast green sky of India filled it entirely, on which the outline of the guru was traced." They spoke in French—Aurobindo's distinguished by "a great purity of expression"—about "the ancient philosophical ideas of India." His approach to mystical matters suited her perfectly. "He belongs to that uncommon category that I so much admire, the reasonable mystics," she later wrote. "He thinks with such clarity, there is such lucidness to his reasoning, such luster in his eyes, that he leaves one with the impression of having contemplated the genius of India such as one dreams it to be after reading the noblest pages of Hindu philosophy." Aurobindo spoke to her about his "experiments" in consciousness. She was struck by the "careful and meticulous control" with which he conducted them.[55]

David-Néel spent only a day or two in Pondicherry. When she arrived in Madras, she was met at the station by a well-dressed European. Thinking he was someone sent by her friends, she followed him to the waiting room. "You must be a member of the Theosophical Society," she remarked. "No," the man replied, "I am the chief of police." She was surprised, but only a little. "I had heard of Aurobindo as a distinguished philosopher," she offered. "He certainly is a very remarkable scholar," the official said, "but he is a dangerous man. We hold him responsible for the recent assassination of Mr. Ashe." David-Néel was unfamiliar with the name. When the chief of police explained, she answered that it seemed "very improbable that the learned man who had spoken to me knowledgeably on philosophical topics was an assassin." The chief of police replied, "He certainly did not kill Mr. Ashe himself. He had him killed."[56] A few weeks later, in Calcutta, she received a letter from the viceroy. Lord Hardinge explained that it was sometimes "difficult for a Government to know whether the relations of an individual with a political refugee are of a political or a philosophical nature."[57]

For David-Néel the matter ended there. Another of Aurobindo's visitors paid more heavily for his indiscretion. D. L. Purohit, an officer in Baroda State, whom Aurobindo had known when he was there, had been asked by the Gaekwar to make a study of religious institutions in India. Why exactly he went to Pondicherry is not clear. The Gaekwar himself may have suggested it. In any event, when Purohit arrived on July 23, 1912 he visited Aurobindo and gave him a copy of his questionnaire. Aurobindo read it but talked mostly about his yoga. Purohit left after a couple of hours. The detective who had followed him from the station continued to shadow him and submitted a report afterward. Two months later, the dewan of Baroda, under pressure from the British political agent, forced Purohit to resign.[58]

The CID clearly had not lost its interest in Aurobindo. This was partly because the revolutionary movement was flourishing, particularly in Bengal. Between April 1911 and April 1913 there were thirty attempted or successful political robberies or murders in India, and all but two were the work of Bengali *samitis.* One of the most active was based in Chandernagore and led by Srish Ghosh and Motilal Roy.

Aurobindo was at least partly aware of Motilal's involvement in the *samiti.* In a note written thirty years later, he observed that while "he dropped all participation in any public political activity" after his arrival in Pondicherry, he did "for some years" keep up "some private communication with the revolutionary forces he had led, through one or two individuals."[59] The reference is to Motilal and his friends. Aurobindo's letters to Motilal contain allusions to "Tantric books," "Tantric kriyas," and the like. These, according to Motilal, were code words for revolutionary actions and equipment. In his letter of August 1912—the one in which he spoke of his *parabrahman* experience—Aurobindo also asked Motilal for particulars about the sending of "Tantric instruments." These "instruments" were six revolvers that Motilal had ordered from France and wanted to be sent to Chandernagore through the French post. It was impossible to arrange a prompt dispatch, and the revolvers had to be buried. When they were unearthed and sent a year later, it was found that they "had become practically useless."[60]

In the letter of 1913 Aurobindo spoke about Motilal's "Tantric Kriyas," that is, revolutionary actions. Several were organized at this time; one of them was the most dramatic assassination attempt in the history of Indian terrorism. Toward the end of 1911 a relative of Srish's named Rashbehari Bose came to Chandernagore. He and others decided to assassinate the viceroy when he made his ceremonial entrance into the new capital of Delhi. Motilal introduced two recruits to Rashbehari, who selected one, Basanta Biswas, to do the job. After a year of planning and training, Rashbehari and Basanta went to Delhi in December 1912, armed with a bomb manufactured in Chandernagore. On December 23, Basanta, dressed as a woman, threw the bomb at Hardinge while he sat with his wife and an attendant on the back of an elephant. The attendant was killed; the viceroy gravely wounded. Basanta and Rashbehari escaped.

Aurobindo referred to this event in a letter of January 1913: "About Tantric Yoga; your experiment in the smashana [cremation ground, i.e., Delhi] was a daring one,—but it seems to have been efficiently and skillfully carried out, and the success is highly gratifying." He went on to say that "in these Kriyas there are three considerations to be held in view," namely, the object, success in attaining it, and *angarakshana,* or "protection of the body" of the practitioner. Aurobindo had taken upon himself the function of repeating an *angarakshana mantra,* or spell of protection. It was up to Motilal to arrange activities in such a way that *bhutas,* or ghosts—that is, the police—did not spoil their plans.[61] It would seem from this that Aurobindo was pleased with the attempt to assassinate the viceroy. But his apparent endorsement of Motilal's activities is hard to reconcile with his evident distress at Hardinge's injuries, which he frequently expressed in his diary.[62] Presumably his attitude toward Motilal's activities was the same as his attitude toward Barin's five years earlier: "it is not wise to check things when they have taken a strong shape" because "something good may come out of them."[63] He certainly never ceased to believe that Indians had the right to use violence to topple a government maintained by violence. But he did not believe in individual terrorism, and he felt more than ever that terrorist acts were against India's long-term interests.

Aurobindo's financial situation remained critical. In April 1913 he and his friends had to leave the house on rue St. Louis when they failed to produce the money to renew their lease. They moved to a place in the center of town, at 59 rue des Missions Étrangères. It was a reasonably good house for the rent they paid, fifteen rupees a month. Built in the old Tamil style, it had three successive courtyards, each surrounded by rooms and a veranda. Aurobindo stayed in a room off of the innermost courtyard, Suresh in the middle, and Nolini, Bijoy, and Saurin in the front. The four young men spent most of their time outside. Aurobindo rarely left the house. In the morning he meditated and wrote; in the afternoon he exercised by walking around the courtyard for three or four hours. Bharati lived nearby and visited every evening, usually with Srinivasacharya. The men talked about literature and politics. Bharati told the latest bazaar gossip. There were stories, jokes, and laughter. If the orthodox Srinivasacharya was absent, the spirit of irreverence extended to religion. When the visitors returned home, people crowded around to hear what Aurobindo had said.

A new addition to the group was Aravamudachari Iyengar, a young friend of Ramaswami Aiyangar's. Because he was not on the British surveillance lists, Aravamuda, soon renamed Amrita, did errands that the others could not do, such as dropping off letters at the French post office. Bijoy's relative Nagen Nag, who suffered from tuberculosis, had begun to live in the house. Amrita sometimes saw Aurobindo visit Nagen in his room. He would "take his seat on the same mat with the sick man, put to him some questions and return to his room." He seemed so preoccupied as he walked past Amrita that the boy believed he did not even notice him. "And yet," he was told, "nothing could escape his notice."[64]

Nagen had some money, and with his help they relocated to a larger place at 41 rue François Martin. The new house had more than enough space for the eight permanent members of the household: Aurobindo, Bijoy, Suresh, Saurin, Nolini, Ramaswami, Nagen, and an attendant of Nagen's named Biren. Aurobindo lived on the first floor in two small rooms. Across the street an enormous silk cotton tree spread its branches.

Life and Yoga

In the early years of Aurobindo's residence in Pondicherry, while he was writing, doing research, corresponding, receiving visitors, balancing the budget, exercising, and feeding the dog, he was also deeply involved in yoga. That "also" may give the wrong idea. The motto of Aurobindo's spiritual practice was "All life is Yoga." Expanding on this in 1914, he wrote that people who followed the traditional paths of yoga, which aim at absorption in the Absolute, tended "to draw away from the common existence and lose [their] hold upon it." His own path aimed instead at reuniting "God and Nature in a liberated and perfected human life." It relied on methods that "not only permit but favour the harmony of our inner and outer activities and experiences in the divine consummation of both."[65]

Aurobindo expressed this aim and method in his daily practice. Rejecting the ascetic life, he did yoga as a "householder." He avoided fixed techniques, spent much of his time reading and writing (and not only about "spiritual" subjects), and passed an hour or two in the evening talking and joking with friends. He lived in a rented house, wore ordinary clothes, observed no dietary restrictions, smoked, and occasionally drank. It became a matter of principle not to reject any human activity, but to incorporate all of life into his yoga. He liked to quote the Latin maxim *nihil humani alienum*, "nothing human is alien to me."[66]

Before he came to Pondicherry, his yoga had proceeded along fairly tradi-tional lines. But by 1912 he could write to a friend of "a new system of Yoga" that had been "revealed" to him. He stressed the unorthodoxy and unexpected-ness of his yoga when he told D.L. Purohit that his was "not the conventional method of Patanjali [the author of the *Yoga Sutras*]," but "the natural method" he had "stumbled upon in his meditations." This makes the discovery seem almost accidental. In a letter to Richard, Aurobindo gave himself more credit by speaking of "the theory and system of yoga which I have formed."[67]

The new system came to him in a series of Sanskrit formulas during his early years in Pondicherry. There were seven main formulas, each of which had four main elements. This gave the system its name: *sapta chatusthaya*, the seven quaternaries. On November 20, 1913 he wrote a synopsis of this system. The summary that follows is based on this and other sources.[68]

The seventh *chatusthaya*, or quaternary of perfection, gives an overview of the system. Its four elements are *shuddhi*, purification; *mukti*, liberation; *bhukti*, beatitude or enjoyment; and *siddhi*, perfection. These are the traditional aims of the practice of tantric yoga. Yogic systems based on the tantras differ from those based on Sankhya and Vedanta in that they take as their central principle not the *purusha* or conscious soul, but rather "Prakriti, the Nature-Soul, the Energy, the Will-in-Power executive in the universe." As a result, there is a difference of approach. The tantric yogi, "instead of drawing back from manifested Nature and its difficulties ... confronted them, seized and conquered."[69] Aurobindo's yoga was not identical to traditional tantric yoga, but like tantric yoga, it aimed at perfection and transformation of the world and life.

The first step on the path toward perfection, Aurobindo wrote, "is some fundamental poise of the soul ... regarding and meeting the things, impacts and workings of Nature," which one can reach "by growing into a perfect equality, *samata*."[70] This is the first element of the first *chatusthaya*. The impacts of the world are met first by indifference, then by rising above them, and finally by accepting them as the will of God. In the end, every touch is experienced as bliss. The next two elements of the first *chatusthaya* are *shanti*, a peace so firm that there is an "absence of all disturbance and trouble," and *sukham*, "a positive inner spiritual happiness and spiritual ease of the natural being which noth-ing can lessen." Finally comes *hasyam*, "an active internal state of gladness and cheerfulness which no adverse experience mental or physical can trouble."[71]

"The next necessity of perfection" in Aurobindo's system "is to raise all the active parts of the human nature"—called, using terms from traditional Indian philosophy, *buddhi*, or intellect; *manas*, or sense-mind; *prana*, or life;

and *sharira*, or body—to their "highest condition and working pitch," their full *shakti* or power. This is the first element of the second *chatusthaya*. Along with *shakti* comes the development of the various types of human personality (*virya*) and the lifting of these types to their divine equivalent (*daivi prakriti*). None of this can be done without the help of the fourth element, *sraddha*, or faith in God and his *shakti*.[72]

Even if raised to a higher power, human nature is at best a reflected image of the divine unless it evolves from a mental into what Aurobindo called a "supramental" being. This is the field of the third or *vijnana chatusthaya*. Supermind or *vijnana* is a power of fully effective knowledge and will. Between the full supermind and ordinary thought lie various powers of vision, inspiration, intuition, and intuitive discrimination. Together these make up *jnana*—higher knowledge or genius. When *jnana* is "applied to the actuality of things, their details of event, tendency etc. in the past, present & future," it is called *trikaldrishti*, the knowledge of the three times, a power held in India to be "a supreme sign of the seer and the Rishi."[73] It was also glimpsed by William Blake, who wrote:

> I see the Past, Present & Future, existing all at once
> Before me.[74]

The various powers of *jnana* and *trikaldrishti* sometimes manifest in *samadhi* or yogic trance. By means of *samadhi* "the range of knowledge & consciousness" can be extended "through all the three states of waking, sleep & dream," enabling the consciousness to awaken to experiences and realizations "to which the ordinary waking consciousness is blind."[75] The full perfection of the *vijnana chatusthaya* includes the development of certain powers, "called specially *siddhis* because of their abnormal nature, rarity and difficulty," though they are not supernatural powers but rather unusual developments of capacities that are latent in all human beings. Following an ancient tradition, Aurobindo spoke of eight *siddhis*: two of knowledge, *prakamya* and *vyapti*; three of power, *aishwarya*, *ishita*, and *vashita*; and three of the body, *mahima*, *laghima*, and *anima*.[76] The *siddhis* of knowledge constitute what is known in the West as telepathy. The *siddhis* of power are applications of will by which one mind can influence another. The *siddhis* of the body overlap with the next *chatusthaya*, the quaternary of the body.

The powers of the fourth or *sharira chatusthaya* manifest when the *vijnana* "brings in a spiritualising and illumination of the whole physical consciousness and a divinising of the law of the body."[77] The first power, *arogya*, is freedom from disease. The second, *utthapana*, is "the state of not being subject to the pressure of physical forces." This comes about by the combined action of the three *siddhis* of the body: *laghima*, or lightness, *anima*, or subtlety, and *mahima*, "an abnormal strength which is not muscular." *Saundarya*, the third element of the *chatusthaya* of the body, is physical beauty. *Vividananda*, the last element, is physical delight in its various forms.

Aurobindo said relatively little about the fifth and sixth *chatusthayas*, the quaternary of divine action and the quaternary of the *brahman*. But he did allude to them in a letter of 1916:

> As [the members of the first and second *chatusthayas*] become firmer and more complete, the system is more able to hold consistently and vividly the settled perception of the One [that is, the *brahman*] in all things and beings, in all qualities, forces, happenings, in all this world-consciousness and the play of its workings. That founds the Unity and upon it the deep satisfaction and growing rapture of the Unity....
>
> When the Unity has been well founded, the static half of our work is done, but the active half remains. It is then that in the One we must see the Master and His Power,—Krishna and Kali as I name them using the terms of our Indian religions.[78]

The first *chatusthaya* was the basis of Aurobindo's yoga; the seventh was its fulfillment. But the course of his yoga was not a linear movement from first to last, but rather an interwoven development of all of the elements of all of the *chatusthayas* simultaneously. This complexity added greatly to its difficulty. An element considered perfectly established on a given level in a given conjunction might need to be established again when the conjunction changed or the *sadhana* rose to a higher level. Each ascent entailed a movement of return, in order to "apply the spiritual knowledge utterly to the world and to the surface psychological and outer life and to effect its transformation both on the higher levels of Nature and on the ordinary mental, vital and physical levels down to the subconscience and basic Inconscience and up to the supreme Truth-Consciousness or Supermind." This application of yoga to life, he wrote years later, would take "decades of spiritual effort to work out towards completeness."[79] In the beginning he thought things would move much faster. In July 1911 he wrote to Richard:

> The principal object of my yoga is to remove absolutely and entirely every possible source of error and ineffectiveness, of error in order that the Truth

I shall eventually show to men may be perfect, and of ineffectiveness in order that the work of changing the world, so far as I have to assist it, may be entirely victorious and irresistible. It is for this reason that I have been going through so long a discipline and that the more brilliant and mighty results of Yoga have been so long withheld.[80]

Here "so long" meant three and a half years. During most of that time, he had given his attention to purification or *shuddhi*. Work on the other parts began in earnest after he came to Pondicherry. By 1911 he was able to report that he could "put himself into men and change them," that he "had been given the power to read men's characters and hearts, even their thoughts" (here he added: "but this power is not yet absolutely complete"), that he could guide action "by the mere exercise of will," and that he was "in communication with the other world" (adding that this was "yet of a troubled character").[81] Although he did not use the terms, these are workings of *vyapti, prakamya, aishwarya, ishita, vashita,* and *samadhi*—all elements of the third *chatusthaya*.

BETWEEN 1912 AND 1920 and again in 1927 Aurobindo kept a detailed record of the state of his *sadhana* in a series of diaries. He gave them various names: "Record of Yoga," "Journal of Yoga," "Notebook of the Sadhana," "Yoga Diary," and so on. Published posthumously between 1986 and 1994, they were grouped under the general title *Record of Yoga*. In a typical *Record* entry, Aurobindo jotted down the day's events, kept track of the fulfillment or lack of fulfillment of various *chatusthayas*, and reflected on his general progress. Most entries are condensed and use terms from Sanskrit, Greek, and other languages, giving the *Record* a cryptic appearance. He did not spend a lot of time describing his inner experiences. When he did, his notations were critical, brief, unpoetic:

Formerly I realised the Impersonal God, Brahma or Sacchidanandam [existence-conscious-bliss] separately from the Personal, Ishwara or Sacchidananda. Brahma has been thoroughly realised in its absolute infinity & as the material & informing presence of the world & each thing it contains, yat kincha jagatyam jagat ["whatever is moving in the moving world," from the Isha Upanishad]. But the sense of the One has not been applicable utterly & constantly,—there have been lacunae in the unitarian consciousness, partly because the Personality has not been realised with equal thoroughness or as one with the Impersonality.... On the other hand the universal Sri Krishna or Krishna-Kali in all things animate or inanimate has been realised entirely, but not with sufficient constancy & latterly with little frequency. The remedy is to unify the two realisations & towards this consummation I feel the Shakti to be now moving.[82]

Such entries are relatively uncommon. More typical are those in which he dealt hour by hour with developments in the various *chatusthayas* as they presented themselves to him. Take for example the entry of December 6, 1912. After waking from a six-hour sleep (during which *swapna-samadhi* or dream-trance was active), he began the day with a feeling that the "obstruction" of the previous day would be continued. He nevertheless was confident that there would be "continued perfection & increasing range & sureness of the praka-mya-vyapti," or telepathy. As the morning progressed, he noted an improved action of *trikaldrishti*, or triple time-vision. A few experiments involving the movements of animals seen from his window gave good results, though the "trikaldrishti of the right event" was "not free from the intrusion of falsity." There was also an improvement in the perfection of the body, but with a persistent sensitivity to cold. Sometime during the morning he saw a one-word *lipi* or etheric writing: "Page." He took this to mean that he would have occasion to remember a page number. This happened a short while later, when he opened his copy of the *Rig Veda* to obtain a sortilege, or reading of the present or future state of his yoga. His eye fell on *Rig Veda* IV.28.1, which he translated: "By thee yoked to him, O Soma, in thy comradeship, Indra poured out that stream on the mind." This he interpreted: "The Mind Force now in contact with Ananda will pour out upon the mentality the stream of the upper knowledge & joy." Returning to his diary after spending the rest of the morning in a variety of occupations, he noted that the bliss in his body (*kamananda*) "has been almost constant at a varying pitch of intensity since the morning except for one interval of an hour or so." This *ananda* came to him spontaneously while he was writing, walking, or engaged in other activities. The other elements of the *sharira chatusthaya* or quaternary of the body were not so well advanced. *Arogya*, or health, was attacked by subtle forces of disease, which he threw out by an effort of will. Imperfect primary *utthapana* tried to return as "the shadow of fatigue," but he still could walk or stand for more than nine hours without tiring. In *saundarya* or beauty there was almost no progress. He had succeeded with some difficulty in changing the form of one of his feet by volition, but the old shape kept returning. Meanwhile, in the third *chatusthaya*, there was progress in *rupa* or vision of forms, "with a number of stable images attaining to the dense developed [condition], far superior in consistency to last

night's forms, appearing straight before the vision, a great frequency of absolutely perfect images which either avoid the eye or only appear for a second
before it, & a number of crude forms." His dreams that night were almost free
"of the element of dream-image & were only a series of mental images & ideas
woven into a connected series of speech and incident."[83]

The above paragraph summarizes four and a half pages of the *Record*. In
printed form, the surviving entries for 1912 to 1913 amount to more than three
hundred, showing in fascinating detail the movement of Aurobindo's *sadhana*.
Beginning a new notebook in November 1912, he wrote: "The regular record
of the sadhana begins today, because now the perceptions are clear enough
to render it of some real value and not merely a record of mistakes and over-
statements."[84] This entry marked the beginning of a long period of progress,
though he remained generally dissatisfied with the state of his yogic practice.
Writing to Richard on December 18, 1912, he noted that "a great silence and
inhibition of action has been the atmosphere of my yoga for the last year." The
"inward struggle," which was "the most serious part of my difficulties," was
complete; but the "outward struggle," that is, the application of the yoga to
the "objective plane," remained. He realized now why he had been obliged to
wait so long before starting his outward work: "It was necessary for me to have
myself a perfect knowledge & power before I seriously undertook it."[85]

In a letter to Motilal written at the end of February or beginning of March
1913, Aurobindo spoke of "a very brilliant advance in January and the early part
of February." The *Record* for those months is filled with varied developments
in the elements of knowledge and power, as well as others such as *dasya*, the
surrender of the personal will to the will of the divine. By January 31, 1913, with
the rapidity of the advance increasing, Aurobindo felt that "finality [was] in
sight." But before the week was out, there was an "attack of pronounced asid-
dhi [imperfection]"; this lasted for as many weeks as the advance, and "seemed
to reverse much of what had already been accomplished and recorded." Looking back on this period in his letter to Motilal, he remarked that "every forward step to be made is violently combated and obstinately obstructed. Our
progress is like the advance of a modern regiment under fire in which we have
to steal a few yards at a run and then lie down under covert and let the storm
of bullets sweep by. I neither hope for nor see yet any prospect of a more successful rapidity."[86]

April proved to be as retrograde as March. "The resistance in all directions still continues," he noted in the middle of the month. For some time his
health was affected: "On the 8th night a swelling on the ankle & foot began, in
the morning the whole of the left foot was attacked & it did not seem as if a

speedy cure were possible." He was apprehensive it might be "the disease common in these parts"—elephantiasis—but received an inner indication that his foot would improve in a couple of days, and so it happened. On the positive side, a "great activity of the poetical power" enabled him to complete a draft of *Ilion* in March.[87]

The rest of 1913 was marked by alternating progress and recoil. In September he set aside the *Record* "because it was found that the habit of miscalculation still persisted, temporary success being mistaken for final fixity etc."[88] Resuming it in November, he provided an update on the state of his *sadhana*: "None of the siddhis are yet finally perfect. Even the first which is nearest to absolute finality has been disturbed yesterday & has not yet recovered its balance." As a result of recent setbacks, "Faith in the rapidity of the Yogasiddhi and in the adeshasiddhi [fulfilment of his work] has been shaken."[89] He would soon recover his "faith in the Yogasiddhi"—his belief that he would achieve perfection in yoga; but he did make a distinction between the "vidya-avidya-siddhi which is constituted by the seven chatusthayas & the higher Amrita [immortality] in which all limitation is removed & Death, etc. entirely cease. Only the first," he was forced to conclude, "will in this life be entirely accomplished."[90]

BEFORE CONTINUING IT IS NECESSARY to consider a question that may have occurred to some readers. In writing and speaking about his *sadhana*, Aurobindo made the following claims: that he saw visions, heard voices, and had other sources of knowledge independent of the senses and reason; that he could read people's minds and had knowledge of the future; that by means of mental power he could change the course of events, cure diseases, and alter the form of his body; that he went into trance; that he felt physical pain as pleasure and experienced spontaneous erotic delight; that he had a sort of supernatural strength; that he was in touch with goddesses and gods; that he was one with God. Those familiar with Indian mythological literature will not be surprised by these powers and experiences, as they are commonplace in the epics and Puranas. Those familiar with the literature of mysticism will observe that Aurobindo's powers and experiences are similar to those that other mystics from Milarepa to Rumi to Saint Teresa are said to have possessed. But those familiar with the literature of psychiatry and clinical psychology may be struck by the similarity between Aurobindo's powers and experiences and the symptoms of schizophrenia.

The question of the relationship between mysticism and madness has been discussed since antiquity. In the folklore of many cultures, a man or woman of exceptional ability has often been thought closer to the lunatic than to the ordinary mortal. Indian tradition offers hundreds of examples of yogis, mystics, and sufis whom others regarded, at least sometimes, as out of their minds. India assigns an honored place to the divine madman and madwoman once their spiritual credentials have been accepted. In the West, someone who acts eccentrically and claims divine influence is more likely to be considered a psychotic with religious delusions. Recent psychiatry has barely amended Freud's idea that "religious phenomena are only to be understood on the pattern of the individual neurotic systems familiar to us."[91] A defender of mysticism would argue that the truth value of mystical experience is so much greater than the truth value of psychiatry—a discipline based on dubious assumptions—that any attempt by the latter to explain the former is absurd. But unless the defender was an experienced mystic, this would just be substituting one set of unverified assumptions for another. When I speak of Aurobindo's experiences, my aim is not to argue either for their veracity or for their delusiveness; I simply present some of the documented events of his inner life and provide a framework for evaluating them.

In his *Varieties of Religious Experience*, William James examined the experiences of "religious geniuses," some of whom were considered unbalanced by their contemporaries. James insisted that such experiences had to be interpreted "in the immediate context of the religious consciousness." The correct criteria for judging them were "immediate luminousness," "philosophical reasonableness," and "moral helpfulness." Later writers continued on similar lines. Anton Boisen felt that there was "an important relationship between acute mental illness of the functional type and those sudden transformations of character" known as conversion experiences. "Certain types of mental disorder and certain types of religious experience" were, he wrote, "attempts at [personality] reorganisation." When successful, such attempts can lead to a new synthesis; when unsuccessful, they lead to insanity.[92] Neither Boisen nor James attempted to erase the line between mysticism and madness. They acknowledged that many people who claimed to have mystical experiences suffered from psychological anguish that made them incapable of leading productive lives. They also noted that certain well-known mystics passed through periods of apparent madness. Sudhir Kakar, who discussed this with reference to Ramakrishna, felt that the distinguishing sign of psychosis in such cases was "painful or anxious affect." In the absence of psychological pain or anxiety, "certain types of mystical experience" could be regarded as having "their ground in creativity, akin to the heightened fantasy of an artist or a writer, rather than in pathology."[93]

Most of Aurobindo's experiences are familiar to the mystic traditions of India and elsewhere. He wrote about them in language that is reasonable and luminous, though often hard to understand. Some of this writing is in the form of diary notations that were concurrent with the experiences. Around the same time he also wrote more than a dozen books on philosophy, textual interpretation, social science, and literary and cultural criticism, along with a mass of miscellaneous prose and poetry. Numerous scholars admire these works for their clarity and consistency; thousands of readers believe that they have been helped spiritually or mentally by them. No contemporary ever remarked that Aurobindo suffered painful or anxious feelings as a result of his experiences. In one or two letters written during the 1930s, he wrote that his life had been a struggle, and hinted at inner dangers and difficulties as great as any "which human beings have borne," but at no time did he give evidence to others of inner or outer stress. Indeed, virtually everyone who met him found him unusually calm, dispassionate, and loving—and eminently sane. The reports to the contrary are so rare that they can be examined individually. As noted earlier, while working as editor-in-chief of *Bande Mataram*, Aurobindo sometimes was severe and occasionally angry. After witnessing a tongue-lashing Aurobindo gave to another, Hemendra Prasad Ghose wrote in his diary that he thought Aurobindo might have inherited "a tinge of lunacy" from his mother. R.C. Dutt, asked by the government for information about Aurobindo, also mentioned Swarnalotta's madness and suggested that her son was "eccentric." After Aurobindo had spoken of his vision of Krishna in the Uttarpara speech, a few of his associates murmured that he had lost his balance. These scattered reports by people out of sympathy with him are hardly significant in themselves; viewed together with every other known report of Aurobindo's character, they stand out as exceptions. Aurobindo's anger was remarkably rare and did not leave scars. A few months after noting down the outburst that had surprised him, Hemendra Prasad wrote to Aurobindo that he would "always look back with pleasure on the period of my life during which I had the privilege of working with you for a cause."[94] That some of Aurobindo's political opponents considered him eccentric or unbalanced is not surprising. When people asked him about his claim to have seen Krishna, the calmness and lack of self-assertion of his answer convinced them that he was anything but unbalanced.

Calm—*shanti*—was the first element of Aurobindo's yoga; balance—*samata*—was its basis. Asked in 1926 about his ability to overcome the difficulties of yoga, he replied: "A perfect yoga requires perfect balance. That was the thing that saved me—the perfect balance. First I believed that nothing was impossible and at the same time I could question everything."[95] *Record of Yoga* is remarkable not only as a chronicle of unusual experiences, but as the self-critical journal of a practitioner who was never satisfied with anything short of perfection.

Annus Mirabilis

The house on rue François Martin that Aurobindo and his companions moved into on October 11, 1913 was in the White Town, a block from the governor's mansion. It was a definite improvement over the place in the rue des Missions Étrangères, but conditions remained primitive. There was a single tap for bathing and only enough soap for use every three or four days. Everyone had to dry himself with the same tattered towel, which was also used for wiping hands after eating. Lacking oil and shampoo, Aurobindo's shoulder-length hair got so dirty and tangled that his combs broke after a month of use. He had neither brush nor stick to clean his teeth; yoga force and an occasional rubbing with cigar ash sufficed. The others were amazed that, despite this treatment, his teeth retained their whiteness and freshness.[96]

The main meal of the day consisted of rice and fish, often with wine, which was cheap in French Pondicherry. The cooking and making of Aurobindo's daily pot of tea was the responsibility of Bijoy and the others. Once Bijoy decided to go to a festival and asked Amrita to give Aurobindo his afternoon meal at three o'clock. Amrita agreed but got so absorbed in what he was reading that he forgot. Rushing out after three o'clock, he found Aurobindo walking on the veranda with a cheroot in his hand. Seeing the boy he exclaimed, "Oh, I have yet to take my bath." After standing under the tap for a while, he went to the kitchen and had his cold meal.[97]

Aurobindo had been a smoker since his student days in England. The Bengalis in the household followed his example to the extent that a measurable portion of the household budget went to cigarettes, cigars, and matches. Aurobindo's conviction that yoga had nothing to do with what one ate, drank, or inhaled made him unwilling to give up the habit. Once when someone suggested that his persistent cough was due to his cigars, he flared up, saying: "If the cigars are going to kill me I am not worthy of living. I would prefer to die."[98] His attitude toward alcohol was similar, and once or twice he drank *bhang*, a cannabis preparation, to see what effect it would have on him. It had no effect at all. Wine enhanced his power of vision, but he never deliberately drank to stimulate what came to him naturally.

THE BRITISH-PAID DETECTIVES who had been watching Aurobindo and his associates followed them to the rue François Martin. Their work became easier when they managed to plant a man inside: Bijoy's relative Nagen Nag, who was staying in the house, had brought a cook and attendant named Biren Roy. At some point Biren began to take money from the CID in exchange for information. After a while he became possessed by the fear that everyone knew what he was up to. One evening while they all were sitting upstairs, Biren said he had an announcement to make. Ready for a joke, everyone grew quiet, then burst into laughter when he exclaimed, "I am a CID man!" Nonplussed, Biren said that if they did not believe him, he would show them the evidence. Rushing into his room, he returned with a large sum of money that his paymasters had given to him. This he placed at Aurobindo's feet. Aurobindo said nothing. Biren was allowed to remain in the household until he returned to Bengal of his own accord.[99]

It was apparently with Biren's help that the CID obtained surprisingly detailed information about Motilal Roy's November 1913 visit to Pondicherry. Motilal brought everyone up to date on revolutionary developments, such as the assassination of two Bengali police officers at the end of September. According to a police report, Aurobindo spoke of Srish Ghose and Amritlal Hazra, the leading revolutionary organizer and the leading bomb maker of Chandernagore, as his "two arms."[100] There is no way to confirm this, though Aurobindo sometimes mentioned Srish in his letters to Motilal. For the most part, their correspondence was confined to financial matters, but in early 1914 Aurobindo devoted a letter to a political case in Chandernagore. Rashbehari Bose had eluded capture after his attempt to assassinate the viceroy. The British police, believing that he was in the French enclave, obtained a extradition warrant for his arrest from the Government of French India and tried to apprehend him on March 8, 1914. Aurobindo saw the British move as "an attack on the security of our position." Drawing on his knowledge of French and British law, he instructed Motilal in the steps to be taken to prevent a precedent from being set. He then suggested for the first time that it might be time for Motilal to scale back his activities. Using their system of yogic code-words, he wrote: "The root of the whole evil is that we have been attempting an extension of Tantric Kriya without any sufficient Vedantic basis"; that is, they had been trying to obtain an outward result, removing British rule, by an outward means, revolutionary activity, without a foundation in inner knowledge and experience. He therefore asked Motilal "to pause, stand on the defensive against your spiritual enemies and go on with your Vedantic

Yoga," that is, the *sadhana* that Aurobindo had given him. A few months later, Aurobindo went further, writing to Motilal that revolution "with its present imperfect basis"—that is, terrorism as opposed to disciplined guerrilla warfare—had become an impediment to his work. Therefore, he wrote, "I call a halt." But by that time the movement had grown so large that Motilal could not restrain it. The robberies and assassinations continued.[101]

AUROBINDO'S ANNUS MIRABILIS came in 1914, but in this year of remarkable events, the one that would be looked back on as the most significant passed all but unnoticed when it occurred. In the evening on March 29, 1914 Aurobindo wrote in his diary: "The afternoon & evening taken up by R's visit, Bh's & translation of Rigveda II.23 & 24."[102] "Bh" was Subramania Bharati making his usual evening visit; "R" was Paul Richard, who had returned to Pondicherry after an absence of almost four years. Aurobindo did not mention Paul's wife Mirra. As the two men spoke of politics, philosophy, and social change, Mirra sat quietly, absorbed in her immediate experience. From the instant she saw Aurobindo, she later explained, she was convinced that he was her spiritual master. A few moments in his presence was enough to overturn all that she had done on her own. Yet she was far from being a novice.[103]

Blanche Rachel Mirra Alfassa was born in Paris on February 21, 1878. Her father Moïse Maurice Alfassa, a banker from Adrianople, had married Mathilde Ismalun in Alexandria in 1874. Both were of Sephardic Jewish origin, though neither was religious.[104] There were no sharp divisions in the Levant of those days, but rather "a dense and intricate interconnectedness" between Arab and Jew, Lebanese and Syrian, Egyptian and Turk.[105] In this cosmopolitan setting, Alexandria was the most cosmopolitan center, with Frenchmen and Italians rubbing shoulders with Egyptians, Arabs, and Greeks. In the 1860s, everybody in town seemed to have something to do with the Suez Canal. Maurice Alfassa had been sent to Egypt by an Ottoman bank with a stake in the multinational venture. He prospered for a while, but things became difficult when the country slipped into political and financial chaos. In 1877, Maurice, Mathilde, and their young son Mattéo settled in Paris. Mirra, who was born the next year, was proud of her Middle Eastern heritage, but she never considered herself anything but French.

Growing up in a comfortable apartment on Paris's boulevard Haussmann, Mirra was educated at home by private tutors. When she was eight, the family moved to 3 square de Roule, just off the elegant rue du Faubourg Saint-Honoré. Around the age of fifteen, she entered the Académie Julien, one of the city's leading art schools; there she developed into a serious painter. At the same time her brother Mattéo was preparing himself for the École Polytechnique, one of the training grounds of French officialdom. He made the grade, and in 1898 became a member of the colonial service.

A year or two before this, Mirra was introduced to a painter named François-Henri Morisset. A student of Gustave Moreau, like Henri Matisse and Georges Rouault, Morisset had been exhibiting in the Paris salons from the age of twenty-one.[106] Unlike Matisse, Rouault, and other artists who are still remembered, Morisset never ventured far from the academic style that dominated the official art of the period. His talent assured him a decent livelihood and Mirra's grandmother thought he would make her a suitable husband. Henri Morisset and Mirra Alfassa were married in October 1897. Ten months later, she gave birth to a son, André.

As a painter and wife of a painter, Mirra associated with artists, musicians, and writers—among them Matisse, Auguste Rodin, César Franck, Anatole France, and Émile Zola—and took an intelligent interest in the issues of the day. In 1898, it seemed to most people in Paris as if "a single matter troubles and fascinates everyone, the question of Dreyfus."[107] In January 1898 Zola published his famous open letter accusing the government of complicity in the framing of the Jewish military officer. Mirra was not one to be absorbed by political matters, but it was impossible for anyone, particularly a woman of Jewish origin, to be indifferent to this inflammatory question.

For the most part, Mirra's life revolved around her family and her art. In 1898 she accompanied Henri to Pau, where they painted a mural in the Church of Saint James. After André's birth, they often went to Beaugency, where the boy passed his youth looked after by his father's sisters. Henri's position in the Paris art establishment was now secure. In 1900 he exhibited a painting in the Universal Exhibition, and the next year won a purse that enabled him and Mirra to spend a number of months in Italy. Few years went by without one or more of his works being accepted by the committees that set the guidelines of state-sponsored art. A few of Mirra's paintings also were exhibited in the salons of 1903, 1904, and 1905. Her works of the period, many of them quiet interior studies, show excellent technique and classical balance, if little originality.

Art, society, and family kept Mirra busy, but they did not fulfill her inner needs. When her brother told her about an esoteric group that was led by his friend Louis Thémanlys, she decided to take a look. Before long, she became one of its most active members. The group, the Mouvement Cosmique, had been founded a few years earlier by the Frenchman Félicien Charles Barlet and a mysterious figure known as Max Théon. Its headquarters were in Tlemcen, Algeria, but it published most of its literature in Paris. Most important was a journal called *La revue cosmique,* which Barlet and Théon had started. Mirra devoted much of her time to the *Revue,* translating the teachings from English into French and contributing an occasional piece of her own.

The Mouvement Cosmique was one of dozens of occult groups that flourished in Paris at the turn of the century. It was a moment of great interest in spiritualism, mysticism, the occult, and Eastern philosophy in the United States, England, France, and other countries. Among the hundreds of organizations started around this time, the most famous was the Theosophical Society. A Paris chapter was opened in 1884—Barlet was a founding member—but it did not have much success. Already active in the French capital were circles of "Kabbalists, Hermeticists, Gnostics, Rosecrucians, Martinists and Mystics" who, in the face of the quasi-Eastern teachings of the Theosophists, held up "the standard of the occidental Tradition."[108] Théon's movement was part of this efflorescence; indeed it claimed to restate in modern language the world's original "Wisdom Tradition," which preceded the "Chaldean tradition," its principal source, the Vedas, the I Ching, and so forth.[109]

Little is known of Théon's early years. He is said to have been born in Poland in 1847. If one is to go by his marriage license, his actual name was Louis-Maxmillian Bimstein. He certainly was of Jewish ancestry, and evidently had been exposed to Kabbalah in his youth, either directly or through Hasidism. It is said that his spiritual instructor encouraged him to take these teachings to the West. No one knows for sure when he left Eastern Europe or where he spent the 1870s (many colorful legends exist), but by 1884 he was established in England. In March 1885 he married an Englishwoman whose name is recorded as Mary-Chrystine Woodroff-Ward, but who was known in London's psychical circles as Una.[110] Later that year Théon began his career teaching practical occultism with the launch of a new society, the Hermetic Brotherhood of Luxor, always referred to as the H.B. of L. Like most such societies, the H.B. of L. claimed ancient origins. Peter Davidson, a Scottish occultist and violin maker, who along with another Scot called Thomas Burgoyne was Théon's collaborator in the venture, wrote that it was "formed into a distinct and Hermetic Order in consequence of a division that took place in the ranks of the Hermetic Initiates 4320 years prior to the year 1881 of our present era." Less grandiosely, the group presented itself as an outgrowth of the Brotherhood of Luxor, a nineteenth-century predecessor of the Theosophical Society. From the beginning the H.B. of L. appealed to those who were dissatisfied by Theosophy's reliance on Hindu mahatmas. For a while it attracted a fair number of members, but its moment in the sun was brief. In 1886 it emerged that Thomas Burgoyne, whose real name was Thomas Henry Dalton, had served time for advertising fraud in Leeds. Threatened with exposure, he and Davidson left England for the United States, where they attracted a handful of followers in Georgia and California.[111] Théon, who seems to have known little or nothing of his partners' past, left for France around this time. He and his wife stayed there for a year and a half before going to Algeria and settling in Tlemcen, where they developed the teachings that a decade later would appear in the *Revue cosmique*.

Mirra was active in the Mouvement Cosmique from 1904 or 1905 to 1907 or 1908. During these years she met frequently with other members of the group and helped with the publication of the *Revue*. She also conducted meetings of a discussion group called Idéa, to which members of the public were invited. "Artists, writers, government officials, critics, philosophers, as well as men and women of the world who wished to improve their conception of life and things" met in the Morissets' studio in the rue Lemercier for conversation. Mirra was the focus of these meetings, but her interests were more spiritual than intellectual. At the end of 1905 she decided that in the year to come she would unite herself with her soul or "psychic being." More than a half a century later she still could remember the intensity of that period: "To enter in contact with the immanent Divine. I was occupied only with that, I thought only of that, I wanted only that. . . . And as it was the thirty-first of December I decided: 'Within the year.'" And before the year was out: "All at once my psychic being was there: 'I am conscious of my psychic being, it is protecting me and I am afraid of nothing.'"[112]

In 1906 Mirra and Henri were invited to spend some time with Théon and his wife in Tlemcen. During their three-month stay, Mirra underwent a profound inner development, but this was due more to Théon's wife than to Théon himself. Madame Théon was "a marvellous woman from the point of view of experience," though her intellect was rather ordinary. Théon, on the other hand, had comparatively little experience, but an encyclopedic knowledge of things occult.[113] A few lines from him was enough to inspire his wife to write pages and pages of what today might be called channeled writings. But these revelations, according to one French critic, were "written in such a bizarre manner that even the most cultivated men (unless of course they were themselves 'Cosmic') quickly abandoned the attempt to read them."[114] Mirra was aware of the deficiencies of Madame Théon's writing, but she felt that this extraordinary woman was in contact with genuine sources of knowledge.

Back in Paris, Mirra continued to conduct the Idéa meetings. A large assortment of people turned up. One was the Russian revolutionary leader Zinovi Pechkoff, the adopted son of Maxim Gorki, about whom Mirra wrote a profile.[115] Another was the lawyer and journalist Paul Richard, who by April 1907 was holding the group captive with his eloquent lectures. In July Mirra went to Tlemcen again, this time without her husband. Her relationship with Henri was unraveling, and in March 1908 the couple obtained a divorce. Soon afterwards, Mirra began to live in an apartment at 49 rue des Lévis, the building where Richard was staying.

Mirra's relationship with Richard led to their estrangement from the Mouvement Cosmique because the Théons did not accept that Richard was Mirra's *dualité* or destined life partner.[116] But the group did not have long to live. In September 1908 Madame Théon died of pneumonia while on a visit to the island of Jersey. Devastated by the loss of his wife, Théon fell into a depression that lasted for several years. Leaving the movement in the hands of Louis Thémanlys, he returned to Tlemcen where he led an inactive life until his death in 1927.

In 1910, just before Richard left for Pondicherry, he and Mirra rented a townhouse at 9 rue du Val-de-Grâce, not far from the Luxembourg Gardens. Neither of them wanted to go through the formalities of marriage, to the scandal of their families and friends. Finally, to placate her mother, Mirra agreed to marry her companion in May 1911.[117] The union was an unusual one. Early in their friendship, Mirra explained to Paul "that the animal mode of reproduction was only a transitional one and that until new ways of creating life became biologically possible her own motherhood would have to remain spiritual." Paul was not ready to go along with this. For him, men—especially men like him—had a duty to bring children into the world. Rather than argue, Mirra encouraged him to look elsewhere for sexual gratification.[118] Their relationship from the beginning was one of intellectual and spiritual collaboration. Encouraged by Mirra, Paul wrote works of spiritual philosophy, or rather dictated works that Mirra wrote down in proper French.[119] *L'éthère vivante* was followed by *Les dieux* (The Gods), which contrasted the despotic personal God of Christianity with the inner divine presence. According to the *Mercure de France*, *Les dieux* had many of the deficiencies of the writings of the Mouvement Cosmique: "There are some beautiful passages in this book, but they unfortunately are spoiled by proximity to other passages ... written in that apocalyptic and Biblical style that Alphonse Daudet called the *patois* of the Promised Land."[120] Among the people who visited the Richards at 9 rue du Val-de-Grâce was Alexandra David-Néel, who was planning her first voyage to the East. In the evenings, she and Mirra went for walks in the Bois de Boulougne, sometimes stopping to watch the early French flying-machines leap like grasshoppers into the air.[121]

Between 1911 and 1913 Mirra gave a number of talks to intellectual and spiritual groups. She also attended meetings where teachers from the East presented their exotic ideas. In November 1912 she and a friend had a talk with Hasrat Inayat Khan, the Indian musician and mystic who introduced Sufism to the West. A few months later, she and Paul became associated with 'Abdu'l-Bahá, the son of the founder of Baha'ism. Both during and after the master's stay in Paris, Paul and Mirra addressed his disciples. The next year, while passing through Egypt on their way to Pondicherry, they received a message from 'Abdu'l-Bahá encouraging them in their spiritual endeavors.[122]

RICHARD HAD COME to India in 1914 to stand for the Pondicherry seat in the Chamber of Deputies. Aurobindo put a lot of energy into his campaign. In the first of three letters he wrote to Motilal in April and May, he explained: "If Richard were to become deputy for French India, that would practically mean the same thing as myself being deputy for French India." He added that "there is no chance, humanly speaking," of Richard's being elected, but he hoped "to stir things a little" in order to form "a nucleus of tendency." In a second letter he gave Motilal a minutely detailed account of the local political situation. On the surface it was the same old story of corrupt candidates using money and gangsters to confirm a preordained outcome. The results, announced in May, were no surprise. Paul Bluysen got 33,154 votes, his rival Jean Lemaire 5,624, J. Laporte 368, and Richard 231. Aurobindo attributed Richard's total to massive electoral fraud, but it is clear that the Frenchman did not have the support of any segment of the electorate. Aurobindo came close to admitting this in his diary: "Aishwarya [will-power] in connection with the elections has been successful in all except the central point—the vote for R^d where it has failed entirely. Knowledge has been clouded owing to the subservience to the suggestions of others."[123]

Undeterred by Paul's failure, the Richards resolved to spend a year or two in India. In May they decided to launch a discussion group on the model of Idéa. It would be called L'idée nouvelle (The New Idea). A week or so later, Paul suddenly asked: "Shall we start a magazine?" Aurobindo, "without hesitating, and with a characteristic movement of the head," agreed. At first they thought of calling it *The New Idea*, but by June they hit on a different name: *Arya*. A few months later, Aurobindo explained the meaning of the Sanskrit word. The *ârya* or Aryan was not a person who belonged to a particular race—a misconception later taken up and distorted by the Nazis—or recognized a particular creed. Rather, the Aryan was a person who "accepted a particular type of self-culture, of inward and outward practice, of ideality, of aspiration."[124]

It does not seem as if the Richards or Aurobindo had thought about starting a group or a journal before May 1914, but it was predictable given their backgrounds. Mirra had been connected with intellectual and occult groups for almost a decade and had helped to edit a journal that one of the groups published. Paul had contributed articles to Parisian newspapers and had been an active member of Idéa. Aurobindo had edited three newspapers, two in English and one in Bengali. While never a starter or joiner of groups, he had occasionally reflected on the help an organization might give to the diffusion of his thought. That June he wrote in the *Record*, under the heading "Work to be done": "A Society to be formed like the Theosophical Society which will support & popularise the Knowledge & the writings which express it."[125]

Soon Aurobindo and his friends were at work on their new projects. The New Idea was registered and a prospectus for the *Arya* printed. Four different kinds of writings would appear in it: "synthetic studies in speculative Philosophy," "translations and commentaries of ancient texts," "studies in Comparative Religion," and "practical methods of inner culture and self-development." The first pieces of speculative philosophy would be "The Wherefore of the Worlds" by Richard, and "an exposition of Vedantic thought in accordance with the Ishopanishad" by Aurobindo. The translations, of the Upanishads and the *Rig Veda*, would be the fruits of "five years of solitary meditation by Sri Aurobindo Ghose." The work in comparative religion would consist of a collection of the sayings of the world's great sages, compiled in France by Paul and Mirra with the help of one of their friends. Finally, there would be "a practical exposition of a new method of inner development, based on personal experimentation, and coordinating results gained through ancient methods."[126] These promises were made in the middle of June 1914. The first issue was scheduled to come out in the middle of August. Of the projected features, only one Vedic translation was ready when the prospectus was sent out.

Aurobindo had plenty of material to draw on. Since his arrival in Pondicherry, he had filled twenty or more notebooks with essays on philosophy and yoga and translations from the Vedas and Upanishads, not to mention linguistic and textual research and various literary writings. But none of his pieces was ready for publication. Rather than selecting some and working them up for print, he decided to write what he needed from scratch in less than six weeks. He finished with time to spare and never returned to his notebook drafts.

The first issue of *Arya* appeared on August 15, Aurobindo's forty-second birthday. There was a small celebration at noon. Later he wrote in the *Record*: "Life has been preparing all this time. Today it begins with the publication of the Review and the continued stream of subscribers." He then summarized the state of his *sadhana*:

> However limited at present the success and the effectivity of the Tapas [will], it has been proved beyond doubt effective and is becoming regularly effective; always as a force among others, sometimes, in varying degrees, as the effective force. So much has been gained, no more.
>
> The organisation of the vijnana [supraintellectual faculty] is now possible. . . . [There is also] faith in the powers that are at work as real powers & the aim as their real aim.
>
> Whether that aim can be worked out by the evolution of the full power needed, has now to be seen. That is the work of 1914–15.[127]

War and Sadhana

On May 28, while Aurobindo was planning the prospectus of *Arya*, Archduke Franz Ferdinand was assassinated in Sarajevo. By the time *Arya* appeared, all of Europe was at war. A confirmed Francophile, Aurobindo had been troubled since his youth by the German occupation of Alsace-Lorraine. When the French advanced in that direction, he wrote of it in detail in his diary, passing over their rapid retreat in comparative silence. He had more reason to be satisfied with developments to the north. On September 15 he wrote: "the great German defeat satisfies at once trikaldrishti and aishwarya."[128] Historians still debate why General von Kluck changed direction just short of Paris, setting up the First Battle of the Marne. Aurobindo and Mirra, who had a vision of Paris being saved, thought that their spiritual intervention had helped the Allied effort. It is of course impossible to confirm such a claim. *Record of Yoga* offers nothing in the way of evidence. In any event, the battle lines in Flanders soon stabilized and soldiers dug in for what would become a bloody four-year stalemate.

The war came to India toward the end of September 1914 when the German cruiser *Emden* sank fifteen British ships in the Bay of Bengal, shelled Madras, and appeared briefly off Pondicherry. Srinivasacharya, Bharati, and Aiyar were walking on the beach when the enemy warship appeared. They noted the half-dozen tiny guns that were the colony's only defense, and watched the city's well-to-do flee to the suburbs. The German captain ordered his gun hatches open, but in the end decided that the tiny French colony was not worth the ammunition.[129] Spared direct involvement, the people of Pondicherry were affected in other ways. The refugees from British India, Aurobindo included, found that they no longer could take the hospitality of the French for granted. British officials pressured their wartime allies to expel the revolutionaries of French India, but at least one bureaucrat in the Government of Bengal did not want to see Aurobindo disturbed. "If he were driven out," he noted, "he would almost certainly make straight for Bengal, and be received with enthusiasm. The risk is too great; and it is understood that there are suitable arrangements for watching him in Pondicherry."[130] Toward the end of the year, Aiyar, Bharati, and others had the idea of waiting out the war in another French colony: Djibouti, perhaps, or Algeria. Bharati went to Aurobindo to explain the plan to him. Aurobindo heard the poet out, then said: "Mr Bharati, I am not going to budge an inch from Pondicherry."[131] In fact he scarcely left the house for the duration of the war. When not writing or sitting in meditation, he walked in his room or on the veranda, putting in so many miles that he wore a channel a few inches deep in the *chunam* (slaked lime) floor.

He met frequently with the Richards to take care of editorial and business matters. Every month, sixty-four pages of text had to be written, translated, typeset, proofread, and printed. In the beginning Aurobindo's articles amounted to around fifty pages, Richard's ten, and other material five. Everything in English had to be translated by Mirra and Paul for the French edition; everything in French had to be translated by Aurobindo into English. After his years in Calcutta, Aurobindo was used to meeting deadlines, and in any event wrote without difficulty. But he was "genuinely surprised" at the way his writing "was taking form, both in terms of the new philosophic trend of his thought and also the 'automatic' manner in which he had come to write." He told Richard once that he had "never written like that before."[132]

On Sundays Aurobindo and others from his house dined with Mirra and Paul, enjoying their vegetarian food, which they rarely had at home. After dinner, they sat on the veranda and spoke. Aurobindo had developed a great regard for the couple. They were, he wrote Motilal, "rare examples of European Yogins who have not been led away by Theosophical and other aberrations." Though he had reservations about parts of Paul's philosophy, he considered him "not only a personal friend" but also "a brother in the Yoga."[133] As for Mirra, she seemed to have a capacity for spiritual surrender that rivaled that of the great Indian *bhaktas* or devotees.

AUROBINDO'S PRINCIPAL INTEREST in the European war was in the effect it would have on India's struggle for freedom. In a letter written to Motilal in August, he discussed the war's three possible outcomes: the defeat of Germany and Austria, the weakening or isolation of Britain, and Britain's defeat. He was under no illusion that the second or third result would benefit India: "in either of these two last cases an invasion of India by Germany, Russia or Japan is only a question of time." India could profit from the war by giving limited cooperation to the British in exchange for military training and other concessions. But India should not, he told Motilal, cooperate to the extent suggested by M.K. Gandhi. Gandhi's aim was "to secure for Indians [in South Africa] the position of kindly treated serfs." India's aim had to be "to create a nation of men fit for independence and able to secure and keep it."[134]

Since Aurobindo departed from Bengal, he had taken little interest in the activities of the Indian National Congress. The purge of the Extremists in 1908 had left that body inactive and moribund. But after the start of the war, even old-line Moderates grasped that India was in a position to ask for real administrative reforms. The session of 1914, held in Madras at the end of December, was the most important since 1907. After it was over, a reporter for the *Hindu* traveled to Pondicherry to ask Aurobindo's opinion of recent developments. Having seen him during his political career, the reporter was surprised to find that he "was much more buoyant and sprightly" than in 1907. "His yogic meditations and self-discipline have had a physical result that is quite contrary to the popular suppositions about yogic practices." Asked about the Congress, Aurobindo replied that, with a single exception—the speech of his former adversary Bhupendranath Bose—the proceedings were "mere repetitions of the petty and lifeless formulas of the past," hardly showing "any sense of the great breath of the future that is blowing upon us." Gaining enthusiasm as he spoke, he went on:

The old, petty forms and little, narrow, make-believe activities are getting out of date. The world is changing rapidly around us and preparing for more colossal changes in the future. We must rise to the greatness of thought and action which it will demand upon the nations who hope to live. . . . We are a nation of three hundred millions inhabiting a great country in which many civilisations have met, full of rich material and unused capacities. We must cease to think and act like the inhabitants of an obscure and petty village. . . .

Only by a general intellectual and spiritual awakening can this nation fulfil its destiny. Our limited information, our second-hand intellectual activities, our bounded interests, our narrow life of little family aims and small money-getting have prevented us from entering into the broad life of the world.... No nation in modern times can grow great by politics alone. A rich and varied life, energetic in all its parts, is the condition of a sound, vigorous national existence.

Aurobindo was glad that British statesmen had begun to speak "of India's proper place in the Councils of the Empire," but, he continued,

it is equally necessary that we Indians should begin to think seriously what part Indian thought, Indian intellect, Indian nationhood, Indian spirituality, Indian culture have to fulfil in the general life of humanity. That humanity is bound to grow increasingly one. We must necessarily be in it and of it. Not a spirit of aloofness or of jealous self-defence, but of generous emulation and brotherhood with all men and all nations, justified by a sense of conscious strength, a great destiny, a large place in the human future—this should be the Indian spirit.

He believed that India could "guide the world" if it reawakened to its spiritual greatness. But if its past was sacred, "the claims of our future with its immense possibilities should be still more sacred." What was important, he concluded, was "that the thought of India should come out of the philosophical school and renew its contact with life, and the spiritual life of India issue out of the cave and the temple and, adapting itself to new forms, lay its hand upon the world." To help this effort along, he had for some time been impelled to turn his energies within, "rather than to the petty political activities which are alone open to us at the present moment." This was the reason for his "continued retirement and detachment from action."[135]

For the moment, however, the thrust of petty politics could still disrupt his plans. In the middle of January 1915 Paul Richard received an order to return to France. According to British intelligence, this was because he had "made himself obnoxious to the Governor by his association with political refugees and anti-British intrigues." But even if he had no such "associations," he would eventually have had to join his regiment. The final order came in February; he had to sail for France at once.

Leaving Pondicherry was more of a shock to Mirra than to her husband. Over the last ten months, she had felt fulfilled in her inner life as never before. Now she was deeply shaken. What did the divine intend for her? After long meditation, she came to understand that "the time of repose and preparation was over"; it was time for her to "turn her regard to the earth." She accepted this, but was still convinced that her place was in Pondicherry. And surely (she told herself) Aurobindo thought so too. If he asked her to stay, she would have done so without hesitation; but far from doing this, he "even appeared to wish that I should go away."[136] When the final order came from Paris, Mirra packed her bags along with Paul. On February 22, 1915 the couple left for Madras. A day or two later, as they boarded their steamer in Colombo, Mirra declared "with great feeling and assurance 'We shall come back.'" As far as Paul could remember, "from that point on, all our thoughts turned towards Europe in the throes of war."[137] Mirra's diary shows that her heart was elsewhere. "Bitter solitude!" she wrote on March 3, "and always that strong impression of having been thrown headlong into a hell of darkness. At no other time, in no other circumstance, have I ever felt myself living in surroundings so totally opposed to all that I am conscious of as true, of all that is the essence of my life."[138]

There is no way of knowing what Aurobindo was thinking at this time. Up to February 6, his entries in the *Record* read as they had for the last ten months, giving details of progress and the occasional setback in his yoga. After February 6 there is a gap of three weeks. When he resumed three days after the Richards departed, he began: "The record has been suspended because of an almost entire suspension of all progress in which the hostile forces have seemed to take possession and only the literary & intellectual activity has continued to progress. In this field the perceptive intuition & creative inter-pretation grow in force." But then he went on to speak of the day's advance in inner experience, intuition, and "the power of work without choice."[139] There is no special mention of Mirra Richard, nor evidence in earlier *Record* entries that he regarded her as more than a "European yogi" of unusual attainments. But it need not be assumed that he put down all he felt in his diary. Years later he explained that he was aware at once that Mirra's aptitude for yoga was ex-traordinary, while Paul's was at best mediocre.[140]

BEFORE LEAVING FOR FRANCE, Paul transferred the ownership of *Arya* to Aurobindo. The French edition was discontinued after the February 1915 issue. The English edition went on without a break. Paul left behind some install-ments of his *Pourquoi des mondes* and the full manuscript of *La sagesse eternelle*, his and Mirra's compilation of spiritual maxims. Translated by Aurobindo, this appeared as *The Eternal Wisdom* over the next six years. During the same six years he wrote from scratch three works of philosophy, one of yoga, six of commentary, three of social science, three of literary and cultural criticism, and dozens of essays. In his spare time he wrote a five-act verse play and the first version of a poetic narrative that would eventually become an epic. He also revised and published a collection of short poems. Whatever else took place during these years, his "literary & intellectual activity" did not fall off.

Aurobindo began *Arya* with the first installments of five different works: *The Life Divine*, *The Synthesis of Yoga*, *The Secret of the Veda*, a series of Vedic translations, and Isha Upanishad. All but the last were still running a year later, when he paused to restate the *Arya's* ideal. The journal had not been conceived as "the mouthpiece of a sect, school or already organised way of thinking." It was an attempt "to feel out for the thought of the future." In recent centuries, human progress had been "almost entirely centred in the twin continents of Asia and Europe." The first of these served "predominantly (not exclusively) as a field for man's spiritual experience and progression," the second "as a work-shop for his mental and vital activities." Europe's material concentration had led it to moral and intellectual bankruptcy and a self-destructive war; Asia's spiritual concentration had resulted in a different sort of bankruptcy, showing "how low a race can fall which in its eagerness to seek after God ignores His intention in humanity." The best hope for the future was "the mutual interpen-etration of the two great currents of human effort." The problem was

> to find out the right idea and the right way of harmony; to restate the ancient and eternal spiritual truth of the Self so that it shall re-embrace, permeate, dominate, transfigure the mental and physical life; to develop the most profound and vital methods of psychological self-discipline and self-development so that the mental and psychical life of man may express the spiritual life through the utmost possible expansion of its own richness, power and complexity; and to seek for the means and motives by which his external life, his society and his institutions may remould themselves progressively in the truth of the spirit and develop towards the utmost pos-sible harmony of individual freedom and social unity.

This is what he intended to do in *Arya*. Conceding that there were "plenty of movements inspired by the same drift," he felt that there was "room for an effort of thought which shall frankly acknowledge the problem in its in-tegral complexity and not be restrained in the flexibility of its search by at-tachment to any cult, creed or extant system of philosophy." The first necessity was "a quest for the Truth that underlies existence and the fundamental Law of its self-expression in the universe." This would be approached in two ways: through "the study and restatement of the ancient Eastern knowledge" and through the development of a new metaphysics. He also would examine "the psychological disciplines of yoga," avoiding "a popular statement of methods and disciplines," but seeking "the principles underlying the methods." Once he had laid this spiritual, philosophical, and psychological foundation, he could show how the truths attainable by yoga could be applied to the problems of social organization and to various forms of cultural expression.[141]

During the six and a half years of *Arya*'s existence, Aurobindo never strayed far from this fivefold project: to reinterpret the Indian tradition, to develop a metaphysics based on the truths of spirit and nature, to uncover the principles of yoga by which these truths could be experienced, to show how the same truths could be applied to political and social life, and to make them the basis of a spiritualized literature and art. These five aspects of his intellectual project are examined in the next chapter.

7. The Major Works

Pondicherry, 1914–1920

In this Review my new theory of the Veda will appear as also a translation and explanation of the Upanishads, a series of essays giving my system of Yoga & a book of Vedantic philosophy (not Shankara's but Vedic Vedanta) giving the Upanishadic foundations of my theory of the ideal life towards which humanity must move. You will see so far as my share is concerned, it will be the intellectual side of my work for the world.

Linking the Future to the Past

The aim of the *Arya*, Aurobindo wrote in 1915, was to discover and give form to "the thought of the future" and to link it "to the best and most vital thought of the past."[1] In the early stages of the project, the linkage with the past predominated. A week before the inaugural issue was published, he wrote out a list of twenty-one works he hoped to complete during his lifetime.[2] Nine were based on the Upanishads, nine on the Vedas; the other three were works of poetry. The scholarly emphasis is consistent with Indian tradition, in which works of philosophy often take the form of commentaries on ancient scriptures. Judging by his writings from 1910 to 1914, Aurobindo was comfortable with this approach. His notebooks are filled with translations of the Vedas and commentaries on the Upanishads. But there are also signs of another, more Western, approach. In an essay of 1912, he insisted on "the importance of original thinking."[3] In other essays from around the same period, he examined the relationship between scripture and experiential truth. A scholarly "enquiry into the meaning of ancient Hindu documents" might be "a worthy object of labour and a patriotic occupation," he wrote, but it was not "a sufficient motive for devoting much time & labour out of a life lived in these pregnant & fruitful times." The reason to study scripture was to gain insight into the nature of the divine and the soul. If scripture, "had not this high utility, if it only brought a philosophical satisfaction or were good for logical disputation," he concluded, "I should not think it worthwhile to write a word about it, much less to delve deep for its meaning."[4]

AT THE TIME he decided to publish *Arya*, Aurobindo was absorbed in the study of the *Rig Veda*, the most ancient and least understood scripture in the Indian tradition. He had begun to read the Vedic texts in connection with his research into the "origins of Aryan speech." This led him to the "discovery of a considerable body of profound psychological thought and experience lying neglected in these ancient hymns."[5] He attempted to bring out this underlying significance in a series of incomplete commentaries, one of which he called "The Secret of the Veda." He used the same title in May 1914 when he began to write material for the *Arya*. The first chapter of this new *Secret of the Veda* was published in the prospectus of the journal and again two months later in its first issue.

In the opening chapter of *The Secret of the Veda*, Aurobindo spelled out what was for him the main problem of Vedic interpretation and proposed a new solution. The problem was why the Vedas, which seemed to be nothing but "the sacrificial compositions of a primitive and still barbarous race written around a system of ceremonial and propriatory rites," were regarded as the fountainhead of the Indian spiritual tradition. He conceded the sacrificial basis of the hymns, but insisted that they had a double meaning: "Their formulas and ceremonies are, overtly, the details of an outward ritual devised for the Pantheistic Nature-Worship which was then the common religion, covertly the sacred words, the effective symbols of a spiritual experience and knowledge and a psychological discipline of self-culture which were then the highest achievement of the human race."[6] So viewed, he concluded, the Rig Veda ceased "to be merely an interesting remnant of barbarism and takes rank among the most important of the world's early scriptures."[7]

In later chapters, Aurobindo explained the significance of several Vedic myths according to his inner vision and experience. In a companion work, *Selected Hymns*, he provided translations to illustrate his theory. Sometimes he contrasted his own reading of a hymn with that of the fourteenth-century commentator Sayana, who codified the ritualistic interpretation. According to Sayana, the first and last verses of *Rig Veda* 1.4 should be read:

> The doer of (works that have) a good shape, Indra, we call daily for protection as (one calls) for the cow-milker a good milch-cow . . .
> Sing to that Indra who is a protector of wealth, great, a good fulfiller (of works) and a friend of the sacrificer.

Aurobindo translated the same verses as follows:

The fashioner of perfect forms, like a good yielder for the milker of the
  Herds, we call for increase from day to day. . . .
He who in his vastness is a continent of bliss,—the friend of the Soma-
  giver and he carries him safely through,—to that Indra raise the chant.[8]

To Sayana wealth was wealth and cows were cows. Aurobindo accepted
this as the exoteric sense of the lines, but he added another, inner sense in
which wealth became spiritual plenitude and cows the divine illumination.

Aurobindo wrote about the Vedas in every issue of the *Arya* until December 1917, and then again in several issues of 1920. His essays and translations provide a sketch of his theory, but he was never satisfied with them and
did not republish the *Secret* during his lifetime. Years later he told a potential
translator: "The 'Secret of the Veda' is not complete and there are besides many
imperfections and some errors in it which I would have preferred to amend
before the book or any translation was published."[9] He never found time to
give the book the revision that it needed. In later years he became less confident that a modern scholar could nail down the meaning of the texts as they
were originally understood. "It is quite impossible to say to what they were
referring in those days," he wrote in a letter of 1933. "We have no longer a clue
to their symbolism."[10] He remained convinced, however, that he had recovered
the inner sense of the Vedas in his own spiritual experience. For him, the seers
of the Vedas were yogis who walked a path he rediscovered and traveled three
thousand years later. A literary critic might observe that in making this claim,
he was—to borrow a phrase from Jorge Luis Borges—creating his precur-
sors.[11] Aurobindo would not have seen it that way, but he accepted that every
reader of a text recreates its meaning in terms of his own experience. As he
wrote in 1919, "even an old thought or truth which I affirm against an opposing
idea, becomes a new thought to me in the effort of affirmation and rejection,
clothes itself with new aspects and issues."[12] What is important to readers of
the *Secret* is whether the "new aspects and issues" that Aurobindo's reading
brought into focus are of living value to them.

WHEN HE BEGAN TO WRITE for the *Arya* in 1914, Aurobindo had been a
student of the Upanishads for more than twenty years. In Baroda he translated most of the shorter texts and wrote commentaries on two of the most
important: the *Isha* and *Kena*. Later, in Pondicherry, he began a commentary
on the *Isha* that he called "The Life Divine." Through successive drafts over
the next two years, this work became less an interpretation of the text than a

sketch of a new philosophy. After he decided to publish the *Arya*, he began a new translation of the *Isha*. Around the same time, he wrote the first chapter of an independent metaphysical study entitled *The Life Divine*. From then on, he kept his textual scholarship and his own philosophy separate.

Aurobindo's new translation of the *Isha* was published in the first issue of the *Arya*. Subsequent issues contained a four-part analysis and an elaborate conclusion. In the first part of the analysis, he presented the main ideas of the text: "the one and stable Spirit inhabiting and governing a universe of movement," "the rule of a divine life for man," and the justification of life and works. He developed these ideas in the second and third parts, showing that the spirit is one with the universe and that the divine rule of life, in which opposites are reconciled, is founded upon this unity. In his conclusion, he showed how immortality—not the survival of death but a status of consciousness beyond both birth and death—could be attained through the practice of yoga.[13]

In a crucial passage of *Isha Upanishad*, Aurobindo showed that the *brahman* or Absolute is unmoving and at the same time present in the activities of the world. "The active Brahman," he wrote, "fulfils Itself in the world by works" but remains forever free. Likewise, when the will of the individual human being is merged in the cosmic will, "one can act with the divine freedom." Thus *brahman* can be realized both "in the universe and in our self-existence." He summed up this ideal in a passage for which he had a special fondness:

> We have to perceive Brahman comprehensively as both the Stable and the Moving. We must see it in eternal and immutable Spirit and in all the changing manifestations of universe and relativity.
>
> We have to perceive all things in Space and Time, the far and the near, the immemorial Past, the immediate Present, the infinite Future with all their contents and happenings as the One Brahman.
>
> We have to perceive Brahman as that which exceeds, contains and supports all individual things as well as all universe, transcendentally of Time and Space and Causality. We have to perceive It also as that which lives in and possesses the universe and all it contains.[14]

Isha Upanishad is the pithiest of Aurobindo's works. Its carefully chiseled sentences leave much for the reader to reflect upon, unlike his ordinary expository prose, in which clause is added to clause and refinement to refinement until the sentences become almost unreadable. Its concision is a result of the amount of work that preceded the final text. The incomplete commentaries written in Baroda and Pondicherry amount to more than three hundred pages in manuscript. By the time he decided to bring out the *Arya*, his interpretation was formed and waiting for expression.

IN 1912, AUROBINDO WROTE that his "religious and philosophical mission" would be "to re-explain the Veda and Vedanta (Upanishads) in the ancient sense which I have recovered." When he began to publish the *Arya* two years later, he still regarded the Veda and Vedanta as the primary sources of his philosophy. But by 1918, when he paused to look back on the first four years of the journal, he took a more self-reliant stand. If he continued to write on Indian scriptures, he said, it was to show that the truths of his own philosophy "were not inconsistent with the old Vedantic truth." The Upanishads remained central to his vision, as he had shown in his analysis of the *Isha* and a commentary on the *Kena* that was published in 1915 and 1916. But he did not accept uncritically all that the Upanishads said. Taken as a whole, he wrote in July 1916, the *Kena* seemed to call for "a rejection of the life of the cosmos." To the extent that it did, it had to be rejected for, after all, "it is only the ignorant soul that will make itself the slave of a book." Where the *Kena* presented the truth of the *brahman*, "its aid to humanity" was "indispensable." But "where anything essential is missing, we must go beyond the Upanishads to seek it,—as for instance when we add to its emphasis on divine knowledge the indispensable ardent emphasis of the later teachings upon divine love and the high emphasis of the Veda upon divine works."[15] In the next issue of the *Arya*, he took up the scripture that harmonized the paths of knowledge, love, and works better than any other: the *Bhagavad Gita*.

Aurobindo had been reading the *Gita* since his early years in Baroda. From the first he was struck by the way its teachings could be applied to an active life. Of the world's great scriptures, only the *Gita* is set on a battlefield. When Arjuna addresses Krishna, it is to ask a practical question: how can he take part in the impending battle if he must face and perhaps kill his relatives and guru? Krishna's initial answer is that a person must act not for the sake of the action, but to fulfill a social duty. Later he gives this teaching a higher turn: a person must perform "the work that is to be done," the *kartavyam karma*, without desire or attachment, accepting it as the will of the divine. This creed of selfless action was never far from Aurobindo's mind during his political career. He brought it out in an *Introduction to the Gita* that he published in his Bengali journal *Dharma* in 1909 and 1910. The *Introduction* is structured in the traditional Indian way, as a chapter-by-chapter translation of the text with a commentary at the end of each chapter. When he returned to the *Gita* six years later, he avoided this scholarly convention. His *Essays on the Gita* follow the text rather closely, but they exploit the freedom of the English form to deal with other questions that interest the author.

Aurobindo began the *Essays* with a statement of purpose. There is "a Truth one and eternal," he wrote, but by its very nature it cannot be "shut up in a single trenchant formula." Each scripture contains two elements, one "belonging to the ideas of the period and country in which it was produced" and another "applicable in all ages and countries." The letter of the text was "subject to the mutations of Time," so one could "never be quite sure of understanding an ancient book of this kind precisely in the sense and spirit it bore to its contemporaries." For this reason Aurobindo held it

> of small importance to extract from the Gita its exact metaphysical connotation as it was understood by the men of the time,—even if that were accurately possible. . . . What we can do with profit is to seek in the Gita for the actual living truths it contains, apart from their metaphysical form, to extract from it what can help us or the world at large and to put it in the most natural and vital form and expression that we can find that will be suitable to the mentality and helpful to the spiritual needs of our present-day humanity.[16]

Here, as in the passage cited above about old texts clothing themselves "with new aspects and issues," Aurobindo anticipated the theories of critics and philosophers who insist on the historicity of interpretation.

Aurobindo divided the *Essays* into two series. In the first, he used the text of the *Gita* as a basis for a general consideration of topics such as equality, sacrifice, philosophical determination, and the theory of the avatar. In the second, he followed the text more closely, painting a memorable picture of Krishna's self-revelation, then taking up the divine teacher's treatment of the elements of Sankhya philosophy. In his two closing essays, Aurobindo encapsulated Krishna's message and tried to place it in context: "The central interest of the Gita's philosophy and Yoga is its attempt . . . to reconcile and even effect a kind of unity between the inner spiritual truth in its most absolute and integral realisation and the outer actualities of man's life and action."[17] In a topical allusion, he referred to those who insist on "Ahimsa, on non-injuring and non-killing, as the highest law of spiritual conduct." For him, such people—he was thinking especially of Gandhi—believed that "the battle, if it is to be fought out at all, must be fought on the spiritual plane and by some kind of non-resistance or refusal of participation or only by soul resistance, and if this does not succeed in the external plane ... the individual will still have preserved his virtue and vindicated by his example the highest ideal." Aurobindo then considered an opposite overemphasis: the ascetic's turning away "from life and its aims and standards of action towards another and celestial or supracosmic state." The *Gita*, he said, goes "beyond all these conflicting positions," justifying "all life to the spirit as a significant manifestation of the one Divine Being" and asserting "the compatibility of a complete human action and a complete spiritual life lived in union with the Infinite."[18]

The *Gita*, Aurobindo concluded, had different messages for the "mind that follows after the vital and material life," for the "mind occupied with the pursuit of intellectual, ethical and social standards," and for the "absolutist seekers of the Infinite." The highest of its messages is that "the Infinite is not solely a spiritual existence remote and ineffable," and that men and women can solve the "inner riddle of Self and God and the outer problem of ... active self-existence" by rising to an integral union with the divine.[19] The sense that Aurobindo extracted from the *Gita* was thus of a piece with his own philosophy. In the penultimate chapter of the *Essays* he wrote, "All the problems of human life arise from the complexity of our existence, the obscurity of its essential principle and the secrecy of the inmost power that makes out its determinations and governs its purpose and its processes."[20] This echoed a much more famous passage he published four years earlier in the first chapter of his principal work of philosophy, *The Life Divine*.

A Divine Life

The prospectus of the *Arya* promised readers "synthetic studies of speculative Philosophy," of which the first would be Aurobindo's "exposition of Vedantic thought in accordance with the Ishopanishad."[21] The philosopher in him was still subservient to the commentator. Most of the writings that fill his notebooks from 1910 to 1914 were based more or less directly on the Upanishads and *Rig Veda*. The most extensive of these were the aforementioned commentaries on the *Isha Upanishad* entitled "The Life Divine." Presumably he intended to draw on them when he wrote the promised "exposition," but when he started a new draft of "The Life Divine" in the middle of May 1914, he hardly mentioned the *Isha Upanishad*. Instead he dealt with Indian philosophy in general, particularly its experiential basis. After working on this draft for about a month, he set it aside and in just three days wrote the opening chapter of another *Life Divine* that would become a thousand-page treatise of spiritual philosophy. He was happy with this chapter when he wrote it and he remained satisfied with it for the rest of his life. In it he presented, in four taut pages, the principal themes of his philosophy:

> The earliest preoccupation of man in his awakened thoughts and, as it seems, his inevitable and ultimate preoccupation,—for it survives the longest periods of scepticism and returns after every banishment,—is also the highest which his thought can envisage. It manifests itself in the divination of Godhead, the impulse towards perfection, the search after pure Truth and unmixed Bliss, the sense of a secret immortality. The ancient dawns of human knowledge have left us their witness to this constant aspiration; today we see a humanity satiated but not satisfied by victorious analysis of the externalities of Nature preparing to return to its primeval longings. The earliest formula of Wisdom promises to be its last,—God, Light, Freedom, Immortality.[22]

These ideals, which are only rarely glimpsed in ordinary life, are affirmed by experiences that are "only to be attained . . . by a revolutionary individual effort or an evolutionary general progression." The goal of this personal effort and cosmic evolution is nothing less than "to know, possess and be the divine being in an animal and egoistic consciousness." The opposition of "realised fact"—all that we take for granted—to these hardly credible aims might seem "a final argument against their validity"; but this opposition is actually part of nature's method. For "all problems of existence are essentially problems of harmony": nature has harmonized, at least partially, life with matter and mind with embodied life. It is therefore not illogical to suppose that a supramental or divine being can take form in "our twilit or obscure physical mentality" and become the basis for a greater harmony. The emergence of life and mind in matter is part of what we call evolution, but life and mind could never have evolved unless they were previously "involved" in matter and impelled to reemerge. That which has involved itself in matter is spirit, or the divine. The human aspiration for "God, Light, Bliss, Freedom, Immortality" is "simply the imperative impulse by which Nature is seeking to evolve beyond Mind" to the divine. If the animal is "a living laboratory" in which nature has worked out the human being, so the human being "may well be a thinking and living laboratory" in which nature "wills to work out the superman, the god." Already the phenomena of "illumined intuition or self-revealing truth" show the direction in which nature is moving. Beyond these "intermittent glancings" lies "the next higher state of consciousness," which Aurobindo called the supermind.[23]

The Life Divine ran in the *Arya* from the first issue in August 1914 to the fifty-fourth issue in January 1919—coinciding almost exactly with the beginning and end of World War I. Aurobindo revised it for book publication in 1939 and 1940, during the early phases of World War II. At that time he divided it structurally into two volumes, or books. Book One, "Omnipresent Reality and the Universe," gives the metaphysical foundations of his worldview. The first chapter, discussed above, affirms the possibility of a divine life on earth. The next two chapters deal with the "Two Negations" that seem to deny this possibility. On the one hand, there is the denial of the materialist, who does not accept the ultimate reality of anything except matter; on the other, there is the refusal of the ascetic, who does not believe that anything but *brahman* is fundamentally true. These two figures, corresponding roughly to a defender of Western science and a proponent of the Adwaita school of Vedanta, remain Aurobindo's principal sparring partners until the end of the book. To the materialist, the monist of matter, he declares that "our enlarging experience" forces us to acknowledge that "there are in the universe knowable realities beyond the range of the senses." He agrees with the Adwaitin, the monist of the spirit, that "consciousness is the great underlying fact," the "universal witness" to whom "the worlds and their objects appeal for their reality." He accepts that it is possible to enter into a state of sheer consciousness that transcends the world and its objects, but he insists that it does not follow that the world and things are nonexistent or illusory, as the Buddhists and Adwaitins declare. In the "completer affirmation" that he proposes, both universe and *brahman*, matter and spirit, have to be given their due.[24]

If Aurobindo is right that matter and spirit are different forms of a single unity, it follows that there is a "scale of substance" that links the two. Aurobindo devotes most of Book One of *The Life Divine* to an examination of this scale. He relies on the terminology of Vedanta to make the necessary distinctions. At the top is "the pure existent" (*sat*), of which the human individual can become aware by spiritual intuition. This being is not different from pure, self-existent consciousness (*chit*), and pure consciousness is not different from pure, self-existent force (*shakti*). Conscious force or *chit-shakti* is the creator of the universe. The purpose of creation is to manifest an impersonal, self-existent delight (*ananda*) that is the very nature of being. *Sat-chit-ananda*, or *sachchidananda*, is the complete description of *brahman*.

Sat, chit, and *ananda* comprise the upper hemisphere of the cosmos. There is also a lower hemisphere made up of three principles: the familiar world of matter, life, and mind. All of these are characterized by division. Mind's analytical action arrives at relative knowledge, which in the end is recognized as ignorance; life's organic limitations result in pain, incapacity, and death; matter's atomic fragmentation ends in the voidness of "the Inconscient." Existence, consciousness, and bliss are present in matter, life, and mind, but owing to an "exclusive concentration of consciousness," when they descend from the higher into the lower hemisphere, they are transformed into their opposites: nothingness, unconsciousness, and pain.

However, Aurobindo argues, it is possible for individuals in the lower hemisphere to break free from the limitations of body, life, and mind. Ascending in consciousness into *sat-chit-ananda,* many such individuals look on matter, life, and mind as creations of *maya,* a mysterious power of illusion. But, according to Aurobindo, the power that creates separate, apparently illusory beings is an inferior form of *maya.* There is also a higher or divine *maya* that is a "power of infinite consciousness to comprehend, contain in itself and measure out, that is to say, to form—for form is delimitation—Name and Shape out of the vast illimitable Truth of infinite existence." This higher *maya,* which Aurobindo calls "supermind," is "the nature of the divine being . . . in its action as the Lord and Creator of its own worlds." Unlike mind, which works by means of division and finds unity only through construction, supermind is simultaneously aware of the unity of *brahman* and the multiplicity of the universe. Standing between the oneness of the higher hemisphere and the divisiveness of the lower, supermind is the principle by which the two can be reconciled.[25]

But if the universe is a creation of the absolute through the intermediary of supermind, how do matter, life, and mind become so obviously undivine, characterized by ignorance, error, evil, incapacity, and pain? Aurobindo deals with these and other classic problems of Western and Indian philosophy in the first part of the second book of *The Life Divine.* The central problem may be stated paradoxically: How did "this division [come] about in the Indivisible"? Aurobindo answers that "the idea of real division" comes from a certain "perversion of the supramental functioning," specifically "from the individualised soul viewing everything from its own standpoint and excluding all others. It proceeds, that is to say, by an exclusive concentration of consciousness, an exclusive self-identification of the soul with a particular temporal and spatial action which is only a part of its own play of being." In some of the most difficult chapters of *The Life Divine,* Aurobindo argues that this "exclusive concentration" is the source not only of the individual's limited view, but also of the cosmic *avidya,* or ignorance, which is the origin of the divisiveness and imperfection of the lower hemisphere. The "wall of separation" that it builds, Aurobindo states, "shuts out the consciousness of each form from the awareness of its own total self, of other embodied consciousness and of universal being."[26]

Exclusive concentration explains how the absolute One becomes a world of multiplicity, with its dual values of truth and falsehood, pleasure and pain, life and death. But the question remains as to why this happens at all. Why must beings in the lower hemisphere become victims not only of ignorance and pain, but also of falsehood and evil? In answering, Aurobindo reminds us that it is *brahman* itself that has become each individual being. The question thus is not "how came God to create for his creatures a suffering and evil of which He is Himself incapable and therefore immune, but how came the sole and infinite Existence-Consciousness-Bliss to admit into itself that which is not bliss, that which seems to be its positive negation." For Aurobindo, the answer is that *brahman* undertakes creation for a purpose: "to trace the cycle of self-oblivion and self-discovery for the joy of which the Ignorance is assumed in Nature." A perfect cosmic manifestation in the higher hemisphere might have been possible, but it would have left certain potentialities unexpressed. The plunge into mind-life-matter was "not a blunder and a fall, but a purposeful descent, not a curse but a divine opportunity.... To achieve a possibility of the divine Existence which could not be achieved in other conditions ... would seem to be the task imposed on the spirit born into the material universe."[27] Put otherwise, *brahman* descends into the lower hemisphere to take part in what Aurobindo calls elsewhere "the adventure of consciouness and joy," to sound the infinite possibilities of existence.[28] The world that is created by *brahman*'s descent, our world of matter, life and mind, is not an aberration or an illusion but part of *brahman*'s purpose.

Up to this point Aurobindo has been dealing with the metaphysical foundations of the divine life. In the second part of the second book, he turns to its psychological conditions.[29] He has traced the origin of the cosmic ignorance (*avidya*) to the involution of the divine in matter. The next step is to explain how the divine re-ascends to knowledge (*vidya*). The knowledge Aurobindo speaks of is "not an intellectual knowledge which can be learned and completed in our present mould of consciousness; it must be an experience, a becoming, a change of consciousness, a change of being." This change can only come about by means of evolution, which would seem to imply "a slow process in Time," similar to that needed for the emergence of life from matter and mind from life. But with the appearance of the higher faculties of mind, "evolution has now become conscious." This means that human will and endeavor have a role to play. Henceforth the ascent to knowledge can proceed swiftly "by a conscious self-transformation."[30]

The ascent to higher levels, the descent of the powers of those levels, and the resultant "transformation of the life of the Ignorance into the divine life of the truth-conscious spirit" are the themes of the concluding chapters of *The Life Divine*. Earlier religious and spiritual worldviews split life "into the spiritual and the mundane," which meant that there could "only be an abrupt transition, not a harmony or reconciliation of these parts of our nature." What they missed, for Aurobindo, was the "spiritual evolution, an unfolding here of the Being within from birth to birth, of which man becomes the central instrument and human life at its highest offers the critical turning-point." A spiritual evolution, Aurobindo insists, "is the link needed for the reconciliation of life and spirit." In the early stages of this evolution, "man"—that is, the human being—needs to "affirm, to make distinct and rich, to possess firmly, powerfully and completely his own individuality." But this is only a preliminary movement. The true individuality is not the ego or separate individual being but the soul, a "psychic being" that carries the gains of one lifetime to another. "For the soul has not finished what it has to do by merely developing into humanity; it has still to develop that humanity into its higher possibilities," and this cannot be done in the course of a single human life. Moreover, "if it is fundamentally an evolution of consciousness that has been taking place in Nature, then man as he is cannot be the last term of that evolution." Man is "a transitional being" and is impelled to "arrive at Supermind and supermanhood or at least lend his mentality, life and body to that greater term of the Spirit manifesting in Nature."[31]

To speak of what is beyond mind using the language of mind involves the writer in, as Aurobindo puts it, "a difficulty which amounts almost to an impossibility." He nevertheless attempts in the last two chapters of *The Life Divine* to explain what supermind is and what a life of supramental or gnostic beings would be. Human life is imperfect because mind is imperfect; mind is not the "native dynamism of consciousness of the Spirit; Supermind, the light of gnosis, is its native dynamism." When mind became an established power on earth, the result was "a race of mental beings"; when supermind similarly becomes active, "there will be established on earth a gnostic Consciousness and Power which will shape a race of gnostic spiritual beings." It will be such beings, and not improved models of humanity, that will bring about the gnostic change. For "a perfected human world cannot be created by men or composed of men who are themselves imperfect." All of the religious, scientific, and political panaceas developed across the centuries failed to produce a perfect society, Aurobindo observes; "It is only the full emergence of the soul, the full descent of the native light and power of the Spirit and the consequent replacement or transformation and uplifting of our insufficient mental and vital nature by a spiritual and supramental Supernature that can effect this evolutionary miracle." Anticipating the objection that a life of gnostic knowledge would have no interest or savor, Aurobindo affirms that a gnostic life would in fact "be more full and fruitful and its interest more vivid than the creative interest of the Ignorance" in which human beings live. "A life of gnostic beings carrying the evolution to a higher supramental status might," Aurobindo concludes, "fitly be characterised as a divine life; for it would be a life of the Divine, a life of the beginnings of a spiritual divine light and power and joy manifested in material Nature."[32]

AUROBINDO HAD LITTLE INTEREST in philosophy and read few of the major Eastern or Western philosophers. At Cambridge he read a few Platonic dialogues as part of his study of Greek literature. He tried to acquaint himself with Hume, Kant, and Hegel, but retained little of the little he read. In general, European philosophy seemed to him to be "a mass of abstractions with nothing concrete or real that could be firmly grasped and written in a metaphysical jargon to which I had not the key." Most of the ideas that he absorbed were "picked up desultorily" in his general reading. This included the works of the English Romantic poets, some books by Friedrich Nietzsche, and secondhand accounts of the theory of evolution. His study of Sanskrit literature led him eventually to the *Bhagavad Gita*, the Upanishads, and the *Rig Veda*, but he did not study the dialectics of Vedanta or other Indian philosophical systems; only some "general ideas" stayed with him.[33] Nevertheless, it would be inaccurate to say that he was innocent of philosophy when he began to write *The Life Divine*. The books he read were enough to introduce him to the classic problems of the discipline and to acquaint him with some of the leading schools.

The only works that Aurobindo regularly cited in *The Life Divine* were the *Gita*, Upanishads, and *Rig Veda*. His philosophy, he explained, "was formed first" by the study of these works, which were also "the basis of my first practice of Yoga; I tried to realise what I read in my spiritual experience and succeeded; in fact I was never satisfied till experience came and it was on this experience that later on I founded my philosophy." But his experience was not confined to confirming the insights of ancient sages. He once wrote in a personal note that as he sat in meditation, ideas from the intuitive levels linking mind and supermind "came down in a mighty flood which swelled into a sea of direct Knowledge always translating itself into experience, or they were intuitions starting from an experience and leading to other intuitions and a corresponding experience. . . . All sorts of ideas came in which might have belonged to conflicting philosophies but they were here reconciled in a large synthetic whole." These ideas and their synthesis were self-validating for Aurobindo, and most of his followers accept them as unquestionable truths. But if a philosophical system is to merit acceptance as philosophy, it has to be defended by logical arguments; otherwise it joins other infallible revelations that depend on faith for acceptance and persuasion or coercion for propagation. In other words, it becomes a religion. Aurobindo did not want his teaching to be regarded as a religion and therefore used logic to present and defend it—but not, he stressed, to arrive at it. In reaching his conclusions, he owed nothing, he said, "to intellectual abstractions, ratiocination or dialectics; when I have used these means it was simply to explain my philosophy and justify it to the intellect of others."[34] If the spiritual value of Aurobindo's system can only be gauged by one who has had the same experiences, its philosophical value is measurable by the usual critical means: studies of sources, arguments, and conclusions, and evaluations of rhetoric and style.

How does Aurobindo rank as a philosopher? Most members of the philosophical profession—those who have read him at all—would be loath to admit him to their club. His methods simply do not fit in with the discipline as it is currently practiced. Even Stephen H. Phillips, the author of a sympathetic monograph on Aurobindo's thought, had to admit that Aurobindo wrote *The Life Divine* not as a philosopher, but as "a 'spiritual preceptor,' in a long tradition of intellectual, but hardly academic 'gurus.'"[35] Yet this preceptorial philosopher created a synthesis of spiritual thought that bears comparison with the best of similar systems: those of Plotinus, Abhinavagupta, and Alfred North Whitehead. Even if his critics deny him the label of philosopher—a label he never claimed for himself—his philosophical writings will continue to be studied by lay and academic readers.

THROUGHOUT THE LIFE OF the *Arya*, Aurobindo published occasional essays in which he dealt with different themes of his thought in an accessible, literary way. "Evolution," which appeared in 1915, considers the ideas of causality and destiny in the light of evolutionary thought. The scientist and the materialist philosopher explain events of all sorts as the mechanical working out of physical cause and effect, but this approach is too cut and dried to account for the complexity of the nonmaterial universe: "Besides the manifest causes there are those that are unmanifest or latent and not subject to our analysis." When the mechanistic approach is left behind, "we move towards the perception of a conscious, supple, flexible, intensely surprising and constantly dramatic evolution by a superconscient Knowledge which reveals things in

Matter, Life and Mind out of the unfathomable Inconscient from which they rise."[36] In another piece of 1915, Aurobindo paid tribute to Nietzsche, who alone among modern thinkers brought back something of the old Greek "dynamism and practical force into philosophy"; but he argued that the German was "an apostle who never entirely understood his own message." Nietzsche's superman, a godhead of power who "fiercely and arrogantly repels the burden of simple sorrow and service," embodied only one of the three qualities of superhumanity: "Power," Aurobindo wrote, "must bow its neck to the yoke of Light and Love before it can do any real good to the race."[37]

The lyrical style that sometimes breaks out in these essays is given full play in "Thoughts and Glimpses," a set of linked aphorisms that owe much to Nietzsche in form, but in expression are vintage Aurobindo: "All religions have saved a number of souls," he wrote, "but none yet has been able to spiritualise mankind. For that is needed not cult and creed but a sustained and all-comprehensive effort at spiritual self-evolution."[38] Aurobindo's name for this effort was yoga, a term he defined at length in an essay of 1916:

> Yoga is a generic name for the processes and the result of processes by which we transcend or shred off our present modes of being and rise to a new, a higher, a wider mode of consciousness which is not that of the ordinary animal and intellectual man. Yoga is the exchange of an egoistic for a universal or cosmic consciousness lifted towards or informed by the supra-cosmic, transcendent Unnameable who is the source and support of all things. Yoga is the passage of the human thinking animal towards the God-consciousness from which he has descended.[39]

To explain the theory and methods of yoga was the second of the tasks he set for himself when he began to publish the *Arya*. The work in which he undertook this explanation ran from the journal's first issue to its last, and even then remained unfinished.

A New System of Yoga

Throughout *The Life Divine*, Aurobindo made it clear that the justification for his philosophical theories lay in spiritual experience rather than logical argument. To him the mind is, at best, an instrument to organize and express "the ignorance," that is, the relative knowledge of words and things. True knowledge, he argued, is knowledge of the absolute, *brahman*, and of the world as an expression of *brahman*'s existence-consciousness-bliss. Such knowledge is available to human beings directly through experiences of identity with *brahman* or its "modes," for example the personal forms of God, or, indirectly, by means of intuition, the power that brings "those brilliant messages from the Unknown which are the beginning of . . . higher knowledge."[40]

Aurobindo did not, as a rule, cite his own spiritual experiences as proofs of his philosophical statements. If he had done so consistently, *The Life Divine* would have been a work of revelatory theology and not philosophy. He did occasionally suggest that he had reached an understanding of some aspect of his system through direct vision or experience, but he did not ask his readers to remain content with his testimony. If his work was to have any value for others, the experiences on which it was based had to be available, in principle, to all human beings, and to be attainable, in practice, by anyone willing to make the necessary effort. Accordingly, in the prospectus of the *Arya*, he said that he would publish "practical methods of inner culture and self-development."[41] Readers hoping for a step-by-step guide to nirvana were destined to be disappointed. *The Synthesis of Yoga*, the work in which he presented his methods, is almost as abstruse as *The Life Divine*, containing no easy-to-follow techniques. Aurobindo explained why in an article published at the end of the *Arya*'s first year:

> Our second preoccupation has been with the psychological disciplines of Yoga; but here also [as in *The Life Divine*] we have been obliged to concern ourselves with a deep study of the principles underlying the methods rather than with a popular statement of methods and disciplines. But without this previous study of principles the statement of methods would have been unsound and not really helpful. There are no short-cuts to an integral perfection.[42]

THE SCOPE OF *The Synthesis of Yoga* is set by its epigraph: "All life is Yoga." Aurobindo meant two different things by this. First, the yoga of the individual must include everything that is essential to life, because life itself "is a vast Yoga of Nature who attempts . . . to realise her perfection in an ever-increasing expression of her yet unrealised potentialities and to unite herself with her own divine reality." Secondly, each system of yoga is just "a selection or compression" of "methods which are already being used loosely, largely, in a leisurely movement" by nature. It follows that yoga is not "something mystic and abnormal which has no relation to the ordinary processes of the

World-Energy"; rather, it is "an intense and exceptional use of powers that she [the *shakti* or World-Energy] has already manifested."[43]

It was necessary to reconsider the traditional paths of yoga because they had, in Aurobindo's view, become excessively formalized, and "all truth and practice too strictly formulated becomes old and loses much, if not all, of its virtue." Aurobindo undertook his investigation with the idea of isolating "the one common principle and the one common power from which all [paths] derive their being and tendency."[44] After considering briefly the mechanical methods of *hatha* and *raja* yoga, he turned to the "triple path" of works, knowledge, and devotion (*karmayoga, jnanayoga,* and *bhaktiyoga*). Each of the paths, or approaches, is based upon a primary function of life: will, knowledge, or love. *Karmayoga, jnanayoga,* and *bhaktiyoga* make use of the energies associated with will, knowledge and love to achieve union with the corresponding form of the ultimate: the divine will, the self, and the divine beloved. Most practitioners, Aurobindo wrote, follow "one of the three parallel paths exclusively and almost in antagonism to the others instead of effecting a synthetic harmony of the intellect, the heart and the will in an integral divine realisation."[45] Aurobindo aimed to effect this harmony; to succeed, he had to find the "common principle" underlying the three.

He located this principle in *shakti*, the divine energy that is emphasized in the Tantras. In the Vedantic paths of works, knowledge, and love, "the lord of the Yoga is the Purusha, the Conscious Soul that knows, observes, attracts, governs." But in tantric yoga, it is "the Nature-Soul, the Energy [*shakti*], the Will-in-Power executive in the universe" that is supreme. Aurobindo noted that tantric yoga had of late "fallen into discredit with those who are not Tantrics," an allusion to the reputation of the "left-hand" path of tantrism, "which not content with exceeding the duality of virtue and sin ... seemed, sometimes, to make a method of self-indulgence, a method of unrestrained social immorality."[46] He rejected this branch of tantrism not because he considered it immoral, but because he shunned fixed practices (*kriyas*) of all sorts. For him, the importance of tantric yoga lay in its fundamental principle, the nature-soul or *shakti*. Combining this dynamic Tantric principle with the static principle of *purusha* or conscious soul, which underlies the philosophies of Sankhya and Vedanta, he arrived at an "integral conception of God and Nature."[47] The integral conception yielded, in turn, an integral method: "to put our whole conscious being into relation and contact with the Divine and to call Him in to transform our entire being into His." This translated "in psychological fact ... into the progressive surrender of the ego with its whole field and all its apparatus to the Beyond-ego with its vast and incalculable but always inevitable workings." Taking up the disparate methods of the paths of works, knowledge, devotion, and perfection, the integral yogi discovers their underlying commonalities and brings about a "perfect harmony" of their results.[48]

IN A STUDY WITH THE MOTTO "all life is Yoga," it is natural that *karmayoga*, the yoga of works, was the first of the traditional paths to be considered. The first necessity in *karmayoga*, as in all forms of yoga, "is to dissolve that central faith and vision in the mind which concentrate it on its development and satisfaction and interests in the old externalised order of things." One must cultivate a "deeper faith and vision" focused on the divine and compel all parts of the being to accept the new orientation. Stated otherwise, one must surrender oneself to what is beyond oneself. The nature "must offer itself in every part and every movement to that which seems to the unregenerated sense-mind so much less real than the material world and its objects."[49] In many forms of yoga, this turning towards the divine is helped along by an ascetic rejection of the world. This is ruled out in the integral yoga. What needs to be rejected is not action and life, but egoism and desire.

In one of the book's most compelling chapters, Aurobindo contrasted the observance of human ethical standards with the freedom of the liberated individual. Taking an almost Nietzschean view of conventional morality, he wrote that from an evolutionary viewpoint "good and evil are . . . shifting quantities and change from time to time their meaning and value."[50] To those incapable of venturing beyond established standards, "this truth may seem to be a dangerous concession which is likely to destroy the very foundation of morality, confuse all conduct and establish only chaos." But "if we have light enough and flexibility enough to recognise that a standard of conduct may be temporary and yet necessary for its time and to observe it faithfully until it can be replaced by a better," we lose not our moral bearings, but "only the fanaticism of an imperfect and intolerant virtue."[51]

In subsequent chapters, Aurobindo examined the liberating concepts of the *Gita*: *samata* or equanimity, the transcendence of the three *gunas*, and freedom from *ahankara* or I-sense, which makes us view ourselves as separate egos. As always, he based himself on an affirmative rather than an ascetic foundation. "Nothing is more difficult than to get rid of egoism while yet we admit personality and adhere to action," he wrote. It is easier "to starve the ego by renouncing the impulse to act or to kill it by cutting away from us all movement of personality." But this was not the road he wanted to take: "Our more difficult problem is to liberate the true Person and attain to a divine manhood which shall be the pure vessel of a divine force and the perfect instrument of a divine action." The final state of the integral yoga of works is one in which "a divine action" arises "spontaneously, freely, infallibly from the light and force of our spiritual self in union with the Divine."[52]

THE "YOGA OF DIVINE WORKS" is the best worked out of the four parts of *The Synthesis of Yoga*, and the only one that was revised for book publication. The next part, the "Yoga of Integral Knowledge," is a sprawling consideration of the principles and practices of *jnanayoga*, the way of knowledge. In the yogic sense, knowledge is the direct awareness of the eternal and absolute being, called self or *atman* when viewed "in relation to the individual" and *brahman* when viewed "in relation to the universe."[53] The knowledge that is brought to us by "the senses and intellectual reasoning from the data of the senses" is "not true knowledge; it is a science of appearances."[54] The status of knowledge envisaged by yoga "is not merely an intellectual conception or clear discrimination of the truth, nor is it an enlightened psychological experience of the modes of our being. It is a 'realisation', in the full sense of the word; it is the making real to ourselves and in ourselves of the Self, the transcendent and universal Divine" and a re-visioning of the various modes of being "in the light of that Self."[55]

The yogi on the path of knowledge "rejects successively the body, the life, the senses, the heart, the very thought in order to merge into the quiescent Self or supreme Nihil or indefinite Absolute."[56] This can lead to an experience of the world as an illusory imposition on the blankness of the self, along with a subjective extinction (nirvana) of the universe and everything in it. But this extinction is not inevitable. The individual's self-realization "in the essence of his conscious being" can also lead to a realization of the absolute's "dynamic divine manifestation."[57]

By means of purification, concentration, and rejection, the practitioner of *jnanayoga* is released from subjection to the body, heart, mind, and I-sense. This makes possible the realization of the self; but the self has more than one poise and more than one mode. The passive self in its immobile poise above the universe is balanced by the active self pervading and upholding the manifestation; the self in its impersonal mode is balanced by the personal divine. According to Aurobindo, an integral realization must include union with the passive and the active self, the impersonal and personal divine, and finally "the Transcendent possessing them both in His being and employing them both as modes for His manifestation."[58]

The *Synthesis* contains few explicitly autobiographical passages, but it is clear that when Aurobindo described the realization of the passive self, the active self, and the transcendent divine, he was sketching his own trajectory. He attained the passive self after silencing his mind in January 1908. The realization of the active, or cosmic, self followed in Alipore a few months later, and the realization of the transcendent took place in August 1912. The last chapters of the "Yoga of Integral Knowledge" deal with what he called his fourth "fundamental realisation," the passage from mind to supermind. It is this that he was concerned with during the years he worked on the *Synthesis*.

The supermind is the level or plane that links the superior planes of existence, consciousness, and bliss with the lower planes of body, life, and mind. A plane, Aurobindo explained in one of three chapters devoted to the subject, is "general settled poise or world of relations between Purusha and Prakriti, between the Soul and Nature."[59] Normally we are acquainted only with the "lower triple Purusha": the soul inhabiting the principles of matter, life, and mind. But it is possible to turn the hierarchy of planes into a "ladder of self-transcendence," rising through the intermediary levels above mind into supermind, and finally into the planes of pure bliss, consciousness, and being. In these superior levels, "there is opened to us an illimitable existence which we feel as if it were an infinity above us to which we attempt to rise and an infinity around us into which we strive to dissolve our separate existence. . . . If this liberation is achieved, its power can take, if so we will, increasing possession of our lower being also until even our lowest and perversest activities are refashioned into the truth of the Vijnana [supermind]."[60]

"LOVE," WROTE AUROBINDO in the first chapter of the third part of the *Synthesis*, "is the crown of works and the flowering of knowledge." By harnessing the power of love, the practitioner of *bhaktiyoga* enters into an intense personal relationship and eventually a state of union with the divine. To the *jnani* or seeker of knowledge, *bhaktiyoga* is an inferior path because it proceeds by worship and always keeps a sense of difference between the devotee and the absolute. The *bhakta*, meanwhile, regards knowledge as joyless and abstract, leading to a union in which both God and aspirant are lost in an impersonal union. And both *jnani* and *bhakta* look down on those who practice the yoga of works, while the worker has little time for the exclusiveness of knowledge or love. In an integral yoga, Aurobindo insisted, these limited visions have to be overcome. Yoga "may commence with the way of love, as with the way of knowledge or of works; but where they meet, is the beginning of its joy of fulfilment."[61]

The yoga of love proceeds on four assumptions: that "the supreme Existence is not an abstraction or a state of existence, but a conscious Being"; that this being "meets us in the universe and is in some way immanent in it as well as its source"; that the same being "is capable of personal relations with us and must therefore be not incapable of personality"; and finally that "when we approach him by our human emotions, we receive a response in kind."[62] To the nondevotee, these assumptions are unwarranted, but they are based on experiences that are as real to the devotee as the relationships of ordinary life are to the rest of us. To the devotee, God is master, friend, father, mother, child, or, most intensely, lover and beloved. Every feeling that can prepare the heart for union is accepted by the devotee and turned to the higher purpose. In the end, the devotee experiences the delight of the divine for the sake of the divine "and for nothing else, for no cause or gain whatever beyond itself."[63] Such delight is felt in every form of union with the divine, from complete merging and mutual presence and nearness "and other wonderful things too for which language has as yet no name."[64] The ineffability of the states makes it difficult to write about *bhaktiyoga,* and Aurobindo gave less space to it in the *Synthesis* than to the other paths. The suggestive language of aphorism may have been more apt to express the intensity of the path of love, as in this example from his posthumously published collection *Thoughts and Aphorisms*:

> What is the use of admiring Nature or worshipping her as a Power, a
> Presence and a goddess? What is the use, either, of appreciating her aes-
> thetically or artistically? The secret is to enjoy her with the soul as
> one enjoys a woman with the body.[65]

THE FIRST THREE PARTS OF *The Synthesis of Yoga* deal with theories and methods that are well known in Indian spiritual literature. The way of works is a primary concern of the *Gita,* the way of knowledge the practical core of Sankhya and Vedanta. The way of love does not lend itself to scriptural treatment, but the *Narada Bhakti Sutras* and similar works attempt to systematize the path's characteristics. But there is no traditional counterpart to the yoga that Aurobindo described in the fourth part of the *Synthesis,* "The Yoga of Self-Perfection." Not until the publication of his *Record of Yoga* did it become clear that the path he was following in Pondicherry, and keeping track of from day to day in the *Record,* was the path that he wrote about in "The Yoga of Self-Perfection." The *Sapta Chatusthaya,* or Seven Quaternaries, form the framework not only of the *Record,* but also of the fourth part of the *Synthesis.*

If *Sapta Chatusthaya* is unique to Aurobindo's yoga, some of its elements are known to other yoga systems. The *siddhis* he speaks of in the third *chatusthaya* are mentioned, with variations, in the *Yoga Sutras* and numerous tantric texts. Tantrism, in fact, provides the general foundation of the yoga of self-perfection. Unlike the Vedantic yogas, "the Tantric system makes liberation the final but not the only aim; it takes on its way a full perfection and enjoyment of the spiritual power, light and joy in the human existence."[66] To use the four terms of Aurobindo's *siddhi-chatusthaya* or quaternary of perfection, tantric yoga aims not only at *shuddhi* (purification) and *mukti* (liberation) but also *bhukti* (enjoyment) and *siddhi* (perfection).

Aurobindo arranged the elements of his yoga of self-perfection into six groupings corresponding to the first six *chatusthayas* of the yoga of the *Record*. He gave an overview of the system in the tenth chapter of "The Yoga of Self-Perfection." The first need, he wrote, is to establish "some fundamental poise of the soul" by "growing into a perfect equality." The second is "to raise all the active parts of the human nature to [the] highest condition and working pitch of their power and capacity." Full development of these two components of the yoga would mean the perfection of our normal human nature; but Aurobindo envisaged "the possession of the divine perfection in the highest terms possible to us." This could only come about by "the evolution of the mental into the gnostic being" and the consequent transformation of the mind and lower faculties into their supramental equivalents; this evolution and transformation are the goals of the third *chatusthaya* and make up the third component of the yoga. When the process of transformation is "pushed to its highest conclusion," it "brings in a spiritualising and illumination of the whole physical consciousness." This is the fourth component of the yoga. What remains, the fifth and sixth components, are "the perfect action and enjoyment of being on the gnostic basis," the harmony of soul and nature and the union of the individual with the *brahman* in all its aspects.[67]

In subsequent chapters of the *Synthesis*, Aurobindo dealt with the various elements of the various groupings in more detail. The first element of the first group is equality, or *samata*, the ability to receive all that happens in the same untroubled way, neither shaken by hardship nor rejoicing in success. The ascetic achieves a precarious equality by avoiding the pressures of the world, but that was not what Aurobindo had in mind. In his yoga, he insisted, there is no question "of an ascetic killing of the life-impulse and its native utilities and functions; not its killing is demanded, but its transformation."[68] Such transformation becomes possible when the practitioner goes beyond the first stage of *samata*, the negative freedom from disturbance, and begins to feel the later, positive, stages: *shanti*, "a firm peace and absence of all disturbance and trouble"; *sukham*, an "inner spiritual happiness and positive ease of the natural being," and finally *hasyam*, "a clear joy and laughter of the soul" in all circumstances.[69]

The second movement of the yoga of self-perfection is the development of "the heightened, enlarged and rectified power of the instruments of our normal Nature."[70] Power means here the perfect functioning of the four lower faculties of the human being: *buddhi*, the intellect; *chitta*, the heart or emotional being; *prana*, the conscious life-force, and *kaya*, the body. Each of these faculties has associated with it an ideal personality, symbolized by one of the *varnas* of the Indian religious tradition: *brahmin, kshatriya, vaishya,* or *shudra.* To Aurobindo these types do not have the values they are given in the corrupt system of caste. Each represents an essential human power that has to be developed for a complete spiritual personality: "a Power for knowledge, a Power for strength, a Power for mutuality and active and productive relation and interchange, a Power for works and labour and service."[71] Each of these powers is associated with a higher, "divine," power, which progressively must replace "our egoistic, our personal, our separatively individual will and energy by a universal and a divine will and energy which determines our action in harmony with the universal action and reveals itself as the direct will and the all-guiding power of the Purushottama [supreme soul]."[72] This seemingly impossible goal can only be achieved through *shraddha,* or faith. What is required is "not a superstitious, dogmatic or limiting credence attached to every temporary support or formula," but rather "a faith fixed on realities [of spiritual experience], moving from the lesser to the completer realities and ready to throw down all scaffolding and keep only the large and growing structure."[73]

Once the aspirant is established in a sure basis of equality and has begun to transform the lower nature, it is safe for him or her to begin the third movement of the yoga: the ascent from mind to supermind. In the lower nature, supermind "is present most strongly as intuition and it is therefore through a development of the intuitive mind that we can make the first step towards the self-existent spontaneous and direct supramental knowledge."[74] The hesitant workings of intuition must be extended so that the ordinary mind can be replaced by a sort of intuitive mentality. From this poise, the aspirant can rise into the lower gradations of the supermind and begin to experience supramental thought and knowledge, even the workings of a supramental sense. The chapters in which Aurobindo introduced these concepts are as difficult as any in *The Life Divine,* but he occasionally included a personal observation that made the transformation seem at least conceivable:

I get the supramental knowledge best by becoming one with the truth, one with the object of knowledge; the supramental satisfaction and integral light is most there when there is no further division between the knower, knowledge and the known.... I see the thing known not as an object outside myself, but as myself or a part of my universal self contained in my most direct consciousness. This leads to the highest and completest knowledge; thought and speech being representations and not this direct possession in the consciousness are to the supermind a lesser form and, if not filled with the spiritual awareness, thought becomes in fact a diminution of knowledge.[75]

The last complete chapter of *The Synthesis of Yoga* deals with *trikaldrishti*, the knowledge of the future, present, and past, the power "held of old to be a supreme sign of the seer and the Rishi."[76] This chapter was published in the January 1921 issue of the *Arya*, which turned out to be the last issue. Aurobindo never wrote in detail on the final element of the third *chatusthaya*, *samadhi* or yogic trance. He also left untreated all of the fourth, fifth, and sixth *chatusthayas*, which deal with the transformation of the body, the divine creation, and the vision of the *brahman*. He always hesitated to take up these subjects in his public writings, and he probably did not regret not having the chance to deal with them in the *Arya*.

The Synthesis of Yoga is a formidable piece of work even in its incomplete state. It surveys familiar and unfamiliar systems of yoga and points out how they can be harmonized. What it gives remarkably little of is what the author promised in the prospectus: "practical methods of inner culture and self-development." It occasionally offers a technique of thought control or a tip about the development of intuition. But there is very little how-to advice. It explains the principles of yoga, but requires the reader to provide the link between principle and practice. To some this is a disappointing approach, but in a way it is the only one possible. As Aurobindo explained in an early chapter, the power of the yoga works differently in each individual. One might almost say that "each man [or woman] in this path has his [or her] own method of Yoga." Nevertheless, there are "certain broad lines of working common to all which enable us to construct not indeed a routine system, but yet some kind of Shastra or scientific method of the synthetic Yoga." These "broad lines" are what he lays down in the *Synthesis*, at the same time acknowledging that "no written Shastra ... can be more than a partial expression of the eternal Knowledge."[77]

Spirituality and Society

In August 1915, at the start of the *Arya*'s second year of publication, Aurobindo reflected on the ideal of the journal and his intentions as author and editor. The first part of his effort was the "quest for the Truth that underlies existence and the fundamental Law of its self-expression in the universe." This was "the work of metaphysical philosophy and religious thought"—and the aim of *The Life Divine*. The second part, "the sounding and harmonising of the psychological methods of discipline by which man purifies and perfects himself," was the work of psychology, in particular "the deeper practical psychology called in India Yoga" and the subject of *The Synthesis of Yoga*. The third part was "the application of our ideas to the problems of man's social and collective life."[78] So far he had avoided any engagement with such problems. When the journal was launched, he excused himself from commenting on current events, in particular on the First World War. He did, however, note that certain aspects of the war were "of supreme importance to a synthetic Philosophy, with which we would have the right to deal" at the appropriate time.[79] A year later—while the British were marching to their doom in Gallipoli, the French were pausing between suicidal offensives in Flanders, the Germans were decimating the Russians in Poland, and the Austrians and Italians were fighting it out on the Isonzo—he began to write on international affairs for the first time since 1910. He was not concerned with the war itself, but with an ideal that, below the clouded surface of events, was "more or less vaguely making its way to the front of our consciousness": ironically, "the ideal of human unity."[80] A work by this name appeared in the *Arya* between September 1915 and July 1918.

In studying *The Ideal of Human Unity*, it is important to keep in mind the nature of the international order before and during the war. A few great imperial powers—notably Britain, France, and Germany—dominated most of the world, and there was little reason to believe that the empires of the victors would not last for centuries. Czarist Russia was powerful but beset by difficulties. The United States and Japan, increasingly important, were still peripheral. While writing the *Ideal*, Aurobindo took this now-vanished order for granted. As a result, although he revised it during the 1930s and 1940s, it is the most dated of his works. Its interest lies not so much in its treatment of contemporary events as in its sketching of large historical trends.

The social and political unity of humanity is "part of Nature's eventual scheme and must come about," wrote Aurobindo in the first chapter of the *Ideal*.[81] The whole course of history could be viewed as the evolution of larger, better-organized groupings. It had become possible to imagine a world in which all empires and nations were combined in a single unit, but this would not necessarily be "a boon in itself; it is only worth pursuing in so far as it provides a means and a framework for a better, richer, more happy and puissant individual and collective life." Such an outcome was far from certain. If union was achieved by "mechanical means," that is, through "social and political adjustments," the result was likely to be an impoverishment of the life of the individual and thus of the collectivity.[82] The world's greatest cultural flowerings took place in small political units, such as the kingdoms of ancient India and the city-states of ancient Greece. Larger units—the Mauryan and Gupta empires in India, the Macedonian and Roman empires in the West—provided stability and a chance for cultural consolidation, but soon became stagnant and uncreative. The problem was how to obtain the benefits of stable organization without sacrificing cultural diversity and richness.

Social life consists of interactions between individuals and collectivities; the perfection of human life, Aurobindo affirmed, required "the elaboration of an as yet unaccomplished harmony between these two poles of our existence." In their dealings with individuals, collectivities had followed one of two main patterns: imposing strict state control, as in ancient Sparta and contemporary Germany, or allowing individuals "as much freedom, power and dignity as is consistent with its control," as in ancient Athens and contemporary France. Strict state control is based on the idea that individual egoism has to be subordinated to the collective good if society is to work efficiently. The problem with this is that "it is this energy of the individual which is the really effective agent of collective progress." If the individual is suppressed, society suffers. Therefore, Aurobindo concluded, the "healthy unity of mankind" cannot be "brought about by State machinery."[83]

It should be remembered that Aurobindo was writing two years before the rise of Communist Russia and two decades before the rise of Nazi Germany. Before those social experiments had run their dreadful course, many believed that an all-powerful state might solve the problems of the individual and society on the national level. And if an all-powerful nation-state was good, might not a supremely powerful world-state be the final answer to the problems of international organization? The purpose of Aurobindo's book was to show the dangers of a coercive world-state and to suggest an alternative: a free world-union.

A world-union that preserved the creativity and diversity of its units would have to be "a confederation of free self-determining nationalities." To survive, it would have to go beyond administrative and economic organization, undergoing an "intellectual and psychological change; for such an inner change could alone give some chance of durability to the unification." The core of such a change "would be the growth of the living idea or religion of humanity." The intellectual religion of humanity grew out of the secular religion of the French Revolution, and was developed by the sociologist Auguste Comte. Its fundamental idea was that "mankind is the godhead to be worshipped and served by man and that the respect, the service, the progress of the human being and human life are the chief duty and the chief aim of the human spirit." But so long as it remained "an intellectual and sentimental ideal," the religion of humanity could never become the basis of a durable world union. For this to be possible, it would have to spiritualize itself and "become the general inner law of human life." The result would not be a "universal religion, a system, a thing of creed and intellectual belief and dogma and outward rite"; rather, it would be based on "the growing realisation that there is a secret Spirit, a divine Reality, in which we are all one, that humanity is its highest present vehicle on earth, that the human race and the human being are the means by which it will progressively reveal itself here. It implies a growing attempt to live out this knowledge and bring about a kingdom of this divine Spirit upon earth."[84] With these words in the closing chapter of *The Ideal of Human Unity*, Aurobindo linked his evolutionary approach in political science to the evolutionary philosophy of *The Life Divine*.

AUROBINDO READ COMPARATIVELY little in Pondicherry. The days when railway parcels filled with books arrived each month were long gone. A few volumes in French and English, mostly for the use of Nolini, Suresh, and the others, were all that his finances would permit. Besides, as he remarked later, "As the Yoga increased, I read very little—for when all the ideas of the world come crowding in from within or from above, there is not much need for gathering mental food from outside sources."[85] His principal study during the early years in Pondicherry was the *Rig Veda*, which he read, took notes on, analyzed, and translated during the entire time that the *Arya* was being published. His more conventional reading included newspapers and a few Indian journals. This ephemeral literature provided him with the themes for several enduring works. Notable among them was *The Psychology of Social Development*, later republished as *The Human Cycle*.

The seed of *The Human Cycle* was an article on the German historian Karl Lamprecht that appeared in the May 1916 issue of the *Hindustan Review*.[86] Going through the article, Aurobindo learned of the stages through which, according to Lamprecht, all human societies pass. First there is a symbolic stage, when thought is ruled by imagination. This is followed by a typal, a conventional, an individualistic, and finally a subjective stage. Although aware that "such classifications are likely to err by rigidity," Aurobindo felt that Lamprecht had grasped an important truth of social evolution. Leaving aside "the Western thinker's own dealings with his idea," he developed it in his own way.[87]

Aurobindo began by applying Lamprecht's theory to the spiritual and intellectual history of India. During the Vedic period, the characteristic institution was the sacrifice, which, according to Aurobindo, symbolized an inner relationship with the divine. The predominantly spiritual culture of the Vedas was later transformed into something "predominantly psychological and ethical." The result was a typal age in which the system of *varnas* or social orders was the key institution. Still later, inflexible conventions replaced the types; the system of *varnas* became the system of castes. According to Aurobindo, India had languished in the last phase for more than two thousand years: "Since the great Buddhistic upheaval of the national thought and life, there has been a series of recurrent attempts to rediscover the truth of the soul and life and get behind the veil of stifling conventions; but these have been conducted by a wide and tolerant spiritual reason, a plastic soul-intuition and deep subjective seeking, insufficiently militant and destructive."[88]

In Europe, rationality was not so inhibited. The emergence of reason was followed by a radical restructuring of society. The objectivity of science replaced the authority of scripture. Individuals claimed the privilege of determining what was true and what was right. To this "passion for the discovery of the actual truth of things and for the governing of human life by whatever law of the truth it has found . . . the West owes its centuries of strength, vigour, light, progress, irresistible expansion." The East felt the thrust of the age of individualism "only by contact and influence," and before it could assimilate the spirit of that age, the West moved on to another. During the subjective age, humanity "begins to gaze deeper, to see and feel what is behind the outside and below the surface and therefore to live from within." But so far subjectivism had "shown itself not so much in the relations of individuals or in the dominant ideas and tendencies of social development . . . but in . . . the nation." The "discovery of the nation-soul," as Aurobindo wrote, was not without its dangers, as shown by the contending national egoisms of Europe. It was necessary to distinguish true from false subjectivism, and to remember that the real object of society was "to provide the conditions of life and growth" by which individuals "according to their capacity" and "the [human] race through the growth of its individuals" could travel toward "divine perfection."[89]

Aurobindo clearly did not believe that the growth of rationality had taken the West to the highest possible level of development. But he admitted that "reason using the intelligent will for the ordering of the inner and the outer life is undoubtedly the highest developed faculty of man at his present point of evolution." For all that, reason was incapable of becoming the "governor of life," because the sources of life are infrarational or suprarational. At best, reason could serve as "a general arbiter and giver of suggestions . . . or as one channel of the sovereign authority. The real sovereign is another than the reasoning intelligence."[90]

According to Aurobindo, this "real sovereign" was the suprarational or spiritual truth behind the changing forms of life. Traditionally, human beings have approached this truth through religion; but religion has not succeeded as a governor of life and often has stood in the way of the growth of truth. It was necessary, therefore, to leave traditional religion behind and to find another approach to suprarational wisdom. Aurobindo took a step in this direction by distinguishing between ordinary religion or "religionism," and spiritual religion or "spirituality":

> True religion is spiritual religion, that which seeks to live in the spirit, in what is beyond the intellect, beyond the aesthetic and ethical and practical being of man, and to inform and govern these members of our being by the higher light and law of the spirit. Religionism, on the contrary, entrenches itself in some narrow pietistic exaltation of the lower members or lays exclusive stress on intellectual dogmas, forms and ceremonies, on some fixed and rigid moral code, on some religio-political or religio-social system.[91]

It is in the former that "we must seek for the directing light and the harmonising law, and in religion only in proportion as it identifies itself with this spirituality."[92]

At this point in *The Human Cycle*, Aurobindo introduced some of the yogic ideas he had been developing in his other works. The true solution for the individual and society would come through an "awakening to our real, because our highest self and nature."[93] Human evolution would move "through a subjective towards a suprarational or spiritual age" in which the human being "will develop progressively a greater spiritual, supra-intellectual and intuitive, perhaps in the end a more than intuitive, a gnostic consciousness."[94] What such an age would be like is difficult to predict, but one thing was certain: "if it limits itself by the old familiar apparatus and the imperfect means of a religious movement, it is likely to register another failure."[95] A religious movement could bring a wave of enthusiasm and uplift, but it would inevitably relapse into conventionality and stagnation. An age of spirituality could only arrive if many individuals underwent an inner change powerful enough to influence society as a whole.

THE LAST INSTALLMENTS of *The Ideal of Human Unity* and *The Psychology of Social Development* (*The Human Cycle*) appeared together in July 1918. The next month, Aurobindo published the first of a group of four essays entitled *The Renaissance in India.* From then on, each issue of the *Arya* included a work on Indian culture. The *Renaissance* was followed by *Is India Civilised?*, which was followed by *A Defence of Indian Culture.* Together these works constitute Aurobindo's main statement on a subject that had absorbed him for more than a quarter of a century: the nature and value of Indian civilization and its expressions.

When Aurobindo returned to India from England at the age of twenty, he decided that Indian culture, taken as a whole, was superior to the culture of the West. Technology and social organization had made Europe and the United States the masters of the material world. Their principal means of conquest was "machinery": mechanical control of physical nature and mechanistic solutions to the problems of society. But as Europe and the United States rose to greatness, they became enslaved to their physical and social machinery, and impoverished aesthetically and spiritually. India, though subjugated politically by Britain, held the key to the full and harmonious development of the various aspects of life. This was why—as Aurobindo often had said in his political writings and speeches—it was necessary for India to be free.

The political and cultural upsurge in India during the early years of the century had lost its momentum after 1910, but eight years later, there were signs that an Indian renaissance might be starting up again. So at least was the hope of James H. Cousins, an Irish poet and critic who was teaching at a college in south India. Cousins published his impressions of Indian artists and writers in a book called *The Renaissance in India.* In an identically titled response, Aurobindo gave his attention not to schools or individuals but to the Indian "spirit" or "mind." An awakening of India's "time-old spirit" would be, he said, "a thing of immense importance both to herself and the world." But before the country could spread its riches, it had to rise from the "inadaptive torpor into which it had lapsed." If it succeeded in this, it would bring about a triple regeneration: "the recovery of the old spiritual knowledge and experience," "the flowing of this spirituality into new forms of philosophy, literature, art, science and critical knowledge," and "an original dealing with modern problems in the light of the Indian spirit and the endeavour to formulate a greater synthesis of a spiritualised society."[96]

Throughout the *Renaissance* and his other writings on India, Aurobindo spoke of India's "ingrained and dominant spirituality." But he also tried to correct the idea, which he attributed to "European writers," that the "Indian mind" was merely "abstract, metaphysical, religious . . . not apt for life, dreamy, unpractical."[97] His own idea was that the Indian mind was practical and spiritual at the same time. But at the moment, what the world most needed was India's spiritual vision. "The work of the renaissance in India," he concluded, "must be to make this spirit, this higher view of life, this sense of deeper potentiality once more a creative, perhaps a dominant power in the world."[98]

Aurobindo championed India's past, but he was far from being a reactionary. He criticized the "revival of orthodox conservatism" as "more academic and sentimental than profound in its impulse or in touch with the great facts and forces of life." It was necessary to "look upon all that our past contains with new eyes" in order "to recover something of their ancient sense" and at the same time "bring out of them a new light which gives to the old truths fresh aspects and therefore novel potentialities of creation and evolution." The cultural monuments he studied belonged mostly to the Hindu tradition, but he insisted that "spirituality is much wider than any particular religion, and in the larger ideas of it that are now coming on us even the greatest religion becomes no more than a broad sect or branch of the one universal religion, by which we shall understand in the future man's seeking for the eternal . . . and his attempt to arrive at some equation . . . of the values of human life with the eternal and the divine values."[99]

Indian civilization had survived colonialism, Aurobindo wrote, because of its inherent strength: "A less vigorous energy of life might well have foundered and perished under the double weight of the deadening of its old innate motives and a servile imitation of alien ideas and habits."[100] The danger that this could still happen had not yet passed. Salvos in the subcontinental conflict of cultures were constantly being fired, and Aurobindo thought it necessary to respond. In 1917 the English critic William Archer published a critique of Indian culture called *India and the Future.* Archer's attitude towards India's political aspirations was relatively advanced: he insisted that Britain had to "acknowledge the duty of giving India, as soon as possible, an equal status in the community of self-governing nations." But he found little to admire in India's social and cultural life, sprinkling his book with supercilious remarks such as "I do not think it important to decide whether India is the most forward of barbarous, or the most backward of civilized, nations."[101] In 1918 John Woodroffe, a judge and scholar best known for his studies of the Tantric tradition, replied to Archer in a book entitled *Is India Civilised?* Later the same year, Aurobindo used Woodroffe's book as the starting-point for a group of three essays, also headed *Is India Civilised?*, in which he examined the question of India's cultural identity and its place in a rapidly changing world. The "passion to imitate English ideas and culture has passed," Aurobindo noted, but something even more dangerous was replacing it: "the passion to imitate continental European culture at large and in particular the crude and vehement turn of revolutionary Russia." This created an "ambiguous situation" out of which there could be "only one out of two issues. Either India will be rationalised and industrialised out of all recognition and she will be no longer India or else she will be the leader in a new world-phase, aid by her example and cultural infiltration the new tendencies of the West and spiritualise the human race."[102]

Much of Aurobindo's *Is India Civilised?* is starkly dualistic, positioning Indian culture as spiritual, aesthetic, and profound and Western culture as rationalistic, mechanistic, and superficial. In a conflict of cultures, one must never lay down ones arms; to do so is "to invite destruction." But toward the end of his treatment, Aurobindo arrived at a broader view. Indians needed "the courage to defend our culture against ignorant occidental criticism and to maintain it against the gigantic modern pressure," but they also needed the "courage to admit not from any European standpoint but from our own outlook the errors of our culture." Pride in the accomplishments of one's motherland did not have to not take the form of an "unthinking cultural Chauvinism which holds that whatever we have is good for us because it is Indian or even that whatever is in India is best, because it is the creation of the Rishis." What India required was not an isolated self-glorification, but "a unity with the rest of mankind, in which we shall maintain our spiritual and our outer independence." In the end, the East-West dichotomy had to be transcended, for "from the view of the evolutionary future, European and Indian civilisation at their best have only been half achievements, infant dawns pointing to the mature sunlight that is to come."[103]

For the moment, however, the most important task was to counter Western cultural imperialism with "a strong, living and mobile defence."[104] The same month in which Aurobindo concluded *Is India Civilised?*, he began his own critique of Archer's book under the title *A Rationalistic Critic on Indian Culture* (he later changed the heading of these essays to *A Defence of Indian Culture*). The first six installments were concerned with the nature of cultural criticism. Long before the term "ethnocentric" came into common use, Aurobindo emphasized the illegitimacy of basing judgments of another culture on the tenets of one's own: "A culture must be judged, first by its essential spirit, then by its best accomplishment and, lastly, by its power of survival, renovation and adaptation to new phases of the permanent needs of the [human] race." Critics such as Archer based their judgments on the criteria of material success. So viewed, Aurobindo wrote, Greece of the philosophers was inferior to the later Roman Empire. India doubtless had fallen from the heights of its "best accomplishment," but this was only a temporary decline. Hostile critics refused "to see or to recognise the saving soul of good which still keeps this civilisation alive and promises a strong and vivid return to the greatness of its permanent ideal." This ideal, the "innermost sense of Indian culture," was "an aspiration to break out in the end from this mind bound to life and matter into a greater spiritual consciousness." But it did not follow that "Indian culture concedes no reality to life, follows no material or vital aims and satisfactions or cares to do nothing for our actual human existence."[105] The finest ages of Indian culture combined spiritual greatness with an outpouring of literary, artistic, social, and political creation.

In answering Archer's negative criticisms, Aurobindo was no more evenhanded than he had been in *Bande Mataram* when writing about the latest utterance of John Morley. *The Defence of Indian Culture* is a polemic from start to finish, as Aurobindo closed his eyes to the critic's positive judgments and blasted him for the slightest negative remark. Archer wrote: "The only characters in the [Indian] epics that can arouse anything like rational admiration are the long suffering and devoted women of whom Sita is the type. Their stories are sometimes really touching, though the heroism they display is too often, like that of Alkestis or Griselda, excessive to the verge of immorality." Illegitimately citing only the last conceit, Aurobindo chastised Archer for writing "that Sita, the type of conjugal fidelity and chastity, is so excessive in her virtue 'as to verge on immorality.'"[106] Archer certainly was colonialist, biased, and condescending, but he made a number of honest points that might have helped early twentieth-century Indians better understand their own culture. Like many other Westerners, Archer was horrified by caste and in particular by untouchability. Without acknowledging Archer's criticisms, Aurobindo admitted in the *Defence* that "the treatment of our outcastes," which condemned "one sixth of the nation to permanent ignominy," was "a constant wound to the social body."[107] But this was just one of those "errors" that Indians had to deal with "not from any European standpoint but from our own outlook." This is not very comforting. Hindu Indians had done nothing about their outcastes for more than a thousand years and were content even in the twentieth century to let the "permanent ignominy" continue.

Archer gave much attention to Indian religion, which to him entailed pessimism, asceticism, and "a flat negation of the value of life."[108] Aurobindo countered that spiritual realization was the fundamental aim of life, that the most perfect systems of spirituality were developed in India, and that Indian spirituality in its true, ancient form encouraged a life expression that "was not wanting in any of the things that make up the vivid interesting activity of human existence."[109] In five pugnacious chapters, he laid down the fundamentals of Indian religion, sketching its evolution from the Vedas to its final flowering in the medieval *bhakti* movement. In laying out this history, he gave most of his attention to what scholars call the Hindu "great tradition": the Vedas, the Upanishads, the epics and philosophers, and the Puranas. To Aurobindo, Buddhism, with its two thousand–year history in India, was just an extreme restatement of the truths of Veda and Vedanta—a characterization that no Buddhist would accept.

Indian art, which Aurobindo took up next, was at its root an expression of Indian spirituality: "Its highest business is to disclose something of the Self, the Infinite, the Divine to the regard of the soul, the Self through its expressions, the Infinite through its living finite symbols, the Divine through his powers."[110] William Archer, not surprisingly, preferred European art. Aurobindo, not surprisingly, preferred Indian. But after the inevitable comparison of Indian and Western artistic motives, Aurobindo at last forgot his "rationalistic critic" and the *Defence* rose to a higher level. The chapters on Indian architecture, painting, and sculpture were insightful and richly detailed. Even better were those on Indian literature. In this field, where India's achievements were self-evident and Aurobindo's expertise broad and deep, his tone became confident and understated, as in this passage on the age of Kalidasa:

> The classical Sanskrit is perhaps the most remarkably finished and capable instrument of thought yet fashioned ... lucid with the utmost possible clarity, precise to the farthest limit of precision, always compact and at its best sparing in its formation of phrase, but yet with all this never poor or bare: there is no sacrifice of depth to lucidity, but rather a pregnant opulence of meaning, a capacity of high richness and beauty, a natural grandeur of sound and diction inherited from the ancient days.[111]

Turning from Indian literature to Indian polity, Aurobindo admitted for the first time that India's achievements did not measure up to those of other civilizations. When judged from the viewpoint of "those activities that raise man to his noblest potentialities as a mental, a spiritual, religious, intellectual, ethical, aesthetic being," Indian civilization had to be considered "one of the half dozen greatest of which we have a still existing record." But in politics, the country's perennial failure to unite and to resist foreign domination meant that "judgment of political incapacity must be passed against the Indian people."[112] The kingdoms of ancient India were admirable creations, but none of the many empires that followed could establish a lasting unity. Somewhat paradoxically given his lack of interest in Muslim India, Aurobindo had a number of positive things to say about the Mughal Empire, "a great and magnificent construction" in whose creation and maintenance "an immense amount of political genius and talent was employed." He noted also that the Muslim dynasties "ceased very rapidly to be a foreign rule." The same could not be said of the British Raj—though the artificial unity established by the British provided the conditions for India's rebirth. The only question that remained was what sort of nation would arise from the current confusion. Would it be, as Aurobindo wrote in the last issue of the *Arya*, "an anglicised oriental people, docile pupil of the West and doomed to repeat the cycle of the Occident's success and failure"? Or would it be a novel expression of "the ancient immemorable Shakti recovering her deepest self . . . and turning to discover the complete meaning and a vaster form of her Dharma [law of being]"?[113]

Poetry of the Past and Future

The *Arya* was published on the fifteenth of every month; each issue contained sixty-four closely printed pages, and Aurobindo did almost all of the writing. He also had to revise the material, prepare it for publication, and correct the proofs. It took him about two weeks each month to do this, leaving him with two weeks for other literary work: Vedic translations and notes, philological research, *Record of Yoga*, poetry, an occasional letter.

During 1915 he wrote comparatively little in the *Record*. There are a fair number of entries from the end of April to the end of August, followed by a gap of almost six months. This was, he later observed, "a period of long torpor and inertia."[114] Nevertheless, he wrote regularly for the *Arya* and also managed to complete, during his two free weeks in October, a five-act comedy in verse, *Vasavadutta*. In most of his earlier plays, the main characters are handsome princes and beautiful, resourceful princesses who have become enslaved. In *Vasavadutta*, the situation is reversed. Vuthsa Udaian, the young king of Cowsamby, is captured by Chunda Meghasegn, the king of Avanty, and forced to become the slave of his daughter, Vasavadutta, who falls in love with her captive in spite of herself. The two escape and in the end rule together over Vuthsa's kingdom. From a literary point of view, Aurobindo's plays are the least interesting of his works. Biographically speaking, they may offer insights into movements in his imaginative life. If his earlier plays suggest that he was searching for his ideal life partner, *Vasavadutta* seems to hint that he had found the woman he was seeking and was waiting for the moment when she would join him.

Nine months after completing *Vasavadutta*, Aurobindo began to work on a poem, *Savitri*, that would become his most extensive literary creation. In its earliest form it is a narrative of about two thousand lines, written on the same Victorian model as *Love and Death*. Like that poem, *Savitri* is based on a legend from the *Mahabharata*. The childless king Aswapati prays to the goddess Savitri for a son. Pleased by the king's devotion, the goddess appears and promises him not a son, but a daughter of unparalleled beauty. The girl, called Savitri after the goddess, grows up to be as remarkable as foretold, so remarkable in fact that no suitor dares ask for her hand. Her father advises her to search for a mate. In a distant forest she comes upon Satyavan, the son of a blind king who has lost his throne, and decides to marry him. Returning to her father's palace, she announces her decision. But the heavenly sage Narad, who happens to be present, reveals that Satyavan is doomed to die in a year. Aswapati asks his daughter to choose again. She refuses. Narad blesses her and advises her father to go ahead with the ceremony. Savitri is married to Satyavan and enjoys a year of bliss. Then one day, while Satyavan is working in the woods, Yama, the god of death, arrives. He throws his noose around Satyavan's soul and departs. Savitri follows silently behind. Yama notices the devoted wife and tells her to return. She replies that her place is with her husband. Moved by her eloquence, Yama offers her boons. She asks that her father-in-law's kingdom be restored, that her father sire a hundred sons, and that she bear the same number herself. Yama grants these wishes. Savitri then informs him that she will not be able to bear a hundred sons without her husband. Forced to agree, Yama releases Satyavan. Returning to the hermitage, the couple discovers that Satyavan's father has regained his sight and that the usurper to his throne has been killed. Satyavan is anointed crown prince, and he and Savitri live together in happiness.

The Savitri legend, Aurobindo later explained, "is recited in the *Mahabharata* as a story of conjugal love conquering death." But it seemed to him that it originally belonged to "one of the many symbolic myths of the Vedic cycle."[115] His reading of the *Rig Veda* had shown him that legends like the killing of Vritra had an outer ritualistic and inner spiritual meaning. In a similar way, the legend of Savitri could be read as a celebration of wifely duty and as a key to the world of yoga. Toward the end of Aurobindo's poem, Death gives Savitri the chance to enjoy "deathless bliss" in a world of celestial beauty. She refuses. Death answers in lines that give expression to a defining characteristic of Aurobindo's yoga:

> Because thou hast rejected my fair calm
> I hold thee without refuge from my will;
> And lay upon thy neck my mighty yoke.
> Now will I do by thee my glorious works. . . .
> For ever love, O beautiful slave of God.[116]

POETRY HAD BEEN IMPORTANT to Aurobindo from his early childhood. As a scholar at St. Paul's and Cambridge, he had read the classics of Greek and Latin literature and the masterpieces of English, French, and Italian poetry and prose. He continued to study these literatures in Baroda, and at the same time read, translated, and wrote criticism on every type of Sanskrit poetry—the epics, the literary classics, the Upanishads—as well as representative works of medieval and modern Bengali literature. Echoing a passage that Aurobindo wrote about himself, one might say that in Baroda poetry was his religion, a cult in which he worshipped and tried to emulate the finest minds of the past.[117]

The idea of poetry as a secular religion was introduced to the English-speaking world by Matthew Arnold, whose essay "The Study of Poetry" was published while Aurobindo was in England. In an age of failing dogmas, the British critic wrote, "more and more mankind will discover that we have to turn to poetry to interpret life for us, to console us, to sustain us. . . . In poetry, as a criticism of life under the conditions fixed for such a criticism by the laws of poetic truth and poetic beauty, the spirit of our race will find . . . its consolation and stay."[118] When Aurobindo defined poetry for his students at Baroda College, he could do no better than to cite Arnold's formula:

> Poetry as generally understood . . . may be defined as a deeper and more imaginative perception of life and nature expressed in the language and rhythm of restrained emotion. In other words its subject-matter is an interpretation of life and nature which goes deeper into the truth of things than ordinary men can do, what has been called a poetic criticism of life; its spirit is one of imagination and feeling, it is not intellectual but imagi-

native, not rational but emotional; and its form is a language impassioned and imaginative but restrained by a desire for perfect beauty of expression; and a rhythm generally taking the form of metre, which naturally suits the expression of deep feeling.[119]

Throughout his stay in Baroda, Aurobindo regarded himself as a poet and produced a large and varied body of poetic literature. Between 1893 and 1906 he wrote two complete and two incomplete verse narratives, two complete and two incomplete verse plays, dozens of poems of various lengths, and many translations from Sanskrit and Bengali. In Pondicherry he continued to write plays, long narratives, short lyrics, and poetic translations. Altogether his literary output between 1893 and 1914 amounted to the equivalent of fifteen hundred printed pages, of which he had published less than two hundred.

In 1915 Aurobindo brought out a collection of twenty-five poems that he had written in Baroda, Calcutta, and Pondicherry. It was called *Ahana and Other Poems.* The title piece is an extended work in dactylic hexameter; as it opens, the Hunters of Joy complain to Ahana, the Dawn of God, that a divine realization consisting only of knowledge and peace would be incomplete:

Is he thy master, Rudra the mighty, Shiva ascetic?
Has he denied thee his world?

Moved by "the voice of the sensuous mortal," Ahana promises to descend:

We two together shall capture the flute and the player relentless.
Son of man, thou hast crowned thy life with flowers that are
   scentless....
Come then to Brindavan, soul of the joyous; faster and faster
Follow the dance I shall teach thee with Shyama for slave and for
   master.[120]

The contrast between the ascetic peace of Shiva and the divine delight of Krishna (Shyama) presents in poetic form a major theme of Aurobindo's philosophy: the insufficiency of the ascetic ideal and the worthiness of a divine life on earth.

A century after its publication, it is difficult to offer a balanced assessment of *Ahana and Other Poems.* All of the pieces in the collection, even those written in Pondicherry, bear the stamp of late-Victorian romanticism. The ideas in them may not have occurred to a Tennyson or Swinburne, but striking ideas in metrical form do not of themselves make poetry. It was considerations such as these that caused the critic James H. Cousins to speak of Aurobindo as an example of "the philosopher as poet." This was the title of an essay on *Ahana and Other Poems* that Cousins published in his book *New Ways in English Literature* in 1917. "Normally there is a high thinking quality in Mr. Ghose's poetry," Cousins wrote, "we feel it is the work of a man who will find salvation, not through song like a poet-philosopher, but through realisation that may or not use verse as a means of expression." The most striking feature of Aurobindo's poetry was its power of vision: "The poet's eyes perpetually go behind the thing visible to the thing essential, so that symbol and significance are always in a state of interfusion." At its best, his poetry stood "self-existent in its own authenticity and beauty"; at its worst it was "poor minted coin of the brain."[121]

Aurobindo was one of several poets that Cousins considered in his book. The other essays gave Aurobindo his first real look at contemporary English poetry. He was particularly intrigued by extracts from the work of two members of the Celtic Revival: W.B. Yeats and A.E. (George William Russell). The Irish poets, with their stress on the supernatural, appealed to his temperament. He was stimulated to read that, in Cousins's opinion, they represented the vanguard of an important new movement in English literature. After finishing Cousins's book, Aurobindo wrote two pages for a review that he planned to publish in the *Arya*, then transformed the review into the opening chapter of what would become a three hundred–page book. The first chapter of *The Future Poetry* was published in the *Arya* in December 1917. From the second installment, Aurobindo left Cousins behind, working out an original theory of poetics based on his "own ideas and his already conceived views of Art and life."[122]

AUROBINDO BEGAN *THE Future Poetry* with a question: What is "the highest power we can demand from poetry" or, more broadly, what is "the nature of poetry, its essential law?" Poetry gives delight, but it is more than an "elevated pastime"; it has a technical side, but "its power soars up beyond the province of any laws of mechanical construction." At its best, the substance and sound of a poem "come entirely as the spontaneous form of [the poet's] soul." All genuine poetry tries to express "something in the object beyond its mere appearances" by drawing on the creative power of word and rhythm. Intellectual language signifies; poetic language evokes. By means of expressive imagery and the "suggestive force of sound," poetry "arrives at the indication of infinite meanings beyond the finite intellectual meaning the word carries." At its highest pitch, poetry has something of the power of the creative word. The Indian name for this power is the mantra. Aurobindo extended the meaning of this term to include supremely evocative poetry on any subject in any language:

> The Mantra, poetic expression of the deepest spiritual reality, is only possible when three highest intensities of poetic speech meet and become indissolubly one, a highest intensity of rhythmic movement, a highest intensity of interwoven verbal form and thought-substance, of style, and a highest intensity of the soul's vision of truth. All great poetry comes about by a unison of these three elements. . . . But it is only at a certain highest level of the fused intensities that the Mantra becomes possible.[123]

Aurobindo devoted a chapter to each of the three powers of poetic speech: rhythm, style, and vision. Rhythm is "the first fundamental and indispensable element without which all the rest . . . remains inacceptable to the Muse of poetry." The technical side of rhythm, of which meter is a part, is only the outer body of a greater energy that impels the finest poetry. This gives us "something as near to wordless music as word-music can get, and with the same power of soul-life, of soul-emotion, of profound supra-intellectual significance."[124] In his consideration of style, Aurobindo often referred to the "level" on which a poem originates. He distinguished a "vital" style uplifted by the life-force, an emotional style, an intellectual style, and on a somewhat higher level, "a genuinely imaginative style, with a certain, often a great beauty of vision in it." Much English poetry was written in this style, but it was "not that highest intensity of the revelatory poetic word from which the Mantra starts." That comes only when "all is powerfully carried on the surge of a spiritual vision which has found its inspired and inevitable speech." The vision-power that characterized the work of the greatest masters—Homer, Valmiki, Kalidasa, Dante, Shakespeare—was "a large and powerful interpretative and intuitive vision of Nature and life and man," giving form to an entire universe.[125]

There is something almost inevitable in the creations of such master poets; but at the same time "poetic vision, like everything else, follows necessarily the evolution of the human mind." The "national spirit" in each literature finds expression according to the characteristics of the age. In the central chapters of *The Future Poetry*, Aurobindo examined the special character of English poetry and sketched a history of its development. "The English language," he began, "has produced . . . the most rich and naturally powerful poetry" of modern Europe. Its superiority came from an unusual combination of elements. There was, on one hand, a "dominant Anglo-Saxon strain" that provided "a strong vital instinct, a sort of tentative dynamic intuition." The dominant strain was quickened and uplifted by a submerged Celtic element, with its "inherent spirituality, the gift of the word, the rapid and brilliant imagination." Together they produced poetry strongly grounded in the outward life but propelled by "a great force of subjective individuality," exhibiting at best "a great intensity of speech" and "a certain kind of direct vision." Developing in isolation from Continental literature, English poetry "followed with remarkable fidelity the natural curve and stages of the psychological evolution of poetry."[126]

The ideas that Aurobindo developed in these chapters need to be placed in historical context. It was a commonplace of European Romanticism that nations had souls that expressed themselves in distinctive cultural forms. Later thinkers, including Karl Lamprecht, combined this notion with that of development through stages. The idea that literatures evolved followed naturally from this. In his "Study of Poetry," Matthew Arnold offered a sketch of the development of English poetry that anticipated Aurobindo's. In *On the Study of Celtic Literature* (1866), Arnold opposed the spiritual and imaginative Celt to the earthy and utilitarian Anglo-Saxon. Aurobindo's originality in dealing with these ideas was to link them with his theory of spiritual evolution and with the idea of poetry as mantra.

The "psychological evolution of poetry" of which Aurobindo speaks begins on the level of the "physical mind," rises to the planes of dynamic life and reflective intellect, and eventually reaches a more consciously spiritual expression. In England the first stage was represented by the poetry of Chaucer, whose motive was "a direct and concrete poetic observation of ordinary human life and character." The next major development was Elizabethan drama, which expressed the "energy, passion and wonder of life."[127] This vital poetry, as Aurobindo called it, reached its apotheosis in Shakespeare:

> He is not primarily an artist, a poetic thinker or anything else of the kind, but a great vital creator and intensely, though within marked limits, a seer of life. . . . His development of human character has a sovereign force within its bounds, but it is the soul of the human being as seen through outward character, passion, action,—the life-soul, and not either the thought-soul or the deeper psychic being, still less the profounder truth of the human spirit. . . . More than any other poet Shakespeare has accomplished mentally the legendary feat of the impetuous sage Vishwamitra; his power of vision has created a Shakespearian world of his own.[128]

The Elizabethan age was followed by a classical and intellectual period with Milton as its primary figure. *Paradise Lost* was "the one supreme fruit left by the attempt of English poetry to seize the classical manner, achieve beauty of poetic expression disciplined by a high intellectual severity." But Milton could not avoid the stumbling block of intellectual poetry: a "failure of vision" that drove him "to poeticise the stock ideas of his religion" rather than reach "through sight to a living figure of Truth and its great expressive thoughts or revelatory symbols." The poets of the eighteenth century emulated Milton's classicism but did not share his power. The work of Dryden, Pope, and the other Augustan poets is dry and mechanical, their verse poetic only in form. They failed to realize that "poetry, even when it is dominated by intellectual tendency and motive, cannot really live and work by intellect alone." Its sources and means are "intuitive seeing and inspired hearing," and these powers "are the characteristic means of all spiritual vision and utterance; they are rays from a greater and intenser Light than the tempered clarity of our intellectual understanding." The poets of the Romantic movement, whom Aurobindo called "the poets of the dawn," gave us "for the first time in occidental literature ... some faint initial falling of this higher light on the poetic intelligence." Blake's mysticism, Coleridge's visions, Wordsworth's nature-communion, Byron's titanism, Shelley's rebelliousness, and Keats's verbal artistry were expressions of this higher light, which for a while seemed ready to usher in a new age of spiritual poetry. But the poets of the Victorian period drew back toward a "dominant intellectualism," although theirs was "an imaginative, artistic intellectualism, touched with the greater and freer breath of modern thought."[129]

While reading recent poetry, Aurobindo was on the lookout for signs that the "dawn" of the early nineteenth century was becoming a spiritual day. He found traces of what he was seeking in Whitman, Carpenter, Tagore's English versions, Yeats, and A.E., but he was not satisfied. "The more perfectly intuitive poetry of the future," he concluded, "will not be a mystic poetry recondite or quite remote from the earthly life of man." Rather, it will aim "at a harmonious and luminous totality of man's being," a "second and greater birth of all man's powers and his being and action and creation."[130]

In the last eight chapters of *The Future Poetry*, Aurobindo returned to poetic theory in an attempt to foreshadow what the poetry of the future would be like. "An intuitive revealing poetry of the kind which we have in view," he began, "would voice a supreme harmony of five eternal powers: Truth, Beauty, Delight, Life and the Spirit." The truth he had in mind was one that would "be able to see, though in another way than that of philosophy and religion, the self of the Eternal, to know God and his godheads, to know the freedom and immortality which is our divinest aim." It would not, however, cut itself off from human life or "the dignity of our labour and action." If the integral spirituality that Aurobindo looked forward to managed to establish itself, one result might be a poetry of spiritual *ananda,* or delight, "making all existence luminous and wonderful and beautiful to us." This new intuitive poetry would help bring about a "change of seeing and aspiration, because what the thought comprehends with a certain abstraction, it can make living to the imagination by the word and a thing of beauty and delight and inspiration for the soul's acceptance." The literature that developed would be something new "to the art of poetic speech, an utterance of the deepest soul of man and of the universal spirit of things … but in the very inmost language of the self-experience of the soul and the sight of the spiritual mind."[131]

Aurobindo wrote *The Future Poetry* between December 1917 and August 1920, that is, during and after World War I. Among its other works of destruction, the war succeeded in killing off the intellectual and artistic assumptions of the nineteenth century. Belief in God, progress, and social stability were replaced by skepticism and irony. The last vestiges of Romanticism were swept away, along with ideas of literary and artistic form that had prevailed for millennia. By 1920 the Modernists were changing the face of European and American literature, and many of the ideas on which *The Future Poetry* was based had become antiquated curiosities before any important poet or critic could read the book. Aurobindo's own poetry, rooted deeply in the soil of the nineteenth century, was out of date before it saw print.

Aurobindo witnessed the rise of Modernism and found it difficult to align with his own ideas of beauty and significance. Reviewing an issue of *Shama'a,* an Indian cultural journal, in September 1920, he noted that modernist poetry, though it had a certain strength, could not compete with traditional formal poetry. The Modernist poems in *Shama'a* were, he wrote, all "of the same stereotyped kind of free verse." He hoped that the journal would publish more "strains that go beyond the present to a greater poetic future,—let us say, like the exquisite rhythm and perfect form of beauty of Harindranath's poem in the first number."[132] Harindranath Chattopadhyay was a young Indian poet whose first volume Aurobindo had praised in the *Arya.* His poem in the first issue of *Shama'a* had lines like these:

> For He shall find our very eyes
> Turned into skies
> And know our human bodies hide
> Fine Gods inside.[133]

It is no surprise that the author of *Ahana and Other Poems* found something to enjoy in such verse. (Aurobindo was honest enough to acknowledge that "a poet likes only the poetry that appeals to his own temperament or taste, the rest he condemns or ignores.")[134] But Chattopadhyay never got beyond his rather insipid beginnings, and his work is now unknown even in India. It certainly did not presage a "greater poetic future"—at least not one that actually happened. Ironically, another item in the first issue of *Shama'a* was a manifesto of the poetry that would dominate the twentieth century, and Aurobindo ignored it completely. The piece was a lecture by the then little-known T. S. Eliot, in which he introduced many of the ideas that he would develop in later essays: tradition and the individual, the importance of French symbolism, the objective correlative.[135] There is nothing in Eliot's lecture that Aurobindo would have especially objected to, but it offers a radically different view of the future of poetry than the one that Aurobindo was developing. Perhaps for that reason, he declined to engage with it. As the Modernist movement progressed, Aurobindo became out of touch with contemporary developments in poetry. As a result his poetry and criticism must now be judged by the standards of the past, or else taken—so far with little support—as harbingers of a future yet to be glimpsed.

Part Five: *Guide*

The monastic attitude implies a fear, an aversion, a distrust of life and its aspirations, and one cannot wisely guide that with which one is entirely out of sympathy, that which one wishes to minimise and discourage.... But a spirituality which draws back from life to envelop it without being dominated by it does not labour under this disability.

8. The Ascent to Supermind

Pondicherry, 1915–1926

After fifteen years [1905–1920] I am only now rising into the lowest of the three levels of the supermind and trying to draw all the lower activities up into it. But when the process is complete there is not the least doubt that God, through me, will give this supramental perfection to others with less difficulty. Then my real work will begin.

Pictures of a Yogic Life

Asked once about the course of his *sadhana* in Pondicherry, Aurobindo replied that it might be said that he was "sitting on the path, so far as sadhana was concerned" during the period "between 1915 and 1920 when I was writing the *Arya*."[1] He certainly made fewer entries in *Record of Yoga* during those years, but when he did write, it often was about progress. Evaluating his position in February 1916, he gave himself good marks in four of the seven *chatusthayas*. In the vital third or *vijnana chatusthaya*, yogic knowledge, *jnana*, was "firm, as also telepathy except that of thought," while triple time vision, *trikaldrishti*, and application of force or will, *tapas-siddhi*, were "drawing towards a first initial perfection."[2]

One of the three *chatusthayas* he was dissatisfied with in February 1916 was the *sharira chatusthaya*, or perfection of the body. Over the next four years, two of the four elements of this *chatusthaya* developed substantially. One was *kamananda*, bliss in the body, which he felt frequently in its various forms and degrees of intensity. The other was *utthapana*, release from "the pressure of physical forces." The primary stage of this power is "liberation from exhaustion, weariness, strain and all their results." Aurobindo "exercised" primary *utthapana* by walking in his room or on the veranda for many hours at a stretch. He also experimented with secondary *utthapana*, in which "the limbs and the whole body can take and maintain any position or begin and continue any movement for any length of time naturally and in its own right."[3] Fully perfected, *kamananda* and *utthapana* could eliminate the hardships of physical embodiment, replacing aches, pains, and exhaustion with unlimited energy and well-being. Aurobindo had a brief experience of this one morning in 1917. He was feeling so tired "that the body insisted on the need of recumbence to ease the back." But after sitting for half an hour he found that "all [exhaustion] had gone, activity returned, wine of anandamaya tapas [blissful energy] was felt in the body and the tables were rearranged, dusted and motion kept up for an hour and a quarter with return of pain in the shoulder and neck and with unease in the physical nerve matter, but without the sense of dominating fatigue, rather of dominating vigour."[4]

There are few long descriptions of psychological or spiritual states in the *Record*. Visions of Krishna or experiences of the formless *brahman* are recorded in the same terse shorthand he used for physical states and activities. Occasionally, however, there is a more explicit paragraph that, despite the obscure terminology, gives the reader a hint of what it is like to be a yogi:

> In the morning [February 5, 1917] sudden efflorescence of a perfect shuddha [pure] anandamaya-vijnanamaya [blissful-gnostic] vision of universal beauty. Every detail is seen in its perfect, divine sense and faery loveliness and in its place in the whole and the divine symmetry of the whole based on its "brihat" [large] Idea, even in what appears to the mind unsymmetrical. This was realised in things yesterday, today in faces, figures, actions, etc. It is not yet stable, but strong and returns in spite of the force that depresses the vision and attempts to return to the diffuse mental view of things.[5]

LIVING CONDITIONS AT 41 rue François Martin remained spartan. Subscriptions to the *Arya* and remittances from Motilal Roy brought in just enough to keep the household running and the journal appearing, but they were not enough to repair the house, mend clothes, or stock up on soap. This "ascetic tendency," Aurobindo wrote in the *Record*, was just something "that circumstances seem to demand."[6]

Aurobindo lived in the house with Nolini, Suresh, Saurin, and others who came and went. Enjoying "utter freedom," the young men let the place fall into "utter disorder"; when Motilal visited, he berated them: "Is this the way you live? And you keep him like this as well?" Aurobindo treated them all as his equals. If one of them brought him proofs for the *Arya*, he would say, "Why do you bring them here? It is my duty to take them, I am not old." If he went to their rooms, he knocked before he entered and asked, "May I come in?"—a courtesy they found remarkable.[7] They visited him in his room as well and spoke about whatever was on their minds. A man named Aiyar, the editor of a local paper, was living in the house around this time. He was terribly in love with a girl named Kamala, who, because she was Christian, was able to accept invitations to walk on the pier. Aiyar, a Brahmin and painfully shy, watched in agony as she talked with his rivals. One day he spoke to Aurobindo about the way that Kamala was behaving. "Is that fair?" he asked when he was finished. "Fair to whom?" Aurobindo replied.[8]

Apart from such casual conversations, Aurobindo had almost no contact with others. He left the house only once or twice a year and received few visitors. Only Bharati was a frequent caller. Aurobindo read the Rig Veda with him and Bharati returned the favor by helping him translate some Tamil devotional hymns. Wartime restrictions made it almost impossible for foreigners to enter French India. One who managed to do so was the Danish artist and writer Johannes Hohlenberg. A friend of the Richards, he had agreed to help them with the *Arya*, but did not arrive until after the Richards had left. In the month he stayed in Pondicherry, he took a snapshot and made some sketches of Aurobindo that became the basis of a portrait he painted in Europe. After the day's sitting was over, he encouraged his subject to "talk of the ineffable."[9] Aurobindo complied with a smile; after all, this was what he was trying to do in *The Life Divine*.

Aurobindo sat for a photographer on at least two other occasions between 1915 and 1918. In one set of pictures he sits or stands in front of a painted backdrop—Corinthian columns, ornamental ironwork—wearing the dhoti that was his constant garment. A much-reproduced shot catches him "working," pen in hand, a pile of *Arya* volumes on the table. Another shows him in profile, a long black shawl wrapped around his body. This was, one imagines, for photographic effect, as he rarely covered his body even in winter. In a second set of portraits he wears a different shawl, light and richly embroidered. One of these portraits, in which he looks like a Roman senator, gives off an extraordinary impression of combined energy and calm, or in the terms of his yoga, *samata* supporting *shakti*.

AUROBINDO KEPT IN touch with Mirra and Paul Richard by letter throughout 1915 and 1916. After departing from Pondicherry in February 1915, the couple traveled by steamer from Colombo to Marseille, and then by train to Paris. Unable to get out of the reserves, Paul returned with his wife to

Lunel, near Montpellier, where he had been posted. In July the couple went to Marsillargues, Paul's birthplace, where they were joined by André, Mirra's eighteen-year-old son. There they received Aurobindo's first letter. "The whole world is now under one law and answers to the same vibrations, and I am sceptical of finding any place where the clash of the struggle will not pursue us," he wrote. "One needs to have a calm heart, a settled will, entire self-abnegation and the eyes constantly fixed on the beyond to live undiscouraged in times like these which are truly a period of universal decomposition."[10] In October Paul was declared unfit for service, and he and Mirra went to Paris. To the east, the French and British were hurling themselves, with little effect, against the German lines in Artois and Champagne. Paul spent his time looking for a job that would take them away from France. At the same time, and with Mirra's approval, he formed a sexual liaison with another woman who later bore him a child. In February 1916 he obtained a letter from the French foreign ministry naming him a delegate of the National Union for the Export of French Products.[11] Armed with this, he and Mirra departed for Japan. Their voyage around the Cape of Good Hope took more than two months. They remained in Japan from May 1916 to the beginning of 1920.

THOUGH AUROBINDO HAD been out of politics for more than seven years, neither political leaders nor the rank and file had forgotten him. Annie Besant, now head of the Indian Home Rule League, asked him to comment on the government's new reform scheme in 1918. Aurobindo wrote that it was "a cleverly constructed Chinese puzzle." India's struggle with British imperialism could not be avoided, but "only be evaded for the moment, and if you evade it now, you will have it tomorrow or the day after."[12] A few weeks later, Congress leader Vithalbhai Patel asked him for his views on another issue: the proposed amendment of the Hindu Marriages Bill. Aurobindo answered in general terms that "everything will have my full approval which helps to liberate and strengthen the life of the individual in the frame of a vigorous society and restore the freedom and energy which India had in her heroic times of greatness and expansion."[13] This was the last opinion on a public issue he would offer for twenty-four years. The role of elder statesman did not suit him.

Another group that had not forgotten Aurobindo was the police. Despite his retirement, he continued to feature prominently in British intelligence reports. The secret *Politico-Criminal Who's Who* gave him a long and flattering entry: "height 5' 6" [two inches too much]; fair [most considered him dark]; medium build; long hair; prominent nose; high forehead.... He is friendly with the gang of anarchists at Pondicherry . . . and believed to be the head and front of the terrorist movement in India."[14] Three secret reports of 1917 emphasized his importance in the history of Indian terrorism and his continued influence on those who were still active. One of them concludes: "The figure of Arabinda Ghosh, now in Pondicherry, is said still to loom large behind Bengal anarchy. . . . He has certainly been in written communication with some of the members since the commencement of the war."[15] The famous *Rowlatt Report*, published in 1918, was a digest of the secret reports of the previous year. It devoted a paragraph to Aurobindo's *Bhawani Mandir* and several pages to the activities of the Maniktala group, which, while unsuccessful, "were subsequently renewed with marked determination in more favourable circumstances."[16]

The revolutionaries involved in the renewed terrorist activity had also not forgotten Aurobindo. The *samitis* of Bengal were extremely active in the early years of the war. In 1915 they carried out eleven assassinations and twenty-four "political dacoities" (gang robberies). This activity fell sharply after the passage of the Defence of India Act, but "revolutionary crime" remained the principal worry of the police throughout the period of the war.[17] Most of the incidents took place in East Bengal, home territory of the Dacca Anushilan *samiti*. Other active groups included Motilal's unit in Chandernagore and the remnants of the Jugantar gang. All of these *samitis* were descended more or less directly from the organization that Aurobindo and his friends had launched in 1902, and members of the groups continued to admire him and probably helped him financially as well. "It is stated by persons in a position to know," asserts a government report of 1917, "that Arabinda in his retreat in Pondicherry is to the present day in receipt of funds especially provided by the Dacca Anushilan Samiti for his support."[18] If true, this would mean that some of the funds that Motilal sent were collected at gunpoint in Bengal, as armed robbery was the *samiti*'s principal means of fundraising.

It is unlikely that Aurobindo knew about the sources of Motilal's remittances. Three years earlier, in 1914, he had told Motilal to draw back from revolutionary activity, and since then he had written nothing about the subject, not even in code. When people asked him in his retirement for advice on revolutionary matters, he told them to desist. One such enquirer was Ambalal Purani, the younger brother of a Gujarati activist to whom Aurobindo had spoken in 1908. The Puranis had organized a revolutionary group following suggestions that Aurobindo had made at that time. Before starting their activities, they "thought it necessary to consult the great leader who gave us the inspiration, as lives of many young men were involved in the plan." After the Armistice of November 1918, the younger Purani met Aurobindo in the rue

François Martin house. Aurobindo sat "in a wooden chair behind a small table covered with an indigo blue cloth." Purani told him that his group "was ready to start revolutionary activity. It had taken us about eleven years to organise." Aurobindo said nothing; then, knowing that Purani was a reader of the *Arya*, he asked him how his *sadhana* was going. "Sadhana is all right," Purani said, "but it is difficult to concentrate on it so long as India is not free." "Perhaps," Aurobindo replied, "it may not be necessary to resort to revolutionary activity to free India." The two talked this over for several minutes. Purani concluded: "But the concentration of my whole being turns towards India's freedom. It is difficult for me to sleep till that is secured." Aurobindo was silent for two or three minutes. Then he said: "Suppose an assurance is given to you that India will be free." "Who can give such an assurance?" Purani asked. "Suppose I give you the assurance," Aurobindo replied. Purani paused. "If you give the assurance, I can accept it." Aurobindo reaffirmed his promise, and Purani passed to other subjects. But before leaving, he could not help blurting out: "Are you quite sure that India will be free?" Aurobindo became serious. He fixed his gaze at the sky, put his fist on the table, and said firmly: "You can take it from me, it is as certain as the rising of the sun tomorrow."[19]

Aurobindo, the revolutionary turned yogi, was a puzzle to his contemporaries and remains one to later generations. When Rabindranath Tagore published his novel *Ghare Bhaire* (The Home and the World) in 1916, some readers thought that the character Sandip, an ostensibly idealistic revolutionary who takes advantage of everyone he meets, was based on Aurobindo. Learning of this, Tagore wrote a letter to set the record straight: "I do not, even to this day, definitely know what is the political standpoint of Aurobindo Ghosh. But this I know positively that he is a great man—one of the greatest we have—and therefore liable to be misunderstood even by his friends. What I feel for him myself is not mere admiration, but reverence for his depth of spirituality, his largeness of vision and his literary gifts, extraordinary in imaginative insight and expression."[20]

The Armistice, which made it possible for people such as Purani to visit Pondicherry, also allowed those who had been cooped up in the town to travel to British India. Subramania Bharati returned to Madras in November 1918 and died there three years later. Two of Aurobindo's attendants, Nolini Kanta Gupta and Saurin Bose, went to Bengal in the summer of 1919. Both ended up getting married. Before Nolini took the step, Aurobindo sent him some tongue-in-cheek advice:

Do you really mean to perpetuate the sexual union dignified by the name of marriage, or don't you? Will you, won't you, will you, won't you—to quote the language of the spider to the fly? . . . To weigh in the subtle scales of amorous thought noses and chins and lips and eyes and the subtleties of expression is no doubt a charming mathematics, but it soars too much into the region of the infinite. . . . Saurin's more concrete and less poetic and philosophic mind seems to have realised this at an early stage and he wrote asking whether it was worth while to marry with our ideas and aims under present social conditions. . . . I have returned a sort of non-committal answer,—that I don't think it is—very, but it may turn out to be and on the whole he had better consult his *antarâtman* [inner soul] and act or not act accordingly.[21]

Also in 1919 the Bengali artist Mukul Chandra Dey came to Pondicherry to paint Aurobindo's portrait. Dey was assembling a portfolio of paintings of the great men of India and felt that Aurobindo, still famous as a political leader and increasingly known for his literary and spiritual achievements, had to be in it. Arriving in French India, Dey approached Aurobindo's residence with trepidation, worried that the British police might learn about his visit. Entering the gate he found himself in the courtyard of "an old two-story dilapidated house. The walls were perhaps once yellow—now there were patches, green with moss—and the lime plaster had fallen off in places, exposing the red bricks." Inside the gate was a row of scraggly banana trees with a half-dozen cats sleeping in the shade. The courtyard was overgrown with grass and weeds; piles of firewood and rubble lay all around. Finding a fellow Bengali, Dey explained his mission, and he was taken to the veranda to wait. After a few anxious minutes, he saw a man approach. "He was wearing a small red-bordered dhoti, rather soiled, which hung down to his knees; there were no pleats; one end was thrown over the shoulder; bare feet; bare body; long hair; bearded; a thin, austere body." Dey knew at once that this was Aurobindo. He explained that he was making a book of paintings of famous Indians, and asked if Aurobindo would let him make a sketch. "How long do I have to sit?" Aurobindo asked. "About half an hour, one hour," Dey replied. "Can you draw if I sit now?" Aurobindo asked. "Yes, I can," Dey answered, taking out paper and pencil. For a full hour Aurobindo "did not move even a bit, nor did I see him bat an eyelid even once." Like so many others, the artist was struck by Aurobindo's eyes, which seemed to him to look into eternity.[22]

At one point during the visit, Dey referred to Aurobindo's wife. In replying Aurobindo did not reveal that Mrinalini had died a few months earlier. The young woman had stayed with her father in Shillong since Aurobindo departed Calcutta in 1910. She spent much of her time reading the works of Sri Ramakrishna and his wife Sarada Devi, to whom she was devoted. When not otherwise occupied, she played with the neighborhood children. During the first few years of their separation, she and her husband exchanged a few letters. According to her father, Aurobindo "lulled her with the hope that someday . . . he would return to Bengal." Later he stopped writing, but "Mrinalini never ceased to hope."[23] More than once her father proposed taking her to Pondicherry. Aurobindo replied that he could not receive her until his finances were more secure. Then the war intervened, making travel impossible. Finally in December 1918, her father sent Mrinalini to Calcutta and arranged for her to go to Pondicherry. It was not the right time to visit Calcutta. The postwar influenza pandemic, which killed tens of millions of people, had just reached India. Mrinalini caught the disease and in two or three days was gone.

Aurobindo must have learned of her death by the end of December. A month and a half later he wrote a letter to his father-in-law, which shows how deeply he was affected:

> I have not written to you with regard to this fatal event in both our lives: words are useless in face of the feelings it has caused, if even they can ever express our deepest emotions. God has seen good to lay on me the one sorrow that could still touch me to the centre. He knows better than ourselves what is best for each of us, and now that the first sense of the irreparable has passed, I can bow with submission to his divine purpose. The physical tie between us is, as you say, severed; but the tie of affection subsists for me. Where I have loved, I do not cease from loving.[24]

Aurobindo and Mrinalini had been married for seventeen years, though they stopped living together from the time of his arrest in 1908. (She relived the terror of that moment during the delirium that preceded her death.) Aurobindo had a good deal of affection for his wife, but he hardly could be called a good husband. He failed to provide for her even when they were together, and made her suffer the indignity of being taken care of in his absence not by his relatives, as custom required, but by her father. About their connubial relations nothing is known. Her father summed up the situation in a sentence: "There was no issue of the marriage."[25] After Aurobindo entered what he called "the sexual union dignified by the name of marriage," he seems to have found the state bothersome and uninteresting. "Marriage," he wrote later to a disciple, "means usually any amount of trouble, heavy burdens, a bondage to the worldly life and great difficulties in the way of single-minded spiritual endeavour." Many of these difficulties, for most people at least, are related to sex and the desires that accompany it. Aurobindo appears to have had few problems in that regard. He was probably alluding to his own experience when he wrote to a disciple that there were "some who can eliminate it [the sexual propensity] decisively by a swift radical dropping away from the nature." On another occasion he said more directly: "I for one have put the sexual side completely aside, it is lying blocked so that I can make this daring attempt" at spiritual transformation.[26]

Endings and Beginnings

In December 1918, while Mrinalini Ghose lay dying of influenza in Calcutta, the pandemic was making its way to Japan. By January the disease was spreading through Tokyo. Among those who were infected was Mirra Richard. One evening, after crossing the city in a tram, she came down with the fever that marked the onset of the disease. A doctor was summoned, but she refused to take any medicine. Fighting inwardly against the source of the infection, she succeeded in driving it away.[27]

Mirra's illness came toward the end of an unhappy four-year sojourn in Japan. Paul's commercial mission had come to nothing, and he and Mirra earned their livelihoods by teaching French. Paul busied himself writing books, articles, and tracts and contacting people who shared his interest in internationalism, pan-Asianism, and similar causes. His past history and present associates put him on the blacklist of the British ambassador, who threatened to have him arrested if he ever set foot in any part of the British Empire.[28] Resigned to remaining in Japan until the end of the war, Mirra spent her time painting, learning a little Japanese, and meditating with a circle of friends. She also wrote a few pieces for publication. "Woman and the War," a mildly feminist article, appeared in a Tokyo newspaper in Japanese translation in 1916. "Impressions of Japan," written in English, was published in India the next year. Mirra admired the Japanese for their "perfect love for nature and beauty" but regretted their lack of spirituality.[29] The artist in her was in a constant state of wonder in Japan, but the seeker in her lived in a spiritual vacuum. The dominant mood of her diary was withdrawal and expectation.

AFTER NOLINI GUPTA and Saurin Bose departed in 1919, life at 41 rue François Martin became even quieter than it had been during the war. Bijoy and Suresh helped to produce the *Arya* and ensured that Aurobindo had regular meals and tea. Amrita, who had gone to college at Aurobindo's insistence, returned to Pondicherry and rejoined the household. The two Bengalis used to patronize the young Tamil until Aurobindo told them to stop. But he said nothing when Haradhan Bakshi, an ex-soldier from Chandernagore, openly insulted Amrita. Later, Aurobindo said that Amrita should have slapped Haradhan in the face.[30]

In this year of few outward events, Aurobindo's *sadhana* was very active. Entries in the *Record* between June and September 1919 show evidence of advancement in all seven *chatusthayas*. Toward the middle of the period he paused to take a "balance of progress." As he had often before, he felt that most of the elements of his yoga were "complete" or nearly so. *Shuddhi* or purification was "practically complete except for the body and the vijnana; essential mukti [liberation] complete, but not the mukti of the Nature," while *bhukti* or enjoyment was "almost complete." As for *siddhi* or perfection, it was "practically perfect in the first [*chatusthaya*], moving towards final perfection in the second, striving towards completeness and a kind of perfection in the third, initial only in the fourth and for the most part obstructed and subject to relapse, busy only with the personal foundation in the fifth, large in the sixth, but not full in its contents or complete in its combination."[31] There is a break in the *Record* after September. It resumes in February 1920 with the *sadhana* of *vijnana* in full flow. On February 4, Aurobindo noted "an extraordinarily rapid development of the whole system into the highest logistic ideality,—first elimination of mental intuivity, confirmation in intuitive revelatory vijnana, then rise to interpretative revelatory, then to revelatory full of founded power of inspiration. The lower forms of vijnana occur from outside."[32] This passage shows the complexity of the planes of *vijnana* as Aurobindo visualized them. "Logistic ideality" is the "lowest total stage of the triple ideal supermind," which lies above mental intuition.[33] Logistic ideality has three levels—intuitive, inspired, and revelatory—each of which, because of their interpenetration, is divided into three sublevels: intuitive, interpretative, and revelatory. The passage describes a movement from the intuitive to the interpretative and revelatory sublevels of the highest or revelatory form of logistic *vijnana*, looking upward to the higher levels of pure *vijnana*, though still troubled by touches of the lower forms.

Aurobindo's *sadhana* continued strongly through March. In a summation written on the last day of the month, he found satisfactory progress in most of the *chatusthayas*, the chief exception being the *sharira chatusthaya*, in which physical *ananda* was weak and scattered and *roga*, illness, had "resumed something of its hold." He set aside April "for the overcoming of the final difficulties in the way of the vijnana," but after a few brief entries he discontinued the *Record* until June.[34]

THE PERIOD BETWEEN March and September 1920 marked a decisive turn in Aurobindo's life. Since 1914 his outward work had been on hold. He rarely met others, answered very few letters, and spent most of his time writing or in concentration. Then, in the course of a few months, he laid the foundations of a spiritual community in Pondicherry, took renewed interest in developments in Bengal, and fended off repeated requests to lead the Indian national movement in the most momentous year of its history.

In March, after the British dropped their objection to the Richards' traveling to India through British ports, Paul, Mirra, and their friend Dorothy Hodgson boarded a steamer in Japan. Three weeks later they disembarked, unmolested, in Colombo. In less than a week they were on a ship bound for Pondicherry, where they arrived on April 24. The three stayed first in one, then another hotel, then briefly in a place in the rue St. Louis, and finally in a house at 7 rue Saint-Martin, close to the sea. They spent much of their time at Aurobindo's place, particularly in the evenings when there was a regular gathering for conversation. Sometimes these sessions became "full of a natural silence verging on meditation."[35] Every Sunday, Aurobindo and members of his household went to the Richards' place for dinner. Mirra prepared some of the dishes herself. Afterward they all went to the terrace for talk and relaxation.

Aurobindo's renewed interest in other people and current events is reflected in the many long letters he wrote this year. In April he wrote to his brother Barin, who had been released from the Andamans two months earlier. Aurobindo began by bringing him up to date on his yoga. What he was doing now was different from what he had received from Lele, different too from what he had done in jail. When he arrived in Pondicherry in 1910, "the indwelling Guru of the world indicated my path to me completely, its full theory." Since then, his inner guide had "been making me develop it in experience." The path was long. "I am only now," Aurobindo wrote, "rising into the lowest of the three levels of the Supermind and trying to draw up into it all the lower activities." But he was certain that when the process was complete "God through me will give this supramental perfection to others with less difficulty. Then my real work will begin."[36]

In his letters to Aurobindo, Barin had written about the state of affairs in Bengal: on one hand a resurgence of traditional religion, on the other an explosion of political ideologies, from communism to Gandhian nationalism. Aurobindo found little of interest in either development. He had left the political field because he saw that what he had been doing "was not the genuine Indian thing," but only "a European import, an imitation of European ways."

If he took up that kind of work again he would be "supporting an alien law of being and a false political life." Politics and society had to be transformed, but the change would only be secure if it was based on spiritually transformed individuals, and for that reason he was concentrating on yoga. When the moment was right, he would establish a spiritual community or *sangha*, but it would not follow any known pattern. "Not a fixed and rigid form like that of the old Aryan society, not a stagnant backwater, but a free form that can spread itself out like the sea with its multitudinous waves." Communal life would have to start slowly. "The *sangha* at first will be in a diffused form," with centers in various places. Gradually the people in these centers would "shape all their activities according to the Self and according to the needs of the age." No activity belonging to a full and healthy life would be excluded: "Politics, trade, social organisation, poetry, art, literature—all will remain, but all will be given a new life, a new form." There would be expansion, but no proselytizing. "I do not want tens of thousands of disciples," Aurobindo insisted. "It will be enough if I can get as instruments of God one hundred complete men free of petty egoism. I have no confidence in guruhood of the usual type. I do not want to be a guru. What I want is for someone, awakened by my touch or that of another, to manifest from within his sleeping divinity and to realise the divine life."[37]

Barin had asked a number of questions about Motilal's group in Chandernagore. Was this what Aurobindo was thinking about when he spoke of a spiritual community? Aurobindo's attitude towards Motilal was similar to his attitude towards Barin twelve years earlier. "I am letting him develop according to his own nature," Aurobindo wrote. "I do not want to fashion everybody in the same mould. . . . Everyone grows from within: I do not wish to model from outside." He told Barin that he had more to say, but he could not put it all in a letter. Barin should come to Pondicherry as soon as possible. As for Aurobindo's going to Bengal, it was not yet the time—"not because Bengal is not ready, but because I am not ready. If the unripe goes amid the unripe, what can he accomplish?"[38]

Motilal also had been thinking about Aurobindo's plans, in particular about what role he might play in the enlarged *sangha*, and whether Barin was likely to upstage him. Aurobindo assuaged his anxieties. In times of expansion, he said, there was a need for multiple approaches, multiple expressions. "India was strongest and most alive when she had many variations of form but one spirit." He asked Motilal to come to Pondicherry so that they could talk about future developments. At the moment Aurobindo had hardly any time, what with the *Arya* and the Richards' daily visits, but "by the time you come I may have a freer atmosphere to attend to the currents of the work and the world about me. There is now the beginning of a pressure from many sides inviting my spiritual attention to the future *karma* [work] and this means the need of a greater outflowing of energy than when I had nothing to do but support a concentrated nucleus of the Shakti."[39]

Barin arrived in Pondicherry before Motilal did. Aurobindo received him "smiling in his usual detached way. Tea with bread and butter were served soon after and we sat down to it with him in his usual chair." In the week that Barin stayed, he spent much of his time in Aurobindo's study. "There were chairs for visitors round one oblong table," he reported. On the walls were a few pictures, and on every side "books were heaped on a table, on chairs, on his sideboard, on the very bed [in Aurobindo's adjoining bedroom]—in every imaginable place and most of them thick with dust." When not talking or laughing, Aurobindo "used to sit there absorbed in thought with his dreamy eyes resting in the blue sky and on the dark tree tops visible through the windows."[40] Among those present were Nolini and Suresh, both "taken up with their football matches in the town, their merry gossip and literary life," and Amrita, less sparkling but more practical. Then there were the foreigners, Paul and Mirra Richard and Dorothy Hodgson. Paul, as usual, made a big impression. "Tall, with large luminous eyes and long flowing beard," he seemed to have "stepped out of the pages of the Rig Veda into this world of ours." Mirra also was striking but in a less showy way: "an exceptionally beautiful woman of medium height,—with a face lit up with power and intelligence and [a] very graceful and active body. Her movements were quick, yet rhythmic and in full control. Her smile was of rare sweetness, which broke out as she looked at you." Though outwardly affectionate and even motherly, she seemed to be holding something back: "Her depth of culture, rare intuitive intellect and yogic powers were seldom manifest to a casual observer." Especially when Mirra and Paul were present, the conversation turned to the fulfillment of Aurobindo's ideal, "the great future when man would bridge the gulf between matter and spirit, by divinising even his body."[41]

Motilal arrived later that summer, and Aurobindo established a division of labor between him and Barin. Motilal, who had published two of Aurobindo's books the previous year, would continue to bring out titles from Chandernagore. Barin, who was in touch with a publishing house in Calcutta, would bring out a series of collected essays from the *Arya*. On the literary side, Barin would write articles for *Narayan,* a Bengali journal published by Chittaranjan Das. Motilal would edit *Prabartak,* his own Bengali journal, and would also launch an English weekly, *The Standard Bearer.* Aurobindo contributed an essay to its first issue in August 1920. The "standard" that the journal carried, he wrote, "is not that of an outward battle, but the ensign of a spiritual ideal and of a life that must be its expression and the growing body of its reality. . . . Our ideal is a new birth of humanity into the spirit; our life must be a spiritually inspired effort to create a body of action for that great new birth and creation."[42]

Aurobindo stressed the spiritual nature of his work because many still expected him to lead the country in its "outward battle" against the British. The Indian national movement, after a decade in the doldrums, had began to pick up again in 1919. In April of that year, M. K. Gandhi, soon to be proclaimed the Mahatma, began a campaign of passive resistance against the so-called Rowlatt Bills, which sought to perpetuate the draconian regulations enacted during the war. The popular response was unprecedented. In Amritsar, the British army was called in to suppress a meeting. Hundreds were killed or injured. To the outrage that followed this massacre was added the insult that Muslims felt over the dismemberment of the Ottoman Empire. Gandhi skillfully combined these grievances, putting together a movement in which Hindus as well as Muslims could take part.

New conditions created new equations of power in the national movement. The old-line Moderates were inactive or dead, Annie Besant was sidelined, and Tilak looked likely to be overshadowed by Gandhi. At such an uncertain juncture, many wanted to know what Aurobindo was thinking. Toward the end of 1919, Gandhi sent his son Devdas to ask Aurobindo to help. Aurobindo told Devdas that independence was certain; what he was concerned with now was the form of life that would develop in independent India. Devdas explained the principles of Gandhian nonviolence. Aurobindo asked him what he would do if the Afghans attacked through the Khyber Pass.[43] Devdas had no reply. Another exchange between the two is apocryphal but often cited. Devdas asked Aurobindo: "Why are you addicted to smoking?" Aurobindo's reply: "Why are you addicted to non-smoking?"

In early 1920 Gandhi gathered the forces of the country around him, and on August 1 he launched a massive noncooperation movement. Tilak died in Bombay the same day. Stunned by their loss, Tilak's followers looked to Aurobindo for leadership. The next regular session of Congress was to be held in Nagpur in December. Balkrishna Shivaram Moonje, a former Extremist associate, wrote to Aurobindo on behalf of the Nagpur Reception Committee asking him to be president of the session. The committee's selection of a man who had been out of action for a decade may be seen as an attempt to put forward an honored figurehead, around whom those who were dubious of Gandhi's approach might gather. Aurobindo's answer to Moonje, written at the end of August, shows that he was unwilling to be used by any faction. "Since my retirement from British India," he explained,

> I have developed an outlook and views which have diverged a great deal from those I held at the time [1906–1910] and, as they are remote from present actualities and do not follow the present stream of political action, I should find myself very much embarrassed what to say to the Congress. I am entirely in sympathy with all that is being done so far as its object is to secure liberty for India, but I should be unable to identify myself with the programme of any of the parties. The President of the Congress is really a mouthpiece of the Congress and to make from the presidential chair a purely personal pronouncement miles away from what the Congress is thinking and doing would be grotesquely out of place.

This would be enough to keep him from accepting Moonje's offer. But the real reasons for his refusal had nothing to do with current politics. "I am no longer first and foremost a politician," he explained, "but have definitely commenced another kind of work with a spiritual basis, a work of spiritual, social, cultural and economic reconstruction of an almost revolutionary kind, and am even making or at least supervising a sort of practical or laboratory experiment in that sense which needs all the attention and energy that I can have to spare."[44]

Despite Aurobindo's refusal, Moonje and his friends were convinced that Aurobindo was the only man for the job. Moonje wrote to him again, then journeyed to Pondicherry to persuade him to reconsider. Aurobindo could only repeat that he was not in a position to accept. Speculation about his political views continued. One newspaper claimed that he supported Gandhi. A former Moderate adversary said that he endorsed the government's reforms. Aurobindo had to issue a denial, making it clear that he had made and would make no statement of his political views. "As regards India," the only work he wanted to be identified with was "the endeavour to reconstitute her cultural, social and economic life within larger and freer lines than [in] the past on a spiritual basis."[45]

At a special session of Congress held that September in Calcutta, Gandhi emerged as the dominant leader. The assembly accepted his policy of noncooperation, and confirmed this decision three months later at the annual session at Nagpur. From the end of 1920 until the beginning of 1922, the noncooperation movement mobilized the country as never before, and even hard-line revolutionaries were tempted to join forces with Gandhi. Sometime in 1920, Jugantar leader Bhupendra K. Dutta came to Pondicherry to ask Aurobindo what he thought of such an alliance. Aurobindo advised him not to make a fetish of Gandhian nonviolence, but to take advantage of the movement to develop on his own lines.[46] Aurobindo could see that revolutionary violence had no further utility in India, as airplanes and other military hardware had made the terrorists' weapons obsolete. On the other hand, he opposed Gandhi's principled nonviolence—"getting beaten with joy," he once called it—and some of his other obsessions, such as *charkha,* or hand-spinning of cotton. He predicted that the noncooperation movement would end "in a great confusion or in a great fiasco." A year and a half later, after Gandhi called it off, Aurobindo admitted that he had been wrong: it had ended in confusion *and* fiasco.[47]

AUROBINDO CONTINUED TO WRITE regularly for the *Arya,* though for the first time since the launching of the journal he sometimes found himself in arrears. Nevertheless, he began the seventh year (1920–1921) on a confident note, asking subscribers to renew without delay. By then he was writing most of the matter directly on a typewriter. Barin was amazed to see him "just ticking away his ideas and thoughts instead of writing them down," and then going through as many as seven sets of proofs to make sure that the printed text was perfect.[48] When he had finished the day's work, a dozen or more people— members of the household, the Richards, visitors from out of town—came to his study for talk and meditation. On Sundays he and other members of his household visited the Richards for dinner and talk. At some of those meetings, people noticed a surprising development. After dinner those present tended to cluster in two groups: Aurobindo and Mirra on one side, Paul and the others on another. Sometimes, when they were alone, Mirra took Aurobindo's hand in hers. One evening, when Nolini found them thus together, Mirra quickly drew her hand away. On another occasion, Suresh entered Aurobindo's room and found Mirra kneeling before him in an attitude of surrender. Sensing the visitor, she at once stood up. There was nothing furtive about these encounters, but they did strike observers as unusual. Neither Mirra nor Aurobindo were in the habit of expressing their emotions openly. The young men, already somewhat unhappy about the inclusion of women in their circle, and the consequent erosion their bohemian lifestyle, were somewhat nonplussed by this turn of events. Paul Richard took it more personally. At times he could be heard muttering a phrase of garbled Tamil, *setth ay pochi,* by which he meant "the calamity has happened."[49] After a while he asked Aurobindo about the nature of his relationship with Mirra. Aurobindo answered that he had accepted her as a disciple. Paul inquired as to what form the relationship would take. Aurobindo said that it would take any form that Mirra wanted. Paul persisted: "Suppose she claims the relationship of marriage?" Marriage did not enter into Aurobindo's calculations, what was important to him was Mirra's autonomy, so he replied that if Mirra ever asked for marriage, that is what she would have.[50]

Paul took up the matter with his wife. According to Mirra, recalling the events forty years later, the confrontation was stormy. Aware more than ever that Mirra had made his literary and spiritual accomplishments possible, Paul demanded that she give her primary loyalty to him. Mirra simply smiled. Paul became violent, came close to strangling her, and threw the furniture out of the window. Mirra remained calm throughout, inwardly calling on the divine. For all intents and purposes this was the end of their relationship. A year later Paul confided to the novelist Romain Rolland that it had been a time of "violent crisis" in his life. He had been forced to fight "a dreadful inner battle, which threw me, alone, face to face with death . . . into the immense and glorious void of the Himalayan 'Ocean.'" In his diary, Rolland translated this into more mundane language: "In fact," he wrote, "his wife . . . left him."[51]

Mirra and her friend Dorothy Hodgson continued to live at 7 rue Saint-Martin. The monsoon was heavy that year, and the roof began to leak. One day a warehouse on the rue d'Orléans collapsed in the incessant rain. Concerned that the same thing might happen at 7 rue Saint-Martin, Aurobindo suggested that the two women move into his house, and they agreed.

In October 1920, for the first time since the start of the *Arya*, Aurobindo was unable to fill an issue. The next to appear was a double number for October and November. The issues of December and January came out as scheduled, but they were the last to be published. Over six and a half years, Aurobindo had produced seventy-seven issues of the journal. The contents were later published in eight large and nine small books, covering a wide range of subjects in philosophy, yoga, textual commentary, political and social science, and cultural criticism. Aurobindo later remarked that a monthly journal was not the best place for such material to appear: "Writing for a magazine month by month, as I did for the *Arya*, you cannot keep the whole thing before you." Because he was unable to restructure while writing, some of the works are unbalanced: one part of *The Synthesis of Yoga* is too long, another too short.[52] Aurobindo hoped to revise the works before reissuing them as books, but he rarely found time for it.

Other criticisms could be leveled at the *Arya* writings. The style is involved and, by modern standards, frequently obscure. Like other writers trained in the classical tradition, Aurobindo loved the periodic sentence, in which clause follows clause follows clause, until sometimes the point of the statement is lost in a maze of qualifications. His was the last generation to write like that in English. The twenty-first-century reader of Dryden, Ruskin, Aurobindo, Virginia Woolf, or continental writers such as Michel Foucault, must develop what British literary critic Philip Davis calls "immersed attention" to be able to profit from this style.[53] The rewards of persistence are a wide understanding that is hard to arrive at when the subject is offered up in the curt, journalistic prose that is favored today.

From a certain point of view, however, Aurobindo wrote the works he published in the *Arya* more for himself than for others. "I wanted to throw out certain things that were moving in my mind," he once said. "If nobody reads and understands, it does not matter."[54] He had remarked, just before starting the *Arya*, that it would be "the intellectual side of my work for the world." Having put his ideas into written form, he was free to attend to other sides of his work, in particular establishing a new way of yoga and a new, spiritualized form of social organization.

Silence and Shakti

Between 1914 and 1920 Aurobindo published some 4,600 pages of philosophy, commentary, translations, and essays in the *Arya;* composed a verse play and a long narrative poem; filled two dozen notebooks with translations, commentaries, and notes on the Veda; wrote diary entries equal in length to a nine-hundred-page book; and corresponded with several associates. Between 1921 and 1926 he wrote practically nothing: no philosophy, no poetry, no *Record of Yoga*, and only a handful of letters. He informed a correspondent in 1921 that he had "written no letters for the last six months to anyone, both on account of lack of time and absorption in Yoga."[55]

In 1926, toward the end of his six-year furlough from writing, Aurobindo remarked that if he had continued to bring out the *Arya*, he would not have been able to advance in *sadhana* to the extent he did during those years.[56] It is difficult to pin down the nature of his progress because he did not document it in the *Record*. One thing is clear, however: the arrival of Mirra Richard had an enormous impact on his practice. With her help, he told Barin, he completed ten years of *sadhana* in one.[57] Her assistance was especially important in turning his *sadhana* outward. If he had been concerned only with his own transformation or with transmitting his yoga to a limited number of people, he could have done it on his own. But for his work to have a lasting effect in the world, he needed a *shakti,* a female counterpart.

Shakti, as Aurobindo explained in *The Synthesis of Yoga,* is the conscious power of the divine. "By this power the spirit creates all things in itself, hides and discovers all itself in the form and behind the veil of its manifestation."[58] Systems of yoga that aim at liberation regard *shakti* as, at best, a force that can help the individual obtain release from the limitations of mind, life and body. But systems aiming for perfection, such as tantric yoga or the way of the *siddhas,* see *shakti* as the power needed to transform oneself and the world. Tantrics and siddhas worship *shakti* in the form of goddesses such as Kali; some also worship women as embodiments of the divine force. This is the rationale behind the esoteric sexuality of certain forms of tantrism. The consecrated union of a human male and female is seen as a reenactment of the cosmic act of creation. Some schools of tantric yoga put so much stress on this relationship that they require male practitioners to have female sexual partners. Aurobindo made it clear that this was not the case in his yoga. "How can the sexual act be made to help in spiritual life?" he asked a disciple who posed the question. It was necessary, in the work he was doing, for the masculine and feminine principles to come together, but the union had nothing to do with sex; in fact it was possible in his and Mirra's case precisely because they had mastered the forces of desire.[59]

For two or three years after her arrival in 1920, Aurobindo's spiritual relationship with Mirra was invisible to those around them. In the little community of eight or ten people, she remained a disciple among disciples, or rather, because no one was called a "disciple," a *sadhak* among *sadhaks.* Although accustomed to a life of comfort in Paris, she accepted the privations of Pondicherry without complaint. She began to wear saris, not of silk but of cotton, and often patched. When there was little money she sewed blouses from pieces of old dhotis.[60] People who came to Aurobindo's study sometimes saw her "with her sweet luminous smile going silently to his room to make it tidy."[61] Otherwise she spent most of her time in her room. This attracted little notice, as many of the *sadhaks* spent a lot of time in their rooms. What did seem strange, at least to some, was that two women, and foreign women at that, were allowed to live in a yogi's house. If such misgivings reached Aurobindo's ears, he paid no attention to them.

In January 1922 Aurobindo asked Amrita to give the keys of the house to Mirra. Under her guidance the place was run more efficiently, but conditions were still austere. There was not enough money to buy chairs and tables for everyone. Clothing, supplied by friends, was often in short supply. Aurobindo, as always, was content with a simple dhoti, worn sometimes with one end across the shoulder. He solved his longstanding footwear problem by going without sandals or shoes. Up to 1921 he was exceedingly thin and looked almost emaciated. Asked why he had allowed himself to get so lean, he replied curtly: "I wanted to become lean."[62] After the arrival of Mirra and Dorothy Hodgson and the consequent improvement in his diet, he filled out somewhat, but remained slim. Many also noticed a sudden lightening of his complexion around this time. Earlier his skin had been dark, though lustrous. But starting in early 1921, people regularly reported that his complexion was fair and luminous: "the whole body glowed with soft creamy white light," "all golden, not figuratively but actually," "a smooth golden body emitting light." In the terminology of the *Record of Yoga,* light, attractive skin is an aspect of *saundarya,* physical beauty, which is a part of the *sharira chatusthaya,* the quaternary of the body. When someone expressed surprise at the change in Aurobindo's appearance, he explained that when the *yoga-shakti* descended from the mind into "the vital," the plane of life, it could produce striking changes in "the nervous and even the physical being."[63]

From 1921 on, most descriptions of Aurobindo read as though they are taken out of the Puranas or other mythological texts: "The atmosphere round the Master was surcharged with pure vibrations of peace, light, power and Ananda [bliss]. One could feel the fragrance of lotuses from his transparent, luminous body"; "His God-like face radiated profound peace and serenity. His intent and faraway look indicated to me that he was not of the earth."[64] Many people remarked that he was tall, though his height remained unchanged at five feet, four inches. Much of the hyperbole may be ascribed to the charisma that was building up around the inaccessible, mysterious Aurobindo, who was reputed, like all certified holy men of India, to possess supernatural powers. Be that as it may, all descriptions of Aurobindo's appearance from this and later periods lay stress on its singularity. He was, A.B. Purani wrote, "cast in a mould of arresting majesty, of regal splendour. We saw that uncommon majesty manifested in every look, in every gesture, in every movement of his. His deportment was kingly yet natural, his voice was melodious yet soft, pleasing yet firm. A born aristocrat, he could be easily spotted in a crowd. He was and looked so uncommon, so out of the ordinary."[65]

Despite an increase in the tempo of life around him, Aurobindo's habits remained unchanged. He rose late, after sleeping from five to nine hours. For the most part his sleep was "perfectly ordinary," though he once remarked that it was "not all sleep," by which he meant that he sometimes passed part of the night in *samadhi*.[66] He spent most of the day in his room, exercising by walking there or on the veranda for as many as six hours a day.[67] He continued to eat meat, though he was no longer the militant nonvegetarian he once had been. Overall he considered food "a secondary matter" in the spiritual life. "We must not imagine," he wrote in *The Synthesis of Yoga*, "that the purity of the mind depends on the things we eat or drink, although during a certain stage restrictions in eating and drinking are useful to our inner progress."[68] He continued to drink wine and to smoke cigars, though perhaps less frequently than before. Mirra was opposed to both habits, blaming Aurobindo's indulgence on those around him: "You people have injured him," she used to say. "Don't give him wine and bad cigars, he may get a cough." Mirra's opposition, and the fact that most of the men in the house had started smoking and drinking after Aurobindo's example, prompted him to reduce and eventually stop using tobacco and alcohol.[69]

In the early 1920s Aurobindo generally set aside two periods per day for interaction with others. From 9:00 to 10:30 in the morning he talked privately with members of the household and with visitors who had appointments to meet him. He received them on the veranda, seated on a chair behind a small, oblong table. His interlocutor sat across from him, on a similar chair. Aurobindo's voice, by all accounts, was soft and melodious, "almost feminine."[70] He never lost his British public school accent. Generally light-hearted and full of laughter, he could be harsh if circumstances seemed to demand it. Once a visitor asked him what he thought of his idea of starting a magazine. Aurobindo replied: "What is it you want to publish, your ignorance?" On another occasion, someone came with a persistent hiccup and wailed: "If this goes on, I will die!" "What does it matter if you die?" Aurobindo asked. The hiccup stopped at once.[71]

Aurobindo was more likely to grant an interview to a young spiritual aspirant than a self-absorbed politician. One public figure who managed to meet him was Colonel Josiah Wedgwood, a descendent of the pottery manufacturer and a so-called friend of India in Parliament. Aurobindo thought him "one of the biggest asses I have ever seen."[72] He was equally uncharitable towards another British visitor, a Mr. Wainscott, whose pate he compared to a cue ball. In 1922 he met with his sister Sarojini, going to the station to receive her and speaking with her happily for some time. To help her out financially, he gave her the rights to an edition of his book *War and Self-Determination*. That was the last time he involved himself in the fortunes of his family. When Sarojini came the next year, he did not exchange a word with her.[73]

The second time in the day when Aurobindo met with others was the late afternoon. This session was restricted to those who had been accepted as serious practitioners of yoga. Just before four, people began to gather on the veranda, where a dozen chairs had been arranged. Aurobindo came out and sat in a chair no different from the others, and the talking began. The topics of conversation were rarely yogic per se. "All kinds of subjects," were taken up, and Aurobindo "freely cracked jokes with a hearty laugh."[74] After a half-hour of talk there was a brief meditation. When it was over, he returned to his room while the others resumed their usual occupations, such as chatting and listening to the gramophone. If Aurobindo thought it might have been better for them to remain quiet for a while, he never let them know.[75] His watchword at the time was democracy. He treated everyone in the house as his equal, and did not allow others to treat him differently. No one made *namaskar*, salutation, when he passed, much less performed *pranam*, bowing, or other acts of reverence. If he needed someone's help, say, to take a telegram to the post office, he would come out of his room and "holding the paper in his hand would say in effect, 'I suppose this must be sent.' A dozen hungry hands would stretch to execute what was neither a request nor a command."[76]

Barin Ghose recalled that Aurobindo "never cared to waste his breath in a long discourse with me on his particular path of yoga." This was true of others as well. Suresh Chakravarty had been a member of the household since 1910, but between then and the mid 1920s, Aurobindo "never even once" spoke to him about yoga. During those years Aurobindo gave "absolute individual liberty" to his companions, and it was only when they decided to take up yoga under his guidance that he began to act as their teacher.[77] And even then he "did not impart instructions or give initiation through a mantra," or provide a fixed method such as *pranayama*, or breath control. Those who came to him "were free to pursue any methods or all methods"—or no method at all. The only suggestion he made to those who came to him for guidance was to try to surrender themselves to the divine and to invoke the *shakti* to purify and illuminate them. His policy toward outward activities was even more *laissez faire*. There was only one rule: strict observance of *brahmacharya*, or celibacy. Otherwise members of the household could do as they liked.

As MENTIONED BEFORE, a number of Aurobindo's visitors during the 1920s were former political or revolutionary associates who tried to coax him back into the field. Upendranath Banerjee and Hrishikesh Kanjilal, both members of Barin's revolutionary group who, like Barin, had passed a decade in the

Andamans, came to Pondicherry to see what kind of leadership Aurobindo might offer. If Upen attended the evening sessions, it was to draw Aurobindo into a discussion of political matters. Aurobindo's position was that a change in government without a general change of consciousness would not bring about any lasting improvement in the country.[78]

Aurobindo was still regarded as one of the most significant political figures in the country. When Subhas Chandra Bose, the future leader of the Indian National Army, was an undergraduate in Calcutta, Aurobindo "was easily the most popular leader in Bengal, despite his voluntary exile and absence since 1909." Bose resigned from the Indian Civil Service in 1921 following Aurobindo's example. "It was widely believed about this time," Bose wrote, that Aurobindo "would soon return to active political life."[79] Such hopes were based largely on Aurobindo's letter to Barin of April 1920, in which he said that his yoga in Pondicherry "may take another two years." Taking this literally, Motilal Roy announced in *The Standard Bearer* that Aurobindo would return to Bengal in February or March 1922.[80] The date came and went, and Aurobindo remained in Pondicherry. He did, however, continue to think that his stay in French India was temporary. In July 1922 he had Amrita tell a correspondent that it was "not true" that he would "not go at all out of Pondy." His stay in French India would "not extend beyond a period of two years."[81] Further postponements were announced in 1924 and again in 1925. Finally he stopped giving dates. Asked in 1926 whether he would return to Bengal anytime soon, he replied that there was "very little chance" of it.[82]

No one was more disappointed by Aurobindo's staying on than Motilal. When the two were together in Chandernagore in 1910, Aurobindo had spoken to the young man about the political and social changes he intended to bring about once his *sadhana* was complete. One project he had in mind was a spiritual commune that would eventually become the nucleus of a gnostic society. He was unsure whether the time was ripe for such an experiment, but at one point he agreed to let Motilal give it a try. The result was the Prabartak Sangha (Pioneer Community) of Chandernagore. For a while it produced positive, if modest, results. Motilal drew back gradually from revolutionary activities, started social service programs, and published journals. As Aurobindo's chief representative in Bengal, he developed a healthy sense of his own importance. He took it for granted that when Aurobindo returned, the Prabartak Sangha would be his center of operations, and he the leader's right-hand man.

The plan began to go awry when Barin was released from his imprisonment. Suddenly Motilal had a competitor for the post of chief disciple. When Aurobindo called them to Pondicherry in 1920, he said that there was more than enough work for both. In 1921 Barin settled down in Pondicherry. The next year Aurobindo asked Motilal to come for an extended stay. He came, but found himself one chick among many instead of the cock of the roost. Besides, it was becoming obvious that if anyone in Pondicherry was going to become Aurobindo's chief disciple, it was Mirra Richard. While Motilal was trying to digest all of this, he received a telegram from his number-two man, Arun Chandra Dutt, asking him to return to Chandernagore before Aurobindo's birthday. Aurobindo advised him to stay. After an agonizing decision, Motilal caught the train for Bengal and never came back.

By 1926 Aurobindo had written off the *sangha* as a failed experiment. In a postmortem discussion he explained: "At that time I was working from the mind and vital," rather than from the higher, supraintellectual faculties. He had some ideas about social and economic organization that he believed were based on truth, and he thought: "Let us begin, change forms as necessary, let us grow." He passed his ideas on to Motilal and Motilal took them up with energy and eloquence, two qualities he had in abundance. (Paul Richard, who met him in 1920, thought he could be a big success in the United States.) But Motilal began to put "an exaggerated dose of egoism" into all he did, and soon got carried away with his own ideas.[83] Eventually, Aurobindo cut off all connection with him. The *sangha* remained active under Motilal's direction for a number of years, but its influence was never more than local.

Rue de la Marine

Aurobindo had been looking for another house for some time, as the place on rue François Martin was in a bad state of repair and not big enough for everyone who wanted to stay. In the summer of 1922 Barin learned that a good house only a minute's walk away was available. Located on the corner of the rue de la Marine, where some government buildings stood, and the rue d'Orléans, where there was an old Ganesh temple, it was owned by a Muslim who worked in the French administration. Anxious to get rid of the current occupant, the mistress of a minor Indian prince, the owner was offering it for a hundred rupees a month. Barin passed this information on to his brother. A few days later, Aurobindo asked him to do all that he could to get the house. By the end of October, the agreement was finalized, and Aurobindo and Mirra, along with Dorothy Hodgson—now known as Dutta—and five others moved into 9 rue de la Marine.[84] They also kept the old place, which soon became known as the Guest House. By August 1923 there were fifteen full-time residents in the two houses. Almost half of them were Bengalis; most of the rest were from Gujarat and the Madras Presidency. Mirra and Datta were the only full-time women, though the wives of two or three of the men were also allowed to stay on the condition that they and their husbands renounced sex.

Two houses were enough for the community's immediate needs, but not enough to allow expansion. Barin, always eager to start big things and unable to stay in one place for long, volunteered to go to Calcutta to collect funds. Aurobindo was not inclined to make a public appeal. When Barin persisted, Aurobindo allowed him to approach selected individuals, but not with a begging bowl. "Make it a point not to accept sums less than a hundred [rupees]," Aurobindo told him, "and when it begins to come in hundreds, then don't take less than a thousand."[85]

Barin went to Calcutta in November and contacted Chittaranjan Das, the barrister who had defended Aurobindo in the Alipore bomb case. At Barin's request, Aurobindo wrote to Das a letter clarifying his plans. For the past several years, he began, he had had practically no contact with the outside world. Now that he was "looking outward again," he was writing to his old friend—his first letter in more than a year—to explain why he needed money. He had remained in retirement for more than a decade because he was convinced that "the true basis of work and life is the spiritual,—that is to say, a new consciousness to be developed only by Yoga." After twelve years' practice, he had been able to touch a higher power of consciousness. The problem before him was to find out how it could be "brought down, mobilised, organised, turned upon life." Until he solved this problem, he would remain in retirement, for he was determined, he wrote, "not to work in the external field till I have the sure and complete possession of this new power of action." But he had reached a point at which he could "undertake one work on a larger scale than before—the training of others to receive this Sadhana and prepare themselves as I have done." He wondered whether Das might use his "recommendation and influence" to help Barin collect money for this purpose.[86]

Aurobindo closed with a reference to Das's political activities. Since 1918 Das had been the leader of the Congress in Bengal. An active participant in the noncooperation movement, he had been arrested and sentenced to six months' imprisonment in February 1922. Gandhi called off the movement shortly afterward. Das was incensed that the Mahatma had "bungled the situation" again.[87] After his release, Das was elected president of the Indian National Congress, and at the Gaya session in December 1922 tried to push through a new policy: Rather than continuing to boycott elections, Congressmen should swamp civic councils and paralyze official business. When Gandhi loyalists defeated his proposal, Das and his supporters formed the Swarajya Party, which became the most active political force in the country between 1923 and 1925. With Gandhi temporarily in jail and the Congress in disarray, Das was briefly the most prominent figure in the Indian national movement.

Das received Aurobindo's letter just before the Gaya Congress. His first reaction was that of a politician. He asked Aurobindo for permission to print portions of the letter that appeared to support his agenda. Aurobindo said he could not allow this. He could not give outright support to Das, any more than he could to Gandhi or to the followers of Tilak. Gandhi's program, he wrote, was not "the true means of bringing out the genuine freedom and greatness of India," but Tilakite nationalism was seriously out of date. His own policy, if he was in the field, "would be radically different in principle and programme from both," but the country was not ready for this. He therefore was "content to work still on the spiritual and psychic plane."[88]

Das had been wanting to speak with Aurobindo for years, and he got his chance in June 1923 when campaigning took him to Madras. Aurobindo reaffirmed his approval of Das's policies and his disapproval of "the fetish-worship of non-cooperation as an end in itself."[89] The Hindu–Muslim problem was again becoming acute; the two agreed that it had to be solved before the British left India. Otherwise, Aurobindo feared, "there will be civil war." In September Das wrote again asking for Aurobindo's endorsement. Aurobindo refused and Das broke off the connection. Das continued to lead his party until 1925, when he died unexpectedly at the age of 54. When the *Bombay Chronicle* asked Aurobindo for a message a short while later, he telegraphed a brief reply: "Consummately endowed with political intelligence, constructive imagination, magnetism, a driving force," Das "was the one man after Tilak who could have led India to Swaraj."[90]

Three days after the telegram was published, a writer for the Anglo-Indian *Times of India* observed with disapproval that Aurobindo had "suddenly been summoned back to [British] India, as the one man who can lead the extremists after the death of Mr. Das." How was it, he asked,

> that Arabindo Ghose is singled out by Mr. Gandhi for the favour of a special summons? And how is it that through all these years he has retained his grip on educated extremists, and is more profoundly admired by these extremists in proportion as they are better educated? One answer which might be given, though it may seem fantastic or trivial, is that he has a reputation as one who beat the Englishman at his own game. . . .

Arabindo Ghose won fame as a writer and speaker of beautiful English, and extremists exulted in the reflection, which was very likely true, that Arabindo was a greater master of English than the leader-writers of the Anglo-Indian Press.

Nevertheless, this Anglo-Indian leader-writer continued, "No man in India has done more to evoke violence while apparently condemning it than Arabindo Ghose, and, when we realise that this is the man whom Mr. Gandhi has asked back to India to take control of the movement against Government we are amazed at Mr. Gandhi."[91] Gandhi's "invitation," which was probably no more than a passing comment, hardly merited this furious denunciation. In any case, Aurobindo was unlikely to say yes to Gandhi after saying no to Moonje and several others. "Do you expect me to fall into the same folly all over again?" he commented when the subject was brought up. At the same time, he admitted that Das's death marked the end of a political epoch.[92] With the collapse of the Swarajya Party, the leadership of the movement passed back to the Gandhi group in the Congress. But Congress's inability to deal with the Hindu–Muslim problem allowed fundamentalist parties such as the Muslim League and Hindu Mahasabha to become more influential. Two Congressmen with Mahasabha leanings, Lala Lajpat Rai and Purushottam Das Tandon, had visited Aurobindo earlier that year. He did not speak with them about Hindu supremacy—an ideology he did not support—but rather Gandhian politics. "*Charkha*," he said, "has its own importance but it cannot bring Swaraj." For Aurobindo, the need of the hour was not any outward program, but the development of discipline and national honor. As for Indian politicians' growing lust for power, he noted, prophetically, that this problem would be "infinitely greater when you get Swaraj."[93]

AT THE END of 1922 Barin rented a house in Bhowanipore, Calcutta, which became the first center for Aurobindo's work outside Pondicherry. Young men came to Barin "seeking a little light and guidance in Yoga."[94] He told them what he knew of Aurobindo's yoga, and sat with them in meditation. If they appeared to be sincere, he wrote to his brother about them, enclosing a photograph when possible. On the basis of Mirra's reading of the photographs and his evaluation of Barin's descriptions, Aurobindo sent detailed guidance by letter. One aspirant had a "highly psychic personality," but had to be careful not to "burn up the body in the intensity of its psychic developments." Another had "an intellectual and philosophic temperament" but "something heavy below." Yet another was "very dull."[95] Barin felt at the time that he was a "live wire" for transmitting Aurobindo's force to others.[96] But he was not sufficiently experienced to deal with spiritual calamities. A young man named Krishnashasi, described by Aurobindo as a "psychic sensitive . . . of a very high though not perhaps the first order," lost his mental balance and within two weeks became a raving lunatic. Aurobindo wrote four letters in quick succession telling Barin how to handle the situation. He closed: "Please keep me constantly informed of his condition until he recovers."[97] The recovery never came, and Aurobindo agreed with Barin that Krishnashasi had to be removed from the Bhowanipore house. Not long afterward, Aurobindo asked Barin to return to Pondicherry. The Bhowanipore center remained open for another two years, finally collapsing due to lack of funds. Aurobindo made no effort to revive it, deciding that such centers "could not function without proper men and the men must first be built up."[98]

AROUND THIS TIME, Aurobindo began to accept the role of guru. The change was due partly to pressure from the *sadhaks,* who wanted to approach him in the traditional way. But it was also the result of his own realization that the democratic ideal he favored in life was not the best for yoga. "I believed in it once," he said. "But now I don't. It is not possible. It will be one man's rule now." Yoga was not always as innocuous as its popularizers made it out to be. Aurobindo complained that at the time "anybody and everybody" was taking up yoga, repeating catch phrases and thinking they had "got the real thing." Many ended up getting into spiritual difficulties. [99]

By the mid 1920s Aurobindo was receiving piles of letters from people known and unknown. Most were requests for cures, for advice, for money, for help in worldly affairs. He left almost all such letters unanswered, but was willing to help people who approached him sincerely for spiritual guidance. Still, he refused to become an oracle on demand. When he felt a letter deserved an answer, he generally called Barin, Purani, or Amrita—his "secretaries" for Bengal, Gujarat, and the South—and told them what to say. The recipients must often have been disappointed. Here is a reply written by Amrita in 1924:

> Sri Aurobindo Ghose asks me to write the following to you:
>
> He does not receive at present any one here either to see him or for anything. Also he does not take disciples to give them Yoga. If you are to get directions for the practising of Aurobindo's Yoga, he says you will get them from within yourself.[100]

Occasionally Aurobindo answered letters himself. Some of the most interesting replies of this period were to U.S. readers of the *Arya* who were trying to practice his yoga. A certain C. E. Lefebvre, from Glenfield, Pennsylvania, wanted to disseminate Aurobindo's teachings using methods like those of Swami Yogananda, a Bengali guru who had settled in America in 1920. The swami, Lefebvre wrote, had had little success until he adopted methods "patterned after American advertising," offering lectures and standardized courses at a fixed rate. "It would seem," Lefebvre concluded, "that America is only ready for elementary instruction."[101] Aurobindo disagreed. Americans had "one great advantage," a "great eagerness and openness of mind to new things." This made them more likely to be open to his ideas than many people in India, who found it difficult "to go beyond ancient ideas and forms." However receptive Indians might be, most were confused by Aurobindo's "departure from the old forms and an absence of the accustomed paraphernalia and a breaking of old barriers and limits." On the other hand, few Indians could be induced to cough up a fee for standardized lessons, as Americans seemed ready to do.[102] The fact of the matter, Aurobindo wrote, was that "Yoga cannot be taught in schools and classes":

> It has to be received personally, it has to be lived, the seeker, *sadhaka*, has to change by a difficult aspiration and endeavour his whole consciousness and nature, his mind, heart, life, every principle of his being and all their movements into a greater Truth than anything the normal life of man can imagine. Those who can do this are not yet many, but some are to be found everywhere, and I see no reason why those in America should be condemned to only an elementary "instruction." The true Truth, the great Path has to be opened to them; how far they will go on it depends on their own personal capacity and the help they receive.[103]

How the knowledge of Aurobindo's path was to be diffused remained an open question. Since the early 1920s publishers in Calcutta and Madras had been putting out collections of essays that had been published in the *Karmayogin* and *Arya*. Lefebvre wanted to publish some titles in the United States. Aurobindo consented, but stressed that books could only lay an intellectual foundation. Real guidance in yoga "must be personal, suited to the recipient and the instruction given can only be effective if it is the channel for a spiritual contact and a guiding or helpful influence." For this reason, he said, "guidance in Yoga by correspondence and without personal contact is a very hampered and not usually in my experience a satisfactory method."[104] He did agree to open a correspondence with one U.S. couple, but it did not last for long. The proposal to publish his works in America also proved unfruitful.

ASKED IN AUGUST 1926 about his "outward work," Aurobindo replied: "I am not doing any outward work at present. I have given up everything, even writing, even the Bhawanipur centre. Unless we realise the thing internally, no outward work will be possible. Only, before we are ready, some attempt may be made. That has its value as a preparatory agent."[105] He said this to a group of fifteen or twenty *sadhaks* who constituted this "attempt." The community had no special name. The word "centre" had "no meaning" in this context, Aurobindo said. "Sangha" and "ashram" were even worse; both terms had been misused for so long, he said, that they ought to be withdrawn from circulation.[106] What existed in Pondicherry was a free assemblage of men and women who lived in his two houses and did yoga under his and Mirra's guidance. What it was called was unimportant.

For the members of the community, the main event of the day was a meeting with Aurobindo in the evening. Much as before, around 4:30 he came out of his room and sat on a chair that had been placed on the veranda. If Kiki, one of the cats who had colonized the house, was curled up in the chair, Aurobindo perched on the edge until Kiki decided to move away. In front of him was a small cloth-covered table with a flower arrangement, ashtray, block-calendar, and clock. Until the end of 1923 the meetings began with a meditation and ended with a talk. The meditations were dispensed with early the next year but the talks continued until 1926. Sometimes instead of asking for questions, Aurobindo just gazed up at the sky. "There were days," Purani recalled, "when more than three-fourths of the time passed in complete silence without any outer suggestion from him, or there was only an abrupt 'Yes' or 'No' to all attempts at drawing him out in conversation." Even when Aurobindo spoke, the others "felt that his voice was that of one who does not let his whole being flow into his words: there was a reserve and what was left unsaid was perhaps more than what was spoken."[107] If the participants managed to get him talking, he continued for a half-hour or more, taking up practically any topic proposed. "Very often," Purani recalled,

> some news-item in the daily newspaper, town-gossip, or some interesting letter received either by him or by a disciple, or a question from one of the gathering, [or] occasionally some remark or query from himself would set the ball rolling for the talk. The whole thing was so informal that one

could never predict the turn the conversation would take. The whole house therefore was in a mood to enjoy the freshness and the delight of meeting the unexpected. There were peals of laughter and light talk, jokes and criticism which might be called personal,—there was seriousness and earnestness in abundance.[108]

The talk moved freely from one subject to another. One evening Aurobindo began with some remarks on the philosophical idea of form, moved on to *samadhi* and the supramental yoga, then compared the Upanishads and European philosophy, calling the latter "a game of words." This led to some remarks on what he felt was the right attitude for discovering truth:

> The first step towards truth is to keep a dissolvant critical attitude, to see things as they are, actually; to dismiss all egoistic nonsense. Things like love and patriotism are vital instincts and it is false to camouflage them as divine emotions. Shaw is an acute thinker who sees things in their actuality. So is Anatole France. But this actuality is not the whole truth. To attain Truth we must look from above, and see what is good and useful in the lower movements and cast off the falsehood and egoism. In mind, knowledge and power are not one. . . . When the mind begins to reflect and rule the vital being, the latter consents so long as it suits its convenience and, when it no longer does suit it, it rushes up. That is why man has not done anything so far but spins in a futile circle, since his knowledge is that of the mind and his will is of the vital and they are separate. To effectuate anything, knowledge and will must be one.

This consideration of "the vital," or life force, led to a discussion of morality. "The moralist," Aurobindo said, "crushes life into a narrow groove and there indulges his movements." To bring about real change, the *sadhak* had to change "the movement of desire, the movement of egoism." He or she had to "psychicise and spiritualise the vital movements—sex, money-force, ambition." But a permanent transformation could only come about by means of supermind. This was why he was "striving to bring down the Supramental on the earth-plane. This has not been done before."

Returning to philosophy, Aurobindo considered the soul and determinism, then the experience of the soul after death. This was followed by some remarks on the occult knowledge of the Egyptians, and the way that certain "powers" manifested in certain countries. "The thoughts and actions of the individual," he said, "are but part of the movement. . . . No individual ever made a country."

He no longer linked his hopes for India to politics, saying, "My one aim is to bring down the Supermind, allow it to organise itself in my being and life. Politics or other work belongs to a lower plane, it uses up much energy." He concluded with some comments on the state of the world:

> Now there seems to be a general awakening in the world, an upheaval, an opening up: the old things are called in question, there is a demand for higher things. Such an awakening is a sign that the higher powers are seeking to manifest themselves in the world. . . . When Christianity first came, there was such an awakening, but the Christians compromised with the vital forces, set about converting people to their religion, and the result was a failure. . . . Unless we now bring down the higher powers here in India, the chance may go to some other country. . . . If people merely go on with their vital aims—patriotism, political work—Truth will not simply follow them into the legislative councils.[109]

Aurobindo was not always interested in discussing such serious topics. Once, asked "what is time?" by a budding philosopher, he glanced at the clock and said, "Eight-twenty."[110] If he commented on Indian politicians, his tone was often ironic. He also could be critical of those who were present: "Don't you see?" he might say, pointing his finger at a questioner, or else: "Don't talk nonsense." In general, however, the mood of the talks was jovial. "I never saw him solemn or serious," recalled V. Chidanandam. "Humour, even light-hearted jokes and jests, used to be there in plenty." Sometimes Aurobindo "would chuckle happily."[111]

AUROBINDO'S BIRTHDAYS BEGAN to be celebrated with some pomp. "From early morning," reads one contemporary account, the house was "humming with various activities. . . . All are eager to go to the Master for his Darshan [formal viewing]. As the time passes there is a tide in the sea of rising emotion. It is 'Darshan'—we see him every day, but today it is 'Darshan'! Today each sees him individually, one after another. In the midst of these multiple activities the consciousness gets concentrated." Climbing the staircase, they found him seated "in the royal chair in the verandah—royal and majestic. In the very posture there is divine self-confidence. In the heart of the Supreme Master, the great Yogin." Those present were filled with emotion: "is it a flood that mounts or a flood that is coming down on humanity? Those alone who have experienced it can know something of its divinity." As they approach, "all doubts get assurance. . . . Love and grace flow on undiminished. The look! enrapturing and captivating eyes! Who can ever forget?—pouring love and grace and ineffable divinity."[112]

There is no way to know what Aurobindo thought about the outpouring of emotion. Basically British in his upbringing, he was always reticent and reserved, never encouraging demonstrations of feeling. He was familiar with the conventions of the Indian *guru-shishya* relationship, such as bowing down before the master and elaborate gestures of devotion, but he resisted attempts by his followers to practice them. He may have regarded such customs as examples of those "ancient ideas and forms" that Indian had such difficulty getting beyond. But if Aurobindo was indifferent or opposed to ceremony, Mirra thrived in it. She was happy to see the *sadhaks* spending hours stringing garlands and preparing special dishes, and later, during the *darshan*, bowing down at Aurobindo's feet.

After the *darshan*, there was a special edition of the evening talk. In August 1923 a disciple began by asking him about the current state of his *sadhana*. He replied in a low, clear voice: "I cannot call it a state or a condition. It is, rather, a complex movement. I am at present engaged in bringing the Supermind into the physical consciousness." It was not an easy task: "One feels as if 'digging the earth,' as the Veda says." He had reached a point at which his whole being had been "made conscious." What remained was to apply the highest level of the supermind to inner and outer things. When this was complete, the body would be immune to attacks by the forces that oppose yoga. The transformation could go so far that "the casting away or retaining of the body would be voluntary."[113]

The above account is the first known document dealing with Aurobindo's *sadhana* since he stopped keeping the *Record* in 1920. On subsequent birthdays it became a tradition to ask him about his practice. In August 1924 he explained that he was still working on the physical level. He was doing "the same thing over and over again," but doing it better each time. It was difficult to bring the supermind down into matter because "the physical layer is a very obstinate thing and it requires to be worked out in detail. You work out one thing then think it is done; something else arises and you have again to go over the same ground. It is not like the mind or the vital where it is easier for the higher power to work." Asked whether his efforts would ultimately prove successful, he could only say: "ask me next August. This time I am more hopeful than I was last year [1923]. . . . Last year was a very hard year for my sadhana. There was an attack from the darkest physical forces on me. This year they are all gone."[114]

Things had improved, but only slightly, by 1925. When the question about his *sadhana* came up, Aurobindo at first tried to avoid it ("My sadhana!— I am doing sadhana? Ask some other question."), then deflected it. Reminded of his statement of the previous year, he made everybody laugh by saying: "I can say now, It is more possible this year than it was last year." It was not a joke, he insisted. "There have been manifestations of it [the supramental light] now that were not there before. The Power is working more directly on the physical plane." But "the more the light and power are coming down, the greater is the resistance," he said. He was doing all he could to bring the supermind into matter, but the *sadhaks* had to cooperate. If they sided with the opposing forces, they would retard their own progress and also the general advance. They could help "by one-pointed aspiration," rejecting "everything that stands in the way of fulfilling the ideal."[115]

To the *sadhaks,* as perhaps to the reader, what Aurobindo was doing remained a mystery. The idea of the supermind was difficult enough to grasp; the *sadhaks* had to take on faith the promise of its "descent" into the physical and the evolutionary changes that were to follow. They were happy to be associated with such an enormous work, but it seemed for the moment to have few discernible effects on their lives. Nevertheless, people continued to join the community, drawn by Aurobindo's writings and his growing reputation as a spiritual leader. By the end of 1926 there were around twenty permanent residents. Two additional houses were rented, one of them just north and the other just east of 9 rue de la Marine. But as the household grew and its activities increased, Aurobindo became less and less accessible. Often he came late to the evening session. Once the *sadhaks* had to sit until two in the morning before he joined them.[116]

Aurobindo spoke little about his progress during the talks, but it seemed to many as though a breakthrough were imminent. Finally, on November 24, 1926 he crossed a threshold. Toward seven o'clock that evening, Mirra summoned the *sadhaks* to the veranda of 9 rue de la Marine. By 7:30 almost everyone was there: the nineteen or twenty permanent residents and five or six others. All sat on mats that had been spread on the floor. "Many saw an oceanic flood of Light rushing down from above. Everyone present felt a kind of pressure above his head. The whole atmosphere was surcharged with some electrical energy." The door of Aurobindo's room was opened from within. First Mirra, then Aurobindo, came out. To some it seemed as if he was half in trance. The two walked slowly across the veranda. Aurobindo sat in his usual chair, Mirra on a stool at his feet. Silence, "absolute, living silence," prevailed. For three-quarters of an hour everyone sat in meditation. Then the *sadhaks* came forward and bowed at Mirra's feet. As each one inclined, Aurobindo held his hand behind her head "as if blessing them through [her]." When all of them had had their turn, Aurobindo and Mirra rose and went back to his room. Breaking the silence, Datta spoke as one inspired. All accounts differ as to what she said, but the substance was: "The Lord has descended into the physical today."[117]

It was clear to the *sadhaks* that something wonderful had happened, but no one knew exactly what it was. In the days that followed, Mirra gave some indications. To one *sadhak* she said that "the Ananda" or plane of cosmic bliss had "descended in the physical." With another she used traditional Hindu terminology: "Sri Krishna had descended and conquered everything in the physical except a few details" that would be worked out by the following August. Aurobindo himself said nothing about the event for almost nine years. Asked in 1935 whether the supermind was going to descend again as it had in 1926, he answered: "The descent of 1926 was rather of the Overmind, not of the Supermind proper."[118] Overmind, a term that he coined in 1927, is a transitional plane between mind and supermind. Its "descent," that is, its manifestation in the physical world, was necessary before the supermind could itself descend. It was this preliminary descent, Aurobindo realized at some point, that had happened on November 24, 1926.

For the members of the household, the exact nature of the experience was less important than its immediate consequences. Three days after the descent, Aurobindo asked Barin to tell the *sadhaks* two things. First: "the power has descended into the unconscious," but it was necessary to work things out in detail "by the help of that power." Second: "Mirra is my Shakti. She has taken charge of the new creation. You will get everything from her. Give [your] consent to whatever she wants to do."[119] What this meant in practice was that he would not see the *sadhaks* any longer. The door to his room remained closed, and no one but Mirra could enter. It was she who would guide the *sadhaks* in their spiritual and practical affairs.

AUROBINDO NEVER WAS an outgoing man. As a student and scholar in England and Baroda, he spent most of his time by himself. If friends came by, he joined them in their talk, but always held something back. Between 1906 and 1910, when he was involved in the nationalist movement, he passed a great deal of time with others, but even when he was writing and addressing public meetings, part of him remained inaccessible. In 1910 he withdrew from outward action and for years saw practically no one. This changed a little in 1914 after the Richards' arrival. He passed time with them and others almost daily, and agreed to their proposal to bring out a philosophical journal. Their return to Pondicherry in 1920 began another period of interaction. His meetings with them and others developed into the evening talks of the 1920s, in which he poured out his thoughts on spirituality, politics, literature, and dozens of other subjects. But in November 1926 the talks ceased. He drew back, beginning a retirement that would last the rest of his life.

As his withdrawal extended from months to years to decades, the *sadhaks* never gave up hope that he would someday reemerge. He never said that he would not. Asked in 1933, "when will you come out of your retirement," he replied: "That is a thing of which nothing can be said at present. My retirement had a purpose, and that purpose must be fulfilled."[120]

9. An Active Retirement

Pondicherry, 1927–1950

My retirement itself was indispensable; otherwise I would not now [1945] be
where I am, that is, personally, near the goal.

Sri Aurobindo and the Mother

Toward the end of 1926 the members of the community that was forming around Aurobindo began to refer to him as Sri Aurobindo. Before then,
people called him A. G. The official form, used in signatures and on the title
page of books, was Aurobindo Ghose, with or without the Sri. The Sanskrit
word *sri,* meaning literally "riches," "majesty," or "beauty," is often used as an
honorific. In modern northern India it is the equivalent of the English honorific "mister." In more formal usage it is placed before the names of gods, saints,
and scriptures. Sri (or Srijut or Sriman) Aurobindo Ghose was in frequent use
during Aurobindo's stay in Calcutta, but Sri Aurobindo without the surname
seems to have first appeared in print in articles published in Chandernagore in
1920. It did not catch on at that time. He first signed his name Sri Aurobindo
in March 1926, but continued to use Sri Aurobindo Ghose for a year or two
more. Sri Aurobindo first appeared on the title page of a book in 1929, and
became the established form in 1933. Since then, the subject of this biography
has always been known as Sri Aurobindo, the two words being regarded as a
single name.

In February 1927 Sri Aurobindo moved to 28 rue François Martin, a house
located in the same block as 9 rue de la Marine and the two buildings that had
been rented in 1925 and 1926. Negotiations to acquire the rue François Martin
house had begun in the summer of 1926, when Barin had taken Mirra to see it.
The landlord asked for 14,000 rupees, a very large sum. Mirra said that "money

wasn't of any consequence as this house meant so much for the future of the [spiritual] colony."[1] On January 8, 1927, Sri Aurobindo and Mirra gave half of the purchase price, and renovation work began. The walls separating the four houses were pierced to make passageways or else torn down entirely. The result was a sprawling complex of rooms, courtyards, and gardens, sufficiently large for most members of the community to live and work. By February 7 enough remodeling had been done for Sri Aurobindo to move into his new quarters. Everyone was asked to leave the houses and Mirra led him from 9 rue de la Marine to 28 rue François Martin. He occupied a spacious second-floor suite consisting of three narrow halls, each nine meters long and three meters wide, with a small square room at the end of each hall. Mirra stayed in an adjoining salon. In July the balance of the purchase price was paid, and Sri Aurobindo signed the title deed for 28 rue François Martin in the presence of the former owner, Mirra, three other French citizens, and S. Duraiswami Iyer, a barrister and disciple from Madras. This was the first time that anyone but Mirra and an occasional *sadhak* had seen him since November.[2]

SRI AUROBINDO'S WITHDRAWAL at the end of November 1926 gave him the chance to concentrate on his *sadhana* in a way that had not been possible for the last few years. In January 1927 he began to make regular entries in *Record of Yoga* for the first time since October 1920. Early notations were upbeat. "The supreme force descends," he wrote on January 3. "The difficulty is finished. The representative imperative [*vijnana*] still obstructs [the higher workings of *vijnana*], but it is ready to disappear." And nine days later: "The final dealings with this body begin from today. The first stage of them finishes with the end of the month." Many entries are concerned with the transformation of "T^3" (telepathy-*trikaldrishti-tapas*) and "T^2" (*trikaldrishti-tapas*) into a superior power "above the Telepathic and above the Tapasic trikalsiddhi [mastery of the three times] and above the combination of these things." This power, called "T" or "Gnostic T," was the true and invincible supermind, which he had been seeking for more than a decade. Around the same time he recorded advances in many other elements of his yoga, such as *samadhi* (yogic trance), *drishti* (the power of vision), and *ananda* (delight on all levels of the being). There was, he noted on January 27, "a vertiginous rapidity of progress in many directions." But, as often before, the intensity could not last. January 31 was "a day of relapse and resistance."[3] A day later he abandoned the *Record* for three months.

Recommencing the diary in April, Sri Aurobindo noted: "There must be an entire submission to the transforming Power and the transforming process.

However tedious it may [seem], each step, each recoil is inevitable, nothing is done unwisely or vainly in the economy of the supreme processes." During the next twelve days there was a steady development in several *chatusthayas*. This was followed by "three days [of] strong obstruction." Then, on April 22, he noted his "first experience of entire gnostic intuition and supramental reason with supramental observation and a supramental recipient in the physical nature."[4] But this was the last entry, or the last one he preserved, for six months.

Between October 24 and October 31, 1927 Sri Aurobindo wrote four pages of *Record* notes. Sometime later he tore them up and threw them in a wastepaper basket. They survive only because A.B. Purani, whose duty it was to burn the trash, recognized Sri Aurobindo's writing and rescued the fragments. Why did Sri Aurobindo throw them away? Did he do the same to other parts of the *Record*? It is impossible to answer either question. Evidently he was dissatisfied with what he wrote in October, though the entries seem as interesting as those of the earlier parts of the year. October 24 was, he wrote, "a day of great and rapid progress," with notable advances in *vijnana*, a name he used in the Record for the higher levels of consciousness and power. The next day there was "something of a recoil into the hampered semi-mental movement," but he progressed in other directions. This mixed advance continued until October 31, when he wrote what would be the last surviving dated entry of *Record of Yoga:*

> Today T^2 (anishwara [without full power]) has acquired the supramental and gnostic character. Not that all movements have entirely eliminated the mental element, but all are supramental or supramentalised or else even (now to some extent) gnostic overmind. Infallible T^2 is beginning more freely to emerge. . . .
>
> Ananda [bliss] is taking possession and becomes automatic, needing only memory or a little attention to act at once. All vision, hearing, smell, taste, touch is now anandamaya [blissful]; even all that is seen, heard, sensed is beginning to be felt as full of ananda and even as if made of Ananda. Sahaituka [stimulated] Ananda of all except event is now automatic. Ahaituka [unstimulated] Ananda within the body shows signs of reaching the same state, but has not quite reached it. This is the only physical siddhi that promises to be soon initially complete; for arogya [health] is still hampered by obstinate minute fragments of illness.[5]

Through *Record of Yoga* we can trace the outlines, if not understand the details, of Sri Aurobindo's *sadhana* between 1912 and 1927. For the next twenty-three years, we have to depend on scattered notes and letters. Three "scripts" or automatic writings from the period just after October 1927 set the pace for what is to follow. "It is true that the most material couch is open and touched, though not yet transformed," one script begins; "But this is not sufficient; for the power that will work in it must be the true supermind, and as yet it is only the supramentalised overmind that has become at all normal in the material consciousness." The passage suggests that the power that descended in November 1926 had stabilized in the months that followed, but it also makes it clear that Sri Aurobindo was aware that what had descended in November 1926 was not the true supermind. "Many things have still to be done before the divine gnosis [the supermind] can manifest in the nature," he wrote in another script. "It is the gnostic overmind in different forms that is now current there; it has to be transformed into the true supermind gnosis." A third fragmentary script, of 1927 or 1928, concludes: "The automatic perfection of supramental overmind thought is the next siddhi [perfection] indicated. It will begin with a progressive elimination of all that remains of supramentalised mind in overmind."[6]

Some readers may feel puzzled by terms such as supermind and overmind, not to mention "supramental or supramentalised or else even (now to some extent) gnostic overmind." What did Sri Aurobindo mean by these levels or powers of consciousness? How and into what do they descend? The goal of Sri Aurobindo's yoga, it will be recalled, was not an escape from a painful or delusive lower world, the *samsara* of the Buddha or *maya* of the Adwaitins, by means of extinction (*nirvana*) or absorption (*samadhi*), but an ascent into a world of self-existent knowledge and power, followed by a descent of the higher knowledge and power into the imperfect lower world. This descent eventually would bring about a transformation of the lower world into a perfect image of the higher. Sri Aurobindo gave the name "supermind" to a power of the higher world between absolute existence-consciousness-bliss (*sat-chit-ananda*) and the lower creation of matter, life, and mind. Although part of the higher world, supermind—unlike pure existence, consciousness, and bliss—can act upon the lower world to change it.

Sri Aurobindo had been trying for many years to ascend through the higher levels of mind, which are characterized by powers such as intuition and inspiration, into the full supermind. As he approached it, he found himself moving in increasingly rarified levels, to which he gave such names as "interpretative logistical vijnana," which was a term he used in June 1920 for the second scale of the highest level of the plane of luminous reason. By 1927, he had dropped most of the terminology that he had been using up until then, much of which was based on words borrowed from Sanskrit and Greek, in favor of a new set of terms such as overmind. He did not explain fully what he meant by overmind until the early 1930s, when he wrote about it in answer to questions from followers. Two points from his answers deserve special notice. First, overmind is the highest of the planes between ordinary mind and supermind. Second, although "full of lights and powers," overmind is still part of mind, which, in Sri Aurobindo's view, is a power of ignorance and not of knowledge. "In its own plane," he wrote in a letter of 1933,

> overmind seems to be only a divided, many-sided play of the Truth, so can easily be taken by the Mind as a supramental province. Mind also when flooded by the overmind lights feels itself living in a surprising revelation of divine Truth. The difficulty comes when we deal with the vital [the life-force] and still more with the physical. Then it becomes imperative to face the difficulty and to make a sharp distinction between overmind and supermind—for it then becomes evident that the overmind Power (in spite of its lights and splendours) is not sufficient to overcome the Ignorance because it is itself under the law of Division out of which came the Ignorance. One has to pass beyond and supramentalise overmind so that mind and all the rest may undergo the final change.[7]

This supramentalizing of the overmind would be the keynote of Sri Aurobindo's *sadhana* after 1927.

ENTRIES FOR *Record of Yoga* were not the only writing that Sri Aurobindo produced in 1927. He took up but soon abandoned several projects that had lain dormant during the 1920s: Vedic research, the poems *Ilion* and *Savitri*, essays on rebirth and karma. He also visited a number of topics that he would return to repeatedly over the next two decades: consciousness, evolution, the nature of the human being. "Psychology," he wrote in one draft, "is the science of consciousness and its status and operations in Nature and, if that can be glimpsed or experienced, its status and operations beyond what we know as Nature."[8] This is straightforward enough. But what is consciousness—or, as Sri Aurobindo wrote, "What is this phenomenon which seems to have so small a part in the vast inconscient mass of things and is yet the sole element here that can give any value to the universe?" Is it really "only a phenomenon, an appearance that has emerged in the course of the workings of an Energy which was, is and will always remain inconscient? Or is it something fundamental, an inherent reality or a latent character or power of that Energy and bound to emerge at some time once it had begun its workings?" If, as he believed, consciousness was bound to emerge more fully, it followed that the human being is only "a transitional being, he is not final. He is a middle term of the evolution, not its end, crown or consummating masterpiece."[9]

Sri Aurobindo also wrote a number of drafts of messages intended for people who wanted to practice his yoga. He did not make his path seem easy. "The way is long, arduous, dangerous, difficult. At every step is an ambush, at every turn a pitfall," he wrote in one such draft. In another he sketched the conditions for the descent of the supreme power: "a total surrender, an exclusive self-opening to the divine influence, and an integral choice of the Truth and rejection of the falsehood."[10] Neither of these pieces were published during his lifetime, but the second, reworked, became the basis of a message that he issued to the members of the community on Mirra's birthday, February 21, 1927:

> There are two powers that alone can effect in their conjunction the great and difficult thing which is the aim of our endeavour, a fixed and unfailing aspiration that calls from below and a supreme Grace from above that answers. . . .
>
> These are the conditions of the Light and Truth, the sole conditions under which the highest force will descend. . . .
>
> There must be a total and sincere surrender; there must be an exclusive self-opening to the divine Power; there must be a constant and integral choice of the Truth that is descending, a constant and integral rejection of the falsehood of the mental, vital and physical Powers and Appearances that still rule the earth-Nature. . . .
>
> This is the true attitude and only those who can take and keep it, preserve a faith unshaken by disappointments and difficulties and shall pass through the ordeal to the supreme victory and the great transmutation.[11]

Apart from this piece, the only writings from 1927 that saw light during Sri Aurobindo's lifetime were letters. Each post brought pleas for cures, appeals to be delivered from misfortune, requests for knowledge of the future. He had to ask his secretary to tell such petitioners that he was not in the business of providing occult goods and services. Requests for guidance in yoga were another matter, though he had no time for correspondents who begged to be accepted as disciples but showed no capacity for inner or outer discipline. To such people he wrote flatly, if he wrote at all, that his path was a specialized one, requiring total dedication and a willingness to leave behind all that hindered a single-minded pursuit of the goal of his yoga.

Four letters that Sri Aurobindo wrote during Summer 1927 dealt with some of the rudiments of his path: personal effort and surrender, the conquest of fear, the right attitude toward money, the egoless way of works. A short while later, he decided to publish these letters and the message of February 21 as a sort of introduction to his yoga. But something more was needed to give the book an ampler scope. Around September he began working on an essay about the four "aspects" of the Divine Mother, *maheshwari, mahakali, mahalakshmi,* and *mahasaraswati,* explaining the importance of these powers in the cosmic order. He concluded: "The supramental change is a thing decreed and inevitable in the evolution of the earth-consciousness," that is, the global consciousness that evolves along with the evolution of life on the planet,

> for its upward ascent is not ended and mind is not its last summit. But that the change may arrive, take form and endure, there is needed the call from below with a will to recognise and not deny the Light when it comes, and there is needed the sanction of the Supreme from above. The power that mediates between the sanction and the call is the presence and power of the Divine Mother.[12]

Sri Aurobindo finished the essay in October and sent it, the four letters, and the February message to a publishing house in Calcutta. The resulting book, entitled *The Mother,* appeared in early 1928. It was his first new work since the suspension of the *Arya* eight years earlier.

AROUND THE TIME that Aurobindo became known as Sri Aurobindo, Mirra became known as Mira and the Mother. In Europe, Mirra and Mira are short forms of the Hebrew name Miriam. In India, Mira is remembered as the name of the fourteenth-century Rajasthani princess and devotee. This homonymy made it possible for Mirra's name to be Indianized by removing a single "r." In letters from 1926 and 1927, Sri Aurobindo referred to her as Mirra Devi, then Mira Devi, then Sri Mira Devi (*devi,* literally "goddess," is sometimes appended to the names of Indian women as a sign of respect). Mira and Sri Mira Devi remained in use well into the 1940s but long before then another form became current among members of the community: the Mother. Sri Aurobindo began referring to her in this way in talks of 1926. By the middle of the next year, the Mother had become the standard form of address.

In his philosophical works, Sri Aurobindo gave special importance to the Mother-force or *shakti.* In *The Life Divine* he wrote: "If we would realise a higher formation or status of being, then it is still through her, through the Divine Shakti, the Consciousness-Force of the Spirit that it has to be done; our surrender must be to the Divine Being through the Divine Mother."[13] Evidently when he began to refer to Mira as the Mother, he regarded her as more than a particularly advanced disciple. He made no claims on her behalf in his published writings, not even in *The Mother.* But it was natural for those who practiced his yoga to take the descriptions in the book as applying to Mira. One reader asked whether "our Mother," that is, Mira, was the individual form of the Divine Mother who, as Sri Aurobindo wrote, "embodies the power of these two vaster ways of her existence [transcendent and cosmic], makes them living and near to us and mediates between the human personality and the divine Nature." Sri Aurobindo replied with a simple "yes."[14]

In letters to disciples in Pondicherry and outside, Sri Aurobindo was more explicit about the role of Mira, the Mother, in the practice of his yoga. "I no longer take direct charge of people's sadhana," he wrote in March 1927, "all is in the hands of Sri Mira Devi."[15] No exceptions to this rule were permitted. A woman from Boston who had been accepted as a disciple but arrived in Pondicherry after Sri Aurobindo had retired pleaded with him for an interview and guidance unmediated by the Mother. His response was unambiguous:

> If you cannot profit by her help, you would find still less profit in mine. But, in any case, I have no intention of altering the arrangement I have made for all the disciples without exception that they should receive the light and force from her and not directly from me and be guided by her in their spiritual progress. I have made the arrangement not for any temporary purpose but because it is the one way—provided always the disciple is open and receives—that is true and effective (considering what she is and her power).[16]

The disciples who accepted the Mother as their guide knew little about the inner status and power that Sri Aurobindo referred to in this letter. To them she was a loving, kind, wise, and mysterious woman with an entrancing smile and penetrating eyes, who seemed to know more about their thoughts and desires than they did themselves. Even visitors were struck by her qualities: one wrote of her in 1927 as "the very embodiment of grace and purity, of love and compassion," transmitting "purity, power and spiritual calm" by her touch. Manifestly "the central figure" of the community, she was "the mother" of the *sadhaks* and "the real soul, the spirit of the whole organisation."[17] This movement to the center marked a decisive change in her place within the community. Between 1923 and 1926 she had spent most of her time in seclusion, seeing and being seen by few. Even then it was clear that Sri Aurobindo considered her his *shakti*, but it did not automatically follow that she was intended to play an important role in the group's collective life. Few could have imagined then that within a few years she would become the point around which the life of the community turned. Looking back on this development thirty years later, the Mother remarked:

> Sri Aurobindo put me in charge of the outer work because he wanted to withdraw into concentration in order to hasten the manifestation of the supramental consciousness and he announced to the few people who were there that he was entrusting me with the work of helping and guiding them, that I would remain in contact with him, of course, and that through me he would do the work. Suddenly, immediately, things took a certain shape: a very brilliant creation was worked out in extraordinary detail, with marvellous experiences, contacts with divine beings, and all kinds of manifestations which are generally considered miraculous. Experiences followed one upon another, and, well, things were unfolding altogether brilliantly.[18]

This brilliant period lasted for a few months. For the *sadhaks* it was a time of extraordinary and sometimes bizarre experiences. Most of them felt that "something great was going to happen."[19] Some were able to bear the pressure; others became disturbed or lost their balance. As the difficulties mounted, the Mother went to see Sri Aurobindo. Years later she recalled what he said: "This is an Overmind creation. It is very interesting, very well done. You will perform miracles which will make you famous throughout the world, you will be able to turn everything topsy-turvy. In fact"—here he smiled—"it will be a *grand* success. But it is an Overmind creation. And this is not the success that we want. We want to establish the Supermind on earth. One must know how to renounce immediate success in order to create the new world, the supramental world, in its integrality." Grasping his meaning, she meditated and within a few hours had torn down all that she had built up since November.[20]

Sri Aurobindo clarified later that the Mother's attempt failed because of the deficiencies of the *sadhaks*. Their lower vital and physical beings had not been able to follow her lead. The power that had been coming down was not the supermind, but it would, he wrote, "have been sufficient for the work of opening the way for the highest action, if it had not been for the irruption" of certain "wrong forces" in the *sadhaks*. As a result, "the Mother had to push the Divine Personalities and Powers, through which she was doing the action, behind a veil and come down into the physical human level and act according to its conditions."[21] From this point forward, progress in the yoga moved at a slower pace.

AFTER SRI AUROBINDO'S RETIREMENT at the end of 1926, it was generally understood that he would reemerge shortly, most likely on his birthday, August 15, 1927. A few days before that date, a message circulated to the effect that he would not be coming out in the foreseeable future. He did, however, agree to give *darshan* on his birthday. Taking his place beside the Mother in one of the outer rooms of his apartment, he sat in silence as the members of the community and a few invited visitors passed before him one by one. Each was allowed a minute or two in his presence. No words were exchanged. Many had powerful experiences. For himself, Sri Aurobindo had a chance to evaluate their progress and to give them his blessings. The *darshan* ceremony was repeated on November 24, 1927, the first anniversary of the overmind descent. Three months later a third *darshan* day was added: February 21, the Mother's birthday. From this time on, the three *darshan* days became the main events in the community's calendar, eagerly awaited and celebrated with solemnity. *Sadhaks* familiar with Hindu ritual were comfortable with the procedure; after all, to most people in India, *darshan* means viewing an image during temple worship. Some Westerners were taken aback to see grown men and women prostrating themselves before Sri Aurobindo and the Mother. Anticipating such a reaction, the Mother warned Philippe Barbier Saint Hilaire, a French engineer who had recently joined the community, not to be surprised or upset by such devotional practices. The Indian disciples, she said, regarded Sri Aurobindo's house as a temple and behaved "as they would in a temple only replacing the idol by a human figure." This gave them "the fullness they need." Saint Hilaire, she allowed, was "brought up differently." He agreed that he had "less need for outer manifestations," but was not put off by the way that the others expressed their devotion.[22]

The Ashram

The community continued to grow, a development that was, as Saint Hilaire wrote to his father, "a little against the wishes of Sri Aurobindo, who wants to arrive at a certain point of [inner] realization before admitting new disciples, to avoid dissipating the effect" of his practice. But people were begging with such intensity to be admitted that Sri Aurobindo was "almost obliged to accept them."[23] When people wrote asking for admission, his usual response was to say that his yoga was a special and difficult path that was not meant for everyone. Those wishing to escape from the problems of the world were advised to look elsewhere. To an aspirant who wanted to lead a peaceful life in Pondicherry, he wrote that attaining inner peace was not the object of his yoga, but "only one of the elementary conditions for it."[24]

When an applicant seemed suitable for his path, Sri Aurobindo asked him or her to come to Pondicherry for a temporary stay. The final decision was left to the Mother. One prospective *sadhak* was told that she had remarked to Sri Aurobindo: "This is a man I can change. *But he is not yet ready.*" The person was advised "to take the right relation to her, to be open and to enter her atmosphere. The most ordinary meeting or talk with her on the physical plane is quite enough for the purpose." Further, he was told that it would be a mistake to make "too rigid a separation" between the Mother and Sri Aurobindo, since "both influences are necessary for the complete development of the sadhana." Sri Aurobindo acted "directly on the mental and the vital being through the illumined mind," while the Mother acted "directly on the psychic being and on the emotional vital and physical nature through the illumined psychic consciousness."[25]

The "psychic being" was a new element in Sri Aurobindo's yoga. In earlier writings, he used the words "self" or "spirit" for the self-existent being that is one in all individuals—what the Upanishads and *Gita* call the *atman*. He used the word "soul" for the divine element in each person, something similar to the *jivatman* of the *Gita*. But the *jivatman*, like the *atman*, neither changes nor evolves. Sri Aurobindo's evolutionary cosmos requires an evolutionary being, a soul that "enters into the body at birth and goes out of it at death," retaining the essence of each incarnation and developing "a physical, a vital, a mental human consciousness as its instruments of world-experience."[26] Up to 1926 Sri Aurobindo had no name for this evolutionary soul. The Mother provided him with one. Théon, her teacher in occultism, had distinguished the *centre divin* or divine center from the *être psychique* or psychic being.[27] When she mentioned the latter term to Sri Aurobindo, he took it up and adapted it to his needs.

Before 1926 Sri Aurobindo emphasized the role of the mind in yoga. "The thinking mind," he wrote in 1915, "is the one instrument we possess at present by which we can arrive at a conscious self-organisation of our internal existence."[28] But he was aware that mind by its very nature could "never be a perfect instrument of the Spirit." Mind is, as he said often in *The Life Divine*, "an instrument of Ignorance," not of knowledge. The seeker has to rise through mind "into some kind of fusing union with the supramental and build up in himself a level of supermind."[29] This is what he had done in his own practice and he thought at first that others could follow his example. Some tried, but lacking his experience and balance, they could not repeat his success. Eventually he realized that the transformation he envisaged would be difficult if not impossible for others without a preliminary awakening of the psychic being, a development of such qualities as sincerity, devotion, and inner discrimination. To bring about this awakening was the primary aim of the *sadhana* under the Mother's guidance.

As the community expanded it attracted more attention, not all of it sympathetic. The British consul in Pondicherry kept a squad of detectives in his pay and sent reports of their findings to his superiors in Delhi. Many of the reports consisted of malicious gossip, for instance the charge that Sri Aurobindo and his followers drank freely and engaged in licentious behavior under the cloak of tantric *sadhana*. The Catholic Church, a powerful institution in the town, also cherished ill feelings towards the Bengali refugee and his mysterious French companion. A certain mother superior told a visiting Englishwoman that entering Sri Aurobindo's house was "polluting the Catholic religion." Madame Alfassa, besides "applying powder and rouge," went out for daily drives in a car and allowed people to kiss her feet. In any event it was just "not good" for Europeans to mix with natives.[30] Outside Pondicherry, Sri Aurobindo was held in higher esteem, but there was still much confusion about his community and plans for future action.

It seemed a good moment to publish an article that would present some factual information about the community and contradict some of the worst rumors. Jatindranath Sen Gupta, a friend of one of the members, offered to write one. His piece, "Sri Aurobindo's Ashram," was published in May 1927 in the *Hindu* of Madras. More an exercise in public relations than an example of balanced reporting, the article provides a useful glimpse into the life of the community at a critical time of its development. "Though everywhere in India and even outside India there is a keen desire to know what is really going on inside this Ashram at Pondicherry," Sen Gupta began, "very few get the opportunity" to find out what was happening, while "on the other hand, all sorts of false and ugly rumours have been assiduously spread by interested persons." Sri Aurobindo's yoga was "chiefly concerned with the inner life." About this the author did not presume to speak. But even as a visitor, he had been struck by "the spiritual atmosphere of calmness and purity that prevails." The members passed the better part of the day "in meditation and sadhana, and the little time they can spare, they devote to all kinds of cultural work": painting, poetry, music, gardening. Everything revolved around Mira Devi, the Mother, who carried out Sri Aurobindo's work with his power behind her. As for the "ugly rumours," Sen Gupta insisted that they were false. "An absolute mastery of the sex movements and entire abstention from the physical (animal) indulgence are the first conditions" of Sri Aurobindo's way of yoga. Accordingly "sensual indulgence" was "absolutely forbidden" and even "such comparatively innocent habits as smoking were discountenanced." Overall the members lived "a very simple and abstemious life. They take vegetarian food and live practically on one frugal meal a day."[31] Nowhere was there evidence of extravagance or waste, but despite this, the community was chronically short of funds. Why this was so, and what others could do to help, was the subject of the article's penultimate paragraph. Drafted by Sri Aurobindo to insert into the article, it was his first public statement of his mission. "Sri Aurobindo's sadhana," he wrote in the third person, "is not merely for himself or a few disciples; it is a foundation for a great spiritual work for India and for all the world." During the early years, when there was only handful of disciples, "much help was not needed" for the expenses were few, but "numbers of disciples are beginning to stream in, and, however economical the style of living, the cost of maintenance is greatly increasing and will go on increasing." For more than fifteen years the center had been supported "by the contributions of a few who are in sympathy with the work and can afford to give some help. But these means are not likely to be sufficient in the future."[32]

The first public announcement of Sri Aurobindo's program is also the earliest known writing in which he referred to the community as an "ashram." He had always disliked the term, which is encumbered with connotations of asceticism and renunciation. Nevertheless, people inside and outside the community had started to refer to it as an ashram, and after Sen Gupta's article appeared, the name became established. Sri Aurobindo himself steered clear of it for another year or two, writing "here" or "at Pondicherry" in letters. When he did begin to use the term "ashram," it was "for want of a better word."[33]

The number of people living in the ashram continued to grow, and as a result, more houses were needed. By the end of 1928 Sri Aurobindo owned or was renting fifteen. People began to complain that the ashram was monopolizing the town's real estate and driving up rents.[34] There were further accusations that the so-called yogis were leading luxurious lives. Were there not five cars in the ashram's garages? Criticisms such as this were based on a conception of yoga that Sri Aurobindo rejected. It was an error, he wrote, to "put a ban on money and riches and proclaim poverty and bareness of life as the only spiritual condition."[35] Besides, all of the property and merchandise he owned was put to practical use. With the number of residents approaching seventy, the fifteen houses were not enough to provide everyone with a separate room. The five vehicles were used for work—and sometimes also for pleasure. The Mother's afternoon drive in her 1925 Lorraine, with Saint Hilaire at the wheel, was about the only time of the day she was able to relax.

ON MAY 28, 1928 Rabindranath Tagore visited Pondicherry. The port still lacked a debarkation facility, so the poet had to be winched from the launch to the pier in a converted barrel. Met by Nolini Kanta Gupta, he was taken to Sri Aurobindo's house, where he but not his companions were received. The next day Tagore wrote about the meeting while on his way to Colombo. Before his arrival in Pondicherry, he had been thinking of the old idea of creation by the Word and the need to develop the entire human being to attain an integral realisation. "While my mind was occupied with such thoughts," he wrote,

> the French steamer on which I was travelling touched Pondicherry and I came to meet Aurobindo. At the very first sight I could realise that he had been seeking for the soul and gained it, and through this long process of realisation had accumulated within him a silent power of inspiration. His face was radiant with an inner light and his serene presence made it evident to me that his soul was not crippled and cramped to the measure of some tyrannical doctrine, which takes delight in inflicting wounds on life. . . .
>
> I felt that the utterance of the ancient Hindu Rishi spoke from him of that equanimity which gives the human soul its freedom of entrance into the All. I said to him, "You have the word and we are waiting to accept it from you. India will speak through your voice to the world."[36]

During their conversation, Tagore asked Sri Aurobindo when he would emerge and give his "word" to the world. Sri Aurobindo said that he could not expand outward until he had established an inner foundation. Tagore concluded that Sri Aurobindo would return to the public sphere in a year or two. When Sri Aurobindo's retirement extended into the 1930s and beyond, the poet felt let down. "He is disappointed," Sri Aurobindo noted dryly in

1936, "that I have not come out and started giving lectures in America and saving humanity."[37]

Another famous Bengali had even less patience with Sri Aurobindo's withdrawal. Subhas Chandra Bose had dropped out of the Indian Civil Service following Aurobindo's example and after his return to India he became a major force in provincial and national politics. As chairman of the All-India Youth Congress in December 1928, he lashed out against "the two schools of thought, which have their centres at Sabarmati and Pondicherry," that is, the "schools" of Gandhi and Aurobindo. The former assumed that modernity was bad, economic development unnecessary, and "that we must endeavour to the best of our ability to go back to the days of the bullock-cart." As for the Pondicherry school, it created "a feeling and an impression that there is nothing higher or nobler than peaceful contemplation." This led "many to forget that spiritual progress under the present-day conditions"—that is, under British colonialism—"is possible only by ceaseless and unselfish action."[38] The Aurobindo whom Bose had admired as a student in Calcutta had called for such a spirituality of selfless action, *karmayoga*. Sri Aurobindo, who remained inactive in his room, had turned his back on his early, inspiring teachings.

Sri Aurobindo ignored Bose's charges, but three of his followers sprang to his defense. It was easy to show that the politician had no real knowledge of Sri Aurobindo's teachings. What Bose had in mind, wrote Nolini Kanta Gupta, was "some of the old schools of spiritual discipline." But "one of the marked aspects of Sri Aurobindo's teaching and practice have been precisely his insistence to put aside the inert and life-shunning quietism, illusionism, asceticism and monasticism of a latter-day and decadent India." What he was trying to do was "conquer a new plane of creative power." If the outer results were of "almost insignificant proportions at present" it was because "the work is still of the nature of experiment and trial in very restricted limits, something in the nature of what is done in a laboratory when a new power has been discovered, but has still to be perfectly formulated in its process."[39]

Bose was unimpressed by Gupta's defense, and from a political point of view one can understand why. India was in the midst of a prolonged struggle with Britain, and selfless action in the country's cause, which Aurobindo had urged in *Bande Mataram* and *Karmayogin,* seemed to be the need of the hour. Other members of Bose's generation, including his rival Jawaharlal Nehru, also expected Sri Aurobindo "to emerge from his retirement and join the great struggle." They were "disappointed at his not doing so."[40] Still, many of those who wrote him off as a leader continued to be inspired by his example. A revolutionary poster entitled "Aurobindo Mandir" ("The Temple of Aurobindo") printed in Allahabad during the 1930s shows the revolutionary martyrs of the previous decade around a picture of "the great philosopher Aurobindo Ghose."

A Period of Expansion

Sri Aurobindo broke his rule about not meeting people on only two occasions after his meeting with Tagore. In August 1928 he spoke briefly with the French Indologist Sylvain Lévy. A year later he gave a private *darshan* to Olive Maitland-March, an Englishwoman who had been staying in the ashram and claimed to be in contact with influential people in Britain. The meeting lasted "for about twenty minutes," Maitland-Marsh later wrote, "during which time no word passed between us, yet the fact of my coming into personal contact with His powerful vibrations, made this a very wonderful personal experience.... For the first time I knew the meaning of spiritual silence, and what can be accomplished in it."[41]

Maitland-Marsh was the last person to have a private meeting with Sri Aurobindo for almost twenty years. All others who asked to see him—rich and poor, famous and obscure, Maharani and clerk, holy man and sinner— were refused. "If the Baba Maharaj asks for an answer," he wrote to his secretary regarding a visiting yogi, "you will tell him that it is impossible for me to satisfy his requests. I am in entire retirement, seeing none, not even my disciples, so I cannot see him." The Harvard philosopher William Ernest Hocking was given the same treatment: "What he wants is evidently to talk with me and that is impossible," Sri Aurobindo wrote to one of his secretaries. "You will have to write to him now regretting that it is not at all likely that I shall come out of my retirement just now." Two years and many rejections later, he responded in similar terms when Mahatma Gandhi wrote asking for an interview. "Perhaps you know," Gandhi began, "that ever since my return to India I have been anxious to meet you face to face.... Now that it is almost certain that I am to be in Pondicherry, will you spare me a few minutes & see me?" Sri Aurobindo replied in his own hand, but in the negative. "I think you will understand that it is not a personal or mental choice but something impersonal from a deeper source for the inner necessity of work and sadhana" that "prevents me from receiving you but I cannot do otherwise than keep to the rule I have adhered to for some years past."[42]

IF SRI AUROBINDO refused to meet people on an individual basis, he allowed more to see him on the public *darshan* days. Most applicants were rejected, but the number of the admitted reached 700 by August 1934. He and the Mother sat with hardly a break from early morning until the middle of the afternoon. This meant that each visitor had a minute or less to make *pranam* and move on. Sri Aurobindo never spoke, rarely smiled, and seemed to most to be as inaccessible as Mount Everest. But he was looking very closely at those who walked by. "I was struck by the rapidity with which your consciousness has grown since last time," he wrote to a disciple after one *darshan*.[43]

Those who saw Sri Aurobindo during *darshans* could not help wondering what he did on the other 362 days of the year. "What has he been doing all these years in his seclusion in Pondicherry . . . is a question frequently heard," one journalist wrote. Sri Aurobindo's followers tried to answer such questions in philosophical terms, but no one except the Mother and one or two attendants had any idea of how he passed the day.[44] From stray remarks in letters one can piece together a rough daily program. He rose late, bathed, ate, concentrated, walked, wrote, spoke with the Mother, worked on his correspondence, went to bed before sunrise, and slept for six or seven hours. The only dated events in his very private life were the writing of letters and poems. His sense of the passing of time as measured by such milestones was unusual. Referring to a letter he had written a couple of months earlier, he might remark that he wrote it "long ago." A poem composed the previous year was, as far as he could remember, "some years old."[45]

During periods of concentration, Sri Aurobindo sat motionless in a chair or on his bed. It does not follow that he was doing nothing. "My concentration is of the nature of action and it is not an easy quietistic contemplation," he wrote to a disciple who envied him his repose.[46] He never spoke at length of what his inner action consisted of, but he occasionally remarked in letters that he used his spiritual force to produce tangible results in the world. When the persons affected were known individuals, they could sometimes vouch for the outcome, as when sick disciples reported that they were cured after he "sent his force" to help them. But Sri Aurobindo believed that his force was "not limited to the Ashram and its conditions"; it also could be used to bring about "change in the [wider] human world." He never claimed to have brought about specific terrestrial effects, but he asserted more than once that he was doing his *sadhana* not for himself but for the earth-consciousness.[47] This obliged him to come down from higher levels of experience to work on "the physical," that is, the physical nature in himself and the world at large.

Up until 1930 or 1931, Sri Aurobindo, the Mother, and a few disciples experienced rapid progress because, as he explained, "the work was on the mental, psychic and higher vital levels." But when the work began on the "lower vital plane"—the level of consciousness that is the field of everyday feelings and de-sires—"it appeared at once that the lower vital and physical nature of human beings (at least of those here) was too obscure and full of rebellious impuri-ties to admit so great a working." As a result the process had to be changed: "instead of doing all from above" by means of spiritual force, "it seemed neces-sary to come down into the lower vital and material nature for a long, slow, patient and difficult work of opening and change."[48] Once he and the Mother descended, "the sadhana as a whole" came down to the lower levels. What this meant for the disciples was a diminution or cessation of higher experiences, such as the awakening of their psychic beings or glimpses of the Self, and a daily confrontation with the desires, obsessions, and inertia of their vital and physical beings. What it meant for Sri Aurobindo and the Mother is harder to pin down. By their own account, they never lost touch with the higher planes of consciousness. After the initial plunge, they took their "station in the physi-cal open to the higher and higher consciousness." Here they "fought it out in the struggle of transformation of the physical consciousness with a view to prepare it for the supramental change."[49]

Sri Aurobindo's task, as he visualized it, was to prepare a "step forward which the evolution of the earth-consciousness has still to make." For a while he thought that he could accomplish the task in a relatively short time. Asked towards the end of 1932 whether the supermind would descend "within a decade," he replied, "I don't know about the date—dates are things that one ought not to fix too rigidly; but I certainly hope we won't have to wait for a decade! Let us be more sanguine and put the beginning of the decade and not the end as the era of the Descent. It is more likely then to make haste." He remained generally sanguine for a year or two more. In November 1933, after noting that "the supramental has not descended into the body or into Matter," he added: "it is only at the point where such a descent has become not only possible but inevitable." And ten months later: "The supramental Force is de-scending, but it has not yet taken possession of the body or of matter—there is still much resistance to that. It is supramentalised Overmind Force that has already touched, and this may at any time change into or give place to the supramental in its own native power." But by the end of 1934 it was becoming clear that the process would take much longer than anticipated. "The descent of the Supermind is a long process," he wrote that October, "or at least a pro-cess with a long preparation, and one can only say that the work is going on sometimes with a strong pressure for completion, sometimes retarded by the things that rise from below and have to be dealt with before further progress can be made."[50]

DESPITE—OR PERHAPS BECAUSE OF—his seclusion, Sri Aurobindo's reputation continued to grow. In August 1929 a short biography of him by Jyotish Chandra Ghose was published in Calcutta. The same year the French writer Romain Rolland wrote eulogistically about him in a book published in Paris and in an article published in Calcutta. Sri Aurobindo was, he said, "the greatest thinker in India today," the latest and greatest in the country's "splendid procession of heroes of Spirit," who "has brought a new message to his countrymen, which completes those preceding it." Winner of the Nobel Prize in literature in 1915, Rolland was one of the first Western thinkers to take contemporary Indian philosophy seriously. He read portions of the *Arya* writings and found in them "the most complete synthesis so far achieved between the genius of the West and the genius of the East." But shortly after he published this opinion, the Frenchman became disenchanted. Sri Aurobindo's later works, he noted in his diary, did not represent any advance over the *Arya*.[51] He based this judgment on a reading of the 1928 edition of *Essays on the Gita*, which was in fact a reprint, with scattered revisions, of the series published in the *Arya* a decade earlier. The *Essays* were hardly an index of Sri Aurobindo's current views; but he had published only one new book, *The Mother,* since the *Arya* folded. Other titles issued during the 1920s were either reprints of essays from the *Arya* or *Karmayogin* or old translations and poems. Sri Aurobindo planned to bring out book editions of his major works—*The Life Divine, The Synthesis of Yoga,* and others—but he wanted to revise them thoroughly beforehand and he found no time to do it. His correspondence was growing at an enormous rate, and soon crowded out all other types of writing.

Aurobindo had never been much of a letter writer. Between 1912 and 1920 he wrote fairly often to Motilal Roy and a few others, but he warned his correspondents that they should not expect regular replies. Between 1921 and 1925 he wrote almost nothing, but after his retirement in 1926 he found time to answer some of the letters that were arriving in ever increasing numbers. Most of his communications with members of the ashram passed verbally through the Mother, but occasionally he read and answered letters from them as well. This changed in early 1930, when he invited letters from a few, then from most of the ashram members. Some of this correspondence was "official": heads of departments (the bakery, the dispensary, the gardens) sent notebooks and reports that kept him and the Mother informed of daily developments. But most of the letters were personal: disciples sent accounts of their inner and outer experiences, along with questions about yoga and life. Sri Aurobindo's replies grew from a trickle during the late 1920s to a flood during the middle

1930s. In all of 1929 he wrote 25 significant replies, meaning sufficiently important to be published in the collected works of 1972. The number more than doubled in each of the three years that followed, approaching 400 in 1932. In 1933 the number more than tripled, touching the daunting figure of 1,350 significant letters for the year. This was the peak. After mid-1934 he slackened his pace somewhat, explaining that the correspondence "interferes with or entirely prevents more important sides of the work."[52] Nevertheless he wrote some 900 significant letters that year. Large as the numbers are, they do not adequately convey his epistolary labors. For every significant reply, he wrote ten not-so-significant ones, consisting of personal advice, remarks on the working of the ashram, and comments on routine problems. And for every letter he answered in one way or another, he read an equal number to which he gave no reply. By the middle of 1933 he was devoting ten to twelve hours daily to reading and writing letters, and his pile of unanswered mail never seemed to diminish. When a *sadhak* became depressed because Sri Aurobindo took a few days to reply to his letter, Sri Aurobindo noted gently: "You do not realise that I have to spend 12 hours over the ordinary correspondence, numerous reports, etc. I work 3 hours in the afternoon and the whole night up to six in the morning over this. So if I get a long letter with many questions I may not be able to answer it all at once."[53]

The disciples' side of the correspondence consisted of loose sheets and notebooks sent to him at fixed intervals, which varied according to the individual (weekly, daily, twice or thrice a day), or else as the need arose. Because the rule of the yoga was to approach Sri Aurobindo through the Mother, the letters were addressed to her. Disciples who knew English wrote in English. Those who did not wrote in Bengali, Gujarati, Hindi, or French. Sri Aurobindo generally answered in English, occasionally in Bengali. Those who could not understand his English got friends to translate for them. Those who could not read his handwriting asked longtime *sadhaks* such as Nolini Kanta Gupta to help them out. Often considered indecipherable, his handwriting nonetheless retained the fineness and deliberateness that had been its characteristic since he had learned penmanship in England. But during this period Sri Aurobindo was writing as many as seventy letters a day, some consisting of a few lines, others a page or more, all dashed off at lightning speed, without reflection or pause, crowding the bottoms and margins and squeezing between the lines of the letters sent to him. It was probably the most spontaneous writing he had ever done. "Whenever I write these letters or replies," he noted in 1935, "I never think or seek for expressions or try to write in good style; it is out of a silent mind that I write whatever comes ready-shaped from above. Even when I correct, it is because the correction comes in the same way."[54]

Most of the letters that Sri Aurobindo received from members of the ashram had to do with quotidian events and problems: the morning's meditation, a quarrel with a neighbor, a sexual infatuation, a feeling of devotion, a cold, a vision seen in dream. The questions were rarely abstract ("What is the meaning of life?" "What is the nature of desire?"), but rather specific and concrete ("Why have I come to the ashram; wouldn't it be better if I just went home?" "I went to sit in the meditation room, but when she looked up at me and smiled I got so excited I had to leave.") He was willing to offer advice on almost any topic, whether spiritual (the right way to meditate, the central process of the yoga), practical (the right way to treat piles, how to deal with a family problem), or trivial (how to clean bathroom tiles, how to cook a half-boiled egg). People outside the ashram also wrote to Aurobindo, but he did not routinely answer their questions. If they wrote about personal problems—an illness in the family, a lawsuit, a business failure—they were told that he refused to get involved in such things, but he sometimes replied to outsiders who wrote to him about their inner lives. When he did, he generally wrote in the third person; his secretary typed the letter and sent it over his own signature.

This indirect way of answering was characteristic of Sri Aurobindo's detached way of dealing with people. Most members of the ashram found him remote, though his correspondence shows that he took a personal interest in all of them, and with some developed ties of surprising intimacy. To a chosen few, instead of writing in his normal way, he began to joke, tease, use persiflage, slang, mild expletives. With one or two he expressed strong paternal affection, giving the lie to the notion, by now deeply entrenched, that he was incapable of human feelings. Asked by one with whom he had built up such a "sweet relationship" what the reason behind it was, he answered, "Cast your plummet into the deep and perhaps you shall find it—or perhaps you will hit something that has nothing at all to do with it." More seriously he explained that while there is "a universal divine love that is given equally to all" there was also a "special relation" with each individual, depending perhaps on relations carried over from past lives. This was something that could not easily be explained, for it was "not the mind that can discover these things."[55]

Some of those with whom Sri Aurobindo developed close relations felt bold enough to ask him questions about his past life and present *sadhana*, which everyone in the ashram was interested in but few had the nerve to bring up. His answers, if he answered at all, were often couched in a mock-exasperated tone that shows his sense of humor to good effect:

NIRODBARAN: You wrote [in an earlier letter] that you had lived dangerously. All that we know is that you did not have enough money in England,—also in Pondicherry in the beginning. In Baroda you had a handsome pay, and in Calcutta you were quite well off.

SRI AUROBINDO: I was so astonished by this succinct, complete and impec-
cably accurate biography of myself that I let myself go in answer! But
I afterwards thought that it was no use living more dangerously than
I am obliged to, so I rubbed all out. My only answer now is ! ! ! ! ! ! !
! ! ! ! ! ! ! ! ! ! ! ! ! ! ! ! ! ! I thank you for the safe, rich, comfortable and
unadventurous career you have given me. I note also that the only danger man can run in this world is that of the lack of money. Karl Marx
himself could not have made a more economic world of it! But I wonder
whether that was what Nietzsche meant by living dangerously?[56]

The same correspondents sometimes vented their doubts and fears, becoming the mouthpieces of ordinary humanity faced with the difficulties of
yoga. His responses to such outbursts are filled with understanding, encouragement, and tenderness:

> The length of your period of dullness is also no sufficient reason for losing
> belief in your capacity or your spiritual destiny. I believe that alternations of
> bright and dark periods are almost a universal experience of yogis, and the
> exceptions are very rare. . . . But in any case the Divine Power is working
> always behind and one day, perhaps when one least expects it, the obstacle
> breaks, the clouds vanish and there is again the light and the sunshine.[57]

Most letters were not so animated. The bulk of his correspondence consisted of brief suggestions about common problems, and equally brief replies
to common questions. Letters dealing with such matters were typed and circulated among members of the ashram, in the hope that he would not have to
write the same letter ten or twenty times over. By the end of 1932 there were
enough typescripts in circulation, and sufficient demand from people outside
the ashram to read them, for Sri Aurobindo's secretary to think about issuing
them in books. The first such compilation consisted of relatively long letters
dealing with the philosophical bases of his yoga. Sri Aurobindo revised the
selected letters and in June 1933 sent the manuscript back to his secretary. Just
at that moment the Mother received a letter from the French novelist Maurice
Magre, posing what is probably the most difficult of all moral conundrums:
What is the purpose of evil and pain in the divine creation? Sri Aurobindo

had dealt with this problem in *The Life Divine,* but instead of sending Magre a chapter from that work, he decided to write something new. His letter, really an extended essay, became the capstone of the new book and gave it its title: *The Riddle of This World.*

Around 1930 some of Sri Aurobindo's disciples began to ask him questions about poetry and to send him poems for evaluation. He seems to have relished this correspondence, writing replies covering a half-dozen literatures and a dazzling variety of writers. He may have been the only critic alive who could write with equal authority on the work of Catullus, Shelley, Homer, Kalidasa, Dante, Madhusudan Dutt, and Victor Hugo. But he gave most of his time not to the great names of the past but to a circle of poet-disciples. Painstakingly correcting their fledgling efforts, he transformed them into readable and occasionally remarkable poems of spiritual aspiration. The labor seems to have prompted him to write poetry of his own after a gap of more than a decade. In 1932, while discussing prosody with a disciple, he wrote a few lines to illustrate his theory of stress-accent:

> A far sail on the unchangeable monotone of a slow slumbering sea,
> A world of power hushed into symbols of hue, silent unendingly;
> Over its head like a gold ball the sun tossed by the gods in their play
> Follows its curve,—a blazing eye of Time watching the motionless day.[58]

This was, he told his correspondent, perhaps "only a curious imagination," but "it came on me strongly, so I put it down on paper." This marked the beginning of his return to poetic activity. A number of other poems written over the next few years also began as experiments in rhythmic technique, but became remarkable expressions of spiritual vision:

> A naked and silver-pointed star
> Floating near the halo of the moon;
> A storm-rack, the pale sky's fringe and bar,
> Over waters stilling into swoon.
> My mind is awake in stirless trance,
> Hushed my heart, a burden of delight;
> Dispelled is the senses' flicker-dance,
> Mute the body aureate with light.[59]

Sri Aurobindo also took up established forms, using them to express his inner experiences with a vividness and immediacy that has few precedents in mystical writing. These lines are from a sonnet called "Transformation":

My breath runs in a subtle rhythmic stream;
It fills my members with a might divine:
I have drunk the Infinite like a giant's wine.
Time is my drama or my pageant dream.
Now are my illumined cells joy's flaming scheme
And changed my thrilled and branching nerves to fine
Channels of rapture opal and hyaline
For the influx of the Unknown and the Supreme.[60]

Sri Aurobindo published this poem and two others in *The Calcutta Review* in October 1934. The same year his secretary Nolini Kanta Gupta compiled and published a collection called *Six Poems of Sri Aurobindo* to commemorate his sixty-second birthday.

THE GENERALLY EXPANSIVE movement of Sri Aurobindo's *sadhana* between 1929 and 1934 was matched by the expanding size and diversity of the ashram. In late 1929 there were around 80 members; by early 1934 there were 150. Though *sadhaks* from Bengal and Gujarat predominated, ashram members came from all parts of the country, and there were also a handful of Europeans and Americans. There were twice as many men as women, due mainly to the difficulties women faced when they tried to abandon their traditional family roles. Most members were between twenty-five and forty-five years of age, though there were a few older people and one or two children. The majority had been raised as Hindus, though there were a small number of Muslims and Parsis and the nominally Christian Westerners. Those from Hindu backgrounds had no difficulty adapting their old beliefs and practices to their new environment. Many had altars in their rooms where photographs of Sri Aurobindo and the Mother replaced, or were surrounded by, pictures or statues of gods. People raised in other religions or no religion sometimes felt that they were being submerged in an ocean of Hindu religiosity. Sri Aurobindo had to explain that the ashram had "nothing to do with Hindu religion or culture or any religion or nationality. The Truth of the Divine which is the spiritual reality behind all religions and the descent of the supramental which is not known to any religion are the sole things which will be the foundation of the work of the future."[61] He must have been surprised when he read in a newspaper that "it is perhaps well known that Sri Aurobindo has established a distinctive religion of his own." He insisted that this was not the case: "It is far from my purpose to propagate any religion, new or old, for humanity in the future. A way to be opened that is still blocked, not a religion to be founded, is my conception of the matter."[62]

Visitors invariably were struck by the order and harmonious functioning of the community. "In the matter of discipline and management under the Mother's direct guidance and supervision," there was "no institution that can even approach Sri Aurobindo's Ashram," wrote one impressed visitor. "Pervaded by a deep spiritual atmosphere," the ashram was a place like no other, "where the beginning is being laid of an altogether new life on the earth full of peace and joy and beauty and love."[63] Insiders took a somewhat less starry-eyed view. They knew for instance there was no lack of friction and conflict between the members. Questioned why this should be so, Sri Aurobindo replied that "in an Ashram which is a 'laboratory'... for a spiritual and supramental yoga" it was necessary that "humanity should be variously represented. For the problem of transformation has to deal with all sorts of elements favourable and unfavourable.... If only sattwic [virtuous] and cultured men come for yoga ... then, because the difficulty of the vital element in terrestrial nature has not been faced and overcome, it might well be that the endeavour would fail."[64]

IN FEBRUARY 1934 the French administration, perhaps prompted by the British consul, began to ask difficult questions about the organization and finances of the ashram. If it was an "institution," why was it not registered? And if there was a "common fund," as some newspapers had reported, where were the books? Complaints were sent to the colonial office in Paris, and the governor of French India was asked to submit a report. Sri Aurobindo took the threat very seriously, calling it a "wanton and brutal attack on my life-work from outside."[65] He issued a public statement in which he set forth what the ashram was and what it was not, and went on to add a column-long summary of his "teaching and method of practice" that remains the best short introduction to his yoga and philosophy. It concludes: "The one aim of his yoga is an inner self-development by which each one who follows it can in time discover the One Self in all and evolve a higher consciousness than the mental, a spiritual and supramental consciousness which will transform and divinise human nature."[66] This statement—along with meetings with local politicians and a letter from the Mother to her brother Mattéo Alfassa, an official in the colonial service—was enough to clear the air. The administration stopped its inquiries, but it insisted that the Mother and Sri Aurobindo stop buying or renting houses. If they wanted more space, they would have to build. To do this, they needed more money than they had. As a result, it became impossible to admit new people for several years. From the beginning of 1934 to the end of 1937 the membership remained stable at 150. This was not altogether a drawback. Sri Aurobindo had "been long wishing to put off further expansion and consolidate the inward life of the Ashram." The Mother too found the current size suitable. Looking back twenty years later, when the membership was six times larger, she remarked that "even till a hundred and fifty ... they were held as though in an egg within my consciousness, so close, you see, that I could direct all their movements, inner and outer, all the time. ... I believe in those days they made some progress."[67]

The mid-1930s were in fact a time of progress for many members of the ashram. For some this meant learning how to work for the good of the community or, in yogic terms, for the sake of the divine; others learned to control their desires and emotions; still others experienced some calm or devotion in meditation. And a few had one or more of the experiences that are the basis of Sri Aurobindo's yoga. Such experiences do not fall from the sky in a flash of lightning, but come with a quiet awareness that this is the way things are and always will be. Here is a report from a disciple's notebook, followed by Sri Aurobindo's comment:

DISCIPLE: My consciousness has been divided into two parts: one above the head and the other from the head downwards. Often I live above the head. Now and then the consciousness pushes upwards with so much intensity that the eyes go inward with an upward push. It seems to me that the consciousness goes very high up and loses itself in a perfect calm limitless place, but it can say nothing about this place. I do not feel so much intensity always. It seems to me something pulls from a higher plane, a sudden push of the consciousness with much force in it; all the consciousness, leaving this world, flies up and seems to seek something in that infinite calm space and remain there motionlessly. What is this experience?

SRI AUROBINDO: It is the Atman, the spiritual being above the mind,—the first experience of it is a silence and calm (which one perceives afterwards to be as infinite and eternal) untouched by the movements of mind and life and body. The higher consciousness lives always in touch with the Self—the lower is separated from it by the activities of the Ignorance.[68]

Such experiences were comparatively infrequent even for those who were advanced enough to have them. As a rule, people spent most of their time in what Sri Aurobindo called the lower consciousness, caught up in the play of ordinary thought and emotion. They did their work, but sometimes argued with their colleagues. They met their neighbors, and sometimes slandered them behind their backs. At home they read Sri Aurobindo's works, or indulged in sexual daydreams. They attended *pranam,* and sometimes were consumed by jealousy because the Mother smiled more warmly at another. Then, while walking on the pier or sitting at home or dusting books in the library, they might again be lifted above the mind and perceive the one soul in all, or plunge into their heart and feel the fire of the psychic being.

In his personal *sadhana,* Sri Aurobindo made satisfactory progress through November 1934. For a moment that month he thought that the event he had been waiting for, "the general descent of the Supermind into Matter," was imminent. Then something unexpected happened. As he later explained, "after November the push for descent stopped and the resistance of material Nature arose." In another letter he was more graphic: "The only result of the last descent was an upsurging of subconscient mud." In Sri Aurobindo's yoga, "the subconscient" is "that quite submerged part of our being in which there is no wakingly conscious and coherent thought, will or feeling or organized reaction, but which yet receives obscurely the impressions of all things and stores them up in itself." When the mind finds itself invaded by "old thoughts, old mental, vital and physical habits or an obscure stimulus to sensations, actions, emotions," or the body's long-forgotten diseases, it is from the subconscient that they rise. Letters written by disciples around this time show that many were troubled by a resurgence of old problems and a general lack of progress. As for Sri Aurobindo, for the next six months he was "busy with the mud of subconscient earth—dredging, dredging, dredging." But, unlike his disciples, he remained in touch with the other end of being, the supermind. "I see it above and know what it is," he wrote around this time, "I feel it ever gleaming down on my consciousness from above and I am seeking to make it possible for it to take up the whole being into its own native power, instead of the nature of man continuing to remain in half-light, half-darkness."[69]

The Tail of the Supermind

In the mid-1930s, Sri Aurobindo continued to spend his days—or rather his nights—writing, reading, and concentrating on his inner work. His attempts to reduce his correspondence were unsuccessful. In 1936 he wrote to someone who suggested the opposite: "Where is the reduction of correspondence? I have to be occupied with correspondence from 8.0 [*sic*] to 12 p.m. (minus one hour), again after bath and meal from 2.30 to 7 a.m. All that apart from afternoon work. And still much is left undone."[70] His routine at this time was as follows: "From 4 p.m. to 6.30 p.m. afternoon correspondence, meal, newspapers. Evening correspondence from 7 or 7.30 to 9. From 9 to 10 p.m. concentration, 10 to 12 correspondence, 12 to 2.30 bath, meal, rest, 2.30 to 5 or 6 a.m. correspondence unless I am lucky."[71]

The hour between nine and ten at night was often the only time that Sri Aurobindo had for concentration. When a disciple expressed amazement that he was spending nine-tenths of his time in "correspondence, works etc." and only one-tenth in concentration, he replied, tongue-in-cheek: "For me, correspondence alone. I have no time left for other 'works etc.'" He went on to clarify: "Concentration and meditation are not the same thing. One can be concentrated in work or bhakti as well as in meditation." From the beginning of his practice of yoga he "had made action and work one of my chief means of realisation," and it remained a central part of his post-realization life. Even his periods of absorbed meditation were "for a particular work"; they were not "for meditation divorced from life."[72]

Sri Aurobindo's "particular work" was to open the way for the descent of supermind into what he called the earth-consciousness. Judging from occasional remarks in letters, his progress was slow through 1935. "One can't advance a single step," he commented that March, without obscure forces "throwing their shells and stink-bombs."[73] Such metaphors imply that he was having a hard time of it, but do not clarify what exactly it was like to struggle against the forces of subconscient nature. It was not, in any event, a solipsistic state of self-absorbed bliss. "No, it is not with the Empyrean that I am busy: I wish it were," he wrote to a disciple in May 1936. "It is rather with the opposite end of things; it is in the Abyss that I have to plunge to build a bridge between the two."[74]

Such references to his inner life are rare because only a few disciples had the temerity to ask him how his *sadhana* was. "What about the uprush of mud?" one of them inquired in the summer of 1935. "It is still there," Sri Aurobindo responded, "but personally I have become superior to it and am travelling forward like a flash of lightning, that is to say zigzag but fairly fast. Now I have got the hang of the whole hanged thing—like a very Einstein I have got the mathematical formula of the whole affair (unintelligible as in his case to anybody but myself) and am working it out figure by figure." Asked about this formula a few months later, he replied that it was "working out rapidly," though only in regard to himself. "The tail of the supermind is descending, descending, descending. It is only the tail at present, but where the tail can pass, the rest will follow." Three years later, recalling this jocular exchange, he implied that what he meant by "the tail of the supermind" was its indirect action through the overmind and other higher mental planes. What he was trying to do at the time he spoke (December 1938) was "to supramentalise the descended Overmind."[75] He had used the same or a similar phrase to describe the current state of his *sadhana* in 1927 or 1928, 1933, 1934, and 1935. The similarity of phrasing suggests that during the 1930s he made little measurable progress. Certainly, as the years went by, he found that supramentalizing the overmind was a larger job than he had thought. The reason, apparently, was that the process was intertwined with the "dredging" of the subconscient. This could explain the slowing down of his *sadhana* during the mid- and late 1930s. But perhaps this was only appearance. Once or twice he spoke of rapid advance and triumph over obstacles. "I am sure of the results of my work," he wrote in 1936, but

> even if I still saw the chance that it might come to nothing (which is impossible), I would go on unperturbed, because I would still have done to the best of my power the work that I had to do, and what is so done always counts in the economy of the universe. But why should I feel that all this may come to nothing when I see each step and where it is leading and every week and day—once it was every year and month and hereafter it will be every day and hour—brings me so much nearer to my goal?[76]

He was sure of the eventual descent of the supermind because he saw it as "an inevitable necessity in the logic of things." Just as life had emerged in matter and mind had emerged in life, so supermind was bound to emerge "in this world of human consciousness and its reasoning ignorance." Others could not see it because they did not "realise the significance of the emergence of consciousness in a world of inconscient Matter." But it made no difference whether others were aware of the process or not; he therefore did not feel that "the [supramental] descent depends on the readiness of the sadhaks of this Asram." Rather, "everything depends on my getting through." But in another letter he acknowledged that his success depended to some extent on the disciples' cooperation. The supermind was descending, he noted in 1936, only "as fast as you fellows will allow." They could not really help him, but they could hold him back by their "revolts, depressions, illnesses, shouts, quarrels and all the rest of it." The disciples' letters of the period are filled with ample evidence of such hindrances, and his answers show his willingness to help them with their difficulties. It is clear that when he accepted someone as a disciple, he assumed that person's real and potential difficulties. With 150 resident *sadhaks* and more than that outside, he had more than enough to keep him busy. Things might have gone better, he once wrote, tongue-in-cheek, "if the sadhaks had been a less neurotic company." But he did not try to lighten his load. Once he was asked whether it might not be better for him to "take an axe of retrenchment and cut off all impeding elements ruthlessly so that among a very few chosen disciples, the whole work may go on most concentratedly and rapidly." He replied: "Things cannot be done like that. You might just as well ask the Mother and myself to isolate ourselves in the Himalayas, get down the supramental, then toss everybody up in a blanket into the Supreme. Very neat but it is not practical." So he continued to spend his days writing letters on every aspect of his yoga, from the emergence of the psychic to the conquest of jealousy and anger.[77]

The consolidation of the ashram that began in 1934 continued. The membership remained at 150; every year a handful of people departed to be replaced at once by others eager to get in. The Mother and Sri Aurobindo never pressured those who wanted to leave. If they saw that a threatened departure was motivated by nothing more than a fit of pique, they might act as indulgent parents, insisting that "your departure and renunciation of sadhana is a thing which nothing in us accepts for a moment." But the choice was always left to the individual: "You must consider yourself entirely free to shape your own course in life by your own independent choice," Sri Aurobindo wrote to a disciple who was in revolt. Even if this person chose to depart, he could be sure that the ashram was "here as your spiritual home so long as you chose to avail yourself of it and our help and consistent support in your difficulties are at your disposal so long as you need and desire them."[78]

Toward the end of 1937 new members were accepted for the first time since 1934. Within a year, the total reached two hundred. The increased number meant increased expenditure. Most newcomers could offer little or nothing to offset the cost of boarding and lodging. Those who had money or possessions were "expected to give what they have." The rationale for this was set forth as follows: "If [members] wish to have the charge of their whole spiritual and material future taken over by us, it is at least fair that they should make the offering of all their possessions."[79] Disciples living outside also gave what they could. Sri Aurobindo refused to appeal publicly for funds, but he encouraged disciples living outside to contact potential donors.

Most donations came from middle-class people of relatively modest means. One exception was a gift of one lakh (100,000) rupees from the government of Hyderabad, arranged for by Sir Akbar Hyderi, the state's prime minister. The Mother had been thinking about constructing a dormitory for ashram members since 1934, when the French government asked her to build rather than buy. After receiving the Hyderabad donation, she was able to begin. Her secretary Saint Hilaire, now known as Pavitra, was acquainted with the Czech-American architect Antonin Raymond, an associate of Frank Lloyd Wright. Pavitra asked him if he would like to design a dormitory. Raymond agreed, and brought in two of his colleagues, František Sammer, a Czech architect who had studied with Le Corbusier, and George Nakashima, an American architect and furniture designer. Preliminary work on Golconde, as the dormitory was named (after the famous Golconda diamond mines, near Hyderabad) began in 1937.

SRI AUROBINDO WROTE more letters in 1936 than in any year except 1933. But he started dropping hints that he could not continue to devote all of his waking hours to this work. Privately he joked that he was being turned into "a correspondence-reading and answering machine."[80] Gradually the volume of his correspondence began to decline; by mid-1937 it had dropped to less than half of the previous year's total. In September an eye problem caused him to stop writing letters for six months. After a brief resumption in the middle of 1938, he had his secretary tell everyone that "all correspondence" would be "suspended until further notice."[81] The reasons, not stated, were his visual problems and desire to devote himself to other work. He had first mentioned his "queasy eye" in the early part of 1935. Another two years of all-night sessions under artificial light is not what an ophthalmologist would have recommended. As always, he regarded the problem as a yogic and not a physical one; because of his dislike of "mechanical" solutions, he never even considered wearing glasses.

The reduced correspondence between 1934 and 1938 allowed him to work on other projects, some of which had been pending for years. In 1935 and 1936 he published two edited collections of letters: *Lights on Yoga* and *Bases of Yoga*. In revising the texts he removed personal references, turning the letters into paragraphs that are full of helpful hints but divested of the warmth that make the originals so remarkable. His publishers also were clamoring for revised texts of his major works. He worked on and off on a number of them without bringing any to a satisfactory conclusion. Around the same time, he took up the poem *Savitri* again. The brief narrative based upon the Satyavan–Savitri story became, through successive revisions, a vast symbolic account of his yoga. But the poem was not just a record of his experiences; it was also a ladder that helped him reach higher levels of poetic expression. As he wrote in a letter of 1936, "I used *Savitri* as a means of ascension. I began with it on a certain mental level, each time I could reach a higher level I rewrote from that level."[82] As a result there are dozens of versions of some of its cantos. By the middle of 1933 he was reasonably content with the poem's opening, but he refused to send a sample to a disciple who had been begging him for one. Finally, in October 1936 he copied out and sent the first sixteen lines of the first canto, "The Symbol Dawn." In the passage, the description of a physical sunrise becomes a symbol for the breaking of the supramental light into the obscurity of the inconscient:

> It was the hour before the Gods awake.
> Across the path of the divine Event,
> The huge unslumbering spirit of Night, alone
> In the unlit temple of immensity,
> Lay stretched immobile on silence' marge.
> Mute with the unplumbed prevision of her change.
> The impassive skies were neutral, waste and still.
> Then a faint hesitating glimmer broke.
> A slow miraculous gesture dimly came,
> The insistent thrill of a transfiguring touch
> Persuaded the inert black quietude
> And beauty and wonder disturbed the fields of God.
> A wandering line of pale enchanted light
> That glowed along the moment's fading brink,
> Fixed with gold panel and opalescent hinge
> A gate of dreams ajar on mystery's verge.[83]

For a few months in 1936 and 1937 Sri Aurobindo sent the disciple dozens of passages of *Savitri* to be typed and returned. Along the way he answered questions, explaining the meaning of passages and lines, but also hinting at his larger intentions. On the technical side, he was trying "to catch something of the Upanishadic and Kalidasian movements, so far as that is a possibility in English." More broadly, he was seeking "to enlarge the field of poetic creation and find for the inner spiritual life of man . . . not a corner and a limited expression such as it had in the past, but a wide space and as manifold and integral an expression . . . as has been found in the past for man's surface and finite view and experience of himself."[84]

Savitri was more than a decade from publication when Sri Aurobindo wrote the above remarks. No new works in either poetry or prose appeared between 1936 and 1939. Nevertheless, his reputation continued to grow. In newspaper stories he was frequently referred to as India's greatest living thinker. Scholars wrote books and articles on his philosophy. There were even some radio talks. Would-be biographers pestered his disciples for material. When one such appeal was sent to him for comment, he noted: "I don't think a reply is necessary. If I am to be murdered in cold print, it had better be done without my disciples becoming abettors of the crime."[85] When the philosopher Sarvepalli Radhakrishnan asked an acquaintance who was a disciple to persuade Sri Aurobindo to contribute something to a volume of essays, Sri Aurobindo replied flatly: "It is impossible for me to write philosophy to order." The disciple was eager for everyone to know about his guru's greatness, but Sri Aurobindo was unenthusiastic. "I do not care a button about having my name in any blessed place," he insisted:

> Then, again, I don't believe in advertisement except for books etc., and in propaganda except for politics and patent medicines. But for serious work it is a poison. It means either a stunt or a boom—and stunts and booms exhaust the thing they carry on their crest and leave it lifeless and broken high and dry on the shores of nowhere—or it means a movement. A movement in the case of a work like mine means the founding of a school or a sect or some other damned nonsense. It means that hundreds or thousands of useless people join in and corrupt the work or reduce it to a pompous farce from which the Truth that was coming down recedes into secrecy and silence. It is what has happened to the "religions" and is the reason of their failure.[86]

Despite his lack of cooperation with would-be publicists, Sri Aurobindo's name became known in Europe, and some intellectuals and writers came to the ashram and wrote about their visits. Others, Maria Montessori and Albert Schweitzer among them, sent warmly inscribed copies of their books. Somerset Maugham, traveling in India to collect material for *The Razor's Edge*, left his card at the ashram gate. Writers on traditional wisdom—Mircea Eliade in Romania, Paul Brunton in England, René Guénon in France—promoted Sri Aurobindo as an authentic representative of the Indian spiritual tradition, and then moved on to other enthusiasms. For the most part, Sri Aurobindo remained unaware of Western interest in him and did nothing to cultivate it.

As had been the case for years, the only time anyone could see him was during the *darshan* celebrations. People now had less than a minute before him, but most went away impressed. A French professor spoke of being filled with "a feeling of certitude, stability—an impression I had received often before on seeing a huge mountain." He was sure, from the first glimpse, that this "was what I had so long searched for, the solution of my problems."[87] A Bengali writer who had admired the political Aurobindo thirty years earlier now found him the very picture of "the venerable 'Rishi' of old which we have in our mind's eye with long grey hairs and beard—a picture of purity, a living deity—calm, collected, serene, cheerful and loving,—at whose sight the head stoops low spontaneously in esteem and reverence."[88]

Whether spontaneous or conventional, a reverential attitude was becoming the only acceptable way to approach Sri Aurobindo. Disciples took it for granted that he was an avatar, or incarnation of God. He never made any such claim on his own behalf; on the other hand, he never dissuaded anyone from regarding him in this way, and wrote openly that the Mother was an incarnation of the *Shakti*. She reciprocated when speaking about him with disciples, but insisted on "great reserve" when people wrote articles for the general public.[89]

AFTER 1936 Sri Aurobindo rarely referred to his *sadhana* in letters. One piece of banter from March 1937 suggests that he was still stuck in the subconscient: "I am not soaring and soaring," he told a disciple who thought he was; "I am digging and digging." The "tail of the supermind" was in sight, but it was of "no use without the head." The full thing was descending but "not so strongly or concentratedly as it ought." Still, the process was going "better than before."[90] A year and a half later, a correspondent wrote teasingly that Sri Aurobindo had "better hurry up" with his supramental descent or "Hitler, Mussolini & Co." would "gunfire it" when it came. Sri Aurobindo's reply was uncharacteristically sharp: "What has Supermind to do with Hitler or Hitler with Supermind.... The descent of S depends on S, not on Hitler or no Hitler."[91] He may have hoped that the descent would happen without regard to world events, but was too well informed about what was going on to be complacent. Besides the newspapers, he had his own intuitive sources of knowledge. Some lines he jotted down in September 1938 suggest more clearly than pages of *The Life Divine* what it might be like to view the world from the perspective of the cosmic consciousness:

I look across the world and no horizon walls my gaze;
I see Paris and Tokio and New York,
I see the bombs bursting on Barcelona and on Canton streets.
Man's numberless misdeeds and rare good deeds take place within my
    single self.
I am the beast he slays, the bird he feeds and saves.
The thoughts of unknown minds exalt me with their thrill,
I carry the sorrow of millions in my lonely breast.[92]

The Impact of Events

The *darshan* of November was reserved for members of the ashram and a few outside disciples. Still, 400 people received permission to attend the ceremony of November 24, 1938. The viewing would begin at 7:30 a.m. and continue, with a few breaks, until the evening. Sri Aurobindo had stopped answering letters three weeks earlier in order to prepare for the event. This also gave him a chance to deal with other projects, such as *Savitri,* which was assuming epic proportions.

Some such work kept him busy until the early hours of November 24. Then he rose from his table and strode across the room where he had lived for the last twelve years. By the north wall, in the center, was his plain wooden bed; on the opposite side, a couch for the Mother to sit on when she came in. A small table occupied the middle of the room. Two others, loaded with papers, stood against the walls at either end. A large bookcase held his set of the *Arya,* inscribed books from admirers, and some dictionaries and odd volumes. On a shelf above one of the tables was a set of Javanese wood carvings. Two pictures, a Chinese landscape and an Indian bodhisattva, hung on the walls. A carpet, the only touch of luxury, covered the floor. On one side was an outspread tiger skin, an offering from a disciple who knew the Indian tradition that animal pelts make excellent seats for yogis. Three or four clocks ticked away on the cabinet and tables, providing the only sound besides the crash of the waves on the seafront three blocks away.[93]

Around two o'clock that morning, while crossing to the bathroom, Sri Aurobindo stumbled over the tiger skin and fell. There was a sudden flash of pain. After years of practice he had developed the ability to transform most types of discomfort into *ananda* or bliss, but the pain he was feeling went beyond his threshold. He tried to get up and failed, then lay back quietly. After a short while, the Mother entered. Attuned inwardly to her partner, she had felt in her sleep that something was wrong. Seeing him on the floor, she went quickly to her room and rang the emergency bell. A.B. Purani rushed up and met her at the head of the stairs. "Sri Aurobindo has fallen down," she told him. "Go and fetch Dr. Manilal." Manilal Parekh, a distinguished physician of Baroda, had come to Pondicherry for the *darshan*. Within a few minutes he was at the patient's side. Each time the doctor turned the injured leg, Sri Aurobindo uttered a short "Ah!" The diagnosis was not long in coming: a fracture of the left thigh close to the knee. Sri Aurobindo heard the verdict in silence.

Other doctors arrived. Putting Sri Aurobindo's leg in a temporary cast, they transferred him gently to his bed. He lay there motionlessly, giving no evidence of the pain he must have been feeling.[94] The *darshan* was cancelled and a shroud of despondency settled over the ashram. None of the disciples had ever imagined that something like this could happen. Life in the ashram went on, but there remained an undercurrent of uneasiness.

Dr. Srinivasa Rao, a government physician who had been called for consultation, suggested that Manilal and the others take the opinion of a specialist from Madras. A car was sent and the doctors spent the rest of the day waiting for it to return. Sri Aurobindo lay silently, giving monosyllabic answers to questions about his condition. Finally the surgeon and a radiologist arrived. When the X-rays were developed the doctors were stunned. It was an especially bad impacted fracture, with two fragments locked together. Forceful or mechanical traction was considered unwise. "I would leave it alone, put the limb in plaster, and by means of the splints exert a steady traction," said the specialist, and his advice was accepted.[95]

The Mother set up a team of attendants: Champaklal, who had been looking after Sri Aurobindo's personal needs for years; Nirodbaran, a doctor and one of his most intimate correspondents; Purani, whom Sri Aurobindo had known since 1918; and Satyendra Thakore, a dentist who had joined the ashram a few years earlier. Each of the attendants was given a shift. The Mother served Sri Aurobindo's meals. Tea became a problem, as he was obliged to drink it from a feeding cup. One day he announced that he would take no more tea, ending at a stroke a lifelong habit.[96]

For the first week or ten days, he hardly spoke with his attendants except to answer questions about his health. But one evening they found that he was willing to talk about other topics, and they clustered around his bed to listen. It was the first time that some of them had heard his voice, "masculine but soft," with a measured delivery and a cultivated British accent. Neither then or at any later time did he look directly at those he addressed.[97]

At first it did not occur to the attendants to note down what Sri Aurobindo said. Then, from December 10, Nirodbaran and Purani made an effort to remember and record the conversations. Their transcripts were later edited and published. Although not perfect records of his talks, they give an idea of the breadth and brilliance of his mind. On December 27, 1938 he began with a comment about a Pondicherry politician, turned to the municipal governments of Pondicherry and Calcutta ("two object lessons against self-government"), and touched on parliamentary democracy in England and France. This led to a consideration of the right form of government for independent India ("a federation, united at the top, leaving ample scope to local bodies"), a discussion of Gandhi's politics ("he made the *charkha* [spinning-wheel] a religious article of faith"), and some thoughts about the role of the English language in India ("all right and even necessary" for education and international relations). From there he jumped to the persecution of the Jews (people were jealous of them "because they are a clever race") and regional rivalries in Europe and India. Questioned about the utility of scientific discoveries, he broadened the discussion to include the possible effects of the supramental descent. Science and politics, he said, had simply "not succeeded in finding a way out of suffering." The descent of the supermind would introduce a new principle in evolution, but it would not abolish all problems, just as mental ability had not eliminated the problems of life and matter. But because supermind was a dynamic creative principle, it eventually would "open the mental, the vital and even the physical to the intuitive and overmental planes."[98]

Sri Aurobindo rarely spoke about his personal *sadhana*. When he did, it was because one of the attendants worked up the courage to ask him a direct question. "Have you realised the Supermind?" Manilal once asked him point-blank. Sri Aurobindo replied: "I know what the Supermind is. And the physical being has flashes and glimpses of it. I have been trying to supramentalise the descended Overmind. Not that the Supermind is not acting. It is doing so—through the Overmind. . . . I am not satisfied with only a part of the Supermind in the physical consciousness. I want to bring down the whole mass of it, pure, and that is an extremely difficult business."[99] On another occasion, Manilal asked what it was like to live in the "divine consciousness." Sri Aurobindo replied:

One feels a perpetual calm, perpetual strength, one is aware of Infinity and lives not only in Infinity but also in Eternity. One feels immortality and does not care about the death of the body. And then one has the consciousness of the One in all. Everything becomes the manifestation of the

Brahman. For instance, as I look round this room, I see everything as the Brahman. No, it is not mere thinking, it is a concrete experience. Even the wall, the books are the Brahman. I see you no more as Dr. Manilal but as the Divine living in the Divine. It is a wonderful experience.[100]

IT TOOK Sri Aurobindo a fairly long time to recover from his accident. The splints on his leg were removed in February 1939, and the leg immediately swelled to twice its normal size. It took several months for the edema to subside, several more for the patient to regain a tolerable amount of flexibility in his knee. For this regular exercise was required: first knee flexions and free-hand movements to restore muscle tone; then walking, first with help from his attendants, then with a walking stick. Owing to the accident there had been no *darshan* in February 1939. Yielding to the requests of devotees, he agreed to appear on April 24, the nineteenth anniversary of the Mother's return to Pondicherry. There was no question of making it a seven-hour marathon, however. The devotees filed past with just a moment's pause in front of him and the Mother. From that point on, April 24 became a fourth *darshan* day.[101]

The Mother was anxious to see Sri Aurobindo resume a regular routine, and with her encouragement, he began the long-postponed task of revising his major works. The first book he took up was *The Life Divine*. His attendants, curious to see how he worked, observed the following:

> No sooner had he begun than followed line after line as if everything was chalked out in the mind, or as he used to say, a tap was turned on and a stream poured down. Absorbed in perfect poise, gazing now and then in front, wiping the perspiration off the hands—for he perspired profusely—he would go on for about two hours. . . . But what shocked me most was when finishing the first [new] chapter, he asked us to tear it and throw it in the wastepaper basket! It needed rewriting! . . . I noticed what a fine calligraphy it was with hardly a scratch.[102]

Book One of *The Life Divine* was sent to the printers toward the middle of 1939. It was issued in November. By then Europe was at war.

SRI AUROBINDO HAD BEEN appalled by the rise of the dictatorships in Germany, Italy, and Russia, but until the late 1930s he could see little to distinguish the new totalitarian states from the old imperial powers. Britain and

France prated about democratic values, but they held on to their colonies and did nothing when Italy invaded Abyssinia or Germany annexed the Sudetenland. Before long, however, he realized that Nazi Germany's rise was too great a price to pay for Britain's fall.[103] Most people in India felt differently. Public opinion in the country was so anti-British that many hoped for a German victory in the war that seemed inevitable. On September 1, 1939 Hitler attacked Poland. Realizing that further appeasement was futile, Britain and France declared war against Germany on September 3. The same day, the viceroy announced that India too was at war.

By the middle of May 1940, German armies controlled Poland, Denmark, and the Low Countries, had a stranglehold on Norway, and had broken through the French line at Sedan. The remnants of the French army and the British Expeditionary Force were trapped at Dunkirk and seemed doomed. It was at this point, Sri Aurobindo later wrote, that he began to act against the German war machine. In public gestures, he and the Mother donated to the French National Defense Fund in May, the Viceroy's War Fund in June, and the Madras War Fund in September. Accompanying the third donation was a letter to the governor of Madras in which they declared their "entire support for the British people and the Empire in their struggle against the aggressions of the Nazi Reich and our complete sympathy with the cause for which they are fighting." They concluded: "We feel that not only is this a battle waged in just self-defence and in defence of nations threatened with the world domination of Germany and the Nazi system of life, but that it is a defence of civilisation and its highest attained social, cultural and spiritual values and of the whole future of humanity."[104]

This declaration attracted a good deal of attention, most of it unfriendly. Leaders of the Congress, including K.M. Munshi, were "very angry" that Sri Aurobindo had chosen this moment to speak.[105] Members of the public were equally irate. "I condemn your contribution to the War-fund," wrote a man from Gujarat, "because your act is against the interests of India and because Germany has greater justice on her side in the present war than Britain." A group of students in Calcutta were "shocked beyond measure" to read of Sri Aurobindo's contribution; they wrote that his statement showed his "utter ignorance of the facts of the world." Even in the ashram, some were puzzled by his support for the British. Several members were openly pro-German, and this put the whole community in danger. "The Government can dissolve the Ashram at any moment," Sri Aurobindo once remarked to his attendants.[106] Seeing the need to clarify his position, he released the texts of two letters he had written about the war. In one, he advised the recipient not to think of the conflict as a fight for certain nations against others or even for India: it is a struggle for an ideal that has to establish itself on earth in the life of humanity, for a Truth that has yet to realise itself fully and against a darkness and falsehood that are trying to overwhelm the earth and mankind in the immediate future.... There cannot be the slightest doubt that if one side wins ... there would be a reign of falsehood and darkness, a cruel oppression and degradation for most of the human race such as people in this country do not dream of and cannot yet at all realise.[107]

Sri Aurobindo was the only important public figure in India to come out unambiguously in favor of the Western democracies. But he considered this only the external side of his work against the Axis. "Inwardly," he noted in a third-person memoir, "he put his spiritual force behind the Allies from the moment of Dunkirk when everybody was expecting the immediate fall of England and the definite triumph of Hitler, and he had the satisfaction of seeing the rush of German victory almost immediately arrested and the tide of war begin to turn in the opposite direction."[108] He made this remark after the end of the war. During the conflict he made no claims on his own behalf. As a general rule, he did not write or speak about his use of yogic force. If he did so, he once remarked, he

would have to propound things that cannot be understood except by reference to other data than those of the physical senses or of reason founded on these alone. I might have to speak of laws and forces not recognised by reason or physical science.... These things are known to some, but they do not usually speak about them, while the public view of much of those as are known is either credulous or incredulous, but in both cases without experience or knowledge.[109]

Occasionally, however, he let slip a comment that those around him took to be claims of success. On May 31, 1940, when the British Expeditionary Force began making its way across the English Channel, he remarked to his attendants: "So they are getting away from Dunkirk?" One offered: "Yes. It seems the fog helped the evacuation." To which he replied: "Yes, fog is rather unusual at this time." Here the attendant who recalled the talk added: "By saying this, it seemed that Sri Aurobindo wanted to hint that Mother and he had made this fog to help the allies."[110] Three years later, he said in passing to a disciple who had asked about the "concreteness" of his force: "I can tell you that I have had to put my force there [in Russia] daily and concretely enough in all conscience." Whereupon the disciple volunteered: "It is most cheering, specially the great Russian victory at Stalingrad."[111] Sri Aurobindo cut this passage from the interview when it was published in an ashram journal, but it did not prevent the disciple from spreading the good news. Within a short while even casual visitors to the ashram were being told that Sri Aurobindo had won the Battle of Stalingrad. The reactions of those who heard it were "either credulous or incredulous": some were convinced that he was a wonder-working *rishi,* while others concluded that he was a megalomaniac.[112]

When Sri Aurobindo wrote to disciples about the workings of his force, he was careful to point out that it acted under conditions, as one among many forces at play. Nevertheless, he took his force and its material effects quite seriously. "The invisible force producing tangible results is the whole meaning of the Yogic consciousness," he once wrote. But, he went on, "it is invisible—not like a blow given or the rush of a motor car knocking somebody down which the physical senses can at once perceive." To become aware of how it worked, one had to "allow the consciousness to go inside, to become aware of inner things, to believe in the experience of the invisible and the supraphysical," and gradually develop the ability to "see, follow and use their workings." Or else one had to "have faith and watch and open oneself" until one was able "to see how things happen" and go on "until the experience becomes daily, regular, normal, complete."[113] To talk about the force without this basis of experience would open the way to credulity or incredulity, both of which he deplored.

SRI AUROBINDO TURNED to the second book of *The Life Divine* after the first was published in November 1939. This time, he saw, it would not be enough to touch up the existing work. He discarded eight full chapters, thoroughly revised the seventeen he kept, and wrote twelve that were entirely new. Especially important were the final six chapters, in which he traced the course of spiritual evolution, surveyed the planes lying between mind and supermind, and described the gnostic individual and the divine life that would come into being after the full supramental transformation. Although densely metaphysical, these chapters bore, to some extent, the impression of current events:

A life of gnostic beings carrying the evolution to a higher supramental status might fitly be characterised as a divine life; for it would be a life in the Divine, a life of the beginnings of a spiritual divine light and power and joy manifested in material Nature. That might be described, since it surpasses the mental human level, as a life of spiritual and supramental supermanhood. But this must not be confused with past and present ideas of supermanhood; for supermanhood in the mental idea consists of an overtopping of the normal human level, not in kind but in degree of the same kind . . . it carries also, commonly implied in it, the idea of a forceful domination over humanity by the superman. That would mean a supermanhood of the Nietzschean type; it might be at its worst the reign of the "blonde beast" or the dark beast or of any and every beast, a return to barbaric strength and ruthlessness and force: but this would be no evolution, it would be a reversion to an old strenuous barbarism. . . . But what has to emerge is something much more difficult and much more simple; it is a self-realised being, a building of the spiritual self, an intensity and urge of the soul and the deliverance and sovereignty of its light and power and beauty,—not an egoistic supermanhood seizing on a mental and vital domination over humanity, but the sovereignty of the Spirit over its own instruments, its possession of itself and its possession of life in the power of the spirit, a new consciousness in which humanity itself shall find its own self-exceeding and self-fulfilment by the revelation of the divinity that is striving for birth within it. This is the sole true supermanhood and the one real possibility of a step forward in evolutionary Nature.[114]

The second book of *The Life Divine* was published in Calcutta in July 1940 and was warmly received in India. It took some time for it to reach England, and readers there had other things on their minds; but to some *The Life Divine* offered hope amid the ruins of Western civilization. Writing in the *Times Literary Supplement* on January 17, 1942, Sir Francis Younghusband found that "the touch of a powerful and subtle mind is evident everywhere in exposition of his philosophy." The most remarkable aspect of this synthesis was its world affirmation: "Mr. Aurobindo does not look upon life on earth as a preparation for life in some distant heaven above the clouds. He would make heaven on earth. He would raise men to the Divine level." "The kingdom of God without," he concluded, "will have to be built upon the kingdom of God that is within us. And in awakening that spirit the philosophy of Aurobindo may play a striking part."[115] Younghusband, a soldier, explorer, and writer of books on mystical subjects, was sufficiently impressed by *The Life Divine* to nominate its author for the Nobel Prize in Literature. The nomination, endorsed by the Royal Society of Literature, was accepted by the Swedish Academy in 1943, a year in which no prize in literature was awarded.[116]

SRI AUROBINDO WROTE a great deal of poetry during the years of the war. In September 1939 he resumed work on a series of sonnets he had begun before his accident. By the time he paused eight weeks later, he had written thirty-eight new sonnets. They are among the most intimate expressions of spiritual experience he ever wrote. On September 18—while Russian troops were pouring into Poland—he described the poise of "the self's infinity":

> I have become what before Time I was.
> A secret touch has quieted thought and sense:
> All things by the agent Mind created pass
> Into a void and mute magnificence.
> My life is a silence grasped by timeless hands;
> The world is drowned in an immortal gaze.
> Naked my spirit from its vestures stands;
> I am alone with my own self for space.[117]

Sri Aurobindo seems to have squeezed the sonnets in between the revising of the first and second books of *The Life Divine*. After the second book was published, he returned to the epic *Savitri*, which he considered his most important literary project. But then, toward the beginning of 1942, his secretary decided to bring out a collection of his previously published poetry, drama, and translations, to be released on his seventieth birthday. Sri Aurobindo went through the typescripts and proofs of these works, some of them written in England more than fifty years earlier (and hardly deserving to be published along with his more mature poetry), and made significant revisions. He also decided to write a note on the metrical system that he used in some of the poems. This grew into a fifty-page treatise on English prosody. *Collected Poems and Plays* was politely reviewed in India after its August publication. The *Times Literary Supplement* gave the book to Ranjee G. Shahani, an Indian writer living in London. Unimpressed by Sri Aurobindo's poetry ("his technical devices are commendable; but the music that enchants or disturbs is not there"), Shahani chose to turn his review into a consideration of the author's entire oeuvre. "As an Indian scholar and critic he is second to none," Shahani wrote, citing such works as *Essays on the Gita* and *The Secret of the Veda*. Sri Aurobindo's literary judgments matched Coleridge's and Heine's in their "piercing and instantaneous insight," while *The Life Divine* was, "it is not too much to say, one of the master-works of our age."[118]

Shahani, like Younghusband, began his review by lamenting that Sri Aurobindo was practically unknown in England and the United States. Both reviewers contrasted this neglect with his growing fame in his own country. Shahani added that in India "there are no criticisms, only praise," which not infrequently rose "to a crescendo of adulation."[119] This was accurately observed. Newspaper articles, pamphlets, and booklets portrayed Sri Aurobindo as a god-man of legendary proportions. "The life of Sri Aurobindo is a wonderful mosaic of all that is beautiful and luminous," declared the author of *Bhagawan Sri Aurobindo, the Superman who Directs India to Life Divine*. "Only the Spirit's aetherial tongue can do full justice to his unfathomable personality that radiates dynamic Truth from the sanctum of an unscalable Silence."[120] Biographers related the miracles of his life and *sadhana*. Even seemingly level-headed publications were filled with distortions and misunderstandings. Perhaps for this reason, Sri Aurobindo agreed to read the manuscripts of biographies by K.R. Srinivasa Iyengar, a professor of English at a south Indian university, and Gabriel Monod-Herzen, a French professor who had settled in the ashram. Seeing that the story of his involvement in politics was ill understood, Sri Aurobindo wrote a twenty-page note stating the facts as he recalled them, contrasting along the way his style of politics with the nonviolent approach of Gandhi and his followers.

GANDHI'S POLICY OF noncooperation had landed the Congress in a predicament in 1939. Miffed at not being consulted by the viceroy when he declared that India was at war, the Congress high command ordered its ministers to quit the provincial governments that they had led since 1937. Non-Congress ministries in Muslim-majority provinces remained in power, and the Muslim League, which had been in decline before the war, regained its influence and asserted its separatist agenda. In March 1940 the League passed a resolution demanding the creation of independent Muslim states in northwestern and eastern India. From that point on, the shadow of Pakistan hung over negotiations between the British, the Congress, and other Indian parties. To most people in India the war seemed very distant. This changed dramatically in December 1941, when the Japanese defeated U.S. and British forces in the Philippines and Hong Kong, occupied Bangkok, and pushed south into the Malay states. In February 1942, "impregnable" Singapore fell. Rangoon followed in March. An attack on India seemed imminent.

Prime Minister Winston Churchill then sent Sir Stafford Cripps, a socialist member of the war cabinet, to Delhi with an offer. After the war India would become a self-governing dominion, like Canada and Australia. Provinces and princely states could opt out if they chose. Meanwhile, "the principal sections of the Indian people" were invited to participate in the counsels of war. Indian members of the Executive Council would control all departments but defense. After meetings with Indian leaders, Cripps announced the proposal over the radio on March 30, 1942. Sri Aurobindo was listening. Breaking his self-imposed rule of keeping silence on political matters, he telegraphed Cripps to say that he welcomed the offer "as an opportunity given to India to determine for herself, and organise in all liberty of choice, her freedom and unity, and take an effective place among the world's free nations"; he concluded by offering his "public adhesion" in case "it can be of any help in your work." Cripps immediately thanked Sri Aurobindo for allowing him to inform the country that one who occupied a "unique position in [the] imagination of Indian youth" felt that the offer "substantially confers the freedom for which Indian Nationalism has so long struggled."[121] A number of newspapers carried Sri Aurobindo's message, which elicited both positive and negative comments. The British editor of *The Statesman,* along with former Bengali Extremists like Bejoy Chandra Chatterji and Amarendranath Chatterjee, advised people in India to follow his advice. Others commented that it would have been better if Sri Aurobindo had not emerged from the isolation he had entered thirty years earlier. "Young India has travelled far in her struggle for freedom since Sri Aurobindo went into voluntary exile," remarked one critic. "The Indian National Congress has become the mouthpiece of the nation" and the country had to look to the leaders of Congress, and not Sri Aurobindo, "for correct lead and guidance."[122]

Sri Aurobindo knew that his advice had to reach the Congress high command if it was going to have any effect. Two days after sending his message to Cripps, he telegraphed C. Rajagopalachari, a member of the Congress Working Committee, and B. S. Moonje, a former Nationalist colleague, now a leader of the Hindu Mahasabha, pointing out the advantages of the offer. He also sent his disciple Duraiswami Iyer, a prominent lawyer of Madras, to Delhi to speak to members of the working committee. By the time Duraiswami reached Delhi, the offer was in mortal danger. The Mahasabha had rejected it because it conceded the possibility of Pakistan. Nehru and others were troubled about the question of defense, and Gandhi opposed anything that might encourage military action. Admitted to a closed meeting of the working committee, Duraiswami presented Sri Aurobindo's position. Gandhi was the first to reply. If Sri Aurobindo thought the situation "so grave and serious that he has departed from his usual rule of not seeing anybody and not speaking to anybody," then "he ought to come out and lead the country." In a letter to Sri Aurobindo, he was even more curt: "Since you have thought it proper to give public advice at this critical juncture in the history of our country, I would request you to come out from your seclusion & give your message to the people. You are especially wanted in Bengal."[123]

Negotiations between Cripps and Indian leaders continued, but on April 10 the working committee delivered its final rejection. When Churchill learned of the outcome, he sighed in relief. He had been against the offer from the start. As he would declare that November, he had not "become the King's First Minister in order to preside over the liquidation of the British Empire."[124] He had gone through the motions to satisfy President Franklin D. Roosevelt, who had been pressing him to grant more self-government to India. Cripps did not know that his mission was meant to fail, or that he, whom some saw as a possible replacement for Churchill, was meant to look bad when it did.

When Sri Aurobindo heard that the offer had been rejected, he remarked to his attendants, "I knew it would fail." They at once pounced on him, asking "Why did you then send Duraiswami at all?" He replied: "For a bit of *nishkama karma*"—the *Gita's* term for selfless action performed without desire for the fruits. In a later conversation he expanded on this. When he heard Cripps's broadcast, he felt there was "very little chance of success"; but he would have urged acceptance even if he was certain that the plan was doomed to failure. It was "a question of play of forces" in the occult planes. But here he paused, because, he said, you "cannot explain these things to people."[125]

What would have happened if the Cripps proposal had been accepted? Many believe that the partition of India might have been averted if the various parties had learned to work together in a wartime national government. Another view is that Congress leaders squandered a once in a lifetime "opportunity of entrenching themselves in the seats of power and also the chance of smothering the Muslim League before it was too late." At least one Congress leader came to agree that refusing the offer had been a mistake. As K.M. Munshi wrote in 1951, "Today we realise that if the first [Cripps] proposal had been accepted, there would have been no partition, no refugees and no Kashmir problem."[126] Such judgments after the fact have to be taken with a grain of salt; but the possibilities that might have opened if the Cripps proposal had been accepted are among the great unanswered questions of modern Indian history.

Up to 1942 Sri Aurobindo had not looked on Tojo's Japan in the same way as he did Hitler's Germany. From the days of *Bande Mataram*, he had regarded the rise of Asian powers as necessary for the new international order he envisaged. But when "it became evident that Japan intended to attack and even invade and conquer India," he "returned to his reliance on spiritual force" and—as he reported after the war—"had the satisfaction of seeing the tide of

Japanese victory, which had till then swept everything before it, change immediately into a tide of rapid, crushing and finally immense and overwhelming defeat."[127] His yoga, he wrote to a disciple, involved not only "union with the Divine or a perception of Him in all things," but also supporting "what has to be supported, even if it means war and strife carried on" through "tanks and cars and American bombs and planes."[128] Allied arms began to prevail in the Pacific in June 1942, but it took three more years for the Japanese to be pushed back to their home islands, and the destruction of Hiroshima and Nagasaki to bring them to their knees. On August 15, 1945, six days after the second atomic bomb was dropped, Emperor Hirohito announced Japan's unconditional surrender. In the ashram, the Allies' victory was observed by a meditation in the evening of that *darshan* day.[129]

THE POPULATION OF the ashram doubled during World War II. As the Japanese advanced toward Assam and Bengal, disciples living outside began clamoring to come to Pondicherry. In a letter written on April 6, 1942 Sri Aurobindo conceded that Calcutta was "now in the danger zone," but warned people to avoid "the illusion that there is any safe place anywhere." Those who were "eager to remove their children could do so." If adults chose to come, they should be ready to face any eventuality.[130] This was enough to open the floodgates. By the end of 1943 there were more than a hundred newcomers, many of them children. Before there had been only a handful of young people in the ashram. Now finding herself with twenty boys and girls to look after, the Mother opened a school, teaching some of the classes herself. A year or two later a playground was acquired. Soon not only the children but also many of the adults were participating in regular sports and exercise.

The increased membership meant a strain on the ashram's finances just when prices were climbing "to a dizzy and fantastic height" on account of the war. As a result Sri Aurobindo and the Mother had to struggle "to make both ends meet and at times to prevent deficit budgets and their results."[131] They managed thanks to the generosity of wealthy disciples and other admirers of their work. The Mother did not believe in investment, so whatever was received was at once put into development. The Golconde dormitory was completed by the mid 1940s, and soon won general acclaim. A printing establishment was set up in 1945, and within a few years was producing books that set a standard for excellence in India. Before long all of Sri Aurobindo's works were being published by the Ashram Press. Around the same time, ashram-related organizations began to bring out quarterly or annual journals. The first canto of *Savitri* appeared in the *Sri Aurobindo Patha-mandir Annual* (Calcutta) in August 1946. Subsequent cantos appeared in *The Advent* (Madras), while poems like "A God's Labour" and "The Infinitesimal Infinite" were published in *Sri Aurobindo Circle* (Bombay). The rest of the material printed in these journals—poems and essays by ashramites and other disciples—are more interesting as examples of devotional expression than as contributions to scholarship or literature. Sri Aurobindo read through some of these productions, but appears to have given little encouragement to intellectual or literary originality. His disciples' poems simply imitate his images and rhythms; their articles summarize or plagiarize his ideas.

THE END OF World War II brought renewed pressure to settle the constitutional and communal problems that stood in the way of Indian self-government. In June 1945 the new viceroy, Lord Wavell, offered a new set of proposals, which Sri Aurobindo thought were "even better than Cripps' in certain respects." But owing to differences between the Congress and the Muslim League, this plan too was rejected. A month later Churchill and the Conservatives were voted out of office. The incoming Labour Party had long been in favor of Indian self-government and immediately took steps to bring it about. A parliamentary delegation was sent to India, followed by a cabinet mission that offered a plan for a free Indian Union. The plan's defining feature was a clause permitting the provinces in the northwest, the northeast, and the balance of the country to form themselves into partly autonomous groups. The idea was to give the substance of Pakistan to the Muslim League without partitioning the country. At first Sri Aurobindo endorsed the plan, taking it as a sign of the imminent liberation of India. But as the details of the "group system" and what it meant unfolded, he felt obliged to express "some very serious misgivings" about a scheme that virtually guaranteed that all of Bengal, Assam, and Punjab would end up in Pakistan. He expressed these reservations in a letter to Surendra Mohan Ghosh, head of the Congress in Bengal and a former Anushilan revolutionary with whom he had been meeting since 1939.[132] He urged Surendra Mohan to work against partition, but events were moving too fast. Sri Aurobindo eventually advised him not to move a resolution in favor of partition, but if it became inevitable, to accept it on the condition that districts that wanted to remain in India would have the right to do so.[133]

At first the Congress and the Muslim League tried to work together in an interim national government, but in mid-1946 the League pulled out and called for "direct action." Soon Bengal and other provinces witnessed the bloodiest communal rioting the country had ever experienced. To a disciple who feared that all Bengali Hindus would be exterminated, Sri Aurobindo wrote, "we must not let our reaction" to the situation "become excessive or suggest despair." He himself was not discouraged "because I know and have experienced hundreds of times that beyond the blackest darkness there lies for one who is a divine instrument the light of God's victory." This attitude did not mean that he advocated nonviolent passivity. "Why don't the Hindus strike?" he asked his attendants more than once when he heard of Muslim atrocities.[134]

While people in Bengal and the North were butchering each other, the leaders of the major Indian parties were attempting to form themselves into a constituent assembly. When their efforts failed, the British took the initiative. In February 1947 Prime Minister Clement Attlee announced that the government intended to complete the transfer of power by June 1948, and that Admiral Lord Lewis Mountbatten would be coming to India with a definite plan of action. Mountbatten arrived in Delhi on March, spoke with leaders of all parties, and returned to Britain in May. On June 3, 1947 Attlee announced the details of the government's final plan of liberation and partition. The next day Mountbatten spoke at a press conference in Delhi. Asked if he had decided on a date to implement the plan, he said: "I think the transfer could be about the 15th of August."[135] This date soon was accepted as final. India would be free in two months.

Sri Aurobindo and the members of the ashram took Mountbatten's choice of date as a sign of the working of divine providence. Writing in a semi-humorous vein in July, he told a disciple that he was happy to be receiving a "birthday present of a free India" on August 15, although he would be happier if it was not "complicated by its being presented in two packets. . . . One free India would have been enough," he thought, "if offered as an unbroken whole."[136] Asked the next month by All India Radio for a message to be broadcast on the eve of the great event, he was even more explicit. "August 15th, 1947 is the birthday of free India," he began. "It marks for her the end of an old era, the beginning of a new age." Then came a personal note, unusual in his public utterances: "August 15th is my own birthday and it is naturally gratifying to me that it should have assumed this vast significance. I take this coincidence, not as a fortuitous accident, but as the sanction and seal of the Divine Force that guides my steps on the work with which I began life, the beginning of its full fruition." He then went on to speak of the five "world-movements he had hoped to see fulfilled in his lifetime," which in his youth had seemed to be "impracticable dreams," but which were now "arriving at fruition or on their way to fulfilment."[137] His message was broadcast by All India Radio in

Tiruchirapalli and Madras on August 14, 1947. The next day was observed not only as Sri Aurobindo's seventy-fifth birthday but also as the first day of India's independence. In the evening the *sadhaks* assembled to listen to a concert of national songs in the ashram's courtyard. Without warning, the ashram was attacked by a band of armed rioters. Several ashramites were injured and one, Mulshankar Jani, was stabbed in the neck and killed. The rioters, mostly paid hooligans, had been instigated by groups that opposed the existence of the ashram, notably Communists and Tamil separatists.[138]

Mulshankar had been one of Sri Aurobindo's attendants, giving him therapeutic massages and participating in the talks. "When the news was brought to Sri Aurobindo that he had been fatally stabbed, the room was filled with gloom and horror," Nirodbaran recalled. "Sri Aurobindo listened quietly and his face bore a grave and serious expression that we had not seen before. The dark forces seemed to have achieved a perilous victory."[139] One might almost suppose that this "victory" was a reflection of the orgy of slaughter that was then sweeping across India. Hindus, Muslims, and Sikhs were killed indiscriminately by their former neighbors. As many as a million people died, staining what ought to have been a joyous celebration of freedom.

Final Flowering

Sri Aurobindo's life fell into a fairly regular pattern in the 1940s. Waking before dawn, he spent some time doing the freehand exercises his doctors recommended. Around 6:30 he sat up to greet the Mother, who came in for a moment before going to give *darshan* to members of the ashram. After she left, he took up the morning papers: *The Hindu* for the news, *The Madras Mail* for its Curly Wee cartoon. By 1945 his eyesight was so bad that he had to rely upon his attendant Nirodbaran for this and other reading. Sometime after nine o'clock, the Mother came in to apply lotion to his hair and to comb and plait it. While she worked, she spoke about affairs in the ashram. When she departed, the attendants took over, washing Sri Aurobindo's face and brushing his teeth. He who had written in the *Record* thirty years earlier that he was able to keep his teeth clean without "artificial means of preservation or cleansing (brush, powder etc.)" now submitted to having them brushed with Neem toothpaste and to having his mouth freshened with Vademecum mouthwash.[140] Once these tasks had been dealt with, he sat quietly by himself for three or four hours. The Mother told the attendants not to interrupt him unless urgent business arose. They wondered what he was doing "wrapped in a most mysterious silence," but got no clue from his actions or gestures:

> All that was visible to our naked eyes was that he sat silently in his bed, afterwards [after his recovery] in the capacious armchair, with his eyes wide open just as any other person would. Only he passed hours and hours thus, changing his position at times and making himself comfortable; the eyes moving a little, and though usually gazing at the wall in front, never fixed *tratak*-like at any particular point. Sometimes the face would beam with a bright smile without any apparent reason . . . as a child smiles in its sleep. Only it was a waking sleep, for as we passed across the room, there was a dim recognition of our shadow-like movements. Occasionally he would look towards the door. This was when he heard some sound that might indicate the Mother's coming.

If the Mother happened to arrive when, contrary to his usual practice, he was "plunged within, with his eyes closed," she would stand beside his bed until he opened his eyes. "Then, seeing her waiting, he would exclaim 'Oh!' and the Mother's lips would part into an exquisite smile." One or more of the attendants were always on call, and he occasionally asked them for something, such as a glass of water. When he did, "his voice seemed to come from a distant cave." When they had to intrude on his privacy, they approached him cautiously and stood near the bed. Without turning he would ask, "in an impersonal tone, 'What is it?'" To Nirodbaran, the voice sounded like "a moment's ripple in the vast even ocean of silence."[141]

Sri Aurobindo's meditation continued until three or four o'clock. Then came his first and principal meal of the day. Various vegetarian dishes prepared by ashram women, along with *luchis*, sweets, savories, and juices, were arranged on a tray and placed before him. The Mother offered him food, keeping up a cheery mealtime banter: "How do you like that dish?" "This is a special brinjal sent from Benares." If he replied at all, it was with an invariable, "Oh, I see! Quite good." The attendants sometimes wondered if he could tell one dish from another. Once they "saw him eat a whole cooked green chili before we could cry halt."[142]

After his meal, Sri Aurobindo rested a little and then walked for a half-hour. Even with his stick he was a bit unsteady, and the Mother sat and watched as he paced back and forth. Then it was time for his bath. "Entirely passive," he "submitted himself to the care of the attendants," who washed his body and rinsed it with a hand-held showerhead. Afterward the attendants helped him dress. His clothes were quite simple: a plain cotton dhoti, worn Bengali style and hitched above his knees when he walked. He wore no body cloth unless it was unusually cold. His feet, like his chest, were bare.[143]

He conversed with his attendants during his bath and the hour or so that followed, but after 1941 talk about anything but routine matters became infrequent and then stopped altogether. Toward the late afternoon, the Mother came in and he spoke with her in private. The rest of the evening was devoted to literary work. In the mid-1940s, as his eyesight deteriorated, his handwriting became so illegible that he began to dictate what he needed to write: passages for *Savitri*, revision of *Arya* works, occasional letters. He waited to take his supper until the Mother returned from her evening activities. If she was late coming back from her drive, he asked about her again and again. He remained awake until two o'clock in the morning, not going to bed until he had been told that the Mother had retired. He slept little: from four to four-and-a-half hours.

Because his talks entirely ceased and his correspondence virtually so, there are no first-hand accounts of Sri Aurobindo's *sadhana* after 1941. One is tempted to mine *Savitri* to make up for the lack. Sri Aurobindo's accounts of Aswapathy's voyage through the worlds of matter, life, and mind before reaching "the kingdoms of the greater knowledge," and Savitri's transit through the "inner countries" until she reaches the inmost soul certainly are based on his and the Mother's experiences; but the poem is a fictional creation, and Sri Aurobindo said explicitly that "the circumstances of this life have nothing to do with" its plot.[144] One is on somewhat firmer ground looking for clues in his lyrical poems, but he wrote only a few after 1943. Those he did write are uncharacteristically dark:

> Is this the end of all that we have been,
> And all we did or dreamed,—
> A name unremembered and a form undone,—
> Is this the end?
> A body rotting under a slab of stone
> Or turned to ash in fire,
> A mind dissolved, lost its forgotten thoughts,—
> Is this the end?

So begins a poem of June 1945. It ends, however, on a brighter note: the "Immortal in the mortal" is "unwilling to cease"

Till all is done for which the stars were made,
Till the heart discovers God
And the soul knows itself. And even then
There is no end.[145]

The same sort of confidence emerges from a letter he dictated in July 1947. This is his last known utterance on the state of his *sadhana*:

My present effort is not to stand up on a high and distant Supermind level and change the world from there, but to bring something of it down here and to stand on that and act by that; but at the present stage the progressive supramentalisation of the Overmind is the first immediate preoccupation and a second is the lightening of the heavy resistance of the Inconscient and the support it gives to human ignorance which is always the main obstacle in any attempt to change the world or even to change oneself.[146]

THE ONLY VARIATIONS in Sri Aurobindo's routine came before the four yearly *darshans,* when there was a noticeable increase in the tempo of activities even in his inner sanctum. On the *darshan* day itself the Mother came in early, bowed before him, told him the program, then rushed off to see that everything was being done as it should. His attendants dressed him in a fine white dhoti, its bottom border crimped in the Bengali fashion. Early in the afternoon the Mother rejoined him, and they walked together to the small outer room where they sat together on a sofa, the Mother on Sri Aurobindo's right. Here they remained for the next few hours as ashramites and visitors—more than three thousand by the end of the 1940s—passed before them one by one. "There is no suggestion of a vulgar jostle anywhere in the moving procession," a visitor noted. "The mystic sits bare-bodied except for a part of his dhoti thrown round his shoulders. A kindly light plays in his eyes." Sri Aurobindo looked directly at each person for a moment. "The moving visitor is conscious of a particular contact with these [eyes] as he bends down to do his obeisance. They leave upon him a mysterious 'feel' that baffles description. The contact, almost physical, instils a faint sense of a fragrance into his heart and he has a perception of a glow akin to that spreading in every fibre of his being."[147] Most visitors had similarly positive experiences. But some, particularly those from the West, were distracted by the theatricality of the setting and the religiosity of the pageantry. Vincent Sheean, a well-known American journalist, had read some of Sri Aurobindo's books before coming and was deeply impressed by them. But as he stood in line to have *darshan,* with incense swirling around him and people throwing themselves at the gurus' feet, he was hit by "a shock of sledge-hammer quality, to see human beings worshipped in this way." Failing to make any sense of it, he at least was glad to see that "whatever others may think or say," Sri Aurobindo did not seem "to be deceived or befuddled by these extravagant manifestations."[148]

SRI AUROBINDO CONTINUED to take an interest in local, national, and international politics. The liberation of British India made the French pocket of Pondicherry an anomaly that had to be dealt with. Shortly after independence, Sri Aurobindo summoned Bengal Congress leader Surendra Mohan Ghosh and gave him a proposal to take to Prime Minister Nehru and other members of the new Indian government. In brief, he wanted the French possessions to be integrated with India, but to retain some measure of autonomy so as to serve as a cultural link between France and India. Nehru expressed interest in the idea, but nothing came of it.[149] A few weeks later, on September 27, 1947, Sri Aurobindo received Maurice Schumann, head of a French cultural delegation, and François Baron, the governor of French India. This was the first time in eighteen years that he had met with anyone from outside the ashram. He endorsed Schumann's plan to make Pondicherry "a meeting place between France and India" and suggested establishing a university at which students from different parts of the world could study Indian culture.[150] The meeting had no immediate effect. A period of tension followed during which the Indian government put a customs cordon around Pondicherry while the pro- and anti-French parties maneuvered and the ashram had to look after its own interests; for a while it was difficult to obtain food and other necessities. In 1950 Sri Aurobindo resumed his efforts to retain Pondicherry's distinctiveness within the Indian union.[151] But the problem remained until 1954, when the colony became a de facto territory of India.

As Sri Aurobindo had prophesied as far back as 1920, freedom did not prove to be a panacea for India's social and economic ills. Less than six months after Independence Day, Mahatma Gandhi was murdered by a Hindu fanatic. Asked for a message by All India Radio, Sri Aurobindo replied:

I would have preferred silence in the face of these circumstances that surround us. . . . This much, however, I will say that the Light which led us to freedom, though not yet to unity, still burns and will burn on till it conquers. . . . The Power that brought us through so much struggle and suffering to freedom, will achieve also, through whatever strife or trouble, the aim which so poignantly occupied the thoughts of the fallen leader at the time of his tragic ending; as it brought us freedom, it will bring us unity.[152]

Many looked to Sri Aurobindo to fill the void left by Gandhi's death. Among them was Jayaprakash Narayan, the militant socialist leader, who called on Sri Aurobindo and Ramana Maharshi "to come out of their seclusion and lead a campaign for the cultural and spiritual regeneration" of the country.[153] Sri Aurobindo would have agreed with Narayan's opinion that India was passing through "an unprecedented spiritual crisis." In a letter issued later as a message, he wrote: "Things are bad, are growing worse and may at any time grow worst or worse than worst if that is possible." All he could offer in consolation was the assurance that "all this was necessary because certain possibilities had to emerge and be got rid of, if a new and better world was at all to come into being."[154]

In June 1948 Sri Aurobindo was offered a National Prize for "eminent merit" in the humanities by Andhra University.[155] After some hesitation, he agreed to accept it. His address for the occasion, read out by another at the presentation ceremony, dealt with the question of linguistic states, an issue then dominating national debate. A month or two later, his political impulses were given an outlet when K. D. Sethna, a close disciple, became the editor of a Bombay newspaper called *Mother India.* Sethna wrote to him for guidance on subjects such as India-Pakistan relations and the Korean War, and incorporated Sri Aurobindo's answers in his editorials. At Sethna's request for advice after the invasion of South Korea, Sri Aurobindo wrote on June 28, 1950:

I do not know why you want a line of thought to be indicated to you for your guidance in the affair of Korea. There is nothing to hesitate about there, the whole affair is as plain as a pike-staff. It is the first move in the Communist plan of campaign to dominate and take possession first of these northern parts and then of South East Asia as a preliminary to their manoeuvres with regard to the rest of the continent—in passing, Tibet as a gate opening to India. If they succeed, there is no reason why domination of the whole world should not follow by steps until they are ready to deal with America.

"For the moment," he concluded, "the situation is as grave as it can be."[156] This message was remembered in 1962 when China attacked India through

Tibet. The next year Sudhir Ghosh, an Indian diplomat in Washington, showed Sri Aurobindo's "last testament"—a *Mother India* article based on his letter—to President John F. Kennedy. After reading it several times, Kennedy remarked to Ghosh: "Surely there is a typing mistake here. The date must have been 1960, not 1950. You mean to say that a man devoted to meditation and contemplation, sitting in one corner of India, said this about the intentions of Communist China as early as 1950?" He concluded with a contrast. "One great Indian, Nehru, showed you the path of non-alignment between China and America, and another great Indian, Aurobindo, showed you another way of survival."[157]

Most of Sri Aurobindo's writing in 1949 and 1950 dealt with subjects far removed from politics. *Savitri,* now more than twenty thousand lines long, was being published canto by canto in ashram journals and in separate booklets. Sri Aurobindo revised each section before publication. Sitting in his armchair with Nirodbaran kneeling at his feet, he listened as the scribe read what had been written already—sometimes a few days, sometimes a few years earlier—and then began to dictate revisions and additions. From mid-1950 he started devoting more time to the poem, putting aside other concerns that were keeping him from what he called his "main work." Each morning at eleven o'clock, Nirodbaran took his place on the floor. Sri Aurobindo would "give a glance of welcome," then take up where he had left off. "Sometimes sitting upright, sometimes leaning on the left side cushion [of his bed], keeping his gaze in front, he would dictate in a quiet, subdued voice slowly and distinctly."[158] Once a canto had been completed, it was sent for typing and then revised further. Another round of revision followed its journal or booklet publication. Finally, in 1950, the first volume of the poem was published by the ashram's press.

Around the same period, Sri Aurobindo revised a number of his *Arya* works. *The Human Cycle* and *The Ideal of Human Unity* had to be brought up to date, accounting for the enormous changes—some of them anticipated in the *Arya*—that had taken place in international politics since 1920. New editions of both books, along with the first part of *The Synthesis of Yoga,* were published in Pondicherry and New York between 1948 and 1950. Sri Aurobindo wrote a series of essays for an ashram journal, *The Bulletin of Physical Education,* in 1949 and 1950. These were his first sustained efforts in expository prose since the revision and enlargement of *The Life Divine* ten years earlier.

Sri Aurobindo's works were now reaching a wider audience in India and abroad. In August 1949 there were public celebrations of his seventy-seventh birthday throughout India and in New York. For his American admirers, he sent a message in which he affirmed the shared destiny of East and West:

> It has been customary to dwell on the division and difference between these two sections of the human family and even oppose them to each other; but, for myself I would rather be disposed to dwell on oneness and unity than on division and difference. . . . There has been a tendency in some minds to dwell on the spirituality or mysticism of the East and the materialism of the West; but the West has had no less than the East its spiritual seekings and, though not in such profusion, its saints and sages and mystics, the East has had its materialistic tendencies, its material splendours, its similar or identical dealings with life and Matter and the world in which we live.

The great need, as the two were drawn together, was to be clear about the ideal and goal to be pursued. Here "there has been, not any absolute difference but an increasing divergence between the tendencies of the East and the West":

> The East has always and increasingly put the highest emphasis on the supreme truth of the Spirit; it has, even in its extreme philosophies, put the world away as an illusion and regarded the Spirit as the sole reality. The West has concentrated more and more increasingly on the world, on the dealings of mind and life with our material existence, on our mastery over it, on the perfection of mind and life and some fulfilment of the human being here: latterly this has gone so far as the denial of the Spirit and even the enthronement of Matter as the sole reality.

But the two ideals "are not incompatible with each other: rather their divergence has to be healed and both have to be included and reconciled in our view of the future." Yoga was the key to the reconciliation:

> The ascent of the human soul to the supreme Spirit is that soul's highest aim and necessity, for that is the supreme reality; but there can be too the descent of the Spirit and its powers into the world and that would justify the existence of the material world also, give a meaning, a divine purpose to the creation and solve its riddle. East and West could be reconciled in the pursuit of the highest and largest ideal, Spirit embrace Matter and Matter find its own true reality and the hidden Reality in all things in the Spirit.[159]

The meeting in New York was chaired by the novelist Pearl Buck and addressed by Pitirim Sorokin, a professor at Harvard and one of the world's leading sociologists. Sorokin said that "from the scientific and philosophical standpoint, the works of Sri Aurobindo are a sound antidote to the pseudo-scientific psychology, psychiatry and educational art of the West."[160] He and other American academics were trying to bring Sri Aurobindo's works into the university curriculum, with limited success. Philosopher Edwin Burtt lectured on *The Life Divine* at Cornell; Frederic Spiegelberg, professor of comparative religion at Stanford, assigned *Essays on the Gita* to his graduate students. The Indian's reach would be wider, Spiegelberg believed, if American philosophy departments were not "under the anti-metaphysical influence of John Dewey and his Instrumentalists, which is the American form of what is called Logical Positivism in Europe."[161] The same influence kept discussions of *The Life Divine* out of philosophical journals in England and the United States, but nonacademics published positive assessments in *World Review* and even the *Chicago Daily News*. Continental thinkers were more open to his thinking than were their Anglo-Saxon counterparts. French scholar Alfred Foucher noted that Sri Aurobindo, like the Existentialists, stressed individual responsibility, but unlike them, condemned egocentrism. One of Foucher's French Academy colleagues, l'Abbé Breuil, wrote that *The Human Cycle* was one of two books that had "interested me most deeply and stimulated the most thought."[162] In the Americas, Sri Aurobindo's influence was felt most by the literary elite. Expatriate English novelist Aldous Huxley considered *The Life Divine* "a book not merely of the highest importance in regard to its content, but remarkably fine as a piece of philosophic and religious literature." Chilean poet Gabriela Mistral regarded Sri Aurobindo as the "highest of mystics," as notable for his spiritual attainments as for his "beautifully austere and classical prose."[163] Both writers supported a snowballing movement to have Sri Aurobindo awarded the Nobel Prize in literature. Mistral, laureate in 1945, joined with Pearl Buck, laureate in 1938, in announcing her willingness to nominate him for the honor, while thirty-six Indian notables—cabinet ministers, governors, premiers, maharajas, vice-chancellors, and others—signed a memorandum to the Swedish Academy outlining his literary and spiritual attainments.[164] Around the same time an Indian academic proposed Sri Aurobindo's name for the Nobel Peace Prize. This was one of thirty-four official nominations considered by the Norwegian Nobel Committee in 1950.[165]

By the end of 1949 Sri Aurobindo was in danger of becoming an international celebrity. Popular U.S. magazines such as *Holiday* and *Life* did illustrated stories featuring him and Ramana Maharshi, a great yogi who lived conveniently close by.[166] The photojournalist Henri Cartier-Bresson visited India and, after shooting the funeral of the Maharshi, turned his sights on Pondicherry. Writing to the secretary of the ashram, he asked for permission to attend the *darshan* and "to make a photographic documentation of the life of the Ashram." Not allowed at first to take pictures of the Mother (much less of Sri Aurobindo), he gradually won her over and shot a few rolls at the daily "balcony darshan" and *pranam*. He found her "a very kind person with a tremendous energy who has absorbed the will of all the disciples." On the day of the *darshan*, he took some unsuccessful shots of Sri Aurobindo and the Mother. The next day he was allowed to enter Sri Aurobindo's room, where he took a series of portraits, the first since 1920. Sri Aurobindo "did not wink an eye during the entire ten minutes I was watching him," Cartier-Bresson noted in his diary. "He did not seem to belong to that impersonal setting."[167] The pictures show Sri Aurobindo in his armchair, looking quietly ahead, with no discernible expression (he appears unaware of the photographer) but conveying a sense of tranquil massiveness.

Cartier-Bresson was one of several outsiders who were allowed in Sri Aurobindo's room after 1947. C.R. Reddy, the vice chancellor of Andhra University, presented a citation and medal in December 1948 when the university awarded Sri Aurobindo its National Prize. Two years later Krishna Kumarsinhji Raol, the Maharaja of Bhavnagar, who as Governor of Madras was ex officio chancellor of the university, was granted an audience. K.M. Munshi, a Congress politician and, member of the central cabinet, who had known Sri Aurobindo at Baroda College forty-five years earlier, had a more substantial interview in July 1950. "I saw before me a being completely transformed, radiant, blissful, enveloped in an atmosphere of godlike calm," he later wrote. Sri Aurobindo seemed to embody "the most beautiful old age imaginable in an atmosphere of inspiring serenity." His "thin white beard and well brushed long white hair framed a radiant face," while "a deep light of calm and wisdom shone in his eyes." Munshi explained what he had been attempting to do for the country, but confessed that he had become so discouraged that he wanted to abandon it all and take up a life of yoga. Sri Aurobindo answered "in a low, clear voice": "You need not give up the world in order to advance in this direction. . . . I will follow your progress. If any help is needed, I shall give it [to] you." At the end of the interview, Munshi asked if there was anything Sri Aurobindo wanted to say. Immediately he asked: "When will India be reunited?" Taken aback, Munshi explained that he could not foresee it in his lifetime. Until 1947 he had worked for a united India, but he considered the partition to have been positive in so far as it allowed India and Pakistan to develop in their own separate ways. Sri Aurobindo insisted that Pakistan was "fraud, force and treachery," and declared: "India will be reunited. I see it clearly." After an exchange of views on local politics, Munshi asked: "When are you coming out of Pondicherry?" Sri Aurobindo replied: "I cannot say. I must first complete my work here."[168]

IN MID-1949, Sri Aurobindo began to experience frequent and difficult urination. Samples revealed an excess of sugar and traces of albumen. Fearing diabetes, the doctors ordered a reduction in starchy food such as *luchis* and sweets. The sugar count dropped, but not the frequency of urination. This made Nirodbaran suspect enlargement of the prostate, a diagnosis confirmed by Dr. Prabhat Sanyal, a Calcutta surgeon who had come to the ashram for *darshan.* For the moment, Sanyal said, there was not much danger, but the situation had to be monitored carefully.[169] He explained to Sri Aurobindo and the Mother the nature and consequences of the condition. As the gland became enlarged, it would exert pressure on the urethra. Frequent, incomplete emptying of the bladder was a first result. If the condition was left untreated, urine would back up into the system, eventually causing infection. The danger may have been greater for Sri Aurobindo because he had a history of kidney-related problems. In England, after he failed his first ICS medical examination, his classmates heard it was because of some "trouble with his urinary organs." Eighteen years later, it was rumored around Pondicherry that he was ill as a result of "kidney trouble."[170] There is no evidence that either of the episodes lasted long, and in 1949, too, the symptoms quickly subsided. When Sanyal returned to the ashram in November and asked about the problem, Sri Aurobindo said emphatically "It is no more troubling me. I have cured it."[171] But he seems to have been more concerned about his health than he let on. On December 7, in one of his rare letters, he mentioned unspecified "personal difficulties," and alluded to "pressure caused by the necessity of hastening the publication of my yet unpublished books." There was, he said, much work that needed to be done "while there is still time."[172]

In mid-1950, Sri Aurobindo's attendants noticed that he was becoming more and more reticent. All of their attempts to draw him out were met by a monosyllabic yes or no. One day Dr. Sanyal got up the courage to ask: "Why are you so serious, Sir?" "The time is very serious," Sri Aurobindo replied.[173] If he was thinking of world events, the allusion may have been to the conflict in Korea. Many feared that it would provoke a third world war. Around the same time, the symptoms of Sri Aurobindo's prostatic hyperplasia reappeared. The doctors were confident that he would use his yogic force to make them subside, and were dismayed when the symptoms worsened. Albumen appeared in the urine, then acetone, "a grave signal." At Sri Aurobindo's request, Nirodbaran reported the news to the Mother. She heard him out in silence.[174]

Sri Aurobindo continued to work on *Savitri* and other literary projects. His publishers decided to release *The Future Poetry,* and for a while he dictated some additions to existing passages. Then, wishing to write a chapter on twentieth-century poetry, he asked for books by the leading writers. These had to be ordered, so he went back to *Savitri.* "I want to finish it soon," he said. This was the first time Nirodbaran had heard him speak in that way. They took up the "Book of Fate." Sri Aurobindo gave his attention to a passage in which Narad tells the Queen that Savitri is strong enough to face her destiny:

> A day may come when she must stand unhelped
> On a dangerous brink of the world's doom and hers,
> Carrying the world's future on her lonely breast,
> Carrying the human hope in a heart left sole
> To conquer or fail on a last desperate verge,
> Alone with death and close to extinction's edge.[175]

The work proceeded slowly. Finally, around the middle of November, Nirodbaran announced that the last proposed passage had been completed. "Ah, it is finished?" Sri Aurobindo said with one of his rare smiles. "What is left now?" "The Book of Death and the Epilogue." "Oh, that," he concluded. "We shall see about that later on."[176]

It was chilly during the monsoon that year, and Sri Aurobindo's discomfort increased. A few days before the November 24 *darshan,* Dr. Satyavrata Sen, another Calcutta surgeon, was consulted. He confirmed the diagnosis. "But what is the remedy?" Sri Aurobindo asked. The only radical remedy, the doctors knew, was to remove the prostate surgically. It was a relatively safe and straightforward procedure, but they were aware that Sri Aurobindo and the Mother would never approve of it.

A suggestion was made to postpone the *darshan* on account of Sri Aurobindo's discomfort. He and the Mother brushed this aside. Some three thousand people had come, and they could not be disappointed. The atmosphere on November 24 was unusually solemn. The visitors stood silently in the street, then entered the building and climbed the stairs to Sri Aurobindo's room. To an American student, a first-time visitor, the whole procedure seemed "a bit ridiculous." What purpose could be served by standing for a moment before the author of *The Life Divine* without saying a word to him? What happened next was unexpected:

> As I stepped into a radius of about four feet, there was the sensation of moving into some kind of a force field. Intuitively, I knew it was the force of Love, but not what ordinary humans usually mean by the term. These two were "geared straight up"; they were not paying attention to me as ordinary parents might have done; yet, this unattachment seemed just the thing that healed. Suddenly, I loved them both, as spiritual "parents."
>
> Then, all thought ceased, I was perfectly aware of where I was; it was not "hypnotism" as one Stanford friend later suggested. It was simply that during those few minutes, my mind became utterly still. It seemed that I stood there a very long, an uncounted time, for there *was* no time. Only many years later did I describe this experience as my having experienced the Timeless *in* Time. When there at the *darshan,* there was not the least doubt in my mind that I had met two people who had experienced what they claimed. They *were* Gnostic Beings. They had realized this new consciousness which Sri Aurobindo called the Supramental.[177]

Two hours into the ceremony, a whisper ran down the line. Sri Aurobindo and the Mother wanted things speeded up. Everyone moved a little more quickly, and by five o'clock it was over. Sri Aurobindo returned to his inner room looking rather tired. "I am very hungry," was the first thing he said. His attendants had never heard such an admission.[178]

Over the next few days Sri Aurobindo's symptoms worsened. The doctors had no alternative than to pass a catheter. This gave immediate relief, but also brought on a fever. Dr. Sanyal was called from Calcutta. Arriving on the evening of November 30, he asked Sri Aurobindo what the trouble was. "Trouble?" he replied. "Nothing troubles me, and suffering—one can be above it." Nirodbaran reminded him of his urinary difficulties. "Well, yes; I had some difficulties, but they were relieved and now I do not feel anything." After consulting with the other doctors and checking the lab reports, Sanyal explained to the Mother that Sri Aurobindo had a mild kidney infection. He hoped antibiotics and normal drainage would set things right.[179]

The next day there was considerable improvement. Sri Aurobindo ate well and cracked jokes with the doctors. When they asked him whether he wanted his blood examined, he replied: "You doctors think only in terms of diseases and medicines, but always there is much more effectual knowledge beyond and above it. I do not need anything."[180] That day and the next were busy ones for the Mother because the school was celebrating its seventh anniversary with a cultural program and physical education display. On the evening of December 2, when she came to Sri Aurobindo's room, Sanyal explained that his condition was slightly worse and asked for permission to try a more aggressive treatment. She did not consent; Sri Aurobindo's body, she said, would not respond to powerful drugs. The doctors could continue to give him simple medicines if they liked. He would "work out whatever is necessary." The next morning he seemed so much improved that Sanyal asked the Mother whether it was necessary for him to stay. He took it back at once when she gave him a serious look. That afternoon Sri Aurobindo's temperature shot up to 102 degrees. He began to have trouble breathing, a sign of reduced kidney efficiency. The doctors insisted that he have a blood analysis. The results were staggering: "all the signs of imminent kidney failure!" That evening Sri Aurobindo was unable to eat, until at length the Mother came and fed him some fruit juice with a spoon. Later she took the doctors aside, and said: "He is fully conscious within but he is losing interest in himself." During the night the attendants kept careful watch. At one point Sanyal told him that Dr. Nirodbaran would change his medicine if needed. "Nirod is no doctor to me," he replied.[181]

The next day, Monday, December 4, Sri Aurobindo felt much better in the morning. The doctors noted with relief that the respiratory distress was gone. His temperature was close to normal. He went to his armchair and sat serenely for a while. The doctors asked whether he was using his yogic power to cure himself. He replied with a simple no. "Why not?" they insisted. "Can't explain. You won't understand." Around noon, his respiratory difficulty reappeared, and his temperature rose above 100 degrees. He rested for a few hours, got up, went to the bathroom, then sat for a while in his armchair. After returning to his bed, he went within. Champaklal sat disconsolately at his feet. From time to time Sri Aurobindo emerged from his drawn-in state, leaned forward, and kissed his faithful attendant on the cheek.[182]

In the evening the Mother returned from her activities. The doctors gave their report, adding that they wanted to arrange for intravenous transfusions. She said: "I told you this is not necessary. He has no interest in himself. He is withdrawing." Around eleven o'clock she came again, gave him some juice, and went away. When she returned an hour later, Sri Aurobindo "opened his eyes and the two looked at each other in a steady gaze." She again left the room, but came back at around one o'clock in the morning of December 5. This time Sri Aurobindo remained withdrawn. "What do you think?" she asked Sanyal. "Can I retire for an hour?" The doctor did not know what to say. "Call me when the time comes," she said, and went to her room.[183] At this point Sri

Aurobindo's breathing was so labored that he had to be given oxygen. Around 1:15, he roused himself, inquired about the time, and asked Nirodbaran for something to drink. After sipping a bit of juice, he plunged within. His attendants huddled anxiously around him. Nirodbaran and Champaklal massaged his feet while Sanyal brushed his hair. Suddenly a tremor ran through his body. He drew up his arms and placed them across his chest. At 1:26 his breathing ceased.[184]

Epilogue

For a half-hour after Sri Aurobindo's death, his attendants sat stunned around his bed. The Mother joined them and stood silently at his feet. Seeing Champaklal sobbing, she silenced him with a look. After a while she went out, and Sanyal, Nirodbaran, and others began to prepare the body for public viewing.[1]

At Sanyal's suggestion, the Mother sent word to the ashram's photographers. They came with their equipment at around three o'clock and spent an hour photographing the body. When they left, the members of the ashram were admitted. Then, at six o'clock, the doors of the ashram were thrown open. Before the end of the day, some sixty thousand people had filed past the body. It lay on a wooden cot, clad in a white silk dhoti and covered with a plain white cloth. "His serene appearance," a newspaper reporter wrote, was more suggestive "of one in sleep than in death."[2]

On the morning of December 6, 1950 all of the major papers of the country announced the passing of Sri Aurobindo with bold headlines, long stories, and obituaries printed as lead editorials. Tributes from his countrymen ran to several columns. President Rajendra Prasad, Prime Minister Jawaharlal Nehru, central and state ministers, governors, legislators, diplomats, and maharajas, together with intellectual, educational, and spiritual leaders, recalled his contribution to the struggle for freedom, his philosophical and other writings, and the example of his yogic discipline. Abroad, his death was noted by newspapers in London, Paris, and New York. A writer in the *Manchester Guardian* called him "the most massive philosophical thinker that modern India has produced" and reminded British readers that he was "a product of the West as much as of the East."[3]

The viewing of Sri Aurobindo's body continued. The funeral, set at first for December 6, was postponed. That evening, the Mother issued a message affirming that Sri Aurobindo's body was "charged with such concentration of supramental light that there is no sign of decomposition"; accordingly it would "be kept lying on his bed so long as it remains intact."[4] She intended "light" to be understood literally: since the morning of December 5, she and others had seen an aura of light around the body. Even those with more mundane powers of vision were struck by its appearance. "The body of Sri Aurobindo is lying majestically on his bed, a marvel of radiance, without any sign that there is no life in it," one reporter wrote.[5]

The laws of French India required funerals to take place within forty-eight hours of the time of death, so permission from the government had to be obtained to delay Sri Aurobindo's internment. On the morning of December 7, Dr. V.P. Barbet, chief medical officer of Pondicherry, together with Dr. Sanyal and Dr. Nirodbaran, examined Sri Aurobindo's body and found "no sign of decomposition."[6] Barbet therefore gave his permission for the viewing to continue. There was talk of sealing the remains in an airtight glass case. At the same time, work continued on a vault in the courtyard of the ashram.

Viewing of the body was by that time reserved for those arriving by car, train, and plane from different parts of India. Visitors were struck by the silence and solemnity in the ashram, notwithstanding the evident distress of some of its members. Many were in a state of inner torment. When they went to the Mother for comfort, she assured them that Sri Aurobindo was still with them and that he would "not leave the earth atmosphere until earth is transformed." "What has happened on the physical plane," she wrote, "affects in no way the truth of his teaching."[7]

On the morning of December 9, more than a hundred hours after the moment of death, the first signs of decomposition appeared. Sri Aurobindo's funeral was set for that evening. At 1:30 in the afternoon, people who had recently arrived were allowed to view the body. Later, the members of the ashram were given a last *darshan*. The body was then placed in a rosewood casket, which was carried down to the courtyard. At five o'clock, it was lowered into the vault. Complete silence prevailed. No religious rites were observed. Nolini and Champaklal threw earth into the vault before it was sealed. Representatives of the Indian and French governments laid wreaths. After a short while, the assembly dispersed.

THE OUTPOURING OF public grief that followed Sri Aurobindo's death was remarkable considering that he had been out of public view for forty years. Only the older generation could remember his writings in *Bande Mataram*. Not many were able to appreciate the thought of *The Life Divine* or the rhythms of *Savitri*. Even fewer felt called upon to follow his path of yoga. Yet great masses of people felt touched by the passing of one who was, as a politician put it, "the last of the great geniuses born in the latter part of the last century."[8] Vivekananda, Tagore, and Gandhi had gone before him. Those who survived were of a different caliber. It was the end of an era.

In the half-century since Sri Aurobindo's death, his reputation has continued to grow. Discussed by historians, philosophers, literary critics, and social scientists, and admired, even worshipped, by thousands of spiritual seekers, he regularly is numbered among the most outstanding Indians of the twentieth century.[9] Like all icons, he is misrepresented by his admirers as well as his detractors, praised or reviled for things he never said or did. Most people allow their opinions of him to be shaped by authorities. His followers and their spokesmen present him as an avatar or incarnation beyond any sort of criticism. Conservative writers and politicians seize on aspects of his thought that appear to support their agendas, ignoring or suppressing other aspects, while other writers and critics cite his works out of context to present him as one of the causes of India's social, political, and literary ills. Still others reject the religiosity of the devout and the zeal of one-sided critics and admirers in an attempt to arrive at a more balanced idea of what Sri Aurobindo was and what his legacy is and will be.

It is difficult to offer a balanced assessment of a man who is regarded by some as an incarnation of God and by others as a social and political reactionary. To accept Sri Aurobindo as an avatar is necessarily a matter of faith, and matters of faith quickly become matters of dogma. Besides, the term "avatar" has lost much of its glow in recent years. Once reserved for "descents" that come "from age to age,"[10] it now is applied to any spiritual leader with a halfway decent following. As for the label "reactionary," it is itself a reaction against Sri Aurobindo's appropriation by members of the Hindu Right, who claim his posthumous endorsement for their backward-looking programs.

The value of Sri Aurobindo's achievements can only be gauged by examining the historical and literary evidence and assessing the nature and effects of his thought and action. For this, assertions of supernatural influence are no more help than assertions of ideological certitude. Sri Aurobindo's role in changing the course of India's freedom struggle is evident from contemporary sources. Before him, no one dared to speak openly of independence; twenty years later, it became the movement's accepted goal. His focus on freedom made him give insufficient importance to social and cultural problems that continue to haunt the country, such as interreligious and intercaste conflict. But there is no contemporary evidence that his actions or words exacerbated these problems. Some of his ideas might, in fact, help to solve them—for example the idea that India's religious and ethnic diversity was "a great advantage for the work to be done" in the future.[11] As an author, Sri Aurobindo looked to nineteenth-century standards that were being overturned as he wrote. As a result, his prose and poetry seem dated today. It is likely, however, that they will continue to be read long after those who excoriate his style have been forgotten. As the fountainhead of a spiritual movement, he undoubtedly has, so to speak, a captive audience. But this is not enough to explain the continuing appeal of his works. Unlike many modernist and postmodernist writers, he did not think questions about the meaning and value of life to be off limits, and he offered ways for people to engage with such questions.

Sri Aurobindo's rank as a thinker and politician appears to be secure. But he did not consider his work in these fields to be the true measure of his worth. As he wrote to a disciple who wanted to spread his fame, "In my view, a man's value does not depend on what he learns or his position or fame or what he does, but on what he is or inwardly becomes."[12] He declined to supply this disciple with any details about his inner life, but his *Record of Yoga* gives an intimate glimpse below the surface of his thought and action. From the time he arrived in Pondicherry, he considered his actual work to be bringing down a new principle into the "earth-consciousness." It is impossible to say anything certain about the success or failure of this endeavor. In the *Record* and in late letters, he indicated that he had made some progress in this direction, but full success seemed always to lie just beyond his current achievement. In November 1926 he had an experience that he called the descent of the overmind, the highest of the powers of consciousness between the ordinary mind and the divine power that he called the supermind. All that remained was to "supramentalise the overmind." This process was still in progress twenty-one years later, when he spoke of it in the last known reference to the state of his *sadhana*.[13] He never announced that the process was complete. During his lifetime, he was often asked to write more about overmind and supermind. "What's the use?" he once replied. "How much would anybody understand? Besides the present business is to bring down and establish the Supermind, not to explain it. If it establishes itself, it will explain itself—if it does not, there is no use in explaining it."[14]

Sri Aurobindo was trying to bring down the power of the supermind because he saw it as the key to transforming the individual and society. While other yogas aimed only at liberating the individual, he foresaw a race of perfected individuals belonging to a gnostic society that "would be a collective soul-power of the Truth-Consciousness, even as the gnostic individual would be an individual soul-power of it." It would be a society that "would be and act not as a mechanical but a spiritual integer."[15] Such a society could only be established if many individuals opened themselves to higher levels of consciousness, but he never believed that this could come about through a popularizing movement or religion. As early as 1918 he wrote in *The Human Cycle,* "A religious movement brings usually a wave of spiritual excitement and aspiration that communicates itself to a large number of individuals and there is as a result a temporary uplifting and an effective formation, partly spiritual, partly ethical, partly dogmatic in its nature. But the wave after a generation or two or at most a few generations begins to subside; the formation remains."[16]

We are now in the second generation after Sri Aurobindo's passing. His work continues in his ashram, in the international community of Auroville near Pondicherry, in centers in India, the United States, and Europe, and in the minds and hearts of thousands of practitioners of his yoga. A superficial look at the organizations he inspired might give the impression that they constitute a movement of the sort he warned against in *The Human Cycle.* But a deeper look, not at organizational forms but at the practice of individuals, might give a different impression. And in the end, any attempt to transform human society must begin with individuals. As Sri Aurobindo wrote to a disciple in the mid 1930s: "After all, the best way to make Humanity progress is to move on oneself;—that may sound either individualistic or egoistic, but it isn't: it is only common sense."[17]

Notes

Part One: Son

Epigraph: Sri Aurobindo, letter to Nirodbaran, June 3, 1935, Nirodbaran, ed., *Correspondence with Sri Aurobindo,* 253.

1. Early Years in India

Epigraph: Sri Aurobindo, "The Awakening Soul of India," published in *Karmayogin,* 61–62.

1. W. W. Hunter, *Statistical Account,* 347–349; Government of Bengal (GOB) General Department (Miscellaneous) 1873, "General Report on the Rajshahye Division for 1872–73," 5, National Archives of Bangladesh.

2. In 1940 Sri Aurobindo said that he was born "in the lawyer Manmohan Ghose's house on Theatre Road" (See Nirodbaran, ed. *Talks with Sri Aurobindo,* 672). He evidently got this information from his family after his return from England in 1893. According to *The Bengal Directory,* Mano Mohun Ghose was living at 14 South Circular Road in August 1872. He lived at 4 Theatre Road between 1880 and 1895. According to two daughters of Mano Mohan Ghose, who presumably got the information from their father, Sri Aurobindo was born at 237 Lower Circular Road (Mrs. Showlata Das [née Ghose] to Nolini Kanta Gupta June 11, 1956, published in *Sri Aurobindo: Archives and Research* 1 (April 1977): 78–79; Nolini Kanta Gupta to Abinash Bhattacharya June 22, 1950 containing information given orally to Gupta by Mrs. Mrigen Mitra [née Ghose]; both letters in Sri Aurobindo Ashram Archives (SAAA). It is clear from entries and maps in *The Bengal Directory,* editions of 1871 to 1882, that the plot numbered 14 South Circular Road in 1872 was given the number 237 Lower Circular Road in 1881. After independence the name of Lower Circular Road was changed to Acharya Jagadish Chandra Road. The plot numbered 14 South Circular Road in 1872 is at present numbered 237 Acharya Jagadish Chandra Road.

3. Aurobindo to D. Roy, quoted in D. Roy, *Sri Aurobindo Came to Me,* 319.

4. Dr. Ghose spelled the name Aravinda. His son followed this practice during his early life, but when he settled in Bengal in 1906, he changed it to Aurobindo; to avoid confusion, I use this spelling throughout. Aurobindo spelled the middle name Acroyd, not Akroyd, before dropping it in 1893.

5. R. Bose, "A Society for the Promotion of National Feeling," 446.

6. R. Bose, *Rajnarayan Basur Atma-charita,* 79–80; S. Sastri, *History of the Brahmo Samaj,* 150–151.

7. K. D. Ghose to J. Bose, December 2, 1890, copy in SAAA.

8. W. Johnston, ed., *Roll of the Graduates,* 192.

9. Manmohan Ghose to Laurence Binyon, July 28, 1887, Laurence Binyon Papers, copy in SAAA.

10. K. Sen, *Keshub Chunder Sen in England,* 1.

11. B. De, "Reminiscences," 180; W. Johnston, ed., *Roll of the Graduates,* 192.

12. A. Purani, *Evening Talks,* 109.

13. K. D. Ghose to J. Bose, December 2, 1890, copy in SAAA.

14. K. Sen, *Keshub Chunder Sen in England,* 393; W. Beveridge, *India Called Them,* 84–85.

15. Annette Akroyd, pocket diary, 1871, Beveridge Papers, India Office Records, Oriental and India Office Library and Records, London.

16. J. Gupta, *Rangpur Today,* 1.

17. GOB *Bengal Civil List,* 1876, West Bengal State Archives; *History of Services of Gazetted Officers,* corrected up to 1887 and 1890, cited in T. K. Mukherjee, Director of Archives, Government of West Bengal, to Sri Aurobindo Ashram Archives, January 20, 1975.

18. Map published with Sir Richard Temple, "Minute," October 31, 1874, in GOB General Department, May 1875, National Archives of Bangladesh; J. Vas, *Eastern Bengal,* 34.

19. GOB Sanitation Department, Proceedings 1876–1878, 69, India Office Records, reference P/895.

20. Diary of Annette Beveridge, December 20, 1877, Beveridge Papers, India Office Records, published in *Sri Aurobindo: Archives and Research* 14 (April 1990): 95.

21. Henry Beveridge to Annette Beveridge, September 1879, Beveridge Papers, India Office Records, published in *Sri Aurobindo: Archives and Research* 14 (April 1990): 99.

22. Sri Aurobindo, *On Himself,* 5; Sri Aurobindo, note published in *Sri Aurobindo: Archives and Research* 1 (December 1977): 87.

23. B. Chakrabarti, "Amader Aurodada," 778.

24. Annette Akroyd to Fanny Akroyd, January 22, 1873, and Henry Beveridge to Annette Beveridge, October 3, 1877, Beveridge Papers, India Office Records, published in *Sri Aurobindo: Archives and Research* 14 (April 1990): 97, 99.

25. Manmohan Ghose to Laurence Binyon, February 18, 1888, Laurence Binyon Papers, copy in SAAA.

26. Annette Beveridge to Henry Beveridge, September 29, 1877, Beveridge Papers, India Office Records, published in *Sri Aurobindo: Archives and Research* 14 (December 1990): 98.

27. A. Purani, *Evening Talks,* 376–377.

28. K. D. Ghose to J. Bose, December 2, 1890 (copy SAAA).

29. B. Ghose, *Amar Atmakatha,* 15.

Part Two: Scholar

Epigraph: Sri Aurobindo, talk in 1938, published in Nirodbaran, ed., *Talks with Sri Aurobindo,* 79.

2. Growing up English

Epigraph: Sri Aurobindo, interview in *Empire*, May 8, 1909, reproduced in *Bengalee*, May 9, 1909.

1. *Manchester Street Directory*, 1881, ref. 914–273 M2, see also microfilm 844 M/C Directory 1874–1876; both items in Manchester Central Library, Local History Collection.

2. Sri Aurobindo, *Early Cultural Writings*, 474.

3. Sri Aurobindo, *On Himself*, 1.

4. Nirodbaran, ed., *Talks with Sri Aurobindo*, 376.

5. British Census Records, ref. RG11, 3918/15, 23, Public Record Office, London.

6. Sri Aurobindo, undated draft letter, published in *Mother India* 23 (February 1971), 15–16.

7. Sri Aurobindo, note published in *Sri Aurobindo: Archives and Research* 1 (December 1977): 88.

8. Purani Talks manuscripts 12: 212–213, in SAAA; Sri Aurobindo, *On Himself*, 137; *Letters on Yoga*, 1237; *Letters on Poetry and Art*, 206.

9. Anonymous [Sri Aurobindo], "Light," *Fox's Weekly*, January 11, 1883, republished in *Sri Aurobindo: Archives and Research* 9 (December 1985): 129.

10. Talk of Sri Aurobindo, in A. Purani, *Life*, 6–7.

11. Sri Aurobindo, *On Himself*, 4.

12. Sri Aurobindo, *On Himself*, 3; Sri Aurobindo, note published in *Sri Aurobindo: Archives and Research* 1 (December 1977): 85; *On Himself*, 4.

13. *Manchester Guardian*, March 21, 1881; church register, cited in A. Purani, *Life*, 7.

14. Interview in *Empire*, May 8, 1909, reprinted in *Bengalee*, May 9, 1909.

15. G. Chesterton, *Autobiography*, 74.

16. E. Bentley, *Those Days*, 58.

17. Nirodbaran, ed., *Correspondence*, 941.

18. Report of Class VII for half-year ending Christmas, St. Paul's School Records, St. Paul's School, London, published in *Sri Aurobindo: Archives and Research* 14 (April 1990): 99.

19. Arthur Wood in Government of India, Home Department Proceedings series D, June 1908, 13: 3, National Archives of India, New Delhi.; L. Binyon, "Introductory," 10; P. Sergeant, *The Ruler*, 140; R. S. Lepper quoted in H. Das, "Sri Aurobindo," 784–785.

20. Report of Class U VIII for half-year ending July 1888, St. Paul's School Records, published in *Sri Aurobindo: Archives and Research* 14 (April 1990): 100.

21. Nirodbaran, ed., *Talks*; Sri Aurobindo, *On Himself*, 1–2.

22. Reports of Class U VIII for half-year ending December 1887 and half-year ending December 1888, St. Paul's School Records, portions published in *Sri Aurobindo: Archives and Research* 14 (April 1990): 100–101.

23. H. Gardner, ed., *The New Oxford Book of English Verse*, 831–850.

24. *Pauline* (1888): 664; *Pauline*, vol. VII & VIII, no. 39 (December 1889): 52, St. Paul's School Records.

25. P. Sergeant, *The Ruler*, 140.

26. Government of India, Home Department Proceedings, series D, June 1908, 13: 3, National Archives of India.

27. Sri Aurobindo, *On Himself*, 4; letter to Mrinalini Bose, August 30, 1905, published in *Bangla Rachana*, 348–352.

28. Purani Talks manuscripts, 22: 9, 12, in SAAA; Government of India, Home Department Proceedings, series D, June 1908, 13: 3, National Archives of India; Sri Aurobindo, *On Himself*, 2.

29. Nirodbaran, ed. *Talks*, 123.

30. M. Ghose to L. Binyon, written at Hastings 1887, Laurence Binyon Papers, copy in SAAA.

31. M. Ghose to Binyon, July and October 1887 Laurence Binyon Papers, copy in SAAA.

32. Nirodbaran, ed. *Talks*, 123; Sri Aurobindo, *On Himself*, 2.

33. Government of India, Home Department Proceedings, series D, June 1908, 13: 3, National Archives of India.

34. Report of Class U VIII for half-year ending Christmas 1889, St. Paul's School Records, published in *Sri Aurobindo: Archives and Research* 4 (April 1990): 101; *Appositions*, Midsummer 1889, St. Paul's School Records.

35. Oscar Browning, quoted in K. D. Ghose to J. Bose, December 2, 1890, copy in SAAA.

36. India Office Records V(21)2174, General Instructions to the Candidates Selected at the Open Competition of June, 1890, reprinted in "Final Examination of Candidates Selected in 1890 for the Civil Service of India, July 1892," 5.

37. India Office Records V(21)2174, 82.

38. Government of India, Home Department Proceedings, series D, June 1908, 13: 3, National Archives of India.

39. Sri Aurobindo, "Sri Aurobindo: A Life-Sketch," published in *Sri Aurobindo: Archives and Research* 9 (April 1985): 66; India Office Records, *Indian Civil Service Open Competition 1890*, 82.

40. Sri Aurobindo, *On Himself*, 2; Tutor's Book, vol. 1, 1874–1918, King's College Records, King's College Library, King's College, Cambridge.

41. Sri Aurobindo, *Early Cultural Writings*, 354.

42. Sri Aurobindo, *Early Cultural Writings*, 354.

43. *Cambridge University Calendar for the Year 1891*, 598, King's College Records.

44. Oscar Browning, quoted in K.D. Ghose to J. Bose, December 2, 1890, copy in SAAA.

45. Room charts 1890–1892, King's College Records.

46. India Office Records V (21) 2174, 3–9.

47. Sri Aurobindo, *On Himself*, 10–11; Nirodbaran, ed., *Talks*, 1016.

48. Sri Aurobindo, *On Himself*, 366.

49. India Office Records V (21) 2174, 5–8.

50. K.D. Ghose to J. Bose, December 2, 1890, in SAAA.

51. India Office Records L/PJ/6/333, Prothero to J. Cotton, November 20, 1892.

52. Sri Aurobindo, *Early Cultural Writings,* 353.

53. R.S. Lepper and anonymous former classmate, quoted in H. Das, "Sri Aurobindo," 784–785.

54. Nirodbaran Talks manuscripts 17: 242, in SAAA; Nirodbaran Talks manuscripts 19: 3.

55. Sri Aurobindo, *On Himself,* 4; Nirodbaran, ed., *Talks,* 955.

56. Sri Aurobindo, *Bande Mataram,* 3.

57. Sri Aurobindo, *On Himself,* 383; *Letters on Poetry and Art,* 522; *Life Divine,* 299; Sri Aurobindo, note published in *Sri Aurobindo: Archives and Research* 7 (December 1983): 163–64.

58. E. Forster, *Dickinson,* 85; B. Russell, *Autobiography,* 56–74.

59. Sri Aurobindo, note published in *Sri Aurobindo: Archives and Research* 7 (December 1983): 164; Sri Aurobindo, *On Himself,* 223, Nirodbaran, ed., *Talks,* 302, 530; Nirodbaran Talks manuscripts 19: 3.

60. India Office Records L/PJ/6/333, Prothero to J. Cotton, November 20, 1892.

61. Sri Aurobindo, *Collected Poems,* 8.

62. E. Forster, *Aspects,* 120.

63. Sri Aurobindo, *Early Cultural Writings,* 110; *On Himself,* 255; *Future Poetry,* 5.

64. Sri Aurobindo, *On Himself,* 254; *Future Poetry,* 5.

65. Sri Aurobindo, *Collected Poems,* 11, 15, 26. In earlier editions "The Lost Deliverer" is entitled "Ferdinand Lassalle."

66. Nirodbaran Talks manuscripts 17: 143.

67. Sri Aurobindo, *Collected Poems,* 18.

68. Sri Aurobindo, *Collected Poems,* 9.

69. Sri Aurobindo, poetic fragment published in *Sri Aurobindo: Archives and Research* 9 (December 1985): 130.

70. Sri Aurobindo, *Early Cultural Writings,* 3–7.

71. Sri Aurobindo, *Early Cultural Writings,* 11–77.

72. *Cambridge University Calendar for the Year 1891,* 599, King's College Records.

73. *Cambridge University Calendar for the Year 1892–1893,* 614–615, 294, King's College Records.

74. Anonymous former classmate, quoted in H. Das, "Sri Aurobindo," 785.

75. Government of India, Home Department Proceedings, series D, June 1908, 13: 3, National Archives of India.

76. Nirodbaran, ed., *Talks,* 39.

77. V. Chirol, *Indian Unrest,* 291.

78. Sri Aurobindo, *Bande Mataram,* 58–59.

79. A. Purani, *Evening Talks,* 547.

80. India Office Records V (21) 2174, 138–139.

81. India Office Records V (21) 2174, 138–139.

82. India Office Records L/PJ/6/326.

83. Government of India, Home Department Proceedings, series D, June 1908, 13: 3, National Archives of India.

84. Lepper quoted in H. Das, "Sri Aurobindo," 484–485.

85. Sri Aurobindo, note published in *Sri Aurobindo: Archives and Research* 1 (December 1977): 88.

86. Nirodbaran, ed., *Talks*, 241.

87. F. Müller, *The Upanishads*, 312.

88. F. Müller, *The Upanishads*, xxx.

89. Sri Aurobindo, note published in *Sri Aurobindo: Archives and Research* 1 (December 1977): 88.

90. F. Müller, *The Upanishads*, xii; quoted by Aurobindo in *Kena and Other Upanishads*, 164.

91. Sri Aurobindo, *Kena and Other Upanishads*, 164.

92. Sri Aurobindo, *On Himself*, 4.

93. India Office Records L/JP/6/333, Memorandum by the Senior Examiner, Civil Service Commission Respecting the Examination in Riding, November 16, 1892; India Office Records L/JP/6/325, Hennell to Under Secretary of State, November 17, 1892.

94. India Office Records L/JP/6/333, Aurobindo to Kimberley, November 21, 1892.

95. India Office Records L/JP/6/325; L/JP /6/327, Kimberley note dated September 9, 1892.

96. India Office Records L/JP/6/333, Kimberley note dated December 2, 1892.

97. Sri Aurobindo, *On Himself*, 3.

98. Sri Aurobindo, note published in *Mother India* 32 (March 1971): 102; Sri Aurobindo, note published in *Sri Aurobindo: Archives and Research* 1 (December 1977): 89.

99. Interview in *Empire*, May 8, 1909, reprinted in *Bengalee*, May 9, 1909.

100. Government of India, Foreign and Political Department, Gen. Conf. B, 1914, no. 2, 9.

101. Sri Aurobindo, *On Himself*, 10, 4.

102. Kimberly and Lansdowne quoted in B. Chandra, *Modern India*, 158.

103. A. Purani, *Evening Talks*, 617; Nirodbaran, ed., *Talks*, 159; Sri Aurobindo, *On Himself*, 6; Sri Aurobindo, note published in *Sri Aurobindo: Archives and Research* 1 (December 1977): 88–89.

104. B. De, "Reminiscences," 181.

105. See P. Heehs, "Genius," 53–54, for a discussion of Swarnalotta's insanity.

106. B. Ghose, *Amar Atmakatha*, 29.

107. B. Ghose, "Sri Aurobindo as I Understand Him," 9.

108. B. De, "Reminiscences," 181. About the lost ship, see the *Times* (London), October 29 and 31, 1892; *Bengalee* (Calcutta) November 5, 1892; note that even in Caluctta the loss of the ship was known six weeks before K. D. Ghose's death. For Sri Aurobindo's version, see Nirodbaran, ed., *Talks*, 123.

109. B. De, "Reminiscences," 181. The exact date of Dr Ghose's death is unknown. Bengal government records give the date of his "retirement" as December 11, a Sunday. His replacement was appointed on December 15. Death notices were published in the *Amrita Bazar Patrika* on the fifteenth and the *Bengalee* on the seventeenth.

110. Sri Aurobindo, note published in *Sri Aurobindo: Archives and Research* 1 (December 1977): 85; Sri Aurobindo, *On Himself*, 7.

111. Nautical Reports 1893–1895, National Maritime Museum; Board of Trade passenger lists (BT 27/135), Public Record Office.

112. H. Nevinson, *The New Spirit*, 118.

113. Nirodbaran, ed., *Talks*, 79.

114. Sri Aurobindo, *On Himself*, 7.

115. Sri Aurobindo, *On Himself*, 7; *Collected Poems*, 28.

116. Purani Talks manuscripts 12: 211; Nirodbaran, ed., *Talks*, 241; 106; Sri Aurobindo, *On Himself*, 50, 98.

3. Encountering India

Epigraph: Sri Aurobindo, "Sri Aurobindo: A Life-Sketch," published in *Sri Aurobindo: Archives and Research* 9 (April 1985): 66–67.

1. Aurobindo's first work order, dated February 18, 1893, says that his service in the state would "commence from the 8th instant," that is, February 8. See Dewan Kutcherry, Vernacular Branch, no. 4762, Baroda State Records, Baroda Record Office, Vadodara.

2. J. R. MacDonald, *The Awakening of India*, 18.

3. Sri Aurobindo, *On Himself*, 7.

4. Dewan Kutcherry, Vernacular Branch, no. 4762, Baroda State Records.

5. Aurobindo to Rajnarain Bose, January 11, 1894, published in *Sri Aurobindo: Archives and Research* 2 (April 1978): 86.

6. Sri Aurobindo, *On Himself*, 9; Sri Aurobindo, note published in *Sri Aurobindo: Archives and Research* 2 (April 1978): 84, 85.

7. Kuvarjee (Diwan) to Sabnis (Huzar Chitnis), January 10, 1895, published in V. Sangave and B. Khane, eds., *Rajarshi Shahu Chhatrapati Papers*, 51.

8. Banerjea quoted by Aurobindo in "New Lamps for Old," published in *Bande Mataram*, 32.

9. Sri Aurobindo, *Bande Mataram*, 7–8.

10. Sri Aurobindo, *Bande Mataram*, 10.

11. Hume quoted in B. Chandra, *Modern India*, 207.

12. A. Mazumdar, *Indian National Evolution*, 100.

13. Sri Aurobindo, *Bande Mataram*, 9.

14. Sri Aurobindo, *Bande Mataram*, 14, 18, 21, 60, 29.

15. Sri Aurobindo, note published in *Sri Aurobindo: Archives and Research* 7 (December 1983): 166.

16. Sri Aurobindo, *Bande Mataram*, 19, 46, 50.

17. B. Ghose, "Sri Aurobindo as I Understand Him," 7; S. Sastri, *History*, 212–214; D. Kopf, *Brahmo Samaj*, 182. The phrase "Hindu Brahmo" is something of an oxymoron, akin to "Jewish Christian."

18. Sarojini Ghose, oral statement to Girijashankar Raychaudhuri, July 5, 1940, quoted in G. Raychaudhuri, *Sri Aurobindo*, 107–108.

19. B. Ghose, "Sri Aurobindo," 11; Sarojini Ghose, oral statement to Girijashankar Raychaudhuri, July 5, 1940, quoted in G. Raychaudhuri, *Sri Aurobindo,* 107–108.

20. Sri Aurobindo, *Supplement,* 420.

21. Sri Aurobindo, *Early Cultural Writings,* 92, 102, 109, 119, 118.

22. Sri Aurobindo, *Early Cultural Writings,* 116, 117, 96, 109.

23. P. Sergeant, *Ruler of Baroda,* 95; S. Karandikar, *Lokamanya,* 115.

24. Telegram from Dorabji to Angre, received May 24, 1895, Baroda State Records.

25. Telegrams from Ghose to Angre, May 26; Ghose to Angre, June 1; Angre to Ghose, June 13, 1895, Baroda State Records.

26. Huzur Order, October 10, 1895 (BSR Huzur Order Book 1895–96, serial number 249), Baroda State Records.

27. Letter to Dewan, January 14, 1897, Baroda State Records.

28. Tippan by Tait February 4, 1898, sanctioned by Dalal February 9, 1898, Baroda State Records.

29. J. R. MacDonald, *Awakening,* 18.

30. Sri Aurobindo, *On Himself,* 31.

31. Purani Talks manuscripts 9: 73, in SAAA.

32. Sri Aurobindo, *Early Cultural Writings,* 125–143.

33. Nirodbaran, ed., *Talks,* 78; Purani Talks manuscripts 9: 73; S. Didmishe, Reminiscences, in SAAA; R. S. Dalal in A. Trivedi, ed., *Baroda College,* 46; M. K. Sharangpani in A. Trivedi, ed., *Baroda College,* 39; Nirodbaran, ed., *Talks,* 79; R. Patkar, Reminiscences, in SAAA.

34. M. N. Kantavala in A. Trivedi, ed., *Baroda College,* 24; R. Patkar, Reminiscences; S. Didmishe, Reminiscences.

35. R. Patkar, Reminiscences.

36. B. Chakrabarti, "Amader Aurodada," 776–777.

37. B. Ghose, "Sri Aurobindo," 7.

38. D. Ray, *Aurobindo Prasanga,* 14–15, 8.

39. Huzur Kamdar to Dewan August 23, 1896, Baroda College Records, Maharaja Sayajirao University, Vadodara, Gujarat, copy in SAAA.

40. D. Ray, *Aurobindo Prasanga,* 6–7.

41. Sri Aurobindo, note published in *Sri Aurobindo: Archives and Research* 2 (December 1978): 194.

42. D. Ray, *Aurobindo Prasanga,* 8; B. Ghose, "Sri Aurobindo," 22.

43. B. Ghose, "Sri Aurobindo," 22; Didmishe reminiscences; Purani Talks manuscripts 16: 691; D. Ray, *Aurobindo Prasanga,* 29.

44. D. Ray, *Aurobindo Prasanga,* 12–13.

45. R. Patkar, Reminiscences.

46. R. Patkar, Reminiscences.

47. D. Ray, *Aurobindo Prasanga,* 29, 20.

48. D. Ray, *Aurobindo Prasanga,* 43.

49. B. Ghose, "Sri Aurobindo," 61.

50. Sri Aurobindo, *Early Cultural Writings,* 107.

51. D. Ray, *Aurobindo Prasanga,* 21–22.

52. Manmohan Ghose to Rabindranath Tagore, October 24, 1894 [error for 1898], Rabindranath Tagore Papers, published in *Sri Aurobindo: Archives and Research* 12 (April 1988): 87.

53. Sri Aurobindo, *Letters on Poetry and Art,* 223.

54. Sri Aurobindo, *On Himself,* 234.

55. Sri Aurobindo, *On Himself,* 267.

56. Sri Aurobindo, *Early Cultural Writings,* 266–270.

57. Sri Aurobindo, *Supplement,* 160.

58. Sri Aurobindo, *On Himself,* 267.

59. Sri Aurobindo, *Collected Poems,* 248.

60. D. Ray, *Aurobindo Prasanga,* 31; Sri Aurobindo, *On Himself,* 9, 10.

61. Tippan by Tait September 5, 1900, followed by Huzur Orders September 29, 1909 and November 4, 1900, Baroda College Records.

62. Huzur Order November 30, 1900, Baroda College Records.

63. Manubhai to Tait April 15, 1901 and Huzur Order April 19, 1901, Baroda College Records.

64. R. Patkar, Reminiscences 14; D. Ray, *Aurobindo Prasanga,* 55; B. Ghose, "Sri Aurobindo," 23.

65. Sri Aurobindo, *Early Cultural Writings,* 153.

66. Information given by Nolini Kanta Gupta to T. V. Kapali Sastry, recorded in Purani Talks manuscripts 5: 97; statement by Sisir Bose (Mrinalini's brother), published in *Sri Aurobindo: Archives and Research* 2 (December 1978): 205.

67. Aurobindo to Acting Principal, Baroda College, July 28, 1900, Baroda College Records.

68. B. Ghose, "Sri Aurobindo," 13.

69. J. Hardie, "A Scamper Round the World," 388.

70. The date is recorded as Baishakh 16, 1308, Bengali era. This corresponds to April 29, 1901.

71. Sri Aurobindo, *Early Cultural Writings,* 332.

72. A. Purani, *Life of Sri Aurobindo,* 50.

73. Sri Aurobindo, Notebook G5, 2, 4, 6, 8, 10, 14, in SAAA.

74. B. Bose, "Mrinalini Ghose" (reminiscences), August 26, 1931, Sri Aurobindo Papers, in SAAA.

75. Sri Aurobindo, *Isha Upanishad,* 138–139.

76. For Sri Aurobindo's general knowledge of human sexuality, see his letters to disciples on sex, which occupy more than forty pages, 1507–1549, of *Letters on Yoga.* For his experience of *maithunananda,* see *Record of Yoga,* 204, 300, 302, 329, 431, 464, 774, and 1456. *Maithunananda* means literally the bliss, *ananda,* of coitus, *maithuna.* In the *Record* it refers to a particular intensity of spontaneous erotic delight, but some references, notably on page 204 ("equal to the first movements of the actual maithuna ananda") seem to imply a knowledge of ordinary *maithuna.* Sri Aurobindo never spoke directly about his experience or lack of experience of sex, but he did refer to the subject indirectly. In 1936 he wrote to his disciple Nirodbaran, who was complaining about the difficulty of overcoming anger and sexual

desire, "I was also noted in my earlier time before Yoga for the rareness of anger. At a certain period of the Yoga it rose in me like a volcano and I had to take a long time eliminating it. As for sex—well. You are always thinking that the things that are happening to you are unique and nobody else ever had such trials or downfalls or misery before." See Nirodbaran, ed., *Correspondence,* 748. When Nirodbaran asked him why spiritual teachers such as Confucius or Sri Aurobindo got married, he replied: "Perfectly natural—they marry before the [spiritual] change—then the change comes and the marriage belongs to the past self, not to the new one." See Nirodbaran, ed., *Correspondence,* 576. A half-century later, Nirodbaran alluded to this exchange in a talk about Mrinalini. He concluded: "Why did Sri Aurobindo marry? As far as I have understood his philosophy of life, he was from the beginning holding the view that life is not an illusion; he refused even to accept a yoga which rejected life. The wholeness, the integrality of the experience of life was his doctrine. . . . And love through marriage playing a very important role could not be excluded from the pursuit of his avataric mission which meant to change the world. That experience left out would not give the seal of completeness to that mission or enable him to say to us, 'This experience also I have had.'" See Nirodbaran, *Mrinalini Devi,* 28. For Sri Aurobindo's own views on the avatar and sex, see Nirodbaran, ed., *Correspondence,* 169, and N. Doshi, ed., *Guidance,* 280–281.

77. R. Patkar, Reminiscences.

78. B. Ghose, "Sri Aurobindo," 33B.

79. Aurobindo to Bhupalchandra Bose June 8, 1906, published in *Sri Aurobindo: Archives and Research* 1 (December 1977): 85.

80. B. Ghose, "Sri Aurobindo," 22.

81. Sri Aurobindo, *Early Cultural Writings,* 284, 305.

82. Sri Aurobindo, *Early Cultural Writings,* 332.

83. Sri Aurobindo, *Kena and Other Upanishads,* 339. Sri Aurobindo crossed out "of Vedanta" but did not complete his revision of the sentence.

84. Sri Aurobindo, *Translations,* 85.

85. Sri Aurobindo, *Early Cultural Writings,* 261–262.

86. Sri Aurobindo, *Early Cultural Writings,* 151.

87. Huzur Order, April 19, 1901, Baroda State Records; K. Singh, *Prophet of Indian Nationalism,* 43; Sri Aurobindo, note published in *Sri Aurobindo: Archives and Research* 2 (December 1978): 197.

88. Huzur Orders November 30, 1900 and April 19, 1901, Baroda State Records; note published in *Sri Aurobindo: Archives and Research* 2 (April 1978): 85.

89. Sri Aurobindo, *Early Cultural Writings,* 725.

90. Aurobindo to Jogindranath Bose, August 15, 1902, published in *Sri Aurobindo: Archives and Research* 1 (April 1977): 68.

91. Sri Aurobindo, *On Himself,* 23.

92. Chapekar quoted in *Source Material for a History of the Freedom Movement in India,* 979.

93. Sri Aurobindo, "To the Boers," published in *Sri Aurobindo: Archives and Research* 2 (April 1978): 23–30.

94. Sri Aurobindo, *On Himself,* 21.

95. See P. Heehs, *The Bomb in Bengal,* 20, for a discussion of the date.

96. Sri Aurobindo, *On Himself,* 23.

97. P. Das, *Amar Jiban Kahini,* 103.

98. Sri Aurobindo, *Bangla Rachana,* 347.

99. Aurobindo to Jogindranath Bose, August 15, 1902, published in *Sri Aurobindo: Archives and Research* 1 (April 1977): 71–72.

100. Huzur Order August 6, 1902, published in *Sri Aurobindo: Archives and Research* 1 (April 1977): 77

101. Aurobindo to Jogindranath Bose August 15, 1902, published in *Sri Aurobindo: Archives and Research* 1 (April 1977): 74; Aurobindo to Mrinalini Bose, August 20, 1902, published in *Sri Aurobindo: Archives and Research* 1 (April 1977): 75.

102. Aurobindo to Mrinalini Ghose August 20, 1902, published in *Sri Aurobindo: Archives and Research* 1 (April 1977): 75.

103. Aurobindo to Jogindranath Bose August 15, 1902, published in *Sri Aurobindo: Archives and Research* 1 (April 1977): 70.

104. Sri Aurobindo, *Bangla Rachana,* 347.

105. Aurobindo to Mrinalini Ghose August 20, 1902, published in *Sri Aurobindo: Archives and Research* 1 (April 1977): 76.

106. Dewan to Aurobindo August 30, 1902, Baroda State Records.

107. India Office Records V/10/197, Oriental and India Office Library and Records, London.

108. T. Sukal, "Such Was Sri Aurobindo and Such the Maharaja," 103.

109. Nivedita to J. MacLeod, July 24, 1902; Nivedita to Swami Brahmananda, July 18, 1902: both published in S. Basu, ed., *Letters of Sister Nivedita,* 482; Atmaprana, *Sister Nivedita,* 141.

110. Sri Aurobindo, *On Himself,* 69, see also 58.

111. Atmaprana, *Sister Nivedita,* 147.

112. Sri Aurobindo, *On Himself,* 4.

113. Nirodbaran, ed., *Talks with Sri Aurobindo,* 952.

114. Sri Aurobindo, *Early Cultural Writings,* 694–721.

115. S. Banerjea, 1902 address reproduced in *Congress Presidential Addresses,* 619.

116. Sri Aurobindo, *On Himself,* 25.

117. Sri Aurobindo, *Bande Mataram,* 65–66.

118. B. Ghose, *Agnijug,* 40, 51.

119. A. Bhattacharya, "Aurobindo," 831. Also A. Bhattacharya, "Baiplabik Samitir Prarambh Kaler Itihas," 190; B. Ghose, *Agnijug,* 58.

120. P. Sergeant, *Ruler of Baroda,* 106.

121. Undated draft letter in reply to Resident's letter of February 11, 1903, Baroda State Records.

122. Sri Aurobindo, *On Himself,* 23.

123. H. Kanungo, *Banglay Biplab Pracheshta,* 19–20.

124. Alipore Bomb Trial Records, Exhibit 291/01, Smaraniyo Bichar Sangraha, Alipore Court Complex, Kolkata.

125. Sri Aurobindo, *On Himself,* 352.

126. Sri Aurobindo, *Kena,* 319.

127. Sri Aurobindo, *Kena,* 163–70; K. Deshpande, "Yoga Mysticism," 302; Sri Aurobindo, note published in *Sri Aurobindo: Archives and Research* 2 (December 1978): 198.

128. Sri Aurobindo, *On Himself,* 50.

129. Sri Aurobindo, *Collected Poems,* 154.

130. Sri Aurobindo, note published in *Archives and Research* 2 (December 1978), 198.

131. Sri Aurobindo, *Collected Poems,* 153.

132. Letter Aravind A. Ghose to Dewan, August 21, 1903, Baroda State Records.

133. Sri Aurobindo, "Sri Aurobindo: A Life-Sketch," in *Sri Aurobindo: Archives and Research* 9 (April 1985): 67

134. Sri Aurobindo, *On Himself,* 21, 14.

135. A. Purani, *Evening Talks,* 601; Sri Aurobindo, *On Himself,* 16; *Bande Mataram,* 824; talk of July 1, 1926, in SAAA.

136. Fraser note, March 28, 1903, quoted in R. Cronin, *British Policy and Administration in Bengal,* 11.

137. Sri Aurobindo, *Bande Mataram,* 70–71.

138. A. Bhattacharya, "Baiplabik Samitir Prarambh Kaler Itihas," 193–194; A. Bhattacharya, "Aurobindo," 833–834.

139. H. Kanungo, *Banglay Biplab,* 29.

140. B. Ghose, "Sri Aurobindo," 37.

141. H. Dalal, Opinion dated August 5, 1904, on Tippan No. 1, dated August 2, 1904, Baroda College Records.

142. B. Ghose, *Agnijug,* 111–12. For Barin's return to Baroda, see *Agnijug,* 106.

143. G. Gokhale, Reminiscences of Sri Aurobindo in Baroda, in SAAA.

144. B. Ghose, "Sri Aurobindo," 13.

145. Aurobindo to the Maharaja, March 29, 1905, with subsequent action, Baroda State Records.

146. G. Natesan, "Japan: Its Message to India," 1.

147. H. Cotton, 1904 address reproduced in *Congress Presidential Addresses,* 14, 18.

148. S. Gaekwar, *Speeches and Addresses,* 174. The quotation is from the seventh chapter of Charles Kingsley's novel *Westward Ho!*

149. B. Ghose, "Sri Aurobindo," 34, P. Chandwani, "Sri Aurobindo: A Few Reminiscences," 468; Chandwani in H. Singh, "Sri Aurobindo through the Eyes of One of His Students," 25; S. Didmishe, Reminiscences.

150. B. Ghose, "Sri Aurobindo," 20.

151. Sri Aurobindo Papers: list of books in Notebook G10, 91, dated August to December; the year is probably 1904.

152. Sri Aurobindo, *Isha Upanishad,* 110–112.

153. Sri Aurobindo, *Early Cultural Writings,* 213; *Kena,* 374, 385.

154. Sri Aurobindo, *On Himself,* 65.

155. Sri Aurobindo, *Record of Yoga,* 128; R. Patkar, Reminiscences.

156. Sri Aurobindo, *On Himself,* 65.

157. Sri Aurobindo, *Bande Mataram*, 79–92.

158. Nirodbaran, ed. *Talks*, 499; see also Sri Aurobindo, *On Himself*, 51.

159. Government of India Home Department Proceedings, series A, February 1904 (Note of December 6, 1904), National Archives of India, quoted in Sumit Sarkar, *The Swadeshi Movement in Bengal*, 18.

160. Lord Curzon, speech at Dacca, February 18, 1904, quoted in J. McLane, "The Decision to Partition Bengal in 1905," 228.

161. *Sanjivani*, July 13, 1906, in Government of Bengal, *Report on Native Newspapers in Bengal*, 1906.

162. Sri Aurobindo, *Early Cultural Writings*, 600.

163. Sri Aurobindo, *Early Cultural Writings*, 600; *On Himself*, 51, 201, 355; Nirodbaran, ed. *Talks*, 473–474; G. Jadhav, Reminiscences of Sri Aurobindo, in SAAA.

164. Sri Aurobindo, *On Himself*, 90.

165. Sri Aurobindo, *Letters on Yoga*, 481; Nirodbaran, ed. *Talks*, 107.

166. Sri Aurobindo, *Isha Upanishad*, 196.

167. Sri Aurobindo, *On Himself*, 352–353.

168. Sri Aurobindo, *On Himself*, 51, 352–353; B. Ghose, "Sri Aurobindo," 41–42.

169. Sri Aurobindo, *Collected Poems*, 139.

170. Nirodbaran, ed. *Talks*, 108; cf. Sri Aurobindo, *On Himself*, 34.

171. Nirodbaran, ed. *Talks*, 107.

172. Sri Aurobindo, *Bangla Rachana*, 348–352.

173. Mrinalini Ghose, annotations to letter from Aurobindo to Mrinalini, August 30, 1905, in SAAA. Her remarks in Bengali are: "*bara mishti shabda*" (referring to *pagali*) and "*dhanya! dhanya!! jiban!!*"

174. Sri Aurobindo, *Early Cultural Writings*, 747–748; Tippan by Aravind A. Ghose July 15, 1905, with Order by Dewan July 29, 1905, Baroda College Records, published in *Early Cultural Writings*, 747–749.

175. Sri Aurobindo, *Bangla Rachana*, 352.

176. Sri Aurobindo, *Bangla Rachana*, 353.

177. R. Patkar, Reminiscences.

178. Sri Aurobindo, *Isha Upanishad*, 215–216.

179. R. Majumdar, *History of the Freedom Movement in India*, 87.

180. Sri Aurobindo, *Bande Mataram*, 100–103.

181. Sri Aurobindo, *On Himself*, 35.

182. S. Deb, "Sri Aurobindo as I Knew Him," 21.

183. G. Khaparde, diary, December 27, 1905 and January 1, 1906, National Archives of India; Tilak to Krishnavarma, February 9, 1906, Lokmanya Tilak Papers, Kesari-Mahratta Office, Pune.

184. S. Didmishe, Reminiscences.

185. P. Chandwani, "Sri Aurobindo," 469; A.B. Clarke quoted in C. Reddy, "Sir C.R. Reddy's Address," 2.

186. K. Munshi, "Kulapati's Letter on Life, Literature & Culture," 10.

187. *Rodogune* (Baroda draft) Act II, scene 1, in SAAA.

188. *Rodogune* (Baroda draft) Act IV, scene 4.

189. R. Patkar, Reminiscences ("answered" is an editorial emendation for "heard").

190. S. Didmishe, Reminiscences.

191. Sri Aurobindo, *Bangla Rachana,* 354–55.

Part Three: Revolutionary

Epigraph: Sri Aurobindo, letter to Balkrishna Shivaram Moonje, August 30, 1920, published in *On Himself,* 433.

4. Into the Fray

Epigraph: Sri Aurobindo, Letter to Joseph Baptista, January 5, 1920, published in *On Himself,* 430.

1. J. Bannerji, "Aurobindo Ghose—A Study," 476.

2. Sri Aurobindo, *On Himself,* 24.

3. Sri Aurobindo, *Amader Rajanitik Adarsh,* published in *Sri Aurobindo: Archives and Research* 15 (December 1991): 234–237 (trans. Richard Hartz).

4. Government of India, Home Department Proceedings, series A, June 1906, 152–168, 26, National Archives of India, New Delhi; S. Deb, "Sri Aurobindo as I Knew Him," 21.

5. Sri Aurobindo, *Bande Mataram,* 291.

6. S. Deb, "Sri Aurobindo," 21.

7. Oral history transcript, Surendra Mohan Ghose Papers, Nehru Memorial Museum and Library, New Delhi.

8. S. Deb, "Sri Aurobindo," 21.

9. A. Roy, ed., "Conversations with Sri Aurobindo," *Sri Aurobindo Circle* 35 (1979): 17.

10. *Bengalee,* May 15 and 16, 1906; J. Armstrong, *An Account of the Revolutionary Organization in Eastern Bengal,* 6; *Second Supplementary Report on Samitis,* 9.

11. National Council of Education Records, *Report of the National Council of Education, Bengal* (1907–1909), Appendix G, National Council of Education, Jadavpur University, Kolkara.

12. Letter from Aurobindo to Bhupalchandra Bose, June 8, 1906, published in *Sri Aurobindo: Archives and Research* 1 (December 1977): 85–86.

13. Sri Aurobindo, *Collected Plays and Stories,* 398, 484.

14. Sri Aurobindo, *Collected Plays and Stories,* 481, 487.

15. National Council of Education Records, manuscript minutes, July 24 and August 11, 1906.

16. Letter from R. N. Madhokar to D. Wacha July 15, 1906, P. Mehta Papers, microfilm, roll 2, National Archives of India, New Delhi; Khaparde cited by Madholkar in the same letter.

17. S. Wolpert, *Morley and India 1906–1910,* 99.

18. S. Deb "When He Was a Political Leader," ix; "Sri Aurobindo," 21–22; Sri Aurobindo, *On Himself,* 28, 42, 59; Diary of Hemendra Prasad Ghose, July 31–August 5, Department of History, Jadavpur University, Kolkata.

19. B. Debsharma, "Aurobindo," 754.

20. National Council of Education Records, Seventh and Fifth Standard Examinations, 1906.

21. S. Deb, "Sri Aurobindo," 22; R. Mookerji, "Some Reminiscences of Sri Aurobindo," 21; "Foreword," viii.

22. Sri Aurobindo, *On Himself,* 45; see also 27, 28, 42; H. Ghose, "Reminiscences of Aurobindo Ghose," 12.

23. Sri Aurobindo, *Bande Mataram,* 175.

24. Sri Aurobindo, *Bande Mataram,* 159.

25. Sri Aurobindo, *Bande Mataram,* September 6, 1906, quoted in the *Times* (London), September 10, 1906, 4.

26. Diary of Hemendra Prasad Ghose, October 24, 1906.

27. Nirodbaran, ed., *Talks with Sri Aurobindo,* 108, 953.

28. Sri Aurobindo, *On Himself,* 29; B. Pal, *Leaders of the Nationalist Movement in Bengal,* 120.

29. Nirodbaran, ed., *Talks,* 111.

30. Sri Aurobindo, Undated memo, published in Sri Aurobindo, *Bande Mataram,* 1134.

31. Sri Aurobindo, *On Himself,* 59; Diary of Hemendra Prasad Ghose, December 12–13, 1906.

32. Sukumar Sen's deposition in sessions court, Alipore Bomb Trial Records, Smaraniyo Bichar Sangraha, Alipore Court Complex, Kolkata; U. Bannerjee, "Aurobindo Prasanga," 6.

33. Diary of Hemendra Prasad Ghose, November 5 and 7, 1906; Government of India, Home Department Proceedings, series A, March 1910: 33–40, 32, 62; Government of Bengal Pol. Conf. 286 of 1908, West Bengal State Archives, Kolkata.

34. Sri Aurobindo, *Bande Mataram,* 201–204.

35. Diary of G. Khaparde, December 31, 1906, National Archives of India, New Delhi.

36. Diary of G. Khaparde, December 31, 1906; Diary of Hemendra Prasad Ghose, December 27, 1906; Sri Aurobindo, *Bande Mataram,* 850; *On Himself,* 15 (footnote), 27, 28, 29; Madan Mohan Malaviya in S. Bapat, *Reminiscences and Anecdotes of Lokamanya Tilak,* 170–171; Lajpat Rai in S. Bapat, *Reminiscences,* 181; From Minto 1907, item 1, Minto Papers, National Archives of Scotland, Edinburgh; D. Tahmankar, *Lokamanya Tilak,* 122.

37. Tilak to Krishnavarma, January 18, 1906, Lokmanya Tilak Papers, Kesari-Mahratta Office, Pune.

38. Bhupendranath Bose to Mehta, January 14, 1907, P. Mehta Papers, National Archives of India, New Delhi; Motilal Nehru to Jawaharlal Nehru, December 27, 1906, quoted in S. Singh, "Moderates and Extremists," 161; *Times* (London) January 2, 1907, quoted in D. Tahmankar, *Lokamanya Tilak,* 121–122.

39. Sri Aurobindo, *Bande Mataram,* 205–208.

40. Minto quoted in M. Minto, *India, Minto and Morley 1905–1910,* 46–47.

41. R. Sethi, *The Last Phase of British Sovereignty in India*, 11.

42. *Jugantar*, October 27, 1906 (official translation in Government of Bengal *Report on Native Newspapers in Bengal*).

43. Sri Aurobindo, *Bande Mataram*, 218, 223.

44. Sri Aurobindo, *Bande Mataram*, 220

45. A. Roy, "Sri Aurobindo Ghose—Memories of Long Ago," 7.

46. Diary of Hemendra Prasad Ghose, January 6–10, 1906; Aurobindo's statement in *Bande Mataram* case, Alipore Bomb Trial Records.

47. Sri Aurobindo, *Collected Plays and Stories*, 864.

48. Sri Aurobindo, *Collected Plays and Stories*, 909.

49. Sri Aurobindo, *Bande Mataram*, 210–211.

50. Sri Aurobindo, *Bande Mataram*, 266.

51. Sri Aurobindo, *Bande Mataram*, 269

52. Sri Aurobindo, *Bande Mataram*, 272, 277, 278.

53. Sri Aurobindo, *Bande Mataram*, 294.

54. Sri Aurobindo, *On Himself*, 21–22.

55. Nirodbaran, ed., *Talks*, 39, 502.

56. H. Kanungo, *Banglay Biplab Pracheshta*, Chapter 11.

57. H. Kanungo, *Banglay Biplab Pracheshta*, 199–200.

58. I discuss this episode at some length in P. Heehs, *Nationalism, Terrorism, Communalism*, 76–83, giving detailed references to the police files (Archives nationales series F/7) that contain information on Hemchandra Das's contact with French and Russian revolutionaries in Paris.

59. J. Ker, *Political Trouble in India*, 73.

60. H. Ghose, "Reminiscences," 12; A. Bhattacharya, "Aurobindo," 835; U. Banerjee, "Aurobindo Prasanga," 6; N. Dutt, "My Recollections of Sri Aurobindo," 601.

61. A. Roy, "Sri Aurobindo Ghose," 7; U. Banerjee, "Aurobindo Prasanga," 6; R. Mookerji, "Some Reminiscences," 21; A. Bhattacharya, "Aurobindo," 835; S. Deb, "Sri Aurobindo," 22.

62. U. Banerjee, "Aurobindo Prasanga," 6; N. Dutt, "My Recollections," 601.

63. A. Bhattacharya, "Aurobindo," 835–6.

64. H. Ghose, "Reminiscences," 11.

65. Sri Aurobindo, *Bande Mataram*, 358.

66. Sri Aurobindo, *Bande Mataram*, 357–358.

67. Sri Aurobindo, *Bande Mataram*, 364.

68. N. Dutt, "My Recollections," 601.

69. J. Bannerji, "Aurobindo Ghose—A Study," 483.

70. Government of India, Home Department Proceedings, series D, July 1907, 3, 2–3.

71. B. Pal, *The New Spirit*, 120.

72. Sri Aurobindo, *On Himself*, 45; see also 44.

73. H. Ghose, *Aurobindo: The Prophet of Patriotism*, 15; Sri Aurobindo, *Bande Mataram*, 395.

74. M. Gilbert, *Servant of India*, 77; Minto to Morley, March 19, 1907, quoted in M. Minto, *India, Minto and Morley*, 109.

75. U. Banerjee, *Nirbasiter Atmakatha,* 5; *Jugantar,* July 16, 1907, quoted in J. Ker, *Political Trouble,* 66 (English idiom modified).

76. Sri Aurobindo, *Bande Mataram,* 554.

77. Government of India, Home Department Proceedings, series A, June 1908: 126–29; Sri Aurobindo, *On Himself,* 24, 41; Bhupendranath Dutt, statement in court, quoted in *Bande Mataram* weekly, August 4, 1907, 6, attributed to Aurobindo by A. Bhattacharya in A. Bhattacharya, "Aurobindo," 840; *Indian Empire,* reproduced in *Bande Mataram* weekly, July 28, 1907, 11.

78. Nirodbaran, ed., *Talks,* 470.

79. Diary of Hemendra Prasad Ghose, August 16–17, 1907; *Bande Mataram* case papers, warrant of arrest, Alipore Bomb Trial Records.

80. *Madras Standard,* reprinted in *Bande Mataram* weekly, August 25, 1907, 9.

81. *Indian Patriot,* reprinted in *Bande Mataram* weekly, August 25, 1907, 9.

82. "Mr. Arobindo Ghose," *Indian Patriot,* reprinted in *Bande Mataram,* September 1, 1907, 13.

83. "Arabinda, Rabindrer laho namaskar," manuscript dated Bhadra 7, 1314 (August 24, 1907), in SAAA; trans. K.M. Sen.

84. Sri Aurobindo, *Bande Mataram,* 655–657.

85. Government of India, Home Department Proceedings, series A, January 1908, 34–37: 5.

86. *Bande Mataram* daily, June 27, 1907.

87. *Bande Mataram* case records, statement by Aurobindo Ghose, Alipore Bomb Trial Records.

88. *Bande Mataram* case records, judgment, Alipore Bomb Trial Records, published in *Bande Mataram* weekly September 29, 1907, 18.

89. H. Mukherjee and U. Mukherjee, *Bipin Chandra Pal and India's Struggle for Swaraj,* 94; J. Lipner, *Brahmabandhab Upadhyay,* 382; Diary of Hemendra Prasad Ghose, September 19 and 23, 1907.

90. Sri Aurobindo, *Bande Mataram,* 692–694.

91. A. Roy, ed., "Conversations," *Sri Aurobindo Circle* 34 (1978): 47; *Sri Aurobindo Circle* 37 (1981): 25. There Aurobindo says "vital enjoyment and satisfaction"; "vital" in his philosophy refers to the movements of the life force (*élan vital*). See also Sri Aurobindo, *On Himself,* 155.

92. Sri Aurobindo, *On Himself,* 433.

93. Aurobindo used this phrase repeatedly in retrospective accounts of his political career. See Sri Aurobindo, *On Himself,* 15, 25–26, 27, 45.

94. Sri Aurobindo, "Sri Aurobindo: A Life-Sketch," published in *Sri Aurobindo: Archives and Research* 9 (April 1985): 68; Sri Aurobindo, *On Himself,* 26, 32, 45, 375; J Bannerji, "Aurobindo Ghose—A Study," 484.

95. Sri Aurobindo, *Bande Mataram,* 743.

96. Sri Aurobindo, *Bande Mataram,* 745–747.

97. Diary of Hemendra Prasad Ghose, October 2–4, 1907.

98. Sri Aurobindo, *Record of Yoga,* 1367–1368.

99. Nirodbaran, ed., *Talks,* 502.

100. Exhibit 293/15, Tilak to Motilal Ghose, December 16, 1907, Alipore Bomb Trial Records; Sri Aurobindo, *Bande Mataram,* 770.

101. Sri Aurobindo, *Bangla Rachana,* 356–357.

102. Aurobindo to Mrinalini Ghose, December 6, 1907, published in Sri Aurobindo, *Bangla Rachana,* 356.

103. Sri Aurobindo, *On Himself,* 32, 45–46; Diary of Hemendra Prasad Ghose, December 9, 1907; Sri Aurobindo, *Bande Mataram,* 790–794; Depositions in sessions court by prosecution witnesses 58, 252, 446, 447, 452, Alipore Bomb Trial Records; H. Nevinson, *The New Spirit in India,* 248.

104. Sri Aurobindo, *Bande Mataram,* 794.

105. Diary of Hemendra Prasad Ghose, December 11, 14, 15, 1907.

106. Nevinson, *The New Spirit in India,* 226.

107. B. Ghose, "Sri Aurobindo as I Understand Him," 45–46.

108. B. Ghose, "Sri Aurobindo," 46.

109. Bombay Presidency Police, *Abstract of Intelligence* 21 (1908): 5, Office of the Deputy Inspector General of Police (Intelligence), Mumbai; S. Karandikar, *Lokamanya Bal Gangadhar Tilak,* 262.

110. S. Chand, *Lajpat Rai: Life and Work,* 210–211. The writer gives Aurobindo's conclusion as: "till you have first emptied it." I take the liberty of deleting the "first."

111. Diary of G. Khaparde, December 25–26, 1907; Nevinson, *The New Spirit in India,* 242–244.

112. Diary of G. Khaparde, December 26, 1907; Nevinson, *The New Spirit in India,* 244–246; Sri Aurobindo, *Bande Mataram,* 850.

113. Nevinson, *The New Spirit in India,* 248.

114. B. Ghose, *Barindrer Atmakahini,* 19–20; B. Ghose, "Sri Aurobindo," 48.

115. B. Ghose, *Barindrer Atmakahini,* 25; Nirodbaran, ed., *Talks,* 470.

116. Sri Aurobindo, *On Himself,* 48; Diary of G. Khaparde, December 28, 1907; B. Ghose, *Barindrer Atmakahini,* 27.

117. H. Nevinson, *More Changes, More Chances,* 270–271; *The New Spirit in India,* 260; Diary of G. Khaparde, December 28, 1907; Bombay Presidency Police, *Abstract of Intelligence* 20 (1908): 19–20.

118. Bombay Presidency Police, *Abstract of Intelligence* 21 (1908): 20; Government of India, Home Department Proceedings, series A, March 1910, 33–40: 70.

119. Nirodbaran Talks manuscripts 14: 53, in SAAA; Sri Aurobindo, *On Himself,* 49; see also 47–48 for a more nuanced account.

120. B. Ghose, letter of 1955, in History of the Freedom Movement Papers IV & V 41/2, National Archives of India, New Delhi.

121. B. Ghose, "Sri Aurobindo," 50; Sri Aurobindo, *On Himself,* 20.

122. B. Ghose, "Sri Aurobindo," 50.

123. Sri Aurobindo, *On Himself,* 77; Nirodbaran, ed., *Correspondence with Sri Aurobindo,* 467, 459–60, 1077; *On Himself,* 78–79; B. Ghose, letter of 1955, History of the Freedom Movement Papers IV & V 41/2.

124. Sri Aurobindo, *On Himself,* 82–84; V. Chidanandam, "Evening Talks," *Mother*

India 24 (April 1972): 165; *On Himself,* 82–83. See also *On Himself,* 80; B. Ghose, "Sri Aurobindo," 50–51; B. Ghose, letter of 1955, History of the Freedom Movement Papers IV & V, 41/2).

125. Sri Aurobindo, *On Himself,* 116, 85–86.

126. Sri Aurobindo, *On Himself,* 116, 101.

127. Sri Aurobindo, *On Himself,* 92. See also *On Himself,* 79, 81, 102.

128. Sri Aurobindo, *On Himself,* 86, 82.

129. W. James, *Essays and Studies,* 374.

130. B. Ghose, "Sri Aurobindo," 51.

131. Bombay Presidency Police, *Abstract of Intelligence* 21 (1908), 324; S. Karandikar, *Lokamanya Bal Gangadhar Tilak,* 279; *Daily Telegraph and Deccan Herald* January 15, 1908; Sri Aurobindo, *Bande Mataram,* 809.

132. Sri Aurobindo, *Collected Poems,* 161.

133. Sri Aurobindo, *On Himself,* 49–50.

134. Sri Aurobindo, *Bande Mataram,* 818–832.

135. Sri Aurobindo, *On Himself,* 50.

136. Sri Aurobindo, *Bande Mataram,* 868–869.

137. T. Sastry, "My First Meeting with Sri Aurobindo," 232; letter from A.K. Chowdhury to Sudha Sundaram, January 10, 1981, in SAAA; P. Chandwani, "Sri Aurobindo: A Few Reminiscences," 469; B. Ghose, "Sri Aurobindo," 33C; A. Purani, Reminiscences, in SAAA.

138. Exhibit 228, Mrinalini Ghose to Aurobindo, December 20, 1907, Alipore Bomb Trial Records.

139. Aurobindo to Mrinalini Ghose February 17, 1907 [error for 1908], published in Sri Aurobindo, *Bangla Rachana,* 355–356.

140. Sri Aurobindo, *On Himself,* 89; S. Deb, "Sri Aurobindo," 22.

141. *Bengalee,* February 12, 1908.

142. Sri Aurobindo, *The Karmayogin,* 369.

143. Sri Aurobindo, *Bande Mataram,* 873.

144. C. Dutt, "My Contact with Revolutionary Independence Movement," 5.

145. Sri Aurobindo, *Bande Mataram,* 1133; Diary of Hemendra Prasad Ghose, February 21, 1908.

146. U. Bannerjee, *Nirbasiter Atmakatha,* 25–27; B. Ghose, *Amar Atmakatha,* 37–40; N. Gupta, *Smritir Pata,* 42.

147. Government of India Home Department Proceedings, series B, March 1909, 181–182: 1–5; Government of India Home Department Proceedings, series D, August 1911, 9: 9; Daly report 9; Kanungo 262–264. Sometime in 1908, a member of Barin's gang, at that time an accused in the Alipore Bomb Trial, told the police about the book-bomb attempt. When another accused person confirmed the story early in 1909, the police asked Kingsford to search his library, which had been shifted to Muzaffarpur when he was transferred there in March 1908. Kingsford made a search, found the package, and, rather rashly, opened it. Finding that the hollowed-out book contained "a metal cylinder," he set it aside. Major Muspratt-Williams, the Chief Inspector of Explosives, was sent to investigate. He identified

the explosive as picric acid and noted that "the mechanism failed to act because the springs [connected to the detonator] had rusted through in the long interval during which the infernal machine had remained in Mr. Kingsford's possession." He also "expressed an opinion that had the bomb been exploded it would have been certain death to Mr. Kingsford and would probably have wrecked the entire house." The hollowed out book and tin, now filled neither with cocoa nor picric acid, are in the Calcutta Police Museum, where I was able to examine and photograph them.

148. Government of India, Home Department Proceedings, series A, May 1908, 104–11: 5; Government of Bengal Pol. Conf. 170 of 1908, Halliday to Chief Secretary, May 16, 1908.

149. A. Bhattacharya, "Aurobindo," 843.

150. Government of India Home Department Proceedings, series A, May 1908, 112–150, 14–15, 28, 34.

151. Sri Aurobindo, *Bande Mataram,* 1033.

152. Sri Aurobindo, *Bande Mataram,* 1003.

153. Sri Aurobindo, *Bande Mataram,* 1047–1051.

154. L. Rai, *India's Will to Freedom,* 119.

155. Sri Aurobindo, *Bande Mataram,* 1056–1060.

156. Sri Aurobindo, *Bande Mataram,* 1067.

157. Sri Aurobindo, *Bande Mataram,* 1070–1072.

158. Exhibit 150 (court translation), Alipore Bomb Trial Records; Alipore Bomb Trial Records, vol. 21, Halliday to Armstrong, April 20, 1908.

159. India Office Records L/PJ/6/871, Oriental and India Office Library and Records, London.

160. Sri Aurobindo, *Bangla Rachana,* 7; *Empire,* May 1, 1908.

161. Nirodbaran, ed., *Talks,* 503–504. The four known accounts of this incident differ considerably; see P. Heehs, *The Bomb in Bengal,* 157–158, footnote.

162. Sri Aurobindo, *Bande Mataram,* 1117–1121.

5. In Jail and After

Epigraph: from Sri Aurobindo, *Karakahini,* published in *Bangla Rachana,* 7.

1. Sri Aurobindo, *Bangla Rachana,* 8.

2. Exhibits 25 and 25A (first series), Alipore Bomb Trial Records, Smaraniyo Bichar Sangraha, Alipore Court Complex, Kolkata.

3. Depositions in magistrate's court of prosecution witness 2 (John Creagan), Alipore Bomb Trial Records.

4. Sri Aurobindo, *Bangla Rachana,* 10.

5. Sri Aurobindo, *Bangla Rachana,* 12.

6. Sri Aurobindo, *Bangla Rachana,* 13.

7. Sri Aurobindo, *Karmayogin,* 5.

8. A. Bhattacharya, "Aurobindo," 845–846.

9. Sri Aurobindo, *Bangla Rachana*, 14–15.

10. Sri Aurobindo, *Bangla Rachana*, 15.

11. Sri Aurobindo, *Karmayogin*, 5.

12. Sri Aurobindo, *Karmayogin*, 5–6.

13. Sri Aurobindo, *Bangla Rachana*, 30–31.

14. *Empire*, May 8, 1908.

15. Government of India, Home Department Proceedings, series D, May 1908, 104–11: 8–9, National Archives of India, New Delhi.

16. Letter Fraser to Minto, May 19, 1908, enclosing confidential note, Minto Papers, National Archives of Scotland, Edinburgh.

17. Government of India, Home Department Proceedings, series A, May 1908, 104–111.

18. Sri Aurobindo, *Bangla Rachana*, 34.

19. Sri Aurobindo, *Karmayogin*, 7.

20. Sri Aurobindo, *Bangla Rachana*, 42–45.

21. Sri Aurobindo, *Bangla Rachana*, 44–45.

22. *Bande Mataram* weekly, June 28, 1908: 2.

23. *Times* (London) May 6, 1908.

24. *Indian World*, quoted in *Review of Reviews* 38 (July 1908): 37.

25. *Eastern Bengal and Assam Era*, May 9, 1908; *Asian*, 11 May 1908, reprinted in *Bande Mataram* daily on May 12.

26. S. Wolpert, *Morley and India*, 113; Minto to Morley, May 27, 1908, Minto Papers.

27. F. Daly, *Note on the Growth of the Revolutionary Movement in Bengal*, 13–15; C. Tegart, *Note on the Chandernagore Gang*, 11–12; B. Ghose, *Barindrer Atmakahini*, Chapter 15; N. Gupta, *Smritir Pata*, 70 (idiom corrected).

28. India Office Records, J&R 4494 of 1908, Oriental and India Office Library and Records, London.

29. *Empire*, August 18, 1908, reprinted in Sri Aurobindo, *Bande Mataram*, 1145–1146.

30. N. Gupta, *Smritir Pata*, 73.

31. Government of India, Home Department (Jails) Proceedings series A, February 1909, 29–32: 62–64; History of the Freedom Movement Papers I 30/2; commitment order reproduced in *Bande Mataram* weekly, September 6, 1908: 17.

32. Government of India, Home Department Proceedings, series B, December 1908, 96–110; Government of Bengal Pol. Conf. 160 of 1908, West Bengal State Archives, Kolkata.

33. Sri Aurobindo, *Karmayogin*, 9.

34. V. Chidanandam, ed., "Sri Aurobindo at Evening Talks," *Mother India* 21 (December 1969): 682; Nirodbaran Talks manuscripts 10: 71–72.

35. U. Banerjee, "Aurobindo Prasanga," 6; S. Sarkar, "Rishi Sri Aurobinder Smriti-katha."

36. *Bande Mataram* daily, August 20, 1908.

37. India Office Records L/PJ/6/922.

38. *Times*, October 22, 1908.

39. India Office Records L/PJ/6/907.

40. Norton's speech reported in the *Bengalee*, October 21 and 22, 1908.

41. Das's speech reported in the *Bengalee*, March 25, 1909.

42. Sri Aurobindo, *Karmayogin,* 8.

43. Sri Aurobindo, *On Himself,* 64; Nirodbaran, ed., *Correspondence with Sri Aurobindo,* 84.

44. Sri Aurobindo, *On Himself,* 64, 68; reply to letter of Josephine MacLeod, December 21, 1938, in SAAA.

45. Purani Talks manuscripts 8: 299; Purani Talks manuscripts 12: 257; V. Chidanandam, ed., "Sri Aurobindo at Evening Talks," *Mother India* 22 (1970): 25–26.

46. Sri Aurobindo, *On Himself,* 58.

47. Sri Aurobindo, *Letters on Yoga,* 1056.

48. Sri Aurobindo, *Letters on Yoga,* 40.

49. Sri Aurobindo, *Record of Yoga,* 76; *On Himself,* 34; *Karmayogin,* 10.

50. N. Gupta, "Sri Aurobinder Jibandhara," 25; *Smritir Pata,* 73; B. Sen, "Sri Aurobindo as I Remember Him," 20; Nirodbaran Talks manuscripts 9: 47–48.

51. *Bengalee,* February 28, 1909.

52. *Bengalee,* May 28, 1909.

53. Government of Bengal Pol. Conf. 194 (C) of 1909.

54. Closing speech of C. R. Das, Alipore Bomb Trial Records.

55. B. Sen, "Sri Aurobindo," 21; *Hindoo Patriot,* May 7, 1909.

56. Government of Bengal Pol. Conf. 194 of 1909 (letter from Daly to Duke, May 6, 1909).

57. Judgment of C. P. Beachcroft, Alipore Bomb Trial Records.

58. Judgment of C. P. Beachcroft, Alipore Bomb Trial Records.

59. F. Daly, *Note on the Growth of the Revolutionary Movement in Bengal,* 11.

60. S. Basu, ed., *Letters of Sister Nivedita,* 1051.

61. *Bengalee,* May 14, 1909, 4.

62. Interview in the *Sanjivani,* published in English translation in *Bengalee,* May 14, 1909.

63. Sri Aurobindo, *On Himself,* 59–60.

64. Act cited in M. Barns, *The Indian Press,* 439–440.

65. S. Wolpert, *Tilak and Gokhale,* 219–225; *Morley and India,* 117–119.

66. Memorandum enclosed in From Minto, December 17, 1908, Morley Papers, India Office Records (MSS Eur D573), Oriental and India Office Library, London; Rash Behari Ghosh, quoted in E. Major, *Viscount Morley and Indian Reform,* 69.

67. *Review of Reviews* 39 (January 1909): 13; Government of India, Home Department Proceedings, series A, July 1909, 40–41, 3.

68. Morley to Minto, August 10, 1908, Morley Papers, India Office Records.

69. Sri Aurobindo, *Karmayogin,* 3–12.

70. Sri Aurobindo, *Karmayogin,* 26.

71. Sri Aurobindo, *Record of Yoga,* 33–34.

72. Sri Aurobindo, *Record of Yoga,* 35.

73. Undated fragmentary letter, published in *Sri Aurobindo's Action* 6 (February/March 1976), 4.

74. Sri Aurobindo, *Karmayogin,* 18–19.

75. Sri Aurobindo, *Karmayogin,* 23–24.

76. Sri Aurobindo, *Karmayogin,* 26–28.

77. C. Taylor, "The Politics of Recognition," 26.

78. Sri Aurobindo, *Karmayogin,* 152–153.

79. Government of Bengal Pol. Conf. 205 of 1909, 3 in notes; Sri Aurobindo, *On Himself,* 34.

80. S. Deb, "Sri Aurobindo as I Knew Him," 23; J. Ghose, *Life-Work of Sri Aurobindo,* 59–60.

81. Sri Aurobindo, *Early Cultural Writings,* 455–459.

82. Sri Aurobindo, *Karmayogin,* 29–31.

83. A. Azad, *India Wins Freedom,* 4.

84. G. Gokhale, speech delivered in Poona, reproduced in *Karmayogin* 4 (July 17, 1909): 14.

85. Sri Aurobindo, *Karmayogin,* 116–121.

86. Sri Aurobindo, *Karmayogin,* 102–104.

87. *Indian Patriot,* July 2, 1909, in Government of Madras, *Report on Native Newspapers in Madras,* 1909.

88. Letter from Nivedita to S.K. Ratcliffe, July 21, 1909, in S. Basu, ed., *Letters of Sister Nivedita,* 986. The editor of the letters has mistranscribed "We can no other," which is of course a translation of Luther's "Ich kann nicht anders."

89. Annie Besant, quoted in *Modern Review,* vol. 6, no. 1 (July 1909): 83, with editorial reply on the same page.

90. Government of Bengal Pol. Conf. 205 of 1909 ("Case against Arabinda Ghose," Chapman's note of May 21, 1909 and sequel).

91. Government of India, Home Department Proceedings, series A, October 1909, 230–48: 3.

92. Morley to Minto, July 7, 1909, Morley Papers, India Office Records.

93. Government of Bengal Pol. Conf. 205 of 1909, Notes, 1–2.

94. Government of Bengal Pol. Conf. 205 of 1909 (Political Notes), 3

95. Sri Aurobindo, *Karmayogin,* 160; S. Basu, ed., *Letters of Sister Nivedita,* 992.

96. *Times,* August 31, 1909; Government of India, Home Department Proceedings, series A, October 1909, 230–248: 72–89; telegrams, August 5–8, 1909, Morley Papers, India Office Records.

97. Sri Aurobindo, *Karmayogin,* 174, 177.

98. Sri Aurobindo, *Karmayogin,* 173; Baker quoted in letter from Minto to Morley, August 5, 1909, 2, Morley Papers, India Office Records.

99. Government of Bengal Pol. Conf. 205 of 1909 (Speeches), 2.

100. B. Ghose, "Sri Aurobindo as I Understand Him," 61.

101. Baker quoted in letter from Minto to Morley, August 5, 1909, Morley Papers, India Office Records; Government of India, Home Department Proceedings, series A, October 1909, 242–243: 74; Minto to Morley, August 5, 1909, Morley Papers, India Office Records; Government of India, Home Department Proceedings, series A, February 1910, 34–42.

102. Government of Bengal Pol. Conf. 205 of 1909, serial nos. 19–27.

103. Government of Bengal Pol. Conf. 205 and 205A of 1909.

104. Government of India, Home Department Proceedings, series A, October 1909, 230–248: 11–14; J.D. Rees, Speech in House of Commons, August 5, 1909 (*Hansard*, House of Commons, vol. 3, 1909, April 19, 1909, col. 1270), quoted in M. Das, *Sri Aurobindo in the First Decade of the Century*, 140.

105. V. Athalye, "Sri Aurobindo in Politics," 503.

106. Government of Bengal Pol. Conf. 13 of 1909, 1–2; Sri Aurobindo, *On Himself,* 35; Government of India, Home Department Proceedings, series B, November 1909, 103–104: 5; Government of India, Home Department Proceedings, series B, November 1909, 103–104: 5, 6; Government of Bengal Pol. Conf. 13 of 1909.

107. Sri Aurobindo, *Karmayogin*, 224.

108. Government of India, Home Department Proceedings, series B, November 1909, 103–104, 2, 5–6, 35; personal interview with Arun Chandra Dutt, Chandernagore, June 4, 1978; Sri Aurobindo, *On Himself,* 32–33.

109. *Dharma* 1 (Ashwin 4, 1316 B.S.): 4. See also Government of India, Home Department Proceedings, series A, December 1909, 15–16: 6–7.

110. N. Gupta, *Smritir Pata*, 82.

111. Sri Aurobindo, *Karmayogin*, 276–278.

112. S. Deb, "Sri Aurobindo as I Knew Him," 23.

113. J. MacDonald, *The Awakening of India*, 49.

114. Advertisement reproduced in the *Karmayogin* 1, no. 11 (September 4, 1909): 12, and subsequent issues.

115. J. Bannerji, "Aurobindo Ghose—A Study," 476–487.

116. Letter from Hiralal Haldar, November 5, 1909, published as "Comment and Criticism" in *Karmayogin* 1 (December 11, 1909): 5.

117. Besant in *Central Hindu College Magazine* 9 (September 1909): 210.

118. Minto to Morley, April 14, 1910, Minto Papers; Diary of R.C. Dutt, August 7, 1909, Baroda State Papers.

119. Government of India, Home Department Proceedings, series B, November 1909, 103–4: 36.

120. Sri Aurobindo, *Karmayogin*, 225–226.

121. Sri Aurobindo, *Karmayogin*, 289, 304.

122. Sri Aurobindo, *On Himself,* 35; Nirodbaran, ed., *Talks with Sri Aurobindo*, 111. See P. Heehs, "Archival Notes," in *Sri Aurobindo: Archives and Research* 7 (December 1983): 212–213 for a discussion of the place and date of this meeting.

123. Sri Aurobindo, "Jukta Mahasabha," *Dharma* 1 (Paush 5, 1316 BS): 4–6, reprinted with translation in *Sri Aurobindo: Archives and Research* 7 (December 1983): 102–107.

124. Sri Aurobindo, *Karmayogin*, 372–376.

125. Government of India, Home Department Proceedings, series A, March 1910, 118–123: 5–6. Information on Satish Sarkar's mission given to me by Nolini Kanta Gupta, Pondicherry, May 1975.

126. Sri Aurobindo, *Karmayogin*, 437; see also *On Himself,* 21.

127. Sri Aurobindo, *Karmayogin*, 434–435.

128. S. Wolpert, *Morley and India 1906–1910*, 127.

129. Government of India, Home Department Proceedings, series A, December 1910, 14–42.

130. Sri Aurobindo, *Karmayogin*, 437, 439–444.

131. Sri Aurobindo, *Essays in Philosophy and Yoga*, 65.

132. Sri Aurobindo Papers, NB R1: 43, in SAAA; S. Srinivasacharya. "Freedom Movement in India," History of Freedom Movement Papers, National Archives of India, copy in SAAA; M. Iyengar, "Forward," 3–4. Relevant extracts from these three documents are published in *Sri Aurobindo: Archives and Research* 11 (December 1987): 209–211.

133. Sri Aurobindo, *On Himself*, 57, 62, 70; B. Ghose, "Sri Aurobindo as I Understand Him," 63, 65; extract from A. B. Purani's transcript of a talk of September 27, 1925, reproduced as Document 1 in *Sri Aurobindo: Archives and Research* 8 (December 1984): 201. I discuss this incident in considerable detail in P. Heehs, "Archival Notes," *Sri Aurobindo: Archives and Research* 8 (December 1984): 221–247.

134. Government of India, Home Department Proceedings, series A, January 1910, 141–142: 4.

135. Sri Aurobindo, *On Himself*, 18.

136. M. Roy, *My Life's Partner*, 174.

137. M. Roy, *My Life's Partner*, 172. N. Bannerjee, *Rakta Biplaber Ek Adhyaya*, 52–59. These two documents are reproduced in *Sri Aurobindo: Archives and Research* 12 (April 1985): 81–86. There are discrepancies between the two accounts. I discuss these in the same issue, 110–111.

138. M. Roy, *My Life's Partner*, 175, translation emended.

139. Sri Aurobindo, *On Himself*, 56, 61, 62–63, 71.

140. M. Roy, *My Life's Partner*, 178, 181.

141. Sri Aurobindo, *On Himself*, 57; *The Secret of the Veda* 36.

142. Sri Aurobindo, *Karmayogin*, 461.

143. All documents bearing on the trip from Chandernagore to Calcutta are reproduced, in English translation, in *Sri Aurobindo: Archives and Research* 9 (April 1985): 86–100. The most important of the narrative sources is N. Guharoy, "Debata Biday," 48–68.

144. A. Chatterjee to N. Guharoy, April 25, 1948, reproduced in N. Guharoy, "Debata Biday," 58.

145. Sri Aurobindo, *Karmayogin*, 461; Sri Aurobindo, letter to the *Hindu* November 7, 1910, published in *Sri Aurobindo: Archives and Research* 8 (April 1984): 61.

146. Sri Aurobindo, "Sri Aurobindo: A Life-Sketch," published in *Sri Aurobindo: Archives and Research* 9 (April 1985): 69. See also Sri Aurobindo, *On Himself*, 35, 54, 55; Sri Aurobindo, note published in *Sri Aurobindo: Archives and Research* 1 (April 1979): 101.

147. Sri Aurobindo, *On Himself*, 35–36, 21–22; see also *On Himself* 400; Nirodbaran, ed., *Talks with Sri Aurobindo*, 227, 238.

148. Nehru, "Foreword," x.

149. Munshi in Shri Kanaialal Munshi Diamond Jubilee Committee, *Munshi: His Art and Work*, 49; B. Ghose, "Sri Aurobindo as I Understand Him," 64; "Sri Aurobindo as I Understand Him," MS II, 122.

150. Government of India, Foreign and Pol. Dept., General, Conf. B of 1914, no. 2, Life Sketch; Deposition of A. C. Banerjea in Sessions Court, Alipore Bomb Trial Records; Charu Chandra Roy, letter to the editor, *Hindusthan Standard*, April 7, 1942.

151. V. Chidanandam, ed., "Sri Aurobindo at Evening Talks," *Mother India* 23 (February 1971): 22; Sri Aurobindo, *On Himself,* 430.

152. K. Munshi, "Sri Aurobindo," 302.

Part Four: Yogi and Philosopher

Epigraph: Sri Aurobindo, letter to Dilip Kumar Roy, August 31, 1934, published in *On Himself,* 374 (text corrected against the original manuscript).

6. A Laboratory Experiment

Epigraph: Sri Aurobindo, letter to Balkrishna Shivaram Moonje, August 30, 1920, published in *On Himself,* 432.

1. S. Chakravarty, *Smritikatha,* 116–119, English translation published in *Sri Aurobindo: Archives and Research* 9 (April 1985): 105.

2. S. Chakravarty, *Smritikatha,* 116–119; Srinivasacharya reminiscences, copy in SAAA.

3. "Rapport général du voyage," *Dupleix*, April 7, 1910, Messageries Maritimes Archives, Le Harvre, France.

4. Sri Aurobindo, *On Himself,* 364.

5. P. Loti, *India,* 133.

6. Telegram from Morley to Minto, May 6, 1910, Morley Papers.

7. Telegram Morley to Minto, April 7, 1910, Morley Papers; *Times* (London), April 7, 1910.

8. Debate in House of Commons April 28, 1910, reported in *Times* (London), April 29, 1910, 7–8.

9. S. Chakravarty, *Smritikatha,* 137–139.

10. Srinivasacharya reminiscences, copy in SAAA.

11. Government of India, Home Department Proceedings, series A, July 1910, 112–13: 3, National Archives of India, New Delhi.

12. S. Chakravarty, *Smritikatha,* 162.

13. Nirodbaran, ed. *Talks with Sri Aurobindo,* 86.

14. V. Ramaswami Aiyangar, "With Aurobindo in those Early Days," 14.

15. Sri Aurobindo, *On Himself,* 373.

16. Sri Aurobindo, *On Himself,* 65.

17. S. Chakravarty, *Smritikatha,* 173–181; A. Neogy, "Pondicherry," 241; Srinivasachaya reminiscences, copy in SAAA.; *Journal officiel des Établissements Français dans l'Inde*, May 6, 1910, 347.

18. P. Richard, "Without Passport," 55.

19. Srinivasacharya reminiscences, copy in SAAA.; S. Chakravarty, *Smritikatha*, 173–188; P. Richard, "Without Passport," 55; History of the Freedom Movement Papers B 1/2, National Archives of India, New Delhi.

20. P. Richard, "Without Passport," 55.

21. Sri Aurobindo, *Collected Poems*, 485–486.

22. Sri Aurobindo, *Collected Plays and Stories*, 533–534, 587, 579.

23. Sri Aurobindo, "Sri Aurobindo: A Life-Sketch," *Sri Aurobindo: Archives and Research* 9 (April 1985): 69.

24. Morley to Minto, May 5, 1910, Morley Papers.

25. Minto to Morley, May 26, 1910, Morley Papers.

26. Sri Aurobindo, "Sri Aurobindo: A Life-Sketch." *Sri Aurobindo: Archives and Research* 9 (April 1985): 69.

27. Srinivasacharya reminiscences, copy in SAAA.

28. Sri Aurobindo, letter to the editor of the *Hindu*, November 7, 1910, published in *Sri Aurobindo: Archives and Research* 8 (April 1984): 61.

29. *Hindu*, November 8, 1910.

30. Diary of British Consul, October 15, 1910, in History of the Freedom Movement Papers, B 1/2.

31 Sri Aurobindo, letter to the editor of the *Hindu*, February 23, 1911, published in *Sri Aurobindo: Archives and Research* 5 (December 1981): 186–187.

32. Sri Aurobindo, *The Secret of the Veda*, 38, 50.

33. Government of India, Home Department Proceedings, series D, January 1912, 47: 3–4.

34. Aurobindo to Paul Richard, July 12, 1911, extracts published in Sri Aurobindo, *On Himself*, 423–424.

35. Crewe to Hardinge January 13, 1911, in Hardinge Papers vol. 117, no. 11, Cambridge University Library, Cambridge.

36. Government of India, Foreign and Political Department, General, Conf. B. 1914, no. 2; R. Padmanabhan, *V. V. S. Aiyar*, 107–115; S. Rowlett et. al., *Report of Committee Appointed to Investigate Revolutionary Conspiracies*, paragraphs. 150–151.

37. *Madras Times*, July 10, 1911, 8.

38. Sri Aurobindo, *On Himself*, 423–424; P. Richard, "Without Passport," 60.

39. Sri Aurobindo, *Supplement*, 500–501.

40. Sri Aurobindo, letter to the editor of the *Hindu*, July 1911, republished in *Sri Aurobindo: Archives and Research* 18 (December 1994): 214–215.

41. Government of India, Foreign and Political Department, General, Conf. series B. 1914, No. 2; Government of Madras, Judicial (1912) Department, G.O. No. 1335, confidential, August 21, 1912, Tamil Nadu State Archives, Chennai.

42. N. Gupta, *Smritir Pata*, 94; R. Padmanabhan, *V. V. S. Aiyar*, 116; A. Purani, *The Life of Sri Aurobindo*, 148.

43. Government of Madras Judicial Department, G.O. no. 1335; Government of India, Home Department Proceedings, series B, May 1912, nos. 14–18: 11 (this gives the date of the search as April 8, 1912); Srinivasacharya reminiscences, copy in SAAA.; Aurobindo to

Motilal Roy, July 3, 1912, published in Sri Aurobindo, *Supplement*, 426–427; "A Note on a Forged Document," published in *Sri Aurobindo: Archives and Research* 9 (December 1985): 190–191; V. Ramaswami Aiyangar, "With Aurobindo," 14; A. Purani, *Life*, 149–150.

44. Motilal Roy, quoted in A. Dutt, "Letters of Sree Aurobindo," 26–27.

45. Sri Aurobindo, *Supplement*, 426.

46. Sri Aurobindo, *Supplement*, 433–435 (the suggested date of this letter in the *Supplement* is certainly incorrect).

47. Sri Aurobindo, *On Himself*, 64.

48. Sri Aurobindo, *Supplement*, 433.

49. Sri Aurobindo, *Supplement*, 433–434.

50. Sri Aurobindo Papers: NB V2:1, V3:1; V4:1, in SAAA.

51. Sri Aurobindo, *Supplement*, 434.

52. Government of India Foreign and Political Dept., General, Conf. B. 1914. no. 2.

53. V. Ramaswami Aiyangar, "With Aurobindo," 16.

54. Sri Aurobindo, *Supplement*, 435.

55. A. David-Néel, *Journal de voyage: lettres à son mari*, 68–69, 75; *Le sortilège du mystère*, 305; *L'Inde où j'ai vécu*, 225.

56. A. David-Néel, *L'Inde où j'ai vécu*, 222–223.

57. Lord Hardinge to David-Néel, March 11, 1912, David-Néel Papers, Fondation Alexandra David Néel, Digne-les-Bains, France.

58. Conf. Files B.R.O.C. 21/Poli Hall, File 5, Baroda State Records 1893–1912, Baroda Record Office, Vadodara; A. Purani, ed., *Evening Talks with Sri Aurobindo*, 18.

59. Sri Aurobindo, *On Himself*, 37.

60. Sri Aurobindo, *Supplement*, 433, 441; Motilal Roy, quoted in A. Dutt, "Letters of Sree Aurobindo," 28.

61. Sri Aurobindo, *Supplement*, 429–430.

62. Sri Aurobindo, *Record of Yoga*, 165–221.

63. Nirodbaran, ed. *Talks*, 39.

64. Amrita, "Old Long Since," 157–160.

65. Sri Aurobindo, *Synthesis of Yoga* before text; *Synthesis of Yoga*, 6–8.

66. Sri Aurobindo, *The Future Poetry*, 70; see also *The Human Cycle*, 266.

67. Sri Aurobindo, *Supplement*, 424; Conf. File. B.R.O.C 21/Poli. Hall, File 5, Baroda State Records; Sri Aurobindo, *On Himself*, 424.

68. Sri Aurobindo, *Record of Yoga*, 3–23. In my summary I rely also on the "scribal version" of Sapta Chatusthaya (*Record of Yoga*, 1467–1481), and Part IV of *The Synthesis of Yoga*, in particular Chapter 10, "The Elements of Perfection."

69. Sri Aurobindo, *Synthesis of Yoga*, 43.

70. Sri Aurobindo, *Synthesis of Yoga*, 692.

71. Sri Aurobindo, *Synthesis of Yoga*, 722; *Record of Yoga*, 5–6.

72. Sri Aurobindo, *Synthesis of Yoga*, 693. I follow this passage in placing *shakti* before *virya*.

73. Sri Aurobindo, *Record of Yoga*, 19; *Synthesis of Yoga*, 886.

74. W. Blake, *The Complete Poetry and Prose of William Blake*, 159 (*Jerusalem*, plate 15).

75. Sri Aurobindo, *Record of Yoga*, 22.

76. Sri Aurobindo, *Record of Yoga*, 19.

77. Sri Aurobindo, *Synthesis of Yoga*, 695.

78. Sri Aurobindo, *On Himself*, 426–427.

79. Sri Aurobindo, *On Himself*, 86.

80. Sri Aurobindo, *On Himself*, 423.

81. Sri Aurobindo, *On Himself*, 423.

82. Sri Aurobindo, *Record of Yoga*, 76–77.

83. Sri Aurobindo, *Record of Yoga*, 132–136.

84. Sri Aurobindo, *Record of Yoga*, 118.

85. Letter of December 18, 1912, in SAAA.

86. Sri Aurobindo, *Supplement*, 436; *Record of Yoga*, 226, 240.

87. Sri Aurobindo, *Record of Yoga*, 241–242.

88. Sri Aurobindo, *Record of Yoga*, 324.

89. Sri Aurobindo, *Record of Yoga*, 324–325.

90. Sri Aurobindo, *Record of Yoga*, 311.

91. Sigmund Freud, *Moses and Monotheism*, quoted in R. Hood, "Mysticism, Reality, Illusion, and the Freudian Critique of Religion," 58.

92. W. James, *The Varieties of Religious Experience*, 24–33; A. Boisen, *The Exploration of the Inner World*, ix.

93. S. Kakar, *The Analyst and the Mystic*, 26.

94. Diary of Hemendra Prasad Ghose, July 28, 1907, in SAAA.

95. Talk of November 11, 1926, quoted in A. Purani, *Life*, 205.

96. Purani Talks manuscripts 5: 82, in SAAA; K. Amrita, "Old Long Since," 163.

97. Purani Talks manuscripts 5: 56.

98. Sri Aurobindo, *Record of Yoga*, 1312–1316; Purani Talks manuscripts, 5: 90.

99. A. Purani, *Life*, 154–55. See also V. Ramaswami Aiyangar, "With Aurobindo," 16; N. Gupta *Smritir Pata*, 103–104; A. Dutt, "Letters," 31–32.

100. J. Armstrong, *An Account of the Revolutionary Organization in Eastern Bengal*, 70.

101. Sri Aurobindo, *Supplement*, 471–73, 458–59. Motilal explains the sense of this letter in M. Roy, "Sri Aurobindo Prasanga," 375.

102. Sri Aurobindo, *Record of Yoga*, 422.

103. The Mother, *L'agenda de Mère* vol. 3, 305–306. See also A. Roy, ed., "Conversations with Sri Aurobindo," *Sri Aurobindo Circle* 32 (1976): 48.

104. Mirra Alfassa spoke little of her origins, and always insisted that her father and mother were nonreligious. There is no doubt, however, that both of them were Jewish. According to Sri Aurobindo's biographer Gabriel Monod-Herzen, who based himself on research in family papers and archives, Moïse Maurice Alfassa's birth was registered with "the Foreign Jewish Community [*Communauté Israélite Étrangère*] of Constantinople, under Italian protection" (G. Monod-Herzen's notes, in SAAA). Alfassa is a fairly common Sephardic Jewish surname, meaning from Fes or Fez, Morocco. Mirra is a short form of Miriam, a very common Jewish forename. One of Mirra's other forenames, Rachel, was the forename of her paternal grandmother, Rachel Hillel. Mirra's maternal grandmother, Mira

Ismalun, née Pinto, wrote in her memoirs that she and her husband Mattéo Ismalun were both "of the Jewish religion" (*de réligion juive*). She also noted "in those days we hardly paid any attention to genealogy and I would have a hard time saying what exactly our origins were. . . . Raised in that religion, I never practiced it." (M. Ismalun, *Mes Mémoirs*, 3, 9). Mirra's brother Mattéo Alfassa received some religious instruction as a boy, and his family celebrated his bar mitzvah (J. Benilan, "Le Gouverneur Alfassa [1876–1942]," 20). None of Mirra Alfassa's writings or recorded talks give evidence that she had any special knowledge of or interest in Judaism, or practiced it at any time.

105. A. Alcalay, *After Jews and Arabs,* 35.

106. See *Catalogue des ouvrages de peinture, sculpture . . . exposés au Grand Palais* (Évreux: Ch. Hérissey, 1898–1912), Paris, Centre Georges Pompidou, for listings of Morisset's paintings in one of the most important Paris salons.

107. General Legrand-Girarde, diary entry, November 27, 1897, quoted in E. Weber, *France, Fin de Siècle*, 121.

108. S. De Guaita, *Essais de sciences maudites,* 24.

109. *Revue cosmique* 7 (March 1908): 182.

110. Madame Théon's name appears on the marriage certificate as Mary-Chrystine Woodroff-Ware, and on her death certificate as "Miriam Lin Woodroff, femme de Max Théon." Modern writers often call her Alma, which is how she is referred to in *Un séjour chez les grands initiés* (1931), a book written by Claire Thémanlys, the wife of Louis Thémanlys. In the book, Claire gave special names to all of the people mentioned. She called Théon l'Aïa, short for Aïa Aziz (Arabic for "the beloved"), a name actually used by Théon, notably as editorial director of the *Revue cosmique* from 1904. Claire gave herself and her husband the pseudonyms Stella and Ary. (Louis Thémanlys and Claire Thémanlys also were pseudonyms: the couple's actual names were Claire Blot, later Madame Louis Moyse, and David Moshe Moyse.) Alma likewise appears to be a pseudonym used only in Claire's book. Teresa (Augusta Rolfe), the devoted secretary of Théon and his wife, always referred to Madame Théon as Théona. In retrospective talks and writings, the Mother and Paul Richard always referred to her as Madame Théon.

111. J. Godwin et al., *The Hermetic Brotherhood of Luxor,* 93, 306, 342–356, 436.

112. J. Benilan, "Le Gouverneur Alfassa (1876–1942)," 48, in SAAA; The Mother, *L'agenda de Mère* vol. 3: 421; *L'agenda de Mère* vol. 13: 154–155.

113. The Mother, *L'agenda de Mère* vol. 2: 392, 422.

114. M. Monestier, *Les sociétés secrètes féminines,* 89.

115. The Mother, *Paroles d'autrefois,* 16–22.

116. Written and oral communications from Pascal Thémanlys, son of Louis and Claire Thémanlys and head of the Cosmic Movement at the time of the communications, to Francis Bertaud (late 1980s). My thanks to Francis Bertaud for sharing this information with me.

117. The information that Mirra married largely under pressure from her mother was given to me by Mirra's granddaughter Janine Panier on November 19, 1988. Mirra herself said (The Mother, *L'agenda de Mère* vol. 2: 404) that another factor was Richard's need to legalize his relationship with her to obtain visitation rights to his children from his previous marriage.

118. P. Richard, "Without Passport," 75–76.

119. P. Richard, "Without Passport," 54; A. Morisset, "Remembrances," 64–65; The Mother, *L'agenda de Mère* vol. 2, 404.

120. *Mercure de France*, May 16, 1914, 371.

121. Diary of A. David-Néel, which records thirteen visits to rue du Val-de-Grâce between December 1910 and February 1911, A. David-Néel Papers.

122. "Tablet" from 'Abdu'l-Bahá (in Haifa) to Paul Richard (in Port Said), March 1914. Summary translation provided to the author by Murray R. Smith, Deputy Secretary-General, Bahá'i International Community, Haifa, July 1995, copy in SAAA.

123. Sri Aurobindo, *Record of Yoga*, 454.

124. Sri Aurobindo, *Essays in Philosophy and Yoga*, 441.

125. Sri Aurobindo, *Record of Yoga*, 508–509.

126. *"Arya": Notre Programme*, in SAAA, reproduced in *Sri Aurobindo: Archives and Research* 13 [April 1889]: 105–106. Translated from the French text as no copy of the English prospectus survives.

127. Sri Aurobindo, *Record of Yoga*, 600.

128. Sri Aurobindo, *Record of Yoga*, 624.

129. Srinivasacharya reminiscences, copy in SAAA.; N. Gupta, *Reminiscences*, 71; Y. Gaebelé, *Histoire de Pondichéry*, 15.

130. Government of India, Home Department Proceedings, series B, September 1915, 145–48: 22, National Archives of India, New Delhi.

131. Purani Talks manuscripts, 5: 75, in SAAA. See N. Gupta, "Sri Aurobinder Jibandhara," 27–28.

132. P. Richard, "Without Passport," 67.

133. Sri Aurobindo, *Supplement*, 442.

134. Sri Aurobindo, *Supplement*, 463–466.

135. Sri Aurobindo, interview published in the *Hindu*, January 4, 1915.

136. The Mother, *Prières et méditations*, 319, 321; A. Roy, ed., "Conversations," *Sri Aurobindo Circle* 33 (1977): 72.

137. P. Richard, "Without Passport," 71.

138. The Mother, *Prières et méditations*, 323.

139. Sri Aurobindo, *Record of Yoga*, 828.

140. N. Gupta, *Reminiscences*, 81; M. Mukherjee, "A Look Behind," 65, reporting a statement by Aurobindo to Barin Ghose.

141. *Arya* 2 (1915): 1–9, published in Sri Aurobindo, *Essays in Philosophy and Yoga*, 140–147, 103–104.

7. The Major Works

Epigraph: Sri Aurobindo, Letter to Motilal Roy, c. June 1914, published in *Supplement*, 456 (text corrected against Sri Aurobindo's manuscript).

1. *Arya* 2, no. 1 (August 1915), 1, published in Sri Aurobindo, *Essays in Philosophy and Yoga,* 103.

2. Sri Aurobindo, *Record of Yoga,* 589.

3. Sri Aurobindo, *Essays Divine and Human,* 38–45; quotation at 504.

4. Sri Aurobindo, *Isha Upanishad,* 339, 342.

5. Sri Aurobindo, *The Secret of the Veda,* 39.

6. Sri Aurobindo, *The Secret of the Veda,* 3, 8.

7. Sri Aurobindo, *The Secret of the Veda,* 7–9.

8. Sri Aurobindo, *The Secret of the Veda,* 257–260.

9. Letter of 1920, published in Sri Aurobindo, *The Secret of the Veda,* 602.

10. Letter of November 4, 1933, in SAAA. Sri Aurobindo made this remark regarding a symbolic passage in the *Brihadaranyaka Upanishad,* but it applies with even more force to the symbolism of the Rig Veda.

11. J. Borges, *Other Inquisitions,* 113.

12. Sri Aurobindo, *The Renaissance in India with A Defence of Indian Culture,* 51.

13. Sri Aurobindo, *Isha Upanishad,* 13–15.

14. Sri Aurobindo, *Isha Upanishad,* 30.

15. Sri Aurobindo, *Supplement,* 424; *Essays in Philosophy and Yoga,* 108; *Kena and Other Upanishads,* 95–96.

16. Sri Aurobindo, *Essays on the Gita,* 4–5.

17. Sri Aurobindo, *Essays on the Gita,* 563.

18. Sri Aurobindo, *Essays on the Gita,* 563–564.

19. Sri Aurobindo, *Essays on the Gita,* 569–570.

20. Sri Aurobindo, *Essays on the Gita,* 564.

21. *Arya* prospectus, published in *Sri Aurobindo: Archives and Research* 13 (April 1989): 106.

22. Sri Aurobindo, *The Life Divine,* 1.

23. Sri Aurobindo, *The Life Divine,* 1–5.

24. Sri Aurobindo, *The Life Divine,* 10, 19, 24.

25. Sri Aurobindo, *The Life Divine,* 115, 132.

26. Sri Aurobindo, *The Life Divine,* 271, 167, 580.

27. Sri Aurobindo, *The Life Divine,* 95, 591–592.

28. Sri Aurobindo, *Savitri,* 2.

29. Sri Aurobindo, *The Life Divine,* 157.

30. Sri Aurobindo, *The Life Divine,* 655–656.

31. Sri Aurobindo, *The Life Divine,* 741, 677, 691, 762, 846–847.

32. Sri Aurobindo, *The Life Divine,* 964, 1018, 967, 1030, 1022, 1059, 1069, 1067.

33. Sri Aurobindo, note published in *Sri Aurobindo: Archives and Research* 7 (December 1983): 164.

34. Sri Aurobindo, note published in *Sri Aurobindo: Archives and Research* 7 (December 1983): 164–165.

35. S. Phillips, "Mutable God: Hartshorne and Indian Theism," 119.

36. Sri Aurobindo, *Essays in Philosophy and Yoga,* 172–175.

37. Sri Aurobindo, *Essays in Philosophy and Yoga*, 244, 151, 152, 157.

38. Sri Aurobindo, *Essays in Philosophy and Yoga*, 211.

39. Sri Aurobindo, *Essays in Philosophy and Yoga*, 119.

40. Sri Aurobindo, *The Life Divine*, 67.

41. Prospectus of the *Arya*; text reproduced on the inside front cover of each issue of the journal.

42. Sri Aurobindo, *Essays in Philosophy and Yoga*, 104.

43. Sri Aurobindo, *The Synthesis of Yoga*, before text, 6.

44. Sri Aurobindo, *The Synthesis of Yoga*, 5, 9.

45. Sri Aurobindo, *The Synthesis of Yoga*, 38.

46. Sri Aurobindo, *The Synthesis of Yoga*, 42–43.

47. Sri Aurobindo, *The Synthesis of Yoga*, 43–44.

48. Sri Aurobindo, *The Synthesis of Yoga*, 45–46, 48.

49. Sri Aurobindo, *The Synthesis of Yoga*, 72.

50. Sri Aurobindo, *The Synthesis of Yoga*, 191.

51. Sri Aurobindo, *The Synthesis of Yoga*, 191–192.

52. Sri Aurobindo, *The Synthesis of Yoga*, 247, 275.

53. Sri Aurobindo, *The Synthesis of Yoga*, 294, 296.

54. Sri Aurobindo, *The Synthesis of Yoga*, 301.

55. Sri Aurobindo, *The Synthesis of Yoga*, 304.

56. Sri Aurobindo, *The Synthesis of Yoga*, 291.

57. Sri Aurobindo, *The Synthesis of Yoga*, 299.

58. Sri Aurobindo, *The Synthesis of Yoga*, 391.

59. Sri Aurobindo, *The Synthesis of Yoga*, 448.

60. Sri Aurobindo, *The Synthesis of Yoga*, 492.

61. Sri Aurobindo, *The Synthesis of Yoga*, 551.

62. Sri Aurobindo, *The Synthesis of Yoga*, 557.

63. Sri Aurobindo, *The Synthesis of Yoga*, 589.

64. Sri Aurobindo, *The Synthesis of Yoga*, 605–606.

65. Sri Aurobindo, *Essays Divine and Human*, 483.

66. Sri Aurobindo, *The Synthesis of Yoga*, 613.

67. Sri Aurobindo, *The Synthesis of Yoga*, 692–695.

68. Sri Aurobindo, *The Synthesis of Yoga*, 703.

69. Sri Aurobindo, *The Synthesis of Yoga*, 722.

70. Sri Aurobindo, *The Synthesis of Yoga*, 729.

71. Sri Aurobindo, *The Synthesis of Yoga*, 742.

72. Sri Aurobindo, *The Synthesis of Yoga*, 754–755.

73. Sri Aurobindo, *The Synthesis of Yoga*, 777.

74. Sri Aurobindo, *The Synthesis of Yoga*, 796.

75. Sri Aurobindo, *The Synthesis of Yoga*, 832.

76. Sri Aurobindo, *The Synthesis of Yoga*, 886.

77. Sri Aurobindo, *The Synthesis of Yoga*, 46–47, 55.

78. Sri Aurobindo, *Essays in Philosophy and Yoga*, 146.

79. Sri Aurobindo, *Essays in Philosophy and Yoga*, 462.

80. Sri Aurobindo, *The Human Cycle, The Ideal of Human Unity, War and Self-Determination*, 280.

81. Sri Aurobindo, *The Human Cycle*, 284.

82. Sri Aurobindo, *The Human Cycle*, 281.

83. Sri Aurobindo, *The Human Cycle*, 285, 293, 297, 302.

84. Sri Aurobindo, *The Human Cycle*, 533, 547, 565, 571, 577.

85. Sri Aurobindo, *On Himself*, 221.

86. G. Salvadori, "The Psychological Interpretation of History," 393–404.

87. Sri Aurobindo, *The Human Cycle*, 6.

88. Sri Aurobindo, *The Human Cycle*, 11, 27.

89. Sri Aurobindo, *The Human Cycle*, 15–16, 44, 33–34, 35, 65–66.

90. Sri Aurobindo, *The Human Cycle*, 102, 112.

91. Sri Aurobindo, *The Human Cycle*, 177–178.

92. Sri Aurobindo, *The Human Cycle*, 181.

93. Sri Aurobindo, *The Human Cycle*, 239.

94. Sri Aurobindo, *The Human Cycle*, 184.

95. Sri Aurobindo, *The Human Cycle*, 263.

96. Sri Aurobindo, *The Renaissance in India with a Defence of Indian Culture*, 3, 5, 15.

97. Sri Aurobindo, *The Renaissance in India*, 10, 5–6.

98. Sri Aurobindo, *The Renaissance in India*, 16.

99. Sri Aurobindo, *The Renaissance in India*, 31, 20, 33.

100. Sri Aurobindo, *The Renaissance in India*, 15.

101. W. Archer, *India and the Future*, xiv, 5.

102. Sri Aurobindo, *The Renaissance in India*, 65–66.

103. Sri Aurobindo, *The Renaissance in India*, 59, 89, 75, 93, 85.

104. Sri Aurobindo, *The Renaissance in India*, 62.

105. Sri Aurobindo, *The Renaissance in India*, 120, 155.

106. W. Archer, *India and the Future*, 209; Sri Aurobindo, *The Renaissance in India*, 103.

107. Sri Aurobindo, *The Renaissance in India*, 89–90.

108. W. Archer, *India and the Future*, 73.

109. Sri Aurobindo, *The Renaissance in India*, 243.

110. Sri Aurobindo, *The Renaissance in India*, 267.

111. Sri Aurobindo, *The Renaissance in India*, 357–358.

112. Sri Aurobindo, *The Renaissance in India*, 384, 426.

113. Sri Aurobindo, *The Renaissance in India*, 443, 441, 444.

114. Sri Aurobindo, *Record of Yoga*, 909.

115. Sri Aurobindo, *Savitri*, before text.

116. First draft of *Savitri*, Sri Aurobindo Papers, NB G35, 113–114, in SAAA.

117. Sri Aurobindo, *The Future Poetry*, 8.

118. M. Arnold, *Selected Essays*, 47, 48.

119. Sri Aurobindo, *Early Cultural Writings*, 126.

120. Sri Aurobindo, *Collected Poems*, 523, 535–536.

121. J. Cousins, *New Ways in English Literature*, 27–31.

122. Sri Aurobindo, *On Himself*, 371.

123. Sri Aurobindo, *The Future Poetry*, 11–15, 19.

124. Sri Aurobindo, *The Future Poetry*, 19, 24.

125. Sri Aurobindo, *The Future Poetry*, 29–30, 32.

126. Sri Aurobindo, *The Future Poetry*, 38, 48, 51–52, 61, 46.

127. Sri Aurobindo, *The Future Poetry*, 66, 70.

128. Sri Aurobindo, *The Future Poetry*, 79–80.

129. Sri Aurobindo, *The Future Poetry*, 93, 95, 101, 103, 148.

130. Sri Aurobindo, *The Future Poetry*, 213–214.

131. Sri Aurobindo, *The Future Poetry*, 222, 240, 223, 263, 270, 302–303.

132. Sri Aurobindo, *Early Cultural Writings*, 631–633.

133. Harindranath Chattopadhyay, "Reverie," *Shama'a* 1, no. 1 (April 1920): 40.

134. Sri Aurobindo, *On Himself*, 273.

135. T. S. Eliot, "Modern Tendencies in Poetry," reprinted in *Shama'a* 1, no. 1 (April 1920): 9–18. Eliot delivered the lecture in England in October 1919.

Part Five: Guide

Epigraph: Sri Aurobindo, *The Human Cycle, The Ideal of Human Unity, War and Self-Determination*, 180.

8. The Ascent to Supermind

Epigraph: Sri Aurobindo, letter to Barindrakumar Ghose, April 1920, published in *Bangla Rachana*, 360.

1. Sri Aurobindo, *On Himself*, 459.

2. Sri Aurobindo, *Record of Yoga*, 909.

3. Sri Aurobindo, *Record of Yoga*, 1477, 948, 1075.

4. Sri Aurobindo, *Record of Yoga*, 949.

5. Sri Aurobindo, *Record of Yoga*, 940–941.

6. Sri Aurobindo, *Record of Yoga*, 456.

7. N. Gupta, *Smritir Pata*, 39; Purani Talks manuscripts 5: 86–88, in SAAA; "May I come in?" anecdote communicated orally by Nolini Kanta Gupta to author via Matri Prasad, January 8, 1983. My thanks to the late Nolini Kanta Gupta and to Matri Prasad for sharing this information.

8. S. Chakravarty, *Smritikatha*, 159.

9. Nirodbaran, ed. *Talks with Sri Aurobindo*, 321.

10. Sri Aurobindo, *On Himself*, 424.

11. P. Richard, "Without Passport," 75–76, 79; letter from French Foreign Ministry, Department of Political and Commercial Affairs, to "all diplomatic and consular agents of

the Republic in Japan and China," in SAAA, reproduced in English translation in *Sri Aurobindo: Archives and Research* 18 (December 1994): 238, cf. *L'agenda de Mère,* vol. 2: 407.

12. Sri Aurobindo, letter to the editor, *New India,* August 10, 1918.

13. Sri Aurobindo, letter to the editor of *Hindustan,* reproduced in *Sri Aurobindo: Archives and Research* 8 (December 1984): 190.

14. Office of the Director, Criminal Intelligence, *Politico-Criminal Who's Who,* 78.

15. J. Nixon, *An Account of the Revolutionary Organisations in Bengal,* 110.

16. S. Rowlatt, *Report of Committee Appointed to Investigate Revolutionary Conspiracies in India,* 19.

17. J. Ker, *Political Trouble in India,* 473–481.

18. J. Armstrong, *An Account of the Revolutionary Organization in Eastern Bengal,* i.

19. A. Purani, *The Life of Sri Aurobindo,* 292–295; see also 166.

20. Letter from R. Tagore to unknown recipient, November 30, 1919, in SAAA.

21. Sri Aurobindo, undated draft letter to Nolini Kanta Gupta, reproduced in *Sri Aurobindo: Archives and Research* 16 (December 1994): 219.

22. M. Dey, "My Darshan of Sri Aurobindo at Pondicherry," 26–28 (translation slightly amended). I have amplified the description of the house using A.B. Purani's description of his visit in December 1918. Dey's visit took place in April 1919.

23. B. Bose, note on Mrinalini Ghose, in SAAA, reproduced in *Sri Aurobindo: Archives and Research* 2 (December 1978): 208.

24. Sri Aurobindo, *Supplement,* 422.

25. B. Bose, note on Mrinalini Ghose, in SAAA, reproduced in *Sri Aurobindo: Archives and Research* 2 (December 1978): 208.

26. Sri Aurobindo, *Letters on Yoga,* 1528, 1512; Sri Aurobindo, talk of December 13, 1923, partly published in *Sri Aurobindo Circle* 9 (1953): 207.

27. The Mother, *Entretiens 1953,* 206–210.

28. The Mother, *L'agenda de Mère,* vol. 2: 407; S. Banerji, "Some Notes on the Mother's Prières et Méditations." *Mother India* 31 (May 1979): 268.

29. The Mother, *Paroles d'autrefois,* 168.

30. Purani Talks manuscripts 2: 310–311.

31. Sri Aurobindo, *Record of Yoga,* 1156.

32. Sri Aurobindo, *Record of Yoga,* 1185.

33. Sri Aurobindo, *Record of Yoga,* 1200.

34. Sri Aurobindo, *Record of Yoga,* 1220–1222.

35. A. Purani, *Life,* 174.

36. Letter to Barindrakumar Ghose, April 1920, translation in *Sri Aurobindo: Archives and Research* 4 (April 1980): 1–9.

37. Letter to Barindrakumar Ghose.

38. Letter to Barindrakumar Ghose.

39. Sri Aurobindo, *Supplement,* 488–495.

40. B. Ghose, "Sri Aurobindo as I Understand Him," 76, in SAAA.

41. B. Ghose, "Sri Aurobindo as I Understand Him," 80.

42. Sri Aurobindo, *Essays in Philosophy and Yoga,* 509.

43. Purani Talks manuscripts 5: 282–283; Sri Aurobindo, *Supplement*, 485; T. Kodandarama Rao, *At the Feet of the Master*, 20.

44. Sri Aurobindo, *On Himself*, 432.

45. Sri Aurobindo, *Supplement*, 499.

46. Bhupendranath K. Dutta, quoted in G. Bandyopadhyay, *Constraints in Bengal Politics*, 116–117.

47. Sri Aurobindo, letter of April 14, 1936, in SAAA.

48. B. Ghose, "Sri Aurobindo as I Understand Him," 79

49. Purani Talks manuscripts 9: 80; 5: 98. Richard, who knew virtually no Tamil, seems to have combined two phrases, *seththup pochchi*, which is colloquial Tamil for "he/she died," and *aypochchu*, which means "it is over."

50. Purani Talks manuscripts 5: 76. In the interest of coherent dialogue, I have expanded and slightly amended Purani's notes regarding this incident, which read: "(One day P.R. came & asked him in what way he (A. G.) related to Mirra. He said she was his disciple. But what was her attitude towards him. He said in whatever way the disciple will aspire for me he will get me as such [possibly an allusion to *Bhagavad Gita* 4.11]—Suppose she claims relations of marriage. 'Well she will have that'—)." In a report of what appears to be a separate conversation between Aurobindo and Richard, Purani writes that in reply to a question from Richard about Mirra "A. G. simply said she had offered herself to him & she had been accepted. It was her lookout to do what she wanted to do.—"

51. The Mother, *L'agenda de Mère*, vol. 2: 409; R. Rolland, *Inde: Journal 1915–1943*, 28.

52. V. Chidanandam, ed., "Sri Aurobindo at Evening Talks," *Mother India* 21 (January 1970): 791.

53. P. Davis, "Summary," xxiii.

54. Talk of August 26, 1926, as recorded by A.B. Purani (Purani Talks manuscripts 11: 132–133), and by V. Chidanandam ("Sri Aurobindo at Evening Talks," *Mother India* 24 [August 1972]: 484). I have quoted partly from one, partly from the other account.

55. Aurobindo to V. Chandrasekhar, April 13, 1921, published in *Mother India* 21 (August 1969): 456.

56. V. Chidanandam, ed., "Sri Aurobindo at Evening Talks," *Mother India* 24 (August 1972): 484 (date of talk July 16, 1926).

57. B. Ghose, "Sri Aurobindo as I Understand Him," II, 123a.

58. Sri Aurobindo, *The Synthesis of Yoga*, 627.

59. A. Purani, ed., *Evening Talks with Sri Aurobindo*, 339.

60. B. Ghose, "Sri Aurobindo as I Understand Him," 93; see also Sri Aurobindo, *The Mother with Letters on the Mother*, 362.

61. B. Ghose, "Sri Aurobindo as I Understand Him," 87.

62. Purani Talks manuscripts 5: 18; V. Chidanandam, ed., "Sri Aurobindo at Evening Talks," *Mother India* 24 (March 1972): 89.

63. A. Purani Papers (Ashram History Collection, alphabetical series), 5a, 12, in SAAA.

64. T. Kodandarama Rao, *At the Feet*, 41; V. Chidanandam, "Sri Aurobindo and the Mother as I Saw Them," 2.

65. A. Purani, "An Intimate Glimpse of the Master," *Sunday Times,* December 17, 1950, 2.

66. Purani Talks manuscripts 12: 377.

67. T. Kodandarama Rao, *At the Feet,* 15, 41.

68. Sri Aurobindo, *The Synthesis of Yoga,* 344.

69. Purani Talks manuscripts 5: 89; T. Kodandarama Rao, *At the Feet,* 17.

70. A. Purani, ed., *Evening Talks,* 9; Chidatmananda, "Towards Peace," 508; V. Chidanandam, "Sri Aurobindo and the Mother," 4.

71. V. Chidanandam, "Sri Aurobindo and the Mother," 1; Purani Talks manuscripts 14: 32.

72. Purani Talks manuscripts 2: 114–15. I have emended Purani's transcription, which reads: "He is one of Big asses I have ever seen."

73. A. Purani, *Life,* 181; T. Kodandarama Rao, *At the Feet,* 33; B. Chakrabarti, "Amader Aurodada," 783.

74. T. Kodandarama Rao, *At the Feet,* 17.

75. Purani Talks manuscripts 5: 58.

76. A. Purani, "An Intimate Glimpse," 2.

77. Purani Talks manuscripts 5: 87.

78. T. Kodandarama Rao, *At the Feet,* 22.

79. S. Bose, *An Indian Pilgrim,* 61, 112.

80. *The Standard Bearer* 1, February 13, 1921, 195.

81. Amrita to Purani July 1, 1922, in SAAA.

82. A. Roy, ed., "Conversations with Sri Aurobindo," *Sri Aurobindo Circle* 35 (1979): 21.

83. Sri Aurobindo, talk of May 12, 1926, Haradhan Bakshi Papers, notebook 3, 125–126, in SAAA.

84. B. Ghose, "Sri Aurobindo as I Understand Him," 87–88.

85. B. Ghose, "Sri Aurobindo as I Understand Him," 88.

86. Sri Aurobindo, *On Himself,* 436–437.

87. H. Das Gupta, *Deshbandhu Chittaranjan Das,* 77.

88. Sri Aurobindo, *On Himself,* 438–439.

89. Sri Aurobindo, *On Himself,* 439.

90. Sri Aurobindo, *On Himself,* 390.

91. *Times of India,* June 25, 1925.

92. Purani Talks manuscripts 8: 87.

93. Purani Talks manuscripts 8: 1–5.

94. B. Ghose, "Sri Aurobindo as I Understand Him," 93.

95. Sri Aurobindo, letter of December 30, 1922, in SAAA.

96. B. Ghose, "Sri Aurobindo as I Understand Him," 95.

97. Sri Aurobindo, letter of January 23, 1923, in SAAA.

98. T. Kodandarama Rao, *At the Feet,* 20.

99. Purani Talks manuscripts 5: 88; 3: 213, 255.

100. Postcard from K. Amrita to N. S. Chidambaram, December 1, 1924, in SAAA.

101. C. E. Lefebvre to Aurobindo, June 13, 1926, in SAAA.

102. Sri Aurobindo, undated letter draft, published in *Bulletin of Sri Aurobindo International Centre of Education* vol. 28, no. 3 (August 1976): 46–47.

103. Sri Aurobindo, undated letter draft, published in *Bulletin of Sri Aurobindo International Centre of Education* vol. 28, no. 3 (August 1976): 48.

104. Sri Aurobindo, undated letter drafts to Mr. and Mrs. Sharman and to C. E. Lefebvre, published in *Bulletin of Sri Aurobindo International Centre of Education* vol. 28, no. 3 (August 1976): 45–46, 48.

105. Sri Aurobindo, talk of May 12, 1926, Haradhan Bakshi Papers, notebook 3, 23, in SAAA. Defective idiom and spelling modified slightly.

106. Purani Talks manuscripts 8: 91–92.

107. A. Purani, ed., *Evening Talks,* 10.

108. A. Purani, ed., *Evening Talks,* 10–11.

109. V. Chidanandam, ed., "Sri Aurobindo at Evening Talks," *Mother India* 23 (February–March 1971): 21–24, 94–97 (talk of August 6, 1926).

110. Purani Talks manuscripts 11: 154.

111. Purani Talks manuscripts 5: 83; V. Chidanandam, "Introduction" to V. Chidanandam, ed., "Sri Aurobindo at Evening Talks," *Mother India* 21 (August 1969): 472.

112. A. Purani, *Life,* 196–197. Purani places this description with events of the year 1924, but it is more likely that it belongs in 1923.

113. Talk of August 15, 1923, published in A. Purani, ed., *Evening Talks,* 484–485.

114. Talk of August 15, 1924, published in A. Purani, ed., *Evening Talks,* 492–494.

115. Talk of August 15, 1925, published in A. Purani, ed., *Evening Talks,* 498–500.

116. A. Purani, *Life,* 214.

117. A. Purani, *Life,* 217.

118. Haradhan Bakshi Papers, notebook 3, 238, 232, in SAAA; letter of August 21, 1935, in SAAA.

119. Sri Aurobindo, reported oral remarks, notation of November 27, 1926, Haradhan Bakshi Papers, notebook 3, 240, in SAAA.

120. Sri Aurobindo, *On Himself,* 189–190.

9. An Active Retirement

Epigraph: Sri Aurobindo, Letter to Dilip Kumar Roy, August 14, 1945, published in *On Himself,* 189.

1. B. Ghose, "Sri Aurobindo as I Understand Him," 99.

2. P. Shah to C. Shah January 11, 1927, in SAAA; B. Ghose, "Sri Aurobindo as I Understand Him," 105; K. Dixit to C. Shah July 14, 1927, in SAAA.

3. Sri Aurobindo, *Record of Yoga,* 1247, 1251, 1254, 1261, 1263.

4. Sri Aurobindo, *Record of Yoga,* 1265–1270.

5. Sri Aurobindo, *Record of Yoga,* 1271–1273.

6. Sri Aurobindo, *Record of Yoga,* 1356–1357.

7. Sri Aurobindo, *Letters on Yoga,* 257, 263.

8. Sri Aurobindo, *Essays Divine and Human,* 316–317.

9. Sri Aurobindo, *Essays Divine and Human,* 284–285, 221.

10. Sri Aurobindo, *Essays Divine and Human*, 155, 373.

11. Sri Aurobindo, *The Mother with Letters on the Mother*, 1–5.

12. Sri Aurobindo, *The Mother*, 40–41.

13. Sri Aurobindo, *The Life Divine*, 356.

14. Sri Aurobindo, *The Mother*, 47, 20.

15. Sri Aurobindo, reply to letter dated March 23, 1927, in SAAA.

16. Sri Aurobindo, *On Himself*, 456.

17. J. Sen Gupta, "Sri Aurobindo's Ashram: Daily Life of Inmates," *Hindu*, May 6, 1927.

18. The Mother, *Entretiens 1957–58*, 168.

19. B. Ghose, "Sri Aurobindo as I Understand Him," 102.

20. The Mother, *Entretiens 1957–58*, 168–69.

21. Sri Aurobindo, *On Himself*, 473–474, 472.

22. Pavitra, ed., *Conversations avec Pavitra*, 141.

23. P. Saint Hilaire to his father, December 6, 1928, published in P. Saint Hilaire, *Itinéraire d'un enfant du siècle*, 138–139.

24. Sri Aurobindo, letter of July 29, 1927, in SAAA.

25. Sri Aurobindo, letter of March 26, 1926, published in *Sri Aurobindo Circle* 32 (1976): 25–26.

26. Sri Aurobindo, *Letters on Yoga*, 276, 438.

27. The Mother, *L'agenda de Mère*, vol. 2 (1961): 93–94.

28. Sri Aurobindo, *Essays in Philosophy and Yoga*, 445.

29. Sri Aurobindo, *The Synthesis of Yoga*, 472; *The Life Divine*, 456; *Synthesis of Yoga*, 785.

30. Report of conversation between A.B. Purani and Olive Maitland-Marsh, 1929, in A. Purani Papers, in SAAA.

31. J. Sen Gupta, "Sri Aurobindo's Ashram: Daily Life of Inmates."

32. J. Sen Gupta, "Sri Aurobindo's Ashram: Daily Life of Inmates." Sri Aurobindo's handwritten manuscript of this paragraph is in SAAA.

33. Sri Aurobindo, *Supplement*, 416.

34. P. Saint Hilaire, *Itinéraire*, 139.

35. Sri Aurobindo, *The Mother*, 12.

36. R. Tagore, "Aurobindo Ghosh," 58–60.

37. Sri Aurobindo, *On Himself*, 162; Nirodbaran, ed., *Correspondence with Sri Aurobindo*, 789.

38. Subhas Chandra Bose, speech of December 1928, reproduced in Hay, ed., *Sources of Indian Tradition*, 306–307.

39. Nolini Kanta Gupta, "Sir [*sic*] Aurobindo and his 'School': Some Misapprehensions Cleared," *Hindu*, January 7, 1929.

40. J. Nehru, "Foreword," x.

41. O. Maitland-Marsh, *Uplifting Humanity*, 160–161.

42. Sri Aurobindo, letter of September 16, 1932; letter of January 1932; letter from M.K. Gandhi to Sri Aurobindo, January 7, 1934; reply of Sri Aurobindo to Gandhi, January 7, 1934, in SAAA.

43. Sri Aurobindo, letter of February 21, 1935, in SAAA.

44. "Sri Aurobindo." *Advance*, August 15, 1937; K. Gandhi, "What is Sri Aurobindo Doing?"

45. Sri Aurobindo, *Letters on Poetry and Art*, 457, 211.

46. Undated fragmentary letter published in *Sri Aurobindo's Action* 6 (February–March 1976), 4

47. Sri Aurobindo, *On Himself*, 196; 144, 145, 147.

48. Sri Aurobindo, letter of September 30, 1929, in SAAA.

49. Sri Aurobindo, *On Himself*, 474, 159.

50. Sri Aurobindo, Undated letter (1930–32, the "decade" mentioned is certainly the 1930s), in SAAA; Sri Aurobindo, *On Himself*, 147, 470, 470–471.

51. R. Rolland *La vie de Vivekananda et l'évangile universel*, 191; "India on the March," 411–412; *La vie de Vivekananda*, 191; *Inde: Journal*, 279, 494.

52. Notice of July 17, 1934, in SAAA.

53. Sri Aurobindo, letter of June 17, 1933, published in *On Himself*, 186.

54. Sri Aurobindo, *On Himself*, 224

55. Nirodbaran, ed., *Correspondence*, 257, 259.

56. Nirodbaran, ed., *Correspondence*, 101.

57. Sri Aurobindo, *Letters on Yoga*, 1665–1666.

58. Sri Aurobindo, *Collected Poems*, 577.

59. Sri Aurobindo, *Collected Poems*, 572.

60. Sri Aurobindo, *Collected Poems*, 161.

61. Sri Aurobindo, undated letter, published in *Bulletin of Sri Aurobindo International Centre of Education* vol. 53, no. 1 (February 2001): 72.

62. V. Ananthakrishan, "Sri Arabindo and his Cult," *Liberty*, April 19, 1933; Sri Aurobindo, *On Himself*, 125.

63. R. Agarwal, "Sri Aurobindo's Asram: Impressions of a Visitor," in SAAA.

64. Sri Aurobindo, *Letters on Yoga*, 856.

65. Sri Aurobindo, letter of February 17, 1934, in SAAA. See also K. Sethna, *Our Light and Delight*, 88–89.

66. "Sri Aurobindo Ashram: Some Misconceptions Cleared." *Hindu* (Madras), February 20, 1934, most reprinted in Sri Aurobindo, *On Himself*, 95–97.

67. Sri Aurobindo, *The Mother*, 360; The Mother, *Entretiens 1954*, 340.

68. Notebook entry dated October 27, 1933 with Sri Aurobindo's comment, published in "Experiences of a Sadhak," *Bulletin of Sri Aurobindo International Centre of Education* vol. 28, no. 3 (August 1976): 74; Sri Aurobindo's reply also published in Sri Aurobindo, *Letters on Yoga*, 1129.

69. Sri Aurobindo, letter of November 6, 1935, in SAAA; letter of February 2, 1935, in SAAA; Nirodbaran, ed., *Correspondence*, 246; Sri Aurobindo, *Letters on Yoga*, 353; letter of June 6, 1935, in SAAA; *On Himself*, 143.

70. Nirodbaran, ed., *Correspondence*, 464.

71. Nirodbaran, ed., *Correspondence*, 553.

72. Nirodbaran, ed., *Correspondence*, 78–80.

73. Nirodbaran, ed., *Correspondence*, 161.

74. Sri Aurobindo, *On Himself,* 153; see also Nirodbaran, ed., *Correspondence,* 852.

75. Nirodbaran, ed., *Correspondence,* 287–288, 388–389; A. Purani, ed., *Evening Talks with Sri Aurobindo,* 543.

76. Sri Aurobindo, *On Himself,* 154–155.

77. Sri Aurobindo, *Letters on Yoga,* 8–9; letter of June 6, 1935, in SAAA; Nirodbaran, ed., *Correspondence,* 590, 594; 222, 221.

78. Sri Aurobindo, letter published in *Mother India* 36 (March 1984): 158; Sri Aurobindo, letters May 24, 1935 and November 5, 1933, in SAAA.

79. Rules of Sri Aurobindo Ashram, in SAAA.

80. Notice of August 31, 1936, in SAAA; Sri Aurobindo, letter of August 19, 1934, in SAAA.

81. Notice of November 2, 1938, in SAAA.

82. Sri Aurobindo, *Letters on Poetry and Art,* 272.

83. Lines appended to letter of October 24, 1936, published in Sri Aurobindo, *Letters on Poetry and Art,* 265.

84. Sri Aurobindo, *Letters on Poetry and Art,* 276, 357.

85. Note to A. B. Purani, June or July 1933, in SAAA.

86. Sri Aurobindo, *On Himself,* 375–376.

87. G. Monod-Herzen, "Reminiscences of Sri Aurobindo," 497.

88. Sri Aurobindo, letter of November 25, 1935, in SAAA.

89. J. Roy, "Sri Aurobindo: Eventful Life Dedicated to Truth," *Advance,* February 21, 1938.

90. Nirodbaran, ed., *Correspondence,* 852, 858, 913, 1067.

91. Nirodbaran, ed., *Correspondence,* 1156–1157.

92. Sri Aurobindo, *Collected Poems,* 120.

93. Nirodbaran, *Twelve Years with Sri Aurobindo,* 7.

94. A. Purani, ed., *Evening Talks,* 12–13; Nirodbaran, *Twelve Years,* 1–5.

95. Nirodbaran, *Twelve Years,* 10–11.

96. Nirodbaran, *Twelve Years,* 11–13.

97. Nirodbaran, *Twelve Years,* 228, 14.

98. Nirodbaran, ed. *Talks with Sri Aurobindo,* 64–70.

99. Nirodbaran, ed. *Talks,* 35–36.

100. Nirodbaran, ed. *Talks,* 19.

101. Nirodbaran, *Twelve Years,* 21–32.

102. Nirodbaran, *Twelve Years,* 36–37.

103. A. Purani, ed., *Evening Talks,* 641–642, 725.

104. "Nazi System Must Go: Sri Aurobindo on the War." *Hindu,* September 19, 1940, partially reprinted in Sri Aurobindo, *On Himself,* 393.

105. K. Munshi, "Sri Aurobindo," 304.

106. Letter from Jayakrishna Manoubhai Patel, Nadiad, September 25, 1940 and letter from students, Scottish Church College, Calcutta, October 30, 1940, in SAAA; Nirodbaran, ed. *Talks,* 641.

107. Sri Aurobindo, undated note, published in *Bulletin of Sri Aurobindo International Centre of Education* 28, no. 1 (February 1976): 26; Sri Aurobindo, *On Himself,* 394.

108. Sri Aurobindo, *On Himself,* 38–39.

109. Sri Aurobindo, *On Himself,* 379.

110. Nirodbaran, ed. *Talks,* 680–681.

111. Partial transcript of interview of Roy with Sri Aurobindo, February 4, 1943, Dilip K. Roy Papers, in SAAA.

112. For negative journalistic views of Sri Aurobindo's supposed claim to have won the battle of Stalingrad, see V. Sheean, "Kings of the Yogis," 75 and C. Hamblett, "Eternity Greets a God," *Illustrated,* January 6, 1951, 28. For a more positive but still incredulous view, see W. Sargeant, "Holy Man," *Life,* May 30, 1949, 92.

113. Sri Aurobindo, *On Himself,* 198.

114. Sri Aurobindo, *The Life Divine,* 1067–1068.

115. F. Younghusband, "An Indian Seer: The Philosophy of Sri Aurobindo," *Times Literary Supplement,* January 17, 1942, 28.

116. Younghusband to Dilip Kumar Roy, December 17, 1941, published in *Mother India* 27 (August 1975): 623; Annika Ekdahl, Nobel Foundation, Stockholm, email to author, March 6, 2003; Sekretariat, Swedish Academy, email to author, April 17, 2003.

117. Sri Aurobindo, *Collected Poems,* 142.

118. R. Shahani, "A Philosopher of Modern India: Aurobindo the Reconciler," *Times Literary Supplement,* July 8, 1944, 330.

119. R. Shahani, "A Philosopher," 330.

120. S. Bharatiar, "Bhagawan Sri Aurobindo: The Superman Who Directs India to Life Divine," 3.

121. Sri Aurobindo, message to Cripps, reproduced in *On* Himself, 399; telegraphic reply from Cripps, reproduced in Sri Aurobindo, *On Himself,* 399.

122. H.K. Basu, "Rejoinder to Mr. G.C. Chatterjee's appeal." *Hindusthan Standard,* April 7, 1942.

123. Gandhi quoted in letter from Duraiswami to Sri Aurobindo, April 5, 1942, in SAAA; Gandhi to Sri Aurobindo, April 5, 1942, in SAAA.

124. W. Churchill, "Speech . . . at the Mansion House," 344.

125. Nirodbaran, *Twelve Years,* 158–159; A. Purani, ed., *Evening Talks,* 747.

126. P. Spear, *A History of India,* 220; K. Munshi, "Sri Aurobindo," 305.

127. Sri Aurobindo, *On Himself,* 39.

128. Sri Aurobindo, *On Himself,* 398.

129. Emperor Hirohito ordered an end to hostilities at noon, local time, on August 15, 1945. The news was announced in Britain shortly after midnight, local time, on the morning of August 15, and in the United States at 7 p.m., local time, on August 14. Since then the day of Allied victory over Japan (V-J Day) has been regarded as August 14 in the United States but as August 15 in Britain and Asia.

130. Message of April 6, 1942; undated message, published in *Bulletin of Sri Aurobindo International Centre of Education* vol. 28, no. 2 (April 1976): 58, 60.

131. Sri Aurobindo, *The Mother,* 231.

132. S. Ghosh, "Two Interviews with Surendra Mohan Ghose," 2.

133. S. Ghosh, "A Talk by Surendra Mohan Ghose," 30.

460 9. An Active Retirement

134. Sri Aurobindo, *On Himself,* 169; Nirodbaran, *Twelve Years,* 251.

135. P. Ziegler, *Mountbatten: The Official Biography,* 386–387, citing Mountbatten's *Time Only to Look Forward: Speeches . . . as Viceroy of India* (London: Nicholas Kaye, 1949), 43.

136. Sri Aurobindo, *On Himself,* 170.

137. Sri Aurobindo, *On Himself,* 404–406.

138. *Hindu,* August 21, 1947; B. Latif, *Her India,* 185.

139. Nirodbaran, *Twelve Years,* 213–214.

140. Nirodbaran, *Twelve Years,* 47–48; Sri Aurobindo, *Record of Yoga,* 276.

141. Nirodbaran, *Twelve Years,* 48–50.

142. Nirodbaran, *Twelve Years,* 51–57.

143. Nirodbaran, *Twelve Years,* 58–59.

144. Sri Aurobindo, *Letters on Poetry and Art,* 276.

145. Sri Aurobindo, *Collected Poems,* 108.

146. Sri Aurobindo, *On Himself,* 170.

147. R. Ganguli, "Pondicherry's Mystic," *Amrita Bazar Patrika,* February 22, 1950.

148. V. Sheean, "Kings," 75.

149. S. Ghose and F. Baron, "Two Personal Documents of Historical Importance," 648–649; S. Ghosh, "A Talk," 30.

150. Press release, Agènce France-Presse, dated September 27, 1947, in SAAA, reported in the *Hindu,* September 29, 1947.

151. Sri Aurobindo, *On Himself,* 417–419.

152. Sri Aurobindo, *On Himself,* 406–407.

153. "Regeneration of India: Aid of Spiritual Leaders Urged: Socialists' Plan." *Times of India,* February 24, 1948; "Aurobindo and Swami Ramana Can Help Build Up Nation," *Indian Express,* April 16, 1948.

154. Sri Aurobindo, *On Himself,* 171.

155. C. R. Reddy to Sri Aurobindo, June 28, 1948, in SAAA.

156. Sri Aurobindo, *On Himself,* 416–417.

157. S. Ghosh, *Gandhi's Emissary,* 314–315. What Ghosh showed Kennedy was a passage from Sethna's editorial "The Truth about Tibet," published in *Mother India* 2 (November 11, 1950): 2.

158. Nirodbaran, *Twelve Years,* 188–189.

159. Sri Aurobindo, *On Himself,* 413–416.

160. Sorokin quoted in *Mother India* 1 (September 17, 1949): 2.

161. Frederic Spiegelberg, "German Savant in India," *Mother India* 1 (April 30, 1949): 5.

162. Alfred Foucher, "A Call to Supermanhood: An Interpretation of Sri Aurobindo," reprinted in *Mother India* 1 (October 15, 1949): 3; Henri Breuil to Sri Aurobindo, December 1, 1950, published in *Mother India* 24 (December 1972): 778–779.

163. Letter Huxley to Dilip Kumar Roy, June 16, 1948, Roy Papers; G. Mistral, "A Few Words on Sri Aurobindo," 142.

164. Petition with signers reproduced in *Mother India* 2 (September 3, 1949).

165. Letter to author from Geir Ludenstad, Director, Norwegian Nobel Institute, May 6, 2003.

166. V. Sheean, "Kings"; W. Sargeant, "Holy Man."

167. Cartier-Bresson to Pavitra, April 13, 1950, in SAAA; notes of Cartier-Bresson on his visit to Pondicherry and the Sri Aurobindo Ashram (from archives of Magnum Photos), published in *Sri Aurobindo: Archives and Research* 14 (December 1990): 207–209.

168. K. Munshi, "Aurobindo Ashram—A Pilgrimage," *Hindustan Times,* Independence Supplement, August 15, 1952; K.M. Munshi, Convocation Address, July 20, 1950, 3, in SAAA; K.M. Munshi, transcript of interview with Sri Aurobindo, July 3, 1950, in SAAA.

169. Nirodbaran, *Sri Aurobindo: "I Am Here, I Am Here,"* 3; *Twelve Years,* 266.

170. Government of India, Home Department Proceedings, series D, June 1908, 13, 3, National Archives of India, New Delhi; Home Department Proceedings, series A, August 1910, 42–43, 6.

171. Nirodbaran, *Sri Aurobindo,* 4; *Twelve Years,* 267.

172. Sri Aurobindo, letter of December 7, 1949, in SAAA.

173. Nirodbaran, *Twelve Years,* 270.

174. Nirodbaran, *Twelve Years,* 270–271.

175. Sri Aurobindo, *Savitri,* 461.

176. Nirodbaran, *Twelve Years,* 272–273.

177. R. Le Cocq, *The Radical Thinkers: Heidegger and Sri Aurobindo,* 199.

178. Nirodbaran, *Twelve Years,* 277.

179. Nirodbaran, *Twelve Years,* 278; P. Sanyal, "A 'Call' from Pondicherry," 181–182. (I follow Nirodbaran where the two accounts disagree.)

180. P. Sanyal, "A 'Call,'" 181–182.

181. P. Sanyal, "A 'Call,'" 182–184; Nirodbaran, *Twelve Years,* 279–281; Nirodbaran's medical report, 14–18, in SAAA. In *Twelve Years,* Nirodbaran places the blood examination on the fourth, but says that this was a Sunday. December 4, 1950 was a Monday. Nirodbaran's medical report gives the results of the blood examination under "Saturday 3rd", but as the notation comes after the other entries for Sunday, "Saturday" must be an error. Sri Aurobindo's blood sugar at that time was 300 mgm; his blood urea was 90 mgm.

182. Nirodbaran, *Twelve Years,* 280–282; P. Sanyal, "A 'Call,'" 185.

183. Nirodbaran, *Twelve Years,* 285–286; P. Sanyal, "A 'Call,'" 185.

184. P. Sanyal, "A 'Call,'" 186; Nirodbaran, *Twelve Years,* 286–287; U. Pinto, "A Report on Sri Aurobindo's Passing," 754–755.

Epilogue

1. P. Sanyal, "A 'Call' from Pondicherry," 186; Nirodbaran, *Twelve Years with Sri Aurobindo,* 287.

2. P. Sanyal, "A 'Call,'" 186; "The Photographs Taken after Sri Aurobindo's Passing on 5 December 1950," *Sri Aurobindo: Archives and Research* 14 (December 1990): 223–227; *Indian Express,* December 6, 1950.

3. K. Panikkar, "The Philosopher of Modern India," *Manchester Guardian,* December 6, 1950.

4. The Mother, message of December 6, 1950, published in *Amrita Bazar Patrika* and other newspapers, December 8, 1950.

5. *Amrita Bazar Patrika* (Allahabad edition), December 8, 1950.

6. *Certificat* dated December 7, 1950, signed by Dr. Barbet, in SAAA.

7. The Mother, *Words of the Mother,* 6–7.

8. J.B. Kripalani, statement reproduced in *Amrita Bazar Patrika* (Allahabad edition), December 8, 1950.

9. See, e.g., "The 100 Indians Who Shaped Our Century," *Gentleman* (February 1986); "100 People Who Shaped India in the Twentieth Century," *India Today,* The Millennium Series, vol. 1 (2000); "Indians of the Century," *The Times of India* (2000), originally published online at http://www.timesofindia.com/century/vote.html, archived at http://web.archive.org/web/20000301113723/http://timesofindia.com/century/vote.html, accessed July 31, 2007.

10. *Bhagavad Gita* 4.8.

11. Sri Aurobindo, letter of November 17, 1932, in SAAA. See also Sri Aurobindo, *Bande Mataram,* 642–643; *Karmayogin,* 23; *The Human Cycle, The Ideal of Human Unity, War and Self-Determination,* 286, 288, 307–308.

12. Sri Aurobindo, letter of June 1930, published in *Sri Aurobindo: Archives and Research* 9 (April 1985): 72.

13. Sri Aurobindo, *On Himself,* 170.

14. Sri Aurobindo, *On Himself,* 152

15. Sri Aurobindo, *The Life Divine,* 1010.

16. Sri Aurobindo, *The Human Cycle, The Ideal of Human Unity, War and Self-Determination,* 263–264.

17. Sri Aurobindo, *Letters on Yoga,* 150.

Bibliography

I. ARCHIVAL SOURCES

I.1. Sri Aurobindo Ashram Archives (SAAA) Collections

Sri Aurobindo Papers
  Manuscripts 1890–1950
  Biographical documents
The Mother (Mirra Alfassa) Papers
  Manuscripts
  Biographical documents
Ashram History Collection
Papers of Followers of Sri Aurobindo
  Haradhan Bakshi Papers
  Nirodbaran Papers (including Nirodbaran Talks manuscripts)
  A.B. Purani Papers (including Purani Talks manuscripts)
  Dilip Kumar Roy Papers
Unpublished reminiscences
  Ismalun, Mira, "Mes Mémoirs," August 1906
  Benilan, Jean, "Le Gouverneur Alfassa (1876–1942)."
  Bose, Bhupalchandra, Reminiscences of Mrinalini Ghose, August 26, 1931
  Didmishe, S.B., Reminiscences of Sri Aurobindo as a teacher, September 18, 1967
  Ghose, Barindrakumar, "Sri Aurobindo as I Understand Him"
  Gokhale, G.H., Reminiscences of Sri Aurobindo in Baroda
  Jadhav, Govindrao, Reminiscences of Sri Aurobindo
  Patkar, R.N., Reminiscences of Sri Aurobindo at Baroda, September 30, 1956
  Purani, A.B., Reminiscences

I.2. Other Personal and Institutional Collections

Personal

Beveridge Papers, 1871–1890, Indian Office Records, London
Laurence Binyon Papers, British Library (copy of letters from Manmohan Ghose in SAAA)

Alexandra David-Néel Papers, Fondation Alexandra David Néel, Digne-les-Bains, France
Hemendra Prasad Ghose Diary, Department of History, Jadavpur University, Kolkata
Surendra Mohan Ghosh Papers, Nehru Memorial Museum and Library, New Delhi
Hardinge Papers, Cambridge University Library, Cambridge
G. S. Khaparde Diary, National Archives of India, New Delhi
Pherozshah Mehta Papers, National Archives of India, New Delhi
Minto Papers, National Archives of Scotland, Edinburgh
Morley Papers, India Office Records, London
Rabindranath Tagore Papers, Rabindra Bhavan Archives, Santiniketan, West Bengal
S. Srinivasachari, "Freedom Movement in India: Some Jottings from My Old Memories," National Archives of India (History of the Freedom Movement Papers), New Delhi
Lokmanya Tilak Papers, Kesari-Mahratta Office, Pune

Institutional

Bahá'í International Community Records, Haifa
Baroda College Records, Maharaja Sayajirao University, Vadodara, Gujarat
History of the Freedom Movement Papers, National Archives of India, New Delhi
King's College Records, King's College Library, Cambridge
Manchester Central Library, Local History Collection, Manchester
Messageries Maritimes Archives, Le Havre
National Council of Education Records, Jadavpur University, Kolkata
St. Paul's School Records, St. Paul's School, London

I.3. Government Records

India

Alipore Bomb Trial Records, Smaraniyo Bichar Sangraha, Alipore Court Complex, Kolkata
Baroda State Records 1893–1912, Vadodara Record Office, Vadodara
Bombay Commissioner of Police Records, Office of the Commissioner of Police, Greater Mumbai
Bombay Presidency Police, *Abstract of Intelligence*, 1908–1911, Office of the Deputy Inspector General of Police (Intelligence), Mumbai
Government of Bengal, West Bengal State Archives, Kolkata
   History of Services of Gazetted Officers
   Intelligence Branch, History Sheets
   Judicial and Judicial/Jails Department Proceedings, 1908–1909
   Political Department, confidential files, 1906–1910
   Quarterly Civil List for Bengal (Bengal Civil List), 1865–1893
   Report on Native Newspapers in Bengal, 1905–1910

Government of India, National Archives of India, New Delhi
    Foreign and Political Department, Proceedings
    Home Department Proceedings, series A, B, D, 1906–1920
Government of Madras, Tamil Nadu State Archives, Chennai
    Judicial Department, Confidential Files, 1912–1915
    Report on Native Newspapers in Madras, 1909–1910

Bangladesh

Government of Bengal, National Archives of Bangladesh, Dhaka
    General Department Proceedings, 1871–1893
    Sanitation Department, Proceedings, 1871–1893
Khulna Municipality, Proceedings, Khulna Town Hall
Rangpur Municipality, Proceedings, Rangpur Town Hall

United Kingdom

Board of Trade Passenger Lists, Public Record Office, London
British Census Records, Public Record Office, London
India Office Records, Public and Judicial, Oriental and India Office Library and Records,
    British Library, London
Nautical Reports, National Maritime Museum, London

France

Police Générale, series F/7, Archives Nationales, Paris

I.4. Government Reports

Armstrong, J.E. 1917. *An Account of the Revolutionary Organization in Eastern Bengal with Special Reference to the Dacca Anushilan Samiti.* Calcutta: n.p.
Daly, F.C. 1911. *Note on the Growth of the Revolutionary Movement in Bengal.* Calcutta: n.p.
Ker, James Campbell. 1917. *Political Trouble in India.* Calcutta: Superintendent Government Printing.
Nixon, J.C. 1917. *An Account of the Revolutionary Organisations in Bengal Other Than the Dacca Anushilan Samiti.* Calcutta: Bengal Secretariat Press.
Office of the Director, Criminal Intelligence. 1914. *Politico-Criminal Who's Who.*
Rowlatt, S.A.T., Basil Scott, C. V. Kumaraswami Sastri, Verney Lovett, P. C. Mitter, and J.D. V. Hodge. 1918. *Report of Committee Appointed to Investigate Revolutionary Conspiracies in India.* London: His Majesty's Stationary Office.
Second Supplementary Report on Samitis in the Dacca Division, Eastern Bengal and Assam.
Tegart, Charles. 1913. *Note on the Chandernagore Gang.* Calcutta: n.p.

II. PUBLISHED MATERIALS

II.1. Sri Aurobindo: Writings and Talks

Writings

Most of the works of Sri Aurobindo were published in 1970–1973 by the Sri Aurobindo Ashram Trust, Pondicherry, under the series title *Sri Aurobindo Birth Centenary Library* (SABCL). In 1995 the same publisher began to bring out the *Complete Works of Sri Aurobindo* (CWSA). References in this bibliography are to the CWSA edition if available at the time of publication, to the SABCL edition if not. For Bengali writings, the 1999 revised edition of *Bangla Rachana* is cited.

Bande Mataram: Political Writings and Speeches 1890–1908 (CWSA vols. 6 and 7)
Bangla Rachana [Bengali Writings]. 1999. Pondicherry: Sri Aurobindo Ashram
Collected Poems (SABCL vol. 5)
Collected Plays and Stories (CWSA vols. 3–4)
Early Cultural Writings (CWSA vol. 1)
Essays Divine and Human (CWSA vol. 12)
Essays in Philosophy and Yoga (CWSA vol. 13)
Essays on the Gita (CWSA vol. 19)
The Future Poetry (CWSA vol. 20)
The Human Cycle, The Ideal of Human Unity, War and Self-Determination (CWSA vol. 25)
Isha Upanishad (CWSA vol. 17)
The Karmayogin: Political Writings and Speeches 1909–1910 (CWSA vol. 8)
Kena and Other Upanishads (CWSA vol. 18)
Letters on Poetry and Art (CWSA vol. 27)
Letters on Yoga (SABCL vols. 22–24)
The Life Divine (SABCL vols. 18–19)
The Mother with Letters on the Mother (SABCL vol. 25)
On Himself (SABCL vol. 26)
Record of Yoga (CWSA vols. 10–11)
The Renaissance in India with A Defence of Indian Culture (CWSA vol. 20)
Savitri (CWSA vols. 34–35)
Supplement (SABCL vol. 27)
The Secret of the Veda (CWSA vol. 15)
The Synthesis of Yoga (CWSA vols. 23–24)
Translations (CWSA vol. 8)

Correspondence

Nirodbaran, ed. 1983. *Correspondence with Sri Aurobindo*, Pondicherry: Sri Aurobindo Ashram.

Talks

Chidanandam, V., ed. 1969–72. "Sri Aurobindo at Evening Talks." *Mother India* vols. 21–24.
Nirodbaran, ed. 2001. *Talks with Sri Aurobindo.* Pondicherry: Sri Aurobindo Ashram (two volumes).
Purani, A.B., ed. 1982. *Evening Talks with Sri Aurobindo.* Pondicherry: Sri Aurobindo Ashram.
Pavitra, ed. 1986. *Conversations avec Pavitra.* Pondicherry: Sri Aurobindo Ashram.
Roy, Anilbaran, ed. 1977–1986. "Conversations with Sri Aurobindo." *Sri Aurobindo Circle,* nos. 33–42.

II.2. The Mother: Writings and Talks

Writings

Paroles d'autrefois. 1983. Pondicherry: Sri Aurobindo Ashram.
Prières et méditations. 1983. Pondicherry: Sri Aurobindo Ashram.
Words of the Mother. 1980. Pondicherry: Sri Aurobindo Ashram.

Talks

L'agenda de Mère. 1978–1982. Paris: Institut de recherches évolutives (thirteen volumes).
Entretiens 1950–51. 1978. Pondicherry: Sri Aurobindo Ashram.
Entretiens 1953. 1978. Pondicherry: Sri Aurobindo Ashram.
Entretiens 1954. 1980. Pondicherry: Sri Aurobindo Ashram.
Entretiens 1957–58. 1978. Pondicherry: Sri Aurobindo Ashram.

II.3. Journals

The Arya (Pondicherry), 1914–1921
The Bengal Directory (Calcutta: Thakur Spink and Co.), 1871–1895
Bulletin of Physical Education/Bulletin of Sri Aurobindo International Centre of Education (Pondicherry), 1949–
Central Hindu College Magazine, 1909
The Indian Review (Madras), 1901–1905
Mercure de France (Paris), 1914
The Modern Review (Calcutta), 1909–1916
Mother India (Bombay/Pondicherry), 1949–
Revue cosmique (Paris), 1901–1908
Shama'a (Madras), 1920–1921
Sri Aurobindo: Archives and Research (Pondicherry), 1977–1994
Sri Aurobindo Circle (Bombay/Pondicherry), 1945–

II.4. Newspapers

Amrita Bazar Patrika (Calcutta), 1892, 1906–1950
Bande Mataram (Calcutta), 1906–1908
The Bengalee (Calcutta), 1892, 1905–1910
Dharma (Calcutta), 1909–1910
Eastern Bengal and Assam Era (Dacca), 1909
The Empire (Calcutta), 1908–1910
Fox's Weekly (Bradford), 1883
The Hindoo Patriot (Calcutta), 1909
The Hindu (Madras), 1910–1950
Hindusthan Standard (Calcutta), 1940–1942
India (Pondicherry), 1909–1910
The Indian Express (Bombay), 1947–1962
Journal officiel des Établissements Français dans l'Inde (Pondicherry), 1910–1914
Karmayogin (Calcutta), 1909–1910
The Madras Times, 1911
The Mahratta (Poona), 1902, 1907–1910
The Manchester Guardian, 1881, 1950
New India (Madras), 1918
The Review of Reviews (London), 1909–1910
The Standard Bearer (Chandernagore), 1920–1921
The Times (London), 1892, 1906–1910, 1950
Times of India (Bombay), 1907–1950

II.5. Printed Books and Articles

Note: B. S. = Bangla samvat, or Bengali era; for the equivalent year in the Gregorian calendar, add 593/594.

Agarwal, R. S. 1934. "Sri Aurobindo's Asram: Impressions of a Visitor." *Advance*, copy in Sri Aurobindo Ashram Archives (SAAA), scrapbook E-1.

Aiyangar, V. Ramaswami. 1950. "With Aurobindo in those Early Days." *Free India* 12 (December 10): 14, 16.

Alcakay, Ammiel. 1993. *After Jews and Arabs: Remaking Levantine Culture*. Minneapolis: University of Minnesota Press.

Amrita, K. 1969. "Old Long Since." In *Reminiscences*. Pondicherry: Sri Aurobindo Ashram Trust.

Ananthakrishan, V. 1933. "Sri Arabindo and his Cult." *Liberty* (April 19), copy in SAAA, scrapbook E-1.

Archer, William. 1917. *India and the Future*. London: Hutchinson & Co.

Arnold, Matthew. 1964. *Selected Essays*, ed. N. Annan. London: Oxford University Press.

Athalye, V.V. 1972. "Sri Aurobindo in Politics" [extract from *Atma-Vritta*], trans. J.S. Kuppuswamy. *Mother India* 24, no. 7 (August): 503.

Atmaprana, Pravrajika. 1967. *Sister Nivedita*. Calcutta: Sister Nivedita Girls' School.

Azad, Abul Kalam. 1984. *India Wins Freedom*. New Delhi: Orient Longman.

Bandyopadhyay, Gitasree. 1984. *Constraints in Bengal Politics, 1921–41*. Calcutta: Sarat Book House.

Bannerjee, Narendranath. 1361 B.S. *Rakta Biplaber Ek Adhyaya*. Chandernagore: Bimalendu Bannerjee.

Banerjee, Upendranath. 1357 B.S. "Aurobindo Prasanga." *Dainik Basumati*, 20 Agrahayan: 6, copy in SAAA, scrapbook B-3.

Banerjee, Upendranath. 1978. *Nirbasiter Atmakatha*. Reprint edition. Calcutta: National Publishers.

Bannerji, Jitendra Lal. 1909. "Aurobindo Ghose–A Study." *Modern Review* 6, no. 5 (November): 476–487.

Bapat, S.V. 1928. *Reminiscences and Anecdotes of Lokamanya Tilak*, vol. 3. Poona: S.V. Bapat.

Barns, Margarita. 1940. *The Indian Press: A History of the Growth of Public Opinion in India*. London: George Allen & Unwin.

Basu, Sankari Prasad, ed. 1982. *Letters of Sister Nivedita*. Calcutta: Nababharat Publishers (two volumes).

Bentley, E.C. 1940. *Those Days*. London: Constable & Co.

Beveridge, Lord William. 1947. *India Called Them*. London: George Allen & Unwin.

Bharatiar, Shuddhananda. 1939. *Bhagawan Sri Aurobindo: The Superman who Directs India to Life Divine*. Pondicherry: Ramanacharanananda (pamphlet).

Bhattacharya, Abinash. 1357 B. S. "Aurobindo." *Galpa Bharati* 6, no. 7 (Paush): 829–850.

Bhattacharya, Abinash. 1949. "Baiplabik Samitir Prarambh Kaler Itihas." In B. Dutta, ed., *Dwitiya Swadhinatar Sangram*, 199–200. Calcutta: Burman Publishing House.

Binyon, Laurence. 1926. "Introductory Memoir." In M. Ghose, *Songs of Love and Death*, 7–23. Oxford: Basil Blackwell.

Blake, William. 1982. *The Complete Poetry and Prose of William Blake*, ed. D. Erdman. Garden City, NY: Anchor Books.

Boisen, Anton T. 1936. *The Exploration of the Inner World: A Study of Mental Disorder and Religious Experience*. Chicago: Willett, Clark & Company.

Borges, Jorge Luis. 1966. *Other Inquisitions 1937–1952*, trans. R. Simms. New York: Washington Square Press.

Bose, Rajnarain. 1861. "A Society for the Promotion of National Feeling among the Educated Natives of Bengal." Reproduced in Jogesh C. Bagal, "Rajnarain Bose and Indian Nationalism." *Modern Review* 75, no. 6 (June 1944): 444–447.

Bose, Rajnarain. 1909. *Rajnarayan Basur Atma-charita*. Calcutta: P.C. Dass.

Bose, Subhas Chandra. 1997. *An Indian Pilgrim: An Unfinished Biography*, ed. S.K. Bose and S. Bose. Delhi: Oxford University Press.

Chakrabarti, Basanti. 1357 B. S. "Amader Aurodada." *Galpa Bharati* 6, no. 7 (Paush): 776–785.

Chakravarty, Suresh Chandra. 1962. *Smritikatha*. Pondicherry: Sri Aurobindo Ashram.

Chand, Feroz. 1978. *Lajpat Rai: Life and Work.* New Delhi: Publications Division, Ministry of Information and Broadcasting.

Chandra, Bipan. 1971. *Modern India.* New Delhi: National Council of Educational Research and Training.

Chandwani, P.B. 1971. "Sri Aurobindo: A Few Reminiscences." *Mother India* 23, no. 7 (August): 468–470.

Chesterton, G.K. 1986. *Autobiography.* London: Hamish Hamilton.

Chidanandam, V. 1973. "Sri Aurobindo and the Mother as I Saw Them." In M.P. Pandit, ed., *Breath of Grace,* 1–17. Pondicherry: Dipti Publications.

Chidatmananda, Swami. 1926. "Towards Peace." *Prabuddha Bharata* 30, no. 11 (November): 506–511.

Chirol, Valentine. 1910. *Indian Unrest.* London: MacMillan and Co.

Congress Presidential Addresses: From the Foundation to the Silver Jubilee. n.d. (1934?) First series. Madras: G. A. Natesan & Co.

Churchill, Winston S. 1952. "Speech at the Lord Mayor's Day Luncheon at the Mansion House, November 10, 1942." In Charles Eade, ed., *The Wartime Speeches of the Rt Hon Winston Churchill,* vol. 2, 342–345. London: Cassell & Co.

Cronin, Richard Paul. 1977. *British Policy and Administration in Bengal: Partition and the New Province of Eastern Bengal and Assam.* Calcutta: Firma KLM Private Ltd.

Cousins, James H. 1917. *New Ways in English Literature.* Madras: Ganesh & Co.

Das Gupta, Hemendranath. 1960. *Deshbandhu Chittaranjan Das.* New Delhi: Publications Division, Ministry of Information and Broadcasting.

Das, Harihar. 1935. "Sri Aurobindo: A Study." *Hindustan Review* 66: 781–785.

Das, Manoj. 1972. *Sri Aurobindo in the First Decade of the Century.* Pondicherry: Sri Aurobindo Ashram Trust.

Das, Pulin Behari. 1987. *Amar Jiban Kahini.* Calcutta: Anushilan Samiti.

David-Néel, Alexandra. 1951. *L'Inde où j'ai vécu.* Paris: Plon.

David-Néel, Alexandra. 1972. *Le sortilège du mystère.* Paris: Plon.

David-Néel, Alexandra. 1975. *Journal de voyage: lettres à son mari (11 août 1904–27 décembre 1917).* Paris: Plon.

Davis, Philip. 1995. "Summary." In John Ruskin, *Selected Writings,* ed. Philip Davis, xxiii–xxvii. London: J. M. Dent.

De, Brajendranath. 1954. "Reminiscences of an Indian Member of the Indian Civil Service." *Calcutta Review* 132, no. 3 (September): 178–181.

Deb, Suresh Chandra. 1949. "When He Was a Political Leader." *Calcutta Municipal Gazette* 50, no. 17 (August 20): viii–ix.

Deb, Suresh Chandra. 1950. "Sri Aurobindo as I Knew Him." *Mother India* 2, no. 13 (August): 21–23.

Debsharma, Balai. 1357 B. S. "Aurobindo." *Galpa Bharati* 6, no. 7 (Paush): 753–759.

De Guaita, Stanislas. 1897. *Essais de sciences maudites: Le serpent de la genése,* vol. 2. Paris: Chamuel.

Deshpande, K.G. 1902. "Yoga Mysticism." *The Indian Review* 3, no. 6 (June): 301–302.

Dey, Mukul. 1988. "My Darshan of Sri Aurobindo at Pondicherry," trans. Manoj Das. *The Heritage* (August): 26–28.

Doshi, Nagin, ed. 1974. *Guidance from Sri Aurobindo: Letters to a Young Disciple*. Pondicherry: Sri Aurobindo Society.

Dutt, Arun Chandra. 1972. "Letters of Sree Aurobindo." In Arun Chandra Dutt, ed., *Light to Superlight: Unpublished Letters of Sri Aurobindo*, 1–111. Calcutta: Prabartak Publishers.

Dutt, C.C. 1952. "My Contact with Revolutionary Independence Movement." *The Mahratta* 72, no. 31 (August 1): 1–7.

Dutt, Nirmal. 1977. "My Recollections of Sri Aurobindo." *Mother India* 29, no. 8 (August): 601–602.

Forster, E.M. 1927. *Aspects of the Novel*. London: Edward Arnold.

Forster, E.M. 1934. *Goldsworthy Lowes Dickinson*. London: Edward Arnold.

Gaebelé, Yvonne Robert. 1960. *Histoire de Pondichéry: de l'an 1000 à nos jours*. Pondicherry: Government Press.

Gaekwar, Sayaji Rao. 1927. *Speeches & Addresses of His Highness Sayaji Rao III*, vol. 1. Cambridge: Cambridge University Press.

Gandhi, K. H. 1945. "What is Sri Aurobindo Doing?" *Sri Aurobindo Circle* 1: 37–56.

Ganguli, Romesh Ch. 1950. "Pondicherry's Mystic." *Amrita Bazar Patrika*, February 22, copy in SAAA, scrapbook E-2.

Gardner, Helen, ed. 1975. *The New Oxford Book of English Verse 1250–1950*. Oxford: Clarendon Press.

Ghose, Barindrakumar. 1338 B. S. *Amar Atmakatha*. Calcutta: Arya Publishing House.

Ghose, Barindrakumar. 1355 B. S. *Agnijug*. Calcutta: Book Publishing Ltd.

Ghose, Barindrakumar. 1379 B. S. *Barindrer Atmakahini: Dhar-Pakader Jug*. Calcutta: D.M. Limited.

Ghose, Hemendra Prasad. 1949. "Reminiscences of Aurobindo Ghose." *Orient Illustrated Weekly* 13, no. 21 (February 27): 10, 11–12.

Ghose, Hemendra Prasad. 1949. *Aurobindo: The Prophet of Patriotism*. Calcutta: A.K. Mitter.

Ghose, Jyotish Chandra. 1929. *Life-Work of Sri Aurobindo*. Calcutta: Atmashakti Library.

Ghosh, Sudhir. 1967. *Gandhi's Emissary*. Boston: Houghton Mifflin.

Ghosh, Surendra Mohan. 1971. "A Talk by Surendra Mohan Ghosh." *Mother India* 23, nos. 1–2 (February–March): 25–31, 108–115.

Ghosh, Surendra Mohan. 1984. "Two Interviews with Surendra Mohan Ghose." *Service Letter* 133 (January 1): 1–4.

Ghosh, Surendra Mohan, and François Baron. 1976. "Two Personal Documents of Historical Importance." *Mother India* 28, no. 8 (August): 648–649.

Gilbert, Martin. 1966. *Servant of India: A Study of Imperial Rule from 1905–1910 as Told through the Correspondence and Diaries of Sir James Dunlop Smith*. London: Longmans.

Godwin, Joscelyn, Christian Chanel, and John Patrick Deveney. 1995. *The Hermetic Brotherhood of Luxor: Initiatic and Historical Documents of an Order of Practical Occultism*. York Beach, ME: Samuel Weiser.

Guharoy, Nagrendrakumar. 1357 B. S. "Debata Biday." *Galpa-Bharati* 5, no. 12 (Jaiystha): 1598–1624; *Galpa-Bharati* 6, no. 1 (Ashadh): 47–68.

Gupta, J. N. 1918. *Rangpur Today: A Study in Local Problems in a Bengal District.* Calcutta: n.p.

Gupta, Nolini Kanta. 1381 B. S. *Smritir Pata.* Calcutta: Sri Aurobindo Pathmandir.

Gupta, Nolini Kanta. 1969. *Reminiscences.* Pondicherry: Sri Aurobindo Ashram.

Gupta, Nolini Kanta. 1973. "Sri Aurobinder Jibandhara." In Nolini Kanta Gupta, *Shatabdir Pranam,* 20–30. Calcutta: Sri Aurobindo Pathmandir.

Hamblett, Charles. 1951. "Eternity Greets a God." *Illustrated* (January 6): 27–29.

Hardie, J. Keir. 1907. "A Scamper Round the World," chapters 1–5. *The Labour Leader,* November 29–December 27.

Hay, Stephen, ed. 1991. *Sources of Indian Tradition, vol. 2: Modern India and Pakistan.* New Delhi: Penguin Books. Reprint edition.

Heehs, Peter. 1993. *The Bomb in Bengal: The Rise of Revolutionary Terrorism in India 1900–1910.* New Delhi: Oxford University Press.

Heehs, Peter. 1997. "Genius, Mysticism and Madness." *The Psychohistory Review* 26, no. 1 (Fall): 45–75.

Heehs, Peter. 1998. *Nationalism, Terrorism, Communalism.* New Delhi: Oxford University Press.

Hood, Ralph W., Jr. 1992. "Mysticism, Reality, Illusion, and the Freudian Critique of Religion." *International Journal for the Psychology of Religion* 2, no. 3: 141–159.

Hunter, W.W. 1876. *A Statistical Account of Bengal, vol. 7: Districts of Maldah, Rangpur, and Dinájpur.* London: Trübner & Co.

Iyengar, M.A. Narayana. 1959. "Forward." In S. Parthasarathy Iyengar, *The Bhagavad Gita: A Simple Paraphrase in English.* Madras: Gnana-Vignana Trust.

James, William. 1912. *Essays and Studies.* New York: Longmans, Green and Co.

James, William. 1961. *The Varieties of Religious Experience: A Study of Human Nature.* New York: Collier.

Johnston, William, ed. 1906. *Roll of the Graduates of the University of Aberdeen 1860–1900.* Aberdeen: n.p.

Kakar, Sudhir. 1991. *The Analyst and the Mystic.* Delhi: Viking.

Kanungo, Hemchandra. 1928. *Banglay Biplab Pracheshta.* Calcutta: Kamala Book Depot.

Karandikar, S.L. 1957. *Lokamanya Bal Gangadhar Tilak: The Hercules & Prometheus of Modern India.* Poona: S.L. Karandikar.

Kopf, David. 1979. *The Brahmo Samaj and the Shaping of the Modern Indian Mind.* Princeton, NJ: Princeton University Press.

Latif, Bilkees. 1984. *Her India: The Fragrance of Forgotten Years.* New Delhi: Arnold-Heinemann.

Le Cocq, Rhoda P. 1969. *The Radical Thinkers: Heidegger and Sri Aurobindo.* Pondicherry: Sri Aurobindo Ashram.

Lipner, Julius J. 1999. *Brahmabandhab Upadhyay: The Life and Thought of a Revolutionary.* Delhi: Oxford University Press.

Loti, Pierre. 1929. *India,* trans. A. Inman. London: T. Werner Laurie Ltd.

MacDonald, J. Ramsay. 1909. *The Awakening of India.* London: Hodder and Stoughton.

McLane, John R. 1965. "The Decision to Partition Bengal in 1905." *Indian Economic and Social History Review* 2, no. 3 (July): 221–237.

Maitland-Marsh, Olive. 1932. *Uplifting Humanity*. Westminster (London): Olive Maitland-Marsh.

Major, E. 1910. *Viscount Morley and Indian Reform*. London: James Nisbet & Co.

Majumdar, R.C. 1975. *History of the Freedom Movement in India*, vol. 2. Calcutta: Firma K.L. Mukhopadhyay.

Mazumdar, Amvika Charan. 1917. *Indian National Evolution*. Madras: G.A. Natesan.

Minto, Mary. 1935. *India, Minto and Morley 1905–1910*. London: Macmillan and Co.

Mistral, Gabriela. 1950. "A Few Words on Sri Aurobindo." *Sri Aurobindo Mandir Annual* 9: 140–142.

Monestier, Marianne. 1963. *Les sociétés secrètes féminines*. Paris: Les Productions de Paris.

Monod-Herzen, G. 1972. "Reminiscences of Sri Aurobindo." *Mother India* 24 (August): 496–502.

Mookerji, Radha Kumud. 1963. "Some Reminiscences of Sri Aurobindo." *Mother India* 25, no. 10–11 (December): 20–21.

Mookerji, Radha Kumud. 1997. "Foreword (To the First Edition)." In H. Mukherjee and U. Mukherjee, eds., *Sri Aurobindo and the New Thought in Indian Politics*, vii–viii. Second edition. Calcutta: Firma KLM Private Ltd.

Morisset, André. "Remembrances." *Sri Aurobindo Circle* 34 (1978): 64–66.

Mukherjee, Haridas, and Uma Mukherjee. 1958. *Bipin Chandra Pal and India's Struggle for Swaraj*. Calcutta: Firma K.L. Mukhopadhyay.

Mukherjee, Mrityunjoy. 1973. "A Look Behind." In M. P. Pandit, ed., *Breath of Grace*, 55–77. Pondicherry: Dipti Publications.

Müller, F. Max, ed. and trans. 1981. *The Upanishads*, Part 1. Vol. 1 of *The Sacred Books of the East*. Reprint edition. Delhi: Motilal Banarsidas.

Munshi, K.M. 1951. "Sri Aurobindo." *The Advent* 8, no. 4 (November): 302–305.

Munshi, K.M. 1952. "Aurobindo Ashram—A Pilgrimage." *Hindustan Times*, Independence Supplement (August 15).

Munshi, K.M. 1962. "Kulapati's Letter on Life, Literature & Culture." *Bhavan's Journal* 8, no. 26 (July 22): 6–11.

Natesan, G. A. 1905. "Japan: Its Message to India." *Indian Review* 6, no. 1 (January): 1–3.

Nehru, Jawaharlal. 1967. "Foreword." In Karan Singh, *Prophet of Indian Nationalism: A Study of the Political Thought of Sri Aurobindo Ghosh 1893–1910*, ix–x. Bombay: Bharatiya Vidya Bhavan.

Neogy, Ajit. 1985. "Pondicherry: A Centre for the Production and Distribution of Seditious Literature." *India Past and Present* 2, no. 2 (December): 241–248.

Nevinson, Henry W. 1908. *The New Spirit in India*. London: Harper and Brothers.

Nevinson, Henry W. 1925. *More Changes, More Chances*. London: Nisbet & Co.

Nirodbaran. 1951. *Sri Aurobindo: "I Am Here, I Am Here."* Pondicherry: Sri Aurobindo Ashram.

Nirodbaran. 1973. *Twelve Years with Sri Aurobindo*. Second edition. Pondicherry: Sri Aurobindo Ashram.

Nirodbaran. 1988. *Mrinalini Devi*. Pondicherry: Sri Mira Trust.

Padmanabhan, R.A. 1980. *V. V. S. Aiyar*. New Delhi: National Book Trust.

Pal, Bipinchandra. 1907. *The New Spirit*. Calcutta: Sinha, Sarvadhikar & Co.

Pal, Bipinchandra. c. 1910. *Leaders of the Nationalist Movement in Bengal*. N.p., n.d.

Phillips, Stephen H. 1989. "Mutable God: Hartshorne and Indian Theism." In R. Kane and S. Phillips, eds., *Hartshorne, Process Philosophy and Theology*, 113–132. Albany, NY: State University of New York Press.

Pinto, Udar. 1972. "A Report on Sri Aurobindo's Passing." *Mother India* 24, nos. 10–11 (December): 754–757.

Purani, A.B. 1950. "An Intimate Glimpse of the Master." *Sunday Times* (December 17): 2.

Purani, A.B. 1978. *The Life of Sri Aurobindo*. Pondicherry: Sri Aurobindo Ashram.

Rai, Lajpat. 1921. *India's Will to Freedom: Writings and Speeches on the Present Situation*. Madras: Ganesh & Co.

Rao, T. Kodandarama. 1969. *At the Feet of the Master (Reminiscences)*. Anantapur, A.P.: P.H. Rao.

Ray, Dinendrakumar. 1379 B. S. *Aurobindo Prasanga*. Calcutta: Sri Aurobindo Pathmandir.

Raychaudhuri, Girijashankar. 1956. *Sri Aurobindo o Banglay Swadeshi Yug*. Calcutta: Navabharat Publishers.

Reddy, C.R. 1948. "Sir C.R. Reddy's Address." In *Sri Aurobindo's Message to the Andhra University*. Pondicherry: Sri Aurobindo Ashram (pamphlet).

Richard, Paul. 1987. "Without Passport." In Michel Paul Richard, ed., *Without Passport: The Life and Work of Paul Richard*, 1–96. New York: Peter Lang.

Rolland, Romain. 1929. "India on the March." *The Modern Review* 45, no. 4 (April): 409–415.

Rolland, Romain. 1948. *La vie de Vivekananda et l'évangile universel*. Reprint edition. Paris: Stock.

Rolland, Romain. 1960. *Inde: Journal 1915–1943*. Paris: Albin Michel.

Roy, Arthur R.S. 1973. "Sri Aurobindo Ghose—Memories of Long Ago." *Bande Mataram* (October 1949). Reprinted in *Sri Aurobindo's Action* 3, no. 10 (July): 7.

Roy, Dilip Kumar. 1952. *Sri Aurobindo Came to Me*. Pondicherry: Sri Aurobindo Ashram.

Roy, Jyotish Chandra. 1938. "Sri Aurobindo: Eventful Life Dedicated to Truth." *Advance* (21 February), in SAAA, scrapbook E-1.

Roy, Motilal. 1357 B. S. "Sri Aurobindo Prasanga." *Prabartak* 35, nos. 9 and 10 (Paush–Magh): 374–383, 439–441.

Roy, Motilal. 1945. *My Life's Partner*, trans. D.S. Mahalanobis. Calcutta: Prabartak Publishers.

Russell, Bertrand. 1967. *The Autobiography of Bertrand Russell 1872–1914*. London: George Allen and Unwin.

Saint Hilaire, Philippe Barbier. 2001. *Itinéraire d'un enfant du siècle: De l'École polytechnique à l'Ashram de Sri Aurobindo (1918–1954)*. Paris: Buchet Chastel.

Salvadori, Guglielmo. 1916. "The Psychological Interpretation of History." *Hindustan Review* 33, whole nos. 201–202 (May–June): 393–404.

Sangave, Vilas, and B.D. Khane, eds. 1983. *Rajarshi Shahu Chhatrapati Papers*, vol. 2. Kolhapur: Shahu Research Institute, Shivaji University.

Sanyal, Prabhat. 1953. "A 'Call' from Pondicherry." *Mother India* 5, no. 11 (December): 180–189.

Sargeant, Winthrop. 1949. "Holy Man." *Life* (May 30): 92ff.

Sarkar, Sudhir. 1952. "Rishi Sri Aurobinder Smriti-katha." *Jugantar* (August 15), copy in SAAA, scrapbook B-2.

Sarkar, Sumit. 1973. *The Swadeshi Movement in Bengal 1903–1908.* New Delhi: People's Publishing House.

Sastri, Sivanath. 1911. *History of the Brahmo Samaj*, vol. 1. Calcutta: R. Chatterji.

Sastri, Sivanath. 1919. *Men I Have Seen.* Calcutta: Modern Review Office.

Sastry, T.V. Kapali. 1979. "My First Meeting with Sri Aurobindo." In *Collected Works of T.V. Kapali Sastry,* vol. 2. Pondicherry: Dipti Publications.

Sen, Biren. 1964. "Sri Aurobindo as I Remember Him." *Mother India* 16, no. 3 (April): 16–24.

Sen, Keshub Chunder. 1938. *Keshub Chunder Sen in England.* Calcutta: Navavidhan Publication Committee.

Sen Gupta, Jatindranath. 1927. "Sri Aurobindo's Ashram: Daily Life of Inmates." *The Hindu* (May 6), copy in SAAA, scrapbook E-1.

Sergeant, Philip W. 1928. *The Ruler of Baroda: An Account of the Life and Work of the Maharaja Gaekwar.* London: John Murray.

Sethi, R.R. 1958. *The Last Phase of British Sovereignty in India.* Delhi: S. Chand. & Co.

Sethna, K. D. 1980. *Our Light and Delight: Recollections of Life with the Mother.* Pondicherry: Amal Kiran (K. D. Sethna).

Shahani, Ranjee G. 1944. "A Philosopher of Modern India: Aurobindo the Reconciler." *Times Literary Supplement* (July 8): 330.

Sheean, Vincent. 1949. "Kings of the Yogis." *Holiday* 6, no. 3 (September): 73–82.

Shri Kanaialal Munshi Diamond Jubilee Committee. 1947. *Munshi: His Art and Work.* Bombay: Padma Publications.

Singh, Har Krishan. 1963. "Sri Aurobindo through the Eyes of One of His Students." *Mother India* 15, no. 7 (August): 25–26.

Singh, Karan. 1967. *Prophet of Indian Nationalism: A Study of the Political Thought of Sri Aurobindo Ghosh 1893–1910.* Bombay: Bharatiya Vidya Bhavan.

Singh, S.R. 1985. "Moderates and Extremists: The Congress till the Surat Split." In *A Centenary History of the Indian National Congress (1885–1985),* vol. 1, 116–179. New Delhi: Vikas.

Source Material for a History of the Freedom Movement in India. 1957–1958. Bombay: Government Central Press (two volumes).

Spear, Percival. 1981. *A History of India,* vol. 2. Harmondsworth, England: Penguin Books.

Sukal, Trambaklal. 1963. "Such Was Sri Aurobindo and Such the Maharaja," trans. Nagin Doshi. *Mother India* 15, no. 1 (February): 38.

Tagore, Rabindranath. 1928. "Aurobindo Ghosh." *The Modern Review* 44, no. 1 (July): 58–60.

Tahmankar, D.V. 1956. *Lokamanya Tilak: Father of Indian Unrest and Maker of Modern India.* London: John Murray.

Taylor, Charles. 1994. "The Politics of Recognition." In A. Gutman, ed., *Multiculturalism: Examining the Politics of Recognition*, 25–73. Princeton: Princeton University Press.

Thémanlys, Claire. 1931. *Un séjour chez les grands initiés*. Paris: Publications Cosmiques.

Trivedi, A.K., ed. 1933. *The Baroda College Golden Jubilee*. Bombay: The Times of India Press.

Vas, J.A. 1911. *Eastern Bengal and Assam District Gazeteers, Rangpur*. Allahabad: Pioneer Press.

Weber, Eugen. 1986. *France, Fin de Siècle*. Cambridge, MA: Belknap Press.

Wolpert, Stanley A. 1967. *Morley and India 1906–1910*. Berkeley and Los Angeles: University of California Press.

Wolpert, Stanley A. 1989. *Tilak and Gokhale: Revolution and Reform in the Making of Modern India*. Reprint edition. New Delhi: Oxford University Press.

Younghusband, Francis. 1942. "An Indian Seer: The Philosophy of Sri Aurobindo." *Times Literary Supplement* (January 17): 28.

Ziegler, Philip. 1985. *Mountbatten: The Official Biography*. London: Fontana/Collins.

Index